CONVERGENCES

MESSAGE · METHOD · MEDIUM

CONVERGENCES

MESSAGE ▪ METHOD ▪ MEDIUM

ROBERT ATWAN

CURRY COLLEGE

BEDFORD/ST. MARTIN'S

BOSTON ▪ NEW YORK

For Bedford/St. Martin's

Executive Editor: Alanya Harter
Production Editor: Bridget Leahy
Senior Production Supervisor: Joe Ford
Senior Marketing Manager: Rachel Falk
Editorial Assistant: Jeffrey Voccola
Copyeditor: Alice Vigliani
Text Design: Delgado and Company, Inc., and Judith Arisman, Arisman Design Studio
Cover Design: Donna Lee Dennison
Cover Art: airport #2. © Rosemary Laing. Courtesy Gallery Lelong, New York
Composition: Monotype Composition
Printing and Binding: R. R. Donnelley & Sons, Inc.

President: Joan E. Feinberg
Editorial Director: Denise B. Wydra
Editor in Chief: Karen S. Henry
Director of Marketing: Karen Melton Soeltz
Director of Editing, Design, and Production: Marcia Cohen
Managing Editor: Elizabeth M. Schaaf

Library of Congress Control Number: 2004102160

For information, write: Bedford/St. Martin's, 75 Arlington Street, Boston, MA 02116 (617-399-4000)

ISBN: 0–312–41291–6
EAN: 978–0–312–41291–3

As series editor of *Best American Essays* and a long-time textbook author, I confess that the essay, as a form and a medium, is my first love. The idea for *Convergences* — a book that pairs the essay with compositions from other media — came from watching my children and my students connect the ideas they discovered in their textbooks to the ideas they saw in other kinds of texts. A television show, a news report, a web site, an image, an advertisement: all these things are compositions, even if they are not traditionally part of the syllabus for a composition course. I found myself playing with this idea of *connections*, and wondering what a composition text might look like that was built around strong essays that were paired with pictures, ads, web sites. As I worked, I realized that convergences were suddenly everywhere — I could connect the dots between everything I saw, read, and watched — and the result is *Convergences*.

    Convergences is built around clusters. Pairing a strong essay with other kinds of texts — a poster, a web site, an essay, and a poem, for example — not only gives students more to think about critically, it also gives those students more to write about. Take the issue of *diversity* as it is treated in this textbook. Rather than re-treading familiar ground in a single essay, *Convergences* includes a dynamic collection of texts in the cluster Us and Them: a controversial essay by David Brooks; a poem by Maya Angelou; images from *America 24/7,* a groundbreaking photographic project to "capture America"; and an ad from the *Islam in America* series. The essay provides a lens with which to read the photographs; the photographs and ad complicate the position Brooks takes in his essay. And as a whole, the cluster brings together a lot of smart people trying to persuade others to their way of thinking about an incredibly important issue using a variety of media. It's powerful stuff.

Students need a coherent methodology to read — and to make — increasingly complex rhetorical choices. As the first edition of *Convergences* came together, it became clear that reading texts in a cluster was, simply, a richer way to think about composition — about *what* people say, *how* they say it, and *why* it matters whether we see something on TV or read it in a book. And there was my methodology: message, method, medium. In these pages are texts that represent multiple media and genres — essays, advertisements, the web, news, comics, television, and film, to name just a few. The purpose of including visual texts in a composition reader is not to pander to students' "MTV" aesthetic; every composition represented in these pages is the result of careful choices made by a writer or designer or artist. Students who use *Convergences* will learn to ask certain questions about what the text is trying to say, how it goes about saying it, and what impact medium has on the message as they read (and compose). What's the best way to tell the story of your life — through words or pictures? How would the Gettysburg Address have been received if Lincoln had delivered it on PowerPoint? Why did Benetton design a marketing campaign around death-row inmates? My hope is that the students using this book will learn to ask these questions, among others.

Convergences is built around themes that vividly connect with the lives of today's students. Students will be invited to consider the film they find most life-altering; they will meet a presumably ordinary guy who sold his entire life on eBay; they will think about fast food as a metaphor for American culture; they will be asked to imagine the inside of their cars as a sacred space; and they'll evaluate the award-winning 9/11 memorial (Reflecting Absence) for its effectiveness as a monument to tragedy. All six chapters mirror the traditional arrangement of the composition reader, starting with the personal and moving to the public. But in this reader, these familiar categories get a new dimension:

1. Staging Portraits outlines the way verbal and visual portraits reveal certain details while hiding others.

2. Telling Stories traces how narrative works across different media — home movies, reality TV, movies, webcams, and the traditional essay.

3. Shaping Spaces focuses on what it means to think spatially — whether the space is a piece of paper, a room, or the world wide web.

4. Making History suggests that describing the past means interpreting it.

5. Dividing Lines shows how different groups of people draw and erase lines between "us" and "them."

6. Packaging Culture unwraps some of the things marketers and advertisers sell beyond products — patriotism, art, health, opinions, youth, and shopping itself.

Convergences is a solid, *traditional* composition reader. An extraordinary collection of essays helps to keep *Convergences* connected with the composition classroom. Though the thematic clusters include a unique array of media and genres, each cluster is solidly anchored to a strong model of writing. For example, this edition features a coming-of-age memoir by John Edgar Wideman in which the noted novelist recalls the first shot he made on a basketball court as a young child; a personal narrative by Louise Erdrich on how a memorable film transformed her adolescent vision of the world; and a historical essay by the noted comic artist Art Spiegelman in which he traces the origins of the comic-book superhero in general and the near-forgotten Plastic Man in particular. Such accomplished essays — and there are many more — will provide excellent models for teaching personal voice, narrative, and expository methods, as well as the skillful use of physical and illustrative detail.

Because *Convergences* is a composition reader, it provides multiple occasions for writing throughout the text.

*   Message, Method, and Medium questions ask what texts say, how they go about saying it, and what impact medium has on message.

*   Questions for Writing, Researching, and Collaborating prompt students to make connections within and outside the text as they write critical responses to what they've read.

New to This Edition

Every cluster now includes a solid essay. I said earlier that the essay was my first love, and one of the things I learned from people who used the first edition of *Convergences* was that they wanted a wider representation of traditional compositions — essays — to serve as examples for their students. I also learned that many instructors feel more comfortable using the essay to lead into the visual material, and that those clusters in the first edition that were composed entirely of images were far more challenging for them to teach. One of the biggest changes in the second edition is that it now includes both more essays and a greater range of essays.

A new design and navigation connect textbook conventions with the principles of web design. Although the general organization of *Convergences* remains the same, the second edition looks different—and my hope is that it's a case in which the handsome design is matched by its functionality. The horizontal navigation bar tells readers which media are represented in each cluster and keeps the reader oriented on each page, in each cluster, and within the entire book.

A systematically revised general introduction better articulates the methodology established in the first edition. First explaining the importance of message, method, and medium, the introduction concretely connects key questions about audience, purpose, and context with the wide range of texts collected in the book. A new section, "Reading and Writing about Texts," includes easy-to-follow annotated models of how to read an essay, a photograph, and an advertisement.

Greater attention is given to visual rhetoric and thinking across media within the text: Visually Speaking Pages throughout *Convergences* focus on key visual and verbal concepts. This new feature offers strategies for reading visual texts and invites students to compose their own multimedia texts.

Greater attention is given to visual rhetoric *outside* the text, because there are some things—and some concepts—you can't explore as well in this medium. Each copy of the second edition of *Convergences* comes with a CD-ROM, *ix visual exercises,* that offers a new way to focus on visual rhetoric. Nine tutorials ask to students to explore fundamental concepts that they can use to analyze and compose multimodal texts: element, contrast, purpose, text, framing, audience, alignment, context, emphasis, color, proximity, organization, and sequence. Each tutorial moves through three steps: an illustrated definition, a model analysis of a real-world text, and an interactive assignment that invites students to make their own rhetorical choices. Ideas for incorporating *ix* into the course are integrated in the text and also in the instructor's manual.

Supplements

Instructor's Manual: *Resources for Teaching CONVERGENCES* gives instructors tips on teaching each selection and ideas for generating class discussion and in-class writing. It also explores additional connections between selections and gives suggestions for further reading, thinking, and writing.

An integrated web site: bedfordstmartins.com/convergences. This site links students to the sites included in the book and offers questions for further exploration and other resources for students and instructors. In addition, Bedford/St. Martin's TopLinks — a topical links database accessible through the above site — guides students to the links with the most useful information on the important authors and complex ideas presented in *Convergences.*

Acknowledgments

I thank those colleagues who offered thoughtful reviews of the first edition of *Convergences*: Kimberly D. Braddock, Idaho State University, English and Philosophy Department; Patricia Burdette, Ohio State University; Dion Cautrell, Ohio State University–Mansfield; Keith Comer, Idaho State University; Clark L. Draney, Idaho State University; Paul Fectueau, Washburn University; Lynda Feldman, Jefferson Community College; Jennifer Firestone, Fordham University; Melody Gough, University of Nevada, Reno; Katherine M. Gray, Lynchburg College; Jefferson Hancock, Cabrillo College; Abigail Martin, Florida International University; Elizabeth Caemasache McKenna, University of Central Florida; Ailish Hopper Meisner, Goucher College; Suzanne E. O'Hop, Northand Pioneer College; Jason A. Pierce, Mars Hill College; Gabe Popovich, Purdue University; Leandra Preston, University of Central Florida; John E. Ribar, Nova Southeastern University; Jeff Rice, University of Detroit; Patricia C. Roby, UW–Washington County; Shant Shahoian, Moorpark College; Kay J. Walter, Idaho State University; Susan Wellington, SUNY–Oswego; and Jennifer Locke Whetham, Bellevue Community College.

Several people helped me shape the revised introduction and offered in-depth comments on drafts of the early chapters, and I want to offer them special thanks: Heidi Wilkinson, California Polytechnic State University; Brock Dethier, Utah State University; Bruce Henderson, Fullerton College; Linda Overman, California State University Northridge; Deborah Coxwell-Teague, Florida State University; and Karen Felts, Orange Coast College.

I am also grateful to Deborah Coxwell-Teague for inviting me to Florida State University to speak with graduate students on using *Convergences* in the composition classroom. I'd like to thank those FSU graduate students for a number of practical suggestions that I was able to incorporate into this edition.

Responding to sample chapters and an early outline for the first edition, several reviewers offered a number of useful suggestions and pointed out some encouraging directions. I remain grateful to Elizabeth Abrams, University of California, Santa Cruz; Angi Caster, Highline Community College; Jeff E. Cravello, California State Polytechnic University; Carrie Heimer, University of New Hampshire; Charles Hood, Antelope Valley College; Priscilla Kanet, Clemson University; David Norlin, Cloud Community College; and J. Wylene Rholetter, Auburn University. Sometimes enthusiastic and sometimes critical, these reviewers helped to keep me focused on practical instructional goals. I tried to follow their advice as much as possible.

I am indebted to the staff of Bedford/St. Martin's for their magnificent support, starting with the publisher Charles E. Christensen and the president, Joan E. Feinberg, who discovered the seeds of this project lying dormant in a proposal I had prepared for a different kind of book. Still, *Convergences* would not have taken root without the energetic support of my editor, Alanya Harter, whose flow of ideas and grasp of cultural and media studies, along with her remarkable sense of design, made it seem as though I had working behind me an entire editorial team. Every page of this book reflects her creative, conceptual, and critical contribution. I'm also extremely grateful to her assistants: Jeff Voccola, who helped in a wide variety of ways and whose research skills proved invaluable, and Kim Hampton, who helped shape the web site. Given our extremely tight schedule, I appreciate the Herculean efforts of all those in production, especially Production Editor Bridget Leahy, who adroitly kept a complicated production process in motion, ensuring that everything flowed smoothly through often challenging channels. Joe Ford oversaw the composition process, and Elizabeth Schaaf managed production concerns. I'm grateful also to Editor in Chief Karen Henry and Editorial Director Denise Wydra for their ideas early on and their continuing support of the project.

I also wish to acknowledge the assistance of several other individuals who work outside of the Bedford/St. Martin's home base. In obtaining the images for the book and clearing permissions, Martha Friedman and Sandy Schechter expertly transformed a possible table of contents into an actual one. Alice Vigliani did a wonderful job copyediting the manuscript; I appreciate her insightful suggestions. Jan Cocker and Courtney Tenz handled the difficult task of proofreading such a wide diversity of material. I also appreciate enormously the work that Christine Nicometo of the University of Wisconsin–Madison put into the Instructor's Manual; as a comprehensive introduction to the ways of reading the convergences of media, messages, and methods, it can stand entirely on its own.

I want to especially acknowledge the contributions of three talented designers: Mark Heffeman, who came up with the concept of horizontal navigation for the book; Lisa Delgado, who helped us redesign the book for greater impact and coherence; and Judith Arisman, who elegantly solved the problem of how to present a complicated table of contents.

I'm also much indebted to Rodes Fishburne, Associate Editor of *Forbes ASAP*, for first calling my attention to the idea of convergence while I was consulting with him on potential contributors to the magazine. *The Big Issue IV: The Great Convergence* (October 4, 1999), with essays by Kathleen Norris, James Burke, Stanley Crouch, Edward O. Wilson, Kurt Vonnegut, and Jan Morris, along with many other distinguished writers and thinkers, remains one of the best introductions to this important concept.

Finally, I appreciate the support I received from my wife, Helene Atwan, and from my children, Gregory and Emily. I dedicate this book to them.

—R. A.

CONTENTS

Preface v

INTRODUCTION 1

1 STAGING PORTRAITS 37

Home Movies 43

MEMOIR Judith Ortiz Cofer: *Silent Dancing*
BOOK COVER *Silent Dancing*
POEM Judith Ortiz Cofer: *Lessons of the Past*

Our Stuff, Our Selves 56

ESSAY John Freyer: *All My Life for Sale*
4 OBJECTS Jacket ■ Thesis ■ Fly-Fishing Patch ■ Bowling Shirt
SCREEN SHOT eBay

Representations 70

ESSAY Dorothy Allison: *What Did You Expect?*
PHOTO *Dorothy Allison, 1958*
BOOK COVER *Bastard Out of Carolina*
FILM STILL *Bastard Out of Carolina*

Confessions 79

RÉSUMÉ Anne Sexton: *Résumé 1965*
POEM Anne Sexton: *Self in 1958*
2 PHOTOS Arthur Furst: *Anne Sexton, Summer 1974* ■ Two photographs of Anne Sexton

Family Photos 89

ESSAY Janet Malcolm: *The Family of Mann*
INTERVIEW Melissa Harris: *Daughter, Model, Muse Jessie Mann on Being Photographed*
4 PHOTOS Sally Mann: *Jessie Bites* ■ *Blowing Bubbles* ■ *Emmett, Jessie, and Virginia* ■ *Candy Cigarette*

The *Mona Lisa* 103

ESSAY Joseph A. Harriss: *Seeking Mona Lisa*
ESSAY Lillian Feldman Schwartz: *The Mona Lisa Identification: Evidence from a Computer Analysis*
7 PORTRAITS Leonardo da Vinci: *The Mona Lisa* ■ *The New Yorker* cover ■ Marcel Duchamp: *L.H.O.O.Q.* ■ Vik Muniz: *Mona Lisa (Peanut Butter and Jelly)* ■ Andy Warhol: *Mona Lisa: 1963* ■ Lillian Schwartz: *Mona/Leo* ■ *Da Vinci Timeline*

Visually Speaking Audience 42 ■ Metaphor 55 ■ Assignments 126
Writing, Researching, Collaborating 128

2 TELLING STORIES 131

Memoir 138

ESSAY David Sedaris: *Ashes*
PHOTO *David and Amy Sedaris*
3 MONTAGES Danny Lyon: *Ernst* ■
Four Generations ■ *Raphe at
Seventeen*

Webcams 155

4 COMIC STRIPS Garry Trudeau: *Alex's
Real-Time Web Site* ■ *She Has Fans in
Finland* ■ *Time for Bed!* ■ *Now Turn
Toward the Camera*
5 SCREEN SHOTS Jennifer Ringley:
jennicam (two shots) ■ Diller +
Scofidio: *Refresh* (three shots)
ESSAY Sara Tucker: *Introduction to
Diller + Scofidio's* Refresh

Reality TV 165

ESSAY Lee Siegel: *Reality in America*
MEMO Anthony Jaffe: *It's a Real,
Real, Real, Real, Real World*
5 PHOTOS *Mr. Personality* ■ *American
Idol* ■ *Extreme Makeover* Before and
After ■ *Fear Factor*

The Movies 180

ESSAY Louise Erdrich: *Z: The Movie
That Changed My Life*
MOVIE POSTER *Z*
5 FILM PROMOS *X-Men 2* ■ *The Wizard
of Oz* ■ *The Matrix* ■ *The Lord of the
Rings: The Return of the King* ■ *The
Passion of the Christ*

Photojournalism 193

ESSAY Wendy Lesser: *Weegee*
ESSAY Nora Ephron: *The Boston
Photographs*
9 PHOTOS Weegee: *Newsboy* ■
Mulberry Street Café ■ *Dancing* ■
Car Crash Upper Fifth Ave. ■ Stanley
Forman: *The Boston Photographs*
(three photos) ■ Bronston Jones:
Missing (two photos)

Videocam 209

SHORT STORY Don DeLillo: *Videotape*
3 FILM STILLS *The Blair Witch Project*
■ *Sex, Lies, and Videotape* ■
American Beauty
PHOTO Jeff Wall: *Man with a Rifle*

Visually Speaking Sequence 136 ■ Assignments 218
Writing, Researching, Collaborating 220

3 SHAPING SPACES 223

Home 229

ESSAY Nicole Lamy: *Life in Motion*
PHOTO-JOURNAL Nicole Lamy: *Life in Motion*
5 PHOTOS Bill Bamberger: *Nancy and Alejandra Camarillo* ▪ *Ada Bennett and daughter Faith* ▪ *Christopher McDonald at home in Orchard Village* ▪ *Charles Evans Hughes* ▪ *The Mobile Gallery*

The Basketball Court 243

ESSAY John Edgar Wideman: *First Shot*
5 PHOTOS Paul D'Amato: *Jump Shot/Tiro con salto* ▪ Brad Richman: *Silver Springs, Maryland* ▪ *Portland, Maine* ▪ *Washington, D.C.* ▪ Dana Lixemberg: *Tamika Catchings*

Roadside Dining 256

ESSAY Nicholas Howe: *Fast-Food America*
AD Horn & Hardart: *Automat*
6 PHOTOS *Ray Kroc Standing outside McDonalds* ▪ David Butow: *Traffic along U.S. Highway 412* ▪ Lauren Greenfield: *Penny Wolfe and daughter Jessica, Santa Monica Place* ▪ *Hot Dog on a Stick employees Dominique King and Wendy Recinos at Baldwin Hills Crenshaw Plaza* ▪ *Keum Ja Chung and Hyung Hee Im in the Koreatown Plaza International Food Court* ▪ *Baldwin Hills Crenshaw Plaza*

Transit Space 265

ESSAY Pico Iyer: *Nowhere Man*
2 PHOTOS Sylvia Otte: *Airport Lounges*
CD COVER Vijay Iyer and Mike Ladd: *In What Language?*

Sacred Spaces 271

ESSAY N. Scott Momaday: *The Way to Rainy Mountain*
POEM Stephen Dunn: *The Sacred*
3 PHOTOS Joan Frederick: *Rainy Mountain, Kiowa Holy Place, Oklahoma* ▪ Jesse DeMartino: *Jason and Mike at the Cabin Near Huntsville, Texas* ▪ Mitch Epstein: *Cocoa Beach, Florida, 1983*

Cyberspace 281

ESSAY Jonathan G. S. Koppell: *No "There" There*
ESSAY Noah D. Zatz: From *Sidewalks in Cyberspace*
BILLBOARD Yahoo! *A Nice Place to Stay on the Internet*
5 SCREEN SHOTS *SimCity 4* (two shots) ▪ *The Sims* (two shots) ▪ *Google*

Visually Speaking Contrast 228 ▪ Assignments 292
Writing, Researching, Collaborating 294

4 MAKING HISTORY 297

Composing America 303

ESSAY Thomas Starr: *The Real Declaration*
ESSAY James Munves: *Going to Press*
5 DOCUMENTS *Declaration of Independence* (draft) ■ *Declaration of Independence* (broadside) ■ *Declaration of Independence* (calligraphy) ■ *Gettysburg Address* (calligraphy) ■ *Gettysburg Address* (PowerPoint)

Indian Ground 318

POEM Sherman Alexie: *The Texas Chainsaw Massacre*
ESSAY Verlyn Klinkenborg: *Sand Creek*
MOVIE POSTER *The Texas Chainsaw Massacre*
2 PHOTOS *Colonel John M. Chivington* ■ *Cheyenne and Arapaho chiefs*
DRAWING *Troops storming the Sand Creek*
MAP Brian Callahan: *Map of Sand Creek*

Chicago's Tenements 331

POEM Gwendolyn Brooks: *Kitchenette Building*
ESSAY Gordon Parks: *Speaking for the Past*
4 PHOTOS Wayne F. Miller: *Rabbits for Sale, 1948* ■ *Two Girls Waiting Outside a Tavern* ■ *One-Room Kitchenette* ■ *Three Teenagers in Kitchenette Apartment*

American Comix 340

ESSAY Art Spiegelman: *Forms Stretched to Their Limits*
8 COMICS *Plastic Man* (cover) ■ *Plastic Man* (interior cells) ■ *True Crime* ■ *Murder, Morphine and Me* (two frames) ■ *Superman* ■ *Green Lama* ■ *Wonder Woman*

Memorial 360

ESSAY Maya Lin: *Between Art and Architecture*
2 PROPOSALS Maya Lin: *Proposal and Sketches for the Vietnam Veterans Memorial* ■ Michael Arad and Peter Walker: *Reflecting Absence* (winning proposal and computer sketch for the WTC 9/11 memorial)
3 PHOTOS *Aerial View of the Vietnam Veterans Memorial* ■ *Vietnam Veterans Memorial* (two views)
AD United States Holocaust Memorial Museum: *Forgetting Would Be A Second Abandonment*

Exposing War 389

ESSAY Susan Sontag: *Watching Suffering from a Distance*
JOURNAL Thomas R. Partsch: *March 16–18, 1968*
TRANSCRIPT William L. Calley: *Court Martial Transcript*
5 PHOTOS Alexander Gardner: *A Harvest of Death, Gettysburg, July 1863* ■ Ron Haviv: *Bijeljina, Bosnia, 1992* ■ Ronald L. Haeberle: *My Lai Villagers before and after being shot by U.S. troops* (three photos)
AD Physicians Against Land Mines: *Emina's Story*

Visually Speaking Context 302 ■ Reading a Monument 359 ■ Assignments 406
Writing, Researching, Collaborating 408

5 DIVIDING LINES 411

Us and Them 417

POEM Maya Angelou: *Human Family*
ESSAY David Brooks: *People Like Us*
4 PHOTOS Dennis McDonald: *Burlington County Times, Berkeley, New Jersey* ■ Kurt Wilson: *St. Ignatius, Montana* ■ Danielle P. Richards: *Teaneck, New Jersey* ■ Gary Fandel: *West Des Moines, Iowa*
AD CAIR: *We're All Americans*

Turf War 430

ESSAY Richard Rodriguez: *Gangstas*
4 PHOTOS Joseph Rodriguez: *Chivo* ■ *Members of Florencia 13 gang outside school* ■ *Mike Estrada holds a photo of his father who is in prison* ■ *Funeral of two-and-a-half-year-old Thomas Regalado III*

Gender 440

ESSAY Penelope Scambly Schott: *Report on the Difference between Men and Women*
SHORT STORY Melanie Sumner: *Marriage*
ESSAY Jan Morris: *Herstory*
2 PHOTOS Roger Ressmeyer: *Crying Infants* ■ Eric James: *School Bus*
LOGO Todd Goldman: *Boys Are Stupid*

On the Margins 451

ESSAY Lars Eighner: *On Dumpster Diving*
ORAL HISTORY Margaret Morton: *Mr. Lee*
5 PHOTOS Jacob Riis: *Homeless Boys, New York City, c. 1890* ■ Mary Ellen Mark: *The Damm Family in Their Car, Los Angeles, California, 1987* ■ *Chrissy Damm and Adam Johnson, Liano, California, 1994* ■ Margaret Morton: *Mr. Lee's House, the Hill, 1991* ■ *Mr. Lee, Chinatown, 1992*

Color Lines 470

ESSAY Orlando Patterson: *Race Over*
4 PHOTOS *Derek Jeter* ■ *Jessica Alba* ■ *Christina Aguilera* ■ *Vin Diesel*

Animal Rights 477

ESSAY Steven M. Wise: *Why Animals Deserve Legal Rights*
ESSAY Vicki Hearne: *What's Wrong with Animal Rights*
2 ADS People for the Ethical Treatment of Animals: *They Called Him Christmas* ■ The Foundation for Biomedical Research: *Animal Research Saves Animals*

Visually Speaking Alignment 416 ■ Assignments 492
Writing, Researching, Collaborating 494

6 PACKAGING CULTURE 497

How to Make an Ad 503
DIRECTIONS Adbusters: *How to Create Your Own Print Ad*
ESSAY Chris Ballard: *How to Write a Catchy Beer Ad*
ESSAY James B. Twitchell: *How to Advertise a Dangerous Product*
PHOTO *The Coors Light Twins*
AD Miss Clairol: *Does she . . . or doesn't she?*

Advertising Morality 518
ESSAY Barbara Ehrenreich: *Dirty Laundry: Benetton's "We on Death Row" Campaign*
6 OP-ADS ONDCP: *Father* ■ *The Enforcer* ■ AICF: *Have You Ever Seen a Real Indian?* ■ NCAYV: *Children Aren't Born Violent* ■ Nike: *The Most Offensive Boots We've Ever Made* ■ Adbusters: *You're Running Because You Want That Raise*

Selling America 536
ESSAY Ian Frazier: *All-Consuming Patriotism*
2 PHOTOS *The American flag as merchandising tool*
4 ADS *I Want You for U.S. Army* ■ *Wake Up, America!* ■ *You'll Be on the Greatest Team in the World!* ■ *When was the last time you got promoted?*
SCREEN SHOT goarmy

The Mall 548
COMIC Peter Bagge: *Malls*
ESSAY David Guterson: *Enclosed. Encyclopedic. Endured.: One Week at the Mall of America*
4 PHOTOS *The Markets of Trajan, Rome* ■ *The Crystal Palace, London* ■ *The Houston Galleria* ■ *The Mall of America, Bloomington*
MIXED MEDIA Barbara Kruger: *I shop therefore I am*

Celebrity 565
ESSAY Neal Gabler: *Our Celebrities, Ourselves*
2 PHOTOS Jeff Koons: *Michael Jackson and Bubbles* ■ Timothy Greenfield-Sanders: *Jeff Koons*
2 ADS L'Oréal, *Celebrity Beauty* ■ Guess/Georges Marciano, *Anna Nicole Smith*
MAGAZINE COVER *Time* magazine: *Diana, Princess of Wales*

The Body 579
ESSAY Eric Tyrone McLeod: *Selling Out: Consumer Culture and Commodification of the Male Body*
2 ADS Charles Atlas: *How Joe's Body Brought Him Fame Instead of Shame* ■ Calvin Klein Pro Stretch: *Fredrik Ljungberg*
BOOK COVER Robert Cameron: *The Drinking Man's Diet*
2 PHOTOS *Two women with mirror and lipstick* ■ *Spilled pink nail polish*

Visually Speaking Emphasis 502 ■ Assignments 596

Writing, Researching, Collaborating 598

Glossary 601
Index 616

INTRODUCTION

INTRODUCTION

■ *Every time you see a term boldfaced or highlighted on the page—in this introduction and throughout the book—it means that the term also appears in the glossary at the end of the book, along with page numbers to help you find examples of the term in action.*

What is **convergence**? The word essentially means "coming together at a single point from different directions." We speak of several roads converging into a single road or opposing views converging into a unified position. In April 1912, the British luxury ship *Titanic* and a colossal iceberg converged in the North Atlantic in one of the twentieth century's most famous disasters. In this book you will find numerous examples of how the ongoing and large-scale convergence of technology, media, and culture is rapidly altering traditional patterns of communication and demanding new critical aptitudes and new perceptual skills. Reading, writing, and the capacity to decipher visual material will be more important than ever before.

MESSAGE

Convergences was designed to help you develop the critical tools necessary for understanding how a wide variety of verbal and visual texts are conceived, composed, targeted, interpreted, and evaluated. To do this, the book—as its subtitle suggests—encourages you to examine every selection from three different, though interrelated, critical approaches: *message, method, medium.*

COMMENT

"Now, as I understand it, *convergence* means that society today is no longer pretending that there is any difference between things like art and nature, science and religion, between the poetry a man makes out of words and the poetry God makes out of time and space, between the fight one man may fight for dignity in a ring and the fight a whole race of people may fight for dignity on the earth."

—Muhammad Ali, three-time world heavyweight champion and civil rights proponent

We want you to look at every text and think about

1. *What* it is saying—its *message.*
2. *How* it goes about saying it—its *method.*
3. *Why* it is delivered to you in a particular way—its *medium.*

These three perspectives are so interdependent that it is difficult to detach one from the others. Your final response to any given work should take all three perspectives into account. But for instructional purposes, we focus on message, method, and medium as separate windows through which we can view a chosen text.

We typically use the word **message** in three ways: as a discrete unit of communication ("You have an important message"); as a condensed moral or central idea ("What's the message of *Oedipus Rex*?"); and, informally, as a strong signal or gesture that drives home an unmistakable point ("Don't worry, he'll get the message"). In each sense, a message—whether verbal or nonverbal—has something to do with **content** and meaning, which is how we will consider it throughout this book.

When we make attempts to interpret any sort of written or visual material, we are usually asking ourselves a series of questions: What is this short story about? What does this painting mean? What is the point of this editorial? In some texts, the message or meaning may be fairly obvious. We are all familiar with reading comprehension tests in which we are asked to identify the main point of a

3

Barbara Kruger, *Untitled* **(Love is something you fall into), 1990.** Kruger mixes text and image to make incredibly strong messages. You can find more of her work on page 563. (Courtesy of the Mary Boone Gallery, New York)

Rigo 95, *Innercity Home.* San Francisco artist Rigo 04 (his name changes with the year) builds his art around the iconography of road signs. *Innercity Home*, a thirty-seven-foot square replica of an interstate sign, is painted on the side wall of a housing project in San Francisco. One tenant said of the piece, "On this street you are either on the way up or on the way down; we want to show which we are." (Photo courtesy of Gallery Paule Anglim)

4

short prose passage. Similarly, a letter to a newspaper, for example, may make a single, unambiguous point, and that's that. In some short essays, the central message may be spelled out in no uncertain terms.

In everyday communication, for convenience, we often boil the content down into its essential message. We reduce a ten-page proposal to its main point or points. We summarize a crime story in a few words. We outline the plot of an action film. But identifying the message or meaning of more complicated works can require more critical effort and even some creativity. The message may not stare us in the face or jump off the page. The main point or central idea may be impossible to state directly. There may even be more than one message. A writer or artist may do something unexpected and you may need to supply missing information to understand the work. For example, the painting on the side of the building shown here looks at first glance like an enormous highway sign. It means more when we learn that San Francisco artist Rigo worked with the people who lived in the community — a newly built project — to come up with the message you see. Rigo had originally planned to paint an arrow pointing up with the message "Sky Here." What does it mean to use the iconography of road signs in public art, and to

COMMENT

"Rigo is one of a growing, informal group of
new artists who, like many before them, tweak
society, either by defacing the symbols of
contemporary America or by inviting that
society in."

— Catherine Berwick, art critic

display the resulting work not in a gallery but in an urban landscape where the
audience is composed of commuters in their cars? If you saw the picture here
without the explanation provided by the caption, what would you think Rigo is
suggesting about community, art, or life?

In trying to identify a work's message or meaning, be careful not to merely
note its subject or theme. To say, for example, that a particular essay is "about
terrorism" is not the same as identifying its message. That requires another step:
What exactly is the essay saying about terrorism? What attitude does the author
have toward that subject? To take another example, saying that Shakespeare's
Hamlet is a play "about revenge" does not in any way tell us what message
Shakespeare wants to deliver on that complicated dramatic subject. Finding the
message can at times require a deep penetration into the text.

We usually know that a work is complex when we cannot easily produce a
brief summary or main point, a caption or callout that conveniently supplies us
with the gist of the entire work. Many works of literature and art (as you will discover in the following chapters) are intricate and contain several levels of meaning
with different and perhaps contradictory messages. In some fiction we may not
be able to find a moral center or a character whose judgments we can rely on. This
is not necessarily the result of an artistic flaw or failure; it is more than likely
intentional. In many creative works the burden of discovering a message or for-
mulating a meaning will seem to fall entirely on the reader or viewer. Many works
of art and literature do not "contain" a message or meaning the way a can of veg-
etable soup contains its ingredients. The individual reader or viewer is responsible
for the construction of meaning. It is good to be wary, of course, of reading more
into a picture or an essay than what is there, making a text more complicated than
it really is. Yet you also have to remember that "reading into" a work is the only
way to establish its meaning, to get at any internal contradictions, and to expose
hidden agendas.

Also as you look for meaning, be careful of too quickly dismissing some
works as simple, trivial, or inconsequential. Many of the texts in this book—
essays, poems, photographs, ads—look simple and casual on the surface, yet their
simplicity often masks an impressive complexity. Many great works can support
an infinite amount of "reading into." Many artists strive for a surface simplicity,

5

Ron English, *Camel Jr's.*
Ron English is an artist who appropriates the methods and media of advertising. In this example he uses colorful, inviting graphics on a billboard to make a statement about the way Camel brands and markets its products. English, who calls himself a landscape painter, began his career actually altering landscapes, painting over billboards and changing the focus of their messages from marketing to social awareness. (© Ron English)

6

even an innocence that camouflages complicated ambitions. And this is true not only of literary and artistic works. In the following chapters you are encouraged to probe deeply into works that may seem unremarkable—advertisements, web pages, maps, news photos, magazine covers, comic strips, posters, and so on. Your effort to find more than meets the eye should lead to insightful observation and productive discussion.

METHOD

The message is *what* a text is saying; the **method** is *how* it goes about saying it. Everything we see, read, or hear is expressed in a particular fashion, no matter how ordinary it seems. "Hello," "Hi," "Hey," "Dude!" "Good morning," "How's it going?" "How are you?" "Whassup?" "What's happening?" and "How you doing?" are all common greetings, but each one represents a different method for delivering a message, with varying levels of formality and tone. A Polaroid snapshot and a black-and-white studio photograph may each be taken of the same subject at the same time and in the same position, but the two pictures will suggest different moods and approaches. As you examine the selections in this book (or any text outside it), ask yourself, *Why did the author or artist choose this means of expression and not another?* Why does the advertising copywriter use just these words or the photographer shoot from just that angle? Why does the poet make just this comparison and not another one, or why does a fiction writer tell a story from one character's perspective instead of another's?

Indeed, there are countless ways to consider methods of expression. Each field—art, literature, photography, film, cartooning, television production, and so on—has developed over time its own professional vocabulary to describe specific procedures and techniques. For example, in Chapter 1 you will see how the nearly universal and mysterious appeal of Leonardo da Vinci's *Mona Lisa* was achieved by his use of a special artistic procedure that enabled him to blur outlines and create an ambiguous effect of shadows and blended colors. As you proceed through this book you will be exposed to various methods used throughout the various media.

One of the most familiar tools used to study methods of expression is **rhetoric**. Developed in ancient Greece, rhetoric was first employed to teach orators the most effective ways to express themselves and persuade audiences. Its formulations were gradually systematized and applied to all kinds of written language, with particular emphasis on the methods of constructing arguments. Traditional rhetoric has lately been brought to bear on the visual arts. We now see the convergence of traditional rhetorical methods with the techniques of film, art, photography, and graphic design. You will find a brief explanation of some of these dominant methods as they apply to various media in the glossary under rhetoric.

When we ask questions about method, we are basically asking about how a text has been composed. **Composition** is a term that can be applied to all sorts of expression. It is a key term in writing, music, art, architecture, photography, film, design, typography, and advertising. It essentially refers to the way something is made or made up (the word means "putting together"), particularly the way in which its parts are arranged and how they relate to the whole. Understanding composition requires an ability to discern the planning that went on behind the scenes. We can observe such internal elements as patterns, balance, harmony, intersecting shapes and lines, symmetry or asymmetry, repeated forms and their variations. In doing so, we are paying attention to how visual or verbal texts are built.

Look closely, say, at Weegee's photograph of two teenagers who just crashed a stolen car (p. 8), and you will see masterly composition. The street-wise photographer eloquently uses the contour of the vehicle's window to frame the incident and at the same time discovers a way to mirror the intimacy of the central image. The more closely you study the photograph, the more you will see. Though the photo may seem spontaneous and natural, that level of composition is no accident. It is artful. It involves seeing with a purpose.

Or consider a typical television news story. It can be composed in many different ways: It could be structured solely by the newscaster speaking directly into the studio cameras, or it could involve a split screen as the newscaster speaks with a reporter on the scene, or it could simply show action accompanied by the newscaster's or reporter's voiceover. Producers are keenly aware of the many possible variations in structure and design, and their decisions determine how a story will generally be positioned and perceived. We experience these broadcasting methods

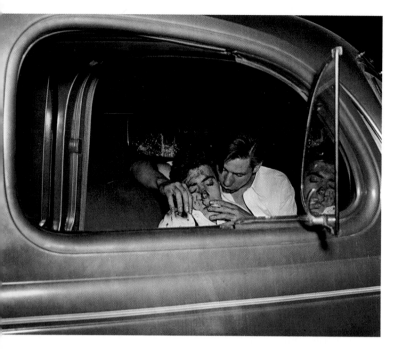

Weegee, *Car Crash Upper Fifth Ave., July 13, 1941*. This black-and-white photograph is a good example of photography as a medium that shows us an event as it actually happened — and as a text that has been carefully composed, framed, and focused on particular details. For more examples of Weegee's photography, see Photojournalism, pages 193–99.

so routinely that as viewers we usually pay no attention to the way someone in charge of production has purposefully decided to structure the news. But every now and then we become aware (sometimes alarmingly) that the same story, perhaps even with identical footage, has been covered differently by different networks. Change the compositional structure of a news story, and you change the viewers' perception of the event.

No matter what sort of text you are considering — whether a newspaper editorial, an automobile advertisement, a rap CD, or a web page — you can be sure that it will exhibit elements that reveal its main compositional characteristics. A single-page color ad for a luxury car that you flip past in *Time* magazine has been composed with the utmost care; the ad's creators paid attention to shading, balance, and textual design. A ten-word advertising headline may be the result of ten staff meetings in which a creative team worked at getting every syllable to sound just right.

In a wholly verbal text like a novel, essay, poem, or short story, composition is largely a matter of arrangement, style, and built-in patterns of sound and imagery. It is through studying composition that we can imagine the writer at work, engaged in the verbal construction of a text and occupied with its development and design. For some creative writers, the art of composition is the central consideration and subsumes all other matters. A novelist may feel that creating interesting characters or devising a compelling plot is secondary to the overall compositional design. The artistic belief is that the composition reveals the writer's genius and originality. The great American novelist Henry James thought that his characters were essentially "compositional resources"; that is, they existed mainly to serve the structure and design that James was interested in most. This is an extreme position, yet it should remind us to consider in any work how the parts are related to the whole.

In visual texts, composition is often a matter of spatial relations: How has the artist, designer, film director, or photographer first framed a space and then arranged the various elements inside it? How are images grouped? How is your eye drawn to particular features? What do you tend to notice first? What is the connection between center and periphery, foreground and background? If the visual material incorporates or is aligned with print (as in most web pages), how do they share the space? Do they seem to be competing for attention? Are they in harmony? Space can also be a decisive factor in printed texts. On one level of reading, we usually visualize **perspective** or **point of view** as well as the actual spaces being described. On another, deeper level, we can visualize a work's architecture, its spatial form as opposed to its linear or narrative structure. In other words, to fully appreciate the composition of a work, especially a serious work of literature, we may need to go beyond its temporal movement and form a mental picture—a map or diagram—of its interrelated themes and imagery. We need to picture its internal networks and circuitry.

An effective way to visualize a work's compositional method is by means of an outline. We tend to be more conscious of how to structure or arrange something when we ourselves need to produce it. Most of us, by our first year of college, have learned that essays and research papers often require an outline. The outline is essentially a planning document that reveals how the various parts of our paper will be arranged. The longer and more ambitious the project, the more complex and layered our outline will be. When we are outlining papers, we are confronting the issue of compositional structure: how our paper should be organized, which points should receive more prominence than others, how topics should be divided and subdivided, and so on. Though most students are taught to construct outlines for their own work, they don't often try outlining the already finished works they are reading. Yet going back over assigned reading texts as we prepare for discussion or writing and then trying to outline them is a very useful way of getting closer to the text (whether fiction or nonfiction) and of discovering the method behind it.

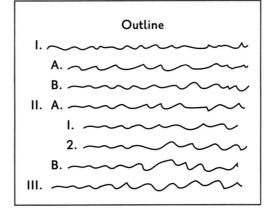

Our outlines needn't be overly detailed or comprehensive, and we can apply them to media other than print. For example, a movie is an incredibly structured visual and aural composition—so much so that one of America's top screenwriters, William Goldman, claims that structure is the single most important and most challenging element of any film script. Quite a few people, it was reported, tried outlining the sequence of Christopher Nolan's *Memento,* the intricately backwards-plotted film about short-term memory loss that captured enormous critical attention in 2001, just to understand what was happening. Such outlines as this, known as plot outlines, can be extremely useful in helping to reconstruct a narrative.

For other visual media like painting and photography, outlining may seem irrelevant because there appear to be no divisible parts: the image is all there in front of us at once, unbroken and nonsequential. Yet the imagery of these texts—especially if they are the work of professional and talented artists—has also been carefully organized and arranged. Certain images are foregrounded while others remain in the background, sometimes very faintly. Often the painting or photograph is composed so that a viewer will follow a particular angle of vision or a deliberate sequence of images that the artist calculated in the planning stage. As you examine, for example, Sally Mann's *Candy Cigarette* (p. 98), try keeping track of how your eyes take in the picture. What elements of the photo are you drawn to first? Which elements take more time to register? If you then try recording in your notes this sequence of movements, you will discover a good deal about the compositional methods of photography.

In understanding a text's method of expression, we should also be careful to observe **patterns**: regular or repetitive arrangements of elements within a text. For example, an artist may have composed a painting by arranging objects in various triangular sets (e.g., three tables, three floral vases, three windows); a piece of popular music will almost always contain regular rhythms and beats, sometimes persistently, so that they run without alteration for several minutes; a film director may show certain images over and over, perhaps using windows or glass to foreshadow ominous moments, as in Sam Mendes's *Road to Perdition* (2003). The use of such repetition may be so unobtrusively integrated into the film as a whole that we might not ever notice it unless it's pointed out to us. But the fact that we aren't conscious of such patterns while experiencing the film doesn't mean they are not exerting an effect on us. Usually, unless we are especially trained in a particular field, we need to experience a text multiple times to thoroughly understand its methods of composition. Once we detect its patterns we can articulate how a painting, song, film, or photograph achieves its effects.

COMMENT

"In a culture like ours, long accustomed to splitting and dividing all things as a means of control, it is sometimes a bit of a shock to be reminded that, in operational and practical fact, the medium is the message. This is merely to say that the personal and social consequences of any medium—that is, of any extension of ourselves—result from the new scale that is introduced into our affairs by each extension of ourselves, or by any new technology."

—Marshall McLuhan, from *Understanding Media* (1964)

MEDIUM

Every expression of meaning we encounter reaches us in some particular way: a song on the radio, a poem on a greeting card, a reminder in an e-mail message, a commercial on television, a speech at a conference, a painting on the wall of a museum. Messages and methods are often shaped for the medium that will convey them. Therefore, in order to understand the full significance of any form of expression, from a newspaper editorial to a web-page advertisement, we need to be attentive to the medium through which we experience it. Listening to a novel on tape is a different experience from reading the book, though every word is identical. Different again is seeing a movie version of the same novel. *Convergences* should help you understand those differences.

Medium is a complex term, with a wide range of connotations. For our critical purposes you need to be aware of two key meanings, both of which are important as you consider and evaluate the selections in this book. First, the word "medium" refers to the physical material an artist uses in the creation or construction of a work: Michelangelo worked with marble; Mary Cassatt with oils and pastels; Winslow Homer with watercolors; Jasper Johns with acrylics. A second, more familiar, use of the term "medium" refers to the various channels of communication by which expression is transmitted. We usually refer to these channels in the plural: "media" or "mass media." These include such print media as newspapers, books, and magazines; such electronic media as radio and television; and such interactive media as world wide web sites and CD-ROMs. It is important to remember that media are normally defined by their processes or equipment, not their content or methodology. Advertising, for example, is not in itself a medium, but it relies on various media—print, broadcasting, billboards, the Internet—to get its messages delivered. Thus, ads prepared for a multimedia campaign will significantly differ according to whether they are

Tibor Kalman, *True Stories,* **1987.** This advertisement was designed by Tibor Kalman for director (and Talking Heads lead singer) David Byrne's movie *True Stories*—movie meets ad meets tabloid, all wrapped up in a poster. (Courtesy of M&Co., New York)

11

intended for radio, television, magazines, or outdoor display—even though the advertised product remains the same.

Artists, writers, critics, and even entertainers expect us to be especially alert to the ways the medium will shape the message or influence the methods behind its creation. They are also attuned to how various media can be combined and refashioned to transform conventional patterns of expression. *Saturday Night Live* once featured an episode of a newscast in which the screen was gradually covered with so many message windows and information bars that viewers could no longer see the news room itself. The episode satirically reveals how television news now blatantly borrows from web-page design. Through its exaggerations, the comedy skit makes us notice—in case we had not before—the appropriation of one medium by another. The skit also forces us to ask some serious questions: Why has television news broadcasting adopted this web-page format? What purpose does it serve? What do television producers think they gain by imitating the Internet? And how does television's appropriation of web-page layout affect the way we receive and interpret the news?

These are the kinds of questions we hope you will ask of the selections in *Convergences.* They are not necessarily new questions—writers, artists, and critics have asked them for generations. But with the enormous growth of digital communications and the rapid convergence of media (along with the merger of mass media industries), such questions have more urgency today than ever before. The boundary lines between advertising and information, news and entertainment, reality and representation, live action and animation grow fainter and fainter with each technological innovation. It has become increasingly harder to tell if a gesture or comment was scripted or spontaneous, whether an event was staged or impromptu. Through digitization, voices can be fabricated, photos can be doctored, film can be altered. Readers and viewers need to be skeptical of claims, reports, and cited evidence; writers need to be especially cautious about the sources of their information.

It is easy to forget that media exist. We often look past the means of communication and think that what we are hearing and seeing is real. A photographic portrait may represent someone we know, but it is not that person—it is first and foremost a photograph. When we watch a breaking story on a news program, we are not witnessing the actual events—cameras and competitive news teams frame and select what we see and hear. A historical movie may be 5 percent fact and 95 percent entertainment. This may seem quite obvious, yet there is a strong tendency to confuse representation with reality. If we are to expand our ability to understand all kinds of verbal and visual texts—as this book encourages us to do—then we must develop an awareness of how media penetrates nearly everything we see and hear. We need to understand how one or another medium is always present, molding and filtering expression, even when it pretends to be invisible. Even when it disguises itself as reality.

UNDERSTANDING TEXTS

In *Convergences,* you will be asked to examine all kinds of written, oral, and visual expressions as though they are "texts" to read—and then you will be asked to write about them. The book invites you to take the concept of reading (and to some degree writing) beyond the printed word. You already read texts that are not written down on paper: you might talk about reading signs and signals, or reading someone's mind, or reading the future. You read music, maps, dials, charts, trails, and thermometers. To confirm reception, airline pilots say "I read you loud and clear." In a famous autobiographical passage, Mark Twain recalled how as a riverboat pilot he learned to "read" the Mississippi River.

Message, method, and medium are the organizing categories of the questions that follow the selections in this book; these questions and categories are formulated to help you read closely. But we also want to introduce you to what might be more familiar categories of questions for talking about *all* texts—audience, purpose, and context.

AUDIENCE

Who is the text written or composed for?

Nearly every type of expression, and certainly all published or displayed works, are designed for an **audience**. A conversation might have an audience of one; a television show, an audience of millions. It helps to think about the identity of an audience in two ways: first as the actual audience that reads, hears, or views a work or performance, and second as the hypothetical audience imagined by the creator of the work. Let's take a magazine article as an example. The actual readers would be found among the subscribers and others who happen to pick up the magazine at a newsstand or perhaps at a dentist's office. This could, of course, be a very mixed lot, with few characteristics in common. Publishers, however, do an enormous amount of costly research in an attempt to obtain at least some general characteristics of their readership. If the magazine article appeared in, say, *Rolling Stone* or *Spin,* there is an excellent chance that the actual audience consists of young males with an interest in rock music and countercultural values. The magazine

COMMENT

"When a word starts to buzz, it vibrates everywhere—as soon as 'convergence' was in the air, the world seemed to be full of things that called out to be described by it. There were now interdisciplinary scientific fields like neurolinguistics and sociobiology; new musical styles like Afropop, jazz-funk, and just plain 'world'; new entertainment genres like infomercials and advertorials. The popularity of such portmanteau words is a sign of the current fascination with hybrids and convergences."

— Geoffrey Nunberg, linguistics professor at Stanford University and usage editor of the *American Heritage Dictionary*

13

Audience Wearing 3-D Glasses, February 5, 1953. An audience watches the screening of *Bwana Devil* in Hollywood. (© Bettmann/Corbis)

Essence is written almost exclusively for African American women. Nearly all magazines (in fact, nearly all commercial media) today are designed around the interests of targeted audiences based on sex, age, race, ethnicity, political views, social and economic status, and so on.

Information about an audience can also be obtained by paying attention to the kinds of advertising or commercials that surround the material. Because advertisers pay dearly for space and time (aside from what it costs to prepare the messages themselves), they devote a great deal of research to making certain they reach precisely those audiences appropriate for their product. You will not see laxatives or luxury cars advertised on children's programs; you will see them featured on the nightly news. An observant survey of the ads in any given magazine will give you a pretty good indication of its anticipated audience.

A more interesting way to consider audience is to proceed inside out instead of outside in. That is, you infer the intended audience from the work itself. Sometimes a work will explicitly identify its audience; an essay might begin: "Are you an American parent who is fed up with the way liberals have taken over our schools?" But more often than not, you will need to consider what the writer's vocabulary level, formality or informality, and range of references tell you about the reader he or she imagines or expects. A scientific essay on the human brain written especially for neuroscientists will contain terms and references that would not appear in a similar essay targeted to a general audience. We can also look at the extent to which authors explain or qualify their references to infer the level of expertise they expect their readers to possess.

With visual works, inferring audiences may present a bit more difficulty. How can we tell from only a photograph itself the kind of audience the photographer wanted to reach? Here, clues can be found by considering the photo's subject and style. Are there elements of either that would turn off, offend, or shock some people? Do any features indicate that the photographer is saying something socially, politically, or artistically that he or she imagines a general public might not find acceptable? Does the photographer appear to identify with his or her subjects, or do you detect a satirical or hostile presence in front of the camera? When photos of the homeless appear in upscale magazines, we know the photographer did not imagine other homeless people as an audience. Also, artworks sometimes contain references and allusions to other works that could indicate a desire on the part of the artist to separate insiders from outsiders—those who get the "quotations" and those who don't.

Another feature to look for—especially in prose fiction and film—is the inclusion of someone in the work who stands in for the intended audience. Movies frequently embody the audience in a particular character; a hero or heroine may represent the values, perspectives, or ideology of the people to whom the moviemakers want to appeal. People often "identify" or have the most sympathy with one particular character in a movie. Print ads and commercials almost always feature characters that represent a vast population of consumers. Whatever kind of text you are examining, always check to see if it contains representations of an audience.

15

PURPOSE

Why was this text written or composed?

A work's **purpose** is its overall goal or aim, the effect it hopes to achieve, the agenda or cause it promotes, the response it expects to receive from an audience. All expression is designed, consciously or unconsciously, to do something—to have some immediate or delayed effect. Someone puts up a sign to warn, draws a cartoon to amuse, writes an essay to explain, pens a letter to console. The famed dramatist and screenwriter David Mamet succinctly, though perhaps extremely, observes: "People only speak to get something."

Identifying a work's purpose will help us evaluate its success or achievement. It is generally unfair to judge a work by criteria that do not apply to it. We should not approach a news story with the same literary expectations that we do a lyric poem. Nor should we judge a lyric poem by the same standards as a news story. The purposes behind the construction of each are not at all similar, even if the topic happens to be the same.

Some works may explicitly state their purpose. A newspaper editorial endorsing a political candidate may ask you directly to go out and vote for that candidate. In some political posters the message and the purpose are identical, as in the

Vietnam Veterans Memorial. As she designed the Vietnam Veterans Memorial, the architectural designer Maya Lin knew her exact purpose, yet she never deviated from making sure the monument would reflect her personal vision of what a war memorial should be and do. For her, purpose and art are the same. For more on the Vietnam Veterans Memorial and issues of representation, see Memorial in Chapter 4 (pp. 360–88). (Image courtesy of Maya Lin Studio)

famous recruiting poster depicting Uncle Sam saying, "I Want You" (p. 539). But as you will note in many of the selections that follow, identifying a work's purpose may require some probing and careful consideration. This is especially true of literary and artistic expression that deliberately avoids the outright declaration of any purpose. A talented painter who produces a work of art in support of AIDS victims may not make that purpose crystal clear—many artists do not believe in editorializing and would prefer that their audiences be hesitant in reducing their work to a slogan. Many works of art do have a political purpose (antiwar, prochoice, fascist) and it is important to recognize that purpose. Yet at the same time we should make sure we have not oversimplified the work's message or its method.

Many works or performances may be said to contain multiple purposes. An entertaining comic strip may be driven by a hidden agenda; readers can be amused even without seeing the more subtle purpose. The jokes of some comedians penetrate more deeply than casual listeners may realize. Most TV infomercials appear to propagate useful information (and the hosts try to maintain this posture), but their primary purpose is to sell something. In fact, given the way commercial realities affect every medium, many published, displayed, or performed works will be enlisted for advertising duty. When someone drinks a Coors beer in a movie, it is not because the character is thirsty but because the brewery paid the filmmakers for what's known in the marketing business as "product placement." Newspapers and magazines practice self-censorship by suppressing or altering stories and articles that might offend their major advertisers. Television shows try to avoid negative comments concerning their sponsors and may even include material that will reinforce the advertising messages. In your reading and viewing, it is a good idea to determine when information or entertainment has an unannounced commercial intent.

CONTEXT

Where has the text come from?

A book reviewer writes, "Can such trash ever be considered enlightening or entertaining?" The publishing company prints an ad with a quote from the review: "enlightening...entertaining." When this sort of distortion occurs, we usually say that something was "taken out of context." What is context? Every work or expression possesses one. The word has two primary meanings, both of which are crucial to understanding what we read, see, or hear. The first meaning pertains to whatever immediately surrounds a word, image, or passage. We often need to know an expression's context to understand it fully. The second meaning refers to a work or expression's surrounding environment or conditions—a text's historical, social, or economic context.

Understanding both meanings of context is essential to interpretation. There was (and to some extent still is) an influential set of art and literary critics who believed a work can be understood only in and by itself—in other words,

www.cnn.com The screen shot taken here is a web page, produced in the context of the news media; the context of CNN specifically; the terrorist attacks of 9/11; media coverage; possible agendas of the American government; and how people use the web to access news. All these elements are part of the context of this page.

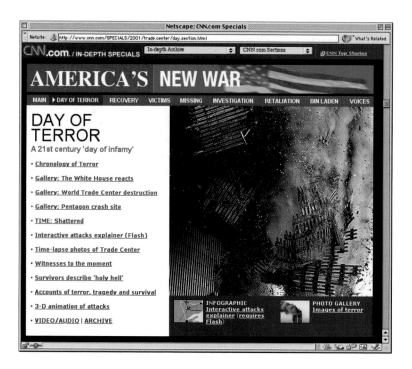

that text and context are identical. According to this school of thought, understanding *Hamlet* requires nothing more than reading the play itself (not that such a reading is nothing). Only the reading matters. No biography of its author, no knowledge of historical events that surrounded its performance, no awareness of class or economic conditions need enter into our criticism. Any references to issues or concerns outside the play might be interesting, but they contribute nothing to our understanding.

Most contemporary critics, however, prefer to work with the broader meaning of context. Thus, the physical characteristics of Shakespeare's stage, the social and economic features of the audience at the time, the acting techniques then in fashion, the political environment

> COMMENT
>
> "Context is crucial in the theater, which only pretends to exist in a world of its own creation. Most mundanely and tangibly, though not insignificantly, a show cannot escape its physical environment. It generally takes place on some kind of stage in some kind of building, the properties of which (size, location, condition) have a palpable effect on the show's artistic strategies and intent, not to mention the expectations of an audience."
>
> — Bruce Weber, theater critic

—all these factors should and would contribute to our understanding of *Hamlet*, just as they would any play from any era. In this sense, the context of a work can seem to expand infinitely. A front-page newspaper photograph can be read in the context of the surrounding stories on that page, the entire paper, the newspaper business in general, global politics, and so on. The context of a web page might be the sum of its links, perhaps the entire Internet. In *Convergences*, we do consider context, but we try to make it a workable idea that stays grounded in the work at hand.

A textbook like *Convergences* has obviously drawn all of its material from other contexts: we found essays, short stories, and poems in magazines, newspapers, books, and on the web. One piece originally appeared in *The Georgia Review*, while another one comes from *Time* or *Newsweek*; the range is wide. We found paintings, art, photographs, and other visual texts in galleries, newspapers, books, magazines, and on the web. Still, you will see most of it retooled and formatted to this context: the textbook. We have tried to give you at least a little background and information about the context for each text, sometimes even showing you how we found it.

READING AND WRITING ABOUT TEXTS

We have seen how any selection in *Convergences* can be approached through a frame that focuses on what it says (**message**), how it is composed (**method**), and how it reaches us (**medium**). We have also seen that in addition to these three key concepts, every selection can be viewed in terms of its **audience** (for whom is the work intended?), its **purpose** (what motives inspired or required it?), and its **context** (what includes or broadly surrounds it?). Throughout *Convergences* you will find questions and assignments designed to reinforce these six critical concepts that apply to all written, artistic, and commercial works.

Because the selections in this book represent so many different types of written and visual texts, from comic strips and web pages to poems and short stories, it would be unwieldy to try to cover each one in a short introduction. You will, however, find relevant information on critical approaches to various kinds of texts in the introductory notes or the accompanying commentary to most of the selections. For now, we will examine in detail approaches to three types of material that will be featured throughout all the chapters in *Convergences*: essays, photographs, and advertisements. This material makes up a large percentage of what we see and read every day. With an emphasis on verbal and visual elements—along with their many combinations—the following examples and lists of questions will be applicable to many other texts from different media that you will encounter in this book, in other courses, and in your daily life.

ESSAYS

Although essays appear in many shapes, sizes, and styles, there are today essentially three dominant types:

1. **Personal essays** in which authors write directly of their own experiences. The personal essay usually contains autobiographic details and is usually written in the first person. But personal essays can—and often do—take a reflective or meditative turn and express the writer's thoughts about certain topics or issues. The personal essay grows out of a long literary tradition and is likely to use more literary techniques than other types of essays. Personal essayists may experiment with structure, style, and compositional methods and frequently concentrate on mood, characterization, dramatic tension, figurative language, and narrative. In many ways, the personal essay can resemble fiction and even poetry. See Judith Ortiz Cofer's "Silent Dancing" on page 44 as an example of a personal essay.

2. **Informative essays** in which authors write about specific topics with the primary purpose of conveying information. Known generally as an "article," this is the most common type of essay published today; it is a staple of most

QUESTIONS FOR READING AND WRITING ABOUT ESSAYS

As with any text, reading an essay should be approached with a dual purpose: identifying the argument or message made in the essay as well as determining how that argument or message is structured. There are many essays and short stories in *Convergences*; the following questions will help you chart the development in a longer, often complicated piece of prose:

- What happens in the course of the essay? What stance is adopted at the beginning, and how does that stance change by the essay's end?

- What tone or voice does the author use? What do word choice and figurative language suggest about the essay's overall message?

- What relationship is assumed between writer and reader? Is the audience already in league with the author, or must readers be convinced to accept the author's position?

- What is the essay's purpose? To inform, persuade, or entertain? A combination of these purposes?

magazines and newspapers, where it is assumed readers turn for news reports, advice, interviews, and other types of information, whether it's a background story on the latest presidential candidate or a short history of the T-shirt. Informative essays may contain some elements of first-person writing, but the main ingredient is information about a topic. Unless it's written by an expert who has all the necessary data at her fingertips or is intended to convey information based on someone's observations as an eye-witness (e.g., a war correspondent), the informative essay is largely research-driven, and therefore writers of informative essays need to be careful about sources. Though in popular periodicals footnotes are often avoided, the writers usually mention in their essays the sources of their information and quotations. (See Joseph A. Harriss's "Seeking Mona Lisa" on p. 105 as an example of an informative essay.)

3. **Opinion essays** in which authors present their own viewpoints on an issue, usually one that is socially, politically, or culturally controversial. Our news-papers and magazines are fueled by opinion essayists who represent a spec-trum of political perspectives and usually deliver their arguments in the space of a 750-word column (which is why they are called "columnists"). Nearly every major newspaper features an editorial page, where it publishes—usually anonymously—the paper's position on a current issue, as well as an "op-ed" page (the page opposite the editorial page) that usually contains diverse opinions of regularly bylined columnists along with opinions sub-mitted to the paper by outside writers. Like personal essayists, opinion essayists often write in the first person singular and rely on personal experi-ences, but their motives are generally far less literary and autobiographical and much more concerned with supporting or denouncing a policy or a position. Columns represent only one type of opinion essay. Many maga-zines, especially those that are closely aligned with a cause or political agen-da, publish long opinion essays. Another common type of opinion essay includes reviews in all fields (e.g., literature, art, science, film) that depend on evaluative judgments supported by critical arguments. (See Lee Siegel's "Reality in America" on p. 166 as an example of an opinion essay.)

The above examples refer mainly to essays we find in print, but it's important to remember that we often hear essays read on radio and experience them being delivered on television or via the Internet. Some of Martin Luther King Jr.'s now famous essays were spoken live to huge audiences. It's important to remember also that many essays contain elements of all three popular types outlined above. Like Stephen Jay Gould's essay presented next, they blend personal experience, information, and opinion. Gould's 9/11 essay, it should be noted, first appeared as an "op-ed" item in *The Boston Globe,* and although he includes a personal episode and some information about ground zero, you will see that these elements are mainly in support of an opinion he holds about human life in general.

September 26, 2001

A TIME OF GIFTS

By Stephen Jay Gould

The patterns of human history mix decency and depravity in equal measure. We often assume, therefore, that such a fine balance of results must emerge from societies made of decent and depraved people in equal numbers. But we need to expose and celebrate the fallacy of this conclusion so that, in this moment of crisis, we may reaffirm an essential truth too easily forgotten, and regain some crucial comfort too readily forgone. Good and kind people outnumber all others by thousands to one. The tragedy of human history lies in the enormous potential for destruction in rare acts of evil, not in the high frequency of evil people. Complex systems can only be built step by step, whereas destruction requires but an instant. Thus, in what I like to call the Great Asymmetry, every spectacular incident of evil will be balanced by 10,000 acts of kindness, too often unnoted and invisible as the "ordinary" efforts of a vast majority.

We have a duty, almost a holy responsibility, to record and honor the victorious weight of these innumerable little kindnesses, when an unprecedented act of evil so threatens to distort our perception of ordinary human behavior. I have stood at ground zero, stunned by the twisted ruins of the largest human structure ever destroyed in a catastrophic moment. (I will discount the claims of a few biblical literalists for the Tower of Babel.) And I have contemplated a single day of carnage that our nation has not suffered since battles that still evoke passions and tears, nearly 150 years later: Antietam, Gettysburg, Cold Harbor. The scene is insufferably sad, but not at all depressing. Rather, ground zero can only be described, in the lost meaning of a grand old word, as "sublime," in the sense of awe inspired by solemnity.

In human terms, ground zero is the focal point for a vast web of bustling goodness, channeling uncountable deeds of kindness from an entire planet — the acts that must be recorded to reaffirm the overwhelming weight of human decency. The rubble of ground zero stands mute, while a beehive of human activity churns within, and radiates outward, as everyone makes a selfless contribution, big or tiny according to means and skills, but each of equal worth. My wife and stepdaughter established a depot on Spring Street to collect and ferry needed items in short supply, including face masks and shoe inserts, to the workers at ground zero. Word spreads like a fire of goodness, and people stream in, bringing gifts from a pocketful of batteries to a $10,000 purchase of hard hats, made on the spot at a local supply house and delivered right to us.

I will cite but one tiny story, among so many, to add to the count that will overwhelm the power of any terrorist's act. And by such tales, multiplied many millionfold, let those few depraved people finally understand why their vision of inspired fear cannot prevail over ordinary decency. As we left a local restaurant to make a delivery to ground zero late one evening, the cook gave us a shopping bag and said: "Here's a dozen apple brown bettys, our

1 Gould uses these words early in the essay—they suggest an image of balancing scales.

2 Many essays arise out a specific occasion; Gould does not disclose the occasion until the middle of the second paragraph.

3 In writing the essay Gould has accepted the responsibility to record the decency and kindness of most human beings. He then goes on to "cite but one tiny story" that encapsulates his central idea.

best dessert, still warm. Please give them to the rescue workers." How lovely, I thought, but how meaningless, except as an act of solidarity, connecting the cook to the cleanup. Still, we promised that we would make the distribution, and we put the bag of 12 apple brown bettys atop several thousand face masks and shoe pads.

Twelve apple brown bettys into the breach. Twelve apple brown bettys for thousands of workers. And then I learned something important that I should never have forgotten—and the joke turned on me. Those 12 apple brown bettys went like literal hot cakes. These trivial symbols in my initial judgment turned into little drops of gold within a rainstorm of similar offerings for the stomach and soul, from children's postcards to cheers by the roadside. We gave the last one to a firefighter, an older man in a young crowd, sitting alone in utter exhaustion as he inserted one of our shoe pads. And he said, with a twinkle and a smile restored to his face: "Thank you. This is the most lovely thing I've seen in four days—and still warm!"

4 *Note how many times in the final two paragraphs Gould repeats this relatively tiny number. He wants us to see how small the restaurant's gesture is in terms of the overwhelming number of rescue workers.*

5 *Note how Gould sets up a transformation by at first thinking the brown bettys were "meaningless" and "trivial."*

1 These words suggest the image of balancing scales. Gould wants us to understand that evil does not tip the scales. By the end of the opening paragraph we know the main point, or central thesis, of the essay: the world contains many more good people than bad. Note that he makes the point but that he hasn't yet demonstrated it; he hasn't provided us with any evidence to believe what he says. When in the essay does he offer the evidence?

2 Gould begins his essay with broad generalities and abstractions about the proportion of good and evil in the world and concludes his essay with small concrete details. Why is this technique effective? Do you think his essay would be just as effective if the opening and conclusion were reversed?

3 This is one of several times Gould explicitly states his purpose in writing the essay—an explicitness that you won't find in most essays. Earlier he says that "we have a duty, almost a holy responsibility, to record and honor the victorious weight of these innumerable little kindnesses." Where else does Gould state his purpose? Does the repetition make his essay stronger?

4 Gould reinforces this discrepancy by letting us know that they placed the twelve apple bettys "atop several thousand face masks." At the same time that he contrasts the disproportion in numbers, he also makes us aware of the contrast between practical necessities and a few delicious treats.

5 Many essays end with a sudden revelation or illumination. The writer learns something new or recognizes something he or she should already have known. Yet Gould doesn't spell out that significance for his readers; instead he ends the essay with the appreciative remarks of one of the rescue workers. How are we supposed to interpret the final quotation?

23

PHOTOGRAPHS

Compared to literature and painting, photography is a fairly recent addition to human art and culture, dating back only to the middle of the nineteenth century, when the technology for taking pictures was initially developed. At first, the general public—though impressed by what photography could achieve—did not consider it an art form because it seemed overly dependent on equipment and mechanical know-how. After all, the photographer didn't "create" a picture the way a painter created one. But toward the end of the nineteenth century, as it grew increasingly associated with painting and was adopted and even promoted by famous painters, photography grew into an accepted art form with its own famous photographers, its magazines, movements, and exhibitions. By 1928, Laszlo Moholy-Nagy, one of the world's leading photographers and critics, would claim that: "The illiterates of the future will not be those who are ignorant of literature but those who neglect photography."

What does it mean to be "literate" in photography? Moholy-Nagy's claim about photographic literacy didn't mean that the public should learn the artistic skills required to be a professional photographer, though at the time he would have had little idea how many millions throughout the entire world would one day be equipped with cameras. He meant instead that the public should learn to "read" a photograph critically, the way a work of literature is customarily read, with an understanding of its design, patterns, purpose, meaning, and methods of composition. As we come to understand photography better, we will be able to discern its aesthetic effects and range of personal creativity as well as its manipulative effects—that is, the ways in which a photograph can be falsified or distorted for political, commercial, sensational, or censorial purposes.

QUESTIONS FOR READING AND WRITING ABOUT A PHOTOGRAPH

- Is the photograph meant for a particular context? Is it solely a work of art, or does it have a commercial purpose?

- How are color choice and linear composition used to convey emotion or symbolism? Remember that no choice is a given—even in photography, the choice of black and white versus color is a deliberate one. You might ask yourself, for example, what a black-and-white photograph suggests, both historically and figuratively. Is the photographer trying to convey a sense of truth, simplicity, or nostalgia?

- Is the subject matter abstract or representational? What does this choice tell us about the relationship between the subjects represented and the idea about the subjects?

- What is the scale of the work? What might this suggest about the photographer's perception of the subject's degree of importance?

Recent advances in digitization have led to new levels of artistry, as professional and even amateur photographers can experiment with pictorial effects as never before. But digitization has also led to an increase in pictorial manipulation that worries critics and journalists, who fear that such falsified or distorted images could be used to misinform the public. Just as a reporter may abuse his responsibility by fabricating quotations, so can a news photographer doctor photos to alter the public's perception of an event or a political figure. Such deliberate manipulation of photos is only an extreme strategy for shaping public sentiment. Many news photos convey a social or political "spin" without any doctoring at all. By choosing to frame an image to include one element and exclude another, to capture a political figure with a grim or puzzled expression instead of a pleased or happy smile, news photographers (and the editors who decide which pictures will be shown) can attempt to manipulate public response.

In *Convergences,* you will find many different types of photographs—some intended to be museum-quality works of art, some professionally snapped for the daily newspaper, some meant to document social conditions, and some designed to be commercially persuasive, to name just a few. How we critically consider and evaluate any photograph will depend upon a number of factors, including its level of artistry, its particular purpose, and the context in which it appears. The more information we have about a photograph, the better equipped we are to analyze it. Despite the wide variety of photographs we experience daily, nearly every photograph we encounter invites us to distinguish certain elements and ask certain questions.

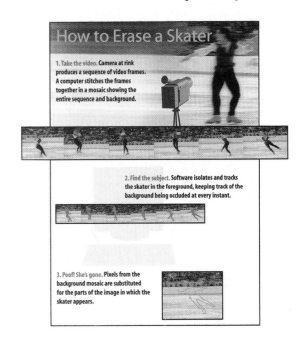

How to Erase a Skater. Technology has made it possible to erase part of a photo or film and add something not originally there — even on a live record of an event, as this clip of skater Katarina Witt shows. The accompanying article, "Lying with Pixels," explores the possible implications of this technology: "Seeing is no longer believing. The image you see on the evening news could well be a fake — a fabrication of fast new video manipulation technology." (Infographic Betsy Hayes. Photos Sarnoff Corp/IOC/USOC)

25

One thing we try to do consistently in *Convergences* is to present images with some information about their context. It helps to know, for example, that the photograph on pages 26–27, *Sara, 19,* was taken by photographer Lauren Greenfield as part of a larger exhibit and book, *Girl Culture* (2002). Greenfield's project grew out of her interest in "the element of performance and exhibitionism that seems to define the contemporary experience of being a girl." But *Sara, 19* can be read as a self-contained text without the context, as we show in the annotations that follow.

1 Framing is one way that a photographer can focus in on a particular subject. The angle of this shot—with the photographer right behind the
young woman—invites us not only to participate in the act of "checking
out" this woman but also to identify with her as the subject of attention.
The gaze of the men, which could be connected by three lines of a triangle
to her body, is another frame for the subject.

2 Lighting is a technique that many photographers use to their advantage.
The way the shadow falls further narrows the space that the young woman
has to walk in down the street (it is narrowed even more by the bodies of
the two men she's about to cross paths with), transforming a wide sidewalk
into a narrow corridor. It's almost as if she's walking a gauntlet.

3 Color choice and linear composition help underscore the impact of this
image. If the image were in black and white it might read as more "arty,"
but color adds a sense of urgency and reality, a sense that this photograph
was taken recently, of real people. The trees, which in another context we

Lauren Greenfield, *Sara, 19*
(© Lauren Greenfield 2002)

might read as a spot of color in an urban setting, are dark and constitute another wall facing the brick wall on the other side of the frame. The only spots of color are the band of exposed skin on the woman's back and the colored T-shirts and hats worn by the men—with the effect that our eye is drawn to that vulnerable exposed space between her shirt and her jeans.

4 The line that the woman is walking seems to recede directly into the space between the twin towers in the distance—the buildings underscoring a sense that this woman's walk will continue indefinitely, as she is hemmed in literally by buildings and figuratively by men looking at her. The only open space is the little patch of sky between buildings and trees.

5 If we did some research to find more about the context for this image, we would discover that Greenfield is well known for her work documenting children who grow up too fast; most of her photographs, like this one, are not posed. Knowing more about Greenfield's artistic projects would inform the way we see this single example.

ADVERTISEMENTS

Advertising represents one of the oldest forms of human communication. Traces of ads can be found throughout ancient civilizations and preliterate cultures, where images painted on walls and signboards served to alert people to trades and products. Later a steady growth of promotional writing accompanied the technological development of the printing press as countless pamphlets appeared throughout Europe trying to persuade people to colonize the New World. In fact, one of the earliest documents in American colonial history was Captain John Smith's 1631 promotional pamphlet *Advertisements for the Unexperienced Planters of New England.*

Advertising as we've come to know it, however, began in earnest around the middle of the nineteenth century with the onset of the Industrial Revolution as manufacturers sought consumers for their latest products. The pages of newspapers and popular magazines of the time were packed from top to bottom with advertisements for everything from corsets and buggies to cast iron stoves and the latest cure for the common cold. The first four-color ads began appearing in the 1890s; since then, with one technological development after another, advertising has become an inseparable part of the human environment. It not only affects the larger economy, as consumer spending fuels production and growth in capitalist nations, but also plays a significant cultural role, as it daily generates new images, symbols, and desires that have an enormous impact on the lives of many millions.

Although the purpose of advertising is largely to persuade someone to buy something, its verbal and visual modes of persuasion have multiple psychological and social effects. For example, a society daily exposed to television commercials for so-called "fast food" restaurants may find its dietary habits permanently altered

---

QUESTIONS FOR READING AN ADVERTISEMENT

As you learn to read advertisements critically, it is important to extend your notion of an ad's purpose beyond that of bottom-line profit for the company. Pairing legitimate ads with the spoof advertisements shown in this book will help you deconstruct advertisers' strategies. The following questions are meant to help you read below the deceptively simple surface of most ads:

- What is actually being sold in the ad? The product itself, or an ideology or image that the advertisers want you to associate with the product?

- Does the ad appeal to your emotions, your sense of logic, or your respect for the company's reputation? Or does it use a combination of these appeals?

- What is the most important element of the ad? Text? Graphics? A catchy slogan or jingle? The company's logo? Where is your eye first drawn? What pieces of the ad pop out?

within a generation. But that alteration, however momentous, is only one effect, for the commercials also shape lifelong attitudes toward food and eating as well as establish in consumers' consciousness a databank of logos, imagery, and psychological associations that can be tapped for other purposes, such as sports or patriotic causes. The persuasive effect of advertising, therefore, does not end with the purchase of a product but reaches deep throughout a society and becomes intricately entangled with other products, values, and sentiments. Every individual commercial for automobiles seen on television during a given evening may be trying to sell you a different car, but the cumulative cultural effect on you—and the general population—will be the prestige value of new-car ownership. After all, one central theme of American advertising has long been that the "new" is better than the "old."

The British cultural critic Raymond Williams once complained that the major problem with advertising wasn't that it promoted a materialistic view of the world but that its message was never materialistic enough. His point was that advertising traded mainly in promoting cultural values, images, and symbols and that it rarely provided useful, specific information about any product that would lead us to make rational decisions about purchasing it. One leading advertising adage is that you don't sell the steak, you sell the sizzle! Because they are so closely linked with social and cultural values, advertisements and commercials can be viewed as complex texts well worth analyzing and decoding. Much time, effort, and money go into the construction of advertisements and especially large-scale advertising campaigns. In every ad there is usally more than meets the eye or ear—visual and verbal tactics designed explicitly or subliminally to influence our individual behavior, to direct our impulses, and to promote certain social and cultural values.

In reading ads, we almost always encounter highly compressed verbal and visual texts. Print ads have little space to capture our attention, and audio commercials must do so in the span of a few seconds. Thus, language and imagery need to be as selective as possible: one phrase may have multiple meanings; one image may contain several levels of suggestion. At first, the words and images may appear so casual or common that no analysis is required. But by taking a closer look at ads and commercials we can usually see how deliberately they are crafted and how artfully they go about their business of persuasion.

In *Convergences* you will find many different kinds of advertisements, some promoting consumer products and others advocating causes or positions on controversial issues. Although these may seem like entirely different cases, both kinds of advertisements employ identical techniques and similar persuasive strategies. Though the advocacy ads may appear to be more ideologically oriented, it's important to remember that an ideology operates to a greater or lesser degree in all commercial texts. Whether the purpose of the ad is to promote a product or to advance a position—for example, to sell cigarettes or to discourage smoking—its underlying motive is persuasion.

Consider the following advertisement sponsored by a national organization founded in 1972 called Negative Population Growth (NPG). This print ad, which appeared in major magazines nationwide, addresses the issue of overcrowding and proposes a solution. The ad consists of both verbal and visual texts, with the visual text also cleverly containing a verbal text.

The Census Bureau projects that there will be 400 million people in the U.S. by 2050.

Remember when this was heavy traffic?

Ask any of your neighbors — things have changed over the past few years. Traffic has gotten worse and schools more crowded. Large developments, eight-lane highways and shopping centers have replaced open fields and wooded areas. Our suburban communities are overwhelmed by the demands of a larger population.

According to the Census Bureau, the U.S. population will grow from 284 million today to over 400 million within the next fifty years — with mass immigration accounting for over 60% of that growth. Every year, our outdated immigration policy brings over 1,000,000 people to the United States. If immigration and population growth continue at these unsustainable levels, a livable America will become a thing of the past.

Negative Population Growth
1717 Massachusetts Avenue, NW
Washington, DC 20036
(202) 667-8950

www.npg.org

1 Effective advertisements often use questions in their headlines. This strategy puts the reader directly into the ad by requiring a response. Although it doesn't look it at first, the headline is a direct address to the reader, but with the "You" implicit rather than explicit. Grammatically the question reads: "(Do you) remember when this was heavy traffic?" Note too that the headline consists of ten syllables, which — known as pentameter — is one of the most common metrical constructions in poetry. The intended effect is to sound smooth and memorable.

2 Advertising often relies on the intentional use of ambiguous words or statements. Note that in the context of the headline we do not know exactly what "this" refers to. It is also somewhat unclear from the photograph, since cars or traffic are not depicted. The reader is asked to infer from the rustic sign and its natural setting that traffic at an earlier time on some unidentified road in some unidentified community was far less of a problem than it is at present. Note that "heavy traffic" in the headline is used ironically to suggest the opposite — that is, that what we might call "heavy traffic" at one time would be considered "light traffic" today.

3 Advertisements are always addressed to some particular audience. That audience is known in the advertising profession as the "target audience." It may be defined by sex, income bracket, age, educational level, hobbies, or other characteristics. Though anyone who saw this ad in a magazine could read it, not everyone who reads it would be part of its intended target audience. For example, the target audience of this ad is someone who very likely owns a home in the suburbs and has neighbors who are worried about overcrowding. The use of "your" targets an individual reader; the later "our" makes that individual a part of a larger group brought together by a common problem. When an ad addresses "you," it wants you to identify with its target audience. This strategy is helped enormously by the English-language convention in which the word "you" can be at the same time both singular and plural.

4 The visual element of the ad shows a handmade sign set in a rural landscape. We have no idea where this place is. We see no traffic or even a road. The sign uses different typefaces, presumably painted from a stencil. It is intended to look homemade and unofficial. It clearly has no legal authority. The sign lets us know that the area is a natural habitat for many creatures. Note that the word "SLOW" on the sign is the most prominent word in the entire ad and that it reinforces the central message of the text that America must slow down its population growth.

5 The ad's first paragraph is closely linked with the headline and picture; it helps establish the image of suburban neighborhoods afflicted with problems of overcrowding due to "the demands of a larger population." But the second paragraph introduces a new point, one that is only loosely connected to the first paragraph. Not only are we presented with statistics that support the sense we may have of overcrowding, but more importantly, we are informed that this rapid growth is due to outdated "mass immigration" policies. The ad's overall purpose, then, is to warn suburban communities that their way of life is being threatened by the nation's current immigration policies. The ad hopes to generate a negative attitude toward America's immigration policies and assumes that in the long run its message will affect voting and community activism. Some versions of the ad invited more immediate action, as they included cut-out coupons that could be sent with a donation to NPG.

HOW TO USE THIS BOOK

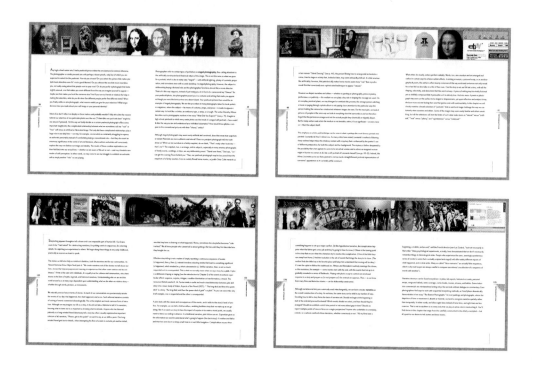

***Convergences* is a composition reader.** That means that it's a collection of material put together by an editor and a publisher to give you something to write about. Tradition has it that you, the student, will be more engaged with your own compositions when you read—or see—something that interests you. Also traditionally, composition readers usually have recognizable and familiar themes: people you know, places you've lived, groups you belong to. *Convergences* is built around some familiar and traditional themes, but when you read the introductions to the six chapters you'll see that these themes are presented in a slightly different way. Part of how the book works is it encourages you to see the layers of meaning in how we portray people, think of places, and tell stories.

***Convergences* brings together readings from different media and genres.** Composition textbooks are traditionally composed of only one medium (and usually one genre): the essay. *Convergences* brings together powerful essays with texts from all kinds of media: movies, television, the web, advertisements, comics, music, and more, helping point out the connections between the writing you do in your college classes and the visual and verbal texts that surround us all.

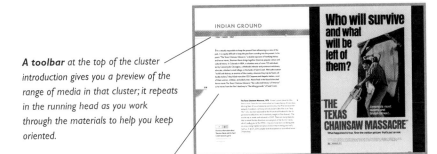

A toolbar at the top of the cluster introduction gives you a preview of the range of media in that cluster; it repeats in the running head as you work through the materials to help you keep oriented.

An introduction to each cluster explains why the editor chose to put the pieces together.

Comments and *call-out questions* throughout the text serve as pop-up windows, bringing in extra voices and direction.

A caption for each text in a cluster gives you a bit of background information about where the piece came from and who created it.

Message, Method, and Medium questions end each cluster. These questions ask you to use those three different critical lenses to consider the material as a group.

33

Six clusters in each chapter group together a wide variety of texts, revealing the layers of our cultural conversations. Here's an example. A traditional composition reader might simply present a reading on diversity. In Chapter 5, an essay by David Brooks, "People Like Us," is grouped with a poem by Maya Angelou, "The Human Family," images from *America 24/7,* a groundbreaking photographic project that set out to "capture America," and an advertisement from the *Islam in America* series. Everything you read in *Convergences* is connected to something else. The shaded "toolbars" mark the beginning of a cluster. A caption for each text in a cluster gives you a bit of background information about where the piece came from and who created it. Comments and call-out questions within clusters serve as pop-up windows, bringing in extra voices and direction. At the end of each cluster are three questions: message/method/medium. These questions ask you to think about what texts say, how they go about saying it, and what impact medium has on message.

Visually Speaking definitions at the beginning of each chapter focus on a fundamental term of visual rhetoric, inviting you to apply it to the materials you're about to read.

Visually Speaking assignments at the end of each chapter offer creative exercises to compose your own multimedia texts.

34

Assignments at the end of each chapter invite you to compose your own texts about what you've read.

In each chapter, there are two or more moments where you're asked to consider Visually Speaking. At the beginning of each chapter is a Visually Speaking concept, like the one for Chapter 2 shown here, on sequence. These pages offer definitions for an important rhetorical concept and invite you to extend your exploration with the CD-ROM of exercises that came with the book, **ix visual exercises**. At the end of each chapter are two Visually Speaking assignments that offer creative exercises to compose your own multimedia texts.

Each chapter ends with Questions for Writing, Researching, and Collaborating, prompting you to make connections within the book and outside it as you write critical responses to what you've read.

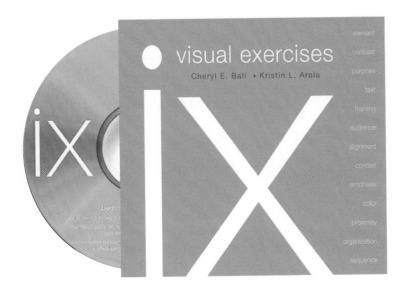

When you see a cube icon ▦ or a go to bar `>` `go` , you're being directed to more content on the CD-ROM of visual exercises that came with your book OR you're being sent to the companion web site, which has lots of useful links and additional content.

At the end of the book, a Glossary defines useful concepts for talking about traditional and visual rhetoric, marketing, or media. **Bold-faced terms** throughout the book highlight concepts that are particularly useful and that you'll find in the glossary.

COMMENT

"In schools and colleges, in these audio-visual days, doubt has been raised as to the future of reading — whether the printed word is on its last legs. One college president has remarked that in fifty years 'only five per cent of the people will be reading.' For this, of course, one must be prepared. But how prepared? To us it would seem that even if only one person out of a hundred and fifty million should continue as a reader, he would be the only one worth saving, the nucleus around which to found a university. We think this not impossible person, this Last Reader, might very well stand in the same relation to the community as the queen bee to the colony of bees, and that the others would quite properly dedicate themselves wholly to his welfare, serving special food and building special accommodations."

—E. B. White, circa 1940

1

STAGING PORTRAITS

Any high school senior who's had a yearbook picture taken has encountered a common dilemma. The photographer or studio presents you with perhaps a dozen proofs, only one of which you are expected to select for the yearbook. How do you choose? Do you select the picture that makes you look most attractive even if it's not a good likeness? Do you choose the one that most resembles you, not really caring about that pimple next to your nose? Or do you prefer a photograph that looks slightly unusual, one that makes you seem different from the way you imagine yourself to appear — maybe one that makes you look like someone else? And if you turn to friends or relatives for help in making the selection, what do you do when five different people prefer five different shots? When you finally settle on one photograph, what *reasons* would you give for your selection? What larger decision have you made about your self-image or your personal identity?

Most of us don't reflect so deeply on these matters and probably wouldn't fully articulate the reasons behind our selection of one particular photo over the rest ("I think this one just looks best" might be our answer if pressed). Yet the way we finally decide on a certain yearbook photograph offers some important insights into the complicated relationship between what we sometimes call our "real" or "true" self versus an artificial or fabricated image. Not only do these complicated relationships play a large role in our daily lives — we may, for example, see ourselves as constantly struggling to express an authentic personality instead of comfortably playing a conventional role — but they also exert an enormous significance in the world of art and literature, where authors and artists self-consciously explore the ways we fashion our image and identity. The results of these creative explorations can then fold back into our actual lives — whether we are aware of the art or not — and may stimulate new modes of self-perception. In other words, we may come to see our struggle to establish an authentic self as simply another "role" we are playing.

Photographers refer to certain types of portraiture as **staged photography**, thus calling attention to the artificially constructed and theatrical nature of the image. This is not the same as when we pose for a portrait, which is also in many ways "staged" — with artificial lighting, plenty of cosmetic preparation, and sometimes even with a scenic backdrop. In staged photography, however, the subject is deliberately playing a fictional role and the photographer functions almost like a movie director. Think of it this way: suppose, instead of just having you sit in front of a camera and say "cheese" for your yearbook photo, the photographer posed you in a costume and setting that made you appear as though you were the lone survivor on a desert island. Your yearbook picture then would be an example of staged photography. We see this procedure in many photographs taken for book jackets or magazines, where the subject — by means of costume, props, and pose — is made to appear a certain way: to look like a scholar, an outdoorsy type, a vamp, or a tough. The writer Dorothy Allison describes such a photographic incident in her essay "What Did You Expect?" (see p. 71). Imagine a high school yearbook in which every senior photo was the result of a staged self-portrait — how would it alter the way you saw and understood your individual classmates? How would these photos compare to the conventional pictures with their "cheesy" smiles?

Although staged photographs may seem overly artificial and contrived, does that mean that snapshots or instant Polaroids are more authentic and natural? Does our passport photograph tell the truth about us? When we see ourselves in a family snapshot, do we think, "That's really what I look like — that's me"? The snapshot, too, is an image, and its subjects, especially in many amateur photographs of family events, weddings, or trips, are very deliberately posed. "Stand over there," Dad says, "so I can get the Leaning Tower behind you." Thus, our yearbook photograph may be less posed than the snapshots of a family vacation. Even in crudely filmed home movies, as Judith Ortiz Cofer reminds us

in her memoir "Silent Dancing" (see p. 44), the person filming tries to arrange and orchestrate a scene, tries to stage an activity that, looked at later, may seem awkwardly artificial. It is that amateur-like artificiality, however, that paradoxically makes home movies seem more "real" than a professional film that consciously uses sophisticated techniques to appear "natural."

However we depict ourselves and others — whether in painting or photography, prose or poetry, performance or publicity — the medium we use plays a key role in shaping the message we send. On an everyday, practical plane, we may disregard or overlook this process; the average person watching a movie or paging through a photo album is not paying close attention to the particular ways the person holding the camera has constructed whatever images she sees. For the most part, we look at pictures of people in the same way we look at everything else that surrounds us and we therefore forget that the pictures are images and not the actual people they chemically or digitally depict. But for many authors and artists the medium is not invisible; rather, it's as significant — or even more so — than the subject itself.

This emphasis on artistry and technique can be seen in what is perhaps the most famous portrait ever painted: Leonardo da Vinci's *Mona Lisa*. As many critics have noted, Leonardo's method of blurring sharp outlines helps imbue the shadowy woman with a mystery that is enhanced by the painter's use of different perspectives for both the subject and her background. The mystery is further deepened by the possibility that what appears to some to be an actual woman and to others an imagined woman might in fact be no woman at all, but a self-portrait of Leonardo himself (see pp. 119–21). Indeed, the *Mona Lisa* invites us to see that a portrait is not so much a straightforward pictorial representation of someone's appearance as it is a totally artful construct.

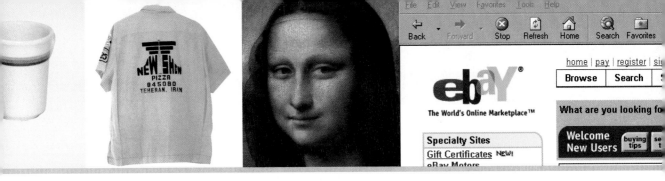

What artists do visually, writers perform verbally. Words, too, are a medium and are arranged and crafted in certain ways to achieve certain effects. In writing a memoir, a personal essay, or an autobiographical poem, the author is often keenly conscious of the way words and sentences not only reveal his or her life but also take on a life of their own. Our life story is not our life but a *story,* with all the shaping, selectivity, and distortions that the word conveys. A piece of writing may be wholly fictional yet so skillfully composed that it persuades us it is entirely true. And vice versa. A poem or photograph may seem on the surface to be staged or dispassionate, yet upon reflection and analysis it may disclose more sincere feeling than one that gushes over with sentimentality. In this chapter we will closely examine a broad selection of "portraits" that in word and image challenge the way we customarily view ourselves and others. Some of the images may seem overly familiar and others unsettling, but all the selections will test the limits of such value-laden terms as "natural" versus "artificial," "real" versus "phony," and "spontaneous" versus "contrived."

Audience

Nearly every visual and verbal text you can imagine is composed for an audience. A portrait might have been commissioned originally for one person or for a small circle of family and friends; hanging in a museum it's shown to a different sort of audience. An NFL game is a spectacle performed for a huge audience, live and at home in front of the television. Every portrait that you see in this chapter has been created for an audience, although it's not always obvious or transparent who that audience might be. As you explore this chapter, ask yourself what clues in the essay or image suggest who was meant to read, see, and/or appreciate that particular text.

Interior view showing art galleries of the Kulturforum in Berlin, 2003. (© Ludovic Maisant /Corbis)

Go to **ix visual exercises** to explore how the concepts of **audience** and **framing** work in visual texts.

HOME MOVIES

Photographs and home movies can both stimulate our memories — sometimes, as is often the case in early childhood, even replacing or reconstructing what we know happened to us. Because so much of childhood occurs in a time when we think primarily in pictures, photographs and poetry are particularly effective media for conveying a time and place. In *Silent Dancing: A Partial Remembrance of a Puerto Rican Childhood* (1990), Judith Ortiz Cofer, a poet and memoirist, collects prose and poetry that play with photographs, home movies, and memories from her childhood, filling in real and imagined details of her bilingual, bicultural experiences in New Jersey and Puerto Rico.

Born in Puerto Rico in 1952, Judith Ortiz Cofer is the author of a number of award-winning books, many of which crisscross the boundaries of poetry, fiction, and nonfiction. In addition to *Silent Dancing,* there are a novel, *The Line of the Sun* (1989); poetry collections, such as *Terms of Survival* (1987) and *Reaching the Mainland* (1986); another memoir, *Woman in Front of the Sun: On Becoming a Writer* (2000); *The Latin Deli: Prose and Poetry* (1993); *An Island Like You: Stories of the Barrio* (1995); and *The Year of Our Revolution: New and Selected Stories and Poems* (1998). Cofer is a professor of English and creative writing at the University of Georgia.

43

> go

For more information about Judith Ortiz Cofer, go to bedfordstmartins.com/ convergences.

COMMENT

"In writing these 'essays' (the Spanish word for essay, *ensayo,* suits my meaning better — it can mean 'a rehearsal,' an exercise or practice), I faced the possibility that the past is mainly a creation of the imagination also, although there are facts one can research and confirm."

—Judith Ortiz Cofer

Judith Ortiz Cofer, *Silent Dancing*. In "Silent Dancing," the title essay of her collection, Judith Ortiz Cofer revisits the Puerto Rican community of her New Jersey childhood by means of a five-minute silent home movie made by one of her relatives at a New Year's Eve party. Though clumsily shot, the film is in color — "the only complete scene in color I can recall from those years," the author says.

Judith Ortiz Cofer
SILENT DANCING

We have a home movie of this party. Several times my mother and I have watched it together, and I have asked questions about the silent revelers coming in and out of focus. It is grainy and of short duration, but it's a great visual aid to my memory of life at that time. And it is in color—the only complete scene in color I can recall from those years.

We lived in Puerto Rico until my brother was born in 1954. Soon after, because of economic pressures on our growing family, my father joined the United States Navy. He was assigned to duty on a ship in Brooklyn Yard—a place of cement and steel that was to be his home base in the States until his retirement more than twenty years later. He left the Island first, alone, going to New York City and tracking down his uncle who lived with his family across the Hudson River in Paterson, New Jersey. There my father found a tiny apartment in a huge tenement that had once housed Jewish families but was just being taken over and transformed by Puerto Ricans, overflowing from New York City. In 1955 he sent for us. My mother was only twenty years old, I was not quite three, and my brother was a toddler when we arrived at *El Building,* as the place had been christened by its newest residents.

My memories of life in Paterson during those first few years are all in shades of gray. Maybe I was too young to absorb vivid colors and details, or to discriminate between the slate blue of the winter sky and the darker hues of the snow-bearing clouds, but that single color washes over the whole period. The building we lived in was gray, as were the streets, filled with slush the first few months of my life there. The coat my father had bought for me was similar in color and too big; it sat heavily on my thin frame.

I do remember the way the heater pipes banged and rattled, startling all of us out of sleep until we got so used to the sound that we automatically shut it out or raised our voices above the racket. The hiss from the valve punctuated my sleep (which has always been fitful) like a nonhuman presence in the room—a dragon sleeping at the entrance of my childhood. But the pipes were also a connection to all the other lives being lived around us. Having come from a house designed for a single family back in Puerto Rico—my mother's extended-family home—it was curious to know that strangers lived under our floor and above our heads, and that the heater pipe went through everyone's apartments. (My first spanking in Paterson came as a result of playing tunes on the pipes in my room to see if there would be an answer.) My mother was as new to this concept of beehive life as I was, but she had been given strict orders by my father to keep the doors locked, the noise down, ourselves to ourselves.

It seems that Father had learned some painful lessons about prejudice while searching for an apartment in Paterson. Not until years later did I hear how much resistance he had encountered with landlords who were panicking at the influx of Latinos into a neighborhood that had been Jewish for a couple of generations. It made no difference that it was the American phenomenon of ethnic turnover which was changing the urban core of Paterson, and that the human flood could not be held back with an accusing finger.

"You Cuban?" one man had asked my father, pointing at his name tag on the Navy uniform—even though my father had the fair skin and light-brown hair of his northern Spanish background, and the name Ortiz is as common in Puerto Rico as Johnson is in the United States.

"No," my father had answered, looking past the finger into his adversary's angry eyes. "I'm Puerto Rican."

"Same shit." And the door closed.

My father could have passed as European, but we couldn't. My brother and I both have our mother's black hair and olive skin, and so we lived in El Building and visited our great-uncle and his fair children on the next block. It was their private joke that they were the German branch of the family. Not many years later that area too would be mainly Puerto Rican. It was as if the heart of the city map were being gradually colored brown—*café con leche*[1] brown. Our color.

The movie opens with a sweep of the living room. It is "typical" immigrant Puerto Rican decor for the time: The sofa and chairs are square and hard-looking, upholstered in bright colors (blue and yellow in this instance), and covered with the transparent plastic that furniture salesmen then were so adept at convincing women to buy. The linoleum on the floor is light blue; if it had been subjected to spike heels (as it was in most places), there were dime-sized indentations all over it that cannot be seen in this movie. The room is full of people dressed up: dark suits for the men, red dresses for the women. When I have asked my mother why most of the women are in red that night, she has shrugged, "I don't remember. Just a coincidence." She doesn't have my obsession for assigning symbolism to everything.

---

[1] *café con leche:* Coffee with cream. In Puerto Rico it is sometimes prepared with boiled milk. [All notes are Cofer's.]

45

The three women in red sitting on the couch are my mother, my eighteen-year-old cousin, and her brother's girlfriend. The novia *is just up from the Island, which is apparent in her body language. She sits up formally, her dress pulled over her knees. She is a pretty girl, but her posture makes her look insecure, lost in her full-skirted dress, which she has carefully tucked around her to make room for my gorgeous cousin, her future sister-in-law. My cousin has grown up in Paterson and is in her last year of high school. She doesn't have a trace of what Puerto Ricans call* la mancha *(literally, the stain: the mark of the new immigrant—something about the posture, the voice, or the humble demeanor that makes it obvious to everyone the person has just arrived on the mainland). My cousin is wearing a tight, sequined, cocktail dress. Her brown hair has been lightened with peroxide around the bangs, and she is holding a cigarette expertly between her fingers, bringing it up to her mouth in a sensuous arc of her arm as she talks animatedly. My mother, who has come up to sit between the two women, both only a few years younger than herself, is somewhere between the poles they represent in our culture.*

It became my father's obsession to get out of the barrio, and thus we were never permitted to form bonds with the place or with the people who lived there. Yet El Building was a comfort to my mother, who never got over yearning for *la isla.* She felt surrounded by her language: The walls were thin, and voices speaking and arguing in Spanish could be heard all day. *Salsas* blasted out of radios, turned on early in the morning and left on for company. Women seemed to cook rice and beans perpetually—the strong aroma of boiling red kidney beans permeated the hallways.

Though Father preferred that we do our grocery shopping at the supermarket when he came home on weekend leaves, my mother insisted that she could cook only with products whose labels she could read. Consequently, during the week I accompanied her and my little brother to *La Bodega*—a hole-in-the-wall grocery store across the street from El Building. There we squeezed down three narrow aisles jammed with various products. Goya's and Libby's—those were the trademarks trusted by *her mamá,* so my mother bought many cans of Goya beans, soups, and condiments, as well as little cans of Libby's fruit juices for us. And she also bought Colgate toothpaste and Palmolive soap. (The final *e* is pronounced in both these products in Spanish, so for many years I believed that they were manufactured on the Island. I remember my surprise at first hearing a commercial on television in which Colgate rhymed with "ate.") We always lingered at La Bodega, for it was there that Mother breathed best, taking in the familiar aromas of the foods she knew from Mamá's kitchen. It was also there that she got to speak to the other women of El Building without violating outright Father's dictates against fraternizing with our neighbors.

Yet Father did his best to make our "assimilation" painless. I can still see him carrying a real Christmas tree up several flights of stairs to our apartment, leaving a trail of aromatic pine. He carried it formally, as if it were a flag in a parade. We were the only ones in El Building that I knew of who got presents on both Christmas day AND *día de Reyes,* the day when the Three Kings brought gifts to Christ and to Hispanic children.

Our supreme luxury in El Building was having our own television set. It must have been a result of Father's guilt feelings over the isolation he had imposed on us, but we were among the first in the barrio to have one. My brother quickly became an avid watcher of Captain Kangaroo and Jungle Jim, while I loved all the series showing families. By the time I started first grade, I could have drawn a map of Middle America as exemplified by the lives of characters in *Father Knows Best, The Donna Reed Show, Leave It to Beaver, My Three Sons,* and (my favorite) *Bachelor Father,* where John Forsythe treated his adopted teenage daughter like a princess because he was rich and had a Chinese houseboy to do everything for him. In truth, compared to our neighbors in El Building, *we* were rich. My father's Navy check provided us with financial security and a standard of life that the factory workers envied. The only thing his money could not buy us was a place to live away from the barrio—his greatest wish, Mother's greatest fear.

In the home movie the men are shown next, sitting around a card table set up in one corner of the living room, playing dominoes. The clack of the ivory pieces was a familiar sound. I heard it in many houses on the Island and in many apartments in Paterson. In Leave It to Beaver, *the Cleavers played bridge in every other episode; in my childhood, the men started every social occasion with a hotly debated round of dominoes. The women would sit around and watch, but they never participated in the games.*

Here and there you can see a small child. Children were always brought to parties and, whenever they got sleepy, were put to bed in the host's bedroom. Babysitting was a concept unrecognized by the Puerto Rican women I knew: A responsible mother did not leave her children with any stranger. And in a culture where children are not considered intrusive, there was no need to leave the children at home. We went where our mother went.

Of my preschool years I have only impressions: the sharp bite of the wind in December as we walked with our parents toward the brightly lit stores downtown; how I felt like a stuffed doll in my heavy coat, boots, and mittens; how good it was to walk into the five-and-dime and sit at the counter drinking hot chocolate. On Saturdays our whole family would walk downtown to shop at the big department stores on Broadway. Mother bought all our clothes at Penney's and Sears, and she liked to buy her dresses at the women's specialty shops like Lerner's and Diana's. At some point we'd go into Woolworth's and sit at the soda fountain to eat.

We never ran into other Latinos at these stores or when eating out, and it became clear to me only years later that the women from El Building shopped mainly in other places—stores owned by other Puerto Ricans or by Jewish merchants who had philosophically accepted our presence in the city and decided to make us their good customers, if not real neighbors and friends. These establishments were located not downtown but in the blocks around our street, and they were referred to generically as *La Tienda, El Bazar, La Bodega, La Botánica.* Everyone knew what was meant. These were the stores where your face did not turn a clerk to stone, where your money was as green as anyone else's.

One New Year's Eve we were dressed up like child models in the Sears catalog: my brother in a miniature man's suit and bow tie, and I in black patent-leather shoes and a frilly dress with several layers of crinoline underneath. My mother wore a bright red dress that night, I remember, and spike heels; her long black hair hung to her waist. Father, who usually wore his Navy uniform during his short visits home, had put on a dark civilian suit for the occasion: We had been invited to his uncle's house for a big celebration. Everyone was excited because my mother's brother Hernan—a bachelor who could indulge himself with luxuries—had bought a home movie camera, which he would be trying out that night.

Even the home movie cannot fill in the sensory details such a gathering left imprinted in a child's brain. The thick sweetness of women's perfumes mixing with the ever-present smells of food cooking in the kitchen: meat and plantain *pasteles,* as well as the ubiquitous rice dish made special with pigeon peas—*gandules*—and seasoned with precious *sofrito*[2] sent up from the Island by somebody's mother or smuggled in by a recent traveler. *Sofrito* was one of the items that women hoarded, since it was hardly ever in stock at La Bodega. It was the flavor of Puerto Rico.

The men drank Palo Viejo rum, and some of the younger ones got weepy. The first time I saw a grown man cry was at a New Year's Eve party: He had been reminded of his mother by the smells in the kitchen. But what I remember most were the boiled *pasteles*—plantain or yucca rectangles stuffed with corned beef or other meats, olives, and many other savory ingredients, all wrapped in banana leaves. Everybody had to fish one out with a fork. There was always a "trick" pastel—one without stuffing—and whoever got that one was the "New Year's Fool."

There was also the music. Long-playing albums were treated like precious china in these homes. Mexican recordings were popular, but the songs that brought tears to my mother's eyes were sung by the melancholy Daniel Santos, whose life as a drug addict was the stuff of legend. Felipe Rodríguez was a particular favorite of couples, since he sang about faithless women and brokenhearted men. There is a snatch of one lyric that has stuck in my mind like a needle on a worn groove: *De piedra ha de ser mi cama, de piedra la cabezera ... la mujer que a mi me quiera ... ha de quererme de veras. Ay, Ay, Ay, corazón, porque no amas.*[3] ... I must have heard it a thousand times since the idea of a bed made of stone, and its connection to love, first troubled me with its disturbing images.

---

[2]*sofrito:* A cooked condiment. A sauce composed of a mixture of fatback, ham, tomatoes, and many Island spices and herbs. It is added to many typical Puerto Rican dishes for a distinctive flavor.

[3]*De piedra ha de ser ... amas:* Lyrics from a popular romantic ballad (called a *bolero* in Puerto Rico). Freely translated: "My bed will be made of stone, of stone also my headrest (or pillow), the woman who (dares to) loves me, will have to love me for real. Ay, Ay, Ay, my heart, why can't you (let me) love...."

The five-minute home movie ends with people dancing in a circle—the creative filmmaker must have set it up, so that all of them could file past him. It is both comical and sad to watch silent dancing. Since there is no justification for the absurd movements that music provides for some of us, people appear frantic, their faces embarrassingly intense. It's as if you were watching sex. Yet for years I've had dreams in the form of this home movie. In a recurring scene, familiar faces push themselves forward into my mind's eyes, plastering their features into distorted close-ups. And I'm asking them: "Who is *she*? Who is the old woman I don't recognize? Is she an aunt? Somebody's wife? Tell me who she is."

"See the beauty mark on her cheek as big as a hill on the lunar landscape of her face—well, that runs in the family. The women on your father's side of the family wrinkle early; it's the price they pay for that fair skin. The young girl with the green stain on her wedding dress is *La Novia*—just up from the Island. See, she lowers her eyes when she approaches the camera, as she's supposed to. Decent girls never look at you directly in the face. *Humilde,* humble, a girl should express humility in all her actions. She will make a good wife for your cousin. He should consider himself lucky to have met her only weeks after she arrived here. If he marries her quickly, she will make him a good Puerto Rican–style wife; but if he waits too long, she will be corrupted by the city—just like your cousin there."

"She means me. I do what I want. This is not some primitive island I live on. Do they expect me to wear a black mantilla on my head and go to mass every day? Not me. I'm an American woman, and I will do as I please. I can type faster than anyone in my senior class at Central High, and I'm going to be a secretary to a lawyer when I graduate. I can pass for an American girl anywhere—I've tried it. At least for Italian, anyway—I never speak Spanish in public. I hate these parties, but I wanted the dress. I look better than any of these *humildes* here. *My* life is going to be different. I have an American boyfriend. He is older and has a car. My parents don't know it, but I sneak out of the house late at night sometimes to be with him. If I marry him, even my name will be American. I hate rice and beans—that's what makes these women fat."

"Your *prima*[4] is pregnant by that man she's been sneaking around with. Would I lie to you? I'm your *Tía Política,*[5] your great-uncle's common-law wife—the one he abandoned on the Island to go marry your cousin's mother. *I* was not invited to this party, of course, but I

---

[4]*prima:* Female cousin.
[5]*Tía Política:* Aunt by marriage.

came anyway. I came to tell you that story about your cousin that you've always wanted to hear. Do you remember the comment your mother made to a neighbor that has always haunted you? The only thing you heard was your cousin's name, and then you saw your mother pick up your doll from the couch and say: 'It was as big as this doll when they flushed it down the toilet.' This image has bothered you for years, hasn't it? You had nightmares about babies being flushed down the toilet, and you wondered why anyone would do such a horrible thing. You didn't dare ask your mother about it. She would only tell you that you had not heard her right, and yell at you for listening to adult conversations. But later, when you were old enough to know about abortions, you suspected.

"I am here to tell you that you were right. Your cousin was growing an *Americanito* in her belly when this movie was made. Soon after she put something long and pointy into her pretty self, thinking maybe she could get rid of the problem before breakfast and still make it to her first class at the high school. Well, *Niña,*[6] her screams could be heard downtown. Your aunt, her mamá, who had been a midwife on the Island, managed to pull the little thing out. Yes, they probably flushed it down the toilet. What else could they do with it — give it a Christian burial in a little white casket with blue bows and ribbons? Nobody wanted that baby — least of all the father, a teacher at her school with a house in West Paterson that he was filling with real children, and a wife who was a natural blond.

"Girl, the scandal sent your uncle back to the bottle. And guess where your cousin ended up? Irony of ironies. She was sent to a village in Puerto Rico to live with a relative on her mother's side: a place so far away from civilization that you have to ride a mule to reach it. A real change in scenery. She found a man there — women like that cannot live without male company — but believe me, the men in Puerto Rico know how to put a saddle on a woman like her. *La Gringa,*[7] they call her. Ha, ha, ha. *La Gringa* is what she always wanted to be...."

The old woman's mouth becomes a cavernous black hole I fall into. And as I fall, I can feel the reverberations of her laughter. I hear the echoes of her last mocking words: *La Gringa, La Gringa!* And the conga line keeps moving silently past me. There is no music in my dream for the dancers.

---

[6]*Niña:* Girl.

[7]*La Gringa:* Derogatory epithet used here to ridicule a Puerto Rican girl who wants to look like a blonde North American.

When Odysseus visits Hades to see the spirit of his mother, he makes an offering of sacrificial blood, but since all the souls crave an audience with the living, he has to listen to many of them before he can ask questions. I, too, have to hear the dead and the forgotten speak in my dream. Those who are still part of my life remain silent, going around and around in their dance. The others keep pressing their faces forward to say things about the past.

My father's uncle is last in line. He is dying of alcoholism, shrunken and shriveled like a monkey, his face a mass of wrinkles and broken arteries. As he comes closer I realize that in his features I can see my whole family. If you were to stretch that rubbery flesh, you could find my father's face, and deep within *that* face—my own. I don't want to look into those eyes ringed in purple. In a few years he will retreat into silence, and take a long, long time to die. *Move back, Tío,* I tell him. *I don't want to hear what you have to say. Give the dancers room to move. Soon it will be midnight. Who is the New Year's Fool this time?*

51

Cover of *Silent Dancing: A Partial Remembrance of a Puerto Rican Childhood,* by Judith Ortiz Cofer. In the last essay of *Silent Dancing,* titled "The Last Word," Cofer describes a "face she's memorized: that of a very solemn two-year-old dressed in a fancy dress. . . . I am not smiling in any of these pictures." (Reprinted by permission of Arte Publico Press)

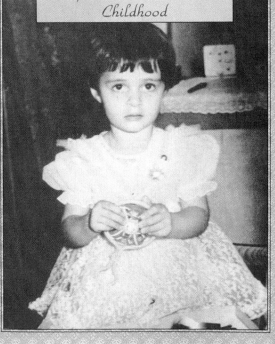

SILENT
DANCING:
A Partial Remembrance
of a Puerto Rican
Childhood

JUDITH ORTIZ COFER

Judith Ortiz Cofer, *Lessons of the Past*. Cofer is best known for her poetry. "Lessons of the Past" describes a significant party of her childhood — like the one recorded in the home movie described in "Silent Dancing," except that this one is also the scene of the recurring argument with her mother described in "The Last Word." Her mother says she did not fall in the fire; Cofer remembers that she did.

Judith Ortiz Cofer
LESSONS OF THE PAST

FOR MY DAUGHTER

I was born the year my father learned to march in step
with other men, to hit bull's eyes, to pose for sepia photos
in dress uniform outside Panamanian nightspots — pictures
he would send home to his pregnant teenage bride inscribed:
To my best girl.

My birth made her a madonna, a husbandless young woman
with a legitimate child, envied by all the tired women
of the pueblo as she strolled my carriage down dirt roads,
both of us dressed in fine clothes bought with army checks.

When he came home,
he bore gifts: silk pajamas from the orient for her; a pink
iron crib for me. People filled our house to welcome him.
He played Elvis loud and sang along in his new English.
She sat on his lap and laughed at everything.
They roasted a suckling pig out on the patio. Later,
no one could explain how I had climbed over the iron bars
and into the fire. Hands lifted me up quickly, but not before
the tongues had licked my curls.

There is a picture of me
taken soon after: my hair clipped close to my head,
my eyes enormous — about to overflow with fear.
I look like a miniature of one of those women

53

■ *In this poem, Cofer refers to a photograph taken of her when she was two years old. That photograph also appears on the cover of her memoir (opposite). If you considered the photograph without reading the poem, how might you describe the child's picture? How does Cofer's poetic reference to the photo affect your response to it? What do you think triggers her comparison to the Parisian women after World War II? Who were these women? What similarities does she suggest between herself and those women? Is it only the cropped hair? (See Visually Speaking: Metaphor, p. 55, for more background to these questions.)*

in Paris after World War II, hair shorn,
being paraded down the streets in shame,
for having loved the enemy.

But then things changed,
and some nights he didn't come home. I remember
hearing her cry in the kitchen. I sat on the rocking chair
waiting for my cocoa, learning how to count, *uno, dos, tres,*
cuatro, cinco, on my toes. So that when he came in,
smelling strong and sweet as sugarcane syrup,
I could surprise my *Papasito*—
who liked his girls smart, who didn't like crybabies—

with a new lesson, learned well.

54

MESSAGE

In an essay, consider the emphasis Cofer places on the silence of the home movie. What role does "silence" play in her essay? How frequently does she refer to the way things sound? What connections does she establish between seeing and hearing? Between visuals and vocals?

METHOD

How does Cofer work the film into the organization of "Silent Dancing"? Why doesn't she summarize the film in one place, say at the beginning, instead of referring to it at different points in the essay? What is the effect of this method?

MEDIUM

What story does the five-minute silent film tell? Does the film have a narrative movement at all, or does Cofer invent one? Whose voices does she use in the extracted paragraphs? Why does she introduce these voices?

Metaphor

Poetry depends for its effects largely on surprising, or even startling, images and **metaphors**. Poets use images to evoke a sensory, physical world, and they frequently tie the individual images together to form a pattern of relations that invites a deeper reading of the poem. Often, the images will be linked by means of a metaphor. Though entire books have been written on metaphor, the word refers essentially to the act of finding resemblances between different kinds of things or ideas. When the resemblance is stated explicitly with a "like" or "as," rhetoricians refer to it as a simile. Technically, to say "He's a rock" is to use a metaphor; to say "He's like a rock" or "He's as hard as a rock" is to use a simile.

Judith Ortiz Cofer's poem "Lessons of the Past" offers an exceptionally vivid use of imagery linked by metaphor and simile. Note especially the fourth stanza, where she introduces the photograph of herself with closely cropped hair and then says about the picture: "I look like a miniature of one of those women / in Paris after World War II, hair shorn, / being paraded down the streets in shame, / for having loved the enemy."

Cofer's reference to the picture of herself ties in with the reference to photographs of her father in the opening lines. And the comparison of her picture to the scenes (which she must have seen in other photographs or newsreels) of punished Parisian women in World War II echoes the military imagery also in the opening lines. Note how her use of the word "parade" recalls the image of her father learning to "march." But the resemblance she discovers between herself and the women surprises us — what connection can there be between an innocent two-year-old Puerto Rican child and French women punished for consorting with the Nazis? In one startling image Cofer makes us aware of the poem's deeper meaning by introducing the notion of treason, punishment, sex, shame, and the idea of loving an enemy. Can you think of metaphors that would help convey a sense of who you are?

Hulton Deutsch, *Women Collaborators Are Punished in Cherbourg.* (© Hulton Deutsch Collection /Corbis)

OUR STUFF, OURSELVES

Do the objects we own describe or define our personalities in any way? What picture can we paint of someone by just knowing what sort of car she drives or what brand of jeans he wears? Could you sneak into someone's room and form a reliable impression of that person by noting his or her possessions? Consumer researchers think that in many ways "we are what we own"; as a result, advertising agencies design **campaigns** that target certain products to certain types of personalities.

For his college thesis, John D. Freyer studied how consumer profiling works: "If you could collect information about how people consume goods and services, you could create a pretty good picture of their personality traits, and might even be able to predict the types of choices that they will make in the future." Later, as a graduate student, Freyer put some of his ideas into action by setting up a web site and selling all his material possessions on eBay. In "All My Life for Sale," he describes his spiritual journey into voluntary dispossession. At the same time, however, he supplies us with an amusing catalogue of those possessions, with information about their origins, their histories, and ultimate destinations. Freyer invites us, as we go through his inventory of what he sold at auction, to consider these varied, sometimes curious but mostly mundane possessions as his own self-portrait. In that sense, they comprise — as Freyer apparently wishes us to see them — a portrait of the artist as a young man.

A graduate of Hamilton College with a degree in political science, John Freyer was born in Syracuse, New York, in 1972. He has worked at nonprofit arts foundations, in cinematography, and in graphic design. He is a Bodine Fellow in the School of Art and Art History at the University of Iowa.

56

John Freyer, *All My Life for Sale*. In 2000, John Freyer made $6,000 auctioning off all of his stuff on eBay. An agent saw an item about his project and invited him to make it into a book. The essay here serves as his introduction to the book and describes his sale and subsequent road trip to visit all his former possessions and their new owners. Freyer has become a minor media celebrity and has inspired numerous similar projects. The essay that follows is taken from Freyer's book *All My Life for Sale* (2002).

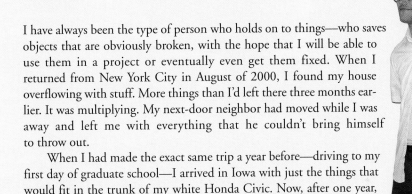

I have always been the type of person who holds on to things—who saves objects that are obviously broken, with the hope that I will be able to use them in a project or eventually even get them fixed. When I returned from New York City in August of 2000, I found my house overflowing with stuff. More things than I'd left there three months earlier. It was multiplying. My next-door neighbor had moved while I was away and left me with everything that he couldn't bring himself to throw out.

When I had made the exact same trip a year before—driving to my first day of graduate school—I arrived in Iowa with just the things that would fit in the trunk of my white Honda Civic. Now, after one year, my apartment was full of stuff that I had collected from the streets and garage sales of Iowa City. I began to wonder why I surrounded myself with the things that I did. I realized that if I didn't have an apartment full of stuff, a lease, and a job in Iowa, I might have stayed in New York City that August. The solution suddenly seemed obvious: I would sell off everything that I didn't need, and would move back to New York by the following January, with all my necessities packed once again into the tiny trunk of my Honda.

When school started that fall, I told my advisers about my plans and started to make arrangements for my return to New York. I looked for another student to take over the classes that I was supposed to teach the following semester, talked to my landlord about ending the lease early, and decided that I would sell some of the stuff I no longer needed on the Internet auction site eBay. I owned a lot of things that people in Iowa wouldn't necessarily appreciate, since they could find much of what I planned to sell in their neighborhood thrift stores and even at their curbsides.

I listed a few items a week on eBay, and was amazed when they sold. I started to photograph the objects and write descriptions, and as I did that I couldn't help but think about where each object came from, and why I even had it in the first place. Many of my friends in New York were working for the booming online catalog industry, and spent their days writing copy for the products in their catalogs. This was the summer of 2000, and everyone I went to college with was making money hand over fist in the dot-com boom doing pretty basic Web design. Every week the news reported on the latest twenty-seven-year-old millionaires, art museums were forming for-profit online businesses, anything and everything was going dot-com.

I decided that I needed my own dot-com, that it would be interesting if I built an online catalog like the one my friends were building for Martha Stewart, but this one would have the lost and found objects that cluttered my Midwestern apartment. In early September, I sat down at my computer and started typing in catchy titles to a domain-registry service. Yardsale.com—not available. Garagesale.com—not available. Junkyard, junksale, housesale, lifesale, lifeforsale, allforsale, everythingsale—all not available. This was the era of people buying up domain names and selling them to corporations for millions of dollars. It seemed like every name was already registered. I eventually entered allmylifeforsale.com and the computer replied AVAILABLE.

Available. I registered it on the spot, thinking that someone else would get it if I didn't snap it up. Who was I kidding? Did I really think that there was someone else out there trying to come up with a domain name to build an online catalog that featured the random objects that occupied his life?

After the name was registered, I wasn't sure what I should do. My original plan was to sell off my unwanted objects and move what I had left to New York, but the domain name that I registered didn't really allow for such maneuvering. It didn't say some-of-my unwanted-stuff-from-the-curb for sale, it emphatically said all. Having sold a few things on eBay, I started looking around my house, thinking about how long it would take for me to actually go through and auction every single thing I owned. I was overwhelmed, and my reasons for the sale in the first place were obscured by the daunting logistics of the task.

58

I knew I would need help if I was going to finish the sale by the end of December, so I invited everyone I knew—and even some total strangers—to my house in October for an inventory party. I handed everyone a clipboard and a handful of tags, and instructed them to tag things that they thought were "representative of my life in Iowa City." The party lasted into the early morning, and in the end more than six hundred items were tagged. This was exactly the structure that I needed. The inventory list included things that were found in boxes under my bed, items from my underwear drawer, things from my bathroom medicine cabinet—objects that I didn't even know I had. I now had a detailed list of possessions that was pretty representative of the "all" that the newly registered domain name specified.

I started to go through all of the items that were tagged—from my favorite shirts to the canned food in my cabinet. As I photographed each item, I reflected on the role that it played in my life and the stories that almost every object made me remember if I spent just a little bit of time with it.

I was immersed in these objects' histories, and started to think about what would happen when I no longer owned them. As an undergraduate political science major, I wrote a thesis about the use of consumer profiling in business and government surveillance. Such profiling presumes that if you could collect information about how people consume goods and services, you could create a pretty good picture of their personality traits, and might even be able to predict the types of choices that they will make in the future.

The dot-com culture thrived on the idea that it could use the Internet to gather such information. All catalog-store business models included layer upon layer of customer-tracking technology. Some dot-coms were setting up businesses that operated at a considerable loss on the consumer-sales side, while selling consumer information to anyone who would buy it to make up the difference.

The histories contained in the objects that I owned could never be uncovered by the consumer profiles that were attached to me. What would happen to my customer profiles when I no longer owned these things? Would I soon have to forward my junk mail to the people who bought my objects on eBay?

In November, I started to sell items on eBay that I had simultaneously posted to the allmylifeforsale site. The first object I sold was my toaster. I sent it to Bill in Illinois. And almost immediately after I sent it, I wondered if Bill even cared about its history. I started to think about the history Bill would attach to my toaster—would it burn his toast, as it did mine? I also realized that the act of

59

selling these objects would start to change my life in subtle ways. After I sold my toaster, I stopped eating toast.

It was also in November that I came to terms with the fact that there was no way I could finish selling everything I owned by the end of the year. I was able to list about ten items during the entire month of November; at that rate it would take me three years to get through all of the tagged items. So the project that grew out of my desire to leave Iowa was now keeping me there. The objects that prevented me from leaving were still doing so, but the other reasons for leaving soon became irrelevant.

The first items I sold ended up all over the country. The simple act of listing an item on eBay had the potential to distribute that item anywhere in the world. I wanted to know more about where all the things I was selling were going, so I started to include a request in the invoice that I sent to high bidders asking them to send me an update on the items they purchased. Some people withdrew from my auctions altogether, but as the sale went on, more and more people were interested in providing information. Over time, I started to receive photographs and stories from the various people who participated in the project, and I posted the updates on the allmylifeforsale site with pictures of the corresponding objects. A genealogy of objects emerged as the project continued, and people who visited the site could get a sense of the histories—old and new—that were attached to my former possessions.

As more people participated, a community seemed to form around allmylifeforsale. I was in almost daily contact with many of the high bidders, and was soon

more interested in the people who bought things from me than I was in the objects I was selling. At about this time, I received an invitation to visit my salt shaker in Portland, Maine. I had never been to Maine, and thought about all the other places my stuff had gone that I had never seen, either.

So, halfway through the project, I sent out another message to all the high bidders saying that I was going to get in my car with whatever was left after the sale, and would like to visit all the people who had bought things from me. Within a week, I had received forty invitations to visit my former possessions. As the project continued, I started to include the prospect of my visit directly into the eBay listings, so the new owner would know in advance that their purchase might lead to a visit from me.

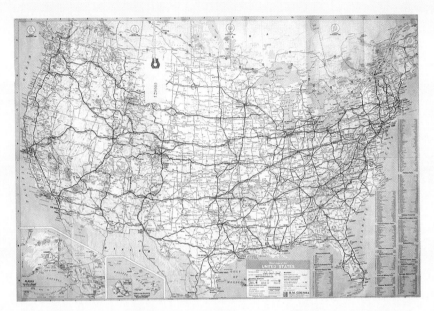

Tag # 000028
Map of USA
Auction Ended: Jan-25-01
Cambridge, Massachusetts
Page: 55

By the end, I had received more than one hundred invitations from all over the world. London, Melbourne, Tokyo, and New York—I didn't know how I would even go about it. On August 1, 2001, my apartment was completely empty; I had sold about six hundred items on eBay, another six hundred or so at a yard sale the week before, and I still had a few boxes of things left. I brought what I could to the local dump and put the remaining items into storage in various friends' basements.

I decided to start my trip in the Midwest and head east from there. The first visits seemed to go pretty well. I really liked the new owners of my things, and was happy to see that my objects were usually more prominently displayed and appreciated than they were when they were in my cluttered apartment. In the first leg of the trip, I tended to stay a few days in each place, trying to meet up with as many people as possible.

As I met more people, the awkwardness of meeting strangers started to wear off. I got comfortable staying in strangers' homes, meeting new people every day. Some might say too comfortable. By the end of the trip, I would help myself to food in the high bidder's refrigerator without a second thought. As I traveled, I posted daily updates on an online travelogue I created at temporama.com.

I was in the Northeast on September 11 in fact, I was in New York City. I had woken up at seven A.M. without an alarm at my friend Maya's house on Canal Street, and had decided to get an early start on my drive to Boston. At eight-forty-five I was sitting in traffic listening to WNYC somewhere just inside the Bronx on

I-95. I listened to news radio during the entire four-hour drive to Boston, and by the time I arrived I was whipped up into the same panic that most of the country was in.

My last posting to Temporama was on September 10 from New York City, and I started to receive messages from random readers of Temporama—complete strangers—asking me if I was OK. Although I had been posting regularly to the travelogue, I guess I never really thought that people were reading what I wrote. I suddenly realized that I wasn't alone on this journey, that many people were traveling along with me. I posted an update so that readers would know that I was OK, and then I tried to figure out what to do next.

I paused the trip for a few days, and eventually canceled my southern itinerary, heading back to Iowa to figure out whether I should continue. I contacted all the people who had invited me to visit and asked them if I was still invited under the current circumstances. Within a day or two, nearly everyone who had invited me to visit sent a new invitation.

I began my tour again, but the nature of my visits changed considerably as I continued. In the beginning, I would spend half my time trying to compose the right photograph of my former object. After September 11, I stopped caring so much about the objects that I was visiting and started caring more about the people who invited me. By the time I made it to Austin, Texas, I had been on the road for nearly three months and had slept on floors, couches, and lawns from coast to coast. The six thousand dollars that I'd made from selling nearly everything I owned had been spent on gas, car repairs, and heart-stopping food. After September 11, I always had a few hundred dollars with me in cash for emergency

gas and lodging. While in Austin I started to spend that reserve, and I decided it was time to go home.

Although I hadn't made it to everyone who had invited me to visit, I knew that it was time to stop driving. That it was time to stop looking. I realized that my sale had done far more than just provide me the means and the freedom to escape and start over. In fact, I no longer wanted to escape. I wanted to return to Iowa City and continue the life I'd started there. All too often in my life I had just picked up and left when things got difficult or overwhelming, and started over somewhere else. Upon returning to Iowa in November, I made a decision to finish my graduate study and to finally finish this project, which had gone on for more than a year. I had spent a year and a half contemplating the things that surrounded me, even after they were long gone. I no longer wanted to move to New York. I now knew that it was possible to engage the broader culture from somewhere besides a big city. After living out of the trunk of my car, location no longer seemed as relevant. I wanted a place to be grounded. I wanted to stop starting over.

COMMENT

"John Freyer personifies an American paradox. . . . He feels the need to collect, consume, and accumulate, and yet also desires a sense of urburdened freedom and the ability to travel at will."

—Will Helfrich, critic

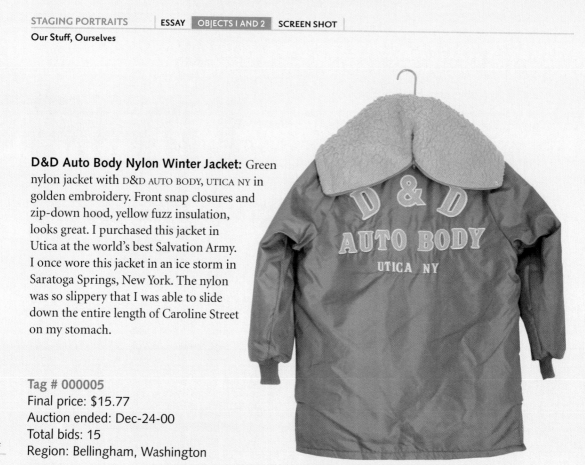

D&D Auto Body Nylon Winter Jacket: Green nylon jacket with D&D AUTO BODY, UTICA NY in golden embroidery. Front snap closures and zip-down hood, yellow fuzz insulation, looks great. I purchased this jacket in Utica at the world's best Salvation Army. I once wore this jacket in an ice storm in Saratoga Springs, New York. The nylon was so slippery that I was able to slide down the entire length of Caroline Street on my stomach.

Tag # 000005
Final price: $15.77
Auction ended: Dec-24-00
Total bids: 15
Region: Bellingham, Washington

Update: Ralph bought my only winter jacket in January of 2001. In one of the last e-mails that I received from him, he said that every time he watched the Weather Channel he felt a little guilty about buying my winter coat. That winter was one of the coldest on record in Iowa, with wind-chill factors averaging about twenty below zero for most of the month of January. Ralph was enrolled in auto-body-repair school last winter. I wonder if my jacket helped him pass his exams.

Jacket, Thesis, Fly-Fishing Patch, Bowling Shirt. Laid out as a catalogue, each object in *All My Life for Sale* is displayed with the original description Freyer wrote about it on eBay, its final price, and an update telling us how it is now. The last thing to sell was the domain name, allmylifeforsale.com, which was bought by the University of Iowa, Museum of Art. These objects are taken from *All My Life for Sale*. (Copyright © 2002 by John D. Freyer. From *All My Life for Sale* by John D. Freyer. Reprinted by permission of Bloomsbury)

My Hamilton College Thesis: *Information Technologies and Their Role in Surveillance Societies.* This paper is a little out of date terminology-wise, but many of the predictions that I made in 1994 have been pretty right on. Back then I still called the Internet "the information superhighway", and most of my interactions with the Net came through the Gopher system and then Mosaic. The paper talks about how information technology is used to gather personal information in an effort to control people. I reviewed literature by Foucault and also looked at Jeremy Bentham's *Panopticon.* My current project, allmylifefor-sale, is informed by my research into informa-tion technologies. Part of this project is to see what happens when all of the information collect-ed about my spending patterns and the like is radi-cally changed. If I no longer own the things that sup-posedly define the type of consumer that I am, will I still consume the same goods and services? Or should the telemarketers start to call the people who have bought my life? It's not a bad read if you can deal with the "information superhighway" language. I still have to thank Trey and Lanethea for proofreading this document.

Hamilton College

Information Technologies
And
Their Role in Surveillance Societies

A thesis submitted in partial fulfillment
of the requirements for
the degree of Bachelor of Arts

Department of Government

by
John Freyer
Clinton, New Y
April 21,

Tag # 000880
Final price: $20.50
Auction ended: Jan-25-01
Total bids: 14
New York, New York

65

Update: After I sold this on eBay I sent the auctions listing to my thesis adviser and to the president of Hamilton College. They both sent rather puzzled responses to my sale. I'm not sure they understood what I was up to, but neither did I at the time. The new owner, Skye, promised to read it. He must have, because I haven't heard from him since. Maybe he wrote the president of my college too, asking how they could have let me graduate.

Fly-Fishing Patch: When I was a kid my family used to spend a week each summer on the St. Lawrence River. Each year my father would try to entertain his four rambunctious boys by attempting to get them all to sit still long enough to fish. I never really liked to fish; it seemed a little pointless to me as a ten-year-old to stand still at the end of a dock and slowly reel in the line over and over and over again. I guess now I'd think it was meditative. My dad used to have his own "Bait of Champions". I'm not sure they will ever sell it in any championship bait shop, but you might be able to get it at your local market in the canned-vegetable section. He used canned corn, and it used to lure the smallest of mini-perch, bony rock bass, and if we were lucky a trout or two.

66

Tag # 000351
Final price: $13.50
Auction ended: Apr-27-01
Total bids: 15
Ridgefield, Washington

Update: I sent this to the same guy who bought my Spa City Rockers shirt (page 174). He said that even though he was disappointed with the shirt, he might hold on to the patch for a while before he throws it out.

Iranian Bowling Shirt: This is my most coveted bowling shirt. When I go bowling, I always bring my collection of bowling shirts, and this shirt is always the first to go. Only the closest of the close have ever worn this shirt. Trey found it for me in some thrift store in San Francisco, and it is from "New Show Pizza" in Tehran, Iran. I wonder if there is still a pizza joint in Tehran. I wore this shirt when I invented "The Butt Dance" at some Skidmore College art opening. The dance includes a slow hip gyration with your butt out to the right side a little for two beats and then to the left side for one beat. Something may tell you that I'm sort of a dork....

67

Tag # 000244
Final price: $66.00
Auction ended: March-10-01
Total bids: 13
London, United Kingdom

Update: I talked to Trey today to see if he would read through the new text I have been working on for this book. He reminded me that about halfway through this project he really started to hate it. For a few months, talking to me was like having to read every page of my project twice: all my life, all the time. Also, as the project went on I started selling the things that I didn't really want to sell—the gifts that I received from friends and family, my cameras, and my books and catalogs. I guess I would hate a project where Trey sold off all the things that I ever gave him. I was wearing this shirt on the day that I went to the post office and received the English money order for the sixty-six-dollar bid.

Our Stuff, Ourselves

eBay. Since its start in 1998, eBay has become the most profitable site for web commerce, today employing 4,500 people and operating in 27 countries. People buy and sell almost everything on the site, as John Freyer showed: collectibles, clothing, kitchen sinks. University of Iowa professor Kendrew McLeod even sold his soul in a 4-ounce glass jar for $1,300. (These materials have been reproduced with the permission of eBay Inc. Copyright © eBay Inc. All Rights Reserved)

MESSAGE

What would you say is the *meaning* of John Freyer's project? Economic? Spiritual? Artistic? Why does he call his project "all my life for sale" and not "all my things for sale"? What connections does he make between his life and his things? How did his undergraduate thesis provide him with the underlying concept for this project? What connections can you see between the point of his thesis (as he summarizes it in his essay) and the goal of his eBay project?

METHOD

The catalogue format gives Freyer a methodology to follow: a clear picture of each object, with a description to the side and pertinent information prominently displayed. In an essay, closely examine Freyer's objects and his account of them and show how they provide you with a portrait of Freyer himself. In what ways do they project his identity and personality?

MEDIUM

Why is eBay so important to Freyer's project? What does it enable him to do? What connections do you see between Freyer's project and a work of art? What connections does he suggest? Do you think that Freyer discovered his project as he proceeded to sell his stuff or that he began the project with the clear idea that it would become both a book and a kind of art exhibit? Why do you think allmylifeforsale.com was purchased by an art museum and not by a retailer?

REPRESENTATIONS

ESSAY | PHOTO | BOOK COVER | FILM STILL

Every portrait, visual or verbal, is a description of a person — a description that includes specific details or implicit clues about that person's race, class, and sex. Whether consciously or not, people make assumptions about strangers based on representations of them — a picture, a biography, a character in an autobiographical novel. Dorothy Allison explores the nature of these assumptions in her essay "What Did You Expect?" when she describes the surprise with which she is greeted as she goes on her book tours, the moment of reconciliation when a desk clerk realizes that the woman before her is a Famous Author. The materials gathered together here — essay, photograph, the book cover for *Bastard Out of Carolina,* and a promotional piece for the Showtime movie based on the book — are all representations of who Allison was and is.

Dorothy Allison has spent her career writing about her experience growing up poor, white, and lesbian in South Carolina. She was born in 1949, the daughter of a fourteen-year-old unwed mother, and while growing up was abused by her stepfather; yet she transcended her circumstances by being the first in her family to finish high school and going on to attend college and earn a master's degree. Her first story collection, *Trash* (1988), won the Lamda Book Award for lesbian fiction. In 1992, her first (largely autobiographical) novel won her mainstream recognition; *Bastard Out of Carolina* went on to be made into a movie for Showtime, directed by Anjelica Huston. Allison has also published a collection of essays, *Skin: Talking about Sex, Class, and Literature* (1994), and a memoir, *Two or Three Things I Know for Sure* (1995). Her most recent novel is *Cavedweller* (1998).

Dorothy Allison, *What Did You Expect?* In "What Did You Expect?"
Dorothy Allison writes on the topic of being photographed for a
magazine; refusing to be pictured "sprinkled with powdered sugar,"
the author settles for a more realistic image. The essay was first
published in *Allure* magazine in April 1998.

Dorothy Allison
WHAT DID YOU EXPECT?

The photographer is a professional; her pictures appear in major magazines. She has two assistants, five cameras, and a no-nonsense attitude toward the people she sets out to capture. She calls half a dozen times, and during each conversation presents more ideas for how she wants to shoot me. Sprinkled with powdered sugar — that is her favorite. I don't think so, I keep telling her. But every time she calls, she brings it up again. "I read some of your stuff, all that food and southern cooking," she tells me. "Really, it would be cool, just a knockout."

"It would be a cliché," I tell her. "Let's just do a regular picture, an everyday picture of a woman writer who doesn't like to have her picture taken at all."

"Do I look like the kind of woman who should be dipped in powdered sugar?" I ask Alix when I get off the phone.

"Absolutely," she says, laughing, and then flashes the smile that is one of the reasons we have lived together for almost ten years.

"You'd look funny, Mama." Our son, Wolf Michael, is right behind Alix. At five years old, he likes the idea of sugar, but he can tell from my expression I am not enthused.

"Well, it's not going to happen, angel-boy."

What was she thinking, this photographer who wanted to sprinkle me with sugar? Who did she think I was? Was she planning some rude joke I only barely comprehended?

Whenever I have to deal with interviewers or photographers, I find myself wondering the same thing. Do they know who I am? Do they know what my work is truly about? I imagine the editor who sends them out, the one who tells them, "A southerner, she writes about rednecks, about child abuse and incest, battered mothers and gospel music. Supposed to be a lesbian with a child. Has a novel coming out. See if you can get her to do something interesting."

It's that word "interesting" that makes me nervous. They all seem to have it in their eyes. Say something interesting. Do something different, something

71

COMMENT

"I did not want to be who the world wanted to make me. . . . I wanted to go to college, not become another waitress or factory worker or laundry person or counter-help woman like all the other women I knew. Everywhere I looked I saw a world that held people like me in contempt — even without the added detail of me being a lesbian."

— Dorothy Allison

Dorothy Allison, 1958. This photograph of a nine-year-old Allison is taken from her memoir, *Two or Three Things I Know for Sure* (1995). (Copyright Dorothy Allison)

redneck or lesbian. What is it you imagine that to be? I want to ask. And always, *Who do you think I am?*

A few years ago I went to Charleston, South Carolina, on behalf of the Last Great Places project for the Nature Conservancy. I had promised to write about the marshes that my family had visited when I was a girl, but by the time I arrived I was, as usual, exhausted and worried about what I could possibly say about birds and rice plantations. I took a taxi from the airport to the inn where I was supposed to stay, getting there near ten o'clock — too late, I knew, for dinner or talking to the man who was to drive me out to the coast the next day. I'll eat some crackers and go right to bed, I promised myself as I staggered up to the checkout desk. The man behind the polished mahogany desk frowned at me. "I'm afraid we have no vacancies," he told me sternly.

"I have a reservation," I told him. I pulled out my confirmation number on a page that had been faxed from the inn two weeks before.

He read the letter closely but kept looking over at me, his eyes moving down from my wrinkled jacket to my black tennis shoes. I travel a lot and have learned the hard way to wear what's comfortable. For this trip I hadn't even brought my usual dress-up outfit. I was, after all, going to be tromping through muddy marshes, not reading at a bookstore or talking to college students.

"Hmm," he said, frowning. "Let me check on this." He stepped into an alcove off to one side and picked up a phone.

I looked around. It was a very nice inn. The mahogany desk matched the breakfront by the staircase. Cut flowers were on every table. The carpet was deep and pale russet, nothing like the industrial carpet I see in most hotels. I felt my shoulders hunch and my neck pull tight. You don't belong here, I thought, and looked again at the man whispering into the phone. When he walked back to where I stood, he looked even more uncomfortable than I felt.

"You're Ms. Allison, the writer?" He looked at my suitcase as if there would be some label on it that would prove I wasn't Ms. Allison at all.

I looked down at my comfortable shoes and loose rayon trousers, the carry-on suitcase with its broken zippers, the satchel beside it with my notebook and emergency supplies of raw peanuts and vitamins. I wondered what kind of writer usually stayed at this inn, maybe the kind who dressed better and freshened their makeup before getting off the plane, maybe the kind who checked their luggage and traveled with their husbands, or even the kind who had matching luggage and a little computer in a snazzy leather bag. Was I really a writer, someone who had a reservation, who was here to do a piece of work and deserved a comfortable bed and a quiet room — or a fraud, a runaway from a trailer park who would steal the hotel towels and peel the shelf liner out of the drawers in the breakfront when no one was watching?

"I am," I told the man. "Is there a problem, or do you have my room?"

He gave me my key, but he did it reluctantly, and for the three days I was there he watched me closely every time I crossed the lobby. I imagined that when I left, he would count the towels and check the drawers to see if the shelf liner remained.

"I thought you were blond," the escorts say when they come to meet me at the airport. "I thought you'd be taller." "Older." "Younger." They hold out my book and look from the picture on the back cover to me. "You're much prettier than your picture," they say sometimes. Some say the picture doesn't look like me at all, though it does. There's my squint, my lips pressed together, my wide cheekbones and tired eyes. I look like my picture but not the picture they expect. Sometimes when I see them looking from me to the picture in their hands, I check myself out in the closest reflective surface. I am always the same, sometimes a little heavier or thinner, but always the same stooped, stubborn shoulders, ready grin, and ragged hair — my mama's replica, only in nicer clothes and better shoes.

For years I've been telling friends that the only place you really see working-class women is in pictures taken at disasters. Car wrecks and mining disasters, that's where you find women who look like me. It's kind of a joke, though it is not funny, and it's not entirely accurate. We're the stars of the tabloid talk shows, and we're typically seen covering our faces or sitting slumped in despair while our husbands, boyfriends, brothers, or cousins are hauled away in handcuffs on *Cops.* The first time I saw that television show, I sat through the whole thing with my mouth hanging open, unable to look away and barely able to stand what I was seeing. Family, community, memory, and my people — vividly rendered on videotape and in simple human anguish. Whenever I meet an escort in an airport, I remember how I felt watching *Cops,* the shame and the outrage. Do they recognize how much I look like those pitiful white girls leaning against the patrol cars? Is that what they see when they come to meet me, the assistant professors who teach my books, the graduate students who want to write their own novels and hope to learn how by making notes on what I say? Is that why they sometimes hesitate and check my picture again? *Are you the writer?* they ask.

This is what I look like, I tell myself when people hesitate at meeting me. This is who I am. This is what a 48-year-old woman looks like when she comes from my family but hasn't worked in a factory all her life, has mostly worked at desk jobs, hasn't given birth to children or had cancer yet, and sees a dentist fairly regularly. I know exactly how much I resemble my mother, and where the difference lies.

I have my mama's hips, full and lush, and her mouth, too often clamped stubbornly tight. I have the same shadows under my eyes she had and her square strong chin, but it is when I smile or laugh that I look most like her. I have trained

Book cover, *Bastard Out of Carolina.* The novel was published in 1992, hailed by critics and rave reviews, and ▶ nominated for a National Book Award. The narrator is a twelve-year-old girl, "Bone" Boatwright, who shares many of Allison's own experiences: illegitimacy, poverty, and rape. Book covers are marketing tools — the representation of the girl here tries to suggest the issues of class and sexuality and also to sell the book as a certain kind of literary fiction. (From *Bastard Out of Carolina* by Dorothy Allison, copyright © 1992 by Dorothy Allison. Used by permission of Dutton, a division of Penguin Group (USA) Inc. Photo by Elizabeth DeRamus)

Now a SHOWTIME ORIGINAL PICTURE™

DOROTHY ALLISON

BASTARD
OUT OF CAROLINA

myself not to drop my eyes, but even when I manage not to do it, I often find myself smiling crooked—an uncertain apologetic smile that is all about feeling uncomfortable with being looked at too closely. My mother would cover her mouth when she smiled, an effort to shield her stained teeth. Years ago I discovered that my version of that was to drop my hair across my eyes as if by doing that I could look out but the world could not see me clearly. I could be safe and hidden, as safe and protected as a woman covering her smile with her hand, or a girl looking away so no one can see her eyes. Not safe at all, not protected, merely pretending to be so.

My mother worked as a waitress or a cook from the time she was a girl till just before she died. My earliest memories are of her sitting at the kitchen table with her little mirror and makeup bag, her short blond hair put up in pin curls, her fingers smoothing foundation over her cheeks. She would pluck her eyebrows into delicate arched lines and carefully fill in the shadows under her eyes with thick makeup. Only when her mask was in place would she release her hair and comb it into shape. Then she would smile at me and my sisters in her mirror.

"Ready for the world," my mother would announce, then flatten her lips together to even out her lipstick. "Ready for anything."

What my mama wore seemed to me like war paint—armor and shield and statement of intent. Don't mess with me, my mama's sculpted eyebrows seemed to warn. I'm ready for you, her dark eyeliner announced.

My sisters adopted the family armor easily, developing the ability to apply mascara while talking on the phone or blush while pulling curlers out of their hair. I never did. I brushed my hair straight back and scrubbed my face, wore my hair long and loose, and declared my independence by refusing to sleep with my hair in curlers. Now and then I would use some black eyeliner or dab my lips with a tangerine lip gloss but with no real enthusiasm. I was going to be different. I wasn't going to be anything like what was expected of me.

Like all the other girls I met in college, I adopted the uniform of blue jeans and T-shirts. I believed myself a new creature, a woman who would never wear a girdle or get up early to put on her makeup before going out into the world. The kind of girl who worried about makeup and split ends and the shape of her butt could never be serious. I wanted to be serious. I wanted to be a revolutionary. I wanted to remake the world. Women who were working at remaking the world were supposed to move through the world as men did, disdainful of foolish obsessions like weight or hairstyle or the size of one's breasts. My ideal of the revolutionary feminist was a fantasy creature—a mixture of Wonder Woman, Joan of Arc, and the drawing of a samurai woman I found in a sketchbook. My ideal might not be beautiful, but she wouldn't care. I wouldn't care either—no matter if I did. I would act like I didn't care what I looked like, what people thought of me. If I acted like that long enough, I believed, sooner or later it would be so. I would get past my embarrassment, my self-conscious smiles and hangdog expressions. I would look like one of the women who carried banners in parades in big cities, with their eyes trained on the horizon and their faces shining with pride

76

■ What does it mean to refuse to be what people expect of you? By the end of the essay, do you think Allison refuses expectations?

◀ **Film still,** *Bastard Out of Carolina.*
Starring Jennifer Jason Leigh as Anney,
the mother, the movie version of the
book was directed by Anjelica Huston
and funded by Ted Turner. Turner
decided it was too graphic to be shown
on his TNT network, however, and
it was subsequently picked up by
Showtime. The book itself has been
banned from classrooms and school
libraries for its graphic nature. The
character of Bone is played by actress
Jenna Malone, shown here. (Photofest)

and determination. A woman who could do the necessary and do it without worrying about what people thought, that was what I aimed to make myself.

I have failed of course. I still worry about what people think. That is why I
have so much trouble standing still for the camera's lens or choosing what to wear
before walking across a stage or even biting my lips before answering the questions put to me by reporters. Who I think I should be and who I am are still not
quite the same, though I try to behave as if that is not so. I show up wherever I
can with my mother's smile but without the makeup she so carefully applied, with
my straightforward fictions of working-class families and the brutal difficulty of
achieving anything like redemption. My persona is as much a conscious rejection

of my mother's armored features as it is an attempt not to cater to the prejudices and assumptions of a culture that seems not to want to look at women like me. It is not seamless, merely stubborn.

I was finally photographed in a Laundromat leaning on a washing machine with a basket propped on one hip. Why am I doing this? I kept wondering. But I had turned down so many of the photographer's requests, this one seemed almost reasonable. I kept laughing at myself and grinning weakly at the women who were actually doing their laundry.

The photographer sighed as she packed up her equipment. "I sure wish you'd let me sprinkle you with powdered sugar," she mumbled one more time.

I pushed my hair back off my face and shifted my aching hips. "Maybe next time," I told her. And then I gave her one of my mother's smiles, strong and stubborn, a smile that, to anyone who knows me, clearly said, No one is ever going to get a picture of me like that.

78

MESSAGE

In the essay, what relationship does Allison establish between her life experiences and her attitude toward being photographed? What connections does she make between social class and photographic expectations? What do you think the essay's title means?

METHOD

Allison resists being constructed by a photographer's **clichéd** appropriations of her background: growing up southern and poor. In a comparative essay, consider the 4 images included in this cluster *as representations:* the essay, the photo of Allison, the book cover, and the DVD cover. Is there a nonclichéd way to represent class? Which representation is the least problematic, do you think? Which method would you choose if you were trying to represent, most concisely, some element of who you are?

MEDIUM

Allison said in an interview that no one in her family read *Bastard Out of Carolina* but that everyone saw the movie: "When the movie happened, it was a big deal. Relatives checked in that had not been heard from in this lifetime. . . . It was a hoot." Which would you say is a bigger deal, a book or a movie? Why is one medium more impressive than another? Who would you cast to play yourself in the story of *your* life?

CONFESSIONS

RÉSUMÉ | 2 PHOTOS | POEM

The **résumé** — a portrait of a potentially desirable employee — is a standard kind of profile. The word comes from the French, meaning to "sum up," and traditionally a résumé is a summary of one's educational background and work experience prepared for a prospective employer. Résumés, as anyone who has composed one knows, typically follow fairly conventional guidelines: information is organized in categories — such as Objective, Education, Experience, and Activities — with the most important information listed first. An especially creative person, however, may break the rules by deviating from the usual impersonal format and content. It's not surprising that a poet like Anne Sexton, known for her intense, confessional poetry, would produce an unusually revealing résumé. Poetry, unlike the résumé, is a medium that is designed to reveal — albeit often an image that requires the reader to fill in its features.

Anne Sexton's "Résumé 1965" includes details about her life and career up to that date. "Self in 1958" is a poem she wrote in the year she "started to write constantly." The victim of depression and several nervous breakdowns, Sexton had spent much time in and out of institutions. The photograph by Arthur Furst was taken the summer before she died, in 1974. Besides the books mentioned in her résumé, Sexton is also the author of *Love Poems* (1969), *Transformations* (1971), *The Book of Folly* (1972), and *The Death Notebooks* (1974). One of her most powerful volumes of poetry, *The Awful Rowing Toward God* (1975), appeared posthumously, and her *Complete Poems* appeared in 1981.

79

Anne Sexton, *Résumé 1965*. Since it includes her life and career up to 1965, Sexton's résumé was most likely written in that year. We do not know its purpose (a grant application? a biographical dictionary?), nor do we know if it was ever submitted anywhere. It was discovered among her papers by her daughter, Linda Gray Sexton, and is printed here just as she originally typed it, with deletions, inserts, and typos. (From *Anne Sexton: The Last Summer* by Arthur Furst. Copyright © 2000 by Arthur Furst)

80

1.

SEXTON, ANNE (November 9th 1928----). American poet writes: I was born in Newton, Massachusetts and have spent most of
                                                    wintering
my life on the coast of Maine in the summer or in Wellesley, Newton and Weston---all suburban towns west of Boston. My ancestor, Willian Brewster, came to America on the Mayflower and sounds like a decent sort of man from what I read of him. My family tree goes back, I have lately found, to assortments of royalty such as Willian The Conqueror, King Edward 111, 11, 1, King Phipid 1V of France, King Ferdinand of Spain, etc. The list amuses me most when I find such notes in the family genealogy as:Edward 111, founded the Knights of the Garter. Married Philipha of Hainault, his mistress age 15. Mistress of 15! Ah, those were the days! Such whisps of information about my lineage make me smile in light of my own puritanical and stifled upbringing.

I was the third and last daughter. As a young child I was locked in my room until the age of five. After that, at school, I did not understand the people who were my size or even the larger ones. At home, or away from it, people seemed out of reach. Thus I hid in fairy tales and read them daily like a prayerbook. Any book was closer than a person. I did not even like my dolls for they resembled people. I stepped on their faces because the resembled me. I think I would have prefered to exist only in a fairy tale where poeple could change reality the way an actor changes his constume. In total, I can say that I learned nothing in any school that I attended and see no point in mentioning places where my body sat at a desk and my soul was elsewhere. I wrote some poems

in high school but stopped when my mother suggested that I
had plagerized them. My mother was brilliant and vital. Her
friends thought of her as a writer although it was only her
father, A.G. Staples, who was a small town, Maine newspaper
editor. Nevertheless, my mother was considered to be a
~~genix~~ genuis. One thought, in meeting her, that she had
written all the first editions in her own library. Of course,
I was unbearable, unhappy and unreachable and as soon as possible,
I became boy-crazy. In fact, I eloped ~~with~~ at nineteen with
Alfred M. Sexton. As a matter of interest I am still married
to him. ~~Perhaps xxxx~~ I have found this somewhat unusual
among writers in general. Fairy tales we all have in common--
but one marriage, seldom.

After I was married I worked as a salesgirl, a fashion
model and a librarian. We lived on a ~~farm~~ farm in Upper
State New York, an apartment in Cochitutate, Mass (between
a pig farm and a chicken farm). Later, when my husband went
into the navy (Korean Conflict) we lived in Baltimore and
San Francsico. In 1954 he got out of the navy and we settled
in our first home in Newton and had our first child, Linda
and two years later a second, Joy. A few months after Joy's
birth I had a severe nervous breakdown (as they are called)
and as I came out of it (and if I ever really came out of it)
I started to write poems.

In 1958 I started to write constantly and then to publish
in such magazines as Harper's, The New Yorker, The Hudson Review,
Partisan Review Etc. I was ~~often~~ often told that my poetry
was too personal, too private. But the art, though it be
suicide or muder, choses you. I let it do this and then I

81

3.

let it continue its path, deeper and deeper. One might call
that <u>style</u>. I think of it as a no-other-choice-project. I
can't give my poems someone's face-lifting-job. Further, I
won't. I've even stopped trying. The critics be damned.
I just let the poems alone. No. Not that I don't rework.
Some poems take years and hundreds of rewrites before they
have their own sound, own face. I remember the long days,
years. of learning to write and that the thing I had to fight
most for was this certain style. For praise or damnation,
the poem must be̶x̶x̶x̶t̶x̶d̶x̶x̶x̶ itself. At best, one hopes to make
something new, a kind of original product. Otherwise, why
bother to hope, to make? And my newest poems are even more
personal. They usually come from a part of me that I don't
know, haven't met and won't understand for a couple of years.
They know things I don't know myself.

    After publication of my first books of poems I was appointed
a Scholar at The Radcliffe Institute for Independent Study for
1961-63. This brought me in touch with other artists and scholars
as well as an informal class of poetry that I taught to
Radcliffe and Harvard students. My second book of poems was
published soon after this period. Some of the painters and
sculptors that met at Radcliffe have influe̶c̶a̶s̶e̶d my work
in hidden ways. After that time I was awarded The First
Traveling Fellowship of The American Academy of Arts and Letters--
1963-64. This opened me up even more. I am something of a
tin can --being opened up all the time. I drove t̶k̶x̶x and walked
throughout Europe and fell in love with Italy, particually its
costal fishing villages. In 1964-65 I was awarded a grant
from The Ford Foundation to be in residence with a theatre

82

4.

in Boston. Of course I wrote a play and learned lots about
the theatre and about loving actors and was, again, opened up
again--tin can me!

In 1965 Oxford University Press in London brought out
my Selected Poems in the UK and I was, at that time, elected
a Fellow of The Royal Society of Literature in London. So
maybe I've come some sort of circle, back again to something
a little xymx royal like my Edward 111 and his mistress (age 15!)
But perhaps it's all a fairy tale and I'm still locked in
my room. I can only speak, from my room, my typewriter,
to say I am just completing a third book of poems, waiting
for someone to produce my play, to either kill it of bring
it forth, and am trying myself on a little prose. But
poetry is my love, my postmark, my hands, my kitchen, my face.

· · · · · · · · · ·
PRINCIPAL WORKS: To Bedlam and Part Way Back 1960, All
My Pretty Ones 1962, Selected Poems 1964, Live or Die,
forthcoming.

· · · · · · · · · · · · ·
ABOUT: The Minnesota Review 1961, Epoch, Fall 1962, Altantic
xi2 Nov. 1962, The New Yorker April 27th 1963, The Nation Feb. 23,
1963, The Reporter Jan 3, 1963, Sewanne Review Summer 1963,
The New York Times April 28th 1963, The Critical Quarerly,
(England) Summer 1964, Spring 1965; London Times March 11, 1965,
The London Magazine March 1964.

◀ **Arthur Furst, *Anne Sexton, Summer 1974.*** Arthur Furst is a prominent New England
photographer who has done portraits of many well-known American authors. He
photographed Sexton in the spring and summer of 1974, just a few months before she
took her own life. (From *Anne Sexton: The Last Summer* by Arthur Furst. Copyright
© 2000 by Arthur Furst)

Anne Sexton
SELF IN 1958

◀ **Anne Sexton, *Self in 1958*.**
From Sexton's third collection
of poems, *Live or Die* (1966),
which won the Pulitzer Prize.

What is reality?
I am a plaster doll; I pose
with eyes that cut open without landfall or nightfall
upon some shellacked and grinning person,
eyes that open, blue, steel, and close.
Am I approximately an I. Magnin[1] transplant?
I have hair, black angel,
black-angel-stuffing to comb,
nylon legs, luminous arms
and some advertised clothes.

I live in a doll's house
with four chairs,
a counterfeit table, a flat roof
and a big front door.
Many have come to such a small crossroad.
There is an iron bed,
(Life enlarges, life takes aim)
a cardboard floor,
windows that flash open on someone's city,
and little more.

Someone plays with me,
plants me in the all-electric kitchen,
Is this what Mrs. Rombauer[2] said?

85

---

[1] I Magnin: A luxurious department store.
[2] Mrs. Rombauer: Irma Rombauer (1877–1962), author of the famous cookbook *Joy of Cooking*.

Confessions

Someone pretends with me —
I am walled in solid by their noise —
or puts me upon their straight bed.
They think I am me!
Their warmth? Their warmth is not a friend!
They pry my mouth for their cups of gin
and their stale bread.

What is reality
to this synthetic doll
who should smile, who should shift gears,
should spring the doors open in a wholesome disorder,
and have no evidence of ruin or fears?
But I would cry,
rooted into the wall that
was once my mother,
if I could remember how
and if I had the tears.

■ *Think about Sexton's use of the word "synthetic" here. If you consult a dictionary, you will find that the word has a number of meanings, some of them philosophical or technical. The word is used in chemistry, for example, to refer to something produced by a chemical process to resemble something natural ("synthetic rubber"). By extension, the term has also come to mean artificial, not real or genuine. In what sense is a doll synthetic? How does Sexton suggest the word can apply to her real self as well as to a doll? What other words and images in the poem reinforce the concept of a synthetic self?*

86

COMMENT

"The intimate details divulged in Sexton's poetry enchanted or repelled with equal passion. In addition to the strong feelings Anne's work aroused, there was the undeniable fact of her physical beauty. Her presence on the platform dazzled with its staginess, its props of water glass, cigarettes, and ashtray. She used pregnant pauses, husky whispers, pseudo-shouts to calculated effect. A Sexton audience might hiss its displeasure or deliver a standing ovation. It did not doze off during a reading."

—Maxine Kumin, poet

Two photographs. Images of the younger and older
Sexton confront each other on the mantel. (From
Anne Sexton: The Last Summer by Arthur Furst.
Copyright © 2000 by Arthur Furst)

COMMENT

"I realize now that while we were taking photographs of her, Anne
was preparing for her imminent death. She was organizing her
estate and image, determining who would be her biographer and
who would handle her writings, and she wanted me to be her
'authorized' photographer. . . . Like an Egyptian queen, she was
planning for the afterlife."

— Arthur Furst, photographer

MESSAGE

What information does Sexton include in "Résumé 1965" that you would expect to find in a standard résumé? What information do you find unexpected? Whom does she appear to be writing the résumé for? Why might she have had to compile this biographical information?

METHOD

Judging from her résumé, what role do fairy tales play in Sexton's life? Recall her final line: "But poetry is my love, my postmark, my hands, my kitchen, my face." How do you interpret this sentence? What other references to "face" can you find in the résumé? In what sense does poetry possess a face?

MEDIUM

Can you find any connections between the self Sexton constructs in her résumé and the image Arthur Furst captures with his camera? What connections can you see between Sexton's "Résumé 1965" and her poem "Self in 1958"? What images, for example, appear in both selections?

FAMILY PHOTOS

ESSAY   4 PHOTOS   INTERVIEW

"They are not your usual pictures of the children to send to the grandparents," the critic Janet Malcolm writes of the photographs in Sally Mann's collection *Immediate Family.* The "usual pictures" are a **genre** we all recognize: children in cute poses, darling outfits, stylized situations. Sally Mann's photographs of her young children are a bit different, Malcolm writes: "pictures to send to the Museum of Modern Art."

Immediate Family collects black-and-white pictures Mann took of her three children (Emmett, Jessie, and Virginia) over the course of several summers in Lexington, Virginia. These beautiful photographs have a languorous, sensual air, and they document child-hood as almost wilderness territory. Some seem unstudied, some use artifice, some confront the direct gaze of the child. Most are taken outdoors as the children fish, sleep, swim, eat — sometimes clothed but often nude. The series has been the subject of much critical acclaim and controversy; some reviewers debate what statements, exactly, Mann is making about art, childhood, family, sexuality, life, and death. And some question Mann personally about her sense of parental responsibility. Mann — and her children, who are by now no longer children — have responded that while the subjects invoked by the photographs are *complicated,* there is nothing *wrong* in them, nor with Emmett, Jessie, and Virginia as a result of modeling for their mother.

Sally Mann began her career as a landscape photographer and has continued to excel in that genre. In 1988 she published *At Twelve: Portraits of Young Women.* In 1992 she published *Immediate Family,* followed by *Still Time,* both focusing on her children. She has returned to her work on landscape photography, producing a series of haunting landscapes around her native Virginia titled *Mother Land: Recent Georgia and Virginia Landscapes* (1997).

89

> go

For more information about
Sally Mann's work go to
bedfordstmartins.com/
convergences.

Sally Mann, *Jessie Bites,* **1985.** From *Immediate Family* by Sally Mann. (© Sally Mann. Courtesy: Edwynn Houk Gallery, New York)

Janet Malcolm, ***The Family of Mann.*** One of the nation's leading journalists, Janet Malcolm was born in Prague, Czechoslovakia, in 1934, and grew up in New York City. Her books cover a wide variety of topics, from psychoanalysis and true crime to photography and biography. She is the author of *Psychoanalysis: The Impossible Profession* (1982), *The Journalist and the Murderer* (1990), *The Silent Woman: Sylvia Plath and Ted Hughes* (1995), *Diana & Nikon: Essays on Photographs* (1997), where "The Family of Mann" is included, and *In the Freud Archives* (2002). Her essays have been collected in *The Purloined Clinic: Selected Writings* (1993).

Janet Malcolm
THE FAMILY OF MANN

The audacity and authority of Sally Mann's work are perhaps nowhere so immediately manifest as on the cover of her first collection of photographs, *At Twelve: Portraits of Young Women* (1988). The cover picture is a sort of double portrait: a girl stands in front of a clapboard house next to a chair on which a torn, oval photograph of another girl, from another time, has been propped. The girl in the old photograph wears a flounced dress and a bow in her hair, and has the stern, fixed, mildly sulky expression that nineteenth-century photographers regularly induced in young subjects; her hands are stiffly, self-protectively crossed over her stomach. The "actual" girl, in contrast, opens herself up to the photographer's scrutiny. Dressed in tight shorts and a T-shirt, she stands in an attitude of trusting relaxation, her legs parted, a hip outthrust, an arm extended to grip the chair holding the torn photograph. We do not see her expression—Mann has cropped the photograph at her chest and her knees—but we don't need to, because the body is so eloquent. Its transfixing feature—you could almost call it its "face"—is the girl's vulva, which plumply strains against the soft stretch fabric of the shorts, creating a radius of creases that impart a sculptural, almost monumental presence to this evocative, slightly embarrassing, slightly arousing sight of summer in America.

Mann uses **framing** to carefully compose her photographs. To explore using the concept of framing to analyze visual texts, go to exercise 03 on **ix visual exercises**.

91

The photograph is radical, however, not because of the truth it renders about twelve-year-old-ness but because of the truth it renders about photography. As if anticipating the criticism that *Immediate Family,* her next book of photographs, was to attract—the charge that she exploits her young subjects—Mann offers an illustration of the medium's innate exploitativeness that is like an impatient manifesto. Of course the girl who posed for Mann in front of her house did not know—everything in the stance of her body tells us she did not—that Mann was taking a picture centering on her pudendum. We can almost see the girl's face squinting against the sun, arranging itself to levelly meet the camera's gaze, the gaze that has treacherously traveled elsewhere. The photograph both unrepentantly enacts and ruefully comments on the treachery. Mann knows, as the major photographers of our time know (the photographers whose company she joins with *Immediate Family*), that photography is a medium not of reassuring realism but of disturbing surrealism.

In *Immediate Family* Mann photographs her own three children, Emmett, Jessie, and Virginia, during warm weather over a period of seven years, in and around the family house in rural southwestern Virginia. The children wear bathing suits or light summer clothes or no clothes. The photographs are beautiful and strange, like a dream of childhood in summer. They are not your usual pictures of the children to send to the grandparents; they are pictures to send to the Museum of Modern Art. During John Szarkowski's tenure as director of the photography department at the Modern, he cultivated a kind of photography that Sally Mann brings to triumphant, sometimes transcendent, fruition. In *On Photography,* Susan Sontag compared the "sleekly calculated, complacently well-made, undialectical" productions of official Surrealism to photography's authentic, natural surrealism. Within photography, Szarkowski distinguished between the calculated, well-made, undialectical art photograph and the artless but vitally interesting snapshot, and he supported photographers who attempted the tour de force of the art snapshot. Of course, every photograph with any claim to interest is a tour de force—all the canonical works of photography retain some trace of the medium's underlying, life-giving, accident-proneness. But the Szarkowski photographers (William Eggleston, Lee Friedlander, Joel Meyerowitz, Garry Winogrand, Emmett Gowin, for example) put greater pressure on the snapshot side of the equation; their pictures are looser, messier, "uglier" than the results of the traditional mediation between the contingent and the premeditated. In Sally Mann's photographs the scale tips back toward the older "beautiful" photograph—without, however, any diminution of the appearance of photojournalistic chanciness and the sense of anxiety, disjunction, invasiveness, uncanniness by which the Szarkowski school is marked.

What mothers who photograph their children normally try to capture (or, as the case may be, create) are the moments when their children look happy and attractive, when their clothes aren't smeared with food, and they aren't clutching themselves. Mann, abnormally, takes pictures of her children looking sulky, angry,

Sally Mann, *Blowing Bubbles,* 1987. From *Immediate Family* by Sally Mann.
(© Sally Mann. Courtesy: Edwynn Houk Gallery, New York)

and dirty, displaying insect bites or bloody noses, and clutching themselves. Reviewers of *Immediate Family* and of the exhibitions that preceded its publication harshly rebuked Mann for her un-motherliness and pitied the helpless, art-abused children. "At moments when any other mother would grab her child to hold and comfort, Mann must have reached instead for her camera," one reviewer wrote in a piece entitled "It may be art, but what about the kids," which concluded with the dictum, "Beauty does not validate exploitation. Motherhood should not give license to activities that are morally wrong. Nor should art." In the *TLS* [*Times Literary Supplement*], Julian Bell wrote, "I don't doubt that Sally Mann's children are doing better than most, but since she offers them for my inspection, I'll say that seems a rotten way to bring them up." Charles Hagen, a *New York Times* photography critic, offered no opinion of his own, but felt constrained to point out that "many people regard photographs of naked children as inherently exploitative and even pornographic, and will reject Ms. Mann's work on those grounds." He went on, "Other viewers will bristle at the sensual, emotionally drenched nature of Ms. Mann's vision of childhood, and will object to her using children to act out the fantasies, some of them sexual, that are central to it."

One of the ways we make ourselves at home, so to speak, in the alien terrain of new art is to deny it its originality, to transform its disquieting strangeness into familiar forms to which we may effortlessly, almost blindly respond. To look at Sally Mann's photographs of her children as unfeeling or immoral is simply to be not looking at them, to be pushing away something complex and difficult (the vulnerability of children, the unhappiness of childhood, the tragic character of the parent-child relationship are among Mann's painful themes) and demanding a cliché in its place. With her summer photographs of Emmett, Jessie, and Virginia, Mann has given us a meditation on infant sorrow and parental rue that is as powerful and delicate as it is undeserving of the facile abuse that has been heaped on it.

"That seems a rotten way to bring them up." Is there a good—or even a good enough—way to bring them up? Mann asks this question in picture after picture. A photograph entitled *The Wet Bed* shows Virginia, the youngest child, at the age of two, lying in bed fast asleep on her back, her arms raised above her head as if they were cherub's wings, her torso stretched out in luxurious relaxation. She is naked; it is a hot night—a chenille bedspread lies in a heap at the foot of the mattress. Like Blake's[1] little girl lost, whose radiant innocence subdued beasts of prey as she slept in the wilderness, Mann's Virginia is the embodiment of invulnerable defenselessness: What harm can befall this beautiful, trusting child? But as

---

[1]The prolific English poet William Blake (1757–1827) is perhaps best known today for his *Songs of Innocence* (1789) and *Songs of Experience* (1794), two remarkable volumes of poetry that explore both the blissful and the bleak sides of childhood. A great illustrator and an early champion of sexual freedom, Blake published these works with intricately arranged hand-colored drawings and decorations that he intended to be viewed as an inseparable part of the text.— ED.

we follow the photographer/mother's gaze and look down with her on the sleeping little girl, we feel her mother's fear. We take in the heavy darkness that frames the whiteness of the child's bed, out of which the image of the sleeping cherub emerges like a hallucinatory vision, and, above all, we are transfixed by the large pale stain that spreads from the child's body over the tautly fitted sheet. The stain is yet another insignia of Blakean innocence, another attribute of the time of life when nothing has yet happened to seriously disturb a child's blameless instinctuality. But the stain is also an augury of Blakean experience. It foretells the time when the child will have to be broken of its habit of trust in the world's benevolence. What Mann, in her introduction, calls "the predictable treacheries of the future" waft out of *The Wet Bed* as they do out of the book as a whole. All happy childhoods are alike: they are the skin that memory has grown over a wound. Children suffer, no matter how lovingly they are brought up. It is in the very nature of upbringing to cause suffering.

Sally Mann's project has been to document the anger, disappointment, shame, confusion, insecurity that in every child attach to the twenty-year-long crisis of growing up. She stalks and waits for, and sometimes stages, the moments that other parents and photographers may prefer not to see. That this anatomy of childhood's discontents is drawn in a paradisal southern summer landscape, and that the family in which the children are growing up is as enlightened, permissive, and affectionate as a family can be, only add to its power and authenticity.

With her pictures of her children's bloody noses, mean insect bites, cuts requiring stitches, faces and bodies smeared with mud and dirt and drips from ice cream, Mann offers striking metaphors for the fall from purity that is childhood's ineluctable trajectory. (We give it the euphemism "child development.") But where *Immediate Family* achieves its great ring of disturbing truth is in the "plot" that emerges from its pages — the plot of how the three children have worked out their respective destinies within their family constellation, how they enact the roles that heredity, chance, and will have written for them in the bitter contest for the parents' love.

This plot is played out in every family, of course, with infinite variations and invariable pathos. In *Immediate Family*, Jessie appears as the tense, self-conscious, younger-sister-haunted older daughter; Emmett as the scowling, withholding, only son, warily stepping through the Oedipal minefield; Virginia as the baby, wearing her belatedness like a blanket against the chill of the others' precedence. The blows and stings of early child–parent and child–sibling relationships do not fade like insect bites and skin punctures but imprint themselves on us forever, determining who we are. Sally Mann's extraordinary contribution has been to give photographic expression to pathetic truths that have hitherto been the exclusive domain of psychologists and authors of great works of fiction. Photography's specificity gives the portrait of the Mann family its arresting, almost abashing intimacy. Its ambiguity — a photograph never says anything unequivocally, even when it most appears to be doing so — allows the family to escape with its secrets.

Sally Mann, *Emmett, Jessie, and Virginia*, 1990. From *Immediate Family* by Sally
Mann. (© Sally Mann. Courtesy: Edwynn Houk Gallery, New York)

Melissa Harris, *Daughter, Model, Muse Jessie Mann on Being Photographed*.
Melissa Harris interviews Jessie Mann about her experience modeling for
her mother and her aspirations for the future.

Melissa Harris

DAUGHTER, MODEL, MUSE JESSIE MANN ON BEING PHOTOGRAPHED

I think what's changed most in the way I feel about my mother's prints is that I don't
look at them as pictures of *me* any longer. There's a point when you just have to look
at them and appreciate what's meaningful about them as photographs rather than
thinking, "Oh, that was the day we caught that really big fish." Because that's how
other people see them. It's interesting now for me to look at their artistic significance. Maybe the pictures are more magical and mysterious and meaningful to me
than they are to other people—although I've spoken to people who seem to pick
up on the magic of that location and of our childhood, and seem to understand it as
if they were there, because they can see it in the photographs. So it's interesting for
me to see if I can feel what other people are getting from the prints.

When we were taking pictures, it created a relationship with Mom that's very
different than other people's relationships—much more powerful. I just read
The Moor's Last Sigh by Salman Rushdie, in which the main character is painted
by his mother through his whole life, and he talks about how this creates a completely different bond between mother and child. Because there already is a very
powerful bond, then add to that the bond between artist and subject, and think
about artists who study one subject for most of their lives, and the bond that they
must have, the artistic bond.... On top of being our mother, she became a whole
lot more. So that made our relationship stronger, but of course more complicated.

At some point, we realized this work was consequential, which I think was
another side effect. Then later on, we became aware of the controversy the work
was creating, and that made us question—well, what were her motives in taking
the photographs? I don't mean anything sexual or negative—but we were hearing
a lot of "bad mother" stuff, so it made us question her more than most children

Sally Mann, *Candy Cigarette,* **1989.** From *Immediate Family* by Sally Mann.
(© Sally Mann. Courtesy: Edwynn Houk Gallery, New York)

might question their mothers. So that added yet another layer of intensity to our relationship.

Up until recently Virginia, Emmett, and I haven't really discussed all of it very much. But now Emmett and I talk about it occasionally. We're at the point where questions have to be asked, as we begin to march out into the future, and we have to look back on our childhood. There's a reconciliation all children have with their parents once they get out of their teenage years. We're getting to it, but with a lot more issues to deal with: about the intensity and the conflict and the mother–child relationship when it's also artist–child. Maybe it was a harder childhood — or a more complicated one — than other children have.

But the other side of the coin is, we *enjoyed* being photographed. It gave us a sense of beauty. When you're around an artist all the time, you're always reminded of what's beautiful and what's special, and you can't forget it. Now, even though we are grown up — and Emmett and I are in college and living apart from her, and Ginna has begun boarding school — we still have that reminder. We got to travel, and meet a lot of great people, and had all this great exposure. So we have to factor those experiences into the moving-out on to our own things.

People don't usually recognize me now. I mean, very rarely. But the three of us have gained this strange status in society. It's different than child movie stars — we're sort of "art stars." But *child* art stars. No one really knows where we stand. But sometimes I'll meet people and they say, "Oh, I've just followed you; you're my favorite one of the kids." And I think, "*Favorite* one?..." It's very odd: the pictures are so significant to so many people that it can be very weird to me.

It's not something we can escape. The best analogy I have for it is the Glass family in the Salinger novels, and how each one of them handled growing out of that childhood celebrity and becoming their own people. Two of them went into the movie business, and one shot himself, and one seemed to drop off the face of the earth. They all had to deal with this child celebrity, childhood significance.

How do you parlay that into your future?

It's weird now when people say, "Well, now what are you going to do?" For so long, what we did was model — that's what we did. And now we have to choose another career, at a time when most people are looking for their first career. We've had this great experience, we've met some of the great minds of our time, and we've *lived* with one of the great minds of our time [LAUGHS] — so how are we going to *use* that? Are we ever going to be able to live up to the significance of the experiences we've had, or live up to our mother?

99

COMMENT

"The inexpensive home-camera may have invented an important part of what we've come to mean in America in the twentieth century by *family* and by all the tangled feelings evoked in the echoes of that most loaded of human nouns."

—Reynolds Price, author

Each of us is dealing with that pressure in a very different way. Emmett is completely daunted by it. He doesn't know what he wants, so he backs away from the whole thing: he's sometimes afraid to have any goals or any aspirations, doesn't want to get too involved or too intense. Mom is a very driven person, and really has little understanding of people who aren't that driven. Emmett has got to sort it out on his own. He and I are very close. Kind of like Franny and Zooey, we keep each other together. We help each other out. Nobody can understand what I'm going through like he can.

Ginna, on the other hand, was a lot younger than Emmett and me when those pictures were taken, so I think the experience for her was completely different. Her attitude right now is: "I want to have a normal life; I want to forget about this; I don't want to have to *use* it to my advantage; I don't want to either be living up to something or living down to something; I'm just going to be *living*." She's trying to go the middle road more than I've ever seen, trying to be "normal." And coming out of our family, that takes a lot of effort.... Ginna wants to be like everybody else, and these pictures have made that difficult. One of the things that Mom did best was always allow us to sort of *go* for it, to find out who we were, no matter what the cost. When I wanted to shave my head, she was there with the clippers. "Do it. Have fun. Explore yourself. I'm not going to tell you who you are." For me, that was a really great freedom, but I don't think Ginna responded to the whole situation like that.

I feel—because I've had all these experiences, and met all these people, and had conversations most other kids my age probably haven't had—that I have a *responsibility* to utilize these experiences in my future. Which is a lot to ask of myself. But not more than I can do. I'm not saying that I'm going to expect to be anything like my mother. I just want to do something that is meaningful, that has a significance outside just making a living. I think that's what I've been taught by all this.

I have a very clear-cut idea about what I want to do with my future, and I think in many ways that's like Mom: we both know exactly what we're going to do and how we're going to get there. I want to be an obstetrician/gynecologist. I think that comes from my feeling of needing to do something significant, outside of just surviving and providing. I think education about birth control and providing birth control and abortion for women is the best thing. . . . It's what our country needs most, because no doctors will become abortion doctors anymore. They're scared. I guess—like Mom's work, in a way—it's doing something that makes people uncomfortable but that needs to be done. She said something that no one wanted to hear, but it had to be said.

There are so many levels to childhood that we as a society ignore, or don't accept. Rather than just saying it, she was able to capture it with photographs. It's easy to discount these things unless you can really see them in the kids' eyes, or see it in their actions.

I also think she brought out a certain sexuality in children that nobody wants to think about. Some people still have real problems with the pictures.... I'll make a friend, and eventually I'll say, "I wonder if I'm ever going to meet your parents?" And the person will answer, "Well, my Mom really opposes your mother's work, so you may not want to come over." I used to get all riled up about it. But now I understand — it's hard for people. I think if you have a certain background or beliefs those photographs could be upsetting or offensive. I don't agree with that point of view, but maybe there's something to their idea that that part of children shouldn't be played up. I can accept someone else's point of view about it. It's only when they start passing judgment about me as a person or my mother as a person that it gets to me.

All three of us are very defensive of Mom because of this, so it's hard to look back and wonder, "Well, what if the photos hadn't been there?" I know, no matter what, there would have been an amazing strain on my relationship with Mom. We're very similar — it's just the way we are made up. There was no way we were going to live together compatibly! But on some level, there's always the question: *Would* things have been easier if it hadn't been for the photographs? Yet at the same time, without them we wouldn't have had these extraordinary opportunities.

With Dad, the best analogy I can come up with is that Mom, Emmett, Virginia, and I — we're all drama queens, actors on a stage, doing our thing and putting on a performance. But Dad is the stage. Without him, we wouldn't have the emotional support we need to keep going. He's there to work between all these strong characters and keep everything together. He's a lawyer; he plays this very simple but absolutely essential role. He keeps us all sane. I can't imagine it's much fun for him. Well, keeping us on peaceful terms is probably good for him, too. He's really needed.

When Aperture published *Immediate Family,* Mom and Dad sat us down, and we had a family meeting. They asked, "Are you going to be okay with this?" Dad was a big part of making sure we *really* were okay; they sent us to a counselor to make sure we were okay with it. We were all pretty young, so I don't think anyone could have had any idea what it was really going to be like. But if I were back at that table today, making the decision, I'd still say, "Go ahead. Show them."

As a result of her upbringing, Mom's a little reserved. She isn't touchy-affectionate. She has a hard time letting us know how much she loves us. But I've also realized that each one of those photographs was her way of capturing, somehow — if not in a hug or a kiss or a comment — how much she cared about us, but obviously didn't have the ability to show us. Each one of those photographs is an affirmation of love. To me, it seems like she's overwhelmed with this feeling of love and she doesn't know what to do with it, so she photographs it.

I think that there's something similar going on with her landscapes. She won't admit to any religious or spiritual tendencies, and laughs at anyone who has them — "Oh, Jessie, you and your spiritual-growth thing again." But I've never seen anything so spiritual as those landscapes. It's her capturing — her understanding of God, her understanding of what life is about. Even though she'd never say it, she'd never tell anyone that's what she's photographing — and she'll probably disagree with me — it's *there.* Because she catches the *meaning* of the beauty around here.

101

COMMENT

"There is absolutely one inarguable statement
you can make about these pictures: they testify
to a maternal passion that is not only natural but
pretty close to universally experienced. Anyone
who finds it 'dichotomous' that a mother should
produce such saturatingly maternal images is
beyond reasoning with."

—Sally Mann

MESSAGE

After you read the interview
with Jessie Mann and study
the photograph, what do
you think *Candy Cigarette,
1989* is attempting to "say"
— if anything? What **caption** might you write for
the photograph? For ex-
ample, how are the issues
of childhood and adult-
hood, innocence and expe-
rience, conveyed visually
by Sally Mann in this photograph of her daughter?

METHOD

As a photograph, *Candy
Cigarette, 1989* seems to
be both a casual snapshot
and an artfully posed portrait. After closely examining the photograph, what
elements would you say
contribute to both effects?
Which aspects of the pho-
tograph appear accidental
or random? Which appear
posed and artificial? Why
would the photographer
want to combine both
kinds of photography — the
snapshot and the studio
portrait — within a single
frame?

MEDIUM

In the interview Jessie Mann
says that she and her siblings "*enjoyed* being photographed." How does it
change the way you read
Candy Cigarette, 1989 to
have Jessie's own words on
being the subject of such
photography? What kind of
a portrait do Jessie's words
paint of her mother?

THE *MONA LISA*

2 ESSAYS   7 PORTRAITS

A superstar is a celebrity whose features we instantly recognize — today, usually because of continuous media coverage. Given today's standards, does Leonardo da Vinci's *Mona Lisa* qualify as a "superstar," as Joseph A. Harriss claims in "Seeking Mona Lisa"? Instantly recognized throughout the world, the portrait has been subjected to endless interpretation; yet much about the painting remains as enigmatic as the mysterious woman's famous smile. Who was the woman Leonardo painted? Was she the young wife of a Florentine official, as is commonly thought? What does her expression signify? And, perhaps most important, why has this particular portrait remained so universally appealing throughout so many centuries? Recent computer analysis suggests a remarkable possibility — that the mysterious Mona Lisa is no actual or imaginary woman but is instead none other than Leonardo da Vinci himself.

Though highly speculative, Lillian Feldman Schwartz's intriguing computer analysis may have been anticipated in 1919 by one of France's earliest modern artists, Marcel Duchamp. On one level Duchamp was commenting on society's blind respect for artistic masterpieces; but on another level was his masculinization of the *Mona Lisa* an indication that he, too, sensed a male presence behind the world's most famous smile?

103

Go to exercise 01 on **ix visual exercises** to explore **element** and **contrast** — then apply those terms to the portraits you see in this cluster's examples of how people have played with an iconoclastic image.

Joseph A. Harriss, *Seeking Mona Lisa*. This informative essay covers the history of what the author calls "the most famous work in the entire 40,000 year history of the visual arts." Joseph A. Harriss is an American writer based in Paris, where he has lived for over forty years. He has contributed to numerous magazines throughout his career but today writes mostly for *Smithsonian* magazine. This essay appeared in the May 1999 issue of *Smithsonian* magazine.

Joseph A. Harriss
SEEKING MONA LISA

Going with the flow, I follow the body heat from the cavernous crypt beneath the Louvre's glass pyramid up past a dying Italian slave and a nude Greek warrior, a diminutive French general directing troops, and a carelessly draped lady with wings. On the second floor, in a room where you could comfortably play tennis, the background murmur grows to a clamor and the air, on this warm August day, is distinctly ripe. Harried tour leaders waving striped sticks or colorful scarves try to corral their polyglot charges. But most of them are busy jockeying and elbowing to get as close as they can to a bullet-proof, air-conditioned showcase for a glimpse of Leonardo da Vinci's 500-year-old portrait of a preternaturally poised Florentine lady.

Largely ignoring the room's other masterpieces of Italian classical painting, its splendid Tintorettos, Veroneses, and Titians, the throng aims high-performance cameras at the showcase and lets fly a fusillade of flashes, pinpoints of light bouncing back from its window. Many stand beside it to be photographed, as if they were in front of the Eiffel Tower. It all reminds me of when, as a young reporter, I occasionally had to cover chaotic, shoving, celebrity press conferences. Except here the superstar says nothing. She merely gazes back with a cool, appraising smile.

◀ **The *Mona Lisa*.** The Italian artist, architect, scientist, and inventor Leonardo da Vinci (1452–1519) painted the *Mona Lisa* five hundred years ago, between 1503 and 1506. Once completed, the painting remained in the artist's possession and was among his personal effects when he died in France. It thus became one of France's most treasured works of art and the leading attraction at the Louvre museum in Paris, where it has been on display since Leonardo's death in 1519. (Réunion des Musées Nationaux/Art Resource, NY)

The New Yorker **cover, February 8, 1999.** In this issue of *The New Yorker,* Monica Lewinsky was named Woman of the Year; an editorial by David Remnick explained why Monica as Mona Lisa made sense: "In Monica we have taken to seeing anything or anyone we care to; the innocent brought low, the sexual independent, the retrograde temptress. She is everywhere. She suits all interpretations." (Dean Rohrer/*The New Yorker* © 1999, Condé Nast Publications. Reprinted by permission. All Rights Reserved)

The *Mona Lisa* is the most famous work in the entire 40,000-year history of the visual arts. And if you don't agree with that, your argument is not with me but with the respected art historian Roy McMullen, who has studied the phenomenon extensively. "It provokes instant shocks of recognition on every continent from Asia to America," he observes, "reduces the Venus of Milo and the Sistine Chapel to the level of merely local marvels, sells as many postcards as a tropical resort, and stimulates as many amateur detectives as an unsolved international murder mystery." Like many celebrities, the *Mona Lisa* today is famous for being famous. Louvre officials estimate that most of the museum's first-time visitors come mainly to stare at this cross between a cultural archetype and an icon of kitsch.[1] Undoubtedly, the painting has become part of our collective subconscious. What they are looking for is the picture that has provoked— and been the object of— more crazy reactions, addled adulation, arcane analysis, gross imitations, scandalous takeoffs, and crass commercialization than any other work of art in history.

The painting's status as a world-class superstar was confirmed beyond any doubt when, in 1963, the French Minister of Culture, André Malraux— who called the painting "the most subtle homage that genius has ever rendered to a living face"— sent it to the United States and, a decade later, to Japan as a sort of itinerant ambassador of French culture, its Italian origins notwithstanding. On arriving in America in January 1963, in its own cabin aboard the SS *France,* the *Mona Lisa* was received more like a potentate than a painting. A tuxedoed President John F. Kennedy and an evening-gowned Jacqueline Kennedy formally welcomed it to Washington's National Gallery of Art, where the director, John Walker, hailed it as "the most famous single work of art ever to cross the ocean." White-gloved U.S. marines guarded the painting around the clock. Even though the museum was kept open evenings for the first time in its history, crowds waited

106

---

[1]A once derogatory term deriving from the German *kitschen* ("to throw together"), **kitsch** referred to art objects that were considered vulgar, inferior, tasteless, sentimental, or highly derivative— such as "collectible" figures of adorable little children, a maudlin portrait of a tearful clown, or paintings of cute kittens or puppies. Kitsch can be found anywhere but is especially plentiful in the souvenir shops of major cities. Wall calendars also commonly display kitsch. As some modern and contemporary artists began dissolving or outright dismissing the boundaries between "high" and "low" art, however, and as they self-consciously incorporated "kitschy" references into their work, the term has become less evaluative and more descriptive of a certain popular style.—ED.

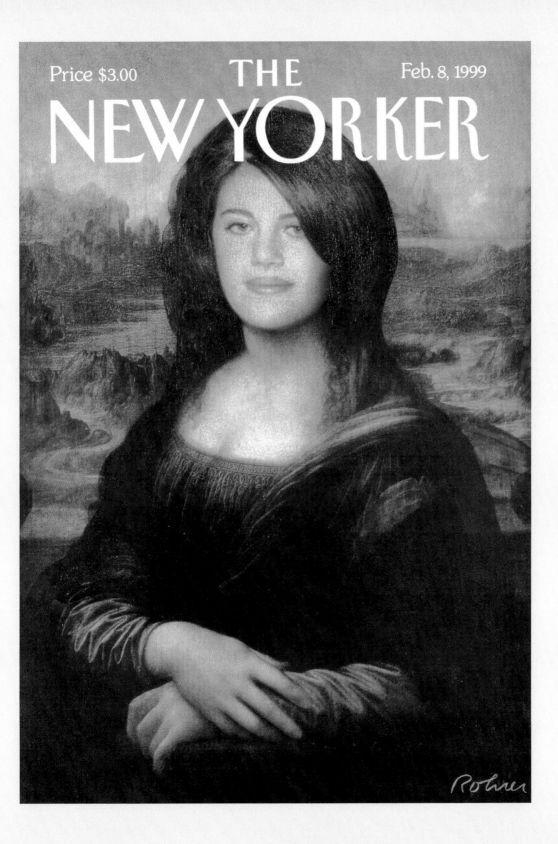

for up to two hours to get a look at the famous face; one man asked a guard, in passing, what the grand building was used for when the *Mona Lisa* wasn't there. It was the same mob scene in February and March at New York's Metropolitan Museum of Art, with lines down Fifth Avenue for blocks in severe winter weather. In all, more than two million Americans ogled the *Mona Lisa.*

But Mona mania in America paled beside the frenzy in Japan, to the hand-wringing despair of some French aesthetes who complained that the work was being exhibited like Brigitte Bardot or a Folies Bergère *danseuse.* When the *Mona Lisa* arrived at Tokyo's National Museum in April 1974, visitors totaling 1.5 million thronged the building and were hustled past the painting for a ten-second look. A uniformed guard atop a podium directed the traffic. Outside, the hype approached hysteria. Dozens of bars and nightclubs changed their names to Mona Lisa, one staging a Mona Lisa Nude Revue. A telephone number yielded a recording of the lady saying, in Italian, how happy she was to be in Japan. Japanese girls wore décolleté dark dresses with long sleeves, and parted their hair in the middle; some even resorted to plastic surgery in order to produce a more convincing Lisa Look.

The look that inspires such bizarre behavior is defined by the enigmatic, tight-lipped smile that has launched a thousand learned interpretations, lucid explanations — and loony analyses. Renowed art critic Bernard Berenson set the tone for serious appreciation when he proclaimed that Leonardo's subtle sfumato[2] technique of modeling light and shade reached its apex with the *Mona Lisa.* For centuries many an artist has tried to equal it as a sort of ultimate challenge, the Everest of oil painting. One, the French artist Luc Maspero, threw himself from the fourth-floor window of his Paris hotel in the mid-19th century, leaving a farewell note: "For years I have grappled desperately with her smile. I prefer to die."

Even when not inducing a death wish, the smile has often generated perplexity. Is it "more divine than human," as a 16th-century Italian writer had it, or "worldly, watchful and self-satisfied," according to British art historian Kenneth Clark? The 19th-century French Positivist thinker Hippolyte Taine seemed unable to make up his mind, variously called it "doubting, licentious, Epicurean, deliciously tender, ardent, sad," while novelist Lawrence Durrell puckishly dubbed it "the smile of a woman who has just eaten her husband." Feminist Camille Paglia went further: "What Mona Lisa is ultimately saying is that males are unnecessary," she opined. Salvador Dalí, ever provocative, even attributed the 1956 attack on the painting, when a young Bolivian threw a rock that put a small scar on the left elbow, to the smile. "Subconsciously in love with his mother, ravaged by the Oedipus complex," Dalí theorized, the young man was "stupefied to

---

[2]Many critics have observed that a large part of the Mona Lisa's enigmatic smile results from Leonardo's innovative use of a technique Italians termed *sfumato,* which noted art historian E. H. Gombrich describes as "the blurred outline and mellowed colors that allow one form to merge with another and always leave something to our imagination."—ED.

discover a portrait of his own mother, transfigured by the maximum female idealization. His own mother, here! And worse, his mother smiles ambiguously at him. . . . Attack is his one possible response to such a smile.

In our less poetic age, the trend has been more to physiological explanations for the smile. Was Mona Lisa, whoever she was, asthmatic? Simply a contented pregnant housewife? Some researchers have concluded that she probably smiled with her mouth closed because she was undergoing 16th-century-style mercury treatment for syphilis; the mercury would have turned her teeth an ugly black, and left her with a sorely inflamed mouth. A Danish doctor found that the model had congenital palsy affecting the left side of her face, backing up his theory by pointing out that she had the typically large hands of such patients. After due study, an orthopedic surgeon in Lyons, France, decided that Mona Lisa's semi-smile resulted from her being half-paralyzed either from birth or as the result of a stroke; one indication of this, he argued, was that her right hand looks relaxed but her left hand is strangely tense.

But more intriguing than why the model is smiling is the mystery of exactly *who* is doing the smiling. An early reference to a woman named Lisa comes from the 16th-century Italian art historian Giorgio Vasari — who himself never actually saw the painting. Writing around 1550, a good 40 years after the work was supposed to have been completed, Vasari says: "Leonardo undertook to paint for Francesco del Giocondo a portrait of Monna [a variation of *mona* or *madonna,* "lady"] Lisa his wife." Historians know that a Lisa Gherardini of Florence was married in 1495, at the age of 16, to Francesco di Bartolommeo di Zanobi del Giocondo, a 35-year-old Florentine official already twice a widower. But there's no evidence at all that del Giocondo commissioned the portrait from Leonardo, no sign he paid the artist, and, most important, no sign the painting was delivered to him, since Leonardo kept it with him until his death in Amboise, France, in 1519. Nor does Leonardo mention the project anywhere in his voluminous notebooks.

So art historians have had a field day trying to guess whose portrait it is. Some plump for Isabella d'Este, who knew Leonardo well in Milan and whose portrait he did in crayon, perhaps as a study for an oil painting. Others hold for Costanza d'Avalos, duchess of Francaville, who is mentioned in a contemporary poem as having been painted in mourning by Leonardo "under the lovely black veil." There's even speculation that a second portrait of Mona Lisa may have existed. That painting may have been commissioned by one Giuliano de' Medici — perhaps because he was so taken with the original portrait that he requested one for himself. Evidence exists that he asked Leonardo to paint her, leading to the intriguing possibility that the artist did two *Mona Lisas*, one for her husband, Francesco, and one for Giuliano, who may have been her lover. Now there's something to smile secretly about.

Then there's the high-tech approach. Lillian Schwartz, a computer graphics consultant at the Lucent Technologies Bell Labs in New Jersey, has applied computer-based techniques to the mystery. After reversing Leonardo's self-portrait so the artist is facing to the left, then scaling the image and juxtaposing it

109

Marcel Duchamp, *L.H.O.O.Q.*, 1930.
Duchamp (1887–1968), who became
a U.S. citizen in 1954, was one of the
first to use ordinary objects as an inspiration for art, a concept of "ready-
mades." Duchamp used bicycle tires,
urinals, snow shovels, and other common, "non-art" objects in work
that ultimately influenced such later
movements as surrealism and pop art.
Wanting to satirize his era's overly reverential attitude toward major works
of art, Duchamp drew a conventional
moustache and goatee on a roughly
8- by 5-inch print of the *Mona Lisa*.
He then added to his appropriation of
Leonardo's famous creation by giving
his work a cryptic, though crude, title.
(Cameraphoto/Art Resource, NY)

110

COMMENT

"The best-known satire on [the worship of high art] was Marcel Duchamp's
L.H.O.O.Q. . . . : the moustache on the *Mona Lisa*, a gesture by now synonymous with
impish cultural irreverence. As is usual with Duchamp's puns, it works on several layers at once. The coarse title — *L.H.O.O.Q.*, pronounced letter by letter in French,
means: 'She's got a hot ass' — combines with the schoolboy graffito of the moustache
and goatee; but then a further level of anxiety reveals itself, since giving male attributes to the most famous and highly fetishized female portrait ever painted is also a
subtler joke on Leonardo's own homosexuality (then a forbidden subject) and on
Duchamp's own interest in the confusion of sexual roles."

— Robert Hughes, from *The Shock of the New* (1991)

with the *Mona Lisa* (whose subject also faces left) on the computer screen, Schwartz found that the noses, mouths, foreheads, cheekbones, eyes, and brows all line up. Conclusion: Leonardo started with an earlier portrait of a woman, then, finding himself without the sitter, used himself as the model—sans beard. She ties it all together with the knotted patterns, resembling basketwork, on the bodice of Mona Lisa's dress. Noting that Leonardo, like many Renaissance poets and artists, loved riddles and puns, she makes the connection between his name, Vinci, and *vinco,* the Italian word for the osier branches used in basketry. Voilà, the case is made. "That famous smile, so tantalizing for so many centuries, is the mirrored smile of da Vinci himself," she says confidently.

Not everyone is convinced. But the possibility of a pun lying at the heart of Leonardo's mystery painting is taken seriously at the Louvre. Giocondo, Lisa Gherardini's married name, means, in Italian, cheerful, merry, joyous, as does "jocund" in English. (A varient of the word supplies the French title for the painting, *La Joconde*). Leonardo had already played with a sitter's name by incorporating a juniper bush in his portrait of Ginevra (similar to "juniper," *ginepro* in Italian) de' Benci that hangs in the National Gallery of Art. "He was punning on Mona Lisa's married name when he gave her a subtle smile in *La Joconde,*" says Cécile Scailliérez, curator of 16th-century French and Italian painting at the Louvre. "He made it emblematic of her. What we really have here is an idea, more than a realistic portrait, the idea of a smile expressed in the form of a painting."

For at least the past 150 years, appreciation of the *Mona Lisa* has veered back and forth between awed Giocondolatry and burlesque Giocondoclasm. The overwrought school of heated, romantic interpretation might have begun, oddly enough, with the Marquis de Sade, who found Mona Lisa full of "seduction and devoted tenderness," and "the very essence of femininity," though given his tastes one wonders exactly what he meant. A bit later the great French historian Jules Michelet admitted, "This painting attracts me, calls me, invades me, absorbs me; I go to it in spite of myself, as the bird goes to the serpent."

The idea of Mona Lisa as femme fatale was launched. Walter Pater, leader of the 19th-century English Aestheticism movement and ardent advocate of art for art's sake, followed up turgidly. "She is older than the rocks among which she sits," he swooned; "like the vampire, she has been dead many times, and learned the secrets of the grave." Not only that; for him this exotic beauty expressed "the animalism of Greece, the lust of Rome, the mysticism of the middle age…the return of the Pagan world, the sins of the Borgias." Pater seemed badly in need of a cold shower, as was the French writer of the same period, Arsène Houssaye, who called her "treacherously and deliciously a woman, with six thousand years of experience, a virgin with an angelic brow who knows more than all the knowing rakes of Boccaccio."

Sigmund Freud, too, pulled out all the stops when trying to figure out the "beautiful Florentine lady." Neatly pigeonholing Leonardo as an obsessive neurotic in his book-length study *Leonardo da Vinci, A Study in Psychosexuality,* Freud decided that Mona Lisa's expression must have resembled the lost, mysterious smile of the artist's mother. As for Mona Lisa herself, he proclaimed her nothing

111

112

Vik Muniz, *Mona Lisa (Peanut Butter and Jelly)*, 1999. Muniz, who was born in Brazil in 1961, uses a quote from the ancient Roman poet Ovid to describe his artistic statement: "My mind is bent to tell of bodies changed into new forms." He uses materials such as chocolate, spaghetti sauce, and PB&J to represent icons of art history and challenges us to see images as "the containers of memory and information." (Art © Vic Muniz/Licensed by VAGA, New York, NY. Courtesy of the Brent Sikkema Gallery, New York)

less than "the most perfect representation of the contrasts dominating the love-life of the woman, namely reserve and seduction, most submissive tenderness and the indifferent craving, which confront the man as a strange and consuming sensuality." (On second thought, perhaps we had better not take the kids to the Louvre after all.)

Twentieth-century ideas on art became more down-to-earth — like, how much is it worth? King Francis I added the *Mona Lisa* to France's royal collections for 4,000 gold *écus,* or about $105,000. Today Louvre officials say that the *Mona Lisa's* monetary value is inestimable. In 1911, however, it was somewhere in between: the painting, though precious, was not yet such a superstar on the world art market that it couldn't be sold. That made it worth stealing.

The biggest art heist in history occurred that year, with Parisians waking up on August 23 to screaming headlines like the one in the daily *Excelsior:* "The Louvre's *Joconde* Stolen: When? How? Who?" The answers were a long time coming, as an army of French, German, Russian, Greek and Italian detectives went on a merry, futile chase for two years. Then, when the public was becoming resigned to the loss of the *Mona Lisa,* an Italian laborer named Vincenzo Perugia got tired of keeping the original in the false bottom of a trunk.

Perugia, who had worked in the museum, used his knowledge of it to lift the painting. He was put up to it by an Argentine con man named Eduardo de Valfierno, who had a skilled art forger knock off six copies. Valfierno then sold the copies to eager, if unscrupulous, collectors — five in North America, one in Brazil — who thought they were getting the real thing straight from the Louvre. The scam made him the equivalent today of $67 million. When Valfierno didn't claim the original — ironically, he didn't need it for the operation — Perugia naively offered it for sale to a Florence art dealer and was promptly pinched. The *Mona Lisa* returned to France on December 31, 1913, ensconced in a special compartment of the Milan-Paris express. Her retinue included an assortment of policemen, politicians, museum bureaucrats, and artists. Incredibly, the painting had suffered no physical damage.

The damage was to the blind veneration and respect in which the portrait had been held for centuries. Somehow the caper and its familiar, irreverent press coverage rubbed off some of the *Mona Lisa's* mystique. The age of Giocondoclasm had begun.

Even Bernard Berenson admitted a change of heart. "To my amazement," he wrote after the theft was announced, "I found myself saying softly: 'If only it were true!' And when the news was confirmed I heaved a sigh of relief....She had simply become an incubus, and I was glad to be rid of her." For this eminent connoisseur of Western art, as surely for many others, all the bowing and scraping over the *Mona Lisa* had become a pain in the neck.

Suddenly the public couldn't get enough of jokey Giocondiana. One postcard showed a grinning, toothy Mona Lisa thumbing her nose at the public and saying, "I'm off to see my Vinci, thanks and good-bye, all you gawkers." Another postcard, after the return, showed her holding a baby with Perugia's picture in the background, as if she'd been on a romantic escapade.

With irreverence and reaction against "bourgeois" values the new order of the day, the painting that had been the image of perfect, inaccessible beauty became the ideal target for desperately modern iconoclastic artists, like the Dadaists, who were sick of the very idea of a masterpiece. Marcel Duchamp, unofficial leader of the Dada anti-art movement, summed up the new zeitgeist[3] in 1919 with a few strokes of his brush. Taking a standard postcard reproduction, he brushed in a pointy mustache and goatee on the sacred face, and added a naughty caption. Now his action looks like no more than a childish prank. But the uptight art establishment, raised on the likes of Pater and the traditions of academic painting, was shocked, *shocked*.

Today the *Mona Lisa* is in the paradoxical situation of being both the symbol of Art and the inspiration for kitsch. Artists vie to see who can do the most outrageous parody; advertising studios labor to come up with the funniest way to use the image to sell everything from aperitifs to airlines, golf clubs to strips that hold your nasal passages open. Collectors of Giocondiana have catalogued nearly 400 advertising uses of the image and counting, along with at least 61 products called Mona Lisa, made in 14 countries.

Want to mock Salvador Dalí's commercialism? Do a montage with his eyes and upraised mustache on Mona Lisa's face, then put his hands overflowing with money in place of hers. Touché! Want to make light of a weighty public figure, from Stalin to De Gaulle to Prince Charles? Caricature him as Mona Lisa. Funn*eee*! The portrait also has become the favorite of computer-age digitizers of images. In Paris, Jean-Pierre Yvaral has done more than 150 synthesized Mona Lisas composed of hundreds of geometric patterns that look abstract up close but become Herself from afar. Next big project: digital images of her on the tails of British Airways jetliners.

Andy Warhol, *Mona Lisa: 1963.* (© 2004 Andy Warhol ▶
Foundation for the Visual Arts/Ars, New York. Photo:
Peter Schalchi, Zurich)

---

[3]In German *zeitgeist* literally means "the spirit of the time." Commonly used in literary and philosophical criticism, the term refers to the ideas that prevail in a particular period and place.—ED.

Though he's no high-flying art critic or historian, Jean Margat has his own answer to the painting's mythic hold on the imagination. A retired geologist, Margat, from his home near Orléans, France, presides over the Friends of Mona Lisa, a club of serious collectors of Giocondiana, of which Louvre director Pierre Rosenberg is a member, along with a woman in faraway Ann Arbor, Michigan.

Margat and other Friends get together once in a while for a convivial lunch in Paris where they discuss and compare their collections. Margat's takes up a good part of his two-story house and ranges from Mona Lisa T-shirts, posters, ballpoint pens, coffee mugs, drink coasters, condoms, panty hose, clocks, matchbooks, and thimbles bearing The Face, to truly rare — and expensive — items like a beaded curtain from Vietnam, a Persian rug, and a life-size Mona Lisa sculptured in two kinds of marble that he paid a pretty penny for in Switzerland. His latest enthusiasm is for a bit of kitsch created in Brooklyn and known as the Giggling Mona Lisa Pillow, which squeals with glee when squeezed in the middle. The Friends now are developing an Internet site and hope to advise the planners of a mega-Mona exhibition, tentatively scheduled to open in Paris, to mark the year 2000.

By then the painting may have its own special room at the Louvre, the better to admire it — and keep the crowd away from the other museumgoers — thanks to a $4.1 million grant from a Japanese television network. This biggest-ever act of cultural sponsorship in France leaves Louvre curators with mixed feelings. Already prisoners of the myth, they can't touch the *Mona Lisa* to clean it for fear of media and public outcry, although it's filthy and covered with thick yellowish varnish that would benefit from cleaning. "The new room will be an improvement," says a resigned Cécile Scailliérez, "but unfortunately it will make the *Mona Lisa* even more of a superstar by setting it apart." As for Jean Margat, the project leaves him cold. "Frankly I don't much like that painting," he says with a shrug. "To me it's not expressive and it doesn't look like a real person. But I guess it's timeless, *hélas.*"

COMMENT

"For Warhol, however, as for the kitsch craftsmen who follow in his wake, the *Mona Lisa* is the quintessential 'celebrity.' While she is famous for being famous, unlike the instant evanescent celebrity of today, she is taken from outside of time — her fame is outside of the ravages of time. She is an icon — an emblem signifying the magical power of images and power of image-making to surpass and ignore style, fad, and even the awkward temporary skills of her many copyists."

— Robert Baron

Lillian Feldman Schwartz, *The Mona Lisa Identification: Evidence from a Computer Analysis*. Lillian Schwartz, one of the pioneers in the field of computer art, concludes that the *Mona Lisa* is really a self-portrait. Combining historical analysis with a computer-based study of the painting in conjunction with a sketch Leonardo did of himself while in his late sixties, Schwartz's analysis suggests an answer to the mystery of the appeal of this painting: "Could it be that both women and men find traits that are physically attractive?"

Lillian Feldman Schwartz

THE MONA LISA IDENTIFICATION: EVIDENCE FROM A COMPUTER ANALYSIS

117

A recent computer-aided study identified the model immortalized in Leonardo da Vinci's celebrated *Mona Lisa* to be none other than the artist himself. A follow-up investigation employing similar techniques identifies the subject of a **second** "Hidden" *Mona Lisa* by the same artist. Analysis of photographic and X-ray images indicates that Leonardo first created a sketch of Isabella, Duchess of Aragon, which he later painted over with the *Mona Lisa,* using himself as the model.

This paper describes a computer-based study supported by historical analysis which indicates that Leonardo da Vinci used himself as the model for the celebrated painting known as the *Mona Lisa,* thereby answering a 500-year-old question and solving the puzzle which has surrounded one of the world's most famous paintings. The results of a second investigation, also described herein, trace the source of contradictory historical evidence surrounding Leonardo's celebrated painting to a second "Hidden" *Mona Lisa* by the same artist, visible to us only in X-rays.

To avoid confusion, the universally acclaimed painting we all know will be referred to as the "Surface" *Mona Lisa,* in order to distinguish it from the second "Hidden" *Mona Lisa* which lies beneath it on the same panel.

An X-ray taken of the *Mona Lisa* early in the twentieth century reveals a second face beneath the "Surface" painting. While uncritical commentators have long assumed that the X-ray image depicts the same face as the one on the "Surface" painting, computer analysis tells us differently. When the two images were superimposed in the study described below, the X-ray's features did not match those of the "Surface" painting. On the other hand, the X-ray seems to match a third image, a cartoon (a full-size preparatory study which is usually copied or transferred to the final surface, in this case a wood panel) portraying Isabella, Duchess of Aragon, and painted with the same composition as the "Surface" painting. Leonardo is known to have sketched this cartoon prior to painting the *Mona Lisa* itself.

Our results suggest that the model who perplexed scholars for so many years posed, not for the celebrated "Surface" *Mona Lisa* itself, but for the second or "Hidden" portrait instead.

Historical analysis described in the subsequent sections of this paper supports the computer-based identification of the two models used in the respective paintings. In the following sections, we describe: the "Surface" *Mona Lisa* and the analytical techniques employed to study it; the "Hidden" portrait and its analysis; and a chronology which tells the story which led to the creation of this two-faced masterpiece.

THE *SURFACE* PAINTING

The identity of Leonardo da Vinci's model for his painting *Mona Lisa* has plagued historians for over 500 years [1]. Early writings stated that she was the wife of Francisco del Giocondo [2], but a number of contradictions question the validity of this candidate and all the others which have been proposed.

The identity is further obscured by a portrait that does not exhibit the clarity of line characteristic of that period [3]. Leonardo blended the figure with the background to make it appear as if we are seeing the figure through a veil [4].

The life-like appearance of the painting [5] leads us to expect it to have been painted from a human model, but much of the portrait appears to be contrived. The strange landscape in the background is half fantasy and half real with two different horizon levels on either side of the figure [6]. The features are submerged so that the corners of the mouth and eyes are not distinct [4]. The lower lids are almost horizontal and the absence of eyebrows is striking [7]. The hands appear boneless [6]. Finally, the dress is timeless and quite plain, with no accompanying emblems, jewelry, or accessories [7], unlike that one would have expected had a conventional model been used.

The circumstances known to surround the creation of the painting raise two objections which act to confound the suggestion of any woman as the model.

First, there was no record pertaining to the *Mona Lisa* [8], or to the identity of the model [1]. Unlike Leonardo's precise notes regarding other commissions, detailed descriptions of their subject matter, sketches, and costs of materials as well as fees [8], there was no trace of a commission, payments, or preliminary studies for this work.

118

Lillian Schwartz, *Mona/Leo,* *1988.* This composite visually describes Schwartz's contention that the *Mona Lisa* is in fact da Vinci's self-portrait; it places the "surface" Mona Lisa next to the "second" face. (*Mona/Leo,* by Lillian F. Schwartz. Copyright © 1987 Lillian F. Schwartz. All rights reserved)

Second, Leonardo spent a number of years (three to ten), to complete this portrait [9], during a period in which he moved many times [9, 3], and lived in households without women [10].

One suggestion which meets many of the known criteria is that Leonardo did paint from life [5, 3], but that he did not use a woman for the sitter but painted from a male model instead [11].

This suggestion would seem to account for the lack of female characteristics in the figure and the contrived dress. Furthermore, the dichotomy of two separate landscapes, artfully blended with the figure, becomes consistent with an ambiguity in the subject.

While the "veil" painting technique would blur most of the male characteristics of a model's face, one distinguishing mark is very difficult to hide, and is indeed apparent on the face of the *Mona Lisa.* The male skulls of sexually dimorphic homminoids typically exhibit supraorbital embellishments. This feature is most pronounced in the large boney masses which protrude from the brows of chimpanzees, gorillas and many of the fossil skulls of human ancestors [12].

Lillian Schwartz, *Da Vinci Timeline*, 1995. Adapted from "The Art Historian's Computer" in *Scientific American*, April 1995, p. 106. (*Leonardo Morphed to the Mona Lisa,* by Lillian F. Schwartz. Copyright © 1995 Lillian F. Schwartz. All rights reserved)

120

While this feature is less pronounced in modern man, personal enquiries by the author [13] indicate that the supraorbital ridge is evident in at least 90 percent of the male skulls of our species, and is almost totally lacking in females. As can be seen from the *Self-Portrait,* Leonardo's face exhibits a markedly prominent orbital ridge. This same feature is also evident in the "female" face of the *Mona Lisa.*

At the same time, using a male instead of a female model would not explain the lack of records, unless the man in question was none other than Leonardo himself, since he could not be expected to make appointments with himself for sittings. Despite the use of androgynous figures in many of Leonardo's paintings, as well as those of other Renaissance artists [14], however, the possibility of a male model for the *Mona Lisa* received little attention prior to the present study.

The work described herein sprang from the accidental discovery of striking facial similarities between Leonardo's *Mona Lisa* and the artist's *Self-Portrait* exhibited in juxtaposed images created as part of an exploratory investigation of artists and their works.

Sequences of images which move gradually from one subject to another have a long history in the world of cinematography. Readers are probably familiar with the scenes in such films as *Dr. Jekyll and Mr. Hyde* and *Dorian Gray,* in which one face dissolves into another. Modern computer-based picture-processing techniques have been adapted to provide a convenient tool for the fusing of such images [15, 16] to provide the intermediate steps. Interactive graphics editors are used to define such transformations and compositions of digitized images [17].

In order to move from one image to another, the two images are first scaled and then aligned with respect to one another. The shape of the image, relative location of features, and the reshaping of features themselves must then be transformed by picture-processing programs. Such a technique was applied to

Leonardo's *Mona Lisa* and his *Self-Portrait.* Both pictures were bisected along vertical lines and the halves aligned using the nose tips. In contrast to other pairs of pictures [16], the two sets of features were found to exhibit a striking similarity. Juxtaposing the *Self-Portrait* with the *Mona Lisa* did not require the usual reshaping of the features to fuse the two images. The relative locations of the nose, mouth, chin, eyes, and forehead in one image matched those of the others as described in detail below.

121

The painting of the *Mona Lisa* and Leonardo's *Self-Portrait* [18] were scanned and digitized [15]. The grey levels were enhanced and the pictures scaled [17]. The image of the *Self-Portrait* was flipped about the vertical axis to make the composite picture, matching the left one-half of [the *Mona Lisa*] with the flipped left one-half of [the *Self-Portrait*].

The separate images exhibit the fine details characteristic of Leonardo's superb draftsmanship [19]. Interestingly, the two noses abut smoothly and exhibit continuity of line. The mouths are continuous except where the corner of Leonardo's mouth turns down. Merely flipping up the corner of the mouth reproduces the mysterious smile [20]. The line of the foreheads and chins falls into place. The eyes and the brows line up. A reduction of the pouch under Leonardo's eye produced a match to the horizontal lid [10] in [the *Mona Lisa*]. When measurements were taken, it was found that the distance between the inner canthi (the inner corners of the eye) deviated by less than 2 percent. To the accuracy of our measurements, the two portraits, one of the old man and the other of a mysterious "woman," portray the same face.

The historical information available to us points out Leonardo's extensive traveling during the period the *Mona Lisa* was painted [10, 4]. It is unlikely that any ordinary model could have accompanied him to Milan in 1506 or remained around during the final years when he worked on the painting without leaving a trace. The one anonymous model always available was himself.

The *Mona Lisa*

Leonardo's anatomical drawings are records in themselves of his superb draftsmanship [18], and yet the lower lids are almost horizontal [10], indicating that he hadn't painted this feature from life. If he painted his own eyes into the *Mona Lisa* he would have had to remove some of the aging from under his eyes. He was about fifty [10] at the time, and his *Self-Portrait,* sketched when he was in his sixties [18], shows a considerable amount of "bagging" under the eyes.

There is a lack of sexuality or clearly defined female beauty for standards of that time [21]. The universal appeal of this painting is a mystery. Could it be that both women and men find traits that are physically attractive? There are a number of sexually ambiguous figures that appear in Leonardo's drawings, in the angel of the *Virgin of the Rocks,* in some of the Apostles and the Christ of the *Last Supper,* and in the *St. John the Baptist* [22]. Such androgynous figures were often seen in Italian, particularly Florentine, fifteenth- and early sixteenth-century art [11, 14]. From his notebooks, we know that Leonardo was familiar with symbolic philosophizing associated with androgyny [11, 14]. Contemporary records support the plausibility of his painting himself in women's clothes [11, 14]. There are records of very persuasive evidence of Leonardo's homosexuality. On two occasions he was accused of sodomy and taken to court [11].

Does the dichotomy of the landscape reflect the dichotomy of the subject? The landscapes on either side of the *Mona Lisa* do not match. The horizon on the left appears much lower than the one on the right. One side is fantasy, the other logical, but neither fits into a time or place [23]. All other portraits generally attributed to Leonardo have some clue as to the subject [24]. The identifying mark in the *Mona Lisa* could well have been the two different landscapes, the two sexes combined into one sitter [25].

These considerations lead to a conclusion which is consistent with all the generally accepted information surrounding the painting and the circumstances of its creation.

1. It resolves the problem of the existence of a human model who was available over a period of years in different locations within a small household which was known to contain no women.
2. It accounts for the dress, no identifying jewelry, and the singular characteristics of the landscape. It explains the veil. The *sfumato* [27] technique was deliberately used to merge the forms, outlines, corners of the mouth and eyes into soft shadows.
3. It is consistent with the absence of records and sketches. There is no mention of a sitter's name, nor any allusions to the picture throughout the unusually long period spent in painting this picture. There is no delivery date and Leonardo never made a delivery [26, 8]. He did not turn it over to Giocondo, whom Vasari reported commissioned the work, or deliver it to some other supposed patron. Instead, he kept it with him in Florence, Milan, Rome, and France. Indeed, it was still with him on the day he died.

Most important, however, is the striking unity of the single image which appears from the fused pair of paintings of what had heretofore been regarded as portraits of two different people [25].

References and Notes

1. R. McMullen, *Mona Lisa* (U.S.A.: Houghton Mifflin, 1975), 31–47; Angela Ottino della Chiesa, *The Complete Paintings of Leonardo da Vinci,* introduction by L. D. Ettlinger (New York: Penguin Classics of World Art, 1967), 103; B. Santi, *Leonardo da Vinci* (U.S.A.: Harper & Row, 1981), 64; A. C. Coppier, *La jaconde est-elle le portrait de Monna Lisa?* (London: Les Arts, 1914), 1–9.

2. G. Vasari, *Lives of the Most Eminent Painters, Sculptors, and Architects,* trans. by Gaston DuC. DeVere (New York: The Modern Library, 1959), 203, 204.

3. B. Berenson, *Italian Painters of the Renaissance* (London: Phaidon, 1952); E. H. Gombrich, *The Story of Art* (N.J.: Prentice Hall, 1984), 224–227.

4. H. Wohl, *Leonardo da Vinci* (New York: McGraw-Hill, 1967), Slide 17: "Leonardo has here used the *sfumato* technique to make it appear that we are seeing the figure through a veil"; "That good and famous painter, who depicts so much beauty under the modest veil, overcomes art and vanquishes himself." E. Irpino, *Poet from Parma* (1505).

5. J. Steer, *A Concise History of Venetian Painting* (New York: Praeger, 1970), 109; E. H. Gombrich, *The Story of Art* (N.J.: Prentice Hall, 1984), 227.

6. J. Canaday, *Metropolitan Seminars in Art,* Portfolio 1, 6. *Mona Lisa* (New York: Metropolitan Museum of Art, 1958), 16, 17.

7. H. W. Janson, *History of Art* (N.J. and Abrams, N.Y.: Prentice Hall, 1963), 352: H. Wolfflin, *Classic Art,* NY Graphic Society publ. (Conn.: Phaidon, 1964), 29.

8. E. MacCurdy, *The Notebooks of Leonardo da Vinci,* vol. 1 (New York: Reynal & Hitchcock, 1939), 1008; R. McMullen, *Mona Lisa: The Picture and the Myth* (U.S.A.: Houghton Mifflin, 1975), 27.

9. R. McMullen, *Mona Lisa: The Picture and the Myth* (U.S.A.: Houghton Mifflin, 1975), 29–32,

10. R. McMullen, *Mona Lisa: The Picture and the Myth* (U.S.A.: Houghton Mifflin, 1975), 16, 18; S. Freud, *Leonardo da Vinci and a Memory of His Childhood,* trans. by A. Tyson. The standard edition of the complete psychological works, vol. 11 (London: 1957).

11. J. G. Griffiths, *Leonardo and the Latin Poets,* Classica et mediaevalia, vol. 16 (1955), 268: G. P. Lomazzo, *Trattato dell'arte della pittura* (Milan: 1584); R. McMullen, *Mona Lisa: The Picture and the Myth* (U.S.A.: Houghton Mifflin, 1975), 82–84.

12. J. H. Schwartz, *The Red Ape* (Boston: Houghton Mifflin, 1987), 195.

13. R. G. Feldman, professor and chairman of the Neurology Department at the Boston University School of Medicine.

14. Botticelli's angels and Verrocchio's *David.*

15. The *Mona Lisa* and the *Self-Portrait* were scanned at 2000 × 2000; D. E. Pearson, *Transmission and Display of Pictorial Information* (London: Pentech Press, 1975); W. B. Green, *Digital Image Processing* (New York: Van Nostrand Reinhold, 1983), 113.

16. L. F. Schwartz, "The Computer and Creativity," *Transactions of the American Philosophical Society 75,* pt. 6 (1985), 30–49; L. F. Schwartz and C. B. Rubinstein, "Film-Making with Computer," *Interdisciplinary Science Reviews 4,* no. 4 (1979), 273, 274, 284, 285.

123

17. G. Holzmann, *AT&T Technical Journal 66,* no. 1 (1987).

18. R. Wallace, *The World of Leonardo* (New York: Time Inc., 1966), 172.

19. L. da Vinci (before 1476), *Study of Drapery.* Brush drawing 26.6 × 23.4 cm (Paris: Louvre); Sala dalle Asse (1498), *Detail of (tempora) decoration by Leonardo* (Milan: Castello Sforzesco); S. A. Cheny, *New World History of Art* (New York: Viking Press, 1956), 365; E. H. Gombrich, *The Story of Art* (N.J.: Prentice Hall, 1984), 228.

20. H. W. Janson, *History of Art* (N.J. and Abrams, N.Y.: Prentice Hall, 1963), 352; Angela Ottino della Chiesa, *The Complete Paintings of Leonardo da Vinci* (New York: Penguin Classics of World Art, 1967), 104.

21. R. Wallace, *The World of Leonardo* (New York: Time-Life, 1966), 126, 127; F. Hart, *Italian Renaissance Art* (Abrams, N.Y.: 1986), 461; K. Clark, *Leonardo da Vinci: An Account of His Development as an Artist* (Md.: Penguin, 1967).

22. Angela Ottino della Chiesa, *Leonardo da Vinci* (Penguin Books, 1967), Plate XXXIII, *The Virgin of the Rocks;* Plates XLIV, XLVI, XLII, *The Last Supper;* Plate LX, *St. John the Baptist.*

23. F. Hart, *Italian Renaissance Art* (Abrams, N.Y.: 1986), 443; J. Canaday, *Metropolitan Seminars in Art,* Portfolio 1 (1958), 17; E. H. Gombrich, *The Story of Art* (N.J.: Prentice Hall, 1984), 228, 229.

24. Angela Ottino della Chiesa, *Leonardo da Vinci* (Penguin Books: 1967), Plates XVII, XXXVII, LXI; B. Santi, *Leonardo da Vinci* (U.S.A.: Harper & Row, 1981), 56; R. McMullen, *Mona Lisa: The Picture and the Myth* (U.S.A.: Houghton Mifflin, 1975), 48–50.

25. D. Merezhkovsky, *Romance of Leonardo da Vinci* (1902): "…she was smiling upon him with his own smile"; R. McMullen, *Mona Lisa: The Picture and the Myth* (U.S.A.: Houghton Mifflin, 1975), 86, 182.

26. Our earliest description of the sitter for the *Mona Lisa* could never have seen the painting for it was at Cloux by 1517, when Vasari was six years old and living in Arezzo. He never visited France. The painting was never delivered but was with Leonardo in France when he died.

27. E. H. Gombrich, *The Story of Art* (N.J.: Prentice Hall, 1986), 228; "Not only did this technique create a mystery around the painting where viewers seem to feel the painting is constantly changing but the age of the model becomes timeless"; R. Huyghe, *Art Treasures of the Louvre* (New York: Dell, 1962), 24, 25.

MESSAGE

In "Seeking Mona Lisa," Joseph A. Harriss says that the subject's "enigmatic, tight-lipped smile" has "launched a thousand learned interpretations." Why do you think critics believe there is a message in Mona Lisa's smile, that her expression contains some deep or hidden meaning? Do you think any of the critics Harriss quotes comes close to solving the enigma? For example, what do you make of Camille Paglia's view: "What Mona Lisa is ultimately saying is that males are unnecessary"? How might someone derive that message from the woman's smile?

METHOD

In what ways would Lillian Schwartz's analysis of how Leonardo da Vinci painted the *Mona Lisa* influence one's "reading" of the subject's smile? Assume that Schwartz's analysis is correct and that the painting is actually a self-portrait of Leonardo. In a short essay, address how this fact affects your interpretation of the famous smile. Be sure to consider a few of the interpretations Harriss cites in his survey. Does Schwartz's scientific observation lend special support to any of the explanations Harriss quotes in his essay?

MEDIUM

Consider Marcel Duchamp's notorious response to the *Mona Lisa* in his 1919 "L.H.O.O.Q." Why do you think he drew what he did? What medium was he imitating in drawing a moustache and goatee? How else might he have altered the image? Also, why do you think he decided to draw these facial hair styles on a postcard of the *Mona Lisa*? Why not paint an exact imitation first and then draw the moustache and goatee? What point is Duchamp making about artistic media?

125

Assignment 1

Traditionally we think of portraits as visual media, usually envisioning a professional photograph or formally posed painting when we hear the term used. In recent decades however, a movement has begun to create and collect audio portraits — especially from those individuals whom history might otherwise tend to forget. One of the pioneer organizations of this movement was Sound Portraits Productions, www.soundportraits.org. Begun in 1994, this organization's mission is "dedicated to telling stories that bring neglected American voices to a national audience." Unlike most traditional visual portraits, these audio portraits attempt to depict "the lives of Americans living in communities often neglected or misunderstood." Explore the Sound Portraits web site, and choose a few portraits to listen to. Record your experiences of listening and compare them to the experiences of viewing the portraits contained within this chapter. How do the experiences differ? What qualities of each medium seem similar? Consider whether it is acceptable to label these audio stories as "portraits" at all, or whether this label is meant as a **metaphor** of what the creators are trying to accomplish. Discuss the historical and social meanings that the portraits within this chapter encompass.

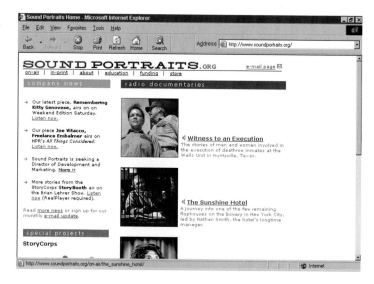

Soundportraits.org. (Courtesy of Soundportraits.org)

Assignment 2

Throughout history, portraits have been used as sentimental **memoirs** as well as historical signposts of their particular time. Reviewing this chapter, we see examples from 1507 (the *Mona Lisa*) all the way to the twenty-first century (John Freyer's eBay images) that capture some aspect of the times in which they were created. The historical and archival significance of artistic and photographic portraits has been long understood. However, what do we know about the artists who create these pieces of history? While the portrait is said to represent the subject, it is really the artist who decides what that representation might suggest. Look back through the chapter and consider what the images tell you about the gaze, or point of view, of their creators. You may also further explore the historical impact of portraits through such web sites as Ken Burns's Civil War portraits archive at pbs.org/civilwar/cwimages/portraits, or other historical collections of images from the past.

Portrait of Boy Soldier, **created between 1860 and 1865.** (Library of Congress, neg. #B8184-10573)

In addition, you may want to research a famous portrait artist or photographer in order to gain an understanding of how he or she conceived of and constructed their images. One site that may be useful is the Library of Congress American Memory Project web site, which contains a link to portraits of famous World War I portrait photographers at memory.loc.gov/ammem/fsahtml/fsap.html. This site also contains one of the world's largest collections of images from American history and may be of use if you are interested in the historical implications of portraits. Follow up on your discussions of the historical impact of portraits by collecting your own archive of images that you see as representative of your place and time in history. Consider the point of view of each of the images you select and what might be left out of the collection. You can then present your work and analyze the meaning that it may have for audiences in the future.

1. Compare the girls in the photographs by Sally Mann (*Candy Cigarette*, p. 98) and Weegee (*Mulberry Street Café*, p. 197). Do these two photographs have anything in common? Which photographer seems more interested in social context? Which photograph seems less "posed" or "staged"? Which do you think better expresses a young girl's personality? Which photograph in your opinion better expresses the photographer's artistic intentions? You needn't prefer one to the other; but weigh the respective merits of each photograph and describe in an essay the ways you think a talented photographer can capture in a moment (or in a "flash") someone's character or personality.

2. Much time and ink have been spent trying to understand the *Mona Lisa*'s smile. In "Seeking Mona Lisa" (p. 105), Joseph A. Harriss surveys some of the explanations critics over the centuries have produced. With these in mind, consider the smile of one of America's most prominent poets, Anne Sexton, as she sat for photographer Arthur Furst in 1974 (see p. 84), just a few months before she took her own life. Using information from Sexton's résumé and poem, write a short essay in which you interpret the meaning of Sexton's smile.

3. In "Seeking Mona Lisa" (p. 105), Joseph A. Harriss refers to Lillian Schwartz's computer analysis that suggests the famous painting is actually a portrait of Leonardo himself (see pp. 119–121). But Harriss adds: "Not everyone is convinced." He offers no reasons, however, why critics or art historians would doubt Schwartz's analysis, nor does he suggest that others have refuted her study. Working in small groups, read Schwartz's analysis carefully and see if you can punch any holes in her argument. Without getting into technical details, can you find places in her discussion of the painting where her argument seems weak, depends on conjecture, or lacks sufficient evidence? Afterwards, each group should research the Internet and report on any professional refutations or endorsements of Schwartz's intriguing thesis.

4. "But is it art?" That question often comes up as people respond to such works as Marcel Duchamp's "L.H.O.O.Q." (p. 110) or John Freyer's "allmylifeforsale.com" (p. 57), a domain name purchased by a university art museum. In an essay, consider why many people question the artistic value of such works. What is it about these works that challenges or even contradicts a general sense

of the nature of an agreed-upon work of art, such as Leonardo's *Mona Lisa*? Select either Duchamp's or Freyer's work, and argue why you do or do not consider it a genuine work of art.

5. In an essay, compare and contrast the cover photographs of Judith Ortiz Cofer's (p. 52) and Dorothy Allison's (p. 75) books. What image of each writer is conveyed by the photos? How do you think each photo is intended to reflect the contents of each book? What moods do the different photos suggest? Why do you think the publishers of Dorothy Allison's book decided to use a staged photo of a model rather than an actual childhood photograph of the author?

6. Who was Marcel Duchamp, and what role did he play in the development of modern art? Using reference sources, including the Internet, write a short profile of Duchamp. What impact did he have on the twentieth century? Why did he become an American citizen? After learning about Duchamp, explain how his ideas about art shape much of what we find in contemporary museums, such as Sally Mann's *Candy Cigarette* and John Freyer's domain name.

7. Regardless of whether Lillian Schwartz is right or wrong in her analysis of Leonardo da Vinci's *Mona Lisa*, in what ways does her essay make you aware of the significance of gender in the portrait? How is this significance echoed in some of the interpretations Joseph Harriss cites in his essay? How is it reflected in Marcel Duchamp's response? Even without Schwartz's computer analysis, do you see signs of ambiguous gender in the portrait? In collaborative groups, form a discussion panel that addresses how this famous sixteenth-century painting suggests gender issues of special relevance today.

8. A collaborative exercise: Imagine that like John Freyer, you have decided to put "all of your life" up for sale. After reviewing Freyer's objects, select three items that you currently own and write a single-paragraph description of each one that would make it appealing to a buyer or an eBay auction. Do not identify yourself. Then submit your descriptions to your instructor, who will blindly exchange them with someone else's. After receiving the other person's descriptions, write a short essay in which you construct a profile of that individual based solely on the objects selected and their descriptions.

129

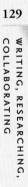

9. The *Mona Lisa* raises a central question of art and literature: Can a work of art be applicable to all cultures? After dividing into several groups, discuss whether a writer or an artist has an obligation to make his or her work universally relevant. You might consider whether all great works of art are automatically universal, even despite the artist's intentions. Also, can a work be universal at all, or do we actually need to be part of a specific culture or language group to appreciate it? Think, too, about whether an advertisement can be universally persuasive. Each group should then identify in this book (or from outside sources) works that illustrate universality or its absence and evaluate them in a panel discussion.

10. Consider the two poems included in this chapter: Judith Ortiz Cofer's "Lessons of the Past" (p. 53) and Anne Sexton's "Self in 1958" (p. 85). What psychological elements do these poems have in common? Examine both of them in an essay in which you discuss how each poem deals with self-image, family tension, and gender issues. Which poem do you think conveys these conflicting tensions more effectively?

2

TELLING STORIES

Storytelling appears throughout all cultures and is an inseparable part of human life. Our brains seem to be "hard-wired" for constructing narratives, for putting events in sequences, for selecting details, for reporting our experiences to others. We begin doing these things in very early childhood, practically as soon as we learn to speak.

The stories we tell also help us construct identities, both for ourselves and for our communities. As Harvard historian Drew Gilpin Faust puts it: "We create ourselves out of the stories we tell about our lives, stories that impose purpose and meaning on experiences that often seem random and discontinuous." If that is the case with individuals, it is equally true for cultures and communities, who share stories in the form of myths, legends, and historical narratives. Understanding who we are and the world around us is in many ways dependent upon understanding what we do when we relate a story—whether through words, pictures, or movements.

We naturally see our lives in terms of stories. In much of our conversation we spontaneously narrate the events of our day: this happened, then that happened, and so on. Such informal narrative consists of a string of events connected chronologically. This is the simplest and most common form of narration. Although we may imagine our life as a story, it should not take a lifetime to tell it! In narration, knowing what to leave out is as important as knowing what to include. Anyone who has listened patiently to a long-winded friend laboriously tell a story has often casually expressed an important criticism of all narration, "Please, get to the point!" we want to say, as we stifle a yawn. Our long-winded friend gets lost in details, often interrupting the flow of events to include yet another detail,

one that may have no bearing on what happened. Worse, sometimes the storyteller becomes "side-tracked." We all know people who cannot tell us about getting a flat tire until they first describe how they bought the car.

Effective storytelling is not a matter of simply repeating a continuous sequence of events (x happened, then y, then z); instead it involves selecting events that lead to something significant (x happened, which resulted in y, which culminated in z). Skillful narrative, then, is not so much sequential as it is *con*sequential. This is what we normally mean when we say a story has a **plot**. A plot is a deliberate shaping or staging (see the introduction to Chapter I) of the events to achieve a particular effect: suspense, surprise, intrigue, a sudden illumination or transformation, a moral. The renowned British novelist E. M. Forster made a useful and much-cited distinction between plot and story in his classic study of fiction, *Aspects of the Novel* (1927): " 'The king died and then the queen died' is a story. 'The king died, and then the queen died of grief' is a plot." As you can see in this very brief example, one is sequential and the other is consequential.

A plot deals with the causes and consequences of the events, and it adds to the story's level of artifice. For example, we can tell a child an artless, rambling bedtime story that we make up as we go along. But if we want our story to have the impact of surprise or to make a moral point, we usually need to know our ending in advance. In a traditional narrative, plot follows an arc. Exposition gives us the information we need to understand what's going to happen (the back story): A mother and father and their two sons live in a sleepy small town in a neat little bungalow. Complication occurs when

something happens to set up a major conflict. (In this hypothetical narrative, the complication happens when the father gets a new job and they're going to have to move.) Climax is the turning point in the story that occurs when the characters try to resolve the complication. (One of the little boys runs away from home.) And the resolution is the set of events that brings the story to its close. (The mother finds the little boy in his favorite place and helps him understand that moving will be okay.) It's rare for a plot to follow this traditional arc. Writers and filmmakers routinely rearrange the climax, or the resolution, for example — some movies start with the end, with the events that led up to it gradually revealed in a series of flashbacks. Playing with plot is a way to control our emotional response to a story and prepare us (or not prepare us!) for reversals or surprises. Plots — as we know from many films and detective stories — can be elaborately constructed.

Although narrative and story are commonly used interchangeably, we can best consider **narrative** as the overall construction of a story. As we know, the same story can be told in any number of ways. Deciding how to tell a story forms the basis of narrative art: Should we begin at the beginning or start at the end and proceed backward? Which events should we select, and how should they be arranged? Should we establish a strict time period or not worry about gaps in time? Should we report multiple points of view or focus on a single perspective? Anyone who undertakes a screenplay, a novel, or a cartoon confronts these decisions, whether consciously or not. "All my films have a

Concept: Sequence

Definition

:: sequence

Sequence refers to the order in which a series of actions, events, words, or images occurs or is shown. We usually think of it as a term that refers strictly to time—a sequence of events or actions. But in film theory, sequence is used to talk about any animated visual text that cuts from scene to scene or from image to image. The question to ask yourself is not what happened first, but rather in what order are things shown and what does the sequence mean.

next ▶

We understand history to be a series of prior events occuring one after the other. Historians and documentary filmmakers call this *sequentiality*.

some examples of sequence

09 · definitions :: analysis :: assignment

ix visual exercis

beginning, a middle, and an end," said the French director Jean-Luc Godard, "but not necessarily in that order." Many psychological experiments, actually, have demonstrated that we don't necessarily remember things in chronological order. People who experience the same, seemingly spontaneous series of events (a series that is actually scripted and staged) will offer widely different reports of what happened, and in what order. Many so-called "false memories" are actually false sequences, which is why trial lawyers are always careful to compare one witness's recollection of a sequence of events with another's.

Narrative structure can be found everywhere: in jokes, lab reports, historical accounts, personal essays, songs and ballads, news coverage, comic books, movies, sitcoms, and ballets. Some television commercials are mininarratives lasting only a few seconds without dialogue or commentary. Even photographers find ways to work with sequential storytelling methods, as Nora Ephron dramatically demonstrates in her essay "The Boston Photographs." In most paintings and photographs, where the depiction of time or movement is absent or minimal, we tend to recognize narrative spatially rather than temporally. In other words, we follow sight-lines instead of time-lines, and sight-lines are less coercive. That is not to say there is no story; only that we play an active role in constructing it. You'll find stories in this chapter that range from the carefully constructed to the utterly unscripted — but all speak to our desire to tell stories and know stories.

135

INTRODUCTION

Sequence

No matter what medium a story is delivered in — film, comics, words — sequence is crucial. Very simply, **sequence** means the order in which things are arranged. In everyday conversation, we usually proceed in chronological order: first A, then B, then C. The end.

In literature and film we often find many variations on chronological sequence. One of the oldest variations, used thousands of years ago by Homer in *The Iliad* and *The Odyssey,* is to begin a story *in medias res* — "in the midst of things." In film, we are accustomed to seeing what is commonly known as a *flashback* — a scene from the past that occurs out of chronological sequence. Some stories are even told backward, in reverse chronological order. Sequences, therefore, can move in many directions: forward, backward, and sideways. A novel, film, or comic strip may juxtapose multiple narrative paths. Comic strip artist and theorist Scott McCloud plays with that idea on the facing page.

 Go to **ix visual exercises** to explore sequence as it applies to visual texts.

Scott McCloud, from *Understanding Comics* (Chapter 4: Time Frames).
Critic Tasha Robinson writes that "McCloud's smart, simple 216-page comic proposed a sort of Unified Field Theory about the comics medium's historical antecedents, unique visual vocabulary, and place in the larger world of art." You can see some of McCloud's experiments with sequence and the conventions of comics at his web site, scottmccloud.com. (© 1993, 1994 by Scott McCloud. Reprinted by permission of HarperCollins Publishers Inc.)

Concept: *Sequence*

exercise 09

Definition

:: sequence

Sequence refers to the order in which a series of actions, events, words, or images occurs or is shown. We usually think of it as a term that refers strictly to time — a sequence of events or actions. But in film theory, sequence is used to talk about any animated visual text that cuts from scene to scene or from image to image. The question to ask yourself is not what happened first, but rather in what order are things shown and what does the sequence mean.

next ▶

We understand history to be a series of prior events occuring one after the other. Historians and documentary filmmakers call this *sequentiality.*

◀ C

some examples of sequence.

TELEVISION AND THE POWER OF VISUAL CULTURE

• Cathode Ray Tube
In late 1800s, the cathode ray tube — foreunner of the TV picture tube — is invented (p. 146).

• First TV Transmission
In 1927, 21-year-old Philo Farnsworth transmits the first TV picture electronically — the image of a dollar sign (p. 147).

• TV F
To sc
dard
assig
the F
deci
on ne
until

Late 1800s   1900

First Public TV Demo •
In 1906, Farnsworth conducts the first public demonstration of television in Philadelphia (p. 147).

09 · definitions ·· analysis ::: assignment

01 02 03 04 05 06 07 08 09

CONTENTS

ix visual exercises

137

MEMOIR

ESSAY | PHOTO | 3 MONTAGES

Family stories are often strung together through bits of repeated information and through old photographs passed around, the faces studied for clues to who our grandfather, great-grandmother, uncles, aunts, and cousins were; how they felt; what their lives were like. When we think about love and family, we tend to focus on the clichés that have evolved to describe strong emotions: *I love you. You can tell me anything. A diamond is forever.* But for many of us, our closest relationships — to our parents, our siblings, the objects of our romantic affections — aren't necessarily the ones in which we express ourselves most freely. Our need to construct coherent family narratives, then, often depends on reading each other and our actions in order to explain our relationships.

David Sedaris uses humor in the essay that follows to tell a piece of the story of his mother's life, his sister's marriage, and the family's way of coping with the news that his mother has cancer. Photographer Danny Lyon takes a more experimental approach to family stories, using montage to put together images to preserve and record a particular time, place, or person, all through a very personal lens.

138

For links to interviews with and articles about David Sedaris as well as audioclips of the author reading from his works on NPR, go to bedfordstmartins.com/ convergences.

David Sedaris, *Ashes.* Sedaris is well known as a commentator on National Public Radio, where he made his debut in 1992 recounting his experiences working as a Christmas elf for Macy's department store. His published collections include *Naked* (1997), *Holidays on Ice* (1997), *Me Talk Pretty One Day* (2000), and *Dress Your Family in Corduroy and Denim* (2004).

COMMENT

"Everyone has their own secrets, you know, in a family. And even if that person's dead, you know, it's still their secrets. . . . Before the book was published, when the galleys came out, I would let them read it and say to them, 'If you don't like your story then we can do something about it.' Of course, I was not going to do anything about it. If they didn't love it, I was going to pay them off or whatever. But they think . . . you know like in any family everybody's got their own take on something and I think my brothers and sisters and my dad too have accepted this as my take."

— David Sedaris

David Sedaris
ASHES

The moment I realized I would be a homosexual for the rest of my life, I forced my brother and sisters to sign a contract swearing they'd never get married. There was a clause allowing them to live with anyone of their choice, just so long as they never made it official.

"What about children?" my sister Gretchen asked, slipping a tab of acid under her tongue. "Can I *not* marry and still have a baby?"

I imagined the child, his fifteen hands batting at the mobile hanging over the crib. "Sure, you can still have kids. Now just pick up your eyebrow pencil and sign on the dotted line."

My fear was that, once married, my sisters would turn their backs on the family, choosing to spend their vacations and holidays with their husbands. One by one they would abandon us until it was just me and my parents, eating our turkey and stuffing off TV trays. It wasn't difficult getting the signatures. The girls in my family didn't play house, they played reformatory. They might one day have a relationship—if it happened, it happened; but they saw no reason to get bent out of shape about it. My father thought otherwise. He saw marriage as their best possible vocation, something they should train for and visualize as a goal. One of my sisters would be stooped before the open refrigerator, dressed in a bathing suit, and my father would weigh her with his eyes. "It looks like you've gained a few pounds," he'd say. "Keep that up and you'll never find a husband." *Find.* He said it as though men were exotic mushrooms growing in the forest and it took a keen eye to spot one.

"Don't listen to him," I'd say. "I think the weight looks good on you. Here, have another bowl of potato chips."

Marriage meant a great deal to our neighbors, and we saw that as another good reason to avoid it. "Well, we finally got Kim married off." This was always said with such a sense of relief, you'd think the Kim in question was not a twenty-year-old girl but the last remaining puppy of an unwanted litter. Our mother couldn't make it to the grocery store and back without having to examine wallet-size photos of someone's dribbling, popeyed grandbaby.

"Now *that's* different," she'd say. "A living baby. All my grandchildren have been ground up for fertilizer or whatever it is they do with the aborted fetuses. It puts them under my feet but keeps them out of my hair, which is just the way I like it. Here's your picture back. You tell that daughter of yours to keep up the good work."

Unlike our father, it pleased her that none of her children had reproduced. She used the fact as part of a routine she delivered on a regular basis. "Six children and none of them are married. I've taken the money we saved on the weddings and am using it to build my daughters a whorehouse."

After living with her boyfriend, Bob, for close to ten years, my sister Lisa nullified our contract when she agreed to marry him. Adding insult to injury, they decided the wedding would take place not at a drive-through chapel in Las Vegas but on a mountaintop in western North Carolina.

"That's nice," my mother said. "Now all I need is a pair of navy blue hiking boots to match my new dress and I'll be all set."

The first time I met my future brother-in-law, he was visiting my parents' home and had his head deep in the oven. I walked into the kitchen and, mistaking him for one of my sisters, grabbed his plump, denim-clad bottom and proceeded to knead it with both hands. He panicked, smacking his head against the oven's crusty ceiling. "Oh, golly," I said, "I'm sorry. I thought you were Lisa."

It was the truth, but for whatever reason, it failed to comfort him. At the time Bob was working as a gravedigger, a career choice that suggested a refreshing lack of ambition. These were not fresh graves, but old ones, slotted for relocation in order to make room for a new highway or shopping center. "How are you going to support my daughter on that?" my father asked.

"Oh, Lou," my mother said, "nobody's asking him to support anyone; they're just sleeping together. Let him be."

We liked Bob because he was both different and unapologetic. "You take a day-old pork chop, stab it with a fork, and soak it in some vinegar and you've got yourself some good eatin'," he'd say, fingering the feathery tip of his waist-length braid. Because of his upbringing and countless allergies, Bob's apartment was a testament to order and cleanliness. We figured that someone who carefully shampooed the lining of his work boots might briefly date our sister but would never go so far as to marry her. Lisa couldn't be trained to scoot the food scraps off her soiled sheets, much less shake out the blanket and actually make the bed. I underestimated both his will and his patience. They had lived together for close to three years when I dropped by unannounced and found my sister standing at the sink with a sponge in one hand and a plate in the other. She still hadn't realized the all-important role of detergent, but she was learning. Bob eventually cut his hair and returned to college, abandoning his shovel for a career in corporate real estate. He was a likable guy; it was the marrying part that got to me. "My sister's wedding" was right up there with "my recent colostomy" in terms of three-word phrases I hoped never to use.

Three weeks before the wedding, my mother called to say she had cancer. She'd gone to a doctor complaining about a ringing in her ear, and the resulting tests revealed a substantial tumor in her lung. "They tell me it's the size of a lemon," she said. "Not a tiny fist or an egg, but a lemon. I think they describe it in terms of fruit so as not to scare you, but come on, who wants a lemon in their lung? They're hoping to catch it before it becomes a peach or a grapefruit, but who knows? I sure as hell don't. Twenty-odd tests and they still haven't figured out what's wrong with my ear. I'm just hoping that whatever it is, it isn't much larger than a grape. This cancer, though, I realize it's my own fault. I'm just sorry your father's still around to remind me of that fact every fifteen goddamned seconds."

My sister Amy was with me when my mother called. We passed the phone back and forth across my tiny New York kitchen and then spent the rest of the evening lying in bed, trying to convince each other that our mother would get better but never quite believing it. I'd heard of people who had survived cancer, but most of them claimed to get through it with the aid of whole grains and spiritual publications that encouraged them to sit quietly in a lotus position. They envisioned their tumors and tried to reason with them. Our mother was not the type to greet the dawn or cook with oats and barley. She didn't reason, she threatened; and if that didn't work, she chose to ignore the problem. We couldn't picture her joining a support group or trotting through the mall in a warm-up suit. Sixty-two years old and none of us had ever seen her in a pair of slacks. I'm not certain why, but it seemed to me that a person needed a pair of pants in order to defeat cancer. Just as important, they needed a plan. They needed to accept the idea of a new and different future, free of crowded ashtrays and five-gallon jugs of wine and scotch. They needed to believe that such a life might be worth living. I didn't know that I'd be able to embrace such an unrewarding future, but I hoped that she could. My brother, sisters, and I undertook a campaign to bolster her spirits and suggest new and exciting hobbies she might explore once she was cured and back on her feet.

"It'll be great," I said. "You could, I don't know, maybe you could learn to pilot small planes or volunteer to hold crack babies. There are a lot of things an older person can do with her time rather than smoke and drink."

"Please don't call me stoned on pot and tell me there are lots of things I can do with my life," she said. "I just got off the phone with your brother, who suggested I open up a petting zoo. If that's what being high does for a person, then what I really need to do is start smoking marijuana, which would be a bit difficult for me since the last time I saw my right lung it was lying in the bottom of a pan."

In truth, her lungs were right where they'd always been. The cancer was too far advanced and she was too weak to survive an operation. The doctor decided to send her home while he devised a plan. The very word sounded hopeful to us, a plan. "The doctor has a plan!" my sisters and I crowed to one another.

"Right," my mother said. "He plans to golf on Saturday, sail on Sunday, and ask for my eyes, kidneys, and what's left of my liver on that following Monday. That's his plan."

We viewed it as a bad sign when she canceled her subscription to *People* magazine and took to buying her cigarettes in packs rather than cartons. She went through her jewelry box, calling my sisters to ask if they preferred pearls or gems. "Right now, the rubies are in a brooch shaped like a candy cane, but you can probably get more money if you have them removed and just sell the stones." In her own way she had already begun to check out, giving up on the plan before it was even announced. *But what about us?* I wanted to say. *Aren't we reason enough to carry on?* I thought of the unrelenting grief we had caused her over the years and answered the question myself. It was her hope to die before one of us landed in jail.

"What's Amy planning on wearing to this little Pepsi commercial," my mother asked, referring to the mountaintop ceremony. "Tell me it's not that wedding dress, please."

Lisa had decided to be married in a simple cream-colored suit, the sort of thing one might wear to work on the day of their employee evaluation. Figuring that at least somebody ought to look the part, Amy had the idea to attend the ceremony dressed in a floor-length wedding gown, complete with veil and train. In the end, she wound up wearing something my mother hated even more, a pink cocktail dress outfitted with detachable leg-o'-mutton sleeves. It wasn't like her to care what anyone wore, but she used the topic to divert attention from what we came to refer to as her "situation." If she'd had it her way, we would never have known about the cancer. It was our father's idea to tell us, and she had fought it, agreeing only when he threatened to tell us himself. Our mother worried that once we found out, we would treat her differently, delicately. We might feel obliged to compliment her cooking and laugh at all her jokes, thinking always of the tumor she was trying so hard to forget. And that is exactly what we did. The knowledge of her illness forced everything into the spotlight and demanded that it be memorable. We were no longer calling our mother. Now we were picking up the telephone to call our mother with cancer. Bad day at work? All you had do was say, "I'm sorry I forgot to vacuum beneath the cushions of your very lovely, very expensive Empire sofa, Mrs. Walman. I know how much it means to you. I guess I should be thinking of more important things than my mother's inoperable cancer."

We weren't the ones who were sick, but still, the temptation was so great. Here we could get the sympathy without enduring any of the symptoms. And we deserved sympathy, didn't we?

Speaking to our mother, we realized that any conversation might be our last, and because of that, we wanted to say something important. What could one say that hadn't already been printed on millions of greeting cards and helium balloons?

"I love you," I said at the end of one of our late-night phone calls.

"I am going to pretend I didn't hear that," she said. I heard a match strike in the background, the tinkling of ice cubes in a raised glass. And then she hung up. I had never said such a thing to my mother, and if I had it to do over again, I would probably take it back. Nobody ever spoke that way except Lisa. It was queer to say such a thing to someone unless you were trying to talk them out of money or into bed, our mother had taught that when we were no taller than pony kegs. I had known people who said such things to their parents, "I love you," but it always translated to mean "I'd love to get off the phone with you."

We gathered together for the wedding, which took place on a clear, crisp October afternoon. The ceremony was held upon a grassy precipice that afforded magnificent views of the surrounding peaks, their trees resplendent in fiery red and orange. It was easy to imagine, looking out over the horizon, that we were it, the last remaining people on the face of the earth. The others had been wiped out by disease and famine, and we had been chosen to fashion a new and better world. It was a pleasant thought until I pictured us foraging for berries and having to bathe in ice-cold streams. Bob's family, hearty and robust, could probably pull it off, but the rest of us would wither and die shortly after we'd run out of shampoo.

My father wept openly during the ceremony. The rest of us studied his crumpled face and fought hard not to follow his example. What was this emotion? My sister was getting married to a kind and thoughtful man who had seen her through a great many hardships. Together they shared a deep commitment to Mexican food and were responsible card-carrying members of the North American Caged Bird Society. The tacos and parrots were strictly between Lisa and Bob, but the rest of her belonged to us. Standing in a semicircle on top of that mountain, it became clear that while Lisa might take on a different last name, she could never escape the pull of our family. Marriage wouldn't let her off the hook, even if she wanted it to. She could move to Antarctica, setting up house in an underground bunker, but still we would track her down. It was senseless to run. Ignore our letters and phone calls, and we would invade your dreams. I'd spent so many years thinking marriage was the enemy that when the true danger entered our lives, I was caught completely off guard. The ceremony inspired a sense of loss directed not at Lisa, but at our mother.

"No booze?" she moaned. My mother staggered toward the buffet table, its retractable legs trembling beneath the weight of sparkling waters, sausage biscuits, and decaffeinated coffee.

"No booze," Lisa had announced a week before the ceremony. "Bob and I have decided we don't want that kind of a wedding."

"Which kind?" my mother asked. "The happy kind? You and Bob might be thrilled to death, but the rest of us will need some help working up the proper spirit."

She didn't look much different than she had the last time I'd seen her. The chemotherapy had just begun, and she'd lost—at most—maybe five pounds. A casual acquaintance might not have noticed any change at all. We did only because we knew, everyone on that mountaintop knew, that she had cancer. That she was going to die. The ceremony was relatively small, attended by both families and an assortment of Lisa's friends, most of whom we had never met but could easily identify. These were the guests who never once complained about the absence of alcohol.

"I just want you to know that Colleen and I both love your sister Lisa so much," the woman said, her eyes moist with tears. "I know we've never been formally introduced, but would you mind if I gave you a big fat hug?"

With the exception of Lisa, we were not a hugging people. In terms of emotional comfort, it was our belief that no amount of physical contact could match the healing powers of a well-made cocktail.

"Hey, wait a minute. Where's *my* hug?" Colleen asked, rolling up her sleeves and moving in for the kill. I looked over my attacker's shoulder and watched as a woman in a floor-length corduroy skirt wrestled my mother into an affectionate headlock.

"I heard what you're going through and I know that you're frightened," the woman said, looking down at the head of thinning gray hair she held clasped between her powerful arms. "You're frightened because you think you are alone."

"I'm frightened," my mother wheezed, "because I'm *not* alone and because you're crushing what's left of my goddamned lungs."

The scariest thing about these people was that they were sober. You could excuse that kind of behavior from someone tanked up on booze, but most of them hadn't taken a drink since the Carter administration. I took my mother's arm and led her to a bench beyond the range of the other guests. The thin mountain air made it difficult for her to breathe, and she moved slowly, pausing every few moments. The families had taken a walk to a nearby glen, and we sat in the shade, eating sausage biscuits and speaking to each other like well-mannered strangers.

"The sausage is good," she said. "It's flavorful but not too greasy."

"Not greasy at all. Still, though, it isn't dry."

"Neither are the biscuits," she said. "They're light and crisp, very buttery."

"Very. These are some very buttery biscuits. They're flaky but not too flaky."

"Not too flaky at all," she said.

We watched the path, awkwardly waiting for someone to release us from the torture of our stiff and meaningless conversation. I'd always been afraid of sick people, and so had my mother. It wasn't that we feared catching their brain aneurysm or accidently ripping out their IV. I think it was their fortitude that frightened us. Sick people reminded us not of what we had, but of what we lacked. Everything we said sounded petty and insignificant; our complaints paled in the face of theirs, and without our complaints, there was nothing to say. My mother and I had been fine over the telephone, but now, face to face, the rules had changed. If she were to complain, she risked being seen as a sick complainer, the worst kind of all. If I were to do it, I might come off sounding even more selfish than I actually was. This sudden turn of events had robbed us of our common language, leaving us to exchange the same innocuous pleasantries we'd always made fun of. I wanted to stop it and so, I think, did she, but neither of us knew how.

After all the gifts had been opened, we returned to our rooms at the Econolodge, the reservations having been made by my father. We looked out the windows, past the freeway and into the distance, squinting at the charming hotel huddled at the base of other, finer mountains. This would be the last time our family was all together. It's so rare when one knowingly does something for the last time: the last time you take a bath, the last time you have sex or trim your toe-nails. If you know you'll never do it again, it might be nice to really make a show of it. This would be it as far as my family was concerned, and it ticked me off that our final meeting would take place in such a sorry excuse for a hotel. My father had taken the liberty of ordering nonsmoking rooms, leaving the rest of us to rifle through the Dumpster in search of cans we might use as ashtrays.

"What more do you want out of a hotel?" he shouted, stepping out onto the patio in his underpants. "It's clean, they've got a couple of snack machines in the lobby, the TVs work, and it's near the interstate. Who cares if you don't like the damned wallpaper? You know what your problem is, don't you?"

"We're spoiled," we shouted in unison.

We were not, however, cheap. We would have gladly paid for something bet-ter. No one was asking for room service or a heated swimming pool, just for something with a little more character: maybe a motel with an Indian theme or one of the many secluded lodges that as a courtesy posted instructions on how to behave should a bear interrupt your picnic. Traveling with our father meant always having to stay at nationally known motor lodges and take our meals only in fast-food restaurants. "What?" he'd ask. "Are you telling me you'd rather sit down at a table and order food you've never tasted before?"

Well, yes, that was exactly what we wanted. Other people did it all the time, and most of them had lived to talk about it.

"Bullshit," he'd shout. "That's not what you want." When arguing, it was always his tactic to deny the validity of our requests. If you wanted, say, a stack of pancakes, he would tell you not that you couldn't have them but that you never really wanted them in the first place. "I know what I want" was always met with "No you don't."

My mother never shared his enthusiasm for corporate culture, and as a result, they had long since decided to take separate vacations. She usually traveled with her sister, returning from Sante Fe or Martha's Vineyard with a deep tan, while my father tended to fish or golf with friends we had never met.

The night before the wedding, we had gone to a charming lodge and eaten dinner with Bob's parents. The dining room had the feel of someone's home. Upon the walls hung pictures of deceased relatives, and the mantel supported aged trophies and a procession of hand-carved decoys. The night of the wedding, Lisa and Bob having left for their honeymoon, we were left on our own. My sisters, stuffed with sausage, chose to remain in their rooms, so I went with my

145

parents and brother to a chain restaurant located on a brightly lit strip of highway near the outskirts of town. Along the way we passed dozens of more attractive options: steak houses boasting firelit dining rooms and clapboard cottages lit with discreet signs reading HOME COOKING and NONE BETTER!

"What about that place?" my brother said. "I've never tasted squirrel before. Hey, that sounds nice."

"Ha!" my father said. "You won't think it's so nice at three A.M. when you're hunched over the john, crapping out the lining of your stomach."

We couldn't go to any of the curious places, because they might not have a sneeze guard over the salad bar. They might not have clean restrooms or a properly anesthetized staff. A person couldn't take chances with a thing like that. My mother had always been willing to try anything. Had there been an Eskimo restaurant, she would have been happy to crawl into the igloo and eat raw seal with her bare hands, but my father was driving, which meant it was his decision. Having arrived at the restaurant of his choice, he lowered his glasses to examine the menu board. "What can you tell me about your boneless Pick O' the Chix combination platter?" he asked the counter girl, a Cherokee teenager wearing a burnt orange synthetic jumper.

"Well, sir, there isn't much *to* say except that it doesn't got any bones and comes with fries and a half-gallon 'Thirsty Man' soda."

My father shouted as if her dusky complexion had somehow affected her hearing. "But the chicken itself, how is it prepared?"

"I put it on a tray," the girl said.

"Oh, I see," my father said. "That explains it all. Golly, you're a bright one, aren't you? IQ just zooming right off the charts. You put it on a tray, do you? I guess that means the chicken is in no position to put itself on the tray, which tells me that it's probably been killed in some fashion. Am I correct? All right, now we're getting somewhere." This continued until the girl was in tears and we returned empty-handed to the car, my father muttering, "Jesus, did you hear that? She could probably tell you everything you needed to know about trapping a possum, but when it comes to chicken, she 'puts it on a tray.' "

Under normal circumstances my mother would have worked overtime to protect the waitress or counter help, but tonight she was simply too tired. She wanted to go somewhere that served drinks. "The Italian place, let's go there."

My brother and I backed her up, and a short time later we found ourselves seated in a dimly lit restaurant, my father looking up at the waitress to shout, "*Rare,* do you know what that means? It means I want my steak the color of your gums."

"Oh, Lou, give it a rest." My mother filled her wine glass and lit a cigarette.

"What are you doing?" He followed his question with an answer. "You're killing yourself is what you're doing."

My mother lifted her glass in salute. "You got that right, baby."

"I don't believe this. You might as well just put a gun to your head. No, I take that back, you can't blow your brains out because you haven't got any."

"You should have known that when I agreed to marry you," she said.

"Sharon, you haven't got a clue." He shook his head in disgust. "You open your mouth and the crap just flies."

My mother had stopped listening years ago, but it was almost a comfort that my father insisted on business as usual, despite the circumstances. In him, she found someone whose behavior would never vary. He had made a commitment to make her life miserable, and no amount of sickness or bad fortune would sway him from that task. My last meal with my parents would be no different than the first. Had we been at home, my mother would have fed him at seven and then waited until ten or eleven, at which time she and I would broil steaks. We would have put away several drinks by then, and if by chance the steaks were over-cooked, she would throw them to the dog and start all over again. Before moving to New York, I had spent two months in Raleigh, painting one of my father's rental units near the university, and during that time our schedule never varied. Sometimes we'd eat in front of the television, and other nights we would set a place for ourselves at the table. I try recalling a single one of those evenings, want-ing to take comfort in the details, but they are lost to me. Even my diary tells me nothing: "Ate steaks with Mom." But which steaks, porterhouse or New York strip? What had we talked about and why hadn't I paid attention?

We returned to the motor lodge, where my parents retired to their room and the rest of us hiked to a nearby cemetery, a once ideal spot that now afforded an excellent view of the newly built Pizza Hut. Over the years our mother had repeatedly voiced her desire to be cremated. We would drive past a small forest fire or observe the pillars of smoke rising from a neighbor's chimney, and she would crush her cigarette, saying, "That's what I want, right there. Do whatever you like with the remains; sprinkle them into the ashtrays of a fine hotel, give them to smart-assed children for Christmas, hand them over to the Catholics to rub into their foreheads, just make sure I'm cremated."

"Oh, Sharon," my father would groan. "You don't know what you want." He'd say it as though he himself had been cremated several times in the past but had finally wised up and accepted burial as the only sensible option.

We laid our Econolodge bedspreads over the dewy grass of the cemetery, smoking joints and trying to imagine a life without our mother. If there was a heaven, we probably shouldn't expect to find her there. Neither did she deserve to roam the fiery tar pits of hell, surrounded for all eternity by the same shitheads who brought us strip malls and theme restaurants. There must exist some middle ground, a place where one was tortured on a daily basis but still allowed a few moments of pleasure, taken wherever one could find it. That place seemed to be Raleigh, North Carolina, so why the big fuss? Why couldn't she just stay where she was and not have cancer? That was always our solution, to go back in time. We discussed it the way others spoke of bone marrow transplants and radiation. We discussed it as though it were a viable option. A time machine, that would solve everything. I could almost see its panel of blinking lights, the control board marked with etched renderings of lumbering dinosaurs and ending with Lisa's

147

wedding. We could turn it back and view our mother as a young girl, befriend her then, before her father's drinking turned her wary and suspicious. See her working in the greeting-card section of the drugstore and warn her not to drop out of school. Her lack of education would make her vulnerable, causing her to overuse the phrase "Well, what do I know" or "I'm just an idiot, but…" We could turn it back and see ourselves as babies, our mother stuck out in the country with no driver's license, wondering whom to call should someone swallow another quarter or safety pin. The dial was ours, and she would be at our mercy, just as she had always been, only this time we would pay attention and keep her safe. Ever since arriving at the motor lodge, we'd gone back and forth from one room to another, holding secret meetings and exchanging private bits of information. We hoped that by preparing ourselves for the worst, we might be able to endure the inevitable with some degree of courage or grace.

Anything we forecasted was puny compared to the future that awaited us. You can't brace yourself for famine if you've never known hunger; it is foolish even to try. The most you can do is eat up while you still can, stuffing yourself, shoveling it in with both hands and licking clean the plates, recalling every course in vivid detail. Our mother was back in her room and very much alive, probably watching a detective program on television. Maybe that was her light in the window, her figure stepping out onto the patio to light a cigarette. We told ourselves she probably wanted to be left alone, that's how stoned we were. We'd think of this later, each in our own separate way. I myself tend to dwell on the stupidity of pacing a cemetery while she sat, frightened and alone, staring at the tip of her cigarette and envisioning her self, clearly now, in ashes.

■ *Sedaris is playing with the idea of changing his mother's story with a time machine. By the end of the essay, though, it's his own past he wishes he could change. How does his perspective shift from the beginning to the end of the essay? How many different family stories can you identify in this essay?*

149

◀ **David and Amy Sedaris.** David Sedaris has collaborated with his comic sister Amy on several theatrical productions, described by one reviewer as "raunchy backyard plays." Calling themselves "The Talent Family," the two have set out to prove that there is something funny about *every* family story. (© Scott Gries/Getty Images)

Danny Lyon, *Ernst*. Documentary photographer Danny Lyon was born in Queens, New York in 1942 to a Russian-born mother and a German father. The photographs collected here include images of the author's father at age five in 1912; crossing the Atlantic in 1934; with relatives in Germany; with Lyon's mother on his shoulders at the beach; and holding hands with his grandson a few months before his death in 1977. Lyon has published several books of documentary photography, including *Knave of Hearts* (1999), a visual memoir from which these montages were taken. (All photos courtesy Magnum Photos, © Danny Lyon)

COMMENT

"How can photographs affect us so, transporting us through time, across continents, and beyond wars? How can they preserve what is gone forever?

—Danny Lyon

Danny Lyon, *Four Generations*. The photographs in this montage include images of Danny Lyon; his grandparents and his father in Kew Gardens around 1950; and, center, his son Raphe with Nanook, the family dog, in New Mexico in 1983.

Danny Lyon, _Raphe at Seventeen, 1992._ This montage is the last in Lyon's collection _Knave of Hearts._ ▶
The last paragraph of prose gives Lyon's answer to his son's question about what he had done during
his first summer break from college: "I told Raphe, 'I hitchhiked west. I had a roommate who lived in
Saint Paul, so I visited him; then I hitchhiked to California.' Raphe sat quietly on the banks, looking
out at the river, wearing my old leather jacket, looking so handsome. 'That's what I want to do, Dad.
You know, have an adventure.'"

MESSAGE

Danny Lyon includes a running narrative with his photo montages in the collection *Knave of Hearts*. Each caption for the three montages includes the information that Lyon gives about that particular image. Study the montages and read the captions carefully. How important is the caption to your understanding of what each montage is presenting? Do the images speak louder than the words, or the other way around?

METHOD

David Sedaris is a performer as well as a writer, and his essays are meant to be read aloud. What verbal elements can you find in "Ashes" that demonstrate the author's ability to make the printed word come alive as speech? For example, how does Sedaris script intonation and vary speech rhythms?

MEDIUM

Both Lyon and Sedaris are telling stories, though in different media. Choose a family story of your own to tell, about an individual family member or occasion. Then pick a medium in which to tell your story: in words, with pictures, or in any combination that makes the most sense to you.

WEBCAMS

In the 1990s the convergence of the computer, the Internet, and the digital video camera allowed people to create live updated imagery that could be accessed through web sites. Webcams (short for "world wide web + camera") became instantly popular for a variety of commercial, personal, and artistic purposes — from businesses that use them for videoconferencing to individuals who set up personal web sites that invite Internet audiences into their daily lives. One of these, jennicam.com, had been a popular autobiographical site from 1996 to 2004, featuring images and journal entries. The site contained years of archival imagery that effectively tells a life story on an everyday basis. Sites like these served as the model for Garry Trudeau's comic strips on "Alex's Real-Time Web Site" show.

A law of contemporary art is as follows: once a technology is in place, an art form will invariably develop out of it. In the mid-nineteenth century, for example, photography was considered no more than another new technology until artists began exploring its aesthetic possibilities. Given the recent explosion of techno-logical developments and gadgetry, it's no surprise, then, that artists have been experimenting with the creative potential of surveillance cameras, cell phones, installation videos, and videocams. The material in this cluster explores the narra-tive power of the webcam.

155

> go

For links to the *Doonesbury* web site, go to bedfordstmartins.com/convergences.
How could you change the medium of the comic strip — designed to run the width of a newspaper — to fit the medium of the web?

Garry Trudeau, *Doonesbury*. *Doonesbury* first appeared on October 26, 1970; it now runs in almost fifteen hundred newspapers and can be found on the Internet. Garry Trudeau, its creator, has won a Pulitzer Prize for editorial cartooning and received the National Cartoonists Society's top award in 1994. He has been satirizing American culture and politics for over thirty years.

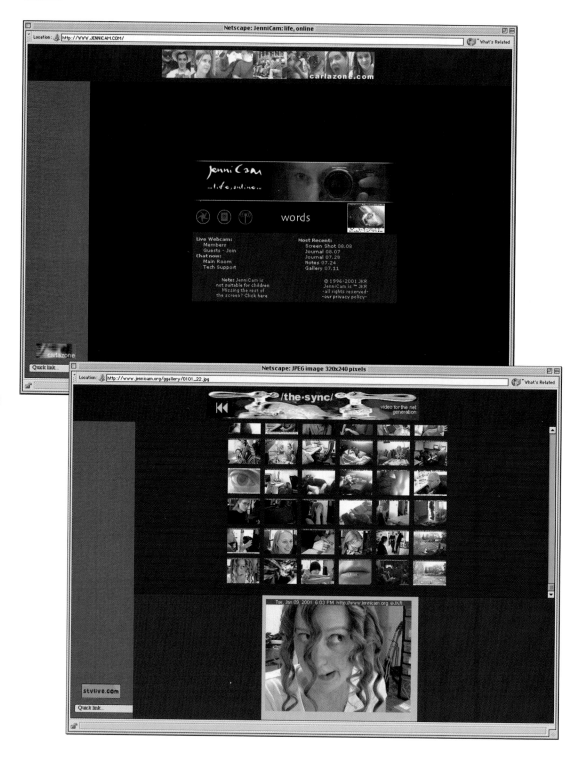

◀ **Jennifer Ringley, jennicam.com.** Jennifer Ringley's site was probably the longest sustained, and most famous, example of someone using a webcam. For five years Ringley's webcams served as windows onto a "virtual human zoo." Anyone could visit the site and get still images every fifteen minutes; subscribing members got images every minute and could access galleries back to 1997. (Reprinted courtesy of jennicam.org)

COMMENT

"Now, with the 'Jennicam,' Ringley has set up a QuickCam which will snap a shot of her bedroom every three minutes and upload it to the Web. Ringley describes the objective: 'The concept of the cam is to show whatever is going on naturally. Essentially, the cam has been there long enough that now I ignore it. So whatever you're seeing isn't staged or faked, and while I don't claim to be the most interesting person in the world, there's something compelling about real life that staging it wouldn't bring to the medium.' And although the JenniCam has uploaded images of Jennifer nude, doing a strip tease, or engaged in sexual activities, she asserts that 'This site is not pornography. Yes, it contains nudity from time to time. Real life contains nudity. Yes, it contains sexual material from time to time. Real life contains sexual material. However, this is not a site about nudity and sexual material. It is a site about real life.' Yet because of the amount of traffic the site receives, this peek into one twenty-year-old white woman's 'real life' comes with a $15 a year subscription fee."

—Kristine Blair and Pamela Takayoshi, from
Feminist Cyberscapes: Essays on Gender in Electronic Spaces

Sara Tucker, *Introduction to Diller + Scofidio's*
Refresh. Sara Tucker is director of digital media
at Dia Center for the Arts in New York. On
Refresh, she explains the artistic impulse behind
this fictional/artistic webcam narrative.

Sara Tucker

INTRODUCTION TO DILLER + SCOFIDIO'S *REFRESH*

Architects Elizabeth Diller and Ricardo Scofidio have worked in many media using the built environment and the visual arts to reveal society norms that operate invisibly to govern and inform daily relationships. One recent area of this investigation has focused on "liveness"—a term that originated in broadcasting and has grown to be synonymous with authenticity and a trusted reality.

For this first project for the web, entitled *Refresh*, Diller + Scofidio have taken office webcams as their point of departure, with the intention of examining the role of live video technologies on everyday life. A webcam is a camera that takes pictures at set intervals, which can range from fifteen times per second to once per hour, then instantly transmits the images to a web server, where the image

go to bedfordstmartins.com/
convergences to explore
Refresh for yourself.

COMMENT

"We are hurtling toward constant electronic scrutiny — of the enemy and of ourselves. Increasingly, ours is a world of ID checks, surveillance cameras, body scans, fingerprint databases, e-mail sifters, and cell phone interceptors designed to ensure that electronic trails don't grow cold. Add to that more mundane domestic gadgets like nanny-cams, wireless heart monitors, swipe-in school and workplace IDs, and E-Z Pass, a tag that attaches to your car windshield and electronically deducts highway tolls from your prepaid account, and you begin to get a whiff of an emerging electronic vigilance, an ever examined, ever watched landscape of total surveillance."

—David Shenk, *National Geographic,* Nov. 2003

160

Their association seems improbable: she is always in severely tailored business suits and silver bracelets, he in ill-fitting shirts and poorly cuffed trousers. While most encounters are extemporaneous -- chance meetings that turn into leisurely conversations -- theirs seems timed to a vague logic. At first, he would arrive shortly after she had already left the vestibule. With military precision he enacted a daily ritual: standing in profile, he would mix a hot concoction, usually with soiled utensils, then with a minimum of movement, he would pivot 180° in the opposite profile and drink, then pivot forward, each time striking a pose for several seconds. Then, he would leave. The timing of his entrances have gradually been shifting closer to hers.

**refresh rate:
10 seconds**

	M	M	M	T	W	W	W	Th	Th	F	F
	9:14 am	10:34 am	10:37 am	10:38 am	10:31 am	10:32 am	10:34 am	10:33 am	10:34 am	10:34 am	10:35 am

LIVE

becomes simultaneously available to anyone on the web. At present, thousands of webcams exist, broadcasting live pictures of fish tanks, traffic conditions, vending machines, private bedrooms, offices....

The artists speculated on the motivations for these cameras: "The live cam phenomenon can be thought of as a public service, or a mode of passive advertisement, or it may be a new type of exhibitionism, or self-disciplinary device. The desire to connect to others in real time may be driven by a response to the 'loss' of the public realm. But, however varied the motives, live cam views always seem casual and lacking dramatic interest and content; they appear unmediated. Despite this apparent innocence, cameras are willfully positioned, their field of vision is carefully considered, and behavior within that field cannot help but anticipate the looming presence of the global viewer."

For each of the dozen sites located in the United States, Europe and Australia that Diller + Scofidio selected for this project, they have constructed fictional narratives using text and fabricated images. For every site there is a grid of twelve images, one of which is live and refreshes when clicked; the other eleven have been constructed for this project with the aid of hired actors and Photoshop. None of the people from the actual location appear in the fabricated images; however, the juxtaposition of the live and the fictional establishes a provocative correspondence. The stories, which range in time from a single day to several seasons, concentrate on subtle changes in behavior as a consequence of the acknowledged presence of the camera in the office: a gradual shift in dress style, the activities of

162

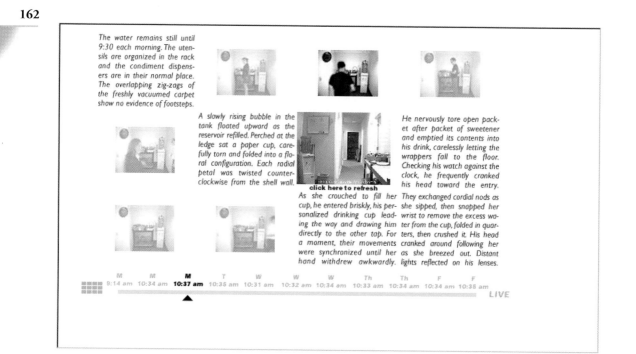

The water remains still until 9:30 each morning. The utensils are organized in the rack and the condiment dispensers are in their normal place. The overlapping zig-zags of the freshly vacuumed carpet show no evidence of footsteps.

A slowly rising bubble in the tank floated upward as the reservoir refilled. Perched at the ledge sat a paper cup, carefully torn and folded into a floral configuration. Each radial petal was twisted counterclockwise from the shell wall.

He nervously tore open packet after packet of sweetener and emptied its contents into his drink, carelessly letting the wrappers fall to the floor. Checking his watch against the clock, he frequently cranked his head toward the entry.

click here to refresh

As she crouched to fill her cup, he entered briskly, his personalized drinking cup leading the way and drawing him directly to the other tap. For a moment, their movements were synchronized until her hand withdrew awkwardly.

They exchanged cordial nods as she sipped, then snapped her wrist to remove the excess water from the cup, folded in quarters, then crushed it. His head cranked around following her as she breezed out. Distant lights reflected on his lenses.

M   M   **M**   T   W   W   W   Th   Th   F   F
9:14 am 10:34 am **10:37 am** 10:35 am 10:31 am 10:32 am 10:34 am 10:33 am 10:34 am 10:35 am

LIVE

an after-hours cleaning crew, a ritual of stacking paper, one person's discreet and incessant ordering of take-out food, and a potential office romance unfolding by the water cooler. There is nothing shocking or dramatic, rather, everyday conventions are slightly modified, either to perform for or to hide from the camera.

The flip side to the performative role chosen or imposed on the people at the live site is the role of the spectator at the other end. Diller + Scofidio argue that liveness appeals to both ends of the technophile/technophobe spectrum: "For technophobes who blame technology for the collapse of the public sphere, liveness may be a last vestige of authenticity—seeing and/or hearing the event at the precise moment of its occurrence. The un-mediated *is* the immediate. For technophiles, liveness defines technology's aspiration to simulate the real...in *real*-time. Lag time, search time, and download time all impair real-time computational performance. But whether motivated by the desire to preserve the real or to fabricate it, liveness is synonymous with the real—an object of uncritical desire for techno-extremes."

Regardless of where one falls on the technophile/phobe spectrum, it is hard not to be captivated by the potential of witnessing something uncensored, no matter how banal. Yet this excitement requires an act of faith that what you are seeing truly is "live," a faith increasingly difficult to achieve given the bag of technical tricks available, especially on the Internet. This skepticism aids, to a degree, these artists' desire to tease the distinctions: to undermine the authority of "live" over mediated experience and to collapse the two into an indeterminate unity.

163

◀ **Diller + Scofidio, *Refresh*.** Husband-and-wife team Elizabeth Diller and Richard Scofidio have been collaborating on interdisciplinary works for the last twenty-five years. Trained as architects, they carry out experimental art projects that marry architectural design with performance and electronic media. This project plays with our expectations about the "liveness" of webcams; the artists used live webcams in offices around the world and scripted a story around each one, putting "live" and fabricated images next to each other. The screen shots you see here show you one such story, about chance (or not so chance) encounters in the office kitchen. (Diller + Scofidio, "Refresh," 1998. A project for Dia Art Foundation at www.diaart.org/dillerscofidio/)

COMMENT

"The live cam phenomenon can be thought of as a public service, or a mode of passive advertisement, or it may be a new type of exhibitionism. . . . But however varied the motives, live cam views always seem casual and lacking dramatic interest and content; they appear unmediated. Despite this apparent innocence, cameras are willfully positioned, their field of vision is carefully considered, and behavior within that field cannot help but anticipate the looming presence of the global viewer."

—Diller + Scofidio

MESSAGE

How much "staging" is there in the texts you've just seen? (How does Alex stage the events in the comic strip? How has Garry Trudeau staged her staging? Is Jennifer Ringley putting on a show or just living her life? How much fiction is there in *Refresh*?) To what degree do you think webcams are recorders of real life?

METHOD

Webcams are on automatic pilot, especially compared with the other means of recorded stories that are represented in this chapter. To what degree does the method of capturing an image determine the kind of stories that get told?

MEDIUM

How would you define "real time"? What other kinds of time are there? What does Alex mean when she says, "The camera continuously records everything that happens"? Does the cartoon exist in continuous time? Does a web site? Write an essay that defines real time, using these examples of webcams — or any of your own that you'd like to bring in — to support your definition.

REALITY TV

Why have "reality TV" shows grown so popular in recent years? And how "real" are such shows as *Survivor, Fear Factor, Temptation Island,* and *The Bachelor,* with their enormous staffs, advanced production techniques, numerous casting specialists, and extensive camera crews? If performing for vast television audiences as a contestant in front of cameras to produce film that is edited, restructured, and enhanced with musical scores is considered "real," then we may well wonder what isn't real.

In "Reality in America," Lee Siegel examines the basic appeal of reality television. He concludes that the "real" in America "comes down to psychology, to the volatile fact that people have emotions." As he puts it, "reality television masters angry and confused emotions with an organizing narrative." It "applies the sophisticated editing and jump-cuts and voice-overs and musical scorings of film to everyday situations, so as to give everyday life the scripted and directed structure of film." The intriguing suggestion here is that for millions of Americans, everyday life somehow isn't real until it is turned into a story.

Lee Siegel, *Reality in America*. Lee Siegel is a frequent contributor to *The New Republic*. His essay starts out as a review of a new
reality show, *Mr. Personality*, but quickly becomes a much
broader meditation on the nature of Americans — how we see
"reality" and what we want from entertainment. This essay first
appeared in the June 23, 2003, issue of *The New Republic*.

Lee Siegel
REALITY IN AMERICA

Four men. Four men left. These are the four finalists, the men among whom
Haley must make the most important decision of her life. They are wearing
masks. Haley must choose the man she is going to marry, which is the most
important decision of her life, among four men who are wearing masks. She will
choose, for this most important of decisions, not on the basis of looks, which is of
course a superficial standard, and a standard that all the other networks are using,
but on the basis of personality. Over the past few weeks, she has gotten to know
these men in an incredibly comprehensive way. They have poured out their
hearts, each one to the other, and vice versa. They have talked about their favorite
wines, and their favorite sports, and their favorite snacks, and their favorite gift
ideas. During a candlelit dinner, at a table beside a glimmering bay, underneath
dark velvet skies, Haley has asked each startled suitor: "So why should I choose
you?" Their answers, though they were all the same, shocked America with their
straightforwardness.

  And now comes the moment of truth, although there is still one episode left,
the heartbreaking segment in which two contestants are suddenly disaggregated
into a lucky winner and a pathetic loser who, America hopes, will bear his crip-
pling, devastating, humiliating rejection with dignity and cheerfulness, two qualities that matter a lot more than being a "winner," which probably just means that
you knew someone on the inside anyway. Standing a little behind Haley is
Monica Lewinsky, who has been advising and consoling and encouraging her
throughout her thrilling odyssey. Yes, Monica Lewinsky. Why Monica Lewinsky?
Because NBC has people eating live cockroaches on *Fear Factor,* and CBS has
people nearly killing each other to prevail on a desert island on *Survivor,* and ABC
has *The Bachelor,* in which a man chooses from a group of women, and *The
Bachelorette,* in which a woman chooses from a group of men. But no one has
thought of getting a celebrity with a racy reputation. Not until *Mr. Personality,*
one of America's newest reality television shows.

166

***Mr. Personality* contestants.** *Mr. Personality*, which ran on the FOX network in
2003, hinges on the question of what's more important, looks or personality,
by taking looks off the table and masking the contestants. Romance reality
shows — *The Bachelor, The Bachelorette, Joe Millionaire, Married by America*,
to date — hinge as much on ego-destroying rejection as on the affirming power
of love. (Photofest)

Only in America could reality become a trend. But then, only in America do we take time out for a "reality check," as if anyone so far gone as to lose his sense of reality would actually know what to check in order to get it back. I mean, get real. Of course, only in America could the admonishment "get real" be a reproach, and "unreality" be a sin. And now that we're on the subject, only in America do we say "I mean" before we say what we mean, as if it was an acceptable convention for people to go around saying what they didn't mean, and it had become another convention to make the distinction, before saying anything of consequence, between meaning and not meaning what you are about to say. Already I'm, like, getting dizzy. Which raises the question of why Americans distance themselves from what they are saying by putting "like" before the description of something, as if people are nervous about committing to a particular version of reality, or to a direct, unmediated, non-metaphorical experience of the real. "Like" is annoying, but it is a powerful tool of detachment and defense; it is verbal armor. So you see the depth of complexity. It is no surprise that "reality television" has become not just a gigantically profitable object of diversion, but also the subject of appalled concern.

The nature of reality in America has been a riddle ever since Europeans started fleeing their own literal conditions by exporting their dreams here in the form of Noble Savages, the Land of Opportunity, and Mahagonny (the last a shy overture disguised as a knowing sneer). Recently, the Europeans have stopped exporting their dreams over here and begun exporting their "reality": *Survivor,* the granddaddy of reality television, came to these shores from England in 2000, and *Big Brother* and *Fear Factor* came over from Holland and Germany around the same time. Or maybe these are new kinds of dreams. As the culture editor of *Die Zeit* said, "People are missing the real life in their lives."

Medieval artists and artisans staged Catholicism for the masses. The painter Jacques-Louis David helped to orchestrate the French Revolution, the Russian avant-garde helped to design the Russian Revolution, the Nazis aestheticized life to cover up the workings of evil. If Baudrillard sounds comical when he complains that reality has disappeared into folds of media-fabricated "simulacra," it is because he thinks that once upon a time, before the media, there used to be something called reality that was available directly and without the interference of interpretation, that existed in isolation, untouched by artifice. But degrees of so-called unreality have always constituted part of so-called reality. That is why reality is so hard to pin down. Which is why they call it reality.

In America, playing around with representations of reality is as commonplace as buying a pair of sunglasses, or getting a cosmetic makeover, or purchasing a cell phone with a clearer video display, or...well, you know what I mean. Melville's *The Confidence-Man* portrayed American reality as so malleable that, after a while, the distinction between art and life in that novel melts like celluloid in fire. In *Huckleberry Finn,* Colonel Sherburne shoots the town drunk dead in the street and the townspeople re-enact the shooting seconds after it happens; there is also the question of whether the drunk was playacting when he threat-

***American Idol* contestants at *Swimfan* premiere.** The final four American idols — Tamyra Gray, Justin Guarini, Kelly Clarkson, and Nikki McKibbin — pose on August 19, 2002, in Los Angeles. Clarkson went on to win the prize. Her bio on her web site begins with an almost strange declaration of gratitude: "Thankfully, Kelly Clarkson's childhood dream to be a marine biologist did not come true and instead in September 2002 she became a household name when her soulful voice captured the hearts and minds of the United States of America and she was voted the 'American Idol.'" (© Reuters NewMedia Inc./Corbis)

ened to shoot Sherburne. Around the turn of the century, immigrant audiences watching the Yiddish version of *King Lear* jumped out of their seats and cried out, "Ungrateful child!" to Cordelia. Orson Wells got everyone hysterical by presenting H. G. Wells's *War of the Worlds* as an actual news event; and people tuning in to the final ride of O.J.'s white Bronco thought that this actual news event was a television drama.

There is more. In the 1960s, people participating in Happenings enacted fragments of life in the context of art, or they enacted fragments of art in the context of life; in the 1980s and 1990s, performance art continued the genre. Back in the '60s, too, everyone was wringing their hands over the so-called New Journalism's conflation of fact and fiction. Remember *In Cold Blood*? Its author proudly called it a non-fiction novel, thereby setting the culture atwitter. The novel, later a movie, was not really a novel but a documentary, or a documentary-like telling, or retelling, of a real event, the murder of a family. But don't worry if you don't remember the book, or the movie. You probably recall that the actor Robert Blake, who starred in the movie as one of the murderers, was recently arrested for cold-blooded murder.

So reality televison did not come out of nowhere. It is as much an exercise in restoration, an echo of the past, a piece of American tradition, as so many other cultural events are now. American popular culture these days seems to be an endless tunnel of such derivative phantoms: revived plays and musicals; revived movies and revived television series; old movies that become new plays; remixed songs; the familiar-looking children of famous actors; old political speeches that make their way into new political speeches. Almost all the contestants on *American Idol,* a talent contest focused exclusively on finding the best singer, are impersonating the styles of famous singers from the past rather than creating an original style themselves.

Way back in 1980, Harry Waters, the acerbic television critic for *Newsweek,* referred to reality television's forerunners—shows such as *Candid Camera, Real People,* and *The Gong Show*—as "actuality programming." The term "reality television" was used the following year in an article in *The Washington Post* describing television news coverage of Anwar Sadat's assassination. Not only does the nature of reality representation keep shifting, so does the language used to describe it.

Television has its own internal history of changing styles of representation. In the early days of television, even scripted dramas were more "real"—forgive the quotation marks, but what do you do with this word?—than reality television, for the simple reason that they were broadcast live. Today's reality television is heavily edited, musically scored, and constructed with overlapping time-frames that present a participant making voice-over analysis as he and the viewers watch him in a situation taped much earlier. Allen Funt, the host of *Candid Camera,* created mildly embarrassing or charmingly awkward situations, let the hidden camera roll without editing, and then revealed to the subject that he or she should smile because "you're on *Candid Camera.*" The contestants who struggle for dominance on their desert island in *Survivor,* by contrast, have agreed to participate in a highly structured game. They see the camerapeople running all around them, and they watch the heavily edited result later.

A later precursor to reality television, MTV's *Real World,* flashier but similar to its own forerunner *Real People,* simply threw the camera into the participants' lives and let them do whatever they wanted. But the people on *Joe Millionaire, The Bachelor,* and *The Bachelorette* are not, strictly speaking, participants—they are contestants in highly calculated and formulaic situations. Their words and their actions are weighed after taping by a team of producers, who decide what to keep in and what to leave out. In the late 1970s and 1980s, *The Gong Show* vulgarized the old *Amateur Hour* by staging a talent show in which people were invited to debase themselves in outrageous ways. The difference between that show and its present-day descendant, *American Idol,* in which three judges decide on the best singer, is that the latter, for all the judges' near-sadistic treatment of the contestants, is much tamer, much more the product of slick camerawork and editing and a big music-sound.

When the word "reality" is used as a modifier, as in "reality television," it means that the thing modified, in this case television, is being adapted to some generally accepted idea of what "reality" means, not that it is being brought closer to reality. It is like encountering a restaurant in Maryland that offers "continental dining." You know that you are not going to be treated to a dining experience of the sort that you would find in Lausanne or Baden-Baden. You are going to get the popular echo of the generic and generally accepted idea of an authentic European dining experience. And the more universally recognizable a quality is the further it gets from its original denotation. Caricature is the price of a universal familiarity. The question is what original element of a thing is being caricatured. Will the continental dining experience consist of waiters in long aprons, a menu in French, dim lights, or merely exorbitant prices? The "reality" in reality television is a caricature of the idea of reality.

And so the question is, what aspect of reality do the producers of these shows seize on and caricature when they confer upon it the honorific "reality"? It isn't the raw, uncut, unedited spontaneity of the original actuality programs. It isn't the banal, tedious texture of life that you find in *cinéma vérité* or Dogma 95, or in the subtle argument seeping up through the accumulation of suggestive quotidian particulars that you get in a documentary by Frederick Wiseman or Errol Morris. The quality of reality that reality television emphasizes and exaggerates exists only in the negative. It is anything that is not physically perfect, not carefully presented, not stylistically flawless, not shiningly successful—anything that is not packaged in the form of an ideal.

Reality television is a gospel of relaxation, a revolt of the *demos*[1] against the oppressive idealizations of celebrity, and against the onerous images of perfection

---

[1]Originally the Greek term for a district, *demos* has come to mean the populace or common people in general. The word democracy derives from it. —Ed.

purveyed by commercial society. Its essential quality is defeat: it celebrates the experience of losing, of being humiliated and rejected, of having your deepest desires unrequited. These become, in reality television, superlative qualities.

It's true that audiences find themselves comforted by the spectacle of other people's rejection or, in the case of shows such as *Survivor, Fear Factor, American Idol,* and *Are You Hot?,* other people's humiliation. In the end, though, reality television consoles people for their daily failures and defeats rather than making

them feel superior to other people's failures and defeats. Reality television replaces the glowing, successful celebrity ideal with gross imperfection and incontrovertible unhappiness. In a ruthlessly competitive society, where the market has become the exclusive arena of success, reality television shames the illusion of meritocracy by making universal the experience of the underdog, the bumbler, the unlucky and unattractive person.

Consider an analogy from American politics. Bush junior, when running for president, misspoke on camera, bumbled, stumbled, got his facts wrong, and generally projected the image of an inferior, inadequate candidate. But he did so with a wink to the audience that acknowledged his inadequacy, and this conspiratorial wink perhaps empowered people by giving them the illusion that they held the secret to his self-presentation. No hidden trickery lay behind the image of Bush on television. He was not a creation of the media; his indictment by the camera was the proof. His magnetism lay in his lack of charisma. He was the antidote to sizzle and buzz, the antihero of the celebrity universe, the encouraging retort to the thronging images of perfection all around us. Who would not prefer true imperfection to false perfection? And so he made universal the viewer's experience of being the underdog, the bumbler, the unlucky and unattractive person. (Never mind that he is one of the luckiest people who ever lived.)

***Extreme Makeover* Before and After.** This woman turned to *Extreme Makeover* for extensive plastic surgery. The show promises "a truly Cinderella-like experience: A real-life fairy tale in which their wishes come true, not just to change their looks, but their lives and destinies." (Photofest)

Doubtless people who participate in reality television hunger to be celebrities—to be beautiful, and excellent, and successful, and rich. But their motivation for being on a particular show is different from the motivation of the show's creators. So, far from being real, reality television shows are, without exception, structured along the lines of a game show. A prize waits at the end of every series: a fiancée, a trip to Hollywood as the "American Idol," a shot at a career in modeling or acting as America's "hottest" physique, a cash prize. Even at the conclusion of *Extreme Makeover,* a reality show that offers three people complete makeovers at the hands of plastic surgeons, cosmetic dentists, and the like, the climactic scene consists of the participants' return home. Will their family and friends be overwhelmed with admiration for their new appearance, thus making the returning participant a winner? ("I can't believe that's my little girl. She's gorgeous.") Or will everyone draw back in horror, thus declaring the hopeful transformee a loser? Whatever happens, the bottom line of reality television's "reality" is winning or losing.

And yet these are game shows with a difference. They combine the competitive formula of the game show with the emotional and psychological nakedness of confessional talk shows—*Let's Make a Deal* meets Jerry Springer. Whatever the category—talent, physical beauty, survivalist skills, or romance, which encompasses them all—the contestants speak throughout the series about their inner states: their anxiety, their frustrations, their hopes, their feelings about the other contestants. And as the losers are announced at the end of various segments of various series, the camera closes in on and lingers over their faces, catching the slightest signs of distress. In the case of the romantic reality shows, the rejected contestants gather together at the end to comment on the winner; in their defeat, they become retrospective judges whose acid analyses, now at an Olympian remove from the fray, have the effect of making them superior to the winners.

But if reality television de-glamorizes the celebrity aura of success and perfection by replacing it with the universality of failure and rejection, it also theatricalizes inner experience. Along with being a revolt against celebrity and commercially driven images of perfection, reality television is a revolt against the worship of "the real." It is a rebellion against the exposure of the dark, gritty side of human life that so much popular art—and "high" art, too—has devoted itself to accomplishing over the past twenty years. As Waters observed in *Newsweek* two decades ago, the advent of actuality programming coincided with—and was a kind of retort to—the rise of issue-oriented sitcoms such as *Lou Grant* and *All in the Family,* shows that grappled with burning topical subjects such as racism and abortion. The advent of today's reality television coincides with the rise of harsh programs such as *Oz* and *The Shield* and *The Sopranos,* which portray psychology as candidly as the earlier sitcoms depicted the social and political issues of the day. Reality television is a retort to this grimy, roiling psychic reality, a great respite from it.

The "real" in America now comes down to psychology, to the volatile fact that people have emotions. Feelings are the last frontier. There is simply nothing to be done with them. So much of present-day life seems organized to yield winnings and controlled to minimize loss. Why should emotional life be any different? Why should feelings be permitted to flow spontaneously and authentically? So the great project of popular culture over the past twenty years has been to unleash unrationalizable, incalculable, uncontrollable feelings into the public arena in hopes of organizing them as neatly as the other areas of our life are organized. Memoirs, talk shows, first-person outpourings of one kind or another—they all toss feeling into public view and cry, "Help! Do something about this! Arrange and order and control this mess!"

In the same way, reality television masters angry and confused emotions with an organizing narrative. Reality television applies the sophisticated editing and jump-cuts and voice-overs and musical scorings of film to everyday situations, so as to give everyday life the scripted and directed structure of film. And not only does reality television organize life into a story, it also analyzes and interprets the story while it unfolds—as in *Blind Date,* where captions gloss each situation in which the daters find themselves. It is so hard to live life without help.

And it all gets absorbed into the competitive paradigm of American society. At one point in *The Bachelor,* the bachelor remarks about one of the contestants, "When she said yes, she would stay the night, I felt really good about it." Score! It is just a good move in what is only a game. And we are supposed to be comforted that this is so, that the life of feeling has been safely objectified for millions into

another game of winning and losing. It turns out that there is something more frightening than the brutality of the market, and it is the brutality of the inner life. As they say on *American Idol:* "You ask an entire country to step forward and audition." Reality television invites an entire country to step forward and be calmed and stupefied and appeased.

At the same time, just as reality television turns inner experience into an impersonal game of winning and losing, it comfortingly turns winning and losing into a game with transparently arbitrary rules. Thus the talent shows such as *American Idol,* and the beauty shows such as *Are You Hot?* and *Extreme Makeover,* demonstrate the arbitrariness of success based on talent and beauty by making the judges so obviously biased and cruel, by proving that all you need to transform your physical appearance is sufficient money for the purpose. And the survivalist shows such as *Fear Factor,* in which women dive underwater to retrieve dead rats with their mouths, are not about survival; they are about finding a structure to house and to console competition anxiety. The contestants break from below the rules of dignity and self-respect, in a society where, as everyone knows, the elites secretly break the rules from above. By bringing your self-respect so low and living to tell the tale, what you really do is prove that your self-respect is invincible. It is a spiteful rebuke to the lucky classes, whose existence weighs so heavily on you. And the "romantic" reality shows are not about romance at all. They are about turning the inexorable and inexplicable losses and setbacks and puzzles of emotional life into another transparent, impersonal game with winners and losers. Better to be a loser, after all, than to find yourself in something that is not a game. Because in the end Eliot was right when he said that humankind cannot bear very much reality. Enter reality television.

175

◀ **Casting call, *Fear Factor,* March 6, 2003.** Natalie Campagna made it to the second stage of the open casting call for the hit reality show *Fear Factor*, held at a Crunch Gym. Further information and a photograph were obtained, putting her in the running for a callback. Producers spend months poring over potential cast members for reality shows. (© Christopher Smith/Corbis)

Anthony Jaffe, *It's a Real, Real, Real, Real, Real World*.
Could it be that everyday life is actually *too real* for
the producers of reality television shows? Anthony
Jaffe makes fun of the format by proposing some new
shows featuring characters who — if reality television
is what Americans mean by "real" — must cope with
the problems of what can only be called an unreal
life. This humorous column appeared in the January
2001 online version of *Mother Jones, Mojo Wire*.

Anthony Jaffe

IT'S A REAL, REAL, REAL, REAL, REAL WORLD

Forget *Temptation Island* and *Survivor II*. What if reality TV were based on, well,
reality? We unearthed one network's internal memorandum outlining some of the
hottest new ideas for gripping television based on real life.

```
Ms. [REDACTED]:
Here are the abstracts, as you
requested. Development should be
making the first cut early next
week. Let us know if you see
something you want to green-light
sooner.

Respectfully,
Bob [REDACTED]
VP, Development

cc: dvt, act, adv, lgl

attch'd: reality_pitch.doc
{converted}
```

BUMS AWAY!

When you're old, mentally ill, or not in possession of a full complement of limbs, remaining unfrozen during a New England winter can be a real challenge, particularly if you live beneath a highway overpass. We'll pick a real-life "Dirty Dozen" of contestants who are just crazy enough to try it! In addition to standing around garbage-fed fires and curling into fetal positions to conserve body warmth, our contestants will compete each week for "Bum Bucks®," which can be exchanged for things like potato chips, cigarettes, malt liquor, or a sock—almost like real money! Spend your Bum Bucks® wisely, and you might come away with nothing more than frostbitten toes. But fritter them away, and your cardboard-box "condo" could be your coffin!

(In regard to the product-placement team's question about fortified wine, a focus group of hobos confirmed that red goes with meat, as well as fish and fowl. It also complements mints, squash, mayonnaise, crackers, stale hoagie rolls, and other fortified wines.)

LORD OF THE FRIES

Our gaggle of downtrodden contestants will think they're sitting in the catbird seat after we give them full-time, minimum-wage gigs plus daily food discounts at a Peoria, Ill., Burger King. But they're in for a real "Whopper" of a surprise when management reveals that one ambitious team member will also receive "Employee of the Month" honors. That means a handsome plaque displayed above the condiment station—and $30 in cold, hard cash! Will it be the lovable senior citizen? The single mom? The recent immigrant? One of the hip teenagers who lives to provide superior levels of customer service? All bets are off as these hard-working fun-loving food-service specialists do whatever it takes to make it to the top!

(Note to Legal: The phrase "sitting in the catbird seat" is not meant to imply that employees may assume a seated position during their assigned shifts.)

LOST IN (A VERY CONFINED) SPACE

Bureaucratic apathy and ineptitude transform contestants' light sentences for jaywalking into indefinite incarceration in a maximum-security penitentiary. One lucky winner will be released after the state discovers its mistake and loses an expensive and protracted legal wrangle. But to get to the outside, contestants will first have to stay alive on the inside! That means our prime-time inmates will learn the subtle arts of shank craftsmanship and improvisational tattooing. They'll hit the weights to prepare for gladiator-style yard fights. Some will find religion; others will find trouble in the showers! One thing's for sure: For these new fish, it's going to be sink or swim!

(We're thinking Shawshank Redemption, *but minus scenes of birds being set free or other metaphorical imagery suggesting redemption, liberation, glints of humanity, etc.)*

177

RUN FOR THE BORDER

Plucked from their comfortable suburban townhouses in the dead of night, our contestants will be blindfolded, transported, and deposited by helicopter into the scorching desert of northern Mexico, where they'll set out on a mad dash to the Arizona border. First person to reach U.S. soil wins! These tough hombres will have to contend with smugglers, bandits, INS agents, vigilante ranchers, desperate thirst, and ignorance of regional geography, ensuring plenty of high-adrenaline high jinks. May the Speediest Gonzales win!

(Legal: Contestants will be provided with tortillas and pond water while off-camera, just to keep things interesting, and to avoid unnecessary and expensive wrongful death suits.)

TOXIC TOWN

Life is pretty sweet for people in Appleville, Neb. That is, until we buy Old Man Johnson's creekside property and sell it to a business consortium that builds a massive petrochemical factory and a pair of industrial-size hog farms. Suddenly our contestants, lifelong residents of Appleville, are getting sicker by the minute! By the fifth episode, the creek is clogged with porcine feces and the local groundwater is toast! Folks will be coughing up blood and sprouting tumors like turnips. The faint of heart will gather up what's left of their families and flee, but our winner will stick it out until the end! What makes a winner? Just good, old-fashioned determination, plus freakish immunity to organ-shredding toxins.

(Possible downside: Advertising can skip pitching ad time to Jimmy Dean or Exxon.)

SOCIAL INSECURITY

Get ready for a terminal case of senioritis! We're going to whisk a dozen ailing octogenarians from the squalid basement apartments and converted family rooms where their offspring have stashed them to the deceptively serene Rainbow Vista ContinuCare Village, where they'll soon realize that only the toughest oldster survives. Alliances will be formed and diabolical measures taken as our contestants coax and connive their way to the medicine, food, and oxygen tanks they crave! Backstabbing desperation and a massive outbreak of bedsores should ensure plenty of humor and drama every week.

(Casting is shooting for a good mix of ambulatory and bed-ridden contestants. Legal is still determining fair market price for contestants who do not win, in order to estimate familial compensation at show's end.)

MESSAGE

"Reality TV" has clearly become a convenient label for a wide range of current television shows. In your opinion, do you think the label accurately describes these shows? In what way do the shows represent reality? Would you propose a different label? Do you agree with Lee Siegel that the ultimate purpose of all these shows is to invite "an entire country to step forward and be calmed and stupefied and appeased"?

METHOD

Note the way Anthony Jaffe pokes fun at reality television. How does he go about satirizing the shows? What format and jargon does he use to make us aware of how the shows represent reality? Using his method, try constructing a few "abstracts" of your own.

MEDIUM

According to Siegel, how does reality television combine elements of other types of TV shows? How does reality television use film-making techniques to achieve the feeling of reality on the shows? What are some of these techniques? Can you explain why these film-making techniques work or don't work?

179

THE MOVIES

Movies tell stories. And they are the narrative form that most of us remember the best, being visually compelling and by nature an engrossing genre (we sit in a darkened theater, surrounded by image, sound, and music, all edited down to a 90-minute story). The movies represented here—whether life-changing or not, as Louise Erdrich describes her experience watching the movie *Z*—have significance for great numbers of people. Different movies speak to different people; in fact, we all can name a movie that we've seen again and again, the teen movie or horror film or action adventure that we love to revisit. How we respond to movies—what makes us say whether a film is good or bad—can reveal a lot about our own stories: where we've come from, where we are, and where we'd like to go.

180

Z poster. The French film *Z* was released in 1969 and received many awards, including ▶ that year's Academy Award for best foreign film. Starring Yves Montand and Irene Papas, and directed by noted film director Constantin Costa-Gavras, the movie, based on an actual incident in 1963, portrays the assassination of a Greek anti-nuclear scientist (played by Montand) and is widely regarded as one of the finest political thrillers in film history. In color and English, it is available in both videocassette and DVD format. (Everett Collection Inc.)

Go to exercise 02 on **ix visual exercises** to explore **purpose**; we often say that the purpose of movies is to entertain, but is that always true?

"Best suspense movie of the year"
—Mystery Writers of America

Z

GP

Louis Erdrich, Z: *The Movie That Changed My Life*. Raised in North Dakota, the daughter of a Chippewa mother and a German father, Louise Erdrich has won many awards for her novels and short story collections. These include *Love Medicine* (1984), *The Beet Queen* (1986), *Tracks* (1988), *The Bingo Palace* (1994), *Tales of Burning Love* (1996), *The Antelope Wife* (1998), and *The Master Butchers Singing Club* (2003). *The Blue Jay's Dance*, a collection of essays, was published in 1995. Her essay on the film *Z* was written for a collection of essays, *The Movie That Changed My Life*, edited by David Rosenberg (1993).

Louise Erdrich

Z: THE MOVIE THAT CHANGED MY LIFE

Next to writing full-time, the best job I ever had combined two passions — pop-corn and narrative. At fourteen, I was hired as a concessioner at the Gilles Theater in Wahpeton, North Dakota. Behind a counter of black marbleized glass, I sold Dots, Red Hot Tamales, Jujubes, Orange Crush, and, of course, hot buttered popcorn. My little stand was surrounded by art deco mirrors, and my post, next to the machine itself, was bathed in an aura of salt and butter. All of my sopho-more year, I exuded a light nutty fragrance that turned, on my coats and dresses, to the stale odor of mouse nests. The best thing about that job was that, once I had wiped the counters, dismantled the machines, washed the stainless steel parts, totaled up the take, and refilled the syrup cannisters and wiped off the soft drink machine, I could watch the show, free.

I saw everything that came to Wahpeton in 1969 — watched every movie seven times, in fact, since each one played a full week. I saw Zeffirelli's *Romeo and Juliet,* and did not weep. I sighed over Charlton Heston in *Planet of the Apes,* and ground my teeth at the irony of the ending shot. But the one that really got to me was Costa-Gavras's *Z.*

Nobody in Wahpeton walked into the Gilles knowing that the film was about the assassination in Greece of a leftist peace leader by a secret right-wing organization and the subsequent investigation that ended in a bloody coup. The ad in the paper said only "Love Thriller" and listed Yves Montand and Irene Papas as the stars.

"Dear Diary," I wrote the morning after I'd seen *Z* for the first time. "The hypocrites are exposed. He is alive! Just saw the best movie of my life. Must remember to dye my bra and underwear to match my cheerleading outfit."

I forgot to rinse out the extra color, so during the week that *Z* was playing, I had purple breasts. The school color of my schizophrenic adolescence. My parents strictly opposed my career as a wrestling cheerleader, on the grounds that it would change me into someone they wouldn't recognize. Now, they were right, though of course I never let anyone know my secret.

I had changed in other ways, too. Until I was fourteen, my dad and I would go hunting on weekends or skating in the winter. Now I practiced screaming S-U-C-C-E-S-S and K-I-L-L for hours, and then, of course, had to run to work during the matinee. Not that I was utterly socialized. Over my cheerleading out-fit I wore Dad's army jacket, and on my ankle, a bracelet made of twisted blasting-wire given to me by a guitar-playing Teen Corps volunteer, Kurt, who hailed from The Valley of the Jolly Green Giant, a real town in eastern Minnesota.

No, I was not yet completely subsumed into small-town femalehood. I knew there was more to life than the stag leap, or the flying T, but it wasn't until I saw *Z* that I learned language for what that "more" was.

After the third viewing, phrases began to whirl in my head. "The forces of greed and hatred cannot tolerate us"; "There are not enough hospitals, not enough doctors, yet one half of the budget goes to the military"; "Peace at all costs"; and, of course, the final words, "He is alive!" But there was more to it than the language. It was the first *real* movie I had ever seen—one with a cynical, unromantic, deflating ending.

At the fourth viewing of the movie, I had a terrible argument with Vincent, the Gilles's pale, sad ticket taker, who was also responsible for changing the wooden letters on the marquee. At the beginning of the week, he had been pleased. He had looked forward to this title for a month. Just one letter. It was he who thought of the ad copy, "Love Thriller." By the middle of the run, he was unhappy, for he sided with the generals, just as he sided with our boss.

Vincent always wore a suit and stood erect. He was officious, a tiger with gatecrashers and tough with those who had misplaced their stubs while going to the bathroom. I, on the other hand, waved people in free when I was left in charge, and regarded our boss with absolute and burning hatred, for he was a pid-dling authority, a man who enjoyed setting meaningless tasks. I hated being made to rewash the butter dispenser. Vincent liked being scolded for not tearing the tickets exactly in half. Ours was an argument of more than foreign ideologies.

Vincent insisted that the boss was a fair man who made lots of money. I maintained that we were exploited. Vincent said the film was lies, while I insisted it was based on fact. Neither of us checked for the truth in the library. Neither of us knew the first thing about modern Greece, yet I began comparing the generals to our boss. Their pompous egotism, the way they bumbled and puffed when they were accused of duplicity, their self-righteous hatred of "long-haired hippies and dope addicts of indefinite sex."

When I talked behind the boss's back, Vincent was worse than horrified; he was incensed.

"Put what's-his-name in a uniform and he'd be the head of the security police," I told Vincent, who looked like he wanted to pound my head.

But I knew what I knew. I had my reasons. Afraid that I might eat him out of Junior Mints, the boss kept a running tab of how many boxes of each type of candy reposed in the bright glass case. Every day, I had to count the boxes and officially request more to fill the spaces. I couldn't be off by so much as a nickel at closing.

One night, made bold by *Z,* I opened each candy box and ate one Jujube, one Jordan Almond, one Black Crow, and so on, out of each box, just to accomplish something subversive. When I bragged, Vincent cruelly pointed out that I had just cheated all my proletarian customers. I allowed that he was right, and stuck to popcorn after that, eating handfuls directly out of the machine. I had to count the boxes, and the buckets, too, and empty out the ones unsold and fold them flat again and mark them. There was an awful lot of paperwork involved in being a concessioner.

As I watched *Z* again and again, the generals took on aspects of other authorities. I memorized the beginning, where the military officers, in a secret meeting, speak of the left as "political mildew" and deplored "the dry rot of subversive ideologies." It sounded just like the morning farm report on our local radio, with all the dire warnings of cow brucellosis and exhortations to mobilize against the invasion of wild oats. I knew nothing about metaphor, nothing, in fact, of communism or what a dictatorship was, but the language grabbed me and would not let go. Without consciously intending it, I had taken sides.

Then, halfway into Christmas vacation, Vincent told on me. The boss took me down into his neat little office in the basement and confronted me with the denouncement that I had eaten one piece of candy from every box in the glass case. I denied it.

"Vincent does it all the time," I lied with a clear conscience.

So there we were, a nest of informers and counterinformers, each waiting to betray the other over a Red Hot Tamale. It was sad. I accused Vincent of snitching; he accused me of the same. We no longer had any pretense of solidarity. He didn't help me when I had a line of customers, and I didn't give him free pop.

Before watching *Z* again the other night, I took a straw poll of people I knew to have been conscientious in 1969, asking them what they remembered about the movie. It was almost unanimous. People running, darkness, a little blue truck, and Irene Papas. Michael and I sat down and put the rented tape of *Z* into the video recorder. Between us we shared a bowl of air-popped corn. No salt. No butter anymore. Back in 1969, Michael had purchased the soundtrack to the movie and reviewed it for his school newspaper. It had obviously had an effect on both of us, and yet we recalled no more about it than the viewers in our poll. My memories were more intense because of the argument that almost got me fired from my first indoor job, but all was very blurred except for Irene Papas. As the credits rolled I looked forward to seeing the star. Moment after moment went by, and she did not appear. The leftist organizer went to the airport to pick up the peace leader, and somehow I expected Irene to get off the plane and stun everyone with her tragic, moral gaze.

Of course, Yves was the big star, the peace leader. We watched. I waited for Irene, and then, when it became clear she was only a prop for Yves, I began to watch for *any* woman with a speaking role.

The first one who appeared spoke into a phone. The second woman was a maid, the third a secretary, then a stewardess, then, finally, briefly, Irene, looking grim, and then a woman in a pink suit handing out leaflets. Finally, a woman appeared in a demonstration, only to get kicked in the rear end.

Not only that, the man who kicked her was gay, and much was made of his seduction of a pinball-playing boy, his evil fey grin, his monstrosity. To the Costa-Gavras of 1969, at least, the lone gay man was a vicious goon, immoral and perverted.

Once Yves was killed, Irene was called in to mourn, on cue. Her main contribution to the rest of the movie was to stare inscrutably, to weep uncontrollably, and to smell her deceased husband's after-shave. How had I gotten the movie so wrong?

By the end, I knew I hadn't gotten it so wrong after all. In spite of all that is lacking from the perspective of twenty years, *Z* is still a good political film. It still holds evil to the light and makes hypocrisy transparent. The witnesses who come forward to expose the assassination are bravely credible, and their loss at the end is terrible and stunning. *Z* remains a moral tale, a story of justice done and vengeance sought. It deals with stupidity and avarice, with hidden motives and the impact that one human being can have on others' lives. I still got a thrill when the last line was spoken, telling us that *Z,* in the language of the ancient Greeks, means "He is alive." I remember feeling that the first time I saw the movie, and now I recalled one other thing. The second evening the movie showed, I watched Vincent, who hadn't even waited for the end, unhook the red velvet rope from its silver post.

Our argument was just starting in earnest. Normally, after everyone was gone and the outside lights were doused, he spent an hour, maybe two if a Disney had played, cleaning up after the crowd. He took his time. After eleven o'clock, the place was his. He had the keys and the boss was gone. Those nights, Vincent walked down each aisle with a bag, a mop, and a bucket filled with the same pink soapy solution I used on the butter machine. He went after the spilled Coke, the mashed chocolate, the Jujubes pressed flat. He scraped the gum off the chairs before it hardened. And there were things people left, things so inconsequential that the movie goers rarely bothered to claim them—handkerchiefs, lipsticks, buttons, pens, and small change. One of the things I knew Vincent liked best about his job was that he always got to keep what he found.

There was nothing to find that night, however, not a chewed pencil or a hair-pin. No one had come. We'd have only a few stragglers the next few nights, then the boss canceled the film. Vincent and I locked the theater and stood for a moment beneath the dark marquee, arguing. Dumb as it was, it was the first time I'd disagreed with anyone over anything but hurt feelings and boyfriends. It was intoxicating. It seemed like we were the only people in the town.

There have been many revolutions, but never one that so thoroughly changed the way women are perceived and depicted as the movement of the last twenty years. In Costa-Gravras's *Missing, Betrayed,* and *Music Box,* strong women are the protagonists, the jugglers of complicated moral dilemmas. These are not women who dye their underwear to lead cheers, and neither am I anymore, metaphorically I mean, but it is hard to escape from expectations. The impulse never stops. Watching *Z* in an empty North Dakota theater was one of those small, incremental experiences that fed into personal doubt, the necessary seed of any change or growth. The country in *Z* seemed terribly foreign, exotic, a large and threatened place — deceptive, dangerous, passionate. As it turned out, it was my first view of the world.

Movie gallery. The five movie images that follow, ▶
and their accompanying comments from a handful of people who enjoy them, give a sense of the
passion that the movies inspire — and of the
power that cinematic stories wield. Can you think
of a movie that changed your life?

X2: X-Men United (2003) aka X-Men 2
Directed by Bryan Singer
Shown: (H) James Marsden, Kelly Hu, Patrick Stewart, Alan Cumming, Halle Berry, Shawn Ashmore, Hugh Jackman, Anna Paquin, Ian McKellen, Rebecca Romijn-Stamos, Aaron Stanford, Famke Janssen

Rentals grant one-time, EDITORIAL use only, unless otherwise negotiated. Please inform us about usage as soon as possible. Research fees may be applicable if no images are used.

PHOTOFEST
(212) 633-6330

Fox, *X-Men 2*, 2003. (Photofest)

COMMENT

"I read comics as a child, although never to the extent Doran [my son] does. My mother thought it was a waste of time that could have been better spent on more intellectual pursuits, but I thought they were fun. My favorites were the X-Men. Teenage superheroes in a special school for 'gifted' youth, the X-Men were 'mutants,' a subgroup of humanity hated and feared by the rest of the human race. That school and those kids felt very real to me, and the stories they told in the comic books were a jumping-off point for myriad stories in my head. I realize now that reading those comics and weaving those fantasies captured and supported my preadolescent feelings that there was something different about me, long before I knew the 'something' was that I was a lesbian, not a mutant superhero."

—Dale Rosenburg, from
"How the X-Men Changed My Life," Advocate.com, May 8, 2003

188

Metro-Goldwyn-Mayer, *The Wizard of Oz*, 1939. (Photofest)

COMMENT

"*The Wizard of Oz* taught me a few things that I still find challenging. That it's okay to be an idealist, that you have to imagine something better and go for it. That you have to believe in something, and it's best to start with yourself and take it from there. At least give it a try. As corny as it may sound, sometimes I am afraid of what's around the corner, or what's not around the corner. But I look anyway. I believe that writing is one of my 'corners' — an intersection, really; and when I'm confused or reluctant to look back, deeper, or ahead, I create my own Emerald Cities and force myself to take longer looks, because it is one sure way that I'm able to see."

— Terry McMillan, novelist

Warner Brothers, *The Matrix,* **1999.** (Everett Collection Inc.)

189

COMMENT

"The original *Matrix* movie was more than just an action flick. Sure, the heroes' new-jack, frozen-time kung fu kicked ass, and the software villains were supremely menacing. But it was the searing social critique, the information-age theology, and the series of head-in-your-palms plot twists that catapulted the film to cult status. . . . By turning 1999 America into a computerized dream world, designed by evil machines to suppress the human race, *The Matrix* put in pictures what so many intuited: that this Bubble-era lifestyle was just a façade, and that the people who swayed to its corporate-worshipping rhythm were sleepwalking through some usurious fantasy."

—Noah Shactman, *Wired* magazine

190

New Line Cinema, *The Lord of the Rings: The Return of the King,* **2003.** (Photofest)

COMMENT

"The film is, by most criteria, an ungainly piece of storytelling. Yet it sweeps you up and hurtles you along like water from an exploded dike. If it's hard to keep hold of the spiraling narrative threads, it's harder still to resist the rush of mythic imagery and cornball heroic dialogue delivered by gorgeously blue-eyed actors and actresses."

—David Edelstein, movie critic for Slate.com

COMMENT

"Despite the fact that the first two installments of *The Lord of the Rings* (and, I imagine, the final one) are overwhelmingly visual, they also seem to belong to a great tradition of oral storytelling."

—Charles Taylor, Salon.com arts critic

COMMENT

"I'm doing what I've always done: telling stories I think are important in the language I speak best: film. I think most great stories
are hero stories. People want to reach out and grab at something
higher, and vicariously live through heroism, and lift their spirit
that way.... There is no greater hero story than this one — about
the greatest love one can have, which is to lay down one's life for
someone. *The Passion* is the biggest adventure story of all time. I
think it's the biggest love-story of all time; God becoming man and
men killing God — if that's not action, nothing is."

—Mel Gibson, director, *The Passion of the Christ*

Newmarket Films, *The Passion of the Christ*, 2003. (Photofest)

MESSAGE

What political message did the young Louise Erdrich take from the movie *Z*? How did she apply this message to her immediate condition at the time? How does the more mature Erdrich respond to the film's message? What parts of that message does she now find dated? What parts does she think are still relevant? How do gender roles play a part in Erdrich's reaction during both time periods?

METHOD

Consider the way Erdrich structures her essay. Why do you think she breaks it into two parts? In what other ways might she have structured her experiences with the movie *Z*? How would the essay affect you differently if she had started with the second part and proceeded back in time? How does her topic — how a movie changed her life — help determine the structure of her essay?

MEDIUM

As everyone knows, movies can exert a powerful influence on our lives. That influence is sometimes a result of the film's message — as we see in the essay on *Z* — but at other times a particular film will strongly influence the way we behave, look, or dress, as well as provoke lifelong fears, beliefs, or desires. In a short essay, tell the story of how a certain film exerted a profound influence on your life. Try, as Erdrich does, to provide a specific time and setting, though you need not examine the film from a later date.

PHOTO|OURNALISM

2 ESSAYS | 9 PHOTOS

Early photographers found themselves severely limited by their cumbersome equipment, and it wasn't until the development of smaller, hand-held cameras that they could go beyond their studios and leave behind their clumsy tripods to adequately cover the daily flow of events. Photojournalism came of age in the 1930s, as big-city newspapers and popular photo magazines like *Life* and *Look* capitalized on the public's appetite for photographs that offered news and entertainment primarily through imagery. Photographers were becoming reporters, and news stories often turned on a photo. Indeed, in effective photojournalism, the picture tells the story without the need for caption or comment; the photo does not simply illustrate or accompany the story. As equipment continued to improve and as the public's demand for sensational pictures grew, photographers not only covered stories but actually created them, as we saw in the death of Princess Diana. Her fatal and extensively reported car crash was (as many commentators have claimed) most probably caused by the motorcycle pursuit of celebrity photographers who went to great extremes to capture her every movement on film.

Although newspapers and magazines today could hardly exist without it, photojournalism as it is often practiced raises a number of ethical issues. How far should the camera be allowed to pry into someone's private life? Does the public really need to see pictures of death and mutilation? Should photojournalists be subjected to stricter professional standards? How far can sensational photographs be trusted to tell the full story? The collection of materials presented in the following pages takes a longitudinal look at sensationalism. It includes a few examples of photographs by Weegee (sometimes credited for being the father of **tabloid** photography) with an essay by Wendy Lesser. Another essay by Nora Ephron, "The Boston Photographs," explores the impact that the now-famous photographs had when they were published in 1975. Finally, two photographs by Bronston Jones suggest an alternate way to handle sensational material in the wake of the terrorist attacks of September 11, 2001.

tabloid: *A newspaper characterized by its small size, condensed stories, popular format, and emphasis on photography. The word often conveys a negative sense (as in "tabloid journalism") due to the way tabloids, or "tabs," have conventionally relied on sensationalism, gossip, celebrity features, and mass appeal.*

Wendy Lesser, Weegee. In the following essay, the critic Wendy Lesser offers some illuminating comments on three Weegee photographs featuring children. Wendy Lesser is the founding editor of the *Threepenny Review*, a Berkeley, California, literary quarterly that frequently covers photography. She is the author of several books, including *His Other Half: Men Looking at Women Through Art* (1991), *Pictures at an Execution: An Inquiry into the Subject of Murder* (1994), *The Amateur: An Independent Life of Letters* (1999), and most recently *Nothing Remains the Same* (2003).

Wendy Lesser
WEEGEE

In Weegee's pictures, we are simultaneously inside and outside. We are given a scene that is spectacular, or stereotypical, or representative, or tabloid-cute; and we are also offered a sense of interiority, in the form of highly individual emotions rendered fleetingly and mysteriously. Weegee's best photos tell us two opposite things at once: that appearances are the only reality, and that the most important knowledge comes through imagining what lies behind appearances.

You can see this quite clearly in the photograph of the tabloid newsboy, which operates as both a sample of tabloid journalism and a commentary on it. Like the tabloids, this picture spells out its message in black and white: stark black letters against white paper, white paper against stark black background. Like the tabloids, it captures and exploits a very particular moment in time, a very particular sort of public event: a confession by a famous murderer (no doubt made famous by the tabloids themselves). But whereas the tabloid front page must show us a face to satisfy us—must let us know what the murderous woman actually looked like—Weegee's photo satisfies by hiding the newsboy's face. The boy, remaining anonymous, becomes both public and private, generic and particular.

And just as the newsboy faces at an oblique angle to us, Weegee's photo stands at an angle to the news it conveys. Looking at the photo, you have to tilt your head sideways to read the headlines and captions, so only one aspect of the double message can be taken in at once. If you can read the tabloid news, you can't "read" the boy, and vice versa.

195

◀ **Weegee, Newsboy.** (Reproduced courtesy of Weegee/ICP/Getty Images)

In another of its versions, this curious mixture of interiority and exteriority, private communication and public message, appears in the Mulberry Street café scene. The image is almost stereotypically Italian: the faces, the hand gestures, the high-waisted pants, the cups of espresso, the knicknacks and gewgaws on the glass-fronted shelves—not to mention all the Italian words, as if to spell it out: *This is Little Italy.* Ethnicity is of great interest to Weegee. (It's even there in the newsboy photo, in that bizarre word "Cohenite.") Ethnic identity is yet another form of inside versus outside, membership versus exclusion. It is also, for Weegee, an essential element of urban life. Ethnic definition—ethnic *self*-definition—is a sign of urbanity, or worldly-wiseness; at the same time, it marks the special provinciality of New York's neighborhoods.

But what makes this picture a Weegee is the little girl who stands on the far left side. She is the only female in the photo, and the only child. She is invisible to everyone else in the scene. (One man even walks right by her without noticing her presence.) She, on the other hand, sees everything. One arm akimbo, the other hand thoughtfully scratching her chin, her dark eyes so wide they are practically all whites, she also seems to be judging everything. Is this how all grown-up men live? Will Mulberry Street always be like this? Am I stuck here forever? *Yes* is the picture's answer. *Not exactly* is our response.

Weegee, *Mulberry Street Café*. One of the earliest photojournalists — and still   ▶
among the most highly regarded — was Weegee (1899–1968). Born into a devout
Jewish family in what is now Ukraine, Weegee (whose legal name was Arthur Fellig)
immigrated to the United States as a child. He grew up in the slums of New York's
Lower East Side, where as a teenager he learned how to take pictures in order to
support himself. He was soon selling his striking flash photographs to various
tabloids and earning a reputation for astonishing close-ups of an unraveling urban
life. In the forward to *Naked City,* a collection of his photographs, Weegee's friend
and editor wrote: "He will take his camera and ride off in search of new evidence
that his city, even in her most drunken and disorderly and pathetic moments, is
beautiful." (Reproduced courtesy of Weegee/ICP/Getty Images)

Weegee, *Dancing*.
(Reproduced courtesy
of Weegee/ICP/Getty
Images)

198

A look of interiority on the face of a female subject also shapes the picture of the dancing woman and girl. Unlike the Caffe Bella Napoli photo, this picture has sprung loose from its setting. We don't know where we are, except that we are outside on the street somewhere, as the paving stones and stray newspapers suggest. In the background is a clot of black and white figures, some of whom are looking at the dancing couple, many of whom are not. The woman and the child are the only ones dancing, as far as we can see. They are, in that sense, making a public spectacle of themselves. But the expressions on their faces define the experience as a completely private one. For the girl, there is pleasure verging on delight. Is it delight at dancing, or at dancing with this woman? Is the woman her sister? Her mother? Her babysitter? A friend? We'll never know.

And for the woman there is also pleasure of a kind, but it is much more pensive. The richly reflective expression on her face is not exactly romantic melancholy, though it contains both sadness and longing. She is listening to a tune that no one else quite hears; she is looking at an empty space and seeing something. She almost seems to be reaching across the impassable gap between her moment in time and ours. The music that guided her steps has long since died, as has the man who took her photograph. But she keeps them alive for us.

COMMENT

"Weegee was a hack—and that was the source of his power. He was raised on the Lower East Side where his father had a pushcart and doubled as the super in their cold-water tenement. He was, in the words of his friend Louis Stettner, 'a guttural egomaniac,' and it shows in all his work."

—Daniel Wolff, *Threepenny Review* 56, Winter 1994

Weegee, *Car Crash Upper Fifth Ave., July 13, 1941.*
This on-the-spot photograph of two boys who
just wrecked a stolen car represents Weegee's
uncanny ability to capture a disturbing moment
and do so with an eye for detail and composition.
(Reproduced courtesy of Weegee/ICP/Getty
Images)

■ *Study this photograph. How has Weegee literally shaped or*
framed the scene? What details inform you that an accident has
occurred? What is the effect of the injured boy's reflection in the
window vent? How does it contribute to Weegee's overall composi-
tion? How does Weegee convey intimacy and vulnerability at the
same time he is recording the news of an accident?

Nora Ephron, *The Boston Photographs.* Nora Ephron takes ethical questions head-on as she examines a dramatic sequence of photos showing a woman falling to her death from a fire escape during an attempted rescue from a burning apartment building. The daughter of two screenwriters, Ephron is now one of Hollywood's leading screenwriters (*When Harry Met Sally, Sleepless in Seattle*) and film directors (*Michael, You've Got Mail,* and *Lucky Numbers*). She began her career as a reporter and media critic for various New York papers and magazines. Ephron, who was born in 1941 and is a graduate of Wellesley College, has also published several collections of essays, including *Crazy Salad* (1975) and *Scribble, Scribble: Notes on the Media* (1978), from which "The Boston Photographs" is taken.

Nora Ephron

THE BOSTON PHOTOGRAPHS

"I made all kinds of pictures because I thought it would be a good rescue shot over the ladder...never dreamed it would be anything else....I kept having to move around because of the light set. The sky was bright and they were in deep shadow. I was making pictures with a motor drive and he, the fire fighter, was reaching up and, I don't know, everything started falling. I followed the girl down taking pictures...I made three or four frames. I realized what was going on and I completely turned around, because I didn't want to see her hit."

You probably saw the photographs. In most newspapers, there were three of them. The first showed some people on a fire escape—a fireman, a woman and a child. The fireman had a nice strong jaw and looked very brave. The woman was holding the child. Smoke was pouring from the building behind them. A rescue ladder was approaching, just a few feet away, and the fireman had one arm around the woman and one arm reaching out toward the ladder. The second picture showed the fire escape slipping off the building. The child had fallen on the escape and seemed about to slide off the edge. The woman was grasping desperately at the legs of the fireman, who had managed to grab the ladder. The third picture showed the woman and child in midair, falling to the ground. Their arms and legs were outstretched, horribly distended. A potted plant was falling too. The caption said that the woman, Diana Bryant, nineteen, died in the fall. The child landed on the woman's body and lived.

The pictures were taken by Stanley Forman, thirty, of the *Boston Herald American.* He used a motor-driven Nikon F set a 1/250, f5.6-S. Because of the motor, the camera can click off three frames a second. More than four hundred newspapers in the United States alone carried the photographs; the tear sheets from overseas are still coming in. The *New York Times* ran them on the first page of its second section; a paper in south Georgia gave them nineteen columns; the *Chicago Tribune,* the *Washington Post* and the *Washington Star* filled almost half their front pages, the *Star* under a somewhat redundant headline that read: SENSATIONAL PHOTOS OF RESCUE ATTEMPT THAT FAILED.

The photographs are indeed sensational. They are pictures of death in action, of that split second when luck runs out, and it is impossible to look at them without feeling their extraordinary impact and remembering, in an almost subconscious way, the morbid fantasy of falling, falling off a building, falling to one's death. Beyond that, the pictures are classics, old-fashioned but perfect examples of photojournalism at its most spectacular. They're throwbacks, really, fire pictures, 1930s tabloid shots; at the same time they're technically superb and thoroughly modern—the sequence could not have been taken at all until the development of the motor-driven camera some sixteen years ago.

Most newspaper editors anticipate some reader reaction to photographs like Forman's; even so, the response around the country was enormous, and almost all of it was negative. I have read hundreds of the letters that were printed in letters-to-the-editor sections, and they repeat the same points. "Invading the privacy of death." "Cheap sensationalism." "I thought I was reading the *National Enquirer.*" "Assigning the agony of a human being in terror of imminent death to the status of a side-show act." "A tawdry way to sell newspapers." The *Seattle Times* received sixty letters and calls; its managing editor even got a couple of them at home. A reader wrote the *Philadelphia Inquirer: "Jaws* and *Towering Inferno* are playing downtown; don't take business away from people who pay good money to advertise in your own paper." Another reader wrote the *Chicago Sun-Times:* "I shall try to hide my disappointment that Miss Bryant wasn't wearing a skirt when she fell to her death. You could have had some award-winning photographs of her underpants as her skirt billowed over her head, you voyeurs." Several newspaper editors

201

Stanley Forman, *The Boston Photographs,* 1975. Photographer Stanley ▶ Forman won the Pulitzer Prize for Spot News Photography for these images, taken in Boston on July 22, 1975, and won a second in 1977 for a picture he took of a riot between whites and blacks over the integration of public schools in Boston. Forman was working for the *Boston Herald American* when he took these photographs, but over four hundred newspapers across the country ran them the next day. (© Stanley J. Forman)

wrote columns defending the pictures: Thomas Keevil of the *Costa Mesa* (California) *Daily Pilot* printed a ballot for readers to vote on whether they would have printed the pictures; Marshall L. Stone of Maine's *Bangor Daily News,* which refused to print the famous assassination picture of the Vietcong prisoner in Saigon, claimed that the Boston pictures showed the dangers of fire escapes and raised questions about slumlords. (The burning building was a five-story brick apartment house on Marlborough Street in the Back Bay section of Boston.)

For the last five years, the *Washington Post* has employed various journalists as ombudsmen, whose job is to monitor the paper on behalf of the public. The *Post*'s current ombudsman is Charles Seib, former managing editor of the *Washington Star;* the day the Boston photographs appeared, the paper received over seventy calls in protest. As Seib later wrote in a column about the pictures, it was "the

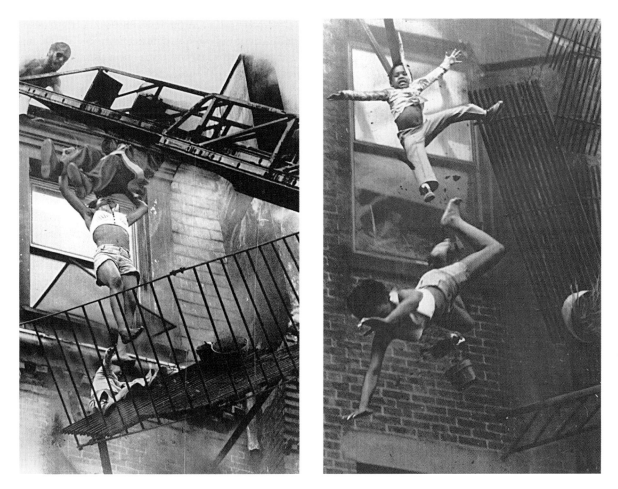

largest reaction to a published item that I have experienced in eight months as the *Post*'s ombudsman....

"In the *Post*'s newsroom, on the other hand, I found no doubts, no second thoughts...the question was not whether they should be printed but how they should be displayed. When I talked to editors...they used words like 'interesting' and 'riveting' and 'gripping' to describe them. The pictures told of something about life in the ghetto, they said (although the neighborhood where the tragedy occurred is not a ghetto, I am told). They dramatized the need to check on the safety of fire escapes. They dramatically conveyed something that had happened, and that is the business we're in. They were news....

"Was publication of that [third] picture a bow to the same taste for the morbidly sensational that makes gold mines of disaster movies? Most papers will not print the picture of a dead body except in the most unusual circumstances. Does the fact that the final picture was taken a millisecond before the young woman died make a difference? Most papers will not print a picture of a bare female breast. Is that a more inappropriate subject for display than the picture of a human being's last agonized instant of life?" Seib offered no answers to the questions he raised, but he went on to say that although as an editor he would probably have run the pictures, as a reader he was revolted by them.

In conclusion, Seib wrote: "Any editor who decided to print those pictures without giving at least a moment's thought to what purpose they served and what their effect was likely to be on the reader should ask another question: Have I become so preoccupied with manufacturing a product according to professional traditions and standards that I have forgotten about the consumer, the reader?"

It should be clear that the phone calls and letters and Seib's own reaction were occasioned by one factor alone: the death of the woman. Obviously, had she survived the fall, no one would have protested; the pictures would have had a completely different impact. Equally obviously, had the child died as well—or instead—Seib would undoubtedly have received ten times the phone calls he did. In each case, the pictures would have been exactly the same—only the captions, and thus the responses, would have been different.

But the questions Seib raises are worth discussing—though not exactly for the reasons he mentions. For it may be that the real lesson of the Boston photographs is not the danger that editors will be forgetful of reader reaction, but that they will continue to censor pictures of death precisely because of that reaction. The protests Seib fielded were really a variation on an old theme—and we saw plenty of it during the Nixon-Agnew years—the "Why doesn't the press print the good news?" argument. In this case, of course, the objections were all dressed up and cleverly disguised as righteous indignation about the privacy of death. This is a form of puritanism that is often justifiable; just as often it is merely puritanical.

Seib takes it for granted that the widespread though fairly recent newspaper policy against printing pictures of dead bodies is a sound one; I don't know that it makes any sense at all. I recognize that printing pictures of corpses raises all sorts of problems about taste and titillation and sensationalism; the fact is, however, that people die. Death happens to be one of life's main events. And it is irresponsible—and more than that, inaccurate—for newspapers to fail to show it, or to show it only when an astonishing set of photos comes in over the Associated Press wire. Most papers covering fatal automobile accidents will print pictures of mangled cars. But the significance of fatal automobile accidents is not that a great deal of steel is twisted but that people die. Why not show it? That's what accidents are about. Throughout the Vietnam war, editors were reluctant to print atrocity pictures. Why *not* print them? That's what that war was about. Murder victims are almost never photographed; they are granted their privacy. But their relatives are relentlessly pictured on their way in and out of hospitals and morgues and funerals.

I'm not advocating that newspapers print these things in order to teach their readers a lesson. The *Post* editors justified their printing of the Boston pictures with several arguments in that direction; every one of them is irrelevant. The pictures don't show anything about slum life; the incident could have happened anywhere, and it did. It is extremely unlikely that anyone who saw them rushed out and had his fire escape strengthened. And the pictures were not news—at least they were not national news. It is not news in Washington, or New York, or Los Angeles that a woman was killed in a Boston fire. The only newsworthy thing about the pictures is that they were taken. They deserve to be printed because they are great pictures, breathtaking pictures of something that happened. That they disturb readers is exactly as it should be: that's why photojournalism is often more powerful than written journalism.

Bronston Jones, *Missing,* 2001. The ethical issues regarding photojournalism have most ▶ recently been explored as people debated what kinds of images were appropriate to show from the destruction of the World Trade Center on September 11, 2001. The photographs taken here, published as part of the September 11 Photo Project, represent a different way to document lives lost other than showing people jumping from the burning towers. Bronston Jones's photographs, taken in the days after the tragedy, are part of the traveling exhibit *Missing: Last Seen at the World Trade Center on September 11, 2001.* The image on page 207 is a contact sheet of 36 missing-person fliers; it would take 160 of these sheets to show the faces of all the missing and deceased. The *Missing* exhibit refocuses emphasis on the lives of those who were lost rather than on the destruction of the towers. As Jones puts it, "the people are real, the buildings are just real estate." (Copyright © 2001 Bronston Jones. All rights reserved)

MESSAGE

Nora Ephron devotes a good portion of her essay to examining the reasons various newspaper editors gave for publishing or not publishing Stanley Forman's photos. What is the central issue here? In your opinion, are the photos newsworthy or not? Certain editors claimed that publication of the photos was justified because they conveyed an important message; what is that message? Does Ephron accept that message? Do you think the photographer intended to convey that message? Many readers who saw the photos on front pages across the nation considered them voyeuristic. Would the photos have had the same impact if a caption had informed us that the woman survived the fall?

METHOD

In many Weegee photographs, we see not only a subject or event but also an audience (sometimes an individual onlooker, often a crowd) that's witnessing it. In which of the four photographs does an audience play a significant role? Why do you think Weegee wants to build an audience into the picture? What effect do onlookers have on the emotional impact of the photographs? How does photographer Bronston Jones create emotional impact?

MEDIUM

In her essay, Ephron praises Forman's photographs by calling them "perfect examples of photojournalism at its most spectacular. They're throwbacks, really, fire pictures, 1930s tabloid shots." Ephron is clearly placing Forman's work in the context of such tabloid photographers as Weegee. In an essay, compare Weegee's *Car Crash Upper Fifth Ave.* with Forman's photographs. What elements do they share? In what ways are they different? Do you agree with Ephron that these are the same type of photographs? In an essay, try to describe the major characteristics of classic tabloid photography.

VIDEOCAM

The most famous home movie ever taken in the United States is the one that shows President John F. Kennedy being shot while riding in an open limousine in Dallas, Texas, on the afternoon of November 22, 1963. It was taken by an onlooker of Kennedy's motorcade, Abraham Zapruder, and though it lasts a mere 30 seconds, it clearly establishes the final and fatal — and still horrible to watch — shot to the young president's head. The amateur film has been the subject of much heated controversy as commentators in their frame-by-frame analyses have found visual support for various conspiracy narratives. Zapruder's home movie, for example, plays a large role in Oliver Stone's controversial film on the assassination, *JFK*. In addition, the video raised the public's consciousness of the intrinsic value of home movies. Could amateurs at times provide us with news and information that on-the-scene television coverage or criminal investigation totally misses? This issue again reached dramatic proportions in 1991 when a Los Angeles resident happened to catch on camera the beating of Rodney King; that videotape became the subject of a hotly disputed frame-by-frame analysis in the subsequent trial of the police officers responsible for the beating.

Around the time of Kennedy's assassination, improvements in hand-held video cameras led to their popularity as a new medium for contemporary artists, who began exploring ways to construct new kinds of visual imagery, much of it based on repetitive patterns that challenged conventions of linear narrative. In the story "Videotape," Don DeLillo creates a strange and disturbing incident involving a twelve-year-old girl who accidentally records a murder as she aims "her camera through the rear window of the family car at the windshield of the car behind her" and produces a tape "realer than real." DeLillo is, of course, punning on the words "reel" and "real" — a verbal pun that reinforces the connection between film and reality. The short story also makes us sensitive to another pun: while a man is being literally shot to death, someone else is also "shooting" the incident with a camera. The photographer Jeff Wall also appears to be guided by this commonly used pun. In *Man with a Rifle* the photographer "shoots" a picture of a man who appears to be aiming an imaginary rifle at an unknown target across a city street.

Don DeLillo, *Videotape*. Widely regarded as one of America's preeminent novelists, Don DeLillo (b. 1936) has long been fascinated by photography and the video arts. The protagonist of his first novel, *Americana* (1971), is a TV executive obsessed with his 16mm movie camera. In *Libra* (1988), DeLillo wrote a fictional account of the Kennedy assassination. From the start of his career, he has examined in fiction the way media shape and alter our sense of reality, become a substitute for it, or even become more real than what we regard as real. DeLillo published "Videotape" in the final 1994 issue of *Antaeus*, a literary journal.

Don DeLillo

VIDEOTAPE

It shows a man driving a car. It is the simplest sort of family video. You see a man at the wheel of a medium Dodge.

It is just a kid aiming her camera through the rear window of the family car at the windshield of the car behind her.

You know about families and their video cameras. You know how kids get involved, how the camera shows them that every subject is potentially charged, a million things they never see with the unaided eye. They investigate the meaning of inert objects and dumb pets and they poke at family privacy. They learn to see things twice.

It is the kid's own privacy that is being protected here. She is twelve years old and her name is being withheld even though she is neither the victim nor the perpetrator of the crime but only the means of recording it.

It shows a man in a sport shirt at the wheel of his car. There is nothing else to see. The car approaches briefly, then falls back.

You know how children with cameras learn to work the exposed moments that define the family cluster. They break every trust, spy out the undefended space, catching Mom coming out of the bathroom in her cumbrous robe and turbaned towel, looking bloodless and plucked. It is not a joke. They will shoot you sitting on the pot if they can manage a suitable vantage.

The tape has the jostled sort of noneventness that marks the family product. Of course the man in this case is not a member of the family but a stranger in a car, a random figure, someone who has happened along in the slow lane.

It shows a man in his forties wearing a pale shirt open at the throat, the image washed by reflections and sunglint, with many jostled moments.

It is not just another video homicide. It is a homicide recorded by a child who thought she was doing something simple and maybe halfway clever, shooting some tape of a man in a car.

He sees the girl and waves briefly, wagging a hand without taking it off the wheel—an underplayed reaction that makes you like him.

It is unrelenting footage that rolls on and on. It has an aimless determination, a persistence that lives outside the subject matter. You are looking into the mind of home video. It is innocent, it is aimless, it is determined, it is real.

He is bald up the middle of his head, a nice guy in his forties whose whole life seems open to the hand-held camera.

But there is also an element of suspense. You keep on looking not because you know something is going to happen—of course you do know something is going to happen and you do look for that reason but you might also keep on looking if you came across this footage for the first time without knowing the outcome. There is a crude power operating here. You keep on looking because things combine to hold you fast—a sense of the random, the amateurish, the accidental, the impending. You don't think of the tape as boring or interesting. It is crude, it is blunt, it is relentless. It is the jostled part of your mind, the film that runs through your hotel brain under all the thoughts you know you're thinking.

The world is lurking in the camera, already framed, waiting for the boy or girl who will come along and take up the device, learn the instrument, shooting old Granddad at breakfast, all stroked out so his nostrils gape, the cereal spoon baby-gripped in his pale fist.

It shows a man alone in a medium Dodge. It seems to go on forever.

There's something about the nature of the tape, the grain of the image, the sputtering black-and-white tones, the starkness—you think this is more real, truer-to-life than anything around you. The things around you have a rehearsed and layered and cosmetic look. The tape is superreal, or maybe underreal is the way you want to put it. It is what lies at the scraped bottom of all the layers you have added. And this is another reason why you keep on looking. The tape has a searing realness.

It shows him giving an abbreviated wave, stiff-palmed, like a signal flag at a siding.

You know how families make up games. This is just another game in which the child invents the rules as she goes along. She likes the idea of videotaping a man in his car. She has probably never done it before and she sees no reason to vary the format or terminate early or pan to another car. This is her game and she is learning it and playing it at the same time. She feels halfway clever and

211

■ *What do you think DeLillo means by "superreal" and "underreal"? Which word do you think more accurately describes home movies, and why?*

Artisan Entertainment,
The Blair Witch Project,
1999. (Photofest)

inventive and maybe slightly intrusive as well, a little bit of brazenness that spices any game.

And you keep on looking. You look because this is the nature of the footage, to make a channeled path through time, to give things a shape and a destiny.

Of course if she had panned to another car, the right car at the precise time, she would have caught the gunman as he fired.

The chance quality of the encounter. The victim, the killer, and the child with a camera. Random energies that approach a common point. There's something here that speaks to you directly, saying terrible things about forces beyond your control, lines of intersection that cut through history and logic and every reasonable layer of human expectation.

She wandered into it. The girl got lost and wandered clear-eyed into horror. This is a children's story about straying too far from home. But it isn't the family car that serves as the instrument of the child's curiosity, her inclination to explore. It is the camera that puts her in the tale.

You know about holidays and family celebrations and how somebody shows up with a camcorder and the relatives stand around and barely react because they're numbingly accustomed to the process of being taped and decked and shown on the VCR with the coffee and cake.

He is hit soon after. If you've seen the tape many times you know from the handwave exactly when he will be hit. It is something, naturally, that you wait for. You say to your wife, if you're at home and she is there, Now here is where he gets it. You say; Janet, hurry up, this is where it happens.

Now here is where he gets it. You see him jolted, sort of wire-shocked—then he seizes up and falls toward the door or maybe leans or slides into the door is the proper way to put it. It is awful and unremarkable at the same time. The car stays in the slow lane. It approaches briefly, then falls back.

You don't usually call your wife over to the TV set. She has her programs, you have yours. But there's a certain urgency here. You want her to see how it looks. The tape has been running forever and now the thing is finally going to happen and you want her to be here when he's shot.

Here it comes, all right. He is shot, head-shot, and the camera reacts, the child reacts—there is a jolting movement but she keeps on taping, there is a sympathetic response, a nerve response, her heart is beating faster but she keeps the camera trained on the subject as he slides into the door and even as you see him die you're thinking of the girl. At some level the girl has to be present here, watching what you're watching, unprepared—the girl is seeing this cold and you have to marvel at the fact that she keeps the tape rolling.

It shows something awful and unaccompanied. You want your wife to see it because it is real this time, not fancy movie violence—the realness beneath the layers of cosmetic perception. Hurry up, Janet, here it comes. He dies so fast. There is no accompaniment of any kind. It is very stripped. You want to tell her it is realer than real but then she will ask what that means.

Miramax Films, *Sex, Lies, and Videotape*, 1989. (Photofest)

The way the camera reacts to the gunshot—a startle reaction that brings pity and terror into the frame, the girl's own shock, the girl's identification with the victim.

You don't see the blood, which is probably trickling behind his ear and down the back of his neck. The way his head is twisted away from the door, the twist of the head gives you only a partial profile and it's the wrong side, it's not the side where he was hit.

And maybe you're being a little aggressive here, practically forcing your wife to watch. Why? What are you telling her? Are you making a little statement? Like I'm going to ruin your day out of ordinary spite. Or a big statement? Like this is the risk of existing. Either way you're rubbing her face in this tape and you don't know why.

It shows the car drifting toward the guardrail and then there's a jostling sense of two other lanes and part of another car, a split-second blur, and the tape ends here, either because the girl stopped shooting or because some central authority, the police or the district attorney or the TV station, decided there was nothing else you had to see.

This is either the tenth or eleventh homicide committed by the Texas Highway Killer. The number is uncertain because the police believe that one of the shootings may have been a copycat crime.

And there is something about videotape, isn't there, and this particular kind of serial crime? This is a crime designed for random taping and immediate playing. You sit there and wonder if this kind of crime became more possible when the means of taping and playing an event—playing it immediately after the taping—became part of the culture. The principal doesn't necessarily commit the sequence of crimes in order to see them taped and played. He commits the crimes as if they

213

were a form of taped-and-played event. The crimes are inseparable from the idea of taping and playing. You sit there thinking that this is a crime that has found its medium, or vice versa — cheap mass production, the sequence of repeated images and victims, stark and glary and more or less unremarkable.

It shows very little in the end. It is a famous murder because it is on tape and because the murderer has done it many times and because the crime was recorded by a child. So the child is involved, the Video Kid as she is sometimes called because they have to call her something. The tape is famous and so is she. She is famous in the modern manner of people whose names are strategically withheld. They are famous without names or faces, spirits living apart from their bodies, the victims and witnesses, the underage criminals, out there somewhere at the edges of perception.

Seeing someone at the moment he dies, dying unexpectedly. This is reason alone to stay fixed to the screen. It is instructional, watching a man shot dead as he drives along on a sunny day. It demonstrates an elemental truth, that every breath you take has two possible endings. And that's another thing. There's a joke locked away here, a note of cruel slapstick that you are completely willing to appreciate. Maybe the victim's a chump, a dope, classically unlucky. He had it coming, in a way, like an innocent fool in a silent movie.

You don't want Janet to give you any crap about it's on all the time, they show it a thousand times a day. They show it because it exists, because they have to show it, because this is why they're out there. The horror freezes your soul but this doesn't mean that you want them to stop.

214

Don DeLillo
ALTERNATE ENDING

■ Alternate ending to "Video-tape." DeLillo embedded "Videotape" (with some alterations) into his award-winning novel Underworld (1997). Here you see the revised ending of the story, with highlighting showing you the parts that he added or changed. How does the revised ending change the impact of this story?

There's a joke locked away here, a note of cruel slapstick that you are willing to appreciate even if it makes you feel a little guilty. Maybe the victim's a chump, a sort of silent-movie dupe, classically unlucky. He had it coming in a sense, for letting himself be caught on camera. Because once the tape starts rolling it can only end one way. This is what the context requires.

You don't want Janet to give you any crap about it's on all the time, they show it a thousand times a day. They show it because it exists, because they have to show it, because this is why they're out there, to provide our entertainment.

The more you watch the tape, the deader and colder and more relentless it becomes. The tape sucks the air right out of your chest but you watch it every time.

Dreamworks Films, *American Beauty*, 1999. (Photofest)

Film stills. Videotapes are now a common appearance in major art museums and a staple of multimedia art. They are also a leading feature in some recent movies, such as *Sex, Lies, and Videotape; The Blair Witch Project;* and *American Beauty*—which all introduce a character who is filming within the film. What is the impact of showing a movie within a movie, either in these films or in another that you've seen? What role have video cameras played in recording your own stories?

216

Jeff Wall, *Man with a Rifle,* **2000.** Jeff Wall was born in Vancouver, British Columbia, in 1946 and studied both fine arts and art history in Vancouver and London. His large-scale photographs have been exhibited in major museums throughout the world. The recipient of numerous awards, he was ranked by the magazine *ArtNews* as one of the world's "Ten Best Living Artists." To accompany a 1997 exhibit in Los Angeles, the museum catalogue described Wall's contribution to art as follows: "Wall creates his works using actors and actresses on location, as in a movie production, and uses a computer to construct elaborate scenes. Just as painters of past ages composed and depicted historic scenes, landscapes, and fashions, Wall portrays our present age fully applying his knowledge of art history and photography." Since his early work, the account goes on, "Wall has continued to picture his hometown, Vancouver, urban life, his stressed-out contemporaries' psychological conflict, and other objects mirroring the society in which we live. His international reputation is that of a storyteller for our age." (Copyright © 2002 Jeff Wall)

COMMENT

"The individual identified by the title of [this] picture acts as if he is aiming and possibly firing a rifle. However, contrary to the title's suggestion, there is no rifle in his hands; he is merely pretending; his hands are empty. Or, to put it differently, he does carry a rifle but it is an invisible one. What else is invisible in this picture? The empty space in the middle ground, framed by a line-up of parked cars, does not give any clue as to what 'the man with a rifle' would be pointing his weapon at. The picture shows an everyday urban street scene, lit by harsh mid-afternoon sunlight, with a few people passing by who do not seem to notice what is going on. The man's aberrant behavior appears to lack external motivation. The camera is aiming in almost the same direction as the rifle, from a position somewhat to the side so that both the gunman and his invisible or imagined target come into view. The convergence of these two 'lines of fire' occurs at some point in the empty middle ground. In fact, *Man with a Rifle* could be read as suggesting that the invisible rifle in the picture acts as some kind of stand-in for the invisible camera — the camera that was 'left out of the picture.'"

—Camiel Van Winkle, art critic, from his foreword to *Jeff Wall: Photographs* (2002)

MESSAGE

What would you say is the message of Don DeLillo's "Videotape"? Can you identify a sentence or short passage from the story that conveys its message? In what ways does the story link message and medium? What similarities can you see between the message of "Videotape" and that of *Man with a Rifle*? Do the similarities extend beyond the subject of each work?

METHOD

Some sources have incorrectly labeled DeLillo's short story as an essay. Can you understand the reason for this mistake? If you were not informed beforehand that it was fiction, would you consider it an essay? Would you accept the Texas Highway Killer as an actual serial murderer? Why or why not? Is there anything about DeLillo's method of composition that would lead you to think his account is fictional? Apply the same questions to Jeff Wall's *Man with a Rifle*. What elements of composition in the photograph would lead you to think the photographer captured a spontaneous moment on a city street? What elements would lead you to think the photographer staged the entire scene?

MEDIUM

Jeff Wall has often been referred to as a "storyteller." Although this label may seem appropriate to the novelist Don DeLillo, do you find it an odd term to use to describe a photographer? In what ways can a photographer tell a story, considering that an individual photograph is extremely limited in its ability to depict narrative process, sequential movement, and the passage of time? In a short essay, consider carefully Wall's photograph and explain how someone could find within it an unfolding story or narrative.

Assignment 1

This chapter focuses on telling stories by offering us some very diverse examples of how present-day stories are told. A number focus on the visual aspects of stories and on how we construct stories from what we observe in the world. Webcams and Diller + Scofidio's *Refresh* project are perfect examples of how we are drawn to create meaning out of seemingly mundane experiences. Capitalizing upon our voyeuristic tendencies are the recent trends in reality TV as well. However, just when we think this is a new phenomenon, we are confronted with Weegee's tabloid photographs, which serve as evidence that what we see on TV today is a somewhat natural evolution of what fascinated us yesterday.

STREET SCENE

ZOOM IN

You may want to investigate our cultural fascination with viewing everyday events by attempting to create your own reality series or pseudo-reality film (think *Blair Witch Project*). Working in creative teams, brainstorm concept ideas and then move to carefully storyboarding the project. Before beginning, you should research storyboarding practices using some of the sites you can link to from the *Convergences* web site. Once the project is storyboarded, your team can move on to production if videocamera equipment is available. If it is not accessible, you should consider how you would stage your project and what sort of casting decisions you would make to complete it. Finally, your team should present the storyboarded ideas to the rest of the class to gather audience feedback before moving on with it. If you are fully producing your project on film (or in digital media), you may want to have another audience screening prior to the final viewing to gauge audience feedback. This experience will help you understand what it is really like to create a film/television show that appeals to audiences today.

Go to bedfordstmartins.com/convergences
for links to storyboarding sites.

Assignment 2

As this chapter shows us, all stories have visual elements, whether they are explicitly focused on (as in Danny Lyon's montages) or implicitly suggested (as in David Sedaris's essay). You may have had the experience of reading a book only to see a movie or television adaptation that failed to live up to the visual images you had created about the story as you read. There can also be a letdown when you read a particular piece by an author and get a visual image of what that author looks like — only to be surprised when you see a real picture of him or her. On the other hand, some people will choose to read a book or see a film simply based on the look of the book jacket or the movie poster. You should consider the film posters included in this chapter and evaluate whether they effectively capture the essence of the films they advertise. Then, working with either a favorite book or a favorite film, redesign the book jacket or film poster to create an image that will provocatively introduce audiences to the essence of the film without giving too much of the plot away. As you will discover, it is a difficult balance that artists must achieve in creating this sort of media; and you might want to document any struggles to share with the class.

If you've ever been disappointed by your favorite book's film or TV adaptation, try storyboarding how you might differently adapt the book to film or television. Carefully consider casting as part of this project, then present the final project to the rest of the class.

Lord of the Rings: The Two Towers, **book cover and DVD case.** These two packagings of the same story dramatically illustrate the choices people make in how to *represent* a story being told (a visual reminder of the cliché that there's more to a book than its cover). (*Book:* Cover of *The Two Towers* by J.R.R. Tolkien [Boston: Houghton Mifflin, 1988]. Reprinted by permission of Houghton Mifflin Company. All rights reserved. *DVD:* © New Line Productions, Inc.)

1. Compare and contrast Weegee's *Car Crash Upper Fifth Ave. July 13, 1941* (p. 199) with both (or either) Mary Ellen Mark's *The Damm Family in Their Car* (p. 458) and Jesse DeMartino's *Jason and Mike at the Cabin Near Huntsville, Texas, 1996* (p. 277). How does the car in each photo serve as an artistic "vehicle" for the photographer? How has each photographer used a car for compositional and framing purposes? In what ways in each photograph does the car contribute to a sense of intimacy? A sense of trouble? Which photo do you think has the most artistic purpose behind it — that is, which photographer wants you to pay more attention to the craft of photography than to his or her subject? In an essay that addresses some of these questions, make a case for the photograph you find most moving.

2. Review Danny Lyon's photographic exploration into his family history (pp. 150–153) in connection with Judith Ortiz Cofer's (p. 44) and Nicole Lamy's (p. 230). How does each individual rely on visual material? After reflecting on all three methods, write an essay in which you describe how you would go about incorporating visual material into your family history. What would your project be like?

What material would you use, and how would it enhance your history? Would you combine text and image, use only text, or use only images?

3. Compare David Sedaris's "Ashes" (p. 139) with Dorothy Allison's "What Did You Expect? (p. 71). What similarities can you find between the two selections? How does each writer connect family matters to storytelling? How does class consciousness enter each essay? In an essay, compare and contrast the ways each writer expresses a personal identity rooted in social and cultural values.

4. Louise Erdrich wrote her personal essay on the film *Z* in response to a book assignment that asked various well-known authors to identify and discuss the movie that changed their lives. But one could easily change the medium. Using Erdrich's essay as a model, in a short personal essay of your own describe a CD or single song, a picture, a story, a poem, a TV show — or perhaps even a letter or greeting card — that changed your life.

5. In small groups identify the differences that occur when you narrate events in a story or essay as opposed to those in a cartoon or comic strip. In

TELLING STORIES

doing so, pay special attention to David Sedaris's "Ashes" (p. 139) and Garry Trudeau's Doonesbury selections (p. 156). Then, each group should attempt to retell Sedaris's personal tale in a comic strip. Your drawn version does not need to look professional (though each group may have members who can draw better than others), but you should rough out the story and characters into frames. Obviously, you will need to compress Sedaris's essay. Try restricting the cartoon to fifteen or twenty frames. Afterward, the groups should compare their productions. How many different ways did the Sedaris story get told? How did each group differ in the events and characters it included and excluded?

6. After re-reading Nora Ephron's "The Boston Photographs," imagine that you are the chief editor of a newspaper and that you have been submitted the photographs in question. Would you or would you not decide to print them? Your staff is divided. You must make the decision. Write a two-paragraph memo to your staff that explains the reasons behind what you ultimately decide to do. Be sure to anticipate the criticism you will receive no matter how you decide.

7. As a research project, break into small groups and learn what you can about what is known as "electronic literature." Each group should try to define the concept, determine how electronic literature differs from other literature, and note several examples. What are the leading features of electronic literature? What could a writer do in this medium that he or she could not do otherwise? Each group should present its findings on the topic to the class, and then in conference format address the issue of how electronic literature will affect traditional methods of storytelling. Groups may also want to address the effects they believe such literature will have on the future of classroom reading and writing.

8. As a research project, several groups of students should rent the film *Z* and watch it in conjunction with reading Louise Erdrich's essay. Each group should also collect some reviews and criticism of the film. After viewing, reading, and discussion, members of each group should collaborate on a short paper that presents the significance of *Z* and looks at it in the context of current films. After full consideration, is it one of the great political thrillers? Does it still have a message for our time?

221

WRITING, RESEARCHING, COLLABORATING

9. Don DeLillo's best selling novel, *Underworld,* which includes the short story "Videotape," has not yet been turned into a Hollywood film. After forming small groups and reading together "Visually Speaking: Sequence," discuss how — if you were working on a movie version of *Underworld* — you would shoot the "Videotape" episode. (In the novel, incidentally, there are repeated references to the Texas Highway Killer). Each group should draft a scenario or sequential outline of how the incident would appear on film and then all groups should share their versions.

10. As mentioned earlier in this chapter, an interesting rule of art, especially contemporary art, is that every new piece of electronic technology will in short time be put to artistic purposes. This process has been going on for some time, from 1960s artists who fashioned sculpture out of television sets to a recent composer who programmed hundreds of cell phones to orchestrate a symphony. Also recently, a French writer composed an entire novel using the slang, abbreviations, symbols, and made-up-words that young people worldwide have adopted for cell phone text-messaging. After breaking into small groups, consider the rapid development as well as convergence of electronic equipment and gadgets — all those new "hot items" at the consumer electronics shows. Select any recent example of one of these "toys" or "tools" and collaboratively draft up some ways you think an artist might re-invent it for aesthetic purposes.

3

SHAPING SPACES

What do a billboard, a web site, an automobile, a basketball court, an airport, and a food court have in common? They are all, in one sense or another, spaces — sites we can visit, inhabit, imagine, reconstruct, escape to, disappear in, fill up. Spaces can be as vast and open as a desert or as small and compact as a wren's nest, as simple as a blank sheet of paper or as complex as a Gothic cathedral. The word "space," of course, means different things to different people. To an astronaut, it can mean everything outside the earth's atmosphere; to a book designer, it may mean the absence of typographical clutter; to a magazine publisher, it represents what can profitably be sold to advertisers.

As cognitive scientists know, the concept of space is fundamental to human thought; the brain is wired for apprehending spatial forms and relations. These relationships, in fact, can be so powerful that people many years later will have forgotten everything about what went on in, say, sixth grade except where they sat. For some reason, spatial orientation exerts an enormous influence on memory. In "Life in Motion" (p. 230), Nicole Lamy alludes to Cicero, a rhetorician in ancient Rome who advised student orators to think of a sequence of places or rooms to help them memorize their speeches. Those of us who remember the assassinations of John F. Kennedy and Martin Luther King Jr. (or perhaps more recently the World Trade Center and Pentagon attacks) can usually recall exactly where we were at the moment we heard the news.

By the time we reach adolescence, we all possess a fairly well developed sense of physical space. We could not function or even survive without it — how could we possibly drive a car or even walk into a classroom? But the larger meanings of space — the ways we conceive of it — are easily overlooked, perhaps because we tend to focus on objects themselves and not on the spaces they inhabit, create, and often transform. For example, how many of us consider the interior of our cars a "sacred space,"

as the poet Stephen Dunn suggests in his poem "The Sacred" (p. 278)? Or, while shopping, how many of us pay close attention to the ways a mall is designed to encourage wandering and discourage a clear sense of destination? In developing spatial literacy, we need to retrain ourselves to observe not only objects but also the way they affect our sense of space or spatial location. Many modern artists now produce museum installations in order to educate the public's perceptual ability to see space not as something that's missing but as something that's always present in one form or another. Furthermore, whereas the average Internet user merely notices a colorful web site, a visually astute designer sees an entirely new medium that's helping to dissolve the boundaries between private and public space.

Because we grow so habituated to spatial forms and perspectives, artists of all kinds — in painting, video, film, architecture, and so on — will deliberately try to challenge the customary ways we view the world around us. When an artist disrupts our conventional spatial orientation — for example, by complicating our mental categories of top/bottom, inside/outside, front/back, or surface/depth — the effect can be one of confusion and disorientation. Writers and artists like to call this effect "defamiliarization," to emphasize the way they have altered our perception of ordinary objects. Even when a work appears to be as realistic as a straight-on photograph, we will probably find on closer inspection some elements of distortion, some degree of artistic contrivance that enables us to observe a scene or object in ways we probably wouldn't notice in actual life.

Look closely, for example, at Mitch Epstein's remarkable photograph *Cocoa Beach, Florida, 1983* (p. 279), and see how many lines of sight you can trace as your eye follows various angles and perspectives. As Epstein photographs it, the scene seems both familiar and unfamiliar. As part of the

defamiliarization process, art also gives us extra eyes, so to speak, shifting us away from the normal frontal perspective that provides nearly all of our visual information. As Richard Estes, another contemporary artist who uses photographic techniques in his paintings, has said, "When you look at a scene or an object, you tend to scan it. Your eye travels around and over things. As your eyes move, the vanishing point moves; to have one vanishing point or perfect camera perspective is not realistic." Estes's comment helps us understand the counter-realism behind Epstein's colorfully realistic *Cocoa Beach* photograph. In its use of intersecting lines with different vanishing points and multiple surfaces crowded together, Epstein's photo—though of a real time and specific space—looks like nothing we've ever noticed before.

As the selections in this chapter (and others throughout the book) will show, reconceiving space is often a matter of dissolving or redrawing boundaries, multiplying or altering perspectives, rearranging or rotating coordinates. It's a matter of seeing and thinking outside the box, learning to perceive outside of our overly rationalistic visual habits. Just as poets and novelists do their thinking through imagery and metaphor, so do architects, sculptors, painters, photographers, film directors, and video artists think spatially as they work out creative problems by means of spatial formulations.

We confront spatial forms not only literally, as physical presences, but figuratively as well. When we read a novel, for example, we envision in a sort of nonphysical space the places and characters evoked by the novelist's language. Because so many writers emphasize narration and storytelling,

// vijay iyer & mike ladd : in what language?

HOW AN AUTOMAT WORKS

FIRST DROP YOUR NICKELS IN THE SLOT

THEN TURN THE KNOB THE GLASS DOOR CLICKS OPEN

LIFT THE DOOR AND HELP YOURSELF

HORN & HARDART

Interior of One of the Fifty Automat-Cafeterias
in Philadelphia and New York

we may overlook the fact that fiction also depends on nonlinear but linked visual elements that contribute significantly to the texture and meaning. Our subjective experience of reading is intensified as we translate the author's words into mental pictures of characters and scenes—visual details and features we will probably recall long after we've forgotten the story's bare chain of events.

The internalized space that we mentally construct when we read is not a real, physical space but rather is akin to the virtual space popularly known as "cyberspace," a term coined by a science fiction writer, William Gibson, in a 1981 short story. Gibson later expanded the concept in his award-winning novel, *Neuromancer* (1984). Unlike the literal space that surrounds and situates us in the three-dimensional world, cyberspace is the abstract realm of electronic data and interactivity, where both vast distances and social boundaries can be instantly annihilated. Cyberspace is a rapidly expanding universe created by the convergence of computers, videos, and telecommunications networking technologies. Entered through our computer screens, cyberspace is the latest conceptualization of space, and its fusion of interdependent media continually and permanently reformats our modes of perception and communication as well as our ideas about what constitutes public space. As the final section of this chapter (Cyberspace) makes clear, a controversial issue today is whether cyberspace is (or soon will be) just as real as any concrete, physical space.

Contrast

How are the pages in a book like a dorm room? They both represent space, something you can fill, visit, imagine. Thinking about space, or place, means visualizing where something is and what its physical dimensions are — whether it's a piece of paper, a computer screen, a room, a building, even the entire earth. The clusters in this chapter all invite you to bring your existing concepts of spatial forms and

relations to bear on the materials

(© Brand X Pictures-Burke/Triolo Productions)

(© Digital Vision)

you are reading about — be it a basket-ball court, someone's home, or a sacred place. Using contrast — exploring how elements are like or not like each other — will invariably be part of the process you go through in considering how spaces are shaped.

 Go to **ix visual exercises** to explore how the concepts of element and contrast work in visual texts.

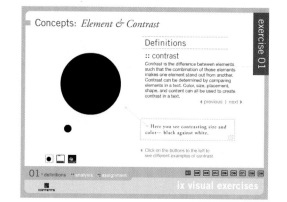

Concepts: *Element & Contrast*

exercise 01

Definitions

:: contrast

Contrast is the difference between elements such that the combination of those elements makes one element stand out from another. Contrast can be determined by comparing elements in a text. Color, size, placement, shape, and content can all be used to create contrast in a text.

◄ previous | next ►

▸ Here you see contrasting size and color— black against white.

◄ Click on the buttons to the left to see different examples of contrast

01 · definitions ·· analysis ·· assignment

ix visual exercises

228

HOME

In *The Poetics of Space* (1958) the French philosopher Gaston Bachelard discusses how vividly our childhood memories are shaped by the houses we lived in. "All our lives we come back to them in daydreams," he claims. The images and essay in this section capture just how powerful the places we live can be — and how much emotion we invest in them.

In "Life in Motion" (2000), Nicole Lamy devises an interesting and imaginative autobiographical plan: she decides to revisit and photograph all the houses she lived in during her childhood. As she assembles this objective visual narrative, she subjectively reconstructs the scattered memories of a highly mobile childhood — she lived in twelve houses before she turned thirteen. "I wanted to gather the photos as charms against fallible memory," she writes, hoping that after binding them in an album she and her mother "could read our lives like straightforward narratives." The photographs by Bill Bamberger that follow, documenting the experiences of first-time, low-income homeowners in the South, are narratives of a new sense of permanence rather than impermanence — but all focus on the four walls, roof, and front door of places people call home.

229

Nicole Lamy, *Life in Motion.* Nicole Lamy (b. 1967) has worked as managing editor of the *Boston Book Review*, freelances as a book reviewer, and is currently living in Cambridge, Massachusetts, and working on a novel. When Lamy's essay was published in *The American Scholar* (Autumn 2000), it appeared with no photographs. She generously supplied us with the photos for this book.

■ *Lamy's essay is divided into 12 numbered sections, corresponding to the 12 photographs. When the essay originally appeared, it contained no photos. In what ways do the pictures add to the essay? Do they depend on the essay as much as the essay depends on them? Explain.*

Nicole Lamy
LIFE IN MOTION

1

Three years ago I took pictures of all the houses I've lived in. The houses impress not in beauty but in number—twelve houses before I turned thirteen. For me the moves had always resisted coherent explanation—no military reassignments or evasion of the law. I wanted to gather the photos as charms against fallible memory, like the list of lost things I used to keep: a plastic purse filled with silver dollars, a mole-colored beret, a strip of negatives from my brother's first day of kindergarten. I planned to bind the photos in an album and give them to my mother. Maybe then, I thought, we could read our lives like straightforward narratives. Wise readers know that all stories follow one of two paths: The Stranger Comes to Town or The Journey. My life in motion suggested both.

2

When idea turned to plan, I asked my father for a list of the addresses I couldn't remember. Instead, as I had hoped, he offered to drive me through Maine, New Hampshire, and Massachusetts himself. My father, too, took photographs, and I wanted to draw him into my life a little, remind him of the times during car trips when, as dusk deepened, he would switch on the light inside the car, without prompting, so that I could continue to read.

3

I photographed the houses and the apartments and the surprising number of duplexes (so often did we live in the left half of a house that I wonder if I've developed a right-hemisphere problem—I imagine the right side of my brain paler

230

and more shriveled than its better half, as atrophied and bleached as an arm that has been in a cast all summer), though I never asked to be let inside. I remembered the flow of rooms in most houses and I could imagine walking through them in a sort of Ciceronian[1] memory system for childhood.

4

The photographs pretend no artistic merit. I centered most of the houses in my viewfinder as I stood on opposite sidewalks. Occasionally a branch or a piece of the neighboring house appears at the edge of the frame. Otherwise the book is a collection of residential mug shots. I wasn't accustomed to snapping pictures of whole buildings without people cluttering the frames, and as I focused before each shot I thought of the pictures my father had taken during his early twenties: ducks and snowdrifts and weathered cottages. Looking through my father's pictures, my mother would squint with mock earnestness at yet another image of a dilapidated barn and ask, "Where were we, behind the barn?"

5

At the first house—125 Wood Street, a gray three-family at the edge of the campus where my father had been a sophomore—I toyed with perspective. I held my camera at my hip; I crouched by the mailboxes, trying to imagine a toddler's vantage point. No preschool impressions came flooding back; I gained nothing but stares from the neighbors. I thought of the family lore about the short time we lived on Wood Street. By 1972, the sixties still hadn't retreated from Lewiston, Maine. The perennial students who shared our building kept the house reeking pleasantly of weed, and our downstairs neighbor wandered up to our apartment now and again to shower, since her bathtub was occupied by her pet duck. Her thesis, my mother insisted, had something to do with roller skates, and she decorated her apartment with black lights and mini-marshmallows, dipped in fluorescent paint, which she stuck to branches that hung from her ceiling. At night, when the lights came on, visitors were treated to an electrifying set of unlikely constellations.

6

From Maine we moved south to New Hampshire. Rooting out the apartments in the freshly overdeveloped landscape of New Hampshire was a trickier prospect; some of the photos of these houses show unfamiliar additions, self-installed sky-

---

[1] We have all experienced the powerful force that place exerts on our memory. Revisit an old apartment, house, neighborhood, or school and specific memories will flash by in an instant, as one association leads to another. This mental phenomenon is so pervasive that in ancient Rome orators were trained to use spatial locations as an aid to memory. Cicero and others recommended that speakers construct in their imagination a spacious house or building and attach associations to particular locations within it so that as they mentally proceed through them in sequence they will visually remind themselves of the separate points they plan to make.—ED.

231

232

Nicole Lamy, *Life in Motion.* Impossible to reproduce here, Lamy's original consists of photographs mounted with old-fashioned photo corners in a handmade accordian book that, when flipped down, shows the houses in progression from first to last. She highlighted different details of the houses — details that stood out in her memory — with colored pencil. (Reprinted by permission of Nicole Lamy; copyright © 2002 Nicole Lamy)

233

■ Why do you think Lamy only colored parts of the photographs? What effect does it have?

lights. Some had new, paved-over driveways, others aluminum siding. One apartment complex in southern New Hampshire remained intact, though the surrounding woods had been leveled to receive three new strip malls. When we wandered closer to the Massachusetts border, images reversed themselves and I found myself remembering the houses' odd absences: an oval of yellow grass showed where an above-ground pool had sat; a chimney stopped abruptly with no fireplace attached.

During each move, after the boxes had been unpacked, my father would turn their openings to the ground and use a pocketknife to cut windows and doors. The refrigerator boxes were best, skyscrapers with grass floors. In my cardboard house I would read cross-legged into the evening, ignoring my parents' invitations to take-out dinners in our new yard until my father lifted the box off me and walked away, bearing my cardboard home, leaving me blinking in the dusk.

7

Now when I leave my apartment for vacation, no matter how anticipated the trip, I experience numbing panic—will I ever see home again? I'm sympathetic to Rilke's Eurydice: What did she care about Orpheus and his willpower? Sure, she had her reasons: hell living had filled her with death and isolated her from human touch. No doubt she could have grown accustomed to the rocks and rivers of Hades. Who among us can get our mind around a move that drastic? From one side of the eternal duplex to the other. Each time I return home from vacation, rooms don't appear the same as I left them. Walls seem to meet floors at subtly altered angles. Careful inspection—heel-toe, heel-toe around each of the rooms—reveals no evidence of the perceived.

8

After my parents split, I kept most of my assorted five-year-old's treasures at the white three-family where I lived with my mother, watched over by a grim, disapproving landlady. My father's wall-to-wall-carpeted bachelor apartment always smelled faintly of hops; he and his two roommates all owned water beds and motorcycles. My personal inventory at my father's new home was limited to a Holly Hobbie nightgown, *The Little Princess,* and Milton Bradley's Sorry!, a game that requires players to apologize without sincerity after forcing their competitors to start again.

9

I found the postdivorce houses on my own. At one address, the brown-stained house I had known in early grade school wasn't there at all. Developers had knocked it down, then paved over the spot to provide parking for the neighboring convenience store and candy shop. On the winter afternoon when I visited, I snapped a photo of a stray shopping cart that had rolled away from the convenience store to the spot where the kitchen had been. The shot, of the lonely shopping cart illuminated by a hazy beam of light, has a Hallmark devotional-card

234

quality. I have no sentimental feelings about the house, though. I even felt satisfaction when I saw the smoothly paved parking lot; it was as though I had willed the destruction of the site of many childhood disappointments (new stepfather! mid-first-grade school switch! dog runs away from home!).

The edges of the photograph give more away. At the top of the frame I can spot a sliver of the foundation of the house that backed up to ours. My friend Annette lived there, an only child whose mother cut women's hair in the pink room adjacent to their dining room and whose father cured meat, hung in strips—dark and pale, meat and fat—in their cellar.

At the left edge of the frame, the tail of an *a* is visible, part of a glowing sign advertising "Gina—Psychic," the fortune-teller who set up shop next door.

10

In a decorative gesture, I planned to hand-color the photographs as if they were pre-Kodachrome portraits of children with blossom-pink cheeks and lips. Armed with the oils and pencils, however, I only touched up a piece of every home—a chimney, a storm door, a front gate. If stacked, they'd make a flip-book composite of a home.

Red shutters and verdant bushes decorate the house after the last fold in the book. There, the three of us—mother, sister, and new brother, aged three—began living alone together for the first time. The stepfather had come and gone, leaving the three of us to find balance in our uneasy triumvirate. Neighbors and shopkeepers looked at us, curious. I could tell that the age gaps perplexed them—too few years between a mother and daughter who chatted like girlfriends and too many between a sister and brother who looked almost like mother and son. Their confusion was compounded by my mother's youth and beauty and by the way at age thirteen I seemed to have passed directly to thirty-five.

The red-shuttered house was home the longest, and it is the only house my brother remembers. When I handed the coloring pencils over to him to spruce up the image of the old house, he colored the whole thing. He and my mother still live in that duplex, formerly the parish house for the Congregational church across the street. We haven't been the only ones comfortable there. Pets and pests flourish: a dog, rabbits, guinea pigs, escaped reptiles, moths and silverfish, hollow shells of worms in macaroni boxes, squirrels in the attic.

The parish house has walls that slant toward the middle and floor-boards that creak too frequently and too loudly to be creepy. During the first year, while discovering the rules and limits of our new family, we cleared the dining-room table each night after dinner and began to play.

The three of us played games from my mother's childhood—tiddledywinks, pick-up-sticks, PIT. And after my brother fell asleep, my mother and I drank tea and played Password, Boggle, and Scrabble, stopping only when the board was almost filled and our wooden racks held two or three impossible consonants. A few years ago, chasing a marble that had slipped through a wrought iron heating grate, my brother lifted the panel by one of its iron curls and found, caught in the

235

black cloth, game pieces of all kinds: dice, tiddledywinks, cribbage pegs, smooth wooden squares with black letters—pieces we had barely missed from games we had continued to play.

II

When the photo project was complete, I felt a historian's satisfaction. I had gathered the proof of my life and given it a shape. To create the album I cut a long strip of black paper and folded and flipped it as if to cut paper dolls. I printed the images small and pasted them in the accordion book. Held from the top, the book tumbles open to reveal twelve homes logically connected.

My mother saw the book as evidence of a life hastily lived. When she unknotted the ribbon around the tidy package and allowed it to unfold, I watched her face seize up.

"Ha, ha," she pushed the sounds out with effort. "All my failures," she said as she held the book away from her in an exaggerated gesture. I had tried to piece a story out of a life that I saw as largely unplanned. For my mother, this life led by reaction had eventually settled into a kind of choice. I was ashamed I thought it was mine to figure out.

■ *The photo album Lamy at last assembles turns out to have different meanings for mother and daughter. What are those two different meanings? Is one more "real" than the other?*

236

I2

One night, a few weeks before I moved out of the parish-house duplex into my own apartment, I returned home and wheeled my bike around to the back of the house. Glancing up at the brightly lit windows, I was afforded an unusual glimpse of the daily theater of my family. From my spot in the yard I saw a woman in the kitchen chopping vegetables and talking on the phone, while a couple of rooms over, a gangly teenage boy sat in a chair by the television. Startled to be given a chance to see the house as a stranger might, I watched for a few moments and tried to imagine the lives of those inside.

Bill Bamberger, *Nancy* **(left)** *and Alejandra Camarillo, Plaza Florencia, 2002.* **For over ten** ▶ years, homes have provided the focus for the camera lens of Bill Bamberger, an award-winning photographer who has been documenting the experiences of first-time, low-income homeowners in the South. Bamberger's photographs were featured at the National Building Museum in the winter of 2003–2004 in an exhibit entitled *Stories of Home.* As the exhibit notes say, "Bamberger's hauntingly beautiful images remind us of the human side of architecture, illustrating how buildings — and homeownership — impact individuals, families, and communities. The sisters pictured here are first-generation Americans whose parents emigrated from Mexico. Here they stand on the front porch of their family home in a subdivision built by Habitat for Humanity of San Antonio. (© Bill Bamberger)

238

Bill Bamberger, *Ada Bennett and daughter Faith, San Antonio, 2002.* They are seated in front of Guadalupe House, a shelter for homeless mothers. (© Bill Bamberger)

COMMENT

"Having a home means you're blessed, means having a home where you can sleep. . . . Having a home is having peace of mind that you have your own place. You can go in without knocking on the door or ringing a bell, without having someone else open the door."

—Ada Bennett, from *Stories of Home*

Bill Bamberger, *Christopher McDonald at home in Orchard Village, 1994.* Orchard Village is a community of fifty-eight newly constructed homes occupied primarily by first-time homeowners. (© Bill Bamberger)

**Bill Bamberger, *Charles Evans
Hughes, Mountainview Courts,
Chattanooga, 1995.*** Hughes became
a first-time homeowner at the age
of seventy-eight. Evans and his wife
had rented for thirty years until
redevelopment made it possible for
them to own. (© Bill Bamberger)

COMMENT

"I've been in this house for so long that I'd
rather be here than anywhere else. This house
is home."

—Charles Evans Hughes

COMMENT

"In these photographs, facial expressions speak volumes—
and the range of emotions is vast. There is angst from heavy
responsibility as well as a sense of tremendous satisfaction,
pride, and accomplishment. There is apprehension of the
unknown as well as enormous relief. There is self-esteem,
self-worth, and validation, and there is the deep sadness that
comes from saying goodbye and leaving familiar and comfortable surroundings. There is a sense of privacy, independence,
security, and control over one's life. There is stability and
continuity and family. There is longing and hope, and there is
great joy."

— From the exhibition script for *Stories of Home*, National Building Museum

241

**The Mobile Gallery,
San Antonio, 2002.**
Bamberger displayed the photographs you see here, as well as
hundreds of others, in a custom-
designed mobile gallery. The
gallery was designed by Gregory
Snyder, associate professor in
the College of Architecture at
the University of North Carolina
at Charlotte. (© Bill Bamberger)

MESSAGE

Bill Bamberger writes, "The meanings of 'home' and homeownership are interwoven with our dreams for the future and of the past." Nicole Lamy spends her essay trying to capture a sense of a childhood home when she lived in twelve different houses in twelve years. What does "home" mean to you? Is it a specific place? Does it represent the past — or the future? Is it people, an address, experiences, or something else?

METHOD

Lamy claims that the "photographs pretend no artistic merit." Why do you think she says this? How does she go about establishing this claim? Do you think Lamy would also claim that her essay pretends "no artistic merit"? What elements of deliberate artistry can you find in her essay? For example, are there extended threads of imagery? How does the reference to "lost things" in section I get picked up in other parts of the essay? How does Lamy use literary allusion?

MEDIUM

The essay by Nicole Lamy and the photographs by Bill Bamberger are each "illustrated" in this text — the first by Lamy's accordian flip book, the second by quotations from photographer and subjects. How important do you think the pictures are to Lamy's essay? How important is the information about Bamberger's subjects to his photographs? Find a picture of the place *you* think of as home. Then write a description of it that conveys what it represents to you. Which medium — words or images — do you think better explores what "home" means?

THE BASKETBALL COURT

As the words and images in this section demonstrate, a basketball court can be almost anywhere there are people with a passion for the game and a ball. When we talk about a sport — basketball, in this case — we're talking about a game that occurs in a circumscribed physical space; but sports space is serious for millions of people. It represents big business, big entertainment, and dreams, triumphs, disappointments, and egos that extend far beyond the lines drawn on a regulation court. For all the players represented here, whether pick-up or professional, basketball occurs in a space bigger than a court.

Throughout his work, the renowned African American novelist John Edgar Wideman displays a remarkable sensitivity to place, always hoping to capture the exact physical surroundings that shape our lives. In "First Shot" (2001), he looks back on the day he first held a basketball and launched it toward a makeshift hoop that seemed "a mile high." Wideman, who later would become a major college player, doesn't at all remember whether the ball went in or not. But he will never forget the actual place where he took that first shot — and in his essay he takes us to the precise spot. Photographers Dana Lixemberg, Paul D'Amato, and Brad Richman all offer portraits of players in action — portraits that capture the place as well as the player.

243

Go to exercise 05 of **ix visual exercises** to explore **context** — and use that concept to examine the materials in this cluster. What specific context was each text taken from?

John Edgar Wideman, *First Shot*. John Edgar Wideman (b. 1941) grew up in the 1940s and 1950s in Homewood, a black section of Pittsburgh, and he has written extensively of his childhood neighborhood in essays and fiction. He returned to it recently in *Hoop Roots* (2001), from which this excerpt is taken. *Hoop Roots*, an autobiography, celebrates his love of basketball and the many ways the sport has permeated his memory and imagination. After the first shot described here, there were many more; Wideman graduated in 1963 from the University of Pennsylvania, where he received the University's creative writing award and starred on its basketball team, eventually becoming a member of the Philadelphia Big Five Basketball Hall of Fame. A Rhodes Scholar at Oxford in the mid-1960s, Wideman has written many award-winning novels and collections of stories, including *A Glance Away* (1967), *Hurry Home* (1970), *The Lynchers* (1973), *Sent for You Yesterday* (1983), *Reuben* (1987), *Philadelphia Fire* (1990), *The Cattle Killing* (1996), and *Two Cities* (1998). He is professor of Africana studies and English at Brown University.

John Edgar Wideman
FIRST SHOT

I could take you there...show you the exact place on Finance Street in Homewood, Pittsburgh, Pennsylvania, where fifty years ago playground basketball began for me, and what would you see. Stand with you on the vacant side of Finance where nobody lives and look through a rusty fence that separates the unpaved sidewalk from a steep hillside overgrown with weeds and stubby trees, whose flat crest bedded railroad tracks when I was a kid and trains still run there and a busway too now, ferrying Homewood people back and forth from downtown Pittsburgh, point through the rusty webbing of twisted wire to a level expanse of ground along the foot of the hillside where no trace remains of a building that once occupied the empty space you see there today, the only structure on this side then, no fence, just this big shedlike building on our negro street where white men arrived to work every weekday, cramming their cars and pickups helter-skelter on the hillside, the bottom row's wheels straddling the curb.

Standing here, we are not far from the T-junction terminating Finance Street at Braddock, an avenue named for a Revolutionary War general, a dead white man as much a stranger to me once upon a time as the white strangers who worked in the factory or warehouse or bottling plant doing whatever they did in the only building on the track side of Finance, a block and a half from Braddock

Paul D'Amato, *Jump Shot/Tiro con salto, 1994.* Paul D'Amato teaches at
the Maine College of Art and is a regular contributor to *DoubleTake*
magazine. This photograph is part of a larger collection called "Crazy
Rhythm: The Mexican Community on the South Side of Chicago."
D'Amato writes of these photographs that he "wanted to make pictures
that were emotionally vivid and irrefutably real — that expressed the
human drama of urban living." (© Paul D'Amato)

Avenue, three and a half from Homewood, the other avenue bracketing our short street backed flush against a jungly hillside. Finance, a street easy to miss if you blinked after the dark, echoing underpasses on Braddock and Homewood below the train tracks, tunnels delivering you here to a community most Pittsburgh people thought of as the wrong side of the tracks, this street marking the beginning and end of the neighborhood in which I was raised, where I used to look for trains in the sky, a street dividing so-called black people from so-called white people, where basketball began for me.

My grandmother's house, 7415, and everybody else's on Finance—Smiths, Conleys, Colberts, Betts, Clarks, etc.—faced the tracks. With my chest pressed into the back of the sofa beneath the front room window, just tall enough on my knees to see out, I'd daydream away hours, waiting for the next train's rumble to fill the house, rattle the window glass I liked to frost in winter with my warm breath and draw on, airplanes, horses, moon faces with slits for eyes, crying eyes that shed real tears when I stroked them right, rivers of tears dripping all the way down the pane, ghost eyes and streaks still visible when the women did their spring cleaning and my grandmother hollered, Look at all this mess, boy. Better stop that scribble-scrabbling on my windows.

No matter how far forward you leaned over the sofa's back, you couldn't see the building farther up the block, on the opposite side of Finance, I could lead you to today and show you where it all began, where fifty-some years ago at a hoop nailed to its outside wall I touched a basketball first time and launched my first shot. And because it couldn't be seen from 7415's front window, the wall, the building were out of bounds. In those days with everybody in the house on edge, a little shaky, a little unhappy because my parents had split up for the first time and we'd moved back to Homewood without my father to live in my mother's mother's house, sometimes it seemed the whole world might be coming apart, especially at 2 or 3 A.M., startled awake by a train crashing through the bedroom walls, me laying eyes wide open for hours worrying about how, piece by piece, anybody could ever put things back together again.

I guess it was easy in that crowded house for everybody to get on everybody else's nerves and I heard a lot of G'wan away from here and play, boy. The words sounding like a prison sentence since going out to play meant occupying myself in the fenced-in back yard or on the porch or sidewalk in front of 7415 so if any adult wanted to check on my whereabouts a loud shout would be enough to get my attention. Just to be sure I wasn't into any mischief, the adult in charge could spy through the front room picture window or the little square window at the back of the house above the kitchen sink. Playing outdoors meant staying close enough so no one ever needed to step out of 7415 to keep an eye on you.

On a good day my mom, grandmother, or one of my aunts might take me by the hand across Finance and let me roam the hillside. Don't you dare try and cross the street till I come back for you. And don't you dare march yourself up near those tracks. Whoever escorted me repeated these commandments and a few others, usually ending with the rule, Better stay where I can see you, young man, or I'll snatch your narrow hips home.

I tried never to be busted for breaking rules because getting caught brought more rules, tighter lockdown, but even in a household of loving, attentive women, an only child, particularly a male child, could slip away. In Homewood boys need to think they can get away with things. And sometimes women encourage boys to believe they can. How else keep alive in their male children the cute, mischievous twinkle racial oppression strives to extinguish. To cut slack for their men the women made allowance for the fact that boys will be boys. Created space, a license for their men to bend rules, a hedge against demeaning rules. The women required this slack as much as the boys if they didn't want to be nailed down too tightly themselves. But the women also had learned from bitter experience that they could be accomplices in crimes against themselves, setting themselves up to be sideswiped or demolished by the first and last rule: you can't trust people, especially men and boys wounded by rules, to respect rules.

As a kid I thought women made up the rules and I resented them for it. I also couldn't help noticing that women were more restricted by rules than men. The rule for instance that kept women home all day and night with us kids. Females (though I'd never have dreamed of calling them *females* or *women* then), my grandmother, aunts, and mother, seemed embodiments of rules and I began to treat them as I treated rules—obstacles to be circumvented, deceived, ignored when I could. If I got caught straying too far out of line, my mother would threaten, Wait till your father gets home. And if and when he did arrive home that day, he might punish me with his hard hand for breaking rules I knew he didn't follow. It seemed to me my father came and went as he pleased. Said whatever to whomever. Closed himself off in the bedroom and nobody better disturb him. Clearly, if I ever grew big enough, strong enough, no one could punish me. I'd be a man, on top like my father, privileged to make my own rules, to slam people for busting rules I wasn't obliged to honor. Men could, perhaps should, I believed, go about their business as if women's rules didn't exist.

I learned I could slip outside the frame of 7415's front window, just so I didn't stay away too long, just so I wasn't invisible when somebody in a bad mood or a big hurry came looking for me. On a tight leash, yes, but it stretched far enough so I could pretend no leash tethered me to the center of the space whose edges I roamed. Part of me, even then, understood that pain-in-the-butt restrictions were linked to being loved and indulged in my grandmother's house and that I couldn't have one without the other. The dread of losing 7415's special sense of well being, even for a short cloudburst of frowns or fussing or tighter rules, of losing the kisses, smiles, and mostly sweet, untroubled rhythm of my days, usually was enough to persuade me to police myself.

Abiding by the women's rules paid off, but some days, boy, you know what I mean, slipping away exerted an irresistible pull. Whatever sensible purposes the rules served—my safety, the convenience and peace of mind of the adults— they were also a challenge, a dare. They existed to be broken. The afternoon I fired my first shot at a hoop I was testing as I did daily in a hundred secret games how much I could get away with. In this instance, how long could I remain out of sight of 7415's front window. Visible within the frame a minute, then gone for

247

248

Brad Richman, *Silver Springs, Maryland—August 1993.* Brad Richman spent nine years traveling across the country taking pictures of basketball courts, games, and players. A collection of these photographs, *America's Game,* from which these three photos are taken, has been exhibited at the Basketball Hall of Fame and has also appeared in *Double Take, Vibe, Fortune,* and *The Washington Post Magazine.* (© Brad Richman. Courtesy of Lee Marks Fine Art)

two, visible again, then absent five minutes, sneaking farther up Finance with each foray and on each trip away longer. I knew whoever was in charge of me would get busy with one thing or another inside the house. Plus, I figured out three facts I could count on. First, I wouldn't be allowed to play on the hillside unless they trusted me. Second, the more I appeared to cooperate, the more trust and less surveillance there would be. Third, the eyes constantly on duty at the window scanning the hillside existed only in my mind. Except for unusual circumstances — my mom maybe, on one of those

days when her eyes were red and puffy, her nose sniffling, a glazed-look day when she might sit at the front window or the kitchen table and stare for hours at nothing, silent, a force field of hurt so palpable around her you bumped into the sting of its barbed wire if you stepped too close — no adult would plant herself on the couch under the window with nothing better to do than maintain unbroken vigilance on the empty hillside where I was playing.

Brad Richman, *Portland, Maine — October 8, 2000.*

249

Brad Richman, *Washington, D.C. — July 10, 1999.*

Once I understood that my imagination endowed the eyes with more power than they deserved, I was ready to begin imagining their absence, begin preparing myself for the great escape, the moment when I could convince myself I had nothing to fear from the patrolling eyes. Minute by minute, day by day, I stretched my leash a little farther. Coached myself to stay away a little longer. No one's watching all the time. Even if Aunt Sis or Aunt Geral or Grandma Freed peeks out and doesn't see you she'll figure you'll be right back in a second, you're a good boy, they trust you and boys will be boys—so she'll go on about her business and when she checks again, sure enough, there you'll be, or at worst, if she's having a worry-wart day, she'll stand at the window a minute or two till you reappear, back safe inside the arc where you're supposed to be. No problem. If she grumbles or cuts her eye at you later—Better stay where I can see you. Mister. Don't be getting too big for your britches—a bit of a smile probably in her sideways glance. Boys will be boys.

No problem as long as the scenarios I constructed inside my boy's pea-brained skull more or less matched what actually transpired inside the house. Of course once I ventured out of sight of 7415, anybody behind the glass was as invisible to me as I was to them. I remember thinking yes, it's a window and through it you're able to watch rain and snow, trains shake-rattle-and-rolling past up on the hilltop, see Freed's roses blooming pink and bloody purple on bushes the neighbors begged her for cuttings from each spring, check out odd looking grownups walking to and from stores on Homewood Avenue, but seeing through

250

COMMENT

"Catchings is the now and the future of the game. I've played and coached against the best players in the world, and no one has played like she does. In the best possible way, she plays like a guy."

—Nancy Lieberman, Olympic, collegiate, and professional basketball player; professional manager and coach; broadcaster; and the first woman to ever play in a men's professional league (USBL)

Dana Lixemberg, *Tamika Catchings*. This photograph illustrated a profile of ▶ Catchings that ran in the May 25, 2003, issue of *The New York Times Magazine*, portraying her as "the brightest hope" for the W.N.B.A. It was taken by celebrated Dutch photographer Dana Lixemberg, who has photographed homeless people, celebrities, and athletes with the same direct lens. Her work has been featured in most major magazines as well as in a collection of her portraits in *United States* (2001). (© Dana Lixemberg)

a window is also being blind as far as it doesn't allow you to look at what it hides beyond the view it commands. I wouldn't have thought the word *commands* then, probably wouldn't have formulated my idea in words at all, but I know I intuited something very precise about how brick walls and windows could function in the same fashion when it comes to keeping you unaware.

I wanted to explore what might be happening farther up Finance Street so I wished away the watching eyes. Pretended I controlled the appearance and disappearance of adult faces in the rectangle of glass, just as I once believed the moon followed me when I ran up and down the street, believed the moon vacated the sky when I paid it no mind, believed, in the darkness of the Bellmawr show, I could entice June Allyson's blue, blue eyes to glance down from the screen and smile at the brown boy curled in his seat, shyly in love with her.

After my Aunt Geral had deposited me on the hillside I'd stare at her back as she recrossed Finance to my grandmother's house, to see whether or not she looked in both directions for oncoming traffic before she stepped into the street. *Stop, look, and listen,* the rule she recited to me each time she took my hand and crossed me to play on the hillside. I was always a little worried and maybe slightly disappointed when she didn't get hit by a car those times she didn't bother to stop, look, and listen. Once she'd made it safely to the paved side of Finance, I'd turn away, hang around at the foot of the hillside as if I needed time to get my bearings. I might even shuffle a couple fake steps away from the direction I intended to scoot in as fast as I could the instant I decided she'd had time to re-enter the house, take a peek at me through the window. I knew better than to turn around like a dumbbell and stare at 7415. Why in the world would I need to know what was happening behind my back. Weren't the dirt, weeds, stones, trees, bushes, and insects of the hillside more than enough to keep my hands busy, my mind occupied.

I pretended, then came to believe, that I didn't need to turn around to see what transpired in the window behind me. I depended on a picture in my mind, my ability to sense the weight of eyes on my shoulders. I drew a square in the empty air in front of me, and it mirrored what hovered behind my back. I could see Aunt Geral's face, see her eyes unaware that I watched them gazing at me, at the scruffy, overgrown hillside, at parcels of cloud in the sky, the emptiness of gleaming rails waiting for a train. My aunt gazing till what's in front of her eyes mingles with what's not there and she stares through it all, past it to the story of whatever she's deciding to do next. I could feel myself becoming transparent, disappearing as her mind fixed on something besides the nephew playing on the hill. As I think back, I can't help comparing my fake view of her in a made-up mirror in the air to her fading view of me, to this view of a fifty-year-old moment flickering on and off in my head while I attempt to represent it for the you—*mirror, mirror on the wall*—I'm imagining reading these words. The you I promised to take by the hand to where it all started, the place basketball began for me.

If I'd sprinted full speed from the spot on Finance opposite my grandmother's house, I bet I could have reached the building where white men were shooting

■ "First Shot" is as much about a young boy testing the limits of his restrictions as it is about holding a basketball for the first time. What significance do you think the window at 7415 has for Wideman? What does it mean to him as a child? What has it come to represent from his adult's perspective?

baskets before my Aunt Geraldine could clomp through the house to a sinkful of dishes in the kitchen. Clomp, clomp, clomp, in her mashed-back houseshoes, glancing at the silent phone, running her finger along the grooved edge of the china cabinet with the cut-glass bowl on top. Sometimes she'd sigh, Wish you were a nice sugar-and-spice girl instead of all snips and snails and puppy tails, you nasty rascal, you. Old enough to stick your arms down in these soapsuds and help your auntie with this mess if you were a sweet little girl child.

From my perspective, an eight- or nine-year-old black boy on stolen time who seldom had much to do with white people, the men up the street in a pool of sunshine in front of the only building on the track side of Finance, launching shots at a hang-dog, netless hoop, seemed huge and old, but it's likely they were in their twenties and thirties, some probably teenagers. A few had stripped off their shirts. I remember pale flesh, hairy chests and armpits, bony rib cages and shoulders, long, lanky arms. They blend into the faces and bodies of guys I played with on mostly white teams in high school and college. For some reason one wears in my memory a full beard like the fair-haired Jesus on a calendar, his blue eyes following you around the Sunday school room of Homewood AME Zion Church.

The men didn't talk much as they took turns shooting, rebounding. Some lounged in the shade smoking, ignoring the ball and basket. Seven or eight guys total, I think, probably on lunch break. Somebody had nailed a rusty hoop to a board above truck size double doors adjacent to the building's entrance. A bright summer day but the interior beyond the partly open double doors in deep shadow. Boxes stacked inside. Machinery too. What little I could see, unfamiliar. Nothing I recognized then nor learned later gave me a clue what work the white men who showed up each weekday performed when they weren't outside shooting baskets.

Once or twice as I watched from the curb the basketball bounced toward me and I retrieved it, rolled it back. Can't tell you whether it was a good, tight, regulation-size ball or some scuffed, lopsided, balloony thing they might kick around or clobber with a bat when they didn't feel like shooting. I don't remember anyone speaking to me. And that was fine because it saved me having to answer. I definitely didn't want to say *yessir* or *nosir* to men without shirts throwing a ball at a basket. I'd been taught at home to be polite to all grownups, especially polite, and as close to silent as I could manage without being impolite, if the grownups happened to be white male strangers. Whether these men shooting hoops spoke or not, I knew I'd better be ready with an appropriate form of address, so I was searching my mind for one. Wonder now if one existed. Or was the point to keep boys like me guessing.

Being unnoticed or ignored allowed me to continue observing them from my spot at the edge of Finance where there could have been a sidewalk if anybody had bothered to pave the no houses side of the street. Since my presence seemed not to matter, I felt comfortably invisible, a ghost who glided into view once or twice, only intruding enough to keep the ball out of the street, guide it back into the circle.

I must have been watching longer than I realized or maybe till that moment I really had been invisible shuttling back and forth from the safety zone opposite

253

7415's front window because one of them said, Kid's not going to leave till he gets a shot. Here, kid. C'mon. Try one. I wish I could describe the man who called me over because remembering him might demonstrate how conscious we made ourselves of white people as individuals, aware of their particular features, character, the threat or advantage a specific person posed. In a way, the last great campaign for civil rights, commencing in the southern states in the early fifties, during the same period this scene on Finance Street occurs, was a demand, a concerted political movement to secure, among other things, the same attentive, circumspect recognition of us as individuals that I was compelled, at my peril, to afford to this white guy who handed or passed me a ball.

I could say the ball felt enormous in my hands, because it probably did. I could say I was suddenly shy, timid, and they had to coax me from the margin where I'd been silently watching. Say once I stepped onto the smooth driveway in front of the hoop with the ball in my hands and the basket a mile high poking out from a board fastened on the brick wall, I could tell you how great it felt then to pat the ball for the first time, feel it rise off the asphalt back to my hand, the thrill of lifting the ball with both hands, sighting over it at the hoop, trying to get all my small weight under it and do what I'd watched the bigger, stronger, pale bodies do. No doubt all the above is true. I could also say the men laughed at the air ball I bricked up or encouraged me and gave me more shots or I heaved the ball high and straight and true that first time so it banked off the board through the rim, *Two*, and everybody whooped and hollered. Could say any damned thing because I don't recall what happened, only that it happened, my first shot in that exact place under the circumstances I'm relating, me AWOL from 7415's front window, suddenly scared I'd lost track of time, shooting and hauling ass back down the track side of Finance because I'd probably been out of sight way too long. The story enlarging, fact, fiction, and something in between, till I become who I am today, the story growing truer and less true as I make it up and it makes me up, but one thing's sure, the spot's still there on Finance and I've never forgotten my first shot.

■ *Why do you think Wideman raises the issue of truth and fiction in this final paragraph? Suppose he had recounted this incident in a short story instead of a memoir. Do you think he would have changed any details about his "first shot"? How do you think memoir is different from fiction based on personal experience? How much of this essay is composed of things Wideman admits he didn't see or can't exactly remember?*

MESSAGE

John Edgar Wideman can't remember what his first shot was like, but he can take us directly to the exact spot where it happened. Why do you think this is important to Wideman? What point is he making about memory and place? Why do you think he spends so much time describing the geography of his neighborhood and the portion of the street where he "stretched my leash a little farther"? What do those details have to do with basketball?

METHOD

Look closely at the photographs by Paul D'Amato, Brad Richman, and Dana Lixemberg. Each is focusing on basketball — but each photograph frames the subject, and the court, differently. Use the concept of *framing* to identify the focus of each photograph. Does basketball represent something different in each, or is the court essentially the same?

MEDIUM

Marketing campaigns surround professional athletics. The N.B.A., in particular is renowned for marketing its talented players as superstar personalities. Using any ad featuring a star athlete, write an essay that considers how the medium of advertising uses individual talent to promote a specific product. Is the person being marketed, or the product? Or something else?

255

ROADSIDE DINING

ESSAY   AD   6 PHOTOS

In the history of American food service, fast-food chains have figured out a distinctive use of commercial space. For example, the earliest McDonald's had no inside seating, so customers took the food out to their cars and ate in the parking lot. Only later, when the franchise noticed that many customers were not teenagers coming in for a snack but rather adults taking their main meal, did the company grow family-oriented by introducing seating. As many new franchises appeared — Burger King, Kentucky Fried Chicken, Pizza Hut, Wendy's, and so on — they collectively and rapidly altered society's concept of eating in restaurants (gone were waiters and waitresses) and the way a restaurant should be designed. They also contributed to a memorable American iconography, as nearly everyone could instantly identify any fast-food chain by its sign and logo. No matter where it was built — in New York City, Milwaukee, or Cheyenne — a McDonald's would display its trademark golden arches.

Such standardization and uniformity disturbed many Americans. As early as 1961, the critic Lewis Mumford, complaining about the effects of suburbanization, angrily wrote that American communities were becoming "a low-grade uniform environment from which escape is impossible." This kind of criticism eventually led to a renewed effort for the preservation of older communities and historical sites as well as a preference among many Americans for all things local and authentic.

Yet, is the longing for the local and authentic in itself a phony quest, fueled by a comforting nostalgia for some past America that may never have existed except in our collective imagination? The essay and pictures in this section capture space that is quintessentially American, authentic or not. In "Fast-Food America" (2002), Nicholas Howe urges us to abandon our sentimentality and nostalgia: we can find the real America of today anytime by pulling off the interstate and sitting down at a Burger King or McDonald's. If we do this with the proper imagination, Howe suggests, we will be on our way to understanding the meaning of place in contemporary America.

Nicholas Howe, *Fast-Food America*. Taking an opposing stand against the quest for authenticity, the travel essayist Nicholas Howe views fast-food franchises, and all that they represent, from a different perspective. Why, he questions, are we repeatedly told that to really see America we need to get off the interstates and drive the back roads, the two-lane blacktops? If we stay on the interstates, are we truly "damned to live in a postmodern hell where everything looks the same and nothing has the savor of its place"? This essay first appeared in the Summer/Fall issue of *The Kenyon Review* (2002).

Nicholas Howe

FAST-FOOD AMERICA

When writers claim to avoid interstates and fast-food restaurants in order to find the real America, get set for foolishness about old-time dialects, country crafts, and characters of the sort they don't make anymore. Or so the writer will assure you, and praise himself (almost always it is a man) for being ballsy enough to turn off the four-lane and find real folks rooted in their region who can't be confused with people three states away or even on the other side of the mountain. These are people, he'll promise you, that it's worth traveling to see because their identities remain rooted in the place and its past.

Most of these books are unbearably certain that you must follow the back-roads or else be damned to live in a postmodern hell where everything looks the same and nothing has the savor of its place. And where, of course, there are no stories. It's not that these travel writers take backroads to find the vivid, the salty, the forgotten that annoys me; it's that they deny other roads lead there. If you read enough of these books, you'll realize that Americans often locate their idea of the exotic in a pastoral world never known this side of the Atlantic. Although less ponderous than most, William Least Heat Moon's *Blue Highways* is the best-known recent example of the genre:

> On the old highway maps of America, the main routes were red and the back roads blue. Now even the colors are changing.. But in those brevities just before dawn and a little after dusk — times neither day nor night — the old roads return to the sky some of its color. Then, in truth, they carry a mysterious cast of blue, and it's that time when the pull of the blue highway is strongest, when the open road is a beckoning, a strangeness, a place where a man can lose himself. (xi)

257

Instead of a raft on the Mississippi or a whaling ship in the South Seas, Least Heat Moon made do with a Ford van he named "Ghost Dancer." He could roam nineteenth-century America because he avoided those interstates that burn their way across the map with only passing regard to topography or culture; he found his curious, gnarled characters by losing himself on blue highways. But you must remember, when reading his book, that he taught English before setting out and knew this country's need to locate the authentic in little hamlets and sleepy burgs: Edwin Arlington Robinson in Maine, Sherwood Anderson in Ohio, Faulkner in Mississippi, Cather in Nebraska, Capote in Kansas. But each of them knew, as few travel writers of the backroads sort ever do, that small-town life is little different from life elsewhere. They put their places on the map precisely because they avoided nostalgia. If we are to follow them today, we must make our route, not on blue highways, but on the main roads of the imagination.

258

HOW AN AUTOMAT WORKS

FIRST DROP YOUR NICKELS IN THE SLOT

THEN TURN THE KNOB THE GLASS DOOR CLICKS OPEN

LIFT THE DOOR AND HELP YOURSELF

HORN & HARDART

Interior of One of the Fifty Automat-Cafeterias
in Philadelphia and New York

Horn & Hardart, *Automat*. Contrary to popular belief, the idea of "fast food" is not a recent innovation but has deep roots in American culture. At the turn of the twentieth century, street vendors sold sausages and frankfurters; by the Depression era, hot dog stands and diners had become part of the American landscape. For convenience food, moreover, nothing could surpass a restaurant like the Horn & Hardart Automat (founded in 1902), where a customer would find an enormous wall of windowed compartments containing a wide variety of meals, sandwiches, and side-orders. All one had to do was select the dish, insert the appropriate change, open the small glass window, remove the plate, and find a seat. Empty compartments were constantly refilled by a behind-the-scenes restaurant staff. The last automat closed in 1991. (© Bettman/Corbis)

Ray Kroc Standing outside McDonald's, 1963. The McDonald brothers (whose first car-hop restaurant opened in San Bernardino, California, in 1940) discovered through trial and error in 1948 how a fast-food restaurant should work. Hot dogs were quick and easy, they realized, but they were also a regional fare, and most people after World War II wanted hamburgers on buns. Until the McDonald brothers came along, no one had figured out how to speed up the process of preparing burgers to satisfy the appetite of a newly suburban society that was just learning to live life in the fast lane. When the entrepreneur Ray Kroc bought out all the rights to McDonald's in 1961, he further streamlined and standardized the process while expanding franchises throughout the United States and eventually throughout the globe. By 1963, the restaurant had sold its one billionth hamburger; today the number is closer to 100 billion. (© Bettman/Corbis)

I think about this sometimes when I'm drinking coffee in a fast-food place along an interstate. Usually, I've driven too far that day and need to slow down; the discipline of hot coffee is that it takes more time than a cold drink. I like chain places because they clean the toilets and keep the place anonymous. They remind me that the most enviable of travelers—adaptable and graceful medievals like Ibn Battuta or Marco Polo—stuck to the main roads, the caravan routes, the pilgrimage ways. On the beaten track, they found what they needed: the exchange of goods, the ebb and flow of human beings moving about for all imaginable reasons, confirmation that life lies in motion and transfer. They knew that routes, like places, have their stories.

And so, on an early winter afternoon in a McDonald's off I-90 in Erie, Pennsylvania, I looked up from my coffee to see a Japanese family settle into the next booth. They negotiated the business of fast-food America with perfect style though limited fluency in English. It was, I guess, little different for them here than in a McDonald's at home. The beauty of chain places is that they keep us from making fools of ourselves when we travel. As the parents spoke to each other in Japanese, I heard "Cleveland" and saw them point to a map; then I heard "Toledo" and they pointed a few inches to the left. "Cleveland" and "Toledo" passed back and forth as they looked at their watches and then at their two kids. I think they decided to stop for the night in Cleveland because they turned to it in their guidebook.

This act of locating oneself on the road, of planning the next stop, occurs millions of times each day around the world. Trivial as the example before me seemed, it made me look at others in that McDonald's and wonder how they located themselves on the edge of the interstate. There were teenagers in sweat-

259

shirts emblazoned "Penn State," "Yale," "Georgia Tech," "Indiana"; a girl in a cheerleader jacket that read "Knoch"; a man in his forties, my age, in a shirt with "Dave" over one pocket and "Master Mold Co." over the other. Some came in with the names of sports teams or sneaker companies across their fronts and were served at the counter by blond teenagers with nametags that said Amy, Katrina, Melissa, and by a Latino named Joe. Yes, it could have been anywhere in America. The colleges and teams would have different names elsewhere, but the need to declare an allegiance would remain. One could say, cynically, that they emblazon themselves with the identities of others because they are displaced and yet still need to belong somewhere. So they choose whatever lies closest to home; in Erie it's "Pirates," "Steelers," "Pitt," "Penn State," "Slippery Rock."

At such moments, it's easy to feel superior to people on the edge of the interstate and to cherish instead the lure of the old days and backroads. But that won't help anyone understand place in America today. Is it the loneliness of these spaces, the certainty that one will meet only strangers along the way, the need to state where one comes from (literally or spiritually), that makes us rely on these emblazonings? Is it that the interstate becomes a metaphor for our condition of being in transit between places and finally at home in none of them? Or are the emblazonings tokens of the journey, like the badges made of base metal that medieval pilgrims back from Saint James of Compestella or Rome or Jerusalem wore on their breasts? These badges testified to the distances pilgrims would go to honor their faith or atone for their sins. They proclaimed that the wearer's business on the highway was holy and thus to be respected. I don't know that the people driving I-90 were searching for some holy shrine of their imagining or that they hoped to find a place with its own savor somewhere along the anonymous road. I could only feel that travelers and writers who turned off the highway for the old roads were distancing themselves from any possibility of speaking about how we travel now.

Fast-food America has its stories. The place itself can seem a never-changing belt along the interstate of neon, grease, sugar, diesel fumes. Most of it is ugly, little is built to last out the decade, and all of it obeys the imperative of speed that is, in America, the creation of space. The traveler's law of thermodynamics, should it ever be written, would relate the desire for speed to the distance that must be traversed. That law would also predict casualties along the way. In a Kentucky Fried Chicken in Sullivan, Missouri, off I-44, I found a graffito on the back of a stall door that could be read only as you sat on the toilet: "Because it's fried shit, that's why." It was, in the idiom of the road, a cautionary message about too much driving and too much fast food. And if you wondered what it meant, you hadn't spent enough time in transient America.

Sentimental travelers speak of old diners as shrines on the highway; they had eccentricities of style, a suspicion of strangers, the best pie for miles. To see this nostalgia for the diner celebrated in, remarkably, a Burger King from the early 1990s is worth a long drive in itself. So go to Sheridan, Wyoming, off I-90 in the eastern and less fashionable part of the state. The place looks like every other Burger King: plastic, easy to clean, comfortable enough for a brief stop. The locals

David Butow, *Traffic along U.S. Highway 412* (2001). In a scene most of us recognize as Anywhere U.S.A., traffic streams along the strip in Springdale, a town north of Fayetteville in northeastern Arkansas. (© David Butow/Corbis)

find it a useful breakfast club. The menu you already know from your hometown. But along one wall hangs a group of pictures meant to remake the place in an older image. "The Runaway" by Norman Rockwell shows a benevolent cop and a little boy sitting next to each other on stools in a diner. Under the boy's stool is his bindle staff, his hobo gear. The story is simple: cop, boy, diner all belong to a time when boys did boys' mischief in running away, cops remembered their own boyhoods when bringing them home, and the counterman was a friend to both. Next is a stark black-and-white photograph of a diner countertop by Paul Hoffman that makes the usual salt-and-pepper shakers, chrome napkin dispensers, ashtrays, and the like seem chic, even monumental. Finally, a poster from the O.K. Harris Gallery in New York's Soho, of all places, shows a painting by Ralph Goings of a diner in a landscape much like that outside this same Burger King.

The message was clear: the diners you miss from your childhood or (more likely) from memories of someone else's have been reconstructed here in the franchise restaurant. The rituals of life continue in the landscape. And so you will discover if you listen to the conversations around you: the exchange of news between a soldier's wife home for a visit and her former high-school teacher; the time-worn stories passed among retired ranchers idling away the June morning when they'd rather have beeen out working; the flow of greetings and news that sustains life and makes for community. If you sit there long enough with your coffee and aren't intrusive—it helps to read the local paper; you will seem less alien above a familiar headline—then you will see that all of this coming and going is the life of the place. Here in a building that looks like thousands of others, the transient is anchored to some sense of home, the international is made local, the stories of the place get told beneath pictures of old diners, the travel writer finds material. It's as close to the real America as anyone will ever get—or could survive finding.

261

Work Cited

Least Heat Moon, William. *Blue Highways: A Journey into America.* New York: Fawcett Crest, 1982.

▲ Lauren Greenfield, *Penny Wolfe and daughter Jessica, Santa Monica Place.*

Lauren Greenfield, *Hot Dog on a Stick employees* ▼
Dominique King and Wendy Recinos at Baldwin Hills
Crenshaw Plaza.

Lauren Greenfield, *Keum Ja Chung and Hyung Hee Im in the Koreatown Plaza* ▲
International Food Court.

Lauren Greenfield, *Baldwin Hills Crenshaw Plaza.* ▼

◀ **Lauren Greenfield, *photos of Los Angeles food courts.*** In these four photos, Lauren Greenfield documents the food courts around Los Angeles and the people who gather there. Greenfield grew up in Venice, California; her photographic documentary on coming of age in Los Angeles, *Fast Forward* (1997), was followed by a study of the different aspects of growing up female in America, *Girl Culture* (2002; see p. 26). Her photographs have appeared in many major magazines, including *Time, Newsweek, Vanity Fair, Life,* and *The New York Times Magazine.* These images first appeared in the January 2004 issue of *Los Angeles.* (© 2004 Lauren Greenfield)

264

MESSAGE

Nicholas Howe mentions a Burger King in Sheridan, Wyoming, that has a display of illustrations and posters of old diners. Why do you think he includes this detail and even describes several of the art works? Why does he find it remarkable that a fast-food franchise would commemorate old diners? What message does Howe extract from the display of art works? In what way is that message similar to the message of his own essay?

METHOD

Note that Howe begins his essay by referring to writers (such as William Least Heat Moon) who hold a different attitude from his toward "interstates and fast-food restaurants." How does Howe summarize these attitudes? What advantage does he gain in starting his essay by presenting an opposing attitude? Suppose he had stated his own position right from the start, without mentioning other writers or other points of view; in your opinion, would his essay have been more or less persuasive? Explain why.

MEDIUM

How do the visual materials in this section support or detract from Howe's argument? Do they make a different argument when you read them as a group? Try to read them as a group and write down what visual argument the editors of this book have made by placing them together with Howe's essay.

TRANSIT SPACE

If you've ever waited to catch a flight at an airport and spent time closely observing your environment, you were paying attention to "transit space" — those special areas of public space where we pause in our journeys from one place to another. In "Nowhere Man" (1997), the noted essayist and travel writer Pico Iyer defines himself as part of a modern group of "transit loungers" who "pass through countries as through revolving doors, resident aliens of the world, impermanent residents of nowhere." As the number of transit loungers has steadily increased, artists and architects have begun exploring — both critically and creatively — the special features of transit space, studying the ways they are designed and their emotional impact on travelers: Are airports designed, for example, to make travelers feel rested and comfortable, or do they instead engender feelings of alienation? Such explorations into transit space have been intensified by travel after the events of 9/11. In fact, a recent underground hip hop–jazz fusion album, *In What Language?*, is devoted to the experiences of dark-skinned people in airports, and a recent film, *Terminal* (starring Tom Hanks), deals with an individual stranded for a year in an airport.

Although in "Nowhere Man" Pico Iyer focuses on airport space, transit space can also be experienced in train and bus stations, elevators, subways, the lobbies of large hotels and corporations, gas stations, motels, parking lots, highway rest stops, and just about any other public space dedicated to the steady human process of coming and going.

Pico Iyer, *Nowhere Man*. As the world becomes more globally connected and multicultural, "an entirely new breed of people," Pico Iyer notes, has come into existence; he includes himself as one of the new "transit loungers." Born in England to Indian parents in 1957, Iyer has been contributing essays regularly to *Time* magazine since 1982. His books include *Video Night in Katmandu* (1988), *The Lady and the Monk* (1991), *Falling Off the Map* (1993), and *The Global Soul: Jet Lag, Shopping Malls, and the Search for Home* (2001). "Nowhere Man" first appeared in the *Utne Reader,* May/June 1997.

Pico Iyer
NOWHERE MAN

By the time I was nine, I was already used to going to school by plane, to sleeping in airports, to shuttling back and forth, three times a year, between my home in California and my boarding school in England. While I was growing up, I was never within six thousand miles of the nearest relative—and came, therefore, to learn how to define relations in nonfamilial ways. From the time I was a teenager, I took it for granted that I could take my budget vacation (as I did) in Bolivia and Tibet, China and Morocco. It never seemed strange to me that a girlfriend might be half a world (or ten hours flying time) away, that my closest friends might be on the other side of a continent or sea. It was only recently that I realized that all these habits of mind and life would scarcely have been imaginable in my parents' youth, that the very facts and facilities that shape my world are all distinctly new developments, and mark me as a modern type.

It was only recently, in fact, that I realized that I am an example, perhaps, of an entirely new breed of people, a transcontinental tribe of wanderers that is multiplying as fast as international telephone lines and frequent flier programs. We are the transit loungers, forever heading to the departure gate. We buy our interests duty-free, we eat our food on plastic plates, we watch the world through borrowed headphones. We pass through countries as through revolving doors, resident aliens of the world, impermanent residents of nowhere. Nothing is strange to us, and nowhere is foreign. We are visitors even in our own homes.

The modern world seems increasingly made for people like me. I can plop myself down anywhere and find myself in the same relation of familiarity and strangeness: Lusaka is scarcely more strange to me than the England in which I was born, the America where I am registered as an "alien," and the almost unvisited India that people tell me is my home. All have Holiday Inns, direct-dial phones, CNN, and DHL. All have sushi, Thai restaurants, and Kentucky Fried Chicken.

This kind of life offers an unprecedented sense of freedom and mobility: Tied down nowhere, we can pick and choose among locations. Ours is the first generation that can go off to visit Tibet for a week, or meet Tibetans down the street; ours is the first generation to be able to go to Nigeria for a holiday—to find our roots or to find that they are not there. At a superficial level, this new internationalism means that I can meet, in the Hilton coffee shop, an Indonesian businessman who is as conversant as I am with Magic Johnson and Madonna. At a deeper level, it means that I need never feel estranged. If all the world is alien to us, all the world is home.

And yet I sometimes think that this mobile way of life is as disquietingly novel as high-rises, or as the video monitors that are rewiring our consciousness. Even as we fret about the changes our progress wreaks in the air and on the air-waves, in forests and on streets, we hardly worry about the change it is working in ourselves, the new kind of soul that is being born out of a new kind of life. Yet this could be the most dangerous development of all, and the least examined.

For us in the transit lounge, disorientation is as alien as affiliation. We become professional observers, able to see the merits and deficiencies of any-where, to balance our parents' viewpoints with their enemies' position. Yes, we say, of course it's terrible, but look at the situation from Saddam's point of view. I understand how you feel, but the Chinese had their own cultural reasons for Tiananmen Square. Fervor comes to seem to us the most foreign place of all.

Seasoned experts at dispassion, we are less good at involvement, or suspen-sion of disbelief; at, in fact, the abolition of distance. We are masters of the aerial perspective, but touching down becomes more difficult. Unable to get stirred by the raising of a flag, we are sometimes unable to see how anyone could be stirred. I sometimes think that this is how Salman Rushdie, the great analyst of this condition, somehow became its victim. He had juggled homes for so long, so adroitly, that he forgot how the world looks to someone who is rooted—in coun-try or in belief. He had chosen to live so far from affiliation that he could no longer see why people choose affiliation in the first place. Besides, being part of no society means one is accountable to no one, and need respect no laws outside

267

COMMENT

"I think America the symbol and America the notion are still very different from America the nation. What's touching and almost regenerative is that whatever is happening in the reality of America, where there is a murder rate worse than Lebanon's and where there is so much homelessness and poverty, still America will be shorthand throughout the world for everything that is young and modern and free."

— Pico Iyer

Transit Space

Sylvia Otte, *Airport Lounges.* (© Sylvia Otte/Photonica)

■ *What do you make of this comparison? Why does Iyer introduce the idea of culpability at all—what is he guilty of? And in what sense is he equivalent to a bystander who snaps a picture of a murder victim? What does the snapshot represent in Iyer's equation? Why is it different from writing an essay?*

■ *Analyze Iyer's final sentence. How does its imagery reinforce his language throughout the essay? What is the comparison in the final metaphor?*

one's own. If single-nation people can be fanatical as terrorists, we can end up ineffectual as peacekeepers.

We become, in fact, strangers to belief itself, unable to comprehend many of the rages and dogmas that animate (and unite) people. I could not begin to fathom why some Muslims would think of murder after hearing about *The Satanic Verses*; yet sometimes I force myself to recall that it is we, in our floating skepticism, who are the exceptions, that in China or Iran, in Korea or Peru, it is not so strange to give up one's life for a cause.

We end up, then, a little like nonaligned nations, confirming our reservations at every step. We tell ourselves, self-servingly, that nationalism breeds monsters, and choose to ignore the fact that internationalism breeds them too. Ours is the culpability not of the assassin, but of the bystander who takes a snapshot of the murder. Or, when the revolution catches fire, hops on the next plane out.

I wonder, sometimes, if this new kind of nonaffiliation may not be alien to something fundamental in the human state. Refugees at least harbor passionate feeling about the world they have left—and generally seek to return there. The exile at least is propelled by some kind of strong emotion away from the old country and toward the new; indifference is not an exile emotion. But what does the transit lounger feel? What are the issues that we would die for? What are the passions that we would live for?

Airports are among the only sites in public life where emotions are hugely sanctioned. We see people weep, shout, kiss in airports; we see them at the furthest edges of excitement and exhaustion. Airports are privileged spaces where we can see the primal states writ large—fear, recognition, hope. But there are some of us, perhaps, sitting at the departure gate, boarding passes in hand, who feel neither the pain of separation nor the exultation of wonder; who alight with the same emotions with which we embarked; who go down to the baggage carousel and watch our lives circling, circling, circling, waiting to be claimed.

COMMENT

"This project takes its title from a pre-9/11 experience of the Iranian filmmaker Jafar Panahi, in spring 2001, while traveling from a festival in Hong Kong to one in Buenos Aires. Transiting through JFK, he was detained by INS officials, shackled to a bench in a crowded cell for several hours, and ultimately sent back to Hong Kong in handcuffs. Panahi's description of this ordeal was widely circulated online. He wanted to explain his story to fellow passengers: 'I'm not a thief! I'm not a murderer! . . . I am just an Iranian, a filmmaker. But how could I tell this, in what language?'

"As fellow brown-skinned travelers, we could not ignore this tale. It became a point of departure for what this project became: a song cycle about people in airports, narratives of lives in transit. Filtered through our hyphenated perspectives, these stories are airport myths, documenting the experiences of the new global worker.

"The airport is not a neutral place. It serves as a contact zone for those empowered or subjugated by globalization. It is a center of commerce and a crossroads of cultures, as well as a place that enforces its own globo-consumer culture. It is a frontier, a place of conflict and quarantine, reception, departure, and detention.

"This is our commentary on the non-neutrality of transit. It is not just a collection of travelers' tales, but also a series of views on history and human migration. It is our attempt to make sense of the tumultuous world around us. We hope that you will do the same."

—Vijay Iyer and Mike Ladd, liner notes from *In What Language?*

269

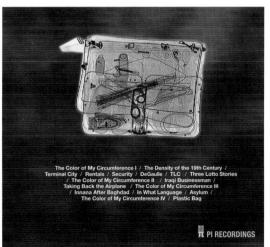

The Color of My Circumference I / The Density of the 19th Century / Terminal City / Rentals / Security / DeGaulle / TLC / Three Lotto Stories / The Color of My Circumference II / Iraqi Businessman / Taking Back the Airplane / The Color of My Circumference III / Innana After Baghdad / In What Language / Asylum / The Color of My Circumference IV / Plastic Bag

PI RECORDINGS

◀ **CD cover for *In What Language?* (2003).** Vijay Iyer (b. 1973) and Mike Ladd (b. 1970) created an entire CD of music — a fusion of hip hop and jazz — devoted to the topic of the post-9/11 airport. Vijay Iyer is the son of Indian immigrants who draws from African, Asian, and European traditions in his music. His other discs include *Panoptic Modes* (2001) and *Blood Sutra* (2003). He collaborated with hip-hop performer Mike Ladd for *In What Language?* Ladd has published in literary magazines and written and produced several other "political" albums, including *Welcome to the Afterfuture* (1999) and *The Infesticons: Gun Hill Road* (2000). (© Nick Zlonis)

270

MESSAGE

How would you define a "transit lounger"? What, literally, does the term refer to? What space would such an individual inhabit? Pico Iyer writes in detail about the negative aspects of transit loungers and very briefly about their pleasures or the advantages of being one. After reading his essay, what advantages do you think he omits?

METHOD

Iyer's essay was written before the events of September 11, 2001, which changed the nature of airport travel. Read the liner notes and study the CD cover for *In What Language?* on p. 269. If you can, go online and listen to a couple of the songs on the CD. What do songwriters do with language when they're trying to express complicated political ideas? How effective is descriptive or metaphorical language when it's used in a song as opposed to in an essay?

MEDIUM

Imagine that you are an architect or interior designer who has been asked to come up with a plan for a new airport. What changes would you make from the existing airports you know? What elements would you leave the same? What would be the overall goal of your design? To what extent would your plan account for comfort, efficiency, accessibility, security? What other concerns would it address?

SACRED SPACES

ESSAY | POEM | 3 PHOTOS

A sacred place is a site that has a spiritual significance for a nation, a people, a community, or even an individual. Sacred places often inspire awe, mystery, and a reverential connection with a charismatic figure or with a key moment of history. Some sacred places are well known in major religions, such as the holy cities Mecca to Muslims and Bethlehem to Christians. Some public sites become sacred to a community because they were the scene of an enormous catastrophe, such as the site of the destroyed World Trade Center or the battlefield at Gettysburg that Lincoln regarded as hallowed ground; or the scene of a great moral achievement, such as the site of Martin Luther King's 1965 civil rights demonstration in Selma, Alabama.

One person's sacred space may be far different from another's — for example, one person may feel a sense of awe in visiting Elvis Presley's Graceland mansion in Memphis, Tennessee, while another may experience a similar emotion in visiting Emily Dickinson's house in Amherst, Massachusetts. But sacred places need not be public sites, as the materials gathered here show. They can be places we privately consider sacred — where we go for solace, serenity, transcendence, or perhaps sheer isolation from the world.

N. Scott Momaday, *The Way to Rainy Mountain*. N. Scott Momaday brings together both the public and private dimensions of a sacred space: Rainy Mountain is a significant ancestral landmark for his people, the Kiowas, as well as the site near which his beloved grandmother is buried. On a visit to Rainy Mountain, which stands in the Oklahoma plains, Momaday reflects on the meaning of a place made sacred by both the habitation of his vanishing people and the enduring legacy of his deceased ancestors. Momaday was born in 1934 in Lawton, Oklahoma, and grew up on an Indian reservation. He has published widely in several media: poetry, prose, memoir, and history. Originally published in *The Reporter* in 1967, "The Way to Rainy Mountain" introduces Momaday's book of the same title, in which he explores the history and mythology of the Kiowa people.

N. Scott Momaday
THE WAY TO RAINY MOUNTAIN

A single knoll rises out of the plain in Oklahoma, north and west of the Wichita Range. For my people, the Kiowas, it is an old landmark, and they gave it the name Rainy Mountain. The hardest weather in the world is there. Winter brings blizzards, hot tornadic winds arise in the spring, and in summer the prairie is an anvil's edge. The grass turns brittle and brown, and it cracks beneath your feet. There are green belts along the rivers and creeks, linear groves of hickory and pecan, willow and witch hazel. At a distance in July or August the steaming foliage seems almost to writhe in fire. Great green and yellow grasshoppers are everywhere in the tall grass, popping up like corn to sting the flesh, and tortoises crawl about on the red earth, going nowhere in the plenty of time. Loneliness is an aspect of the land. All things in the plain are isolate; there is no confusion of objects in the eye, but *one* hill or *one* tree or *one* man. To look upon that landscape in the early morning, with the sun at your back, is to lose the sense of proportion. Your imagination comes to life, and this, you think, is where Creation was begun.

I returned to Rainy Mountain in July. My grandmother had died in the spring, and I wanted to be at her grave. She had lived to be very old and at last infirm. Her only living daughter was with her when she died, and I was told that in death her face was that of a child.

I like to think of her as a child. When she was born, the Kiowas were living the last great moment of their history. For more than a hundred years they had controlled the open range from the Smoky Hill River to the Red, from the headwaters of the Canadian to the fork of the Arkansas and Cimarron. In alliance with the Comanches, they had ruled the whole of the southern Plains. War was their sacred business, and they were among the finest horsemen the world has ever known. But warfare for the Kiowas was preeminently a matter of disposition rather than of survival, and they never understood the grim, unrelenting advance of the U.S. Cavalry. When at last, divided and ill-provisioned, they were driven onto the Staked Plains in the cold rains of autumn, they fell into panic. In Palo Duro Canyon they abandoned their crucial stores to pillage and had nothing then but their lives. In order to save themselves, they surrendered to the soldiers at Fort Sill and were imprisoned in the old stone corral that now stands as a military museum. My grandmother was spared the humiliation of those high gray walls by eight or ten years, but she must have known from birth the affliction of defeat, the dark brooding of old warriors.

Her name was Aho, and she belonged to the last culture to evolve in North America. Her forebears came down from the high country in western Montana nearly three centuries ago. They were a mountain people, a mysterious tribe of hunters whose language has never been positively classified in any major group. In the late seventeenth century they began a long migration to the south and east. It was a journey toward the dawn, and it led to a golden age. Along the way the Kiowas were befriended by the Crows, who gave them the culture and religion of the Plains. They acquired horses, and their ancient nomadic spirit was suddenly free of the ground. They acquired Tai-me, the sacred Sun Dance doll, from that moment the object and symbol of their worship, and so shared in the divinity of the sun. Not least, they acquired the sense of destiny, therefore courage and pride. When they entered upon the southern Plains they had been transformed. No longer were they slaves to the simple necessity of survival; they were a lordly and dangerous society of fighters and thieves, hunters and priests of the sun. According to their origin myth, they entered the world through a hollow log. From one point of view, their migration was the fruit of an old prophecy, for indeed they emerged from a sunless world.

Although my grandmother lived out her long life in the shadow of Rainy Mountain, the immense landscape of the continental interior lay like memory in her blood. She could tell of the Crows, whom she had never seen, and of the Black Hills, where she had never been. I wanted to see in reality what she had seen more perfectly in the mind's eye, and traveled fifteen hundred miles to begin my pilgrimage.

Yellowstone, it seemed to me, was the top of the world, a region of deep lakes and dark timber, canyons and waterfalls. But, beautiful as it is, one might have the sense of confinement there. The skyline in all directions is close at hand, the high wall of the woods and deep cleavages of shade. There is a perfect freedom in the mountains, but it belongs to the eagle and the elk, the badger and the bear. The Kiowas reckoned their stature by the distance they could see, and they were bent and blind in the wilderness.

Descending eastward, the highland meadows are a stairway to the plain. In July the inland slope of the Rockies is luxuriant with flax and buckwheat, stonecrop and larkspur. The earth unfolds and the limit of the land recedes. Clusters of trees, and animals grazing far in the distance, cause the vision to reach away and wonder to build upon the mind. The sun follows a longer course in the day, and the sky is immense beyond all comparison. The great billowing clouds that sail upon it are shadows that move upon the grain like water, dividing light. Farther down, in the land of the Crows and Blackfeet, the plain is yellow. Sweet clover takes hold of the hills and bends upon itself to cover and seal the soil. There the Kiowas paused on their way; they had come to the place where they must change their lives. The sun is at home on the plains. Precisely there does it have the certain character of a god. When the Kiowas came to the land of the Crows, they could see the dark lees of the hills at dawn across the Bighorn River, the pro-fusion of light on the grain shelves, the oldest deity ranging after the solstices. Not yet would they veer southward to the caldron of the land that lay below; they must wean their blood from the northern winter and hold the mountains a while longer in their view. They bore Tai-me in procession to the east.

A dark mist lay over the Black Hills, and the land was like iron. At the top of a ridge I caught sight of Devil's Tower upthrust against the gray sky as if in the birth of time the core of the earth had broken through its crust and the motion of the world was begun. There are things in nature that engender an awful quiet in the heart of man; Devil's Tower is one of them. Two centuries ago, because they could not do otherwise, the Kiowas made a legend at the base of the rock. My grandmother said:

274

> Eight children were there at play, seven sisters and their brother. Suddenly the boy was struck dumb; he trembled and began to run upon his hands and feet. His fingers became claws, and his body was covered with fur. Directly there was a bear where the boy had been. The sisters were terrified; they ran, and the bear after them. They came to the stump of a great tree, and the tree spoke to them. It bade them climb upon it, and as they did so it began to rise into the air. The bear came to kill them, but they were just beyond its reach. It reared against the tree and scored the bark all around with its claws. The seven sisters were borne into the sky, and they became the stars of the Big Dipper.

From that moment, and so long as the legend lives, the Kiowas have kinsmen in the night sky. Whatever they were in the mountains, they could be no more. However tenuous their well-being, however much they had suffered and would suffer again, they had found a way out of the wilderness.

My grandmother had a reverence for the sun, a holy regard that now is all but gone out of mankind. There was a wariness in her, and an ancient awe. She was a Christian in her later years, but she had come a long way about, and she never forgot her birthright. As a child she had been to the Sun Dances; she had taken part in those annual rites, and by then she had learned the restoration of her people in the presence of Tai-me. She was about seven when the last Kiowa Sun Dance was held in 1887 on the Washita River above Rainy Mountain Creek. The buffalo were gone. In order to consummate the ancient sacrifice—to impale the head of a buffalo bull upon the medicine tree—a delegation of old men journeyed into Texas, there to beg and barter for an animal from the Goodnight herd. She was ten when the Kiowas came together for the last time as a living Sun Dance culture. They could find no buffalo; they had to hang an old hide from the sacred tree. Before the dance could begin, a company of soldiers rode out from Fort Sill under orders to disperse the tribe. Forbidden without cause the essential act of their faith, having seen the wild herds slaughtered and left to rot upon the ground, the Kiowas backed away forever from the medicine tree. That was July 20, 1890, at the great bend of the Washita. My grandmother was there. Without bitterness, and for as long as she lived, she bore a vision of deicide.

Now that I can have her only in memory, I see my grandmother in the several postures that were peculiar to her: standing at the wood stove on a winter morning and turning meat in a great iron skillet; sitting at the south window, bent above her beadwork, and afterwards, when her vision failed, looking down for a long time into the fold of her hands; going out upon a cane, very slowly as she did when the weight of age came upon her; praying. I remember her most often at prayer. She made long, rambling prayers out of suffering and hope, having seen many things. I was never sure that I had the right to hear, so exclusive were they of all mere custom and company. The last time I saw her she prayed standing by the side of her bed at night, naked to the waist, the light of a kerosene lamp moving upon her dark skin. Her long, black hair, always drawn and braided in the day, lay upon her shoulders and against her breasts like a shawl. I do not speak Kiowa, and I never understood her prayers, but there was something inherently sad in the sound, some merest hesitation upon the syllables of sorrow. She began in a high and descending pitch, exhausting her breath to silence; then again and again—and always the same intensity of effort, of something that is, and is not, like urgency in the human voice. Transported so in the dancing light among the shadows of her room, she seemed beyond the reach of time. But that was illusion; I think I knew then that I should not see her again.

Houses are like sentinels in the plain, old keepers of the weather watch. There, in a very little while, wood takes on the appearance of great age. All colors wear soon away in the wind and rain, and then the wood is burned gray and the grain appears and the nails turn red with rust. The windowpanes are black and opaque; you imagine there is nothing within, and indeed there are many ghosts, bones given up to the land. They stand here and there against the sky, and you approach them for a longer time than you expect. They belong in the distance; it is their domain.

Once there was a lot of sound in my grandmother's house, a lot of coming and going, feasting and talk. The summers there were full of excitement and reunion. The Kiowas are a summer people; they abide the cold and keep to themselves, but when the season turns and the land becomes warm and vital they cannot hold still; an old love of going returns upon them. The aged visitors who came to my grandmother's house when I was a child were made of lean and leather, and they bore themselves upright. They wore great black hats and bright ample shirts that shook in the wind. They rubbed fat upon their hair and wound their braids with strips of colored cloth. Some of them painted their faces and carried the scars of old and cherished enmities. They were an old council of warlords, come to remind and be reminded of who they were. Their wives and daughters served them well. The women might indulge themselves; gossip was at once the mark and compensation of their servitude. They made loud and elaborate talk among themselves, full of jest and gesture, fright and false alarm. They went abroad in fringed and flowered shawls, bright beadwork and German silver. They were at home in the kitchen, and they prepared meals that were banquets.

There were frequent prayer meetings, and great nocturnal feasts. When I was a child I played with my cousins outside, where the lamplight fell upon the ground and the singing of the old people rose up around us and carried away into the darkness. There were a lot of good things to eat, a lot of laughter and surprise. And afterwards, when the quiet returned, I lay down with my grandmother and could hear the frogs away by the river and feel the motion of the air.

Now there is a funeral silence in the rooms, the endless wake of some final word. The walls have closed in upon my grandmother's house. When I returned to it in mourning, I saw for the first time in my life how small it was. It was late at night, and there was a white moon, nearly full. I sat for a long time on the stone steps by the kitchen door. From there I could see out across the land; I could see the long row of trees by the creek, the low light upon the rolling plains, and the stars of the Big Dipper. Once I looked at the moon and caught sight of a strange thing. A cricket had perched upon the handrail, only a few inches away from me. My line of vision was such that the creature filled the moon like a fossil. It had gone there, I thought, to live and die, for there, of all places, was its small definition made whole and eternal. A warm wind rose up and purled like the longing within me.

The next morning I awoke at dawn and went out on the dirt road to Rainy Mountain. It was already hot, and the grasshoppers began to fill the air. Still, it was early in the morning, and the birds sang out of the shadows. The long yellow grass on the mountain shone in the bright light, and a scissortail hied above the land. There, where it ought to be, at the end of a long and legendary way, was my grandmother's grave. Here and there on the dark stones were ancestral names. Looking back once, I saw the mountain and came away.

Jesse DeMartino, *Jason and Mike at the Cabin Near Huntsville, Texas, 1996*.
This photograph is from DeMartino's three-year project of photographing
skateboarders. The exhibit, called *Keep on Rolling: The Skateboarders of
Houston,* was shown at Rice University. Jesse DeMartino's work has been
featured in *DoubleTake, Aperture, Shots,* and *Creative Camera.* (© Jesse
DeMartino)

Stephen Dunn, *The Sacred*. In Stephen Dunn's poem, "The Sacred," a teacher asks the students "if anyone had a sacred space." After the usual squirming that such a question triggers, there's an unexpected answer. Is it possible a *car* could be a sacred space? Not a religious site, not a historical monument, not a favorite wilderness spot — but your own *car*? Dunn's poem reminds us that once we begin seriously to consider the full meaning of sacred places, we may discover more than we anticipated. Stephen Dunn teaches creative writing at the Richard Stockton College of New Jersey. He has received numerous awards for his poetry, including the 2000 Pulitzer Prize for Poetry for *Different Hours* (2000).

Stephen Dunn
THE SACRED

After the teacher asked if anyone had
a sacred place
and the students fidgeted and shrank

in their chairs, the most serious of them all
said it was his car,
being in it alone, his tape deck playing

things he'd chosen, and others knew the truth
had been spoken
and began speaking about their rooms,

their hiding places, but the car kept coming up,
the car in motion,
music filling it, and sometimes one other person

who understood the bright altar of the dashboard
and how far away
a car could take you from the need

to speak, or to answer, the key
in having a key
and putting it in, and going.

Mitch Epstein, *Cocoa Beach, Florida, 1983.* Born in Holyoke, Massachusetts, in 1952, Mitch Epstein studied at the Rhode Island School of Design and Cooper Union in New York City. Epstein is one of the principal figures of the New Color Photography, a movement that borrows principles from *abstract art* and helps give color photographs the artistic status previously accorded only to black and white. His widely published work appears in a number of international collections, including the Museum of Modern Art. His books include *In Pursuit of India* (1987), *Fire, Water, Wind* (1996), *Vietnam: A Book of Changes* (1996), and *The City* (2001). (© 1983 Black River Productions, Ltd./Mitch Epstein, courtesy of Brent Sikkema, New York)

MESSAGE

How would you summarize the meaning of Stephen Dunn's "The Sacred"? Why, for instance, do you think the setting is a classroom? When someone finally answers that his sacred place is his car, why do others know "the truth / had been spoken"? We often speak of knowing a meaning as "having the key" to something. How does that metaphor become literal in the last lines of the poem? What is the "key" to this poem?

METHOD

How does N. Scott Momaday in "The Way to Rainy Mountain" layer a sense of space with the act of storytelling? How is his writing stimulated by a link between the Kiowa landscape and ancestral legends and stories? What similarities do you see between the Kiowa tales he relates and his own method of composition?

MEDIUM

Painters, writers, poets, philosophers, and others have explored the sacred for thousands of years — usually focusing on religious iconography or narratives from the Bible and other holy books. What is your sacred space, whether personal or public? What medium would you choose to show it to others (a photograph, a poem, a CD, or something else) — and why would that medium work best?

CYBERSPACE

Does cyberspace consist of real places such as San Francisco, Florida State University, and your local pizzeria? Or, as Jonathan G. S. Koppell argues in "No 'There' There," is it merely a figure of speech, a common way of talking with no basis in physical reality? When you visit an e-store and fill up your "shopping cart," you aren't literally in a store or actually wheeling a cart. Or are you? Some new media thinkers — and futurists — believe we are heading toward a "convergence" of cyberspace and the physical environment as new technology rapidly blurs the boundaries between the real and the virtual. In other words, we're heading toward the fictional world of William Gibson's 1984 science fiction classic, *Neuromancer.* As Gibson writes, "I coined the term 'cyberspace' in 1981 in one of my first science fiction stories and subsequently used it to describe something that people insist on seeing as a sort of literary forerunner of the Internet."

The question of just how real are the electronic places we visit on the Internet is becoming a controversial topic for artists, academics, and legal scholars, who see a number of issues — ranging from the legitimacy of art works to free speech — arising from our increasingly frequent travel into cyberspace.

281

> go

Go to the Yahoo! home page at www.yahoo.com. Does the home page give you the same invitation as the billboard?

Yahoo! *A Nice Place to Stay on the Internet.* Yahoo! is, by some counts, the most popular search engine on the web — it offers a starting page for people who want to conduct research online, shop, chat with others about common interests or issues, or take part in any of the other myriad activities the Internet offers. There is also a *Yahoo!* print magazine that features the best sites and describes other web-related content. This image was taken from the November/December 2000 issue of *Print: America's Graphic Design* magazine, as part of an article about Black Rocket, the agency in charge of advertising for Yahoo!

Jonathan G. S. Koppell, *No "There" There.* Jonathan
Koppell teaches at the Yale School of Management
and has published widely on public administration
and politics. In this essay, he argues that cyberspace
is really no place at all. This essay first appeared in
the *Atlantic Monthly* in August 2000.

Jonathan G. S. Koppell
NO "THERE" THERE

I'm a pretty Net-savvy guy. I read my morning newspaper online. I buy discount
airline tickets online. I participate in animated sports banter online. I even manage my finances online (if transferring money to cover checks qualifies as "managing my finances"). Still, I have never been to the magical land called cyberspace.

Cyberspace isn't on any map, but I know that it must exist, because it is
spoken of every day. People spend hours in *chat rooms.* They visit *web sites.* They
travel through this electronic domain on an *information superhighway.* The
language we use implies that cyberspace is a place as tangible as France or St.
Louis or the coffee shop on the corner. But why, exactly, should we think of the
Internet as a geographic location? I recently participated in a telephone conference call with people in several other states and countries. Were we all together in
another "place"? I doubt that any of us thought so.

Many would say that it isn't just the act of communicating that makes cyberspace a place but the existence of a community consisting of broadly dispersed
people. But that characteristic is not particularly distinctive. There are communities big and small that do not exist within any physical jurisdiction. Professional
associations, alumni groups, and religious orders are among them. Members of
such groups feel a kinship with other members with whom they have never interacted, in either the real or the virtual sense.

Some would respond, "Those people all had something in common before
they forged connections across boundaries. But cyberspace communities were
created online. There were no prior affinities to bring them together. That's
unique." Is it? Ham radio operators have a global network of friends and acquaintances who came together solely through their use of that instrument. Do they
exist in "hamspace"? And why is the manner in which people make first contact
so significant? Do pen pals exist in "penpalspace"?

One reason that cyberspace is described as a place is to avoid downgrading it
to the status of a mere medium, and perhaps especially to avoid comparisons with

283

SimCity 4. Many video games attempt to create a sense of space, of "there." In Sim City, players manage a cityscape — they fight disasters, plan budgets, and govern hundreds of thousands of people. (*SimCity*™4 © 2003 Electronic Arts Inc. SimCity is a trademark or registered trademark of Electronic Arts Inc. in the U.S. and/or other countries. All rights reserved)

284

COMMENT

"Every SimCity is an ideal city, a site of pure subjectivity. The city you end up with will be a projection of nothing but you, your sublimity and goofiness included. Choose your terrain, alter the landscape in accordance with whatever inner vision satisfies you, select the basic architectural style you want and start zoning. Whatever happens will be a result of your choices. The game offers an odd mix of vulnerability and power, and it is deeply satisfying."

—Jeffrey Hammond, critic, essayist

television. Those who would distinguish the Internet from television point out that Web denizens are not mere passive recipients of electronic signals. That may be (partly) true. But telephones and the postal system are also communications media that allow two-way communication. We don't regard them as places.

Thinking of the Internet as a place certainly makes it seem more intriguing. The idea of logging on and entering another space is suggestive in all sorts of ways. It raises issues of consciousness, allows us to think of ourselves as disembodied cybernauts, and sets us apart not just from our primitive ancestors but also from our recent ones. Not incidentally, representing the home computer and AOL membership as a gateway to another dimension helps to sell home computers and AOL memberships. The various Web sites, IPOs, and dot-coms-of-the-day feed on the fervor surrounding our exploration of this strange new land. By morphing the Internet into a destination, cyberspace has become the Klondike of our age. (Curiously, Seattle is reaping the benefits this time around, too.)

Metaphors matter: they can help to shape our views and actions. Consider the widespread acceptance of the term "marketplace of ideas" as a metaphor for free speech. This representation emphasizes one's freedom to enter the arena of discourse, rather than one's ability to be heard. Thus, in the context of campaign-finance regulation, protection of free speech means that unlimited campaign expenditures are sacrosanct, but guaranteeing equal opportunities to reach the electorate is not a consideration. If, in contrast, we imagined not a marketplace but a classroom, enabling the quietest voice to be heard would be more important than protecting the rights of the loudest. Another example is the ill-fated "war on drugs." By conceiving of drugs as an enemy to be defeated in combat, we blind ourselves to many potential solutions. In the context of war the legalization of drugs amounts to capitulation to the enemy—even if it might address many of the problems, such as crime, disease, and chronic poverty, that were used to justify the war in the first place.

For its part, the cyberspace-as-place metaphor raises issues of logic and psychology that may ultimately impede wise management of the Internet. Lawrence Lessig, of Harvard Law School, argues in his book *Code and Other Laws of Cyberspace* (1999) that the government should not sit by while private code (software) writers define the nature of the Internet. Such a seemingly neutral stance, Lessig says, is not neutral but irresponsible. In the case of cyberspace, laissez-faire government simply defers decision-making authority to profit-seeking companies. Guided only by commercial interests, the development of the Internet is skewed to favor the corporation rather than the individual or society as a whole.

The problem, Lessig explains, is that legislatures and courts are reluctant to regulate the Internet. He lays out some compelling reasons why this is so, but he skips a crucial one. Because we think of the Internet as a place, the prospect of "going there" takes on an extra dimension. Legislatures are wary of bringing government to cyberspace—as if it somehow existed in some pure state beyond ordinary society. Judges are reluctant to bring law into this "new" arena, as if applying existing laws to Internet transactions would be tantamount to colonizing

285

Antarctica or the moon. In the context of legal discussions, cyberspace is seen not as a potentially anarchic realm but as a virginal Eden; the introduction of law would not so much bring order as corrupt utopia. Republicans in Congress have vowed to "stand at the door to the Internet" to defend its sanctity. Their "E-Contract 2000" would, for example, prohibit sales taxes in cyberspace for at least five years — as if such a moratorium were needed to nurture the most dynamic sector of the economy. Many Democrats, equally eager to win favor in the industry, also support the concept of an online duty-free "zone."

As it happens, Lessig himself reinforces cyberspace-as-place thinking. He argues that the Internet user exists simultaneously in two "places," a physical location and cyberspace — thus making the application of law somewhat difficult. In reality, the problems created by Internet transactions simply involve making decisions about jurisdiction. Should a criminal computer user, for example, be subject to the laws of the state in which he resides, or to the laws of the state in which the victim resides? This can be a knotty question, but it is not a new problem — not a "cyberspace problem." Such determinations are made every day with respect to telephone and postal transactions. Are these problems more common because of the Internet? Yes. Do they involve more jurisdictions because of the Internet? Yes. But they do not involve their own jurisdiction, any more than matters initiated or conducted through the mails involve "postalspace."

That is not to say that the Internet will have no consequences for governance. The growth of the Internet may gradually shift the locus of authority upward, from local and state governments to the federal government or even international institutions, because as human interactions transcend political boundaries, only governments with broad jurisdictions will be able to monitor certain kinds of behavior and enforce certain kinds of laws. Law and government will adapt accordingly.

The cyberspace-as-place metaphor is probably here to stay. And it has its uses, as do the many other fanciful metaphors we use in everyday speech. But let's not be misled. The regulation of cyberspace — in areas from copyright to taxation to privacy — hardly represents the spoliation of a pristine and untamed land.

Noah D. Zatz, ***Sidewalks in Cyberspace.*** The way widespread use of the Internet affects our democratic society is the subject of a highly influential essay that appeared in the *Harvard Journal of Law and Technology* (Fall 1998), in which Noah D. Zatz addresses a wide range of difficult issues stemming from the ways that cyberspace has altered our concepts of public forums, assembly, and free speech. Although the essay is too technical and lengthy to include in this text, the argument did require Zatz to add a section ("Mapping Physical and Electronic Space") that briefly and systematically clarifies what he considers to be the similarities and differences among the various kinds of space we currently inhabit. His concise classification of spatial concepts—such as distance, adjacency, and fixity—serves as a useful starting point for all subsequent discussion of the issue.

Noah D. Zatz
SIDEWALKS IN CYBERSPACE

MAPPING PHYSICAL AND ELECTRONIC SPACE

Relationships among ordinary, physical places are primarily structured by relationships of distance and direction. Places occupy fixed locations in space, and although the significance of fixed relative location is substantially influenced by technological interventions and social practices,[1] geography matters nonetheless.[2] All other things being equal, places that are geographically close are causally intertwined more tightly than those far apart, though the extent to which this is true varies substantially with the nature of the causal mechanisms.[3]

In the material environment, spatial relationships are not symmetrical in all directions. A store should generally be far more concerned by garbage in front of its entrance than by the same garbage an equal distance above, below, or behind it. Perhaps more important, when moving a given distance *between* places, one always travels *through* other places.[4] Our efforts to move through space efficiently create bottlenecks, such as streets, sidewalks, and airport terminals, where people

287

---

[1] New York and Los Angeles may, in many senses, be closer to one another than to many points intermediate on the map.

[2] A store in downtown Manhattan would generally be wise to spend its money advertising in New York City rather than Buenos Aires, even if the people of Buenos Aires might be equally interested in its wares.

[3] For the purposes of the shared effects of a chemical spill, the Upper East Side and East Harlem will be tied to each other much more closely than either is to the Lower East Side, while changes in New York City policy toward abandoned buildings would yield a different ordering.

[4] Driving from New York to Delaware is not simply a question of traversing a given distance, but of going through New Jersey.

The Sims. In The Sims, the game is life — you have a body, a house, a job, relationships; and you have to get up in the morning and get stuff done. (*The Sims*™2 © 2003 Electronic Arts Inc. SimCity is a trademark or registered trademark of Electronic Arts Inc. in the U.S. and/or other countries. All rights reserved)

gather simply because they are on their way someplace else, and locations such as malls and business districts, where people congregate to take advantage of shared needs and low transportation costs. All of these bottlenecks are potential sites of blockade. Anything that enters a given place must pass through some other place adjacent to it. Any shopper who enters the store must pass by the picketer standing out front.

Cyberspace is different. Although within its bounds a discrete cyber-place may be substantially similar to analogous "real world" places, the relationships *among* cyber-places are vastly different. Three features are particularly salient: distance, adjacency, and fixity.

1. Distance

The most widely heralded spatial characteristic of cyberspace is its erasure of distance. Cyberspace, like many communication and transportation technologies before it, in significant ways eliminates and therefore equalizes distance. The distance between any two websites, for instance, is just the entry of a new Uniform Resource Locator ("URL," for example, <http://jolt.law.harvard.edu/>), as is the distance between home and the airline ticket counter, library, or fashion boutique. This conclusion, however, is somewhat misleading because it assumes that one already knows where one is going. Nonetheless, cyber-distance is at least highly contingent and compressible. Although your first journey might require a long and winding road, a simple "bookmark" makes your second visit just a step across the street.

2. Adjacency

Except that there is no street to cross. The lack of direction and continuity in cyberspace means that there are no fixed spaces that lie between any other two, nor is the environment of one place affected much by any other. There are no neighbors in cyberspace and, therefore, no blockades, no loud noise bothering you from the disco next door, and no neighbor's tree dropping fruit on your side of the fence.

Of course, there *are* important and interesting relationships of adjacency on the Web via hypertext links between sites. These relationships, however, are neither symmetrical nor exclusive, unlike in the material environment. That site A has a link to site B creates a limited spatial relationship between them, in the sense that visitors to A are more likely to travel to B than they would be in the absence of the link. In contrast to movement between neighboring plots of land, the ease of moving from A to B says nothing about the ease of moving from B to A. Moreover, since one can always go directly to B from any other point on the Web simply by entering its URL directly or by using a bookmark, there is no site through which one must pass in order to reach B.

3. Fixity

As is apparent from the preceding discussion, cyberspace is not simply a disordered set of places. There are important spatial relationships among sites, but they are of a different character than those among places in our material environment. Of particular import is the relative contingency of cyberspatial orderings. Relative to the physical environment, the spatial relationship between two places in cyberspace can easily shift based on how one arrives at a given place, or through the passage of time.

First, they are contingent upon one's course and means of travel. Not only is the relationship of adjacency asymmetrical, and thus contingent upon which of two sites one visits first, but the distance between two sites may be modified by a path through a third. Thus, site C may link to site A, while site D links to A and B. If one comes to A via C, the spatial relationship of A to B is different than if one comes to A via D, having passed an alternate path toward B. This sort of relationship is readily apparent in search engines — the closest thing cyberspace has to a highway system and whose function is to facilitate travel to other places. A search for "Corps" might place AmeriCorps and the Marine Corps in close proximity, while one could easily compose searches which would yield one but not the other.

Secondly, spatial relationships are highly subject to change over time. Whereas building a new road or airport, tearing down or building walls, or relocating the site of a store are time-consuming and costly affairs, adding or deleting links, changing keywords for search engines, bookmarking (or memorizing) an address, and moving a website to a new Internet Protocol ("IP") address are much less capital- and labor-intensive undertakings. When purchasing a parcel of land, "location is everything"; a substantial fraction of its price will reflect not the material characteristics of the place itself but its spatial relationships to other sites. Cyberspace, by contrast, disaggregates internal features of the place from its spatial characteristics.

While this feature renders the spatial ordering of cyberspace less reliable, it also leaves it more open to purposeful intervention. Although the spatial ordering of our physical landscape is a social construction in the sense that its particular form can be explained in terms of social processes of decision-making, the spatial ordering of cyberspace has far less permanence. Once built, a website's *persistence* over time far more reflects a continuing social choice than the permanence of a bridge at a given site, despite subsequent regrets. Having built an information superhighway without sidewalks, we can still add them on without displacing either the roadway or the places abutting it.

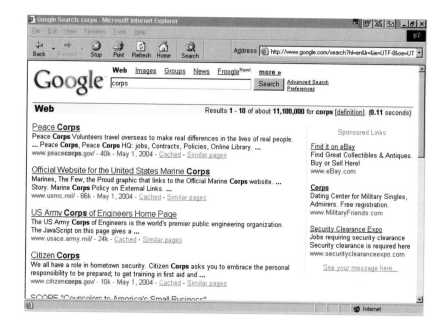

Google. This search for "Corps" demonstrates what Zatz is saying: "a search for 'Corps' might place AmeriCorps and the Marine Corps in close proximity, while one could easily compose searches which would yield one but not the other." (Google Inc.)

MESSAGE	METHOD	MEDIUM
What differences does Noah D. Zatz find between physical and electronic space? Do you think he considers the differences to be more critical than the similarities? Make a list of the key differences and similarities. Do you think Jonathan Koppell and Noah Zatz are basically in agreement about the "reality" of cyberspace? Can you detect any fundamental differences between their assessments of both spaces?	Note that Zatz's classification system is largely abstract. How does he help you visualize the concepts of distance, adjacency, and fixity? Why do you think he titles this section of his essay "Mapping Physical and Electronic Space"? In what sense is he mapping— or is that, as Koppell might argue, itself only a metaphor?	"One reason that cyberspace is described as a place," says Koppell, "is to avoid downgrading it to the status of a mere medium." Is that what Koppell believes it is? If so, in what way would the Internet be a medium rather than a place? In what sense would thinking about cyberspace as a medium be a "downgrading"? In your opinion, is the Internet a medium like television? Or is it something much different? Do *you* think of it as a place?

291

Assignment I

This chapter focuses on the spaces we tend to spend most of our lives occupying, such as home, transit spaces, food and sports venues, even cyberspace. However, these categories are by no means all-inclusive of the places we inhabit and help to shape in the world. What other kinds of categories could have been used in this chapter? You might cite shopping malls or grocery stores (consumer spaces) or schools (educational spaces) as broad categories that could have been included. You might argue that nature (as a space) should occupy a separate category from "sacred spaces" for some important reasons. In creative teams, gather materials to help others think about the importance of some alternate spaces — your goal is to pull together a new cluster for this chapter. What kinds of genres should you represent? Draw from a variety of sources to encourage the most lively discussion and thought from your readers. When you've pulled together a collection of interesting material, present your concept and cluster to the class. Choose your submissions thoughtfully, and design your presentations persuasively — because your classmates will vote on which cluster is the most thought-provoking cluster and best choice for inclusion in the chapter.

Steve Satushek, *Boy Running in Field* (iconica image bank, A0018-000109)

Assignment 2

You've seen a wide variety of images in this chapter: artistic and journalistic photography, digital graphics, and advertising, to name a few. As the clusters show us,
images play a large role in shaping spaces in our world. In virtually no other area
are they more influential than that of advertising, as we glimpse through the
images offered in this section of the book. In the Home cluster, however, we see
refreshingly candid photos of the spaces some of us call home. These images
touch us with their truth and simplicity in many ways. Look for images featured in
advertising and media that represent home to consumers. You might start your
search in home/lifestyle publications like *Better Homes and Gardens* or *Martha
Stewart Living*—or explore the recent media trend in home decorating/design
programs (*Trading Spaces, Queer Eye for the Straight Guy, Clean Sweep, Home
Free,* to name a few). Analyze your examples carefully: What concepts or ideals
are being sold to consumers? How is the modern "American Dream" of homeownership being represented? What does it mean to be a homeowner today?
What sort of homes are we expected to live in, and what are we supposed to fill
them with? Who is responsible for creating these home spaces? What do the
images project about how we are to live, and how do they relate to Nicole Lamy's
mother's reaction to her project, or Bill Bamberger's captioned photos of new
homeowners presented in this chapter? What do the recent remodeling programs
say about the current ways in which we live? Explore your answer to these questions in the medium of your choice: an essay, collage, poetry, or something else.

Federal Home Loan Bank of Seattle, *Report on lending initiatives.* The lending report for this bank, which
has a unique policy that gives 10 percent of yearly
earnings to affordable housing projects, focuses on
portraits of people that have purchased homes. It's
organized around the question "What does it mean to
thrive?" and is a nice example of the ways that marketing portrays the space of safe home and family.
(Design and photo: Methodologie, Seattle)

1. Using John Edgar Wideman's "First Shot" (p. 244) as a model, write a short autobiographical narrative that describes as accurately as possible the precise place where you did something for the first time. Choose an event, as Wideman does, that would come to have significance for you over time. For example, basketball came to be an extremely important part of his life.

2. Do you think that an advertising agency would agree with Nicholas Howe's feelings about fast-food franchises? If so, how might they use Howe's warm assessment of franchises as the basis for a new advertising campaign? After reading "Fast-Food America" (p. 257) carefully, meet in small groups and try to design either a print ad or a TV commercial that would be grounded in Howe's appreciation. Imagine, for example, that you represent one of America's many fast-food franchises (or make up your own). What visuals would you create to support Howe's positive attitude? What would your headline or tagline be? Remember, all the ads we see now for such franchises are already positive: what *new* positive features would your campaign emphasize?

3. Both Nicole Lamy in "Life in Motion" (p. 230) and Judith Ortiz Cofer in "Silent Dancing" (p. 44) write personal essays in which they review their lives in

relation to visual material — Lamy's photographs and Cofer's home movie. What similarities are there between the essays? In an essay of your own, discuss how visual material can be introduced in writing. Do you think it always enhances the text? For example, should some stills from Cofer's home movie have been included with her essay? Remember, when Lamy's essay was first published, it did not feature the photographs. Which essayist is better at handling visual information? What standards would you use to make this evaluation? Consider, too, which writer is more influenced by visual media in constructing her essay.

4. Artists and travel writers are often accused of trying to make places more appealing or glamorous than they truly are — that is, of "romanticizing" them. Why do you think they do this? Find a selection in this chapter (or in the book as a whole) in which you think the author or artist has romanticized a place. Do you think N. Scott Momaday (p. 272) romanticizes the Kiowa landscapes or Nicholas Howe (p. 257) the fast-food franchises? Does Bill Bamberger (p. 236) do the same in his photographs of first-time homeowners?

5. Consider Mitch Epstein's *Cocoa Beach, Florida, 1983* (p. 279). How does your eye process that photograph? In an essay, discuss the photo. What

SHAPING SPACES

information do you think Epstein wants it to convey? How is the picture angled and structured to best convey that information? After studying the photograph detail by detail, describe any information you found that you did not process at first but rather sensed, perhaps subconsciously. Did you screen out some details when you initially looked at the photo? Try to articulate the process by which certain subconscious elements eventually became part of your conscious interpretation. (This exercise, of course, could be applied to any other photograph in the book as well.)

6. The ad for Yahoo! (p. 282) plays on the idea that the Internet offers places to stay (like a hotel) where you meet new friends or romantic partners (who tell you that you look cute today). Using specific examples of sites that offer communities, write an essay about whether or not the Internet is "a nice place to stay." Do the groups that exist in chat rooms or other virtual communities indeed share a sense of place and connection? Or is the medium, as some people have claimed, always one of isolation, one where people actually interact less than they would without it?

7. After reading the cluster introduction to "Sacred Spaces" (p. 271) and after considering the selections, try this thought experiment: What do you

think would be the *opposite* of a sacred space? In a short essay, try describing one such space. Would it necessarily be a public site? Can you provide a concrete example? Can you find examples of such spaces in this chapter or elsewhere in the book?

8. As explained at the start of this chapter, the word "cyberspace" was coined by novelist William Gibson, author of the 1984 science fiction novel *Neuromancer*. Locate a copy of the novel and read it; then, in a research paper, discuss the significance of that term to Gibson's novel. What particular meaning does it have in the novel? How is the word mainly used today? Has its meaning changed? Do you view cyberspace as a real place or an imaginary one? Explain, using screen shots from this book or the web to support your points.

9. Imagine that you are in film school and a group of your classmates has decided, after reading John Edgar Wideman's "First Shot" (p. 244), to make a short documentary of the event. How would you go about doing this? What details of the essay would you select to expand? Would you eliminate anything? At what moment would you begin? How would you conclude? Would you introduce Wideman himself into the film? How many characters would you need? Would your film's general

WRITING, RESEARCHING, COLLABORATING

tone be realistic, gritty, or poetic? Would you shoot in color or black and white? What dialogue, if any, would you include? Form several small groups, and after breaking the essay down into approximately ten "shots," briefly describe in the outline form of a rough script or a storyboard what each shot would look like so that someone could visualize the sequence and imagery of your short film.

10. Consider Pico Iyer's "Nowhere Man" (p. 266) and Nicholas Howe's "Fast-Food America" (p. 257) in relation to each other and to the excerpt to

Noah D. Zatz's "Sidewalks in Cyberspace" (p. 287). After reading the essays, work in small groups to collaboratively construct a working definition of "transit space." Try to articulate a brief definition — several sentences long — that will account for all the kinds of spaces that you agree belong to that category. For example, though neither Iyer nor Howe mentions them, are sidewalks an example of transit space? Afterwards, the groups can compare definitions and discuss their relative inclusiveness and effectiveness.

SHAPING SPACES

4

MAKING HISTORY

As Americans, we seem to toggle between two diametrically opposed attitudes toward history. On the one hand, we feel that history is — as the industrialist Henry Ford once said — "more or less bunk." This dismissive attitude encapsulated the sentiment of a young, pragmatic nation that believed in the unlimited promise of future progress and the futility of dwelling on the past. Today educators and professional historians regularly complain about the average citizen's woeful lack of historical knowledge, often referring to it as a "national amnesia."

On the other hand, why is the History Channel one of the country's most successful cable TV stations? Founded in 1995 and running twenty-four hours a day, with almost all original programming, the channel reaches nearly eighty million households. Its managers believe that they have tapped into a phenomenal surge in historical interest, and the ratings prove it. Add to this the enormous popularity of such historical films as *Titanic, The Patriot, Gladiator,* and *The Passion of the Christ,* and it seems reasonable to conclude that, despite the concerns of educators, we have an almost obsessive interest in history, both our own and the world's.

Historians, however, may argue that public interest in historical programs and movies only proves their point: what Americans want is not genuine history but history packaged as popular entertainment. If you distort the facts, play fast and loose with accuracy, introduce box-office stars, and invent a romantic relationship to drive a story line, then the public might digest a few spoonfuls of history. But does anyone really believe that what actually occurred during the *Titanic*'s fateful cruise bears any resemblance to what happens in the film, with its fabricated love story and facile moralizing? The commercial pressure to entertain a large audience, many historians argue, inevitably leads to carica-

ture and oversimplification. History then becomes just another commodity. In fact, the History
Channel capitalizes on its popularity and familiar logo by selling a variety of merchandise, from videotapes to home furnishings.

Since the past has vanished, how do we accurately recover it? How can we capture what it was like
to live in another time? Films, photographs, and preserved or restored sites can offer some sense of
the texture of the past — and some blockbusters budget astronomically for sets and costumes trying
to make us feel the physical presence of the past — but the problem with trying to encounter an
authentic past is that history, even just yesterday's, can only be imagined. It cannot truly be relived
because for that to occur the past itself would need to become present, a condition that so far
remains only within the realm of science fiction. This basic, insurmountable fact leads to a substantial
amount of historical distortion, no matter what the medium. We see actors in films set in Elizabethan
times displaying the cosmetically bright smiles of modern dentistry, while also speaking, gesturing,
and behaving like contemporary Americans. We visit ancient sites wearing audio-tour headsets. We
visit restored eighteenth-century villages equipped with wheelchair ramps and smoke detectors, and
we find signs that no individual from that era could possibly make sense of: No Smoking, Rest Rooms,
Ye Olde Gift Shoppe.

Because we are locked into our shared present, it is virtually impossible to know the past. This is
true not only of our material re-creations of history but of our interpretive renditions as well. We read
popular romances, some set in medieval or even ancient Europe, whose heroines are miraculously
endowed with the insights and values of contemporary feminism. Some historians believe that this

single-perspectivism is unavoidable, that objectivity is unattainable or possibly even politically sinister. For them, the chief task of history is to understand the present by learning how we arrived at where we are. Other historians believe they have an obligation to suspend (or multiply) their own viewpoints and get as close as possible to the mind-set of another era. The great Dutch scholar Johan Huizinga wrote that historians must constantly put themselves "at a point in the past at which the known factors will seem to permit different outcomes." After all, those who fought at the Battle of Gettysburg did not know how it would end.

To what extent is the history we see, hear, know, or read objective and reliable? And to what extent is it biased and fabricated? These are questions that every educated citizen asks at one time or another, whether watching a television documentary, enjoying a movie, reading a historical novel, visiting a museum, or touring a restored colonial town. How much should contemporary attitudes affect how history is portrayed? Should Maya Lin (p. 362) have modified her design for the Vietnam Veterans Memorial because certain military groups considered it inappropriately pacifist? What part should multicultural sensitivities play in our reconstructions of history? That is, in the interests of truth and accuracy, should old enemies be depicted in the racist fashion they once were? Does "softening" the picture so as not to offend distort the record?

As more visual information becomes increasingly available and as new electronic technologies make factual data more accessible than ever before, the line between popular and academic history may grow even fuzzier. Over time, the movie versions of events, it seems, become as attached to those events as do any of the legitimate historical sources and documents; for some critics and historians,

Vietnam films like *The Deer Hunter*, *Apocalypse Now*, *Platoon*, or *Full Metal Jacket* are as much a part of our collective Vietnam experience as the My Lai Massacre or the evacuation of Saigon. The Internet has also opened historical "channels" that allow many people outside the customary academic or publishing hierarchies to put their own (or their community's) memories, stories, documents, and images on public record. Though this still leaves us with the obligation to sift the significant from the trivial or the factual from the fictive, it nevertheless advances the possibility of what socially minded historians have long been calling for: a less elitist history, a "history from below."

Whatever approach we take to history — whether we view it as an interpretation of the present, a reconstruction of the past, or a prophetic window into the future — it will continue to exert a powerful presence in our lives. We can now safely say that Henry Ford's famous dictum is self-refuting "bunk" — if it had been correct, it would not have been remembered. And we can also safely say that history's power can be the source of great understanding or great misery. Three months before he blew up the Alfred P. Murrah Federal Building in Oklahoma City in 1995, Timothy McVeigh — who saw history as prophesy — wrote to the American Legion: "Does anyone even STUDY history anymore???"

Context

The image you see here is the cover to the official program for a march for women's voting rights that took place in 1913. To understand this image, you have to read it in its historical **context**. That means knowing something about the social, economic, and political situation in 1913, the accepted roles of women and men, the history of black suffrage (African American men got the vote in 1867) — even the iconography of Joan of Arc marching into battle, which this image echoes. Thinking about history means thinking about context. All the clusters in this chapter invite you to explore a historical moment, problem, or idea; the way individual pieces are grouped provides some context for reading. But when reading history, remember that the more you know about context, the clearer — or more complicated — the picture becomes.

Official Program, Woman Suffrage Procession, 1913.
(Library of Congress, digital id #CPH3A21392)

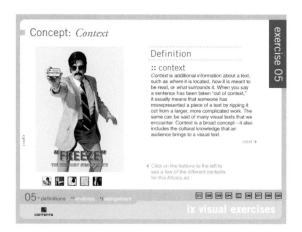

 Go to **ix visual exercises** to explore context as it applies to visual texts.

(Reprinted with permission of Callard & Bower-Suchard, Inc.)

COMPOSING AMERICA

2 ESSAYS | 5 DOCUMENTS

The Library of Congress is a repository for many important documents that are almost synonymous with the United States of America: the Declaration of Independence, the Emancipation Proclamation, the Bill of Rights. We tend to think of such official statements as polished manifestos created by a united government. Each of these documents, however, represents a composition: an argument or statement drafted first by one person, then revised by committee. This cluster considers the history of the composition of one of America's most precious historical documents, the Declaration of Independence. Anyone can view the Declaration at the National Archives in Washington, D.C. Yet many citizens who visit this iconic display are unaware that the impressive document in front of them is not the original Declaration, but rather the third, "official" calligraphic version. Essays by Thomas Starr and James Munves reconstruct the history of this founding document and the implications and impact of the medium of its delivery—whether longhand, typography, or calligraphy. A PowerPoint presentation that converts another priceless document, the Gettysburg Address, into bulleted talking points invites us to consider our evolving ideas about effective composition and presentation.

303

To explore these and other important documents archived by the Library of Congress, go to bedfordstmartins.com/ convergences.

3 Declarations. *From left to right:* draft, print, calligraphy. ▶ Jefferson's hand-corrected draft was rushed to printer John Dunlap, who typeset the broadside that was published throughout the colonies. Most Americans at the time who were politically informed and persuaded by the Declaration saw only the typeset text. On the right is a facsimile of the calligraphic, "official" document that we know today as the iconic Declaration. (*draft:* Library of Congress, negative #LC-MSS 27748-i; *broadside:* Courtesy of The Massachusetts Historical Society; *calligraphy:* National Archives)

A Declaration by the Representatives of the UNITED STATES OF AMERICA, in General Congress assembled.

When in the course of human events it becomes necessary for one people to dissolve the political bands which have connected them with another, and to assume among the powers of the earth the separate and equal station to which the laws of nature & of nature's god entitle them, a decent respect to the opinions of mankind requires that they should declare the causes which impel them to the separation.

We hold these truths to be self-evident; that all men are created equal & independent; that from that equal creation they derive rights inherent & inalienable, among which are the preservation of life, & liberty, & the pursuit of happiness; that to secure these ends, governments are instituted among men, deriving their just powers from the consent of the governed; that whenever any form of government shall becomes destructive of these ends, it is the right of the people to alter or to abolish it, & to institute new government, laying it's foundation on such principles & organising it's powers in such form, as to them shall seem most likely to effect their safety & happiness. prudence indeed will dictate that governments long established should not be changed for light & transient causes: and accordingly all experience hath shewn that mankind are more disposed to suffer while evils are sufferable, than to right themselves by abolishing the forms to which they are accustomed. but when a long train of abuses & usurpations [begun at a distinguished period, &] pursuing invariably the same object, evinces a design to reduce them under absolute Despotism, it is their right, it is their duty, to throw off such government & to provide new guards for their future security. such has been the patient sufferance of these colonies; & such is now the necessity which constrains them to expunge their former systems of government. the history of the present king of Great Britain is a history of unremitting injuries & usurpations, [among which appears no solitary fact to contradict the uniform tenor of the rest but all have] in direct object the establishment of an absolute tyranny over these states. to prove this, let facts be submitted to a candid world, for the truth of which we pledge a faith yet unsullied by falsehood.

IN CONGRESS

A DECLARATION

BY THE REPRESENTATIVES OF THE

UNITED STATES OF AMERICA,

IN GENERAL CONGRESS ASSEMBLED.

WHEN in the Course of human Events, it becomes necessary for one People to dissolve the Political Bands which have connected them with another, and to assume among the Powers of the Earth, the separate and equal Station to which the Laws of Nature and of Nature's God entitle them, a decent Respect to the Opinions of Mankind requires that they should declare the Causes which impel them to the Separation.

WE hold these Truths to be self-evident, that all Men are created equal, that they are endowed by their Creator with certain unalienable Rights, that among these are Life, Liberty, and the Pursuit of Happiness—That to secure these Rights, Governments are instituted among Men, deriving their just Powers from the Consent of the Governed, that whenever any Form of Government becomes destructive of these Ends, it is the Right of the People to alter or to abolish it, and to institute new Government, laying its Foundation on such Principles, and organizing its Powers in such Form, as to them shall seem most likely to effect their Safety and Happiness. Prudence, indeed, will dictate that Governments long established should not be changed for light and transient Causes; and accordingly all Experience hath shewn, that Mankind are more disposed to suffer, while Evils are sufferable, than to right themselves by abolishing the Forms to which they are accustomed. But when a long Train of Abuses and Usurpations, pursuing invariably the same Object, evinces a Design to reduce them under absolute Despotism, it is their Right, it is their Duty, to throw off such Government, and to provide new Guards for their future Security. Such has been the patient Sufferance of these Colonies; and such is now the Necessity which constrains them to alter their former Systems of Government. The History of the present King of Great-Britain is a History of repeated Injuries and Usurpations, all having in direct Object the Establishment of an absolute Tyranny over these States. To prove this, let Facts be submitted to a candid World.

HE has refused his Assent to Laws, the most wholesome and necessary for the public Good.

HE has forbidden his Governors to pass Laws of immediate and pressing Importance, unless suspended in their Operation till his Assent should be obtained; and when so suspended, he has utterly neglected to attend to them.

HE has refused to pass other Laws for the Accommodation of large Districts of People, unless those People would relinquish the Right of Representation in the Legislature, a Right inestimable to them, and formidable to Tyrants only.

HE has called together Legislative Bodies at Places unusual, uncomfortable, and distant from the Depository of their public Records, for the sole Purpose of fatiguing them into Compliance with his Measures.

HE has dissolved Representative Houses repeatedly, for opposing with manly Firmness his Invasions on the Rights of the People.

HE has refused for a long Time, after such Dissolutions, to cause others to be elected; whereby the Legislative Powers, incapable of Annihilation, have returned to the People at large for their exercise; the State remaining in the mean time exposed to all the Dangers of Invasion from without, and Convulsions within.

HE has endeavoured to prevent the Population of these States; for that Purpose obstructing the Laws for Naturalization of Foreigners; refusing to pass others to encourage their Migrations hither, and raising the Conditions of new Appropriations of Lands.

HE has obstructed the Administration of Justice, by refusing his Assent to Laws for establishing Judiciary Powers.

HE has made Judges dependent on his Will alone, for the Tenure of their Offices, and the Amount and Payment of their Salaries.

HE has erected a Multitude of new Offices, and sent hither Swarms of Officers to harrass our People, and eat out their Substance.

HE has kept among us, in Times of Peace, Standing Armies, without the consent of our Legislatures.

HE has affected to render the Military independent of and superior to the Civil Power.

HE has combined with others to subject us to a Jurisdiction foreign to our Constitution, and unacknowledged by our Laws; giving his Assent to their Acts of pretended Legislation:

FOR quartering large Bodies of Armed Troops among us:

FOR protecting them, by a mock Trial, from Punishment for any Murders which they should commit on the Inhabitants of these States:

FOR cutting off our Trade with all Parts of the World:

FOR imposing Taxes on us without our Consent:

FOR depriving us, in many Cases, of the Benefits of Trial by Jury:

FOR transporting us beyond Seas to be tried for pretended Offences:

FOR abolishing the free System of English Laws in a neighbouring Province, establishing therein an arbitrary Government, and enlarging its Boundaries, so as to render it at once an Example and fit Instrument for introducing the same absolute Rule into these Colonies:

FOR taking away our Charters, abolishing our most valuable Laws, and altering fundamentally the Forms of our Governments:

FOR suspending our own Legislatures, and declaring themselves invested with Power to legislate for us in all Cases whatsoever.

HE has abdicated Government here, by declaring us out of his Protection and waging War against us.

HE has plundered our Seas, ravaged our Coasts, burnt our Towns, and destroyed the Lives of our People.

HE is, at this Time, transporting large Armies of foreign Mercenaries to compleat the Works of Death, Desolation, and Tyranny, already begun with circumstances of Cruelty and Perfidy, scarcely paralleled in the most barbarous Ages, and totally unworthy the Head of a civilized Nation.

HE has constrained our fellow Citizens taken Captive on the high Seas to bear Arms against their Country, to become the Executioners of their Friends and Brethren, or to fall themselves by their Hands.

HE has excited domestic Insurrections amongst us, and has endeavoured to bring on the Inhabitants of our Frontiers, the merciless Indian Savages, whose known Rule of Warfare, is an undistinguished Destruction, of all Ages, Sexes and Conditions.

IN every stage of these Oppressions we have Petitioned for Redress in the most humble Terms: Our repeated Petitions have been answered only by repeated Injury. A Prince, whose Character is thus marked by every act which may define a Tyrant, is unfit to be the Ruler of a free People.

NOR have we been wanting in Attentions to our British Brethren. We have warned them from Time to Time of Attempts by their Legislature to extend an unwarrantable Jurisdiction over us. We have reminded them of the Circumstances of our Emigration and Settlement here. We have appealed to their native Justice and Magnanimity, and we have conjured them by the Ties of our common Kindred to disavow these Usurpations, which, would inevitably interrupt our Connections and Correspondence. They too have been deaf to the Voice of Justice and of Consanguinity. We must, therefore, acquiesce in the Necessity, which denounces our Separation, and hold them, as we hold the rest of Mankind, Enemies in War, in Peace, Friends.

WE, therefore, the Representatives of the UNITED STATES OF AMERICA, in General Congress, Assembled, appealing to the Supreme Judge of the World for the Rectitude of our Intentions, do, in the Name, and by Authority of the good People of these Colonies, solemnly Publish and Declare, That these United Colonies are, and of Right ought to be, FREE AND INDEPENDENT STATES; that they are absolved from all Allegiance to the British Crown, and that all political Connection between them and the State of Great-Britain, is and ought to be totally dissolved; and that as Free and Independent States, they have full Power to levy War, conclude Peace, contract Alliances, establish Commerce, and to do all other Acts and Things which INDEPENDENT STATES may of right do. And for the support of this Declaration, with a firm Reliance on the Protection of divine Providence, we mutually pledge to each other our Lives, our Fortunes, and our sacred Honor.

Signed by ORDER and in BEHALF of the CONGRESS,

JOHN HANCOCK, PRESIDENT.

ATTEST.

CHARLES THOMSON, SECRETARY.

PHILADELPHIA: PRINTED BY JOHN DUNLAP.

IN CONGRESS, JULY 4, 1776.

The unanimous Declaration of the thirteen united States of America,

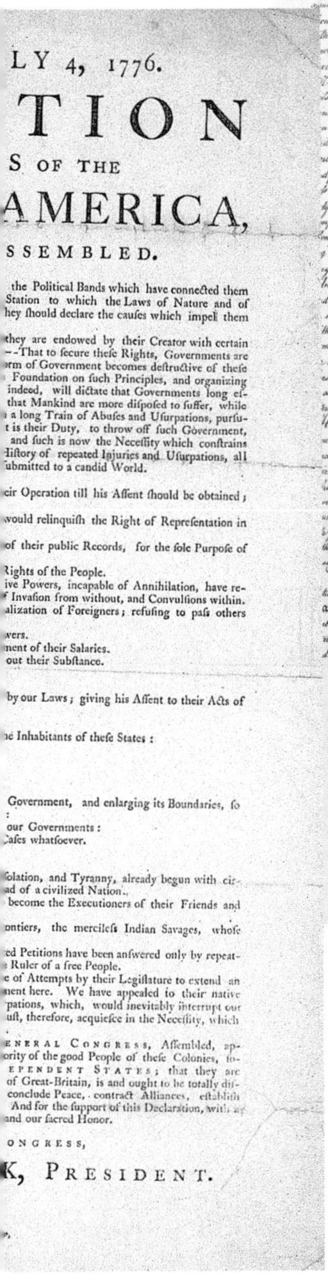

LY 4, 1776.

TION

S OF THE

AMERICA,

SSEMBLED.

the Political Bands which have connected them
Station to which the Laws of Nature and of
hey fhould declare the caufes which impel them

they are endowed by their Creator with certain
--That to fecure thefe Rights, Governments are
orm of Government becomes destructive of thefe
Foundation on fuch Principles, and organizing
indeed, will dictate that Governments long ef-
that Mankind are more difpofed to fuffer, while
a long Train of Abufes and Ufurpations, purfu-
t is their Duty, to throw off fuch Government,
and fuch is now the Neceffity which conftrains
Hiftory of repeated Injuries and Ufurpations, all
ubmitted to a candid World.

eir Operation till his Affent fhould be obtained;

would relinquifh the Right of Reprefentation in

of their public Records, for the fole Purpofe of

Rights of the People.
ive Powers, incapable of Annihilation, have re-
Invafion from without, and Convulfions within.
alization of Foreigners; refufing to pafs others

wers.
ment of their Salaries.
out their Subftance.

by our Laws; giving his Affent to their Acts of

e Inhabitants of thefe States:

Government, and enlarging its Boundaries, fo

our Governments:
Cafes whatfoever.

folation, and Tyranny, already begun with cir-
ad of a civilized Nation.
become the Executioners of their Friends and

ontiers, the mercilefs Indian Savages, whofe

ed Petitions have been anfwered only by repeat-
Ruler of a free People.
e of Attempts by their Legiflature to extend an
ment here. We have appealed to their native
pations, which, would inevitably interrupt our
uft, therefore, acquiefce in the Neceffity, which

ENERAL CONGRESS, Affembled, ap-
ority of the good People of thefe Colonies, fo-
EPENDENT STATES; that they are
of Great-Britain, is and ought to be totally dif-
conclude Peace, contract Alliances, eftablifh
And for the fupport of this Declaration, with a
and our facred Honor.

ONGRESS,

K, PRESIDENT.

Thomas Starr, *The Real Declaration*. Thomas Starr, an associate professor of graphic design at Northeastern University, points out that the "official" handwritten document on display appeared some two months after a hastily printed version was distributed throughout the thirteen colonies. Why did Congress commission a calligraphic version in the first place? What does that decision say about democracy? (From *The Boston Globe*, June 29, 2003, p. D5)

Thomas Starr

THE REAL DECLARATION

At a time when the United States is attempting to spread democracy abroad, the Declaration's promise of "life, liberty, and the pursuit of happiness" seems more important than ever. We uphold the iconic calligraphy on parchment as the very document that expresses the principles on which our country is based. But in fact, that document expresses something quite different.

In early June 1776, Thomas Jefferson, Benjamin Franklin, John Adams, Robert R. Livingston, and Roger Sherman were appointed by the Continental Congress to collectively prepare a declaration on independence. Jefferson composed the text. It was revised by committee members before being presented to Congress on June 28. Although the vote for independence took place on July 2, the entire Congress then spent two days deleting a third of the text and making 39 additions and alterations. The text completed on July 4, like the government of the country it founded, was a collective effort.

The manuscript, which must have been so heavily edited as to be almost indecipherable, was sent that day to a typographer, not a calligrapher. John Dunlap, printer to Congress, took on what was surely the most important overnight printing job in history. The "Dunlap prints" were sent to the colonies, where they were often reset in type and republished locally. No holiday is more specific about its date than "the Fourth." What we commemorate that day is the first complete assembly of the Declaration's words, in type.

The work of declaring independence throughout the 13 colonies was the work of either a Dunlap print or one of its typographic descendants. Within two weeks the typographic text had already been republished in 24 newspapers, including two in Boston on July 18. That same day, at 1 P.M., the Declaration was proclaimed from the balcony of what is now the Old State House, an event re-enacted each July 4th at 10 A.M.

The calligraphic document was created only afterward; it was ordered on July 19 and not completed and signed until August 2. In 1776, Congress used calligraphy as a formalizing medium to add legitimacy to its most important papers, a tradition left over from monarchy. Publishing in type, however, was the medium of democracy. It is contradictory, then, that the symbol of our independence is the regal calligraphic document, rather than the humble, pluralistic Dunlap prints.

Calligraphy reveres the hand of the author by idealizing handwriting, which is not uniformly legible to readers. Typography idealizes and standardizes the letters of the alphabet, making them more accessible. Calligraphy implies a single author, and the product of the calligrapher is a singular document. Typography easily accommodates and assumes multiple authorship by merging many collaborators and edits into a seamless whole; type exists to produce multiple documents. Calligraphy is exclusive, elite, and vulnerable to loss or destruction; the calligraphic Declaration is now so faded that it is completely unreadable, more an image than a text. Typography is inherently plural and democratic. And because they are multiples, typeset texts are difficult to lose or destroy.

Collectivity is the essence of a democracy. The Declaration was collective in authorship, audience, and content. Its authors worked collaboratively and as representatives of others. Its audience comprised inhabitants of 13 distinct colonies distributed over a wide area. Its content fused readers into a union of equals. Its form of identical typographic prints perfectly reflected this. To underscore the role of typographic publication, Congress included it among its alterations to the Declaration: "We therefore . . . solemnly *publish* and declare . . ."

This July 4, as in 1776, all Americans are in equality with the Declaration. None of us will have access to the icon. But we all have equal access to the text. Through typography it remains ubiquitous, readily available to every American. We can find it in our homes in encyclopedias and almanacs. It is in libraries and bookstores. And, of course, it can be printed endlessly from the Web.

In January 1776, an ordinary citizen published a pamphlet that turned the tide of public sentiment in favor of independence. Thomas Paine's "Common Sense," which sold 100,000 copies that year alone—the equivalent of 9 million copies in contemporary America—paved the way for Congress to act that summer. Today, with technology on our desks that would be the envy of John Dunlap, we can all join in the collective debate that is democracy. We are all typographers and printers.

307

James Munves, *Going to Press*. Thomas Jefferson began working on the first draft of the Declaration in June 1776. By the end of the month he submitted it to a small committee (which included Benjamin Franklin and John Adams) for revision before it went to the entire Continental Congress, which made major changes. It was that manuscript—full of deletions, additions, and alterations—that went to the printer on July 4, 1776. In "Going to Press," James Munves provides a narrative history of the document's transformation from manuscript to print to calligraphy. Munves has written numerous historical narratives for young adults and older audiences; his most recent publication is *The Kent State Coverup* (2001). He has also written a novel, *Andes Rising* (1999). This chapter is reprinted from his book on the Declaration's composition, *Thomas Jefferson and the Declaration of Independence* (1978).

James Munves
GOING TO PRESS

There is no record of which of the five committee members went to the shop of John Dunlap to oversee the printing. Was it Jefferson, Adams, or that old printer and former employer of John Dunlap's uncle William, Benjamin Franklin? The printing was a rush job. As propaganda, the Declaration would be treated as a broadside (poster) printed on one side of a sheet of paper for display, with capital letters used to attract attention rather than in accordance with grammatical rules.

The rules of grammar in the eighteenth century were, in any case, not as firmly fixed as they are now. Nouns were capitalized haphazardly for emphasis. Jefferson went to the other extreme and used capital letters very sparingly—only at the beginnings of paragraphs and in the names of nations (Great Britain) or peoples (Indians). He used even fewer capital letters than we do today (leaving even *god* in lowercase). With all this, his style was closer to what came later than that of his contemporaries.

In setting the Declaration in type, Dunlap first of all put a new heading at the top:

IN CONGRESS, JULY 4, 1776.

In the body of the Declaration, Dunlap capitalized the entire first word of each paragraph and the first letter of most of the nouns. He also got rid of the ampersands (&), spelling out *and* in all cases....

Draft Declaration of Independence (detail). Thomas Jefferson was assigned the job of drafting the declaration by the Continental Congress. Here you see the numerous edits and additions — eighty-six in all — that were made by John Adams, Benjamin Franklin, and the other members of the committee. This is the document that was delivered to the printer for an overnight rush job. (Library of Congress, negative #LC-MSS 27748-1)

Dunlap's apprentice dipped the leather roller into the greasy ink and squeaked it across the type. Paper was put into position, and the printer pulled the lever. The proof was examined, corrections were made, and the press run began, powered by the brawny arms of the apprentice.

The following morning a copy was glued into the Journal of Congress and others were dispatched to the states and to the troops in the field. The next day, Saturday, July 6, the Declaration appeared in a Philadelphia newspaper, the *Evening Post.*

There still had been no celebration. The members of Congress had little enough time for thoughts about their decision, let alone gaiety. They could think only of the fact of independence and its consequences. They made grim jokes

IN CONGRESS, JULY 4, 1776.

A DECLARATION

BY THE REPRESENTATIVES OF THE

UNITED STATES OF AMERICA,

IN GENERAL CONGRESS ASSEMBLED.

WHEN in the Course of human Events, it becomes neceſſary for one People to diſſolve the Political Bands which have connected them with another, and to aſſume among the Powers of the Earth, the ſeparate and equal Station to which the Laws of Nature and of Nature's God entitle them, a decent Reſpect to the Opinions of Mankind requires that they ſhould declare the cauſes which impell them to the Separation.

We hold theſe Truths to be ſelf-evident, that all Men are created equal, that they are endowed by their Creator with certain unalienable Rights, that among theſe are Life, Liberty, and the Purſuit of Happineſs--That to ſecure theſe Rights, Governments are inſtituted among Men, deriving their juſt Powers from the Conſent of the Governed, that whenever any Form of Government becomes deſtructive of theſe Ends, it is the Right of the People to alter or to aboliſh it, and to inſtitute new Government, laying its Foundation on ſuch Principles, and organizing its Powers in ſuch Form, as to them ſhall ſeem moſt-likely to effect their Safety and Happineſs. Prudence, indeed, will dictate that Governments long eſtabliſhed ſhould not be changed for light and tranſient Cauſes; and accordingly all Experience hath ſhewn, that Mankind are more diſpoſed to ſuffer, while Evils are ſufferable, than to right themſelves by aboliſhing the Forms to which they are accuſtomed. But when a long Train of Abuſes and Uſurpations, purſuing invariably the ſame Object, evinces a Deſign to reduce them under abſolute Deſpotiſm, it is their Right, it is their Duty, to throw off ſuch Government, and to provide new Guards for their future Security. Such has been the patient Sufferance of theſe Colonies; and ſuch is now the Neceſſity which conſtrains them to alter their former Syſtems of Government. The Hiſtory of the preſent King of Great-Britain is a Hiſtory of repeated Injuries and Uſurpations, all

Broadside Declaration of Independence (detail). John Dunlap, the printer, added the new heading at the top of the document: "In Congress, July 4, 1776." This is what we celebrate on Independence Day — the printing of the Declaration. John Hancock sent a copy of the initial printing to George Washington, who had it read to his assembled troops in New York on July 9. (Courtesy of The Massachusetts Historical Society)

about being hanged for treason. "Congress," a New Jersey delegate noted, might soon be "exalted on a high gallows."

On Monday, July 8, the *Pennsylvania Packet* announced, "This day, at twelve o'clock, the Declaration of Independence will be proclaimed at the State House." A small crowd of idlers, unemployed sailors, and a few others gathered around the platform in the State House yard to hear the Declaration read by Colonel John Nixon of the Philadelphia Committee of Safety. Bells were rung all day throughout the city. But the Liberty Bell, then in the State House steeple, probably was not rung. The rickety wooden steeple would have collapsed. The bell had been cast more than twenty years before, to celebrate the fiftieth anniversary of the Pennsylvania Assembly. Its strangely prophetic legend, *Proclaim liberty throughout the land and to the people thereof,* was taken from the Bible (Leviticus 25, 10). The verse referred to the Hebrew custom of leaving the land idle every half-century.

That evening the Declaration was read again on the Commons, at the head of each battalion of Associators (Philadelphia militia), and there was more celebration. John Adams described the scene to his wife:

> Three cheers rended the welkin [sky]. The battalions paraded...and gave us the *feu de joie* [firing of guns in token of joy], notwithstanding the scarcity of powder.

The next evening the Declaration was heard by each brigade of the army in New York, arousing, in Washington's words, "hearty assent" and "warmest approbation." As news of the Declaration spread through the city, a crowd, uncowed by the British fleet—now 130 ships strong—in the harbor, overturned a gilded lead statue of King George III. It was later melted into bullets. Everywhere, in the days that followed, boisterous mobs tore down the symbols of royal authority, whether coats of arms on public buildings or scepters and crowns on the signboards of inns.

Jefferson remained annoyed at the way his Declaration had been edited. He spent many hours making copies of his version to send to Virginia friends to show them what Congress had done to the document. He sent copies to Richard Henry Lee; to the president of the Virginia convention, Edmund Pendleton; to his mentor George Wythe; to his neighbor, the Italian, Philip Mazzei; and probably to his old friend John Page. In some cases, he indicated Congress's changes right on the copies. To Richard Henry Lee, he sent a copy of his final draft along with the Dunlap broadside for comparison. "You will judge," he wrote Lee, "whether it is the better or worse for the Critics."

His friends, as writers' friends are wont to do, sympathized with him. Edmund Pendleton thought that the members of Congress had treated the Declaration just as badly as they had Jefferson's draft of the 1775 Declaration of Causes. They had, Pendleton said, changed it "much for the worse."

Lee wrote back that he wished

> sincerely, as well for the honor of Congress, as for that of the States, that the Manuscript had not been mangled as it is. It is wonderful, and passing pitiful, that the rage of change should be so unhappily applied.

Consolingly, he added that the piece was

> in its nature so good, that no Cookery can spoil the Dish for the palates of Freemen.

The cookery certainly spoiled the dish for the palate of Thomas Jefferson, who put his draft away and scarcely thought about the Declaration for many years. He did, however, along with a number of other members of Congress, sign an ornately hand-lettered (engrossed) copy on August 2, 1776.

311

312

Official Declaration of Independence (detail). Timothy Matlack, who was known for his skill at calligraphy, was given the job of recopying the print version for the "signers." He seems to have run out of room for the long title; he made *of the thirteen united* much smaller so he could fit *States of America* on one line. (National Archives)

This copy, with the signatures of fifty-five signers, is enshrined in the National Archives in Washington. The engrossing was probably done by one of Secretary Thomson's assistants, Timothy Matlack. Matlack had been assigned the hand-lettering job on July 19, when Congress heard that New York had voted in favor of independence.

The new copy reflected New York's action in its title. The document could now boast that the states were unanimous:

The unanimous Declaration of the thirteen united States of America;

instead of, as before:

A DECLARATION By THE REPRESENTATIVES OF THE UNITED STATES OF AMERICA, in GENERAL CONGRESS ASSEMBLED.

(In none of its official transformations has the document borne the title *Declaration of Independence*.)

In copying the Declaration, Matlack accidentally left out two letters of one word and also an entire word. He had to correct these omissions with carets and interlining:

> *en*
> He has dissolved Represtative Houses...
>   ^

>   *only*
> Our repeated petitions have been answered by...
>   ^

He also put an extra *t* in *Brittish,* eliminated all the paragraphing, and used capital letters in a completely haphazard fashion. Dunlap, in following broadside usage, had capitalized almost all the nouns. Matlack capitalized some and not others, following no sort of rule at all.

The signers of the Declaration, fearing hanging, kept their names secret. The engrossed, signed parchment copy was carefully hidden away by Charles Thomson....

313

Gettysburg Address* and Peter Norvig, *PowerPoint Presentation for the Gettysburg Address. On these pages you see two versions of the Gettysburg Address: the calligraphic text of the speech as read by Abraham Lincoln at Gettysburg, and a PowerPoint version created by using the AutoContent Wizard. Try putting the opening of the Declaration of Independence into PowerPoint or any other presentation program: What happens to the message as a result? (*Lithograph:* Rare Books and Special Collections Division, McGill University Libraries, Montreal, Canada; *PowerPoint:* Peter Norvig)

Lincoln's Gettysburg Address

1809 — 1865

November 19, 1863

Four score and seven years ago our fathers brought forth on this continent, a new nation, conceived in liberty, and dedicated to the proposition that all men are created equal.

Now we are engaged in a great civil war, testing whether that nation, or any nation so conceived and so dedicated, can long endure. We are met on a great battlefield of that war. We have come to dedicate a portion of that field, as a final resting place for those who here gave their lives that that nation might live. It is altogether fitting and proper that we should do this.

But, in a larger sense, we can not dedicate ~ we can not consecrate ~ we can not hallow ~ this ground. The brave men, living and dead, who struggled here have consecrated it, far above our poor power to add or detract. The world will little note, nor long remember what we say here, but it can never forget what they did here. It is for us the living, rather, to be dedicated here to the unfinished work which they who fought here have thus far so nobly advanced. It is rather for us to be here dedicated to the great task remaining before us ~ that from these honored dead we take increased devotion to that cause for which they gave the last full measure of devotion ~ that we here highly resolve that these dead shall not have died in vain ~ that this nation, under God, shall have a new birth of freedom ~ and that government of the people, by the people, for the people, shall not perish from the earth.

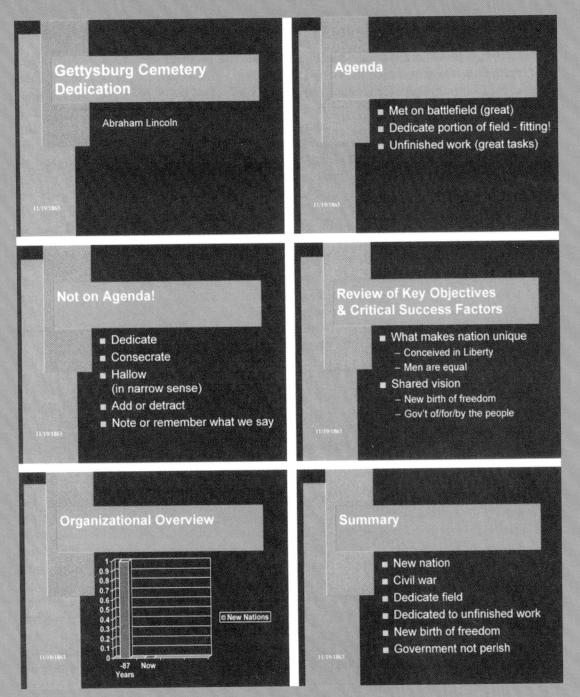

COMMENT

"Imagine a world with almost no pronouns or punctuation. A world where any complex thought must be broken into seven-word chunks, with colorful blobs between them. It sounds like the futuristic dystopia of Kurt Vonnegut's short story 'Harrison Bergeron,' in which intelligent citizens receive earsplitting broadcasts over headsets so that they cannot gain an unfair advantage over their less intelligent peers. But this world is no fiction — it is the present-day reality of a PowerPoint presentation, a reality that is repeated an estimated 30 million times a day.

"Stanford University's Cliff Nass was quoted in the *New Yorker* saying that PowerPoint 'lifts the floor'; it allows some main points to come across even if the speaker mumbles, forgets, or is otherwise grossly incompetent. But PowerPoint also 'lowers the ceiling'; it makes it harder to have an open exchange between presenter and audience, to convey ideas that do not neatly fit into outline format, or to have a truly inspiring presentation. This is what I was getting at when I created the Gettysburg PowerPoint presentation, a parody that has been viewed by hundreds of thousands of frustrated PowerPoint sufferers. I used PowerPoint's AutoContent Wizard, adding only the slide 'Not on Agenda!' to the standard format."

— Peter Norvig, director of search quality at Google

MESSAGE

According to Thomas Starr, how do the typographic and calligraphic texts of the Declaration of Independence send different messages? Why do you think the National Archive displays the calligraphic text? Which text does Starr seem to prefer, and why? He only considers two texts; in your opinion what message would be sent by the manuscript of the first draft, which retains all the committee and congressional revisions?

METHOD

James Munves tells the story of the Declaration as if he were there to see it, as a narrative. How effective is this method of recounting history? Which account do you find more compelling; Munves's narrative or Starr's more academic description? Why?

MEDIUM

Both the draft and the printed versions of the Declaration are similar in that they consist of words on paper (in contrast, the calligraphic text is on parchment). Can you think of other ways the document might be displayed today? For example, would putting the Declaration into electronic media alter its meaning in any way? If so, how?

317

INDIAN GROUND

POEM | 5 IMAGES | ESSAY

If it is virtually impossible to keep the present from influencing our view of the past, it is equally difficult to keep the past from crowding into the present. In his poem "The Texas Chainsaw Massacre," a double exposure of horrifying history and horror movie, Sherman Alexie brings together American popular culture and cultural history. In Colorado in 1864, a volunteer army of some 725 individuals led by Colonel John Chivington, a Methodist minister and prominent antislavery advocate, attacked a small village on the banks of Sand Creek. With authorization "to kill and destroy, as enemies of the country, wherever they may be found, all hostile Indians," they killed more than 125 Cheyenne and Arapaho Indians, most of them women, children, and elderly men. Alexie finds in the blood-drenched horror movie *The Texas Chainsaw Massacre* "the collected history / of America" as he moves from the film's butchery to "the killing grounds" of Sand Creek.

318

The Texas Chainsaw Massacre, 1973. Alexie's poem takes its title from a now-classic horror movie about an insane family of cannibals. Moving from drive-in feature to cult favorite, this film has been the subject of academic and pop culture acclaim (the film is on "top 100" lists, has been selected by the Museum of Modern Art for its permanent collection, and is routinely taught in film classes). The movie was remade and released in 2003. There are many theories that account for the American consumption of the horror movie, which really grew in the 1970s — the most common one being that we enjoy being frightened when we know that nothing can really hurt us. In short, some people want to experience *controlled* terror. (Photofest)

> | go

For more information about Sherman Alexie and the Sand Creek massacre, go to bedfordstmartins.com/ convergences.

Sherman Alexie, *The Texas Chainsaw Massacre.* A Spokane/Coeur d'Alene Indian, Sherman Alexie (b. 1966) grew up on the Spokane Indian Reservation in Wellpinit, Washington. His career as a writer began almost immediately after his graduation from Washington State University in Pullman, where he majored in American studies. Since then he has received many prestigious literary awards, including the Lila Wallace–Reader's Digest Writers' Award and the PEN/ Hemingway Award as well as several awards for screenplays. He wrote the screenplay for the film *Smoke Signals* (1998). "The Texas Chainsaw Massacre" was published in the Summer 1992 issue of *The Kenyon Review*.

320

Sherman Alexie

THE TEXAS CHAINSAW MASSACRE

> What can you say about a movie so horrific even its title scares
> people away?
>
> —Stephen King

I
have seen it
and I like it: The blood,
the way like *Sand Creek*
even its name brings fear,
because I am an American
Indian and have learned
words are another kind of violence.

This vocabulary is genetic.

When Leatherface crushes the white boy's skull
with a sledgehammer, brings it down again and again
while the boy's arms and legs spasm and kick wildly
against real and imagined enemies, I remember

another killing floor

in the slaughter yard from earlier in the film,
all the cows with their stunned eyes and mouths
waiting for the sledgehammer with fear so strong
it becomes a smell that won't allow escape. I remember

the killing grounds

of Sand Creek
where 105 Southern Cheyenne and Arapaho women and children

and 28 men were slaughtered by 700 heavily armed soldiers,
led by Colonel Chivington and his Volunteers. *Volunteers.*

Violence has no metaphors; it does have reveille.

Believe me, there is nothing surprising
about a dead body. This late in the twentieth century
tears come easily and without sense:
taste and touch have been replaced
by the fear of reprisal. I have seen it

and like it: The butchery, its dark humor
that thin line "between art and exploitation,"
because I recognize the need to prove blood
against blood. I have been in places
where I understood *Tear his heart out*
and eat it whole. I have tasted rage
and bitterness like skin between my teeth.

I have been in love.

I first saw it in the reservation drive-in
and witnessed the collected history
of America roll and roll across the screen,
voices and dreams distorted by tin speakers.

Since then, I have been hungry
for all those things I haven't seen.

This country demands that particular sort of weakness:
we must devour everything on our plates
and ask for more. Our mouths hinge open.
Our teeth grow long and we gnaw them down
to prevent their growth into the brain. I have

seen it and like it: The blood,
the way like music
it makes us all larger
and more responsible
for our sins,
because I am an American
Indian and have learned

hunger becomes madness easily.

■ *Horror is a genre that often borrows elements from comedy* —witness the popularity of Scream *and* Scary Movie, *both of which have combined the two. In these lines Alexie refers to "its dark humor / that thin line 'between art and exploitation.'" What do you think he means by that? What do you think Alexie thinks about the horror movie as a genre—he equates* The Texas Chainsaw Massacre *to a real-life massacre, but does he really think they are on the same scale?*

321

COMMENT

"I always tell people that the five primary influences in my life are my father, for his nontraditional Indian stories, my grandmother for her traditional Indian stories, Stephen King, John Steinbeck, and *The Brady Bunch.* That's who I am. I think a lot of Indian artists like to pretend that they're not influenced by pop culture or Western culture, but I am, and I'm happy to admit it. . . . It's a cultural currency."

—Sherman Alexie

Verlyn Klinkenborg, *Sand Creek*. This essay, with accompanying photographs, appeared as the first in a series "on forgotten places that stirred the American conscience" in the November/December 2000 issue of *Mother Jones*. Klinkenborg is one of America's leading nonfiction writers; his work appears in many magazines, including *The New Republic, Harper's, Esquire, National Geographic, The New Yorker, Smithsonian, Audubon*, and *Mother Jones*, where he often contributes the text to photo-essays. A recipient of the Lila Wallace–Reader's Digest Writers' Award and a National Endowment for the Arts Fellowship, he is the author of *Making Hay* (1997) and *The Last Fine Time* (1991).

Verlyn Klinkenborg
SAND CREEK

In southeastern Colorado, about 130 miles from Pueblo, there is a small town called Chivington. Once, it had railroad shops and saloons and as many as 1,500 residents. There was even an East Chivington. But then the railroad shops moved away, taking the people with them, and all that remains of Chivington today is a Friends Church and the ruins of a brick schoolhouse, its roof caved in, its rafters collapsed upon each other like the ambitions of this civic corpse.

Chivington is named after a man who turned from the ministry to the military and made a reputation for himself fit only for a ghost town. The first time Colonel John M. Chivington came through the region he was at the head of some 725 men, members of the 3rd and 1st regiments of the Colorado Cavalry. It was early morning, well before daylight, and the date was November 29, 1864. He passed that way a second time two days later, on his way back southward to Fort Lyon and thence to Denver, where he received a hero's welcome. In the interval, Chivington and his men had ridden down at daybreak upon a village of 500 or 600 Cheyennes and Arapahos camped a few miles north of present-day Chivington on Sand Creek. There, the Colorado troops—most of them volunteers commissioned for a 100-day term of service—murdered between 125 and 160 Indians, mostly women, children, and the elderly. Black Kettle, the chief of one of the Cheyenne clans, had met with Chivington and other military leaders at Camp Weld in Denver in late September, and he believed that his village was at peace with the whites. At the sight of the troops riding toward him, Black Kettle raised a large American flag and a white flag on a lodge pole and stood holding it aloft. When the troops began firing, he fled.

The attack rolled northward from a sharp bend in Sand Creek, and when the shooting was over, Chivington's men returned to the Indian village to mutilate the bodies of the dead and burn their lodges and, almost incidentally, to murder a half-breed prisoner named Jack Smith. Nearly four years later, General William T. Sherman, passing through, stopped at Sand Creek to collect relics. One of his men later wrote, "We found many things, such as Indian baby skulls; many skulls of men and women; arrows, some perfect, many broken; spears, scalps, knives, cooking utensils, and many other things too numerous to mention. We laid over one day and collected nearly a wagon load."

Two of the Cheyennes killed at Sand Creek, War Bonnet and Standing in the Water, had visited Washington the year before and were photographed in the White House conservatory. They had been given a short course in geography and addressed by President Lincoln. "It is the object of this Government to be on terms of peace with you, and with all our red brethren," Lincoln said. "We make treaties with you, and will try to observe them; and if our children should sometimes behave badly, and violate these treaties, it is against our wish."

Lincoln's words must be contrasted with those of a proclamation issued on August 11, 1864, by the territorial governor of Colorado, John Evans. Evans authorized "all citizens of Colorado, either individually, or in such parties as they may organize, to go in pursuit of all hostile Indians on the plains, scrupulously avoiding those who have responded to my call to rendezvous at the points indicated; also, to kill and destroy as enemies of the country, wherever they may be found, all such hostile Indians."

Almost 136 years to the day after that proclamation was issued and Colorado volunteers began to form the 100-day militia, I stood on a sand bluff overlooking the site of the Sand Creek massacre. It is now private property, but legislation has been introduced in Congress by Senator Ben Nighthorse Campbell, who is a Northern Cheyenne, to create a Sand Creek Massacre National Historic Site here.

This is the kind of place, common in the rural West, where you might almost believe that nothing has changed since the event that made it memorable. There are a thousand — ten thousand — shallow washes like it on the high plains: a grassy flood zone, now thickly shaded with cottonwoods, the waters of Sand Creek nearly always in abeyance, except for pools here and there grown round with rushes where cattle stand flank-deep on hot days. Sand Creek flows to the southeast, but just below the massacre site it makes a long eastward bend before turning south again. On a plain near the crook of that bend and to the north of it, Black Kettle's village had stood, one hundred and more buffalo-skin lodges, pony herds grazing on the high ground above the village. Now, in August, the shrill sound of grasshoppers rang out across the undulating flatland beyond Sand Creek. In November, they would have been silent.

It's always an illusion to believe that you can see the past unchanged. In the mid-1970s, a gas company ran a pipeline right through Sand Creek, just above the bend. The 1864 soil level is buried under some ten inches of new soil that has drifted in over the years. In 1887, a town called New Chicago lived for a grasshopper's lifetime just beyond the massacre site, sustained only by the hopes of a railroad coming through someday. Around 1910, local citizens formed the

Colonel John M. Chivington.
Chivington led the cavalry attack at
Sand Creek. (From the Denver
Public Library, Western History
Collection)

324

Cheyenne and Arapaho chiefs. This photo was taken after conversations about peace with U.S. military leaders in Denver. (From the Denver Public Library, Western History Collection)

Chivington Canal Company and dug a canal that angles toward Brandon, a small town just east of Chivington. You can still see the line of the canal where it edges the massacre site. For several years, a farmer tried to raise a crop in the creek bend. New Chicago failed. The canal failed. The crop failed.

And over time, a clear sense of the location of Black Kettle's village had eroded as well. Relics of the kind that General Sherman found in abundance on the surface at Sand Creek had long since disappeared. An inconclusive archaeological study was conducted in 1997 by the state of Colorado. In 1999, the National Park Service—conducting an archaeological reconnaissance with local landowners and tribal representatives from the Northern and Southern Cheyennes and Northern and Southern Arapahos—rediscovered the village site, though there is still some dissent about its actual extent.

In 1950, local citizens placed a stone monument to the massacre on the sand bluff where I stood, a bluff that allows a view of much of the land that would be included in the Sand Creek Massacre historic site. The monument reads "Sand Creek Battle Ground Nov. 29 & 30. 1864," and it shows the head of a generic Indian in profile, looking almost like Liberty in her Indian headdress on the old copper cent, which could have been found in the pockets of Chivington's cavalry. People used to drive to this monument to park and drink and smoke dope and dump their trash and ferret out relics until Bill Dawson, the owner of much of the massacre site and the land that the monument sits upon, closed the access road, partly to stop an unruly traffic but also out of respect for the wishes of the Cheyennes and Arapahos, to whom this site is sacred.

I tried to imagine the running slaughter—it was never really a battle—that began in the slow light of late November, the pony herds cut off, the melee among the lodges, the sullen mutilation that began later that day and continued during the night and into the following day, the scalps flayed from the dead, the breasts cut from women and the scrotums from men to be used as tobacco bags, all attested by witnesses who appeared before military and congressional investigations of Sand Creek in 1865. But the day I stood there, it was too peaceful a place to sustain such memories, and besides, those are memories that belong to the descendants of the people who camped there long ago. The night of November 29, 1864, wrote George Bent, a mixed-blood Cheyenne who survived the attack, "will never be forgotten as long as any of us who went through it are alive." It still lives, vividly, among the Cheyenne and Arapaho.

But before the running slaughter began, there had been a running argument, and that was much easier to imagine. Chivington did not ride down upon a peaceful village in hot blood. Nor did he attack peaceable Cheyennes in ignorance. He had just run for office and lost on a ticket that would have admitted Colorado to statehood. No sooner was the election over than Chivington began laying out his campaign against Black Kettle's village.

Political ambition and intractable moral ferocity drove Chivington, that and a panic caused by Confederate raids in southeastern Colorado and by the murder of the Hungate family—father, mother, and two young children—near Denver by four Arapahos. Two weeks after the Hungate murders, Governor Evans directed "all friendly Indians of the Plains" to separate themselves from hostile Indians and to rendezvous at assigned places of safety. It was precisely such a friendly village, camped in accordance with Evans' directive, that Chivington planned to attack.

He was forcefully confronted at every stage by men who opposed his plan because it meant betraying Black Kettle and the assurances of peace that had been made in council in late September. Though he rode with Chivington, Captain Silas Soule refused to take part in the killing, and he testified against Chivington during the military investigation of Sand Creek in early 1865, an act for which he was shot down on the streets of Denver by a Chivington supporter. The night before the massacre, Lieutenant Joseph Cramer told Chivington that the raid he was planning was murder and a violation of their word as officers and men. "Colonel Chivington's reply," Cramer wrote, "was, that he believed it to be right or honorable to use any means under God's heaven to kill Indians that would kill women and children, and 'damn any man that was in sympathy with the Indians.'" Again that evening Chivington was confronted by a group of officers and civilians, and again he damned their sympathy. Then he ordered his men to mount and ride northward through the night to Sand Creek.

Chivington had decided upon war and upon the deaths of the Cheyennes and Arapahos who favored peace. In the aftermath of Sand Creek, a man named J. W. Wright, outraged at Chivington's actions, neatly summed up the purpose of the massacre in an open letter. "An Indian war is on the country," he wrote. "Every effort has been made for two years to produce it." That war erupted on the Plains the following year. It took Chivington and Sand Creek to make it happen, to set in motion the machinery that would eventually kill Black Kettle, still seeking peace four years later, at Washita, in what is now Oklahoma. There, at dawn, George Armstrong Custer rode down upon Black Kettle's village again, employing Chivington's brutal tactics and his unswerving convictions.

327

Troops storming the Sand Creek. When Chivington's
men rode in, Black Kettle raised an American flag and a
white flag as a sign of peace. (From the Denver Public
Library, Western History Collection)

328

Brian Callahan, *Map of Sand Creek.* (Originally printed in *Mother Jones*)

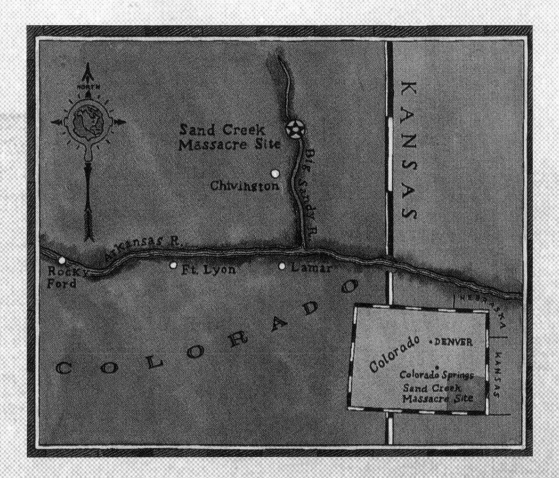

330

MESSAGE

What connection does Sherman Alexie establish between *The Texas Chainsaw Massacre* and the massacre at Sand Creek? Why does the film evoke these historical memories? Alexie says several times that he has seen the movie and liked it — why? What appeals to him about it? Why do you think he repeats the phrase throughout? Do you think his poem is in favor of violence? Try putting the poem's final sentence into your own words.

METHOD

How much information do you need to read this poem? What does Alexie expect you to know? What if you have never seen *The Texas Chainsaw Massacre* or know nothing about Sand Creek — can you still appreciate the poem? Explain how important the historical background is to your understanding. For example, did reading Klinkenborg's "Sand Creek" help you better understand Alexie's poem and position? Does the poem add anything to your reading of the essay?

MEDIUM

Suppose you were creating a documentary film to commemorate the Sand Creek massacre. What elements from Klinkenborg's essay would you want to incorporate? How would you introduce visual information? What Native American artifacts would be important to your vision of the incident? Would you want to include Alexie's poem? Why or why not? What does a poem supply that a documentary film does not, and vice versa?

CHICAGO'S TENEMENTS

One of the prime shaping forces of twentieth-century America was the Great Migration of the late 1930s and 1940s, when African Americans left their rural southern and heartland roots and settled in the northern cities. As thousands came to Chicago's South Side, they permanently altered the city's social and cultural atmosphere, an alteration that can be traced in the novels of Richard Wright, the prose and poetry of Gwendolyn Brooks, and the drama of Lorraine Hansberry, each of whom vividly brings us into impoverished neighborhoods with their crowded "kitchenette" apartments, storefront churches, beauty parlors, pool halls, nightclubs, and saloons. What these writers captured in words was also — around the same time — being permanently documented visually by Wayne F. Miller, a white photographer who decided to document the Great Migration as it affected his native Chicago. Miller's photographs have been praised as an important part of American urban history — but not "headline history." As critic Robert Stepto says of Miller's imagery, "This is news from the street presented in most of its variety."

Wayne F. Miller, *Rabbits for Sale, 1948*. Wayne F. Miller (b. 1918) served as a photographer in the U.S. Navy during World War II and in an illustrious career has worked for many magazines. He helped establish one of the world's major photography shows, *The Family of Man*. Robert Stepto writes that images like this one "record the fact that some migrants worked not in the industries but in the alleyways, selling ice and vegetables and peddling whatever they could from the backs of wagons." All photographs are reproduced from Miller's collected photographs in *Chicago's South Side: 1946–1948* (2000). (All photos © by Wayne F. Miller, courtesy of Wayne F. Miller/Magnum Photos, Inc.)

Wayne F. Miller, *Two Girls Waiting Outside a Tavern.*

Wayne F. Miller, *One-Room Kitchenette*. Kitchenettes often consisted of only one room, like that depicted in this photograph. In her novella *Maud Martha* (1953), Gwendolyn Brooks describes a kitchenette that may have been more comfortable than most: "Their home was on the third floor of a great gray stone building. The two rooms were small. The bedroom was furnished with a bed and dresser, old-fashioned, but in fair condition, and a faded occasional chair. In the kitchen were an oilcloth-covered table, two kitchen chairs, one folding chair, a cabinet base, a brown wooden icebox, and a three-burner gas stove. . . . There was a bathroom at the end of the hall, which they would have to share with four other families who lived on the floor."

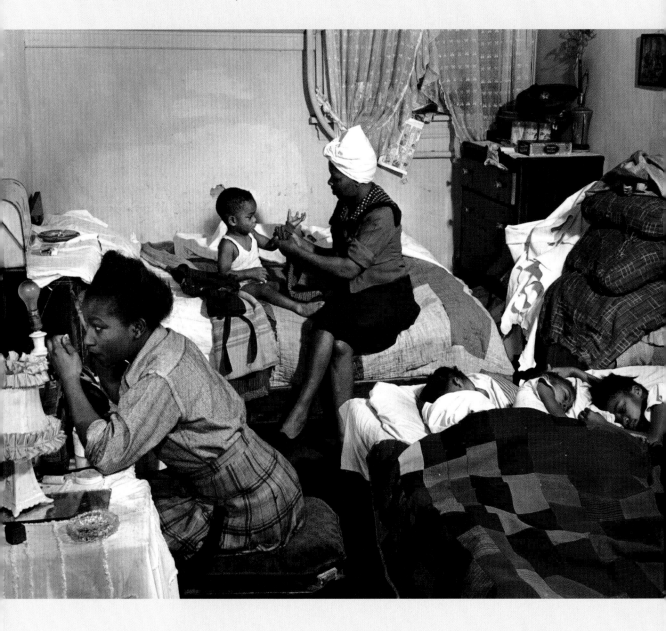

Gwendolyn Brooks, *Kitchenette Building* (1945). One of the nation's most prominent poets, Gwendolyn Brooks (1917–2000) grew up on Chicago's South Side, the setting of the prize-winning collection *A Street in Bronzeville* (1945), which included "Kitchenette Building." The volume garnered much literary attention just about the time Wayne Miller began his photographic project, and Brooks's verbal imagery of crammed apartments and segregated neighborhoods may have stimulated Miller's visual interest in the South Side community.

Gwendolyn Brooks
KITCHENETTE BUILDING

We are things of dry hours and the involuntary plan.
Grayed in, and gray. "Dream" makes a giddy sound, not strong
Like "rent," "feeding a wife," "satisfying a man."

But could a dream send up through onion fumes
Its white and violet, fight with fried potatoes
And yesterday's garbage ripening in the hall,
Flutter, or sing an aria down these rooms

Even if we were willing to let it in,
Had time to warm it, keep it very clean,
Anticipate a message, let it begin?

We wonder. But not well! not for a minute!
Since Number Five is out of the bathroom now,
We think of lukewarm water, hope to get in it.

COMMENT

"[I was convinced] that after the war, with a camera, I might be able to document the things that make this human race of ours a family. We may differ in race, color, language, wealth, and politics. But look at what we all have in common — dreams, laughter, tears, pride, the comfort of home, the hunger of love. If I could photograph these universal truths, I thought that might help us better understand the strangers on the other side of the world — and on the other side of town."

— Wayne F. Miller

Wayne F. Miller, *Three Teenagers in Kitchenette Apartment.*

Gordon Parks, *Speaking for the Past.* Gordon Parks (b. 1912) is an award-winning photographer, composer, and filmmaker; he is also the author of twelve books. This essay is one of three that introduce Wayne F. Miller's *Chicago's South Side, 1946–1948.*

Gordon Parks

SPEAKING FOR THE PAST

I was born a black boy inside a black world. So, like moments rising out of my unfathomed past, many of Wayne Miller's images slice through me like a razor. And I'm left remembering hunks of my time being murdered away as I suffered blistering hot summers or ate the salt of equally cruel winters. For me those crowded kitchenettes, the loneliness of rented bedrooms, and the praying in left-over churches remain an ongoing memory. Here, far from the Kansas prairies where I was spawned, I just couldn't melt into the ghetto's tortuous ways—unlike so many others who, after a hard day's work, numbed the misery with booze and soothing music. "Hello blues. Blues, how do you do?"

New York's Harlem, Chicago's South Side—both cities of blackness crammed inside larger cities of whiteness—offered mostly hunger, frustration, and anger to their tenement dwellers. And those same tenements that imprisoned thousands are still there, refusing to crumble. I recall swarms of slow-moving people passing the chili shacks, rib joints, storefront churches, and funeral parlors—all with the same skin coloring but rarely speaking to one another. When you left your door you walked among strangers. Now there are a few new buildings going up to look smugly down at the old ones. Good music, laughter, and prayers are still in the air, but for many young blacks music, laughter, and prayers offer at most an uneasy peace.

At times I became disgruntled with this social imprisonment, even became angry with myself for not finding a way out. But eventually that anger grew tired of hanging out with me day and night, and little by little it left me alone. And for a long time I remained alone—still desperately searching for bread in the rubbish. That search was awful. I was constantly reaching for something denied me, or perhaps longing for something lost along the way.

338

Slowly the shadow of hope had spread its presence. Anger had fled — running as though it were escaping the violence festering inside me. Then gradually the light that avoided so many other hearts began falling on mine. But be free of doubt. Wayne Miller shows us what I remember most — those garbaged alleys and wintry streets where snowflakes fell like tears, those numberless wooden fire-traps called home, the homeless gathered around flaming trash cans to escape the hawk of winter, those crudely worded signs — COAL 50 cents, WOOD 25 cents — those old men reclining in forgotten chairs left at curbside for moving vans that never showed up. There where funerals had become a habit and hardship never seemed to be out of order.

How feeble the uncertainty! Wayne's camera appears to be inexhaustible as it goes from life to life — abruptly leaving one door to arrive at another. Then somewhere, perhaps a short distance away in a pool hall or restaurant, he finds brothers and sisters of the soul muddling through the grime and sipping Fox Head beer. Yet to some of their fortunate kinfolk that was a small thing. Having swum through the dust, they were now in tuxedos and ball gowns, dancing to the strains of Ellington's uptown music in a softly lit ballroom. "Hug me, sugar, and let the good times roll."

Where, one might ask, does Wayne Miller fit into this chaos that plagued my youth? A good question. Did he possess an insatiable curiosity that had to be fed, or was he perhaps treading the path of any competent photographic journalist? A close acquaintance with him for many years gives shape to my own answer. He was simply speaking for people who found it hard to speak for themselves. And that trait takes full measure of any journalist who is worth his salt. Once when a reporter wrapped that question around his neck, he answered unhesitatingly, and rather bluntly, "I am interested in expressing my subjects. I won't turn a nice guy into a son-of-a-bitch or a son-of-a-bitch into a nice guy. There are people who make pictures and people who take them. I take them. At times I have been so busy capturing what I was seeing that it was impossible to cry and work at the same time. Good images emerge from good dreaming. And, to me, dreaming is so important."

Wayne went to wherever his conscience called him, and his camera's eye baptized whatever confronted him. Earthbound and free of any shadowy miscellany, he made contact with the roots. And as no one can stop the waters flowing, neither can one eliminate his powerful images from our past. They will still be here with us, even if those tenements crumble in time, exhausted.

MESSAGE

What idea does Wayne F. Miller portray in *Rabbits for Sale, 1948*? How does it establish an urban environment? How does it convey the history of the migrant — the rural areas from which many of the new Chicagoans had recently come? What other connotations can you find in Miller's urban image? In what way can this picture be called a slice of history?

METHOD

Compare Wayne F. Miller's *One-Room Kitchenette* with Gwendolyn Brooks's well-known "Kitchenette Building." Remember that these two works were produced at nearly the same time. What verbal and visual images do they share? Gordon Parks quotes Miller as saying, "Good images emerge from good dreaming. And, to me, dreaming is so important." How does this comment help illuminate both photograph and poem? How is dreaming captured literally and figuratively?

MEDIUM

Gordon Parks says in his essay that Miller was "simply speaking for people who found it hard to speak for themselves." How do photographs "speak"? What do you think Miller's *Three Teenagers in Kitchenette Apartment* is saying — both to those represented and to us as viewers?

339

AMERICAN COMIX

The historical and artistic status of America's comic-book superheroes — such popular figures as Spider-Man, Superman, Wonder Woman, and Batman — was vitally enhanced in the summer of 2003 when the History Channel featured them on a special show called *Comic Book Superheroes Unmasked*. Stimulated by the success of such films as *Daredevil* and the Spider-Man and X-Men movies, along with the perennially remade Superman, the documentary (available on DVD) reveals the stories behind the creation of the superheroes as well as the historical contexts in which they performed their astonishing feats. The documentary begins with the creation of Superman in 1938 as the Great Depression was slowly ending and a second world war was looming. Superman ushered in what is now considered the Golden Age of comic books.

Another reason for producing a documentary history of superheroes is that comic books had long been considered trash and their artistry overlooked. As one of today's leading figures in the field, Art Spiegelman, writes: "'comic'" is a misleading word that "often keeps my medium of choice from getting any respect." "Many otherwise literate people," he argues, "even those who have long since crossed the high-low divide and welcomed comic strips like 'Krazy Kat' and 'Little Nemo' into the canon of twentieth-century achievement — right up there next to Picasso's paintings and Joyce's novels — remained predisposed against comic *books*." To demonstrate how artistically outstanding comic books can be, Spiegelman profiles in "Forms Stretched to Their Limits" the "tragically short-lived comic-book giant," Jack Cole (1914–1958), the creator of Plastic Man. Along with the profile of Cole, Spiegelman provides an astute description of how all great art synthesizes the artist's method, medium, and message.

340

> go

To explore the history of other superheroes and their creators, go to bedfordstmartins.com/ convergences.

Plastic Man. Plastic Man is not a superhero who has survived to appear in a blockbuster hit (at least not yet); he did, however, spring from the same mold as his better-known crime fighters. ("Police Comics" #38 © 1945 DC Comics. All Rights Reserved. Used with Permission)

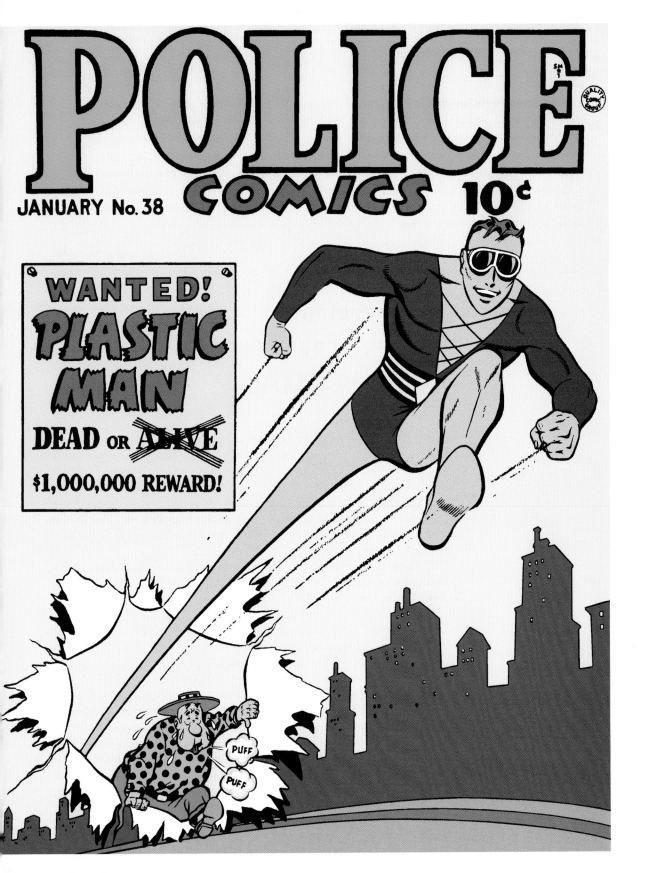

American Comix

Art Spiegelman, *Forms Stretched to Their Limits.* Spiegelman (b. 1948), winner of the 1992 Pulitzer Prize for his graphic memoir *Maus I: A Survivor's Tale (My Father Bleeds History)* (1986), is a leader in the art of avant-garde comics. His work has appeared in numerous periodicals, and the Museum of Modern Art has exhibited his drawings. He published a sequel to the memoir, *Maus II: A Survivor's Tale (And Here My Troubles Began)* in 1992. Sections of both memoirs originally appeared in *Raw*, an acclaimed magazine he co-founded and edits. In 2004, Spiegelman published *In the Shadow of No Towers*, which chronicles his experience of September 11 and its aftermath. "Forms Stretched to Their Limits" was first published in *The New Yorker* (April 19, 1999) and has been excerpted here.

Art Spiegelman
FORMS STRETCHED
TO THEIR LIMITS

Disguised as a red, black, and yellow throw rug, our hero cocks one ear up to listen in on two hoods huddled at the table that rests on him. In the next panel he literally hangs out at an art museum, above a label that says "Abstract," his body now distorted into a red, black, and yellow bebop-Cubist composition, in order to eavesdrop on two cheap gunsels out gallery-hopping. And in the panel after that two molls gossip from tenement windows across an alley while our protean hero continues his stakeout camouflaged as a red, black, and yellow line of laundry flapping between them.

This manic spritz of images appeared in a 1950 issue of "Plastic Man," one of the last issues written and drawn by Jack Cole, a tragically short-lived comic-book giant. "Plastic Man" can be found mainly in those plastic bags collectors use to stash their rare, slow-burning forest fires of newsprint, although DC Comics has at last published "The Plastic Man Archives, Volume 1," which at least reprints the first twenty "Plastic Man" stories, published between 1941 and 1943, when the developing artist was just beginning to stretch. (Incidentally, the reproduction in this deluxe, $49.95 hardcover stinks—or maybe it simply doesn't stink enough, managing somehow to look both blurry and shrill. Anyone with a spare twenty-six thousand four hundred and fifty dollars should consider seeking out near-mint copies of the original pulp-paper comic books.) I'm embarrassed to confess to being in love with a superhero comic, but Jack Cole's "Plastic Man" belongs high on any adult's How to Avoid Prozac list, up there with the best of S. J. Perelman, Laurel and Hardy, Damon Runyon, Tex Avery, and the Marx Brothers. Cole's comics have helped me feel reconciled to the misleading word "comic," which often keeps my medium of choice from getting any respect.

342

Many otherwise literate people, even those who have long since crossed the high-low divide and welcomed comic strips like "Krazy Kat" and "Little Nemo" into the canon of twentieth-century cultural achievement—right up there next to Picasso's paintings and Joyce's novels—remain predisposed against comic *books.* Of course, most comic books really *are* junk, just as our parents said, but so is most painting and literature. The lowly comic book has a lot of strikes against it, not least a residual public distaste left over from Senator Kefauver's 1950s crime hearings, which scapegoated the whole medium as a species of pornography for tots. The hearings forced a draconian "self-regulating" Comics Code Authority on the publishers; the edict stamped out the reckless excesses of the crime, war, and horror comics (categories that tended to appeal to an older audience of G.I.s and other adults) and left lobotomized superheroes and innocuous funny animals as virtually the only survivors on the newsstands. We've committed some of our most censorious follies in the guise of protecting our children.

It's a tribute to the medium's appeal that the comic book has bounced back from the grave several times in its history, though the industry has never been as close to death as now. Near-suicidal publishing and marketing decisions—for example, aiming at a narrow collectors' market rather than reaching out to mainstream audiences—have left the industry in a depressed state. Television almost killed what remained of comics in the mid-fifties; now new computer-generated special-effects technologies have robbed comics of even their near-monopoly on primal visual fantasy. Comic books must reposition themselves—possibly as Art—in order to survive as anything more than part of the feeder system for Hollywood. Otherwise, like vaudeville, they will vanish.

Art? It now seems natural to see Orson Welles's "Touch of Evil" or a Howard Hawks Western at MOMA, but a generation of aestheticians like Manny Farber had to show people how to see movies for such programming to become plausible. In a landmark 1962 essay in *Film Culture,* Farber looked at B movies with a painter's eyes and championed the neglected genre films he loved. He contrasted "the idea of art as an expensive hunk of well-regulated area . . . shrieking with preciosity, fame, ambition" with art made "where the spotlight of culture is nowhere in evidence, so that the craftsman can be ornery, wasteful, stubbornly self-involved, doing go-for-broke art and not caring what comes of it." This he called a "termite-tapeworm-fungus-moss art . . . that goes always forward, eating its own boundaries and likely as not leaves nothing in its path other than signs of eager, industrious unkempt activity." The comic-book form has always swarmed with termites, never more so than in the Golden Age, which collectors date from the spring of 1938, when Superman first turned the ephemeral periodicals into a major fad, until the devastation brought by the Comics Code, in late 1954. It was a time when comics always traveled below critical radar and offered a direct gateway into the unrestrained dream life of their creators—lurid, violent, funny, and sometimes sublime.

Jack Cole, whose comic-book career started a year before that Golden Age and ended precisely with it, was born in December 1914 in the small coal-mining

343

and industrial town of New Castle, in western Pennsylvania. His father, a Methodist Sunday-school teacher for twenty years, owned a drygoods store and was a popular local performer, playing the bones in King Cole's Corn Crackers; his mother had been a grade-school teacher. Jack, the third of six children, was introspective, imaginative, high-spirited, and graced with a pronounced sense of humor. A childhood passion for newspaper strips like Elzie Segar's "Thimble Theater" (featuring Popeye), George McManus's "Bringing Up Father," and Rube Goldberg's "Boob McNutt" blossomed into a lifelong desire to draw a syndicated strip of his own. His formal art training, beyond copying his favorites to crack their physiognomic code, consisted of mail-order lessons from the Landon School of Cartooning. When he was fifteen, he secretly saved up his school-lunch money to pay for the course, smuggling sandwiches from home in the hollowed-out pages of a book. Two years later, he again proved his strength of character by bicycling alone to Los Angeles and back, a seven-thousand-mile adventure that he later recounted in his first sale, an illustrated feature for *Boy's Life.*

After graduating from high school, Cole eloped with his childhood sweetheart, Dorothy Mahoney. Drawing cartoons at night and working at the local American Can factory by day, he remained in his parents' home until his mother found out about the secret marriage and suggested that he live with his wife. Dick Cole, his youngest brother, still remembers the Pop-Art-before-its-time furniture Jack playfully improvised out of printed tin sheets brought home from his job. American Can, however, clearly didn't offer him the creative outlet he was searching for, and in 1936, at the age of twenty-two, he quit. Borrowing five hundred dollars from family friends and local merchants, he moved to Greenwich Village with Dorothy to seek his fortune as a cartoonist. In a dutiful letter that he sent home after settling in, he put a positive spin on his career prospects, praising Dorothy's steadfastness and reassuring his parents that he hadn't been corrupted by the big city:

> Every kid wants to grow up to be as good as his parents, and I, being no exception, have about as high a goal as could be possible to strive for. Have tried to do things as you would do them, but unfortunately I am ruled by my heart rather than my head, and sometimes slip up. (or rather, many times) I have never told you this before, but in case you are interested, I have never taken a drink of beer or liquer yet and never mean to—don't smoke—cuss some but have never used HIS name in a vain expression.

Though he eventually smoked, drank moderately, and possibly even took God's name in vain, Cole was always conscientious. In time, he paid his debts to the New Castle folk who sponsored him, although in his first year of trying to break into magazines and newspapers he had whittled his stake down to five cents. According to the comics historian Ron Goulart—whose brief but invaluable "Focus on Jack Cole" (Fantagraphics; 1986) is the closest the cartoonist has come to having a biography—Cole found himself working for about twenty dollars a week in a factory again: in Harry "A" Chesler's comicbook "sweatshop," at Fifth Avenue and Twenty-ninth Street, set up to provide new material for publishers unable to find any newspaper strips worth reprinting. The first ten-cent comic book, "Famous Funnies," published in 1934, consisted of reduced-scale color reprints of "Mutt and Jeff," "The Bungle Family," and other popular syndicated features; green-kid cartoonists worked elbow to elbow with old pulp illustrators, down-on-their-luck painters, and other has-beens and never-wases to pioneer a new art form at cut rates that could compete with the low-priced syndicate retreads. Marshall McLuhan has written that every new medium cannibalizes the content of the medium that preceded it (the movies, for example, were once called "photoplays"), and the comic book bears this idea out: pale imitations of "Dick Tracy" and "Mandrake the Magician" were the anemic norm until 1938, when the first issue of Action Comics presented a caped *Übermensch* who fought for Truth, Justice, and the American Way—a crack-brained idea by two Jewish kids from Cleveland that really made the new medium fly. *Action!* The title nails the basic appeal of the new four-color heroes: Crimson Avengers, Purple Zombies, Green Masks, Blue Beetles, Blue Bolts, Blue Streaks, White Streaks, and Silver Streaks started zipping through the sky, hitting the newsstands and one another.

Cole thrived, first in the Chesler shop and then as a freelancer, working against tight deadlines and learning in print how to take advantage of the flexible panel layouts and dynamic pages that these books demanded. He was an "all-around man," writing as well as drawing, even lettering and sometimes coloring his own material. He started out doing screwball filler pages and then graduated to the longer and more lucrative "straight" stuff, though even his most illustrative work happily betrayed his roots in loopy-doodle cartooning. His early straight work was crazily bent: "Mantoka" (a supernaturally empowered Native American medicine man who takes revenge on evil Caucasians), "The Comet" (whose disintegrating rays shoot out of his eyes whenever he crosses them to melt down bad guys), and, for Silver Streak Comics, "The Claw" (the ultimate Yellow Peril, a fanged Asian warlord who can get taller than King Kong when aroused) all displayed a feverish imagination, verve, and a cheerful streak of perverse violence.

By the end of 1940, Cole had begun working for Quality Comics, Everett (Busy) Arnold's newly launched line of publications. Quality became home base for the rest of Cole's comic-book career. The feel and look of the Quality Comics house style had been established by Will Eisner, creator of "The Spirit," whose work was to have a major influence on Cole. Eisner, who is now in his eighties and still doing significant comics, had studied painting and hoped to become a theatrical set designer; he was more culturally sophisticated than Cole, who had been shaped mainly by pulps, movies, comic strips, and the other early comic books—which were mostly influenced by more of the same. Cole's first sustained work for Quality was "Midnight," a feature intended by the pragmatic Arnold as a clone of "The Spirit"—just in case Eisner, who was in the unique position of owning his own character, were to be drafted and die or otherwise leave Quality. Cole learned important lessons in narrative and structural coherence from this apprenticeship, and brought his singular sense of humor and fantasy to the project.

A few months after "Midnight" came "Plastic Man," starting as a minor feature in Police Comics but soon to become the star of that anthology. Inspired by sideshow freaks, Cole planned to call the character the India Rubber Man. Arnold, however, astutely suggested that it might be bouncier to name him after the miracle substance that was reshaping the modern world. In 1943, when Plastic Man expanded into his own book, Cole explained the morphing hero to new readers: "If you should see a man standing on the street and reaching into the top window of a sky-scraper...that's not astigmatism—it's Plastic Man!...If you happen upon a gent all bent up like a pretzel...don't dunk him...it's Plastic Man! All this and bouncing too, you'll see when the rubber man and his pal Woozy Winks gamble their lives in—The Game of Death."

Plastic Man. Comic book interior cells. ("Police Comics" #1 © 1941 DC Comics. All Rights Reserved. Used with permission)

Plastic Man wore a V-necked red rubber leotard accessorized by a wide black-and-yellow striped belt and very cool tinted goggles. He started life as Eel O'Brian, a lowlife gangster accidentally doused by some unnamed acid while committing a robbery. He was saved by a reclusive order of monks who recognized that his villainy was the result of an unhappy childhood. They nursed him back to health and in a memorable couple of panels [at left] he discovered his gift:

The acid bath had given him the ability to violate the laws of physics; the monks gave him the will to defend the laws of men, first as part of the police force and later as a special agent for the F.B.I. His F.B.I. chief, sporting one of the most peculiar comb-overs in comics, was the authority figure in Plastic Man's tiny nuclear family. Nobody knew that Plastic Man and the gangster Eel O'Brian were the same person. His secret identity—as a public enemy he himself was supposed to capture—was too limiting a concept for a hero who could be literally anything he wanted to be. Superman and the tribe that grew from that template have a mere two identities: they're binary. Plas, as his friends called him, was multiphrenic and illimitable, and soon forgot about being Eel O'Brian.

It says something about Cole's superego, if not his superhero, that he often cast reformed villains as his principals. Woozy Winks, Plastic Man's Robin, was hardly a Boy Wonder. He entered the series as a miscreant, the Man Who Can't Be Harmed, having chosen a life of crime on the basis of a coin toss. Several issues later his powers diminished, so that he became the Man Whom Nature Protects (Sometimes), and he eventually settled in as an all too mortal bungler, a skirt-chaser, and an occasional pickpocket. He was a slovenly, scrotum-cheeked rube in a straw hat and green polka-dot shirt who looked a bit like Alfred Hitchcock. Providing a meatball-shaped counterweight to Plastic Man's spaghetti, his direct forebear was Popeye's pal Wimpy. In a more "straight" comic-book reality, Woozy would have provided comic relief.

Naturally enough, Cole resembled both his leads: like Woozy, he was soft-bodied, somewhat disheveled, and no city slicker; like Plastic Man, he was tall, pointy-nosed, and "very likable...a straight arrow—sort of a Boy Scout in some ways," as Gill Fox, Cole's close friend and his editor at Quality, described him to me.

Cartoonists "become" each character in their comics, acting out every gesture and expression; it's in this sense that Cole most resembles Plastic Man—as the Spirit of Cartooning. Cole successfully performed the one magic act at the heart of the craft: believing so profoundly in the reality of the world conjured up with lines on paper that, against the odds, the marks gain enough authority to become a real world for the reader. Cole's world teems with invention, gags, and an amazing number of hyperactive characters tucked into every nook and cranny of a panel. Plastic Man never stretches exactly the same way twice. While Cole's work is often overloaded with ideas, the drawing is never overwrought; the art displays a Midwesterner's laconic mastery. What remains most remarkable is his ability to be so fully present in his comic-book work from moment to moment, always following his lines of thought with the same curiosity the reader might have—as astonished as any reader by where they take him.

If the going rate for pictures is still only a thousand words per, most "Plastic Man" panels are worth at least two or three pictures. Each panel seems to swallow several separate instants of time whole, as if the page were made up of small screens with different, though related, films whizzing by at forty-eight frames a second. Cole's is an amphetamine-riddled art: Tex Avery on speed! And it's not just Plastic Man who bounces and twists; any one of Cole's incidental figures would seem as kinetic as Plastic Man if it were transplanted into someone else's comic book. Each page is intuitively visualized to form a coherent whole, even though the individual panels form a narrative flood of run-on sentences that breathlessly jump from one page to the next. The art ricochets like a racquetball slammed full force in a closet. Your eye, however, is guided as if it were a skillfully controlled pinball, often by Plastic Man himself acting as a compositional device. His distended body is an arrow pointing out the sights as it hurtles through time. In just a single panel, our hero chases along a footpath in a park, trailing a mugger. Running from the rear of the picture, Plastic Man's S-curved body echoes the path itself as he loops around one pedestrian in the distance and extends between two lovers about to kiss—lipstick traces are on his elongated neck as he passes them—to swoop up between an old man's legs like an enormous penis wearing sunglasses and stare into his startled face. Plastic Man had all the crackling intensity of the life force transferred to paper. Pulpier than James Cameron's Terminator, more frantic than Jim Carrey in "The Mask," and less self-conscious than Woody Allen's "Zelig," "Plastic Man" literally *embodied* the comic-book form: its exuberant energy, its flexibility, its boyishness, and its only

347

■ What do you think Spiegelman means when he says that "'Plastic Man' literally embodied the comic-book form"? Why is there emphasis on the word "embodied"? The writer Marshall McLuhan famously said that "the medium is the message." How does Spiegelman's analysis of Cole's work support McLuhan's dictim?

partially sublimated sexuality. Cole's infinitely malleable hero, Clinton-like in his ability to change shape and squeeze through tiny loopholes, just oozed sex. It was never made explicit — the idea of a hard-core version of "Plastic Man" boggles the mind — but there was a polymorphously perverse quality to a character who personified Georges Bataille's[1] notion of the body on the brink of dissolving its borders. Cole let it all hang out as Plastic Man slithered from panel to panel — sometimes shifting from male to female, and freely mutating from erect and hardboiled to soft as a Dali clock.[2]

Most of the plots are as twisted and swervy as Plastic Man himself. They're convincing enough in their mad, moment-to-moment flow, but they're as hard to reconstruct and as elusive as dreams, with their vividly improvised incidents. Gender-bending and cross-dressing were the least of it. In a 1942 story, Plastic Man is swallowed whole by one Cyrus Smythe, a seventeenth-century mad doctor whose brain has been transplanted into a dying Army pilot's body. Symthe, who has learned how to grow hundreds of feet tall, but who must walk on his hands since the body he possesses is paralyzed from the waist down, chokes to death when Plastic Man climbs out of his stomach to lodge himself in the giant's windpipe. The early stories, while bizarre, don't feel psychopathic, sadistic, or even particularly mean-spirited in Cole's telling. In his postwar period, the "Plastic Man" stories are totally nuts in a different way, prefiguring the idea-per-minute vaudeville zaniness of the early *Mad* comics. In all his stories, heavily populated by shape-changing villains, mad scientists, and monsters, as well as by more mundane murderers, con men, and saboteurs, Cole demonstrates the termite go-for-broke quality that made his friend Gill Fox exclaim admiringly, "That's Jack, he'd let his mind go anywhere!"

Gill Fox told me that he remembers starring in an 8-mm home movie that Cole shot sometime in the early forties, after Jack and Dorothy became his neighbors in Stamford, Connecticut, in order to be closer to Quality's studio there. Cole's improvised film scenario, about an ambitious young comic-book artist fighting a deadline, had Fox dragging his drawing table into the bathroom, pulling his pants down, and continuing to work while seated on the toilet. Cole was always behind schedule, a procrastinator and a perfectionist who took pride in his craft and managed to turn out his monthly quota only by working for punishing all-night stretches. Fox recalls a sweltering summer day in the Quality studio that has become legendary among his generation of comic-book artists: Only the nasty buzz of horseflies broke the silence of cartoonists sweating at their desks over some exceptionally brutal deadline when a disturbance broke their concentration. Something was fluttering and streaking by above their heads. All work stopped

348

---

[1]Georges Bataille (1897–1962), an influential French intellectual and one of the founders of postmodernism, is known largely for his philosophical explorations of eroticism.—ED.
[2]A reference to the famous surrealist painting *The Persistence of Memory* by the Spanish artist Salvador Dali (1904–1989). The 1931 painting shows a barren landscape with four melting timepieces.—ED.

until they caught what turned out to be one very angry horsefly hauling a long, tissue-paper banner with the words "Drink Pepsi Cola!" that Cole had patiently lettered and glued to the insect's back. A genius at work!

Creig Flessel, an intimate colleague of Cole's, visited the Quality offices around that time, wanting to observe an old letterer there who could ink in text balloons perfectly without penciling. He noticed Busy Arnold with large scissors at a nearby desk cutting old "Plastic Man" originals to ribbons: "I nudged Jack and pointed it out to him, and he just shrugged sheepishly." After the art was used, Arnold routinely destroyed it to prevent unauthorized reprinting. The disposability of the art was a given, but it makes Cole's pride in his craft seem downright existential!

The pressure to produce lots of pages quickly, in a situation that offered little prestige and relatively small rates for the skills involved, took its toll. "A number of the artists I knew back then cracked," says Fox, who still draws a Sunday feature for the *Herald Press,* in New Britain, Connecticut. "Al Bryant, who drew Doll Man, drove himself into an abutment on the Long Island Expressway shortly after a nervous breakdown. Another guy at Quality, a writer, threw himself in front of a subway, but somehow survived." John Spranger, an exceptionally gifted artist who assisted on "Plastic Man" in the postwar years, had a severe breakdown; Bob Wood, like many of the other artists, drank heavily. It was a tough business, making funny books, but Cole flourished in that environment.

At the start of the Second World War, Cole doubled his workload to put money aside for Dorothy in case he got drafted. Although he never had children, and was apparently in good health, he wasn't taken. As one of the best cartoonists left on the home front at a moment when publishers were selling all the comics their newsprint rations let them print, Cole made out well. He even briefly ghosted the daily newspaper version of "The Spirit" when Will Eisner got drafted. By the end of the war, Cole was getting the top rate for comic books (about thirty-five dollars per page) as well as occasional bonuses of up to twenty-five hundred dollars when his books broke the two-hundred-thousand point. He and Dorothy bought property and settled into a series of houses in New England. "Their Stamford place was a fourteen-room mansion that had once belonged to the Masked Marvel, a famous pool shark," Flessel told me. "Dorothy was horrified by the cold marble tiles when she first saw the house, so Jack put in some wall-to-wall carpeting. It must have set him back plenty, but he absolutely doted on his wife." Flessel remembers Cole with great affection as an acute, thoughtful, and gentle guy, a "pussycat," with a screwy smile and an irrepressible streak of humor. When I visited the Flessels' Long Island home, he conjured up one small Jacques Tati–like[3] moment when the Coles were leaving after a weekend visit there in the mid-forties: Stooping to get behind the wheel of his pint-sized car, the oversized

349

---

[3]The legendary French film director Jacques Tati (1908–1982) was known for his brilliant use of mime in a number of silent visual comedies.— ED.

Cole knocked his homburg to the ground. He scooped it up while shutting the car door, then casually put the hat back on top of the roof and drove off waving.

Cole worked at home, sending in his popular fifteen-page lead stories for Police Comics every month, as well as material for his "Plastic Man" solo title and occasional humor pieces for other comics. Fox has said, "Jack insisted on doing everything himself.…He didn't even clear his plot lines with anyone. The only thing we did was copy-read for mistakes." Cole was elated to get his own book; but when he was told that it would mean having assistants and ghosts do some of the stories he burst into tears. (Neither Flessel nor Fox could verify what might be an apocryphal story, but both independently said it sounded like the Cole they knew.) The problem of Cole's ghosts and assistants plagues anyone who admires his work. Since some of his assistants—most notably his worshipful friend Alex Kotzky and John Spranger—were very skillful mimics, and since Cole didn't always sign his own art, the "forgeries" are sometimes as hard to spot as Plastic Man himself in disguise. When the characters tilt and sway, unable to hold themselves upright at a mere ninety degrees, when that extra blaze of invention—a few more ideas than any sane artist would dare squeeze into a panel—shines through, one can surmise that one is in the hands of the master.

"Plastic Man" was totally ghosted after 1950, when Cole reached his giddiest heights before burning out on the character. The ghosts who remained behind lost their inspiration, but the buoyant originality of the basic concept kept "Plastic Man" afloat through 1956. Subsequent attempts to revive the character haven't been especially distinguished, nor have imitations that recycle the notion of a stretchable hero, though the character's virtual DNA lives on in the leader of MarvelComics' Fantastic Four, a "straight" Plastic Man with way too much starch.

In 1947, Cole hired Alex Kotzky to help him package True Crime Comics, a new publisher's short-lived attempt to cash in on the crime comics then dominating the field; a story in the second issue, "Murder, Morphine and Me," has become notorious as one of the most intense and delirious examples that the lurid genre had to offer. One small panel—so charged that it has tremor lines around it and tilts, almost tumbling off the page—was enshrined as Exhibit A in Dr. Fredric Wertham's *Seduction of the Innocent,* the book

Jack Cole, *Murder, Morphine and Me.*

(Courtesy of Benjamin S. Samuels)

351

◀ ***True Crime.*** Cole took crime comics to a special level in gore and drama. (Courtesy of Benjamin S. Samuels)

Jack Cole, *Murder, Morphine and Me.* As this frame shows, Cole plays with narrative and medium in creative and effective ways. (Courtesy of Benjamin S. Samuels)

that triggered the Senate hearings and thereby toppled the industry: it shows a closeup of Mary Kennedy, the dope-dealing protagonist, being stabbed in the eye by a junkie with a hypodermic needle. I concede that this isn't Mother Goose, but I find the panel (part of a dream sequence, incidentally) emblematic of the comic book's visceral power to pass the reader's analytical defenses and pierce the brain. Dr. Wertham, on the other hand, focussed on the depraved image as an example of "the injury-to-the-eye motif... [that] shows perhaps the true color of crime comics better than anything else. It has no counterpart in any other literature of the world, for children or adults." I suspect that Dr. Wertham never saw Buñuel and Dali's "Un Chien Andalou" (the 1929 film shocker that featured a closeup of a woman's eye getting slashed by a razor), but that it had made a strong impression on Cole. On the other hand, Cole's True Crime capers point out the continuum between his manic humor and plain old mania. As Kotzky recalled, "Jack was a wild man mentally."

The New York State Legislature thought enough of "Murder, Morphine and Me" to reprint eight pages of blow-ups and excerpts in its 1951 report on comic books and censorship. As a young teen in the arid comic-book landscape of the early sixties, I stumbled onto this report in Manhattan's Donnell Library. It was my first exposure to Cole, and I checked the report out repeatedly. The story included ethnically stereotyped Scandinavians and Italians, lingerie shots of Mary Kennedy, and more gangland gunplay than there is in a John Woo Hong Kong action flick, all delivered with Cole's signature velocity. It is also among the most formally sophisticated comics stories I've ever seen; all the elements, including the panel shapes and the lettering are deployed for narrative effect. When Mary, working as a hash-slinger, spills coffee on Tony, seated at her lunch counter, it's love at first sight. Through two progressive closeups, moving from profiles of their faces to their twitching lips, they exchange a machine-gun volley of speech balloons with dialogue worthy of James M. Cain. Tony departs ("Be seein' ya, honey eyes"), leaving Mary almost swooning, her heart banging against her chest like a five-hundred-pound canary trying to break out of its cage. (Cole's body language is priceless.)

Cole's last comic-book work was for Web of Evil, Quality's entry into the horror comics of the early fifties. Unlike most of his output, these horror comics, often scripted and barbarically inked by others, look as if they were done for the money. One noteworthy tale, clearly by Cole, "The Killer from Saturn," is about a serial murderer from outer space who terrorizes the city but turns out to be a mousy municipal window clerk who has gone postal. Wearing an imposing monster costume and stilts, he takes revenge on those who abused him. He's put in a mental institution where, in the closing panel, two detectives outside the barred door peer in at the pathetic wimp who still insists that he's the omnipotent killer from Saturn. One cop says, "He always will be . . . up here . . . where he can safely kill . . . in his *imagination*." The story, laced with fifties psychological jargon, seems to be Cole's hymn to the power of fantasy and the need to keep that power contained.

If Cole was through with comics, comics were also through with him. Searching for work in the fifties, he is said to have brought his portfolio to DC Comics, one of the few publishers that survived past 1954, and was summarily turned away. As early as the mid-forties, he had been preparing to leave the field, more out of ambition and restlessness than remorse. He began to put much of his energy into reshaping himself as a gag cartoonist, selling occasional drawings to the *Saturday Evening Post, Collier's,* and *Judge.* A knack for drawing genuinely sexy women made his cartoons, signed "Jake," a fixture of the down-market girlie-cartoon and pin-up magazines. Cole was struggling as a mid-echelon gag cartoonist at the end of 1953 when he submitted a batch of gags to *Stag Party,* a planned men's magazine that announced its need for cartoons in trade journals. Cole's drawings began appearing in the fifth issue of the magazine, after it was launched as *Playboy.* At least one full-page drawing by him appeared in *Playboy* every month thereafter for the rest of his life.

353

Superman, **Action Comics #1, 1938.** Superman was the brainchild of two friends from Cleveland, ▶ Ohio: Jerry Siegal and Joe Shuster. They met on the staff of their high school newspaper in 1930 and then moved to New York to break into comics. DC Comics bought the story, and all the rights to the character, for $130. Before DC bought Superman, every major comic syndicate in the country had rejected him. The character was widely successful and spawned a host of caped crusaders. ("Action Comics" #1 © 1938 DC Comics. All Rights Reserved. Used with Permission)

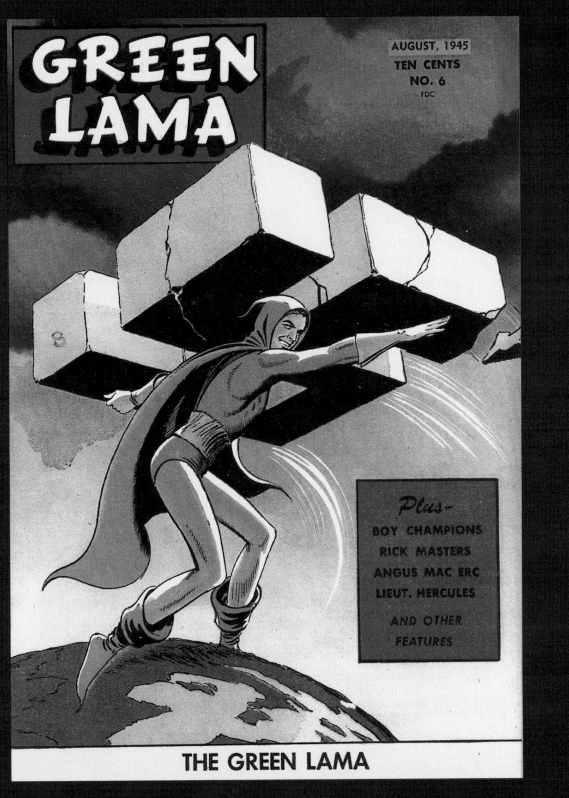

◀ **Green Lama, August 1945.** The Green Lama first appeared in the pulp magazine *Double Detective* in 1940. His alter ego is a multimillionaire who travels to Tibet for postgraduate work and becomes a priest. Returning to America, he uses his superhuman powers to fight crime with nonviolent methods (he never uses a gun and never kills anyone). (Courtesy of Benjamin S. Samuels)

Ms. Magazine, July 1972. Wonder Woman was created by Wil Marston in 1941. ▶ Marston was hired by DC Comics as an educational consultant. He proposed to DC that he create a female superhero, a character "with all the strength of Superman plus all the allure of a good and beautiful woman." It was fitting that the first magazine for women run entirely by women — *Ms.* magazine — featured Wonder Woman on its cover. At the time journalist Harry Reasoner joked that it would have a limited life, saying, "I'll give it six months before they run out of things to say." Its 300,000 copies sold out in eight days; today the magazine remains the most influential feminist publication in the world.

356

COMMENT

"It's too bad for us 'literary' enthusiasts, but it's the truth nevertheless — pictures tell any story more effectively than words. . . . if children read comics . . . why isn't it advisable to give them some constructive comics to read?"

— Will Marston, creator of Wonder Woman

■ *Look carefully at the cover of the first issue of* Ms. *magazine, bearing the title "Wonder Woman for President." What does this choice of cover art claim or suggest about feminism? What is significant about using Wonder Woman as the cover art, rather than, say, a picture of Gloria Steinem or Simone de Beauvoir, both of whom were featured in this edition? Why do you think women responded to this magazine with such enthusiasm?*

358

MESSAGE

Many of the superheroes mentioned in this cluster — Plastic Man, Wonder Woman, Batman, Super-man — were conceived of in a particular historical moment. In the 1930s and 1940s, when Americans were enduring the Great Depression and facing the daunting prospects of a second world war, the superhero conveyed a message of power against insurmountable circumstances that resonated with Americans' sense of powerlessness. A few of these characters are still popular, as illustrated by the recent spate of movies based on comics. What message do you think superheroes send today? Is there something about *this* historical moment that the superhero speaks to?

METHOD

Art Spiegelman's essay is jam-packed with references to popular culture, literature and film, along with critical and philosophical commentary. What is the overall effect of Spiegelman's essayistic method? Could you follow all the references? Most of them? Few of them? What connections can you find between Spiegelman's method of writing and the audience he is writing for? Can you detect any similarities between his compositional methods and the comic-book styles he admires? If so, what are they?

MEDIUM

A noted comic-book artist, Spiegelman chooses the essay form to express his enthusiasm for and analysis of Jack Cole's genius. What if Spiegelman had decided to express his ideas through his own favorite medium — comics? How might he have gone about this? Do you think a comic-book format that both profiles Cole and assesses his work would be a more appropriate medium? Why or why not? What would be the advantages and limitations of each medium, given the author's purpose?

Reading a Monument

When reading a sculpture, monument, or installation, it is important to keep in mind that the piece's artistic meaning is often linked to the interplay of several different media. The following questions will help guide your reading of the material in Memorial and other texts that mix media:

- What materials are used in the piece, and what associations do they embody? A choice between black granite and white marble might at first seem arbitrary, but it can indicate the tone the artist wishes to convey.

- Is the subject portrayed in an abstract fashion or a realistic one? Does this choice reflect cultural attitudes about the subject matter, or does it challenge them?

- Where is the artwork meant to be seen? A museum exhibit? A mall? A park? What does this choice suggest about the work's purpose and its level of seriousness?

Vietnam Veterans Memorial. This photograph of the Vietnam Veterans Memorial designed by artist/architect Maya Lin is both an example of a particular view of a monument and also a reminder about how difficult it is to record a single representation of a three-dimensional, enormous text. (Image courtesy of Maya Lin Studio)

MEMORIAL

"What exactly is a memorial? What should it do?" Maya Lin asks (and answers) these questions in her essay on the Vietnam Veterans Memorial, "Between Art and Architecture." The *American Heritage Dictionary* offers this **definition** for "memorial": "Something, such as a monument or holiday, intended to celebrate or honor the memory of a person or event." Andrew Butterfield's comment on the facing page offers a definition for "monument": a permanent physical structure that serves to make the memory of an event tangible. Memorials and monuments are part of how we collectively remember history. The materials presented here offer several answers to Lin's question, for three separate events: The Vietnam War, the Holocaust, and September 11, 2001. As you read through these materials, consider what *you* think a memorial should be.

360

memorial
Vietnam Veterans Memorial,
Washington, D.C.; designed
by Maya Ying Lin

mem·o·ran·dum (měm′ə-răn′dəm) *n., pl.* **-dums** or **-da** (-də) **1.** A short note written as a reminder. **2.** A written record or communication, as in a business office. **3.** *Law* A short written statement outlining the terms of an agreement, transaction, or contract. **4.** A business statement made by a consignor about a shipment of goods that may be returned. **5.** A brief, unsigned diplomatic communication. [Middle English, to be remembered (used as a manuscript notation), from Latin, neuter sing. gerundive of *memorāre*, to bring to remembrance. See MEMORABLE.]

me·mo·ri·al (mə-môr′ē-əl, -mōr′-) *n.* **1.** Something, such as a monument or holiday, intended to celebrate or honor the memory of a person or an event. **2.** A written statement of facts or a petition presented to a legislative body or an executive. ✧ *adj.* **1.** Serving as a remembrance of a person or an event; commemorative. **2.** Of, relating to, or being in memory. [Middle English, from Old French, from Late Latin *memoriāle*, from neuter of Latin *memoriālis*, belonging to memory, from *memoria*, memory. See MEMORY.] —**me·mo′ri·al·ly** *adv.*

Me·mo·ri·al Day (mə-môr′ē-əl, -mōr′-) *n.* May 30, observed in the United States in commemoration of those members of the armed forces killed in war. It is officially observed on the last Monday in May. Also called *Decoration Day.*

me·mo·ri·al·ist (mə-môr′ē-ə-list, -mōr′-) *n.* **1.** A person who writes memoirs. **2.** A person who writes or signs a memorial.

COMMENT

"What is a monument? The word comes from the Latin noun *monumentum,* which is derived from the Latin verb *moneo.* The primary meaning of *moneo* is 'to bring to the notice of, to remind, or to tell of.' *Monumentum* consequently is a thing with this function, specifically something that stimulates the remembrance of a person or an event. *Monumentum* could be used for anything with this purpose — a text, a building, a work of art; but its primary denotation was a tomb or a funerary memorial. In English, the word 'monument' retains this basic meaning; it has special reference to a tomb, a cenotaph, or a memorial.

"Monuments provide an enduring physical demonstration of the fact of the existence of a person or an event. It marks a spot and it says who. And it says so forever. It is an object that serves as the locus of the memories of a person or a group, and it makes those memories tangible — literally so. Hence the most basic component of a monument is its marker: the physical object erected to mark a locus in perpetuity. Owing to the emphasis on permanence, survival, and continuity, the marker naturally is made of the most durable materials — stone and metal."

— Andrew Butterfield, From "Monuments and Memories:
What history can teach the architects at Ground Zero"
(*The New Republic*, February 3, 2003)

361

■ *Read through Maya Lin's proposal and carefully examine her sketches. Do you think the committee weighed the visual and verbal parts of the proposal equally when they were making the decision about who would design the memorial? Or do you agree with Lin's assessment that they paid more attention to the written proposal?*

Maya Lin, Proposal and sketches. These are the materials that Maya Lin (b. 1959) created as part of the design class she was taking at Yale. She writes that "the drawings were in soft pastels, very mysterious, very painterly, and not at all typical of architectural drawings. . . . But ultimately, I think it was the written description that convinced the jurors to select my design." (Courtesy of the Library of Congress, copyright Maya Lin)   ▶

>   go

For another view of the Vietnam Veterans Memorial — and a virtual walk around it — go to a "digitial, interactive legacy memorializing the men and women who gave their lives in Vietnam" at www.thevirtualwall.org. How effective is the web site at giving you a sense of how the memorial works?

Walking through this park-like area, the memorial appears as a rift in the earth- a long, polished black stone wall, emerging from and receding into the earth. Approaching the memorial, the ground slopes gently downward, and the low walls emerging on either side, growing out of the earth, extend and converge at a point below and ahead. Walking into the grassy site contained by the walls of this memorial we can barely make out the carved names upon the memorial's walls. These names, seemingly infinite in number, convey the sense of overwhelming numbers, while unifying those individuals into a whole. For this memorial is meant not as a monument to the individual, but rather as a memorial to the men and women who died during this war, as a whole.

The memorial is composed not as an unchanging monument, but as a moving composition, to be understood as we move into and out of it; the passage itself is gradual, the descent to the origin slow, but it is at the origin that the meaning of this memorial is to fully understood. At the intersection of these walls, on the right side, at this wall's top is carved the date of the first death. It is followed by the names of those who have died in the war, in chronological order. These names continue on this wall, appearing to recede into the earth at the wall's end. The names resume on the left wall, as the wall emerges from the earth, continuing back to the origin, where the date of the last death is carved, at the bottom of this wall. Thus the war's beginning and end meet; the war is "complete", coming full circle, yet broken by the earth that bounds the angle's open side, and contained within the earth itself. As we turn to leave, we see these walls stretching into the distance, directing us to the Washington Monument to the left and the Lincoln Memorial to the right, thus bringing the Vietnam Memorial into historical context. We, the living are brought to a concrete realization of these deaths.

Brought to a sharp awareness of such a loss, it is up to each individual to resolve or come to terms with this loss. For death is in the end a personal and private matter, and the area contained within this memorial is a quiet place meant for personal reflection and private reckoning. The black granite walls, each 200 feet long, and 10 feet below ground at their lowest point (gradually ascending towards ground level) effectively act as a sound barrier, yet are of such a height and length so as not to appear threatening or enclosing. The actual area is wide and shallow; allowing for a sense of privacy and the sunlight from the memorial's southern exposure along with the grassy park surrounding and within it's wall contribute to the serenity of the area. Thus this memorial is for those who have died, and for us to remember them.

The memorial's origin is located approximately at the center of this site; it legs each extending 200 feet towards the Washington Monument and the Lincoln Memorial. The walls, contained on one side by the earth is are 10 feet below ground at their point of origin, gradually lessening in height, until they finally recede totally into the earth at their ends. The walls are to be made of a hard, polished black granite, with the names to be carved in a simple Trajan letter, 3/4 inch high, allowing for nine inches in length for each name. The memorial's construction involves recontouring the area within the wall's boundaries so as to provide for an easily accessible descent, but as much of the site as possible should be left untouched (including trees). The area should be made into a park for all the public to enjoy.

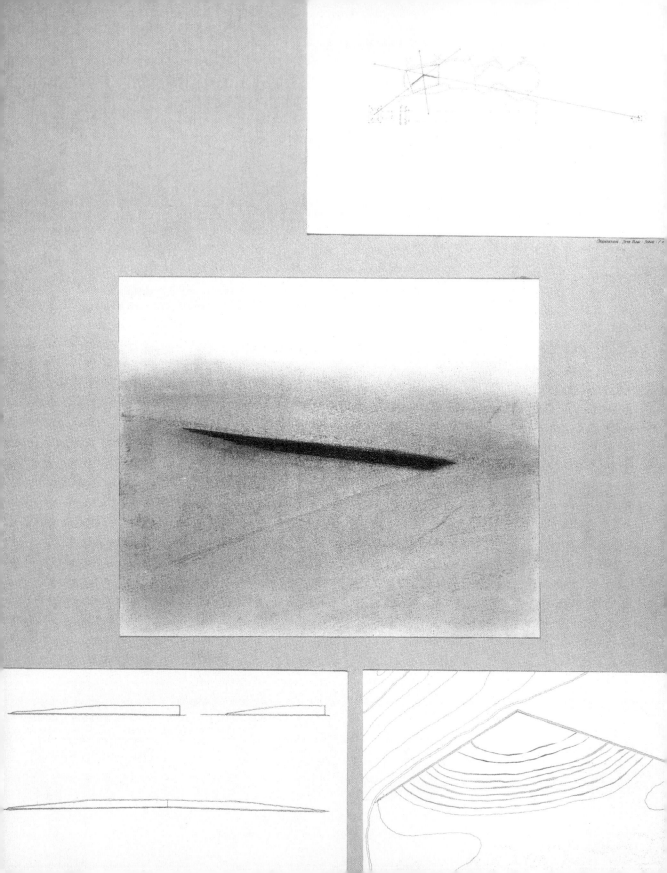

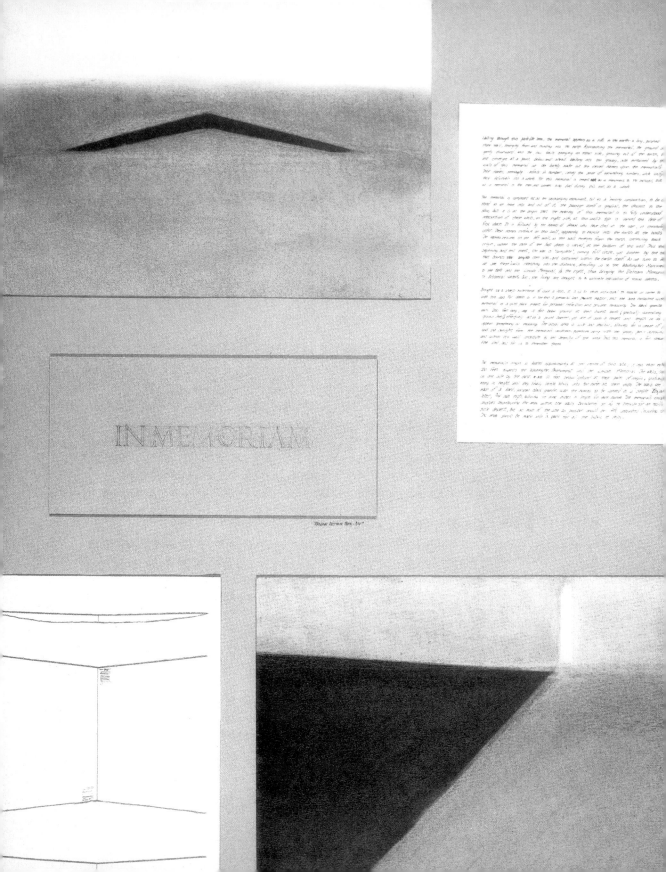

"I consider the monuments to be true hybrids, existing between art and architecture, they have a specific need or function, yet their function is purely symbolic."

Maya Lin, *Between Art and Architecture.* Probably no prolonged episode in recent American history was more divisive than our nation's military involvement in Vietnam. With highly publicized anti-war rallies and massive organized protests, the war created a cultural rift that can still be felt throughout the nation. Given the extreme positions maintained during the long course of the conflict, it would have been surprising if the drive afterward to construct a fitting memorial to the war had escaped controversy. What would this memorial memorialize? Victory or defeat? Patriotism, courage, and commitment — or national dishonor and disgrace? Maya Lin (b. 1959) was a senior at Yale when her design, the result of an architectural seminar, won the national competition for a Vietnam veterans memorial. She has subsequently designed the Civil Rights Memorial (1989) in Montgomery, Alabama; the Langston Hughes Library (1999) in Clinton, Tennessee; and other private and public projects. This essay is the fourth chapter of Maya Lin's book, *Boundaries* (2000). She writes that her book is "an extension of my art — and like my other works, it sits between two identities . . . a visual and verbal sketchbook, where image can be seen as text and text is sometimes used as image." We have reproduced the text of the essay here, with some of the images included.

Maya Lin

BETWEEN ART AND ARCHITECTURE

It's taken me years to be able to discuss the making of the Vietnam Veterans Memorial, partly because I needed to move past it and partly because I had forgotten the process of getting it built. I would not discuss the controversy surrounding its construction and it wasn't until I saw the documentary, *Maya Lin: A Strong Clear Vision,* that I was able to remember that time in my life. But I wrote the body of this essay just as the memorial was being completed — in the fall of 1982. Then I put it away . . . until now.

I think the most important aspect of the design of the Vietnam Veterans Memorial was that I had originally designed it for a class I was taking at Yale and not for the competition. In that sense, I had designed it for me — or, more exactly, for what I believed it should be. I never tried to second-guess a jury. And it wasn't until after I had completed the design that I decided to enter it in the competition.

The design emerged from an architectural seminar I was taking during my senior year. The initial idea of a memorial had come from a notice posted at the school announcing a competition for a Vietnam veterans memorial. The class, which was on funereal architecture, had spent the semester studying how people, through the built form, express their attitudes on death. As a class, we thought the memorial was an appropriate design idea for our program, so we adopted it as our final design project.

At that point, not much was known about the actual competition, so for the first half of the assignment we were left without concrete directions as to what "they" were looking for or even who "they" were. Instead, we had to determine for ourselves what a Vietnam memorial should be. Since a previous project had been to design a memorial for World War III, I had already begun to ask the simple questions: What exactly is a memorial? What should it do?

My design for a World War III memorial was a tomblike underground structure that I deliberately made to be a very futile and frustrating experience. I remember the professor of the class, Andrus Burr, coming up to me afterward, saying quite angrily, "If I had a brother who died in that war, I would never want to visit this memorial." I was somewhat puzzled that he didn't quite understand that World War III would be of such devastation that none of us would be around to visit any memorial, and that my design was instead a prewar commentary. In asking myself what a memorial to a third world war would be, I came up with a political statement that was meant as a deterrent.

I had studied earlier monuments and memorials while designing that memorial and I continued this research for the design of the Vietnam memorial. As I did more research on monuments, I realized most carried larger, more general messages about a leader's victory or accomplishments rather than the lives lost. In fact, at the national level, individual lives were very seldom dealt with, until you arrived at the memorials for World War I. Many of these memorials included the names of those killed. Partly it was a practical need to list those whose bodies could not be identified—since dog tags as identification had not yet been adopted and, due to the nature of the warfare, many killed were not indentifiable—but I think as well the listing of names reflected a response by these designers to the horrors of World War I, to the immense loss of life.

The images of these monuments were extremely moving. They captured emotionally what I felt memorials should be: honest about the reality of war, about the loss of life in war, and about remembering those who served and especially those who died.

I made a conscious decision not to do any specific research on the Vietnam War and the political turmoil surrounding it. I felt that the politics had eclipsed the veterans, their service and their lives. I wanted to create a memorial that everyone would be able to respond to, regardless of whether one thought our country should or should not have participated in the war. The power of a name was very much with me at the time, partly because of the Memorial Rotunda at Yale. In Woolsey Hall, the walls are inscribed with the names of all the Yale alumni who have been killed in wars. I had never been able to resist touching the names cut

369

into these marble walls, and no matter how busy or crowded the place is, a sense of quiet, a reverence, always surrounds those names. Throughout my freshman and sophomore years, the stonecutters were carving in by hand the names of those killed in the Vietnam War, and I think it left a lasting impression on me...the sense of the power of a name.

One memorial I came across also made a strong impression on me. It was a monument to the missing soldiers of the World War I battle of the Somme by Sir Edwin Lutyens in Thiepval, France. The monument includes more than 100,000 names of people who were listed as missing because, without ID tags, it was impossible to identify the dead. (The cemetery contains the bodies of 70,000 dead.) To walk past those names and realize those lost lives—the effect of that is the strength of the design. This memorial acknowledged those lives without focusing on the war or on creating a political statement of victory or loss. This apolitical approach became the essential aim of my design; I did not want to civilize war by glorifying it or by forgetting the sacrifices involved. The price of human life in war should always be clearly remembered.

But on a personal level, I wanted to focus on the nature of accepting and coming to terms with a loved one's death. Simple as it may seem, I remember feeling that accepting a person's death is the first step in being able to overcome that loss.

I felt that as a culture we were extremely youth oriented and not willing or able to accept death or dying as a part of life. The rites of mourning, which in more primitive and older cultures were very much a part of life, have been suppressed in our modern times. In the design of the memorial, a fundamental goal was to be honest about death, since we must accept that loss in order to begin to overcome it. The pain of the loss will always be there, it will always hurt, but we must acknowledge the death in order to move on.

What then would bring back the memory of a person? A specific object or image would be limiting. A realistic sculpture would be only one interpretation of that time. I wanted something that all people could relate to on a personal level. At this time I had as yet no form, no specific artistic image.

The use of names was a way to bring back everything someone could remember about a person. The strength in a name is something that has always made me wonder at the "abstraction" of the design; the ability of a name to bring back every single memory you have of that person is far more realistic and specific and much more comprehensive than a still photograph, which captures a specific moment in time or a single event or a generalized image that may or may not be moving for all who have connections to that time.

Then someone in the class received the design program, which stated the basic philosophy of the memorial's design and also its requirements: all the names of those missing and killed (57,000) must be a part of the memorial; the design must be apolitical, harmonious with the site, and conciliatory.

These were all the thoughts that were in my mind before I went to see the site.

370

Without having seen it, I couldn't design the memorial, so a few of us traveled to Washington, D.C., and it was at the site that the idea for the design took shape. The site was a beautiful park surrounded by trees, with traffic and noise coming from one side — Constitution Avenue.

I had a simple impulse to cut into the earth.

I imagined taking a knife and cutting into the earth, opening it up, an initial violence and pain that in time would heal. The grass would grow back, but the initial cut would remain a pure flat surface in the earth with a polished, mirrored surface, much like the surface on a geode when you cut it and polish the edge. The need for the names to be on the memorial would become the memorial; there was no need to embellish the design further. The people and their names would allow everyone to respond and remember.

It would be an interface, between our world and the quieter, darker, more peaceful world beyond. I chose black granite in order to make the surface reflective and peaceful. I never looked at the memorial as a wall, an object, but as an edge to the earth, an opened side. The mirrored effect would double the size of the park, creating two worlds, one we are a part of and one we cannot enter. The two walls were positioned so that one pointed to the Lincoln Memorial and the other pointed to the Washington Monument. By linking these two strong symbols for the country, I wanted to create a unity between the nation's past and present.

The idea of destroying the park to create something that by its very nature should commemorate life seemed hypocritical, nor was it in my nature. I wanted my design to work with the land, to make something with the site, not to fight it or dominate it. I see my works and their relationship to the landscape as being an additive rather than a combative process.

On our return to Yale, I quickly sketched my idea up, and it almost seemed too simple, too little. I toyed with adding some large flat slabs that would appear to lead into the memorial, but they didn't belong. The image was so simple that anything added to it began to detract from it.

I always wanted the names to be chronological, to make it so that those who served and returned from the war could find their place in the memorial. I initially had the names beginning on the left side and ending on the right. In a preliminary critique, a professor asked what importance that left for the apex, and I, too, thought it was a weak point, so I changed the design for the final critique. Now the chronological sequence began and ended at the apex so that the time line would circle back to itself and close the sequence. A progression in time is memorialized. The design is not just a list of the dead. To find one name, chances are you will see the others close by, and you will see yourself reflected through them.

The memorial was designed before I decided to enter the competition. I didn't even consider that it might win. When I submitted the project, I had the greatest difficulty trying to describe it in just one page. It took longer, in fact, to write the statement that I felt was needed to accompany the required drawings than to design the memorial. The description was critical to understanding the design since the memorial worked more on an emotional level than a formal level.

371

Aerial view of Vietnam ▶
Veterans Memorial.
(Courtesy of the
National Park Service)

Coincidentally, at the time, I was taking a course with Professor Vincent Scully, in which he just happened to focus on the same memorial I had been so moved by—the Lutyens memorial to the missing. Professor Scully described one's experience of that piece as a passage or journey through a yawning archway. As he described it, it resembled a gaping scream, which after you passed through, you were left looking out on a simple graveyard with the crosses and tombstones of the French and the English. It was a journey to an awareness of immeasurable loss, with the names of the missing carved on every surface of this immense archway.

I started writing furiously in Scully's class. I think he has always been puzzled by my connection to the Lutyens memorial. Formally the two memorials could not be more different. But for me, the experiences of these two memorials describe a similar passage to an awareness about loss.

The competition required drawings, along with the option to include a written description. As the deadline for submission approached, I created a series of simple drawings. The only thing left was to complete the essay, which I instinctively knew was the only way to get anyone to understand the design, the form of which was deceptively simple. I kept reworking and reediting the final description. I actually never quite finished it. I ended up at the last minute writing freehand directly onto the presentation boards (you can see a few misprints on the actual page), and then I sent the project in, never expecting to hear about it again.

The drawings were in soft pastels, very mysterious, very painterly, and not at all typical of architectural drawings. One of the comments made by a juror was "*He* must really know what he is doing to dare to do something so naive" (italics mine). But ultimately, I think it was the written description that convinced the jurors to select my design.

On my last day of classes my roommate, Liz Perry, came to retrieve me from one of my classes, telling me a call from Washington had come in and that it was from the Vietnam Veterans Memorial Fund; they needed to talk to me and would call back with a few questions about the design. When they called back, they merely said they needed to ask me a few questions and wanted to fly up to New Haven to talk to me. I was convinced that I was number 100 and they were only going to question me about drainage and other technical issues. It never occurred to me that I might have won the competition. It was still, in my mind, an exercise—as competitions customarily are for architecture students.

And even after three officers of the fund were seated in my college dorm room, explaining to me that it was the largest competition of its kind, with more than fourteen hundred entries, and Colonel Schaet, who was talking, without missing a beat calmly added that I had won (I think my roommate's face showed more emotion than mine did at the time), it still hadn't registered. I don't

374

COMMENT

"I begin by imagining an artwork verbally. I try to describe in writing what the project is, what it is trying to do. I need to understand the artwork without giving it a specific materiality or solid form. . . . I try not to find the form too soon. Instead, I try to think about it as an idea without a shape."

—Maya Lin

think it did for almost a year. Having studied the nature of competitions, especially in Washington (for instance, the FDR Memorial, still unbuilt in 1981, nearly forty years after it was first proposed, or the artwork Robert Venturi and Richard Serra collaborated on for L'Enfant Plaza, which was completely modified as it went through the required Washington design process of approvals), my attitude about unusual projects getting built in Washington was not optimistic. Partly it's my nature—I never get my hopes up—and partly I assumed the simplicity of the design, and its atypical form and color, would afford it a difficult time through the various governmental-approval agencies.

After the design had been chosen, it was subject to approval by various governmental agencies at both the conceptual and design development phases. I moved to Washington and stayed there throughout these phases. I expected the design to be debated within the design-approval agencies; I never expected the politics that constantly surrounded its development and fabrication.

I was driven down to D.C. the day of my college graduation, and I immediately became part of an internal struggle for control of the design. I think my age made it seem apparent to some that I was too young to understand what I had done or to see it through to completion. To bring the design into reality would require that I associate with an architect of record, a qualified firm that would work with me to realize the design. I had a very difficult time convincing the fund in charge of the memorial, the VVMF, of the importance of selecting a qualified firm that had experience both in architecture and landscape-integrated solutions, and that would be sympathetic to the design.

I had gone to Cesar Pelli, then dean of Yale's School of Architecture, for the names of some firms that could handle the job. A firm by the name of Cooper-Lecky was the one he recommended, and I presented its name to the fund, unaware that the competition's adviser was the fund's choice as architect of record. I was told by the fund that this person was the architect of record, and that was that.

After a few weeks of tense and hostile negotiations (in which at one point I was warned that I would regret these actions, and that I would "come crawling back on my hands and knees"), I was finally able to convince the fund to go through a legitimate process of selecting a firm to become the architect of record. The then architecture critic for the *Washington Post,* Wolf Von Eckardt, was instrumental in pressing the fund to listen to me. But the struggle left a considerable amount of ill will and mistrust between the veterans and myself.

Through the remaining phases of the project I worked with the Cooper-Lecky architectural firm. We worked on the practical details of the design, from the addition of a safety curb to a sidewalk to the problems in inscribing the names. Many of the issues we dealt with were connected to the text and my decision to list the names chronologically. People felt it would be an inconvenience to have to search out a name in a book and then find its panel location and thought that an alphabetical listing would be more convenient—until a tally of how many Smiths had died made it clear that an alphabetical listing wouldn't

375

be feasible. The MIA groups wanted their list of the missing separated out and listed alphabetically. I knew this would break the strength of the time line, interrupting the real-time experience of the piece, so I fought hard to maintain the chronological listing. I ended up convincing the groups that the time in which an individual was noted as missing was the emotionally compelling time for family members. A system of noting these names with a symbol[1] that could be modified to signify if the veteran was later found alive or officially declared dead would appease the concerns of the MIA groups without breaking the time line. I knew the time line was key to the experience of the memorial: a returning veteran would be able to find his or her time of service when finding a friend's name.

The text of the memorial and the fact that I had left out everything except the names led to a fight as to what else needed to be said about the war. The apex is the memorial's strongest point; I argued against the addition of text at that point for fear that a politically charged statement, one that would force a specific reading, would destroy the apolitical nature of the design. Throughout this time I was very careful not to discuss my beliefs in terms of politics; I played it extremely naive about politics, instead turning the issue into a strictly aesthetic one. Text could be added, but whatever was said needed to fit in three lines — to match the height of the dates "1959" and "1975" that it would be adjacent to. The veterans approved this graphic parameter, and the statements became a simple prologue and epilogue.

The memorial is analogous to a book in many ways. Note that on the right-hand panels the pages are set ragged right and on the left they are set ragged left, creating a spine at the apex as in a book. Another issue was scale; the text type is the smallest that we had come across, less than half an inch, which is unheard of in monument type sizing. What it does is create a very intimate reading in a very public space, the difference in intimacy between reading a billboard and reading a book.

The only other issue was the polished black granite and how it should be detailed, over which I remember having a few arguments with the architects of record. The architects could not understand my choice of a reflective, highly polished black granite. One of them felt I was making a mistake and the polished surface would be "too *feminine.*" Also puzzling to them was my choice of detailing the monument as a thin veneer with barely any thickness at its top edge. They wanted to make the monument's walls read as a massive, thick stone wall, which was not my intention at all. I always saw the wall as pure surface, an interface between light and dark, where I cut the earth and polished its open edge. The wall dematerializes as a form and allows the names to become the object, a pure and

■ *Why was Lin determined to use a "highly polished black granite"? What mood do the various materials and design ultimately suggest? In what ways is Lin's design (as she says) "experiential and cathartic"?*

376

[1]Each name is preceded (on the west wall) or followed (on the east wall) by one of two symbols: a diamond or a cross. The diamond denotes that the serviceman's or servicewoman's death was confirmed. The cross symbolizes those who were missing in action or prisoners at the end of the war. When a serviceperson's remains were returned, the diamond symbol is superimposed over the cross. If a serviceman or woman returns alive, a circle will be inscribed around the cross. [Lin's note.]

reflective surface that would allow visitors the chance to see themselves with the names. I do not think I thought of the color black as a color, more as the idea of a dark mirror into a shadowed mirrored image of the space, a space we cannot enter and from which the names separate us, an interface between the world of the living and the world of the dead.

One aspect that made the project unusual was its politicized building process. For instance, the granite could not come from Canada or Sweden. Though those countries had beautiful black granites, draft evaders went to both countries, so the veterans felt that we could not consider their granites as options. (The stone finally selected came from India.) The actual building process went smoothly for the most part, and the memorial was built very close to my original intentions.

As far as all of the controversy, I really never wanted to go into it too much. The memorial's starkness, its being below grade, being black, and how much my age, gender, and race played a part in the controversy, we'll never quite know. I think it is actually a miracle that the piece ever got built. From the very beginning I often wondered, if it had not been an anonymous entry 1026 but rather an entry by Maya Lin, would I have been selected?

I remember at the very first press conference a reporter asking me if I did not find it ironic that the memorial was for the Vietnam War and that I was of Asian descent. I was so righteous in my response that my race was completely irrelevant. It took me almost nine months to ask the VVMF, in charge of building the memorial, if my race was at all an issue. It had never occurred to me that it would be, and I think they had taken all the measures they could to shield me from such comments about a "gook" designing the memorial.

I remember reading the article that appeared in the *Washington Post* referring to "An Asian Memorial for an Asian War" and I knew we were in trouble. The controversy exploded in Washington after that article. Ironically, one side attacked the design for being "too Asian," while others saw its simplicity and understatement, not as an intention to create a more Eastern, meditative space, but as a minimalist statement which they interpreted as being nonreferential and disconnected from human experience.

This left the opinion in many that the piece emanated from a series of intellectualized aesthetic decisions, which automatically pitted artist against veterans. The fact that I was from an Ivy League college, had hair down to my knees, further fueled this distrust of the design and suspicions of a hippie college liberal or aesthetic elitist forcing her art and commentary upon them.

Perhaps it was an empathetic response to the idea about war that had led me to cut open the earth—an initial violence that heals in time but leaves a memory, like a scar. But this imagery, which some detractors would later describe as "a black gash of shame and sorrow" in which the color black was

Vietnam Veterans Memorial, two views. Lin writes, "I have often felt that a still photograph of my works does not afford an understanding of the piece, unless one has already seen it. Sometimes I think a film or sequence of still frames pieced together allows one to walk through the piece, giving one a clearer understanding of the work. But these works are hard to capture in a single image." (Images courtesy of Maya Lin Studio)

called the "universal color of shame and dishonor," would prove incredibly diffi-cult to defend. The misreading of the design as a negative political statement that in some way was meant to reflect upon the service of the veterans was in part fueled by a cultural prejudice against the color black as well as by the misreading or misinformation that led some veterans to imagine the design as a ditch or a hole. It took a prominent four-star general, Brigadier General George Price, who happened to be black, testifying before one of the countless subcommittee hear-ings and defending the color black, before the design could move forward.

But the distrust, the fact that no veterans had been on the jury, the uncon-ventionality of the design and the designer, and a very radical requirement made by the Vietnam veterans to include all the names of those killed made it inevitable that the project would become controversial. I think ultimately that much of the negative response goes back to the very natural response to cover up or not acknowledge that which is painful or unpleasant. The very fact that the veterans themselves had required the listing and therefore the acknowledgment of the more than 57,000 casualties, which is a landmark in our country in terms of see-ing a war via the individual lives lost, was very hard for many to face. I remember Ross Perot when he was trying to persuade the veterans that it was an inappro-priate design, asking me if I truly didn't feel that the veterans would prefer a parade instead, something happy or uplifting, and I can remember thinking that a parade would not in the long term help them overcome the enormous trauma of the politics of that war.

I do not think I fully realized until the dedication and homecoming parade that the veterans needed both. In effect the veterans gave themselves their own homecoming. In November 1982, I was in tears watching these men welcoming themselves home after almost ten years of not being acknowledged by their coun-try for their service, their sacrifice.

But until the memorial was built I don't think they realized that the design was experiential and cathartic, and, most importantly, designed not for me, but for them. They didn't see that the chronology of the names allowed a returning veteran the ability to find his or her own time frame on the wall and created a psy-chological space for them that directly focused on human response and feeling. I remember one of the veterans asking me before the wall was built what I thought people's reaction would be to it. I realized then that these veterans were willing to defend a design they really didn't quite understand. I was too afraid to tell him what I was thinking, that I knew a returning veteran would cry.

An architect once told me to look always at what was originally envisioned and try to keep it. I left Washington before ground breaking. I had to. The fund and I knew that we had to accept a compromise. The closer you watch something grow, the less able you are to notice changes in it. When I saw the site again, the granite panels were being put up and the place was frighteningly close to what I thought it should be. It terrified me. It was a strange feeling, to have had an idea that was solely yours be no longer a part of your mind but totally public, no longer yours.

There was always the expectation that since the war had been controversial, the memorial must be also. It wasn't so much an artistic dispute as a political one. The choice to make an apolitical memorial was in itself political to those who felt only a positive statement about the war would make up for the earlier antiwar days, a past swing to the left now to be balanced. It was extremely naive of me to think that I could produce a neutral statement that would not become politically controversial simply because it chose not to take sides.

Anyway, the push, as one congressman put it, to "politicize" the design didn't really affect the memorial in this way. The addition of the statue of infantrymen and then the addition of the female statue to make them equal are to me sad indicators that some politicians believe that you can please all of the people all of the time by compromise and conglomerate works. These statues leave only the false reading that the wall is for the dead and they are for the living, when the design I made was for the returning veterans and equally names all who served regardless of race, creed, or sex. I am only glad that the three infantrymen are not where they had been originally intended, right in the center of the memorial, heads sticking up higher than the walls, converting the walls to a backdrop and violating that private contemplative space. Ironically, the compromise memorializes the conflict in the building of the piece.

People cannot resolve that war, nor can they separate the issues, the politics, from it. As for me, the first time I visited the memorial after it was completed I found myself searching out the name of a friend's father and touching it. It was strange to realize that I was another visitor and I was reacting to it as I had designed it.

383

Michael Arad and Peter Walker, *Reflecting Absence*. The question of what a memorial should be and do has been actively debated during the last few years, since the tragic events of September 11, 2001. A jury appointed by the Lower Manhattan Development Corporation (LMDC) sifted through 5,201 proposals to determine what should happen to the space where the World Trade Center once stood. This is the winning proposal and computer "sketch." (Copyright 2004 LMDC. Rendering by dbox)

Michael Arad and Peter Walker
REFLECTING ABSENCE

This memorial proposes a space that resonates with the feelings of loss and absence that were generated by the destruction of the World Trade Center and the taking of thousands of lives on September 11, 2001, and February 26, 1993 [when the World Trade Center was first bombed, though with far less devastating effect]. It is located in a field of trees that is interrupted by two large voids containing recessed pools. The pools and the ramps that surround them encompass the footprints of the twin towers. A cascade of water that describes the perimeter of each square feeds the pools with a continuous stream. They are large voids, open and visible reminders of the absence.

The surface of the memorial plaza is punctuated by the linear rhythms of rows of deciduous trees, forming informal clusters, clearings, and groves. This surface consists of a composition of stone pavers, plantings, and low ground cover. Through its annual cycle of rebirth, the living park extends and deepens the experience of the memorial.

Bordering each pool is a pair of ramps that lead down to the memorial spaces. Descending into the memorial, visitors are removed from the sights and sounds of the city and immersed in a cool darkness. As they proceed, the sound of water falling grows louder, and more daylight filters in from below. At the bottom of their descent, they find themselves behind a thin curtain of water, staring out at an enormous pool. Surrounding this pool is a continuous ribbon of names. The enormity of this space and the multitude of names that form this endless ribbon underscore the vast scope of the destruction. Standing there at the water's edge, looking at a pool of water that is flowing away into an abyss, a visitor to the site can sense that what is beyond this curtain of water and ribbon of names is inaccessible.

The names of the deceased will be arranged in no particular order around the pools. After carefully considering different arrangements, I have found that any arrangement that tries to impose meaning through physical adjacency will cause grief and anguish to people who might be excluded from that process, furthering the sense of loss that they are already suffering.

The haphazard brutality of the attacks is reflected in the arrangement of names, and no attempt is made to impose order upon this suffering. The selfless sacrifices of rescue workers could be acknowledged with their agency's insignia

next to their names. Visitors to the site, including family members and friends of the deceased, would be guided by on-site staff or a printed directory to the specific location of each name. For those whose deceased were never physically identified, the location of the name marks a spot that is their own.

In between the two pools is a short passageway that links them at this lower level. A single alcove is located along this passageway, containing a small dais where visitors can light a candle or leave an artifact in memory of loved ones. Across from it, in a small chamber, visitors might pause and contemplate. This space provides for gatherings, quiet reflection, and memorial services.

Along the western edge of the site, a deep fissure exposes the slurry wall from plaza level to bedrock and provides access via a stairway. Descending alongside its battered surfaces, visitors will witness the massive expanse of the original foundations. The entrance to the underground interpretive center is located at bedrock. Here visitors could view many preserved artifacts from the twin towers: twisted steel beams, a crushed fire truck, and personal effects. The underground interpretive center would contain exhibition areas as well as lecture halls and a research library.

In contrast with the public mandate of the underground interpretive center is the very private nature of the room for unidentified remains. It is situated at bedrock at the north tower footprint. Here a large stone vessel forms a centerpiece for the unidentified remains. A large opening in the ceiling connects this space to the sky above, and the sound of water shelters the space from the city. Family members can gather here for moments of private contemplation. It is a personal space for remembrance.

The memorial plaza is designed to be a mediating space; it belongs both to the city and to the memorial. Located at street level to allow for its integration into the fabric of the city, the plaza encourages the use of this space by New Yorkers on a daily basis. The memorial grounds will not be isolated from the rest of the city; they will be a living part of it.

386

United States Holocaust Memorial Museum, *Forgetting Would Be A Second Abandonment.* How much did the ▶ United States and its World War II allies know about the Nazi concentration camps and the extermination of Jews? Holocaust scholars worldwide have spent decades investigating this question. One widely acclaimed study, David Wyman's *The Abandonment of the Jews* (1984), argues that the U.S. government's failure to act on the information it had about the death camps made it a "passive accomplice" to the Nazi regime. It is this first moral failure to act that the United States Holocaust Memorial Museum echoes in its advertisement headlined "Forgetting Would Be A Second Abandonment."

The United States Holocaust Memorial Museum opened in April 1993 — its goal is to perpetuate the memory of the destruction of European Jewry. The museum's collections include over 35,000 objects, archival documents, photographs, oral histories, films, and books, and the museum regularly offers lectures, a registry, research facilities, and special exhibits and events. In addition, Congress has established annual National Days of Remembrance to commemorate victims of the Holocaust. The museum is committed to the belief that "remembrance of the past will influence the course of the future." The announcement shown here advertised the National Days of Remembrance for the year 2000.

Forgetting Would Be A Second Abandonment

What message do you think this headline sends? What is it asking you to do?

"History will not forgive us if we fail. History will not forget us if we succeed."

—Report of the President's Commission on the Holocaust, September 27, 1979

NATIONAL DAYS OF REMEMBRANCE

APRIL 30 – MAY 7, 2000

UNITED STATES HOLOCAUST MEMORIAL MUSEUM

100 Raoul Wallenberg Place, SW • Washington, D.C. 20024-2126 • (202) 488-0400 • www.ushmm.org

> go

To visit the online Holocaust
Memorial Museum, go to
www.ushmm.org/museum.

MESSAGE

How does Maya Lin's
proposal for the Vietnam
Veterans Memorial com-
pare with Michael Arad's
and Peter Walker's proposal
for a 9/11 memorial? Lin
has said that she thinks the
Vietnam memorial judges
were swayed by her written
description rather than by
her sketches; how impor-
tant do you think the written
description "Reflecting
Absence" is to being
chosen as the winning proposal to commemorate
9/11? What message does
each verbal proposal send,
beyond the physical
description of what each
memorial would look like?

METHOD

The Holocaust Memorial
Museum holds annual Days
of Remembrance; the print
ad on page 387 promotes
the days of remembrance
for 2000. Such methods
of advertising are obviously
different from the methods
of building a physical monument, though in some
respects one could say the
purpose is the same. Try to
use advertising methods
to design a print ad for this
year's 9/11 anniversary. How
would you combine print
and image? What kind of
image would you choose?
The burning tower? The
photos and posters of the
missing? Something else?
What do you want people to
remember, and what
method would you use to
send that message?

MEDIUM

Lin compares the Vietnam
Veterans Memorial to a
book. In what ways do
these very different media
resemble each other? How
does the comparison help
you conceive of Lin's
memorial? Does it alter the
way you visualize it? How
else does writing enter into
Lin's thinking about the
memorial's design? What
connections can you see
between her verbal and
visual processes? What
other media does she introduce for comparisons?

EXPOSING WAR

ESSAY | JOURNAL | TRANSCRIPT | 5 PHOTOS | AD

"Central to modern expectations, and modern ethical feeling," writes the renowned critic Susan Sontag, "is the conviction that war is an aberration, if an unstoppable one. That peace is the norm, if an unattainable one. This, of course, is not the way war has been regarded throughout history. War has been the norm and peace the exception." In our time, Sontag notes in her book *Regarding the Pain of Others* (2003), the public sees war largely through photographs and video clips. What do these images tell us about the reality of combat? What sense do we make of the harrowing pictures and atrocious images displayed in magazines and on our TV screens? Do we turn away from them, or do we—as Sontag suggests—let "the atrocious images haunt us"? For Sontag, the images "perform a vital function." They say: "This is what human beings are capable of doing—may volunteer to do, enthusiastically, self-righteously. Don't forget."

Although *Regarding the Pain of Others* covers a wide array of war images, from the Civil War through the war in Iraq, the book includes no photographs. In this chapter we have included a few of the significant photographs Sontag mentions—Alexander Gardner's grim photograph of the battlefield at Gettysburg, and Ronald L. Haeberle's astonishing photos of the My Lai massacre during the Vietnam War. Gardner's comments on his Gettysburg photo accompany the photograph, and the My Lai photos are supplemented by two documents from the subsequent military trial of the officer responsible for the massacre. Also included here is an advertisement that pertains to the argument Sontag makes in "Watching Suffering from a Distance," an excerpt from one of the final chapters of her book.

 Go to exercise 06 on **ix visual exercises** on **emphasis** and **color** and use these concepts to think about the material in this chapter. What does color do to photographs of war?

389

COMMENT

"One of the great platitudes of our epoch is that images, in particular photographic or filmed images, transmit messages that are much clearer and stronger than words, which disguise the truth more than they reveal it. But in truth nothing could be less certain: a photograph can stun us, but taken out of context it may not convey any significant meaning. You see a mutilated corpse, you are moved and overcome by shock or pity; but you do not yet know who this corpse is, nor why this person has been killed, nor by whom; nor whether this is a case that warrants an appeal to vengeance, or on the contrary an appeal for peace, or whether it is only an incitement to meditate on the fragility of human existence. Sentences have a subject and a predicate, a part that delimits what is being discussed and another part that says something about it. But images are subjects without predicates: they evoke the world intensely, but they do not tell us, of themselves, what we should think about it."

— Tzvetan Todorov, from "Exposures"
(*The New Republic,* April 21 and 28, 2003)

Susan Sontag, *Watching Suffering from a Distance*. One of America's best known and most admired writers, activists, and theorists, Susan Sontag was born in New York City in 1933; she grew up in Tucson, Arizona, and attended high school in Los Angeles. She received her B.A. from the College of the University of Chicago and did graduate work in philosophy, literature, and theology at Harvard University and Saint Anne's College, Oxford. Her publications include fiction, plays, screenplays, and eight important works of nonfiction, including *Against Interpretation* (1966), *On Photography* (1978), *Illness as Metaphor* (1979), *Where the Stress Falls* (2001), and *Regarding the Pain of Others* (2003). Sontag has recently written on the photographs from the notorious Abu Ghraib prison in Iraq. She has won numerous awards, including the National Book Award. This essay is taken from Chapter 8 in *Regarding the Pain of Others*. In this book Sontag explores war, as we know it through images; along the way she reconsiders some of the ideas she laid out in her highly influential book *On Photography*.

Susan Sontag

WATCHING SUFFERING FROM A DISTANCE

To designate a hell is not, of course, to tell us anything about how to extract people from that hell, how to moderate hell's flames. Still, it seems a good in itself to acknowledge, to have enlarged, one's sense of how much suffering caused by human wickedness there is in the world we share with others. Someone who is perennially surprised that depravity exists, who continues to feel disillusioned (even incredulous) when confronted with evidence of what humans are capable of inflicting in the way of gruesome, hands-on cruelties upon other humans, has not reached moral or psychological adulthood.

No one after a certain age has the right to this kind of innocence, of superficiality, to this degree of ignorance, or amnesia.

There now exists a vast repository of images that make it harder to maintain this kind of moral defectiveness. Let the atrocious images haunt us. Even if they are only tokens, and cannot possibly encompass most of the reality to which they refer, they still perform a vital function. The images say: This is what human beings are capable of doing—may volunteer to do, enthusiastically, self-righteously. Don't forget.

This is not quite the same as asking people to remember a particularly monstrous bout of evil. ("Never forget.") Perhaps too much value is assigned to memory, not enough to thinking. Remembering *is* an ethical act, has ethical value in and of itself. Memory is, achingly, the only relation we can have with the dead. So the belief that remembering is an ethical act is deep in our natures as humans, who know we are going to die, and who mourn those who in the normal course of things die before us—grandparents, parents, teachers, and older friends. Heartlessness and amnesia seem to go together. But history gives contradictory signals about the value of remembering in the much longer span of a collective history. There is simply too much injustice in the world. And too much remembering (of ancient grievances: Serbs, Irish) embitters. To make peace is to forget. To reconcile, it is necessary that memory be faulty and limited.

If the goal is having some space in which to live one's own life, then it is desirable that the account of specific injustices dissolve into a more general understanding that human beings everywhere do terrible things to one another.

Parked in front of the little screens—television, computer, palmtop—we can surf to images and brief reports of disasters throughout the world. It seems as if there is a greater quantity of such news than before. This is probably an illusion. It's just that the spread of news is "everywhere." And some people's sufferings have a lot more intrinsic interest to an audience (given that suffering must be acknowledged as having an audience) than the sufferings of others. That news about war is now disseminated worldwide does not mean that the capacity to think about the suffering of people far away is significantly larger. In a modern life—a life in which there is a superfluity of things to which we are invited to pay attention—it seems normal to turn away from images that simply make us feel bad. Many more would be switching channels if the news media were to devote more time to the particulars of human suffering caused by war and other infamies. But it is probably not true that people are responding less.

That we are not totally transformed, that we can turn away, turn the page, switch the channel, does not impugn the ethical value of an assault by images. It is not a defect that we are not seared, that we do not suffer *enough,* when we see these images. Neither is the photograph supposed to repair our ignorance about the history and causes of the suffering it picks out and frames. Such images cannot be more than an invitation to pay attention, to reflect, to learn, to examine the rationalizations for mass suffering offered by established powers. Who caused what the picture shows? Who is responsible? Is it excusable? Was it inevitable? Is there some state of affairs which we have accepted up to now that ought to be challenged? All this, with the understanding that moral indignation, like compassion, cannot dictate a course of action.

The frustration of not being able to do anything about what the images show may be translated into an accusation of the indecency of regarding such images, or the indecencies of the way such images are disseminated—flanked, as they may well be, by advertising for emollients, pain relievers, and SUVs. If we could do something about what the images show, we might not care as much about these issues.

Images have been reproached for being a way of watching suffering at a distance, as if there were some other way of watching. But watching up close—without the mediation of an image—is still just watching.

Some of the reproaches made against images of atrocity are not different from characterizations of sight itself. Sight is effortless; sight requires spatial distance; sight can be turned off (we have lids on our eyes, we do not have doors on our ears). The very qualities that made the ancient Greek philosophers consider sight the most excellent, the noblest of the senses are now associated with a deficit.

It is felt that there is something morally wrong with the abstract of reality offered by photography; that one has no right to experience the suffering of others at a distance, denuded of its raw power; that we pay too high a human (or moral) price for those hitherto admired qualities of visions—the standing back from the aggressiveness of the world which frees us for observation and for elective attention. But this is only to describe the function of the mind itself.

There's nothing wrong with standing back and thinking. To paraphrase several sages: "Nobody can think and hit someone at the same time."

COMMENT

"The first full-scale attempt to document a war was carried out during the American Civil War, by a firm of Northern photographers headed by Mathew Brady, who had made several official portraits of President Lincoln. The Brady war pictures — most were shot by Alexander Gardner and Timothy O'Sullivan, although their employer was invariably credited with them — showed conventional subjects, such as encampments populated by officers and foot soldiers, towns in war's way, ordnance, ships, and also, most famously, dead Union and Confederate soldiers lying on the blasted ground of Gettysburg and Antietam. Though access to the battlefield came as a privilege extended to Brady and his team by Lincoln himself, the photographers were not commissioned, [. . .] Their status evolved in rather typical American fashion, with nominal government sponsorship giving way to the force of entrepreneurial and freelance motives.

"The first justification for the brutally legible pictures of a field of dead soldiers was the simple duty to record. 'The camera is the eye of history,' Brady is supposed to have said. And history, invoked as truth beyond appeal, was allied with the rising prestige of a certain notion of subjects needing more attention, known as realism, which was soon to have a host of defenders among novelists as well as photographers. In the name of realism, one was permitted — required — to show unpleasant, hard facts. Such pictures also convey 'a useful moral' by showing 'the blank horror and reality of war, in opposition to its pageantry,' as Gardner wrote in a text accompanying O'Sullivan's picture of fallen Confederate soldiers, their agonized faces clearly visible. 'Here are the dreadful details! Let them aid in preventing another such calamity falling upon the nation.' But the frankness of the most memorable pictures in an album of photographs by Gardner and other Brady photographers, which Gardner published after the war, did not mean that he and his colleagues had necessarily photographed their subjects as they found them. To photograph was to compose (with living subjects, to pose); the desire to arrange elements in the picture did not vanish because the subject was immobilized, or immobile."

—Susan Sontag, from *Regarding the Pain of Others*

Alexander Gardner, *A Harvest of Death, Gettysburg, July, 1863*. For three days in
July 1863, members of the confederate and Union armies confronted each other at
Gettysburg. An estimated 51,000 men died. That battle remains the bloodiest con-
frontation ever fought on North American soil. Alexander Gardner was the official photographer of the Union's Army of the Potomac until the end of the Civil War. He traveled with the army and documented scenes of the camps and the battlefields. (Library
of Congress, negative #LC-B8184-7694-A)

Ron Haviv, *Bijeljina, Bosnia, 1992.* Sontag refers to this picture by Ron Haviv; Haviv documented the beginning of the Serbian brutalities against Muslims in Bosnia. Haviv says of his photography, "it's a cliché but it's important that the photojournalists are out there, documenting what's happening and holding people accountable. The work does become evidence." (© Ron Haviv/VII)

COMMENT

"Harrowing photographs do not inevitably lose their power to shock. But they don't help us much to understand. Narratives can make us understand. Photographs do something else: they haunt us. Consider one of the most unforgettable images of the war in Bosnia, a photograph of which the *New York Times* foreign correspondent John Kifner wrote, 'The image is stark, one of the most enduring of the Balkan wars: a Serb militiaman casually kicking a dying Muslim woman in the head. It tells you everything you need to know.' But of course it doesn't tell us everything we need to know.

"From the identification supplied by the photographer, Ron Haviv, we learn that the photograph was taken in the town of Bijeljina in April 1992, the first month of the Serb rampage through Bosnia. From behind, we see a uniformed Serb soldier, a youthful figure with sunglasses perched on the top of his head, a cigarette between the second and third fingers of his raised left hand, rifle dangling in his right hand, right leg poised to kick a woman lying face down on the sidewalk between two other bodies. The photograph doesn't tell us that she is Muslim, but she is not likely to have been labeled in any other way, or why would she and the two others be lying there, as if dead (why 'dying'?), under the gaze of some Serb soldiers? In fact, the photograph tells us very little — except that war is hell, and that graceful young men with guns are capable of kicking in the head overweight older women lying helpless, or already killed.

"The pictures of Bosnian atrocities were seen soon after they took place. Like pictures from the Vietnam War, such as Ron Haeberle's documents of the massacre by a company of American soldiers of some five hundred unarmed civilians in the village of My Lai in March 1968, they became important in bolstering indignation at this war which had been far from inevitable, far from intractable; and could have been stopped much sooner. Therefore one could feel an obligation to look at these pictures, gruesome as they were, because there was something to be done, right now, about what they depicted. Other issues are raised when the public is invited to respond to a dossier of hitherto unknown pictures of horrors long past."

—Susan Sontag, from *Regarding the Pain of Others*

◀ **Ronald L. Haeberle,** *My Lai villagers before and after being shot by U.S. troops.*
Combat photography became part of military life in the mid-nineteenth century,
changing the nature of the public's relation to national conflicts. Photographs of
war satisfied public curiosity far more than sketches or words had previously, and
the military quickly learned that photographs could be incredibly useful in sway-
ing public opinion. During World War II, photographs were carefully released
and controlled — sometimes even staged — to satisfy the military's need to control its image and to celebrate American heros in the field.

The Vietnam War, however, was as different for photographers as it was for
the soldiers in the field — photojournalists played an important role in exposing
the space between what the American government wanted to claim and what was
actually happening. Haeberle, a combat photographer, accompanied Charlie
Company to My Lai and recorded the massacre on both his official black-and-
white army camera and his personal color camera. When his personal photographs appeared in *Life* magazine on December 5, 1969, they provoked international outrage and enormous media coverage. The pictures of the My Lai massacre are only one example — albeit some of the most famous — of the images
that sparked anti-war sentiments in the United States. (Reprinted by permission
of Ronald S. Haeberle/TimePix)

400

Thomas R. Partsch, *March 16–18, 1968.* Early in the morning of March 16, 1968, Captain
Ernest Medina's Charlie Company attacked the small village of My Lai (the troops also
referred to it as "Pinkville") expecting to encounter an enemy battalion. But Charlie
Company found no resistance and saw only civilians. For the next four hours they killed
between four and five hundred Vietnamese — mostly women, children, babies, and the elderly. According to eyewitnesses, many women and girls were raped and then brutally executed. Not all the soldiers participated; some refused to fire, and some tried to stop what
would become one of the most disgraceful episodes in American military history. The army
tried to keep the incident secret, but there were too many leaks; in November 1969, the
government launched an official investigation. Many Americans disbelieved the rumors or
excused them as an unfortunate part of warfare until they saw the shocking photographs
released by *Life* magazine a month later. One of the men in Charlie Company who kept a
war journal was Thomas R. Partsch. During the subsequent military trial, the relevant parts
of his journal (March 16–March 18, 1968) were introduced as evidence.

Thomas R. Partsch
MARCH 16–18, 1968

<u>Mar 16 Sat</u>. got up at 5:30 left at 7:15 we had 9 choppers. 2 lifts first landed had mortar team with us. We started to move slowly through the village shooting everything in sight children men and women and animals. Some was sickening. There legs were shot off and they were still moving it was just hanging there. I think there bodies were made of rubber. I didn't fire a round yet and didn't kill anybody not even a chicken I couldn't. We are know suppose to push through 2 more it is about 10 A.M. and we are taken a rest before going in. We also got 2 weapons M1 and a carbine our final desti[na]tion is the Pinkville suppose to be cement bunkers we killed about 100 people after a while they said not to kill women and children. Stopped for chow about 1 P.M. we didn't do much after that. We are know setting up for the night 2 companies B and someone else we are set up in part of a village and rice patties had to dig foxhole area pretty level are mortars are out with us. Are serving hot chow tonite I looked in my pack for dry socks and found out they were stolen from the time we were out in the field the name of the villages are My Lai 4, 5, and 6. I am know pulling my guard for night. 1 1/2 hours I am with the 1st squad had pop and beer. Sky is a little cloudy but it is warm out.

    <u>Mar 17 Sun</u>: got up at 6:30 foggy out. We didn't go to Pinkville went to My Lai 2, 3, and 4 no one was there we burned as we pushed. We got 4 VC and a nurse. Had documents on them yesterday we took 14 VC. We pushed as far as the coast to the South China Sea there was a village along the coast also a lot of sailboats we stayed there for about an hour we went back about 2 kilometers to set up camp its in a graveyard actually we didn't pull guard but awake most of the night.

    <u>Mar 18 Mon</u>: moved back to another area 1 VC said he would take us to a tunnel he took us all over didn't find any after that we met with other platoons as we were going 2 guys hit mines there flack jackets saved them not hurt bad Trevino and Gonzalez. . . . [T]here is a lot of fuss on what happened at the village a Gen was asking questions. There is going to be an investigation on Medina. We are not supposed to say anything. I didn't think it was right but we did it but we did it at least I can say I didn't kill anybody. I think I wanted to but in another way I didn't.

■ *What elements make Partsch's journal authentic? How do spelling and grammatical errors contribute? What details does he introduce that persuade you he is an actual participant and witness to the event? Why do you think he's keeping this journal? What does his attitude appear to be toward the massacre?*

401

William L. Calley Court Martial Transcript, 1970. In this excerpt from his court-martial trial, Calley talks about his combat experiences before My Lai. After the investigation and trials, Lieutenant Calley, a platoon leader who claimed he acted under direct orders, was the only defendant found guilty of war crimes. In March 1971, he was sentenced to life imprisonment for multiple murders. He was pardoned and released in 1974.

William L. Calley
COURT MARTIAL TRANSCRIPT

Q: Every time that the company would go, at least a company-sized unit, to try to get in that area and stay there, they encountered hostile fire, enemy fire, suffered casualties, and were driven out?

A: Yes, sir. [Calley was asked about an incident that occurred when he was returning to his company from in-country R and R. As he was waiting for a helicopter to take him to his men, he helped unload a chopper filled with casualties caused by a mine field.]

Q: What did you see and what did you do in connection with that helicopter when it landed back there and before you boarded up to go to meet your company?

A: The chopper was filled with gear, rifles, rucksacks. I think the most — the thing that really hit me hard was the heavy boots. There must have been six boots there with the feet still in them, brains all over the place, and everything was saturated with blood, rifles blown in half. I believe there was one arm on it and a piece of a man's face, half of a man's face was on the chopper with the gear.

Q: Did you later subsequently learn that those members that were emaciated in that manner were members of your company or your platoon?

A: I knew at the time they were.

Q: What was your feeling when you saw what you did see in the chopper and what you found out about your organization being involved in that kind of an operation?

A: I don't know if I can describe the feelings.

Q: At least try.

A: It's anger, hate, fear, generally sick to your stomach, hurt.

Q: Did it have any impact on your beliefs, your ideas, or what you might like to do in connection with somehow or other on into combat and accomplishing your mission? Am I making that too complicated for you?

A: I believe so.

Q: I'm trying to find out if it had any impact on your future actions as you were going to have to go in and if you did go in and reach the enemy on other occasions and if so, what was the impact?

A: I'm not really sure of what my actual feelings were at that time. I can't sit down and say I made any formal conclusions of what I would do when I met the enemy. I think there is an—that instilled a deeper sense of hatred for the enemy. I don't think I ever made up my mind or came to any conclusion as to what I'd do to the enemy.

Q: All right. Now did you have any remorse or grief or anything?

A: Yes, sir, I did.

Q: What was that?

A: The remorse for losing my men in the mine field. The remorse that those men ever had to go to Vietnam, the remorse of being in that situation where you are completely helpless. I think I felt mainly remorse because I wasn't there, although there was nothing I could do. There was a psychological factor of just not being there when everything is happening.

Q: Did you feel sorry that you weren't there with your troops?

A: Yes, sir.

COMMENT

"I think most Americans understood that the My Lai massacre was not representative of our people, of the war we were fighting, or of our men who were fighting it; but from the time it first became public the whole tragic episode was used by the media and the antiwar forces to chip away at our efforts to build public support for our Vietnam objectives and policies."

—Richard Nixon

Physicians Against Land Mines, *Emina's Story*. Although used primarily for military ▶ purposes, land mines exact a horrifying toll on civilian populations, primarily in developing nations. It is estimated that over 80 percent of all land-mine victims are civilians. Of these, 30 to 40 percent are children under age fifteen. In 1999, 137 countries signed a treaty prohibiting the use, stockpiling, and production of land mines, but the United States, along with Russia and China, refused to sign. Physicians Against Land Mines (PALM) describes itself as a "nongovernmental organization whose mission is to end the death, dismemberment and disability caused by land mines." A program of the Center for International Rehabilitation in Chicago, PALM sponsors public information initiatives, advocates reforms in international law, and runs numerous disability programs. It also educates the public through advertisements such as the one reprinted here, designed by advertising company Leo Barnett for use in magazines, in bus shelters, and inside buses and trains. Several magazines—including *Harper's, Atlantic Monthly, Bomb,* and *People*— have donated space for this ad campaign.

Emina Uzicanin was just 5 years old. Her family was living on the outskirts of Sarajevo. On a sunny afternoon in May, Emina was playing in a field behind her Uncle's house. There, she spotted two little rabbits. As soon as she started toward them, the rabbits took off. So she began running. Five feet. Ten feet. That's when it happened. An ear-shattering explosion ripped through Emina's body — severing her left leg and leaving the rest of her badly scarred. Every 22 minutes another innocent civilian is killed or maimed by a land mine. Right now there are over 60 million unexploded land mines waiting just beneath the earth in nearly 70 countries. We need your help to rid the planet of land mines and to help its victims like Emina.

Physicians Against Land Mines
Member of the International Campaign to Ban Land Mines

www.banmines.org

COMMENT

"Emina Uzicanin was just 5 years old. Her family was living on the outskirts of Sarajevo. On a sunny afternoon in May, Emina was playing in a field behind her Uncle's house. There, she spotted two little rabbits. As soon as she started toward them, the rabbits took off. So she began running. Five feet. Ten feet. That's when it happened. An ear-shattering explosion ripped through Emina's body — severing her left leg and leaving the rest of her badly scarred. Every 22 minutes another innocent civilian is killed or maimed by a land mine. Right now there are over 60 million unexploded land mines waiting just beneath the earth in nearly 70 countries. We need your help to rid the planet of land mines and to help its victims like Emina."

— "Emina's Story," from the PALM web site (www.banmines.org)

■ *Consider what the pronoun "its" refers to. Would you have expected the word "their" instead? Given the grammatical structure, what is Emina Uzicanin a victim of? How do you interpret the phrasing? Do you think the copywriter made a grammatical error?*

MESSAGE

Susan Sontag raises an ethical issue in "Watching Suffering from a Distance." How would you describe that issue in a single sentence? In your opinion, does she find the display of atrocious images indecent or morally wrong, or does she think there is a value to seeing them? In what ways do you find her position complicated?

METHOD

Sontag deliberately includes no photographs in her book. The editors of this book, however, made a decision to include a few of the pictures she refers to. Which method do you find most effective in this particular case — visually illustrating an argument, or choosing not to and having words speak for themselves? Explain your answer.

MEDIUM

Though Sontag focuses on photography as a medium for recording war and suffering, today we are more likely to see such images on television. What do you think is the strongest and most responsible medium for capturing the horror of war or the pain of others? Can you think of a moving picture that has lingered in your heart and mind as deeply as a still photograph? Or do words have a greater effect? Explain your answer.

Assignment 1

After enjoying more than a decade of relative peace, America was first assaulted with the violent attacks of September 11, 2001, and shortly thereafter entered into wars in both Afghanistan and Iraq. These military actions of today will eventually take their places in the history books, alongside other wars you have studied and we — as a nation — have commemorated. You may personally know someone who fought, who is taking part in current military action, or who is simply waiting for a loved one to return home safely from fighting overseas. Conversely, you might have very strong convictions against the actions that have taken place in Iraq and Afghanistan — or you may not have followed the news coverage and political debates over the wars much at all. Take some time to free write about your understanding of and feelings about America's actions, and about what impact you think they might eventually have on the history of the nation. Next, research the Iraq war and the events surrounding it, as well as the continued operations in that country to restore peace and stability. Begin gathering images and parts of the story that would help commemorate this wartime in America's history. How do you think this war, and the servicemen and women who fought in it, should be commemorated? What details will be important for future generations to know about these actions, and about the people taking part in them? Adopt the role of a historian to gather information, images, interviews, and television and web site coverage of the Iraq war. Create your own chapter for a history book that tells the story of what has happened and is happening in Iraq today. Decide what level of audience your chapter will be written to and the issues it will need to discuss to fully communicate a sense of the war and the time period that spawned it. Determine the balance of text, images, and web and video resources you would include to engage your audience and make this time period come to life for your future readers. How will your chapter illustrate, commemorate, and document this war for history?

Laurent Rebours, *Statue of Iraqi President Saddam Hussein Being Pulled Down in Downtown Baghdad, Wednesday, April 9, 2003.* This photograph appears on a web site for the U.S. Department of State's Office of International Information Programs (usinfo.state.gov). It is one of many images that you could choose to represent the Iraq war. (© 2003 AP/WideWorld Photos)

Assignment 2

There have been many 20th-century genocides such as those in Armenia, Bosnia, Cambodia, Rwanda, Sri Lanka, Ukraine, and Zimbabwe, to name a few. You are most likely not as familiar with the details of these events in recent history as you are with the Holocaust — and yet, the devastation to certain peoples and cultures was often just as significant. Research one of these episodes of genocide in small groups. What explicit and implicit tensions, rivalries, or racist agendas led up to these events? Who was involved, and what happened? How have the people involved and those affected moved on? What changes have resulted in the country, and how is the healing process evolving there? In your groups, gather as many resources as you can in order to create a summary proposal for some type of memorial to the genocide victims that will help raise awareness of what took place (such as the Holocaust Memorial poster). Your proposals can focus on a print ad campaign, poster campaign, video documentary, audio documentary, or other public awareness vehicle to bring your message of awareness to the larger public. Your teams will need to utilize your knowledge and research of the events in order to carefully and respectfully represent the genocide victims.

Human Rights Watch, _Remembering Rwanda: Africa in Conflict, Yesterday and Today._ This publication from Human Rights Watch commemorates the ten-year anniversary of the genocide in Rwanda. In 1994, at least half a million Tutsi and moderate Hutu were killed in Rwanda over a three-month period. (© 2004 Corinne Dufka/Human Rights Watch)

407

> **go**

Go to bedfordstmartins.com/ convergences to find links to web resources that will be useful to you in undertaking this research project.

1. Note some of the similarities between the urban photographs of Weegee in Chapter 2 and those of Wayne F. Miller in this chapter. How would you describe the resemblance? What similarities can you find, say, between Weegee's *Mulberry Street Café* (p. 197) and Miller's *Two Girls Waiting Outside a Tavern* (p. 333)? After examining Wendy Lesser's reading of Weegee's photos, write an essay in which you apply her analytical methods to one of Wayne Miller's pictures. How does the analysis contribute to your understanding of the photo's historical value?

2. Using the Internet, find out what you can about the Sand Creek massacre. Then, after your class reads Maya Lin's essay on designing the Vietnam Veterans Memorial (p. 368), form several small groups to work independently on an appropriate design for a Sand Creek Memorial. Be sure to touch on the relationship between the materials you would use and the site you would choose. Be sure also to anticipate criticisms you may receive from various interested parties. Afterward, form a panel in which a designated member of each group exhibits a rough sketch and provides a verbal description of the memorial's design.

3. In an essay, compare and contrast Susan Sontag's "Watching Suffering from a Distance" (p. 391) with Nora Ephron's "The Boston Photographs" (p. 200). In what ways are the essays similar? In what ways are the ethical issues similar? Which writer, in your opinion, deals with the ethical issues more effectively? Which set of photos do you find more disturbing? Why?

4. After reading James Munves's "Going to Press" (p. 308) and Art Spiegelman's essay on Plastic Man (p. 342), along with Scott McCloud's lesson on sequence (p. 137), break into small groups and imagine how Munves's essay might be transformed into a historical comic strip that portrays the publishing process behind The Declaration of Independence. What details from Munves's account would you use? How would you begin and end? Each group should select its most skilled "artist" and prepare a rough draft of eight to ten frames.

5. The Holocaust was a central event of the twentieth century for the Western world. In class discussion, develop a list of questions regarding what U.S. leaders did and did not know about the death camps at the time. After coming up with several well-defined questions, form small groups and research information relevant to each question. The United States Holocaust Memorial Museum's web site (www.ushmm.org) provides data and relevant

MAKING HISTORY

links. Then, select members of each group to participate in a panel that addresses to what extent the United States "abandoned" victims of the Holocaust.

6. Through the process of class discussion, collectively select a historical film (for example, *Malcolm X, Gandhi, The Patriot*) to watch as part of a class exercise. Watch it closely, especially noticing its use of historical details. Afterward, break into small groups and talk about the relation between the value of historical accuracy and the special demands of film. What aspects of the movie do you think were contrived or fabricated to serve the interests of entertainment — storytelling, emotional drama, and so on? What aspects do you think were handled accurately and truthfully? Did you think the movie was using an episode or character from the past mainly to reflect present-day values? Did you feel you had sufficient information beforehand to make these evaluations? In a paper, discuss how well the film you watched stacked up as history.

7. A good number of books and articles have been written about the My Lai massacre. The investigation and trial captured the attention of the entire world. Using as much information as you can gather from library and Internet sources, write a research paper in which you describe how the facts of the incident leaked out. In your paper explore the following questions, though you need not answer them all or in any particular order: What sequence of events immediately followed the massacre? Who talked and to whom? How did the army try to cover up the killings? How important were the eyewitness reports, and whose reports seemed most trustworthy? Did any Vietnamese testify? How important were the photographs in establishing the facts? Remember: the object is to narrate the step-by-step process of disclosure. Be sure to document your sources.

8. Can the Internet provide the groundwork for a new social history in which people without credentials or influence tell their personal or communal stories? Can such sites become the foundation for what the historian Howard Zinn has called a "people's history" of the world? In a paper that reflects your research of web sites and bulletin boards, identify those that now perform this historical function (or could possibly do so) and discuss how important these sites can be for future historians. You might take, for example, the Sand Creek massacre (p. 322): Can you find oral histories that give the perspectives of American Indians?

409

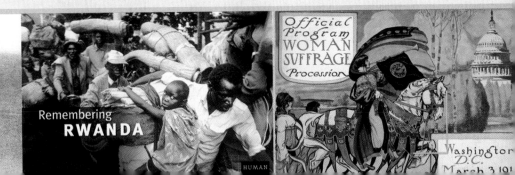

Remembering
RWANDA

Official Program WOMAN SUFFRAGE *Procession*

Washington D.C.
March 3 191

9. Pretend that you have just won a national lottery to be the person to travel into the past in a time machine. The conditions: you can return to any moment you choose, but only for an hour, and though you will be invisible, you will retain your present consciousness. Write an essay about your imaginary voyage into the past. What moment did you select? How difficult was it to decide? Why did you finally choose that moment? Was there something you wanted to know? What do you think you could tell the world when you returned?

10. For a research project, read Gwendolyn Brooks's first volume of poetry, *A Street in Bronzeville* (1945), in conjunction with viewing whatever photographs of Chicago's South Side during that era you can find in the library or on the Internet. In a paper, discuss the ways in which the poet and the photographer(s) converged toward the same subject matter. Do you think this convergence is accidental, or can you find reasons for the similarities? In your paper, make an attempt to show how these two different media can work toward similar artistic goals.

5

DIVIDING LINES

Knowing who we are usually means knowing also who we are not. As individuals or in groups, we habitually define ourselves by our differences from others, drawing a line between "us" and "them." What are these powerful lines? Are they wholly imaginary, or do they have a concrete existence? To what extent do these lines shape personal identity and social behavior? How do they partition the world around us? Wherever you happen to be, if you pay close attention, you will notice dividing lines — both visible and invisible — everywhere. They include everything from the property boundaries of a suburban subdivision to the police barriers at a political demonstration, from a roommate's portion of a bookshelf to the variously priced seating sections of a stadium.

At certain points in our nation's history, religious differences — even relatively small ones between sects — led to widespread discrimination and violent conflict. The American Civil War was fought largely over the issue of slavery, which had been a constant source of regional and ideological tension since the nation's founding. In the 1960s, generational differences became heated, as counterculture leaders famously advised their followers not to trust anyone over the age of thirty, which meant essentially not to trust the authority of parents, political leaders, or teachers. In the 1990s, during the Clinton presidency, both the Senate and the House were almost always divided according to strict party lines. The popular news media continue to present belligerent, polarized coverage of serious problems that — if you believe the commentators — have only two competing solutions, one liberal and the other conservative. The political terms "right" and "left" themselves originally referred to a sharp dividing line: conservative delegates to the French National Assembly, formed after the 1789 revolution, sat on the right side of the meeting hall, while radical delegates sat on the left.

The news media, which for the most part today frame the public issues, thrive on high drama and conflict: men versus women, black versus white, poor versus rich, gay versus straight, religious versus secular, blue-collar versus elite, human versus nonhuman. The model is invariably adversarial, as hard lines are drawn between opposing perspectives. Every story must have a conflict, and the more that conflict can be personalized — portrayed by individuals who instantly personify the various views — the better. Public discourse is reduced to extreme expression and accusation, as nuanced or moderate views find little air time. Complex or abstract stories are simplified by being physically embodied in a character who clearly stands for a position; thus, the news media find themselves every day rounding up the "usual suspects" for interviews and sound bites. This process has become so entrenched that it's difficult to tell when cultural, social, or political divisions are genuine and threatening or when they're fabricated or fueled by a news industry hungry for another juicy conflict.

Identifying serious divisions does, of course, play a major role in the maintenance of a just society. In the United States today, largely because of continuing legislation stemming from the Civil Rights Act of 1964, we are keen to detect unequal treatment based on "race, color, religion, sex, or national origin." We have also grown increasingly sensitive to the rights of the disadvantaged and disabled. Much of what popularly goes under the name "multiculturalism" is a corrective response to the exclusionary practices of the past. Yet even as we strive to be inclusive and nondiscriminatory, the ideal of "diversity" depends on affirming differences. As citizens, we are asked to ignore differences but at the same time to recognize or even celebrate them. This seemingly contradictory state of mind often fuels contentious debates on race and gender matters or issues related to any victimized or marginalized group.

Many divisions have been intensified over the past several decades by what has become popularly known as "identity politics," a political position or perspective based on an individual's identification with a particular group, one typically based on gender, race, ethnicity, or sexual orientation. Since we all belong to multiple groups and have several allegiances, identity politics can lead to personal conflict, especially when we feel pressured to choose one allegiance over the rest. Within the earlier civil rights and antiwar movements, for example, young women frequently felt they had to subordinate their feminist agenda to bolster the other efforts and to endure the entrenched chauvinism of male leaders. What happens when the lines that divide one group from another are internalized within a single person? How do we decide whether ethnic heritage trumps gender or whether class matters more than race?

The convergence of multiculturalism and identity politics troubled many moderate-to-conservative political thinkers, who criticized the general movement for its simplistic relativism, archaic tribalism, and naive anti-Americanism, which recognized marvelous human values everywhere on earth except at home. With political correctness added to the mix, even prominent liberals went on the offensive, criticizing the censorship and intimidation on college campuses that took the form of "speech codes." Though defenders of these codes believed they were contributing a much-needed sensitivity to minority perspectives and were helping to curtail "hate speech," many others worried that writers, entertainers, artists, and even scholars were becoming increasingly controlled by the fear of offending one group or another.

The so-called culture wars were — and still are — vigorously fought on numerous fronts: in class-rooms, press rooms, museums, and publishing houses. The broadcast media have found that they can turn the various culture wars into profitable entertainment by designing antagonistic talk shows that regularly feature diametrically opposed political views. The success of these shows usually depends on one of the media's favorite conflicts: the hostility between the average citizen and the elite establishment. The conflict of "us" against "them" is, as we all know, one of life's persistent struggles, no matter who we are or what we believe. Urban gangs have little to do with establish-ments — elite or otherwise — yet their boundaries and turfs can be as violently disputed as those of hostile nations. Gang zones, however, are not official; they are not like the zoning laws that configure our towns and suburbs, where land use is strictly coded in order to benefit all who live and work within their limits. In this chapter we will explore several kinds of dividing lines, large and small, hard and soft, public and private, with selections covering America's sexual, ethnic, political, and socioeconomic conflicts.

Alignment

The cartoon you see here plays with the idea of dividing lines, analyzing a child's lunch for what it reveals about his parents' membership in various religious and political groups. The materials you'll encounter in this chapter all have to do with different ways of belonging, whether the context is a formal organization or a less codified kind of group, like people with a similar way of dressing or a shared love of a certain kind of music. We all have alignments — or relationships — with people who share values, interests, or activities. What kinds of people or groups do you align yourself with? Can you analyze the way you dress, or what you read or watch or do, or even eat for lunch — to reveal the groups you belong to?

Roz Chast, _Deconstructing Lunch_. (© The New Yorker Collection 2000 Roz Chast from cartoonbank.com. All Rights Reserved)

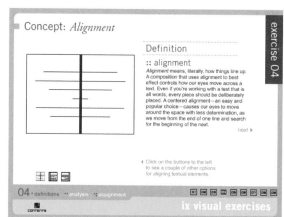

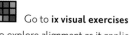 Go to **ix visual exercises** to explore alignment as it applies to visual texts.

416

US AND THEM

POEM | 4 PHOTOS | ESSAY | AD

The word "diversity" has become, like the word "community," one of those terms with a plus-sign hovering over it: the word automatically suggests something that everyone is supposed to value. It is a key term in the media, in education, and in politics; in fact, many corporations have established departments in "diversity training."

Yet is diversity really what Americans want, or is it a fashionable concept that people merely say they want? If it is truly desired, then why, asks David Brooks in "People Like Us," are Americans so un-diverse in so many ways? Does the idea of diversity go against the grain of human nature? As Brooks claims: "what I have seen all around the country is people making strenuous efforts to group themselves with people who are basically like themselves" — and the photographs from *America 24/7,* reproduced here, document a few of those groups. However, is focusing on diversity really not the point, as Maya Angelou suggests in her poem "Human Family"?

417

◀ **Dennis McDonald,** *Burlington County Times,* **Berkeley, New Jersey, 2003.** This photograph and the four that follow are taken from a recent best-selling and comprehensive photographic project, *America 24/7* (2003), the "largest collaborative photography project in history." Thousands of amateur and professional photographers were invited to go out during the week of May 12–18, 2003, and "show the world what it means to be American." The resulting collection captures a highly diverse nation. But as these photos show, our melting pot is also a country in which people tend naturally to form groups and share space on the basis of self-selection, social distinctions, and cultural affinity. (Photos from *America 24/7.* New York: DK Publishing, 2003)

419

Kurt Wilson, *St. Ignatius, Montana, 2003.* "The Amish usually marry within their own communities, which tends to reduce the pool of surnames. Heidi Miller, Hannah Miller, Naomah Miller, and Emily Miller (holding cat) are actually from three separate families. Their solid-colored dresses and white caps are designed to encourage humility and separateness from the outside world."

Maya Angelou, *Human Family*. Poet, playwright, and novelist Maya Angelou was born Marguerite Johnson in St. Louis, Missouri, on April 4, 1928. She grew up in St. Louis and in Stamps, Arkansas. With many books to her credit, she is best known for her autobiographical *I Know Why the Caged Bird Sings* (1969) and her poetry, including *I Shall Not Be Moved* (1990), from which "Human Family" was taken. In 1993, Angelou wrote and read a poem at the inauguration of President Bill Clinton, at his request.

Maya Angelou
HUMAN FAMILY

I note the obvious differences
in the human family.
Some of us are serious,
some thrive on comedy.

Some declare their lives are lived
as true profundity,
and others claim they really live
the real reality.

The variety of our skin tones
can confuse, bemuse, delight,
brown and pink and beige and purple,
tan and blue and white.
I've sailed upon the seven seas
and stopped in every land,
I've seen the wonders of the world,
not yet one common man.

I know ten thousand women
called Jane and Mary Jane,
but I've not seen any two
who really were the same.

Mirror twins are different
although their features jibe,

and lovers think quite different thoughts
while lying side by side.

We love and lose in China
we weep on England's moors,
and laugh and moan in Guinea,
and thrive on Spanish shores.

We seek success in Finland,
are born and die in Maine.
In minor ways we differ,
in major we're the same.

I note the obvious differences
between each sort and type,
but we are more alike, my friends,
than we are unalike.

We are more alike, my friends,
than we are unalike.

We are more alike, my friends,
than we are unalike.

■ *Why do you think the speaker repeats the last two lines three times? What is the effect of this repetition?*

421

Danielle P. Richards, *Teaneck, New Jersey, 2003.* "Girls at the co-ed 220-student Muslim junior-senior high school, Al-Ghazaly, jump rope during lunch break. Muslim religious and cultural beliefs prohibit girls from appearing in public without their headcover, or 'hijab.'"

David Brooks, *People Like Us*. In this essay, David Brooks examines the difference between what people *say* about diversity and what they *do*. Brooks has been a journalist and cultural commentator for over twenty years, since his graduation from the University of Chicago in 1983. He worked first as a police reporter and then at *The Wall Street Journal*, where he was variously the book review editor, movie critic, and op-ed editor. For the last ten years he has been the editor of *The Weekly Standard*, a contributing editor at *Newsweek* and *The Atlantic Monthly*, and a commentator on NPR and *The NewsHour with Jim Lehrer*. He is now a columnist with the *New York Times*. He is also the editor of *Backward and Upward: The New Conservative Writing* (1996), and the author of *Bobos in Paradise: The New Upper Class and How They Got There* (2001). "People Like Us" first appeared in the September 2003 issue of *The Atlantic Monthly*.

David Brooks
PEOPLE LIKE US

Maybe it's time to admit the obvious. We don't really care about diversity all that much in America, even though we talk about it a great deal. Maybe somewhere in this country there is a truly diverse neighborhood in which a black Pentecostal minister lives next to a white anti-globalization activist, who lives next to an Asian short-order cook, who lives next to a professional golfer, who lives next to a post-modern-literature professor and a cardiovascular surgeon. But I have never been to or heard of that neighborhood. Instead, what I have seen all around the country is people making strenuous efforts to group themselves with people who are basically like themselves.

Human beings are capable of drawing amazingly subtle social distinctions and then shaping their lives around them. In the Washington, D.C., area Democratic lawyers tend to live in suburban Maryland, and Republican lawyers tend to live in suburban Virginia. If you asked a Democratic lawyer to move from her $750,000 house in Bethesda, Maryland, to a $750,000 house in Great Falls, Virginia, she'd look at you as if you had just asked her to buy a pickup truck with a gun rack and to shove chewing tobacco in her kid's mouth. In Manhattan the owner of a $3 million SoHo loft would feel out of place moving into a $3 million Fifth Avenue apartment. A West Hollywood interior decorator would feel dislocated if you asked him to move to Orange County. In Georgia a barista from Athens would probably not fit in serving coffee in Americus.

It is a common complaint that every place is starting to look the same. But in the information age, the late writer James Chapin once told me, every place becomes more like itself. People are less often tied down to factories and mills, and they can search for places to live on the basis of cultural affinity. Once they find a town in which people share their values, they flock there, and reinforce whatever was distinctive about the town in the first place. Once Boulder, Colorado, became known as congenial to politically progressive mountain bikers, half the politically progressive mountain bikers in the country (it seems) moved there; they made the place so culturally pure that it has become practically a parody of itself.

But people love it. Make no mistake—we are increasing our happiness by segmenting off so rigorously. We are finding places where we are comfortable and where we feel we can flourish. But the choices we make toward that end lead to the very opposite of diversity. The United States might be a diverse nation when considered as a whole, but block by block and institution by institution it is a relatively homogeneous nation.

When we use the word "diversity" today we usually mean racial integration. But even here our good intentions seem to have run into the brick wall of human nature. Over the past generation reformers have tried heroically, and in many cases successfully, to end housing discrimination. But recent patterns aren't encouraging: according to an analysis of the 2000 census data, the 1990s saw only a slight increase in the racial integration of neighborhoods in the United States. The number of middle-class and upper-middle-class African American families is rising, but for whatever reasons—racism, psychological comfort—these families tend to congregate in predominantly black neighborhoods.

In fact, evidence suggests that some neighborhoods become more segregated over time. New suburbs in Arizona and Nevada, for example, start out reasonably well integrated. These neighborhoods don't yet have reputations, so people choose their houses for other, mostly economic reasons. But as neighborhoods age, they develop personalities (that's where the Asians live, and that's where the Hispanics live), and segmentation occurs. It could be that in a few years the new suburbs in the Southwest will be nearly as segregated as the established ones in the Northeast and the Midwest.

Even though race and ethnicity run deep in American society, we should in theory be able to find areas that are at least culturally diverse. But here, too, people show few signs of being truly interested in building diverse communities. If you run a retail company and you're thinking of opening new stores, you can choose among dozens of consulting firms that are quite effective at locating your potential customers. They can do this because people with similar tastes and preferences tend to congregate by ZIP code.

The most famous of these precision marketing firms is Claritas, which breaks down the U.S. population into sixty-two psycho-demographic clusters, based on such factors as how much money people make, what they like to read and watch, and what products they have bought in the past. For example, the "suburban sprawl" cluster is composed of young families making about $41,000 a year and living in fast-growing places such as Burnsville, Minnesota, and Bensalem, Pennsylvania. These people are almost twice as likely as other Americans to have three-way calling. They are two and a half times as likely to buy Light n' Lively

423

Kid Yogurt. Members of the "towns & gowns" cluster are recent college graduates in places such as Berkeley, California, and Gainesville, Florida. They are big consumers of DoveBars and *Saturday Night Live.* They tend to drive small foreign cars and to read *Rolling Stone* and *Scientific American.*

Looking through the market research, one can sometimes be amazed by how efficiently people cluster—and by how predictable we all are. If you wanted to sell imported wine, obviously you would have to find places where rich people live. But did you know that the sixteen counties with the greatest proportion of imported-wine drinkers are all in the same three metropolitan areas (New York, San Francisco, and Washington, D.C.)? If you tried to open a motor-home dealership in Montgomery County, Pennsylvania, you'd probably go broke, because people in this ring of the Philadelphia suburbs think RVs are kind of uncool. But if you traveled just a short way north, to Monroe County, Pennsylvania, you would find yourself in the fifth motor-home-friendliest county in America.

Geography is not the only way we find ourselves divided from people unlike us. Some of us watch Fox News, while others listen to NPR. Some like David Letterman, and others—typically in less urban neighborhoods—like Jay Leno. Some go to charismatic churches; some go to mainstream churches. Americans tend more and more often to marry people with education levels similar to their own, and to befriend people with backgrounds similar to their own.

Gary Fandel, *West Des Moines, Iowa, 2003.*

425

My favorite illustration of this latter pattern comes from the first, noncontroversial chapter of *The Bell Curve.* Think of your twelve closest friends, Richard J. Herrnstein and Charles Murray write. If you had chosen them randomly from the American population, the odds that half of your twelve closest friends would be college graduates would be six in a thousand. The odds that half of the twelve would have advanced degrees would be less than one in a million. Have any of your twelve closest friends graduated from Harvard, Stanford, Yale, Princeton, Caltech, MIT, Duke, Dartmouth, Cornell, Columbia, Chicago, or Brown? If you chose your friends randomly from the American population, the odds against your having four or more friends from those schools would be more than a billion to one.

Many of us live in absurdly unlikely groupings, because we have organized our lives that way.

It's striking that the institutions that talk the most about diversity often practice it the least. For example, no group of people sings the diversity anthem more frequently and fervently than administrators at just such elite universities. But elite universities are amazingly undiverse in their values, politics, and mores. Professors in particular are drawn from a rather narrow segment of the population. If faculties reflected the general population, 32 percent of professors would be registered Democrats and 31 percent would be registered Republicans. Forty percent would be evangelical Christians. But a recent study of several universities by the conservative Center for the Study of Popular Culture and the American Enterprise Institute found that roughly 90 percent of those professors in the arts and sciences who had registered with a political party had registered Democratic. Fifty-seven professors at Brown were found on the voter-registration rolls. Of those, fifty-four were Democrats. Of the forty-two professors in the English, history, sociology, and political-science departments, all were Democrats. The results at Harvard, Penn State, Maryland, and the University of California at Santa Barbara were similar to the results at Brown.

What we are looking at here is human nature. People want to be around others who are roughly like themselves. That's called community. It probably would be psychologically difficult for most Brown professors to share an office with someone who was pro-life, a member of the National Rifle Association, or an evangelical Christian. It's likely that hiring committees would subtly — even unconsciously — screen out any such people they encountered. Republicans and evangelical Christians have sensed that they are not welcome at places like Brown, so they don't even consider working there. In fact, any registered Republican who

426

■ *How persuasive do you find Brooks's claim (mentioned several times) that diversity goes against "human nature"? What evidence does he use to support this claim? How persuasive do you find his evidence?*

CAIR, *We're All Americans.* **This advertisement was the first of fifty-two in the Islam in America series created by the Council on American-Islamic Relations after September 11, 2001. The ad makes a different argument about diversity than Brooks's essay does; the ad stresses that "people like us" is a larger category than just one particular religion. (Courtesy of the Council on American-Islamic Relations)**   ▶

WE'RE ALL AMERICANS...

BUT, WHICH ONE OF US IS A MUSLIM?

We all are...we're American Muslims. It's impossible to make general assumptions about Muslims because we represent more than one billion people from a vast range of races, nationalities and cultures – from the South Pacific to the Horn of Africa. Only about 18 percent of Muslims live in the Arabic-speaking world. The largest Muslim community is in Indonesia. Substantial parts of Asia and most of Africa have Muslim majority populations, while significant minorities are to be found in the countries of the former Soviet Union, China, North and South America, and Europe.

American Muslims are an equally diverse group of people. We're immigrants from across the globe who came here seeking freedom and opportunity. We're the children of immigrant parents, and descendants of Africans who have called America home for generations. We're converts of varied nationalities and ethnic backgrounds. We're doctors, lawyers, teachers, politicians, civil rights activists, mothers, fathers, students... making our homes and raising our families in communities across America.

What we all have in common is a shared faith and a shared commitment to our nation's safety and prosperity. We're Americans and we're Muslims.

WE'RE AMERICAN MUSLIMS

Number one of fifty-two in the *Islam in America* series.
To learn more about the series, visit www.americanmuslims.info

CAIR
COUNCIL ON AMERICAN-ISLAMIC RELATIONS

contemplates a career in academia these days is both a hero and a fool. So, in a semi-self-selective pattern, brainy people with generally liberal social mores flow to academia, and brainy people with generally conservative mores flow elsewhere.

The dream of diversity is like the dream of equality. Both are based on ideals we celebrate even as we undermine them daily. (How many times have you seen someone renounce a high-paying job or pull his child from an elite college on the grounds that these things are bad for equality?) On the one hand, the situation is appalling. It is appalling that Americans know so little about one another. It is appalling that many of us are so narrow-minded that we can't tolerate a few people with ideas significantly different from our own. It's appalling that evangelical Christians are practically absent from entire professions, such as academia, the media, and filmmaking. It's appalling that people should be content to cut themselves off from everyone unlike themselves.

The segmentation of society means that often we don't even have arguments across the political divide. Within their little validating communities, liberals and conservatives circulate half-truths about the supposed awfulness of the other side. These distortions are believed because it feels good to believe them.

On the other hand, there are limits to how diverse any community can or should be. I've come to think that it is not useful to try to hammer diversity into every neighborhood and institution in the United States. Sure, Augusta National should probably admit women, and university sociology departments should probably hire a conservative or two. It would be nice if all neighborhoods had a good mixture of ethnicities. But human nature being what it is, most places and institutions are going to remain culturally homogeneous.

It's probably better to think about diverse lives, not diverse institutions. Human beings, if they are to live well, will have to move through a series of institutions and environments, which may be individually homogeneous but, taken together, will offer diverse experiences. It might also be a good idea to make national service a rite of passage for young people in this country: it would take them out of their narrow neighborhood segment and thrust them in with people unlike themselves. Finally, it's probably important for adults to get out of their own familiar circles. If you live in a coastal, socially liberal neighborhood, maybe you should take out a subscription to *The Door,* the evangelical humor magazine; or maybe you should visit Branson, Missouri. Maybe you should stop in at a megachurch. Sure, it would be superficial familiarity, but it beats the iron curtains that now separate the nation's various cultural zones.

Look around at your daily life. Are you really in touch with the broad diversity of American life? Do you care?

MESSAGE

What is David Brooks saying about "diversity" in his essay? Does he define the word precisely? What do you think his position is? Is he opposed to the ideal of diversity, or would he prefer that Americans actually become more diversified than they are? Explain his position as accurately as you can. Then do the same for each of the other texts in this cluster: What is Maya Angelou saying about diversity? What do the images from *America 24/7* say? What does the ad from the *Islam in America* series say? Try to summarize each text's position in a single sentence.

METHOD

Each of the texts uses examples — some verbal, some visual — of specific people or kinds of people to make its points about how we are alike or different. Evaluate the examples offered by each text for their effectiveness. Which method do you find most persuasive?

MEDIUM

The photographs, advertisement, poem, and essay in this section all make claims about diversity in America. To what degree do you think our commitment to diversity grows from our history as a melting pot? In what medium would you portray your own philosophy about diversity — in a photograph, a movie, an essay, a cartoon, or something else? Imagine that you're trying to reach as many people as possible. Then outline or sketch out how you would convey this complicated idea in the most direct, persuasive way possible.

429

TURF WAR

One of the most intense group identities a young person can develop is with a gang, especially in cities where a gang offers both protection and an escape from anonymity. In the 1940s and 1950s, street gangs were commonly white and were drawn around neighborhood lines. Authorities regarded them as training camps for "juvenile delinquency" and a subsequent life of crime. By the 1960s urban gangs were growing increasingly divided along racial and ethnic lines, a social phenomenon depicted in the popular musical and film, *West Side Story.* By the 1980s, gangs had grown more violent; members were equipped with high-powered weapons and were increasingly connected with drug trafficking. More recently, gangs have been responsible for generating an explosion in popular culture — their clothing and gestures can be seen, and their music and slang heard, in every suburban shopping mall in the United States. In "Gangstas," the noted National Public Radio commentator Richard Rodriguez uses the photographs of Joseph Rodriguez to take a close though unromanticized view of Latino gang life in Los Angeles in the early 1990s.

> go

For the full photo-essay on L.A. gangs by Joseph Rodriguez, go to bedfordstmartins.com/ convergences.

Richard Rodriguez, *Gangstas*. Richard Rodriguez was born in San Francisco in 1944 into a working-class Mexican American family. He graduated from Stanford University in 1967, then received an M.A. from Columbia University two years later. A prize-winning reporter and essayist for *The NewsHour with Jim Lehrer*, Rodriguez has published widely in magazines and newspapers. He is the author of a well-known memoir, *The Hunger of Memory: The Education of Richard Rodriguez* (1982), a collection of essays, *Days of Obligation: An Argument with My Mexican Father* (1992), and *Brown: The Last Discovery of America* (2002), a discussion about the "browning" of America that completes Rodriguez's "trilogy on American public life." "Gangstas" first appeared in a special issue of *Mother Jones* on the subject of guns in January/February 1994.

Richard Rodriguez
GANGSTAS

Oh, how I hate their stupid sign language, occult and crooked palmings, finger-Chinese. I hate their Puritan black. Their fat heads shaved like Roundheads in the age of Cromwell—the penitentiary look—not Cavalier. I hate their singlets. I hate their tattoos, sentimental prick-roses. I hate their jargon. I hate their bandannas. I hate rap.

Anyway, there I was at my sissy gym the other day—read the *Wall Street Journal*, lose a few pounds on the StairMaster—and what do you think accompanied me through the canyons of Wall Street, but insidious black, male, heterosexual rap. There it was—the music of thump—blasting through the blond pagan house of abs and pecs.

I hate the rhymed-dictate. Rap dictates not thought but rhyme, encourages rhythmic sloganing and jingle—monotony posing as song, attitude posing as thought.

Is there a more complicated love affair going on in America? We know for a fact, those of us who read the *Wall Street Journal*, that white middle-class children buy more rap than black children. We don't know why. Or we say we don't.

Forget the sociological abstraction! The other day, I was looking through some snapshots of my niece and nephew that my sister had left on the drainboard. Snow. Tent. Skis. Birthday party. Clowns. Balloons. And then this: the nine-year-old boy and the six-year-old girl are posing in the backyard of their suburban house as gangstas. The boy with a bandanna on his head, a mustache and goatee painted on. The girl with a T-shirt and dangling earrings. They were both signing with their fingers. They had dead eyes.

My initial reaction was amusement at their charade. Even pride. They got it so right. MTV, I guess. But to what reality are my niece and nephew drawn?

431

432

Joseph Rodriguez, *Chivo.* Boyle Heights, 1993. On Joseph Rodriguez's web site, he tells us that this photo was taken "the morning after a rival gang tried to shoot Chivo for the fourth time. Chivo teaches his daughter how to hold a .32-caliber pistol while her mother looks on." The winner of a 1993 Mother Jones International Fund for Documentary Photography award, Joseph Rodriguez has had his photography published in many magazines. His books include *East Side Stories: Gang Life in East L.A.* (1996), from which all the photographs shown here are taken. (All photos courtesy of Joseph Rodriguez/Black Star)

We adults do most heartily deplore what is happening in the "inner city." Those of us who live elsewhere are shocked by the mayhem—little pops and flares in the night and answering sirens, far away. We deplore all of it. And when something hideous happens, which it does, in the morning paper or on the news, then we mutter something, a thought—not a thought—a blank bubble, like an unmarked van, passes through our consciousness and its freight is obscene loathing we dare not enunciate: ANIMALS. SCUM.

The commercial on the eleven o'clock news is a rap for cola, with black children in black, mouthing a mindless jingle which celebrates the elixir. And the eleven o'clock news, which leads with an "Animals on the Loose" story, ends with five minutes of contract mayhem—pro football and ice hockey fights and baseball teams in Baltimore or basketball players in Boston duking it out before cheering fans.

I went to a fancy benefit for some Mexican American charity. The entertainment, alternating with the sentimental mariachis, included several famous comics and actors doing "street stuff"—Edward James Olmos, for example, did his famous pachuco bit, the slouch, hands in his pocket, the head cocked back, the legs far out in front. HEY MANNNNN, WHA'S HAPPENIIIIING? The standard black jargon with an East L.A. whine. Like, "no steenkin' badges, mannnnn."

What I like best about Joe Rodriguez's photographs is that they are devoid of middle-class *nostalgie de la boue.*[1] Still, part of the turn-on of these photos is that we can stare without fear of being killed. None of us should stare at such faces in real life.

They get on the bus in their Raiders jackets, their ears plugged with huge brainstorms of rap—that's what they hear; we hear a tiny, metallic tish, tish, tish leaking from their earphones—they board the city bus in groups, talk loud, for they are giants, pirates . . .

It would be a smart idea not to look at them—no, I mean it—these are children, but they are children with machetes and guns and no point of reffrance, so betta show me def-france, or you are outta breff, once I blow your brains to hell.

Keep your eyes to yourself. Read your paperback. Read your magazine. Do not make eye contact. They are children so wary of any "dis" they might "smoke" you for staring.

Stare instead at Joe Rodriguez's photos, the Mexican American chapter of youthful offenders. Examine their four-block piece of L.A. Look at the neat houses of some of them, not exactly lead-peeling, stinkin' tenements in Spanish Harlem. East L.A. is not Spanish Harlem. And L.A., like Miami, has a better climate for child murder than New York or Chicago. On a sweetly scented January night one can hang out, throw rocks at buses or at the cars on the freeway.

Some of these children are good-looking, some not. (They seem, in either case, unaware of the difference.) They look more American than Mexican to my eye, with an American irony on their faces, especially the child-women who look like they are made up for *Elektra.*[2]

Clearly, Joe Rodriguez has put in his time with these children. What his camera does not explain is why they look so dead to conscience. Mother Church had

---

[1] *nostalgie de la boue:* French, "yearning for slime."—ED.
[2] *Elektra:* Richard Strauss's opera based on Sophocles' tragedy *Elektra.* The combination of tragedy and opera would, in most productions, mean heavy, masklike makeup for the performers.—ED.

always told us that the "age of reason" begins around the age of seven, well before hormones sprout domes. Is it that they know we are watching? Gangsta life reduces to an attitude, a pose. These children appear prisoners of street theater, even when they are in the family kitchen. Only one, the child staring into the Los Angeles night sky, has an expression to which a caption of "wonder" might fit.

As actors, they seem only to exist in the plural. Dress the same. Spell identically with their fingers. They shave each others' heads and watch each others' backs. The gang regards the greatest sinner to be the member who wants out.

These children of East L.A. puzzle us for being so intensely communal. We Americans honor the idea of the youthful rebel. We have taken our meaning from the notion of adolescent rebellion. (James Dean rebels against the mad British king.) Huck Finn is the nineteenth century's romantic hero, free of the schoolmarm, free of his drunk pappy, free as a runaway slave on a raft.

Joseph Rodriguez, *Members of Florencia*
13 gang outside school. South Central, 1992.

If within the neighborhood the lost-boy brotherhood is the only society going, outside — in the city of adults — the child appears solitary, defiant. It is in this defiance the child is most interesting to the city. The rapster becomes Huck Finn. The stance, the dress, the music of this outsider exercise erotic appeal.

In the fall 1993 issue of *Esquire Gentleman,* a magazine of no distinction or exception, there is an article by Mark Leyner called "Gangsta Allure." ("What becomes a man most? Evil, of course. Smug, sinister dudes get all the hot action. Here's how to look like a real Reservoir Dog.") In Paris recently, at a show of Jean Colonna's "outlaw chic," the models fired blank cartridges at the photographers at the foot of the runway.

Bang! The theatrical turns real and then we of the audience are horrified. *Look, my God, look, the baby in his tiny coffin, draped with gauze.*

MONSTERS! ANIMALS!

On the other side of the fascination with the rebel is this high moral distancing. Consign the gangsta to subhumanity. But when this child falls, he leaks blood. They are not monsters, after all.

If, as God's silence to Job suggests, there is something inexplicable about evil — either the evil the night commits against us or the evil we inflict on each other — there is also less mystery to the cruelty in East Los Angeles than we otherwise pretend.

Is it so inexplicable that a child never embraced might be seduced by the cult of power? An Oakland cop says to me: "Have you ever been in a physical fight? It may be the only moment in your life when you can control the outcome."

These photographs do not tell us about crack mothers or schools that don't work or pappy dead or in prison. Documentary without a hint of narrative comes dangerously close to the vision Diane Arbus[3] saw in her madness. Children appear grotesques. Spawn of some hideous neighborhood (not ours) without trees or sun or air. A land of roaches and rats and unnatural mothers.

No man is an island entire of itself. Didn't we learn that in high school? There is no possibility of a healthy suburb radiant from a corrupt inner city. The children of East L.A. live in the same city as Madonna and Tom Bradley and Harvard-educated screenwriters who use coke for inspiration to sell a believably tarnished vision of the world to the children of the crack mother in Compton. In this Los Angeles an Austrian muscle man becomes kin to the Kennedys and a movie mogul who kills with dead eyes.

And look: there is always a TV in the houses of East L.A. And it's always on. In the suburbs we use TV to watch the mayhem of the inner city. But on the TV in the inner city, they watch us. The bejeweled pimp in his gold BMW parodies the Beverly Hills matron on Rodeo Drive. The baby with the gun in his chubby fist is spiritual heir to John Wayne and his feminist cowgirl wife Annie Oakley,

435

---

[3] Diane Arbus (1923–1971), American photographer, now famous for her gritty pictures of urban alienation and the socially marginalized. — ED.

436

**Joseph Rodriguez, *Mike Estrada holds a photo
of his father who is in prison.*** Boyle Heights, 1993.

COMMENT

"One picture ran today in the *New York Times:* the
two and a half year old in the coffin at the funeral.
I was really depressed. I can't understand why one
must always show violence or famine to be recognized as an accomplished photojournalist."

— Joseph Rodriguez

and to the country that was settled with guns in the cowboy movies, and in truth.

The political left used to speak of "community" when Americans were more interested in the separation of the rich from the poor. But lately the left has gotten involved with the self-actualization movement, a most American movement for being so centered on the individual. Now the talk is all about my right to do my own thing with my own body and it's nobody's business if I do. The right responds with a nostalgic creak about "family values," as though this country was ever a place of family values, and not a country where healthy families prepared their children to leave home.

We are people who believe in the first-person singular pronoun—which is our strength. But our weakness is that we don't comprehend our lives in common,

Joseph Rodriguez, *Funeral of two-and-a-half-year-old Thomas Regalado III.* East Los Angeles, 1992.

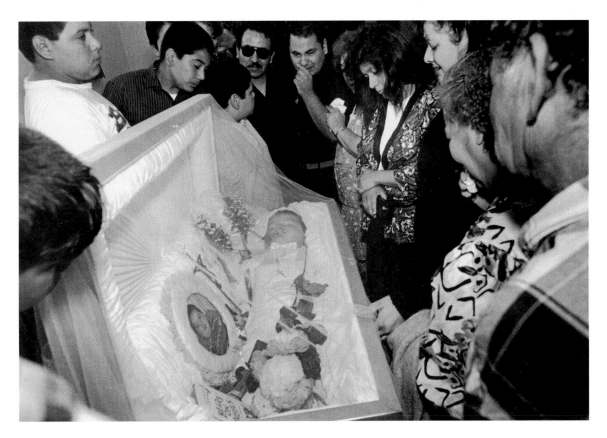

the ways we create one another in the American city. As Americans we have always feared the city; with Huck we have always wanted to escape. Thus do we look at the faces of East L.A.: we consign the children to some remote kingdom of THEM.

Thirty years ago, I grew up listening to the black Protestant hymns of the civil rights movement. In the 1960s, black America was perceived by most Americans as the moral authority of this nation. Today we are to believe that the inner city is so bereft of moral life that children must be taken out of town — taken where? To moral Walnut Creek? Moral Evanston?

Even black intellectuals and smart filmmakers propose that what is needed is to get the children out of the city. It is a romantic notion that has survived into our century. Transport street children, get them away from concrete and broken glass and piss smell, expose them to a redemptive green world. This notion credits to trees powers that we used to assign to the soul. And it assumes that what is needed to heal the children of East L.A. is something leafy rather than the human touch.

We do not believe in souls. We believe in pecs and abs. We do not believe in the city. We believe in nightmares and monsters. Finally, these photographs do not embarrass us, though they should. Looking at these faces, we never guess why we use the music of violence to build up our skinny arms.

438

COMMENT

"This is the view of the barrio we need — human and complex, the black and white as well as the grey. Through our media we usually only receive a fragment of the neighborhood, a slice of narrative. . . . The media's sensationalism easily divides barrio and suburb into 'us' and 'them.' We need the rest of the story to be told, as in these photographs. Then it won't be so easy to deny that the barrio kids are 'our' children too."

—Ruben Martinez, from the introduction to
Joseph Rodriguez's *East Side Stories*

M E S S A G E	M E T H O D	M E D I U M
Richard Rodriguez says that he is puzzled by the "communal" aspects of the gangs. What does he mean by this? In his essay, what does he oppose to the communal? After reading his essay, which do you think he regards as most important: the individual or the community?	Richard Rodriguez praises Joseph Rodriguez's photographs for lacking "middle-class *nostalgie de la boue*" (French, "yearning for slime"), meaning that they don't romanticize their subject. Do you agree with him? Do you find in the photography a different attitude toward the gang members than you find in the essay? In your opinion, who portrays the gangs better: the essayist or the photographer?	Richard Rodriguez admits right from the start of his essay that he hates the gang subculture. What does he especially hate about it? What features does he seem to dislike most of all? How do the photographs capture these features? Do the photos support the text and the text the photos? Explain your assessment of how they work together.

GENDER

2 PHOTOS | 2 ESSAYS | SHORT STORY | LOGO

Throughout history and cultures, the differences between males and females have accounted for a seemingly endless amount of discussion, drama, and stereotyping. Although the subject is hardly new, we might think — judging from the continual stream of coverage it receives in the media — that the topic had only recently emerged as one of the central issues of our time. Nearly every day, on radio and TV shows, in magazine and newspaper features, and in comic strips and cartoons, we encounter some version of the popular notion that "Men Are from Mars and Women Are from Venus."

The idea that males and females seem to come from two different planets is counterbalanced today by the opposing notion that the differences between the sexes are socially and culturally constructed. This controversy cuts across many boundaries and disciplines — feminist studies, education, sports, the social and biological sciences, law and medicine, and so on. The material that follows explores just a few of the angles that writers and artists have taken when examining the issue of gender.

440

Roger Ressmeyer, *Crying Infants, 1984.* Some experts claim that if we changed ▶ our patterns of childhood socialization and our expectations of what each sex is capable of, then we would discover that males and females are far more similar than we currently think. Others, however, claim that because sex is biologically determined, gender roles are more or less hard-wired from infancy, if not earlier. (© Roger Ressmeyer/CORBIS)

Penelope Scambly Schott, *Report on the Difference between Men and Women.* Although the literature surrounding the subject is vast, the writers of this text and the next have brilliantly managed to encapsulate their views in miniature. In Schott's mini-essay we see a lifetime of marital experience distilled into a few paragraphs. Penelope Scambly Schott is a poet who also teaches college correspondence courses for adults. She is the author of a book-length historical poem, *Penelope: The Story of the Half-Scalped Woman* (1994).

Penelope Scambly Schott

REPORT ON THE DIFFERENCE BETWEEN MEN AND WOMEN

After thirteen years and twenty-seven days of marriage, my husband turns to me and asks, "How come we never have lemonade?" He pauses. "That kind that comes frozen in a can?"

It's not like he's never been to the grocery store or I haven't asked him regularly if there's anything he'd like me to pick up, anything special he's in the mood for.

So on the twenty-eighth day of our fourteenth year of marriage, I go to the store and buy lemonade, that kind that comes frozen in the can. At the checkout, I push the frozen pale yellow cylinder onto the conveyor belt and look into the eyes of the middle-aged woman who is ringing up my groceries. Without preliminary, I announce, "After all the time we've been married, my husband just asked me yesterday, out of the blue, 'How come we never have lemonade?' "

She looks back at me. The edges of her mouth flicker in and out. First the whole bottom of her face and then her shoulders begin to tremble. She convulses into giggling. Neither of us needs to say another word.

I go home, unbag, defrost the can, mix up his lemonade in a tall jar, shake it well, and put it in the refrigerator, front and center on the top shelf where even he can't miss it. When he comes in from work and starts browsing for something to drink, I say, "I bought lemonade today. It's right here in the front," and I point to it. He pours an enormous glass.

I wonder what else he secretly wants.

Melanie Sumner, *Marriage*. Melanie Sumner is a writer and reporter who has served in the Peace Corps, taught English in Senegal, and published a novel on growing up rich, female, and wild in the South, *The School of Beauty and Charm* (2001). Her mini-short story, like Schott's mini-essay, tells a great deal in a small space.

Melanie Sumner

MARRIAGE

"Every night," she told the marriage counselor, "he drinks a glass of milk. When he's finished, he sets the empty glass on the kitchen counter and goes to bed. He does not rinse it out. I have asked him and asked him. I've asked nicely, and I've screamed. Why should I rinse his glass out for him every night? If I don't do it, it's the first thing I see in the morning, this disgusting milk scum. I've even asked him, 'Will you just put the glass in the sink?' But he won't."

The counselor looked at the husband, a balding, middle-aged man who sat with his hands in his lap, a pleasant expression on his face.

"Did you hear what she was saying?" asked the counselor.

"Yes," said the man, nodding first at him, and then at his wife, to acknowledge everyone present.

A moment of silence passed. The counselor made a note on his pad, reminding himself to pick up a gallon of milk after work. Then he made eye contact with the wife.

"There is something you need to understand," he said. "He will never, never stop drinking that glass of milk before he goes to bed, and he will never rinse it out. There is absolutely nothing you can do."

The woman looked surprised. Sometimes even after the divorce, she would think about the counselor's words, marveling at his wisdom.

443

■ *The photographer asks of this image, "Why presume the person behind you on the bus is some abstract stereotype you think they should be? At the time of this photo, these two were dating. Did you think that first?"*

444

Eric James, *School Bus, 2003*. This photograph was taken by a nineteen-year-old photographer and was published in *Look-Look*, a magazine for young writers, photographers, and artists. (© Look-Look Magazine/Eric James 2003)

Jan Morris, *Herstory*. Jan Morris takes a broader view than Penelope
Scambly Schott and Melanie Sumner, introducing us to significant
gender differences and similarities. Having experienced life as both
a man and a woman, Morris isn't so sure how opposite our polarized
categories of male and female really are. Morris, a travel writer, has
written books on places around the world, including works of history, biography, memoir, and fiction. "Herstory" was published in the
October 4, 1999, issue of FORBES ASAP.

Jan Morris

HERSTORY

446

Twenty-seven years ago, almost on the cusp between the third and fourth quarters
of the 20th century, I completed what was then simplistically called a change of
sex. Nowadays it is more often euphemized as gender reassignment, and this shift
of words is not simply semantic. It recognizes that across the civilized world, sex
is no longer being seen as something absolute, and that the old immovable opposites of Male and Female may be converging after all.

When this happened to me—for I certainly did not ask for it, only obeyed
an irresistible organic urge—it seemed to many people utterly astonishing, if not
actually incredible. I was not the first person to undergo such a metamorphosis,
but I suppose I seemed an unlikely candidate for it. I was a foreign correspondent
and an established author, I had been a soldier, I was happily married with children, I was a staunch advocate of the stiff upper lip, grinning and bearing it,
pulling myself together, and many another attitude popularly supposed to be particularly masculine. When it emerged that I had abandoned maleness and would,
in the future, be known not as James but as Jan, some of my male acquaintances
thought I must have gone off my head. Otherwise, why on earth would anybody
rather be a woman than a man?

Gradually, though, it turned out that I was not crazy. I did not run away with
a property tycoon or appear topless in nightclubs. My family life remained happy
as ever, and I continued to write books. Now the quandary facing people was no

longer how best to humor me but how to deal with me as a woman rather than as a man. And that is how it was that I first experienced for myself, in the world of the 1970s, the great gulf that then still lay between the two halves of mankind. The women's movement had long been stirring, but the great mass of people still thought of male and female almost as separate species and treated them as differently as they would a dog and a cat.

Men, in those days, seem to me to have been much more courteous to women (opening doors, taking hats off in elevators), but the dullards among them were also much more condescending. They really did not take women very seriously. I happened at that time to know rather a lot about oil politics in the Arab world (I had been the Middle East correspondent for the *Times* of London), but I remember all too clearly with what patronizing contempt my opinions were dismissed by men I met on airplanes. It just did not seem possible to them that a woman could even be interested in, let alone conversant with, such grown-up, undomestic matters, and the extraordinary thing was that men I had known for years now instantly changed their personalities in my presence.

Women by and large were far less fazed. My change of life did not seem to them so astonishing. They welcomed me as a recruit to the oppressed classes, and they kindly helped me with the transition. Besides, I think some were attracted by the very idea of a conjunction between male and female—for I did not try to disguise the traits of temperament and intellect that remained with me from my previous existence.

And in this they were, I think, far more responsive to the changing times than most men were. For as the last decades of the century passed, that gap between the sexes narrowed, and I began to be seen—to feel myself, too—not just as symbiotic but as symbolic, too. What was so unutterably bizarre, after all, in a sex change? Which is the profounder entity: sex, which is a matter of hormones and ovaries, or gender, which is spirit and taste, the form of talent, and the nature of love? And anyway, are we not all an amalgam of male and female, in one degree or another?

Of course, by then the historic rise of feminism was changing all the world's attitudes. I could measure in male responses the tremendous shift of balance between the sexes that was happening all around us—a redistribution of power far greater and more fateful than any political revolution. No longer would male mediocrities sweetly change the course of a conversation, if I ventured to insert a thought about the possibilities of glasnost in the Soviet Union, or the historical origins of Serbian intransigence. (And alas, perhaps only gentlemen of very uncertain age would remove their bowler hats when one entered the elevator.)

Slowly, tentatively, often reluctantly, the world was recognizing as nonsense the antique inequality between the sexes, and the relationship between men and women was achieving a new rationality. All revolutions are violent, and there was certainly an element of brutal intolerance to this one. Often enough, standing in the middle as I did, I felt myself sympathizing first with one party, then with another, as women rebelling against centuries of unfairness conflicted with men

447

dazed by the collapse of so many inherited convictions. I could sympathize with women still scorned by damn fool bureaucrats and disgracefully underpaid; I felt sorry for men obliged to admit women into their cherished clubs, and willy-nilly to adapt their age-old conceptions. But I knew that such discomforts were only incidental to a vast beneficial rearrangement of humanity, not to be completed for another generation at least, and I felt a sort of undeserved pride to be standing as a living symbol of a great reconciliation.

For convergence, of course, is generally reconciliation. When you come up close, most things are not as bad as they looked from a distance, and men and women turn out to be not so different after all. Even physically, at the end of the 20th century, they are growing more alike: the women taller and stronger as they lead newer, freer lives; the men less macho as the organic need for brute force subsides.

Who would have thought, 50 years ago, that women would be playing soccer, let alone boxing? Or that men would habitually be sharing the housework—or for that matter, if we are to believe the hi-sci pundits (who are generally right), that they might one day be bearing babies? Who could have foreseen that the toughest politician in 1980s Europe would be female (Thatcher), and the most conciliatory in 1990s Africa, male (Mandela)?

Divinities of older times were sternly sexist, creating one sex first, elevating one above the other, obliging them to sit in separate parts of the temple. The deities of technology don't give a damn, and today's men and women bow down in perfect equality before the cybergods.

In the age of sperm banks and genetic engineering, nobody is much surprised by my life story. It is no big deal anyway: simply a matter, so the scientists say, of some birth anomaly of the brain. In another half century, I do not doubt, the convergence of the genders will have gone much further, and a good thing, too. By then I shall no longer be able to claim, even to myself, the status of a symbol. For one thing, switching between the sexes will be commonplace. For another, I shall be dead.

david & goliath

BOYS ARE STUPID, THROW ROCKS AT THEM!

449

Boys Are Stupid. This logo, which appeared on T-shirts and other products, is but one example of how gender stereotyping gets reflected in popular culture. Designed by Todd Goldman, the graphics became controversial when they came to the attention of a radio commentator named Glenn Sacks, who urged listeners to boycott the stores that carried the shirts. Sacks has argued that these products promote anti-male violence and are simply not funny. (Courtesy of David & Goliath, Inc.)

MESSAGE

Explain what you think Jan Morris means when she writes that "the old immovable opposites of Male and Female may be converging after all." Could she mean that the two sexes are evolving biologically toward a new, third sex? Or that people can change their sex, as she has? Or that because of the feminist movement, women are becoming more like men and vice versa? Explain which of these summaries you think best conveys the message of Morris's essay, and why. Alternatively, do you think a different statement — or a combination of them all — works as a better summary of her viewpoint?

METHOD

What aspect of Melanie Sumner's method of writing in "Marriage" helps convey that her story is fictional? For example, if you rewrote the story in the first person — using the perspective of any one of the three characters — what information or details would you not be able to include? And if you turned Penelope Scambly Schott's essay into a story told in the third person, what information or details might you decide to include? How would the exclusion or inclusion of these elements affect your ability to produce an effective narrative?

MEDIUM

Look carefully at Eric James's photograph of teenagers on a school bus. In what ways does the photograph convey visually the dividing lines of gender? Using Sumner's story or Schott's essay as a model, try writing a very short story or essay (no more than several paragraphs) in which you transform James's photograph into a brief prose narrative that dramatizes gender roles.

450

ON THE MARGINS

ESSAY | 5 PHOTOS | ORAL HISTORY

Homelessness has been a national problem for well over a century, repeatedly offering visible proof that not every American participates in the American Dream. The situation grows worse in periods of recession and low employment, when many workers and families who already live on the edge lose their basic means of support and find themselves on the street. A major concern throughout the Great Depression of the 1930s and again in the late 1980s during Ronald Reagan's second term, the issue has returned once more to the forefront since the collapse of the 1990s economy and the subsequent loss of many jobs. Though the homeless population also consists of the mentally ill and substance abusers — along with those who are inveterate drifters — it nevertheless always climbs when the job market dwindles and social services are curtailed. The materials that follow document the lives of just a few of those people who live outside of a world many of us take for granted — a world where you have a comfortable place to go at the end of the day.

Go to exercise 05 on **ix visual exercises** to explore **audience** and **framing** and apply those concepts to the materials in this cluster.

> go

For links to more information about Mary Ellen Mark and Margaret Morton, go to bedfordstmartins.com/convergences.

COMMENT

"Whence this army of homeless boys? is a question often asked. The answer is supplied by the pro-cession of mothers that go out and in at Police Headquarters the year round, inquiring for missing boys, often not until they have been gone for weeks and months, and then sometimes rather as a matter of decent form than from any real interest in the lad's fate. The stereotyped promise of the clerks who fail to find his name on the books among the arrests, that he 'will come back when he gets hungry,' does not always come true. More likely he went away because he was hungry. Some are orphans, actually or in effect, thrown upon the world when their parents were 'sent up' to the island or to Sing Sing, and somehow overlooked by the 'Society,' which thenceforth became the enemy to be shunned until growth and dirt and the hardships of the street, that make old early, offer some hope of successfully floating the lie that they are 'sixteen.' A drunken father explains the matter in other cases, as in that of John and Willie, aged ten and eight, picked up by the police. They 'didn't live nowhere,' never went to school, could neither read nor write. Their twelve-year-old sister kept house for the father, who turned the boys out to beg, or steal, or starve. Grinding poverty and hard work beyond the years of the lad; blows and curses for breakfast, dinner, and supper; all these are recruiting agents for the homeless army. Sickness in the house, too many mouths to feed."

— Jacob Riis, from *How the Other Half Lives* (1890)

◀ **Jacob Riis, *Homeless Boys, New York City, c. 1890.*** "Half the world knows not how the other half lives," wrote the great English poet George Herbert, whose memorable phrase was borrowed by photographer/social reformer Jacob Riis "for his classic exposé of the New York slums. Skilled in both print and photo-journalism, Riis published *How the Other Half Lives* (from which this photo was taken) in 1890, and over the course of several editions it quickly became a model of how photography could reveal to the public what the public would perhaps rather not see. Throughout the twentieth century, photographers like Lewis Hines, Dorothea Lange, Walker Evans, and into the present, Mary Ellen Mark, followed in Riis's tradition of documentary photography, offering penetrating visual records of lives on the margins of society — the poor, the homeless, the addicted, the abandoned, the desperately ill. (Copyright Museum of the City of New York; part of the Jacob A. Riis Collection [image 121])

Lars Eighner, *On Dumpster Diving*. Lars Eighner (b. 1948) lost his job as a mental-hospital attendant in Texas and found himself trying to survive on the street. He not only survived, but went on to write what is now a classic essay on the subject of homelessness. In "On Dumpster Diving," an essay that has retained its relevance for over a decade, Eighner, without self-pity and with sly wit, describes the fine art of scavenging for survival. His account is full of practical advice: "By far the best way to go through a Dumpster is to lower yourself into it. Most of the good stuff tends to settle at the bottom because it is usually weightier than the rubbish." Eighner now supports himself by writing essays and short stories; he is the author of *Travels with Lizbeth* (1994), a memoir of his homeless years wandering with his dog. "On Dumpster Diving" first appeared in the Fall 1991 issue of *Threepenny Review*.

Lars Eighner
ON DUMPSTER DIVING

Long before I began Dumpster diving I was impressed with Dumpsters, enough so that I wrote the Merriam-Webster research service to discover what I could about the word "Dumpster." I learned from them that "Dumpster" is a proprietary word belonging to the Dempsey Dumpster company.

Since then I have dutifully capitalized the word although it was lower-cased in almost all of the citations Merriam-Webster photocopied for me. Dempsey's word is too apt. I have never heard these things called anything but Dumpsters. I do not know anyone who knows the generic name for these objects. From time to time, however, I hear a wino or hobo give some corrupted credit to the original and call them Dipsy Dumpsters.

I began Dumpster diving about a year before I became homeless.

I prefer the term "scavenging" and use the word "scrounging" when I mean to be obscure. I have heard people, evidently meaning to be polite, using the word "foraging," but I prefer to reserve that word for gathering nuts and berries and such which I do also according to the season and the opportunity. "Dumpster diving" seems to me to be a little too cute and, in my case, inaccurate because I lack the athletic ability to lower myself into the Dumpsters as the true divers do, much to their increased profit.

I like the frankness of the word "scavenging," which I can hardly think of without picturing a big black snail on an aquarium wall. I live from the refuse of others. I am a scavenger. I think it a sound and honorable niche, although if I could I would naturally prefer to live the comfortable consumer life, perhaps—

and only perhaps—as a slightly less wasteful consumer owing to what I have learned as a scavenger.

While my dog Lizbeth and I were still living in the house on Avenue B in Austin, as my savings ran out, I put almost all my sporadic income into rent. The necessities of daily life I began to extract from Dumpsters. Yes, we ate from Dumpsters. Except for jeans, all my clothes came from Dumpsters. Boom boxes, candles, bedding, toilet paper, medicine, books, a typewriter, a virgin male love doll, change sometimes amounting to many dollars: I acquired many things from the Dumpsters.

I have learned much as a scavenger. I mean to put some of what I have learned down here, beginning with the practical art of Dumpster diving and proceeding to the abstract.

What is safe to eat?

After all, the finding of objects is becoming something of an urban art. Even respectable employed people will sometimes find something tempting sticking out of a Dumpster or standing beside one. Quite a number of people, not all of them of the bohemian type, are willing to brag that they found this or that piece in the trash. But eating from Dumpsters is the thing that separates the dilettanti from the professionals.

Eating safely from the Dumpsters involves three principles: using the senses and common sense to evaluate the condition of the found materials, knowing the Dumpsters of a given area and checking them regularly, and seeking always to answer the question "Why was this discarded?"

Perhaps everyone who has a kitchen and a regular supply of groceries has, at one time or another, made a sandwich and eaten half of it before discovering mold on the bread or got a mouthful of milk before realizing the milk had turned. Nothing of the sort is likely to happen to a Dumpster diver because he is constantly reminded that most food is discarded for a reason. Yet a lot of perfectly good food can be found in Dumpsters.

Canned goods, for example, turn up fairly often in the Dumpsters I frequent. All except the most phobic people would be willing to eat from a can even if it came from a Dumpster. Canned goods are among the safest of foods to be found in Dumpsters, but are not utterly foolproof.

Although very rare with modern canning methods, botulism is a possibility. Most other forms of food poisoning seldom do lasting harm to a healthy person. But botulism is almost certainly fatal and often the first symptom is death. Except for carbonated beverages, all canned goods should contain a slight vacuum and suck air when first punctured. Bulging, rusty, dented cans and cans that spew when punctured should be avoided, especially when the contents are not very acidic or syrupy.

Heat can break down the botulin, but this requires much more cooking than most people do to canned goods. To the extent that botulism occurs at all, of course, it can occur in cans on pantry shelves as well as in cans from Dumpsters. Need I say that home-canned goods found in Dumpsters are simply too risky to be recommended.

From time to time one of my companions, aware of the source of my provisions, will ask, "Do you think these crackers are really safe to eat?" For some reason it is most often the crackers they ask about.

This question always makes me angry. Of course I would not offer my companion anything I had doubts about. But more than that I wonder why he cannot evaluate the condition of the crackers for himself. I have no special knowledge and I have been wrong before. Since he knows where the food comes from, it seems to me he ought to assume some of the responsibility for deciding what he will put in his mouth.

For myself I have few qualms about dry foods such as crackers, cookies, cereal, chips, and pasta if they are free of visible contaminates and still dry and crisp. Most often such things are found in the original packaging, which is not so much a positive sign as it is the absence of a negative one.

Raw fruits and vegetables with intact skins seem perfectly safe to me, excluding of course the obviously rotten. Many are discarded for minor imperfections which can be pared away. Leafy vegetables, grapes, cauliflower, broccoli, and similar things may be contaminated by liquids and may be impractical to wash.

Candy, especially hard candy, is usually safe if it has not drawn ants. Chocolate is often discarded only because it has become discolored as the cocoa butter de-emulsified. Candying after all is one method of food preservation because pathogens do not like very sugary substances.

All of these foods might be found in any Dumpster and can be evaluated with some confidence largely on the basis of appearance. Beyond these are foods which cannot be correctly evaluated without additional information.

I began scavenging by pulling pizzas out of the Dumpster behind a pizza delivery shop. In general prepared food requires caution, but in this case I knew when the shop closed and went to the Dumpster as soon as the last of the help left.

Such shops often get prank orders, called "bogus." Because help seldom stays long at these places pizzas are often made with the wrong topping, refused on delivery for being cold, or baked incorrectly. The products to be discarded are boxed up because inventory is kept by counting boxes: a boxed pizza can be written off; an unboxed pizza does not exist.

I never placed a bogus order to increase the supply of pizzas and I believe no one else was scavenging in this Dumpster. But the people in the shop became suspicious and began to retain their garbage in the shop overnight.

While it lasted I had a steady supply of fresh, sometimes warm pizza. Because I knew the Dumpster I knew the source of the pizza, and because I visited the Dumpster regularly I knew what was fresh and what was yesterday's.

The area I frequent is inhabited by many affluent college students. I am not here by chance; the Dumpsters in this area are very rich. Students throw out many good things, including food. In particular they tend to throw everything out when they move at the end of a semester, before and after breaks, and around midterm when many of them despair of college. So I find it advantageous to keep an eye on the academic calendar.

The students throw food away around the breaks because they do not know whether it has spoiled or will spoil before they return. A typical discard is a half jar of peanut butter. In fact nonorganic peanut butter does not require refrigeration and is unlikely to spoil in any reasonable time. The student does not know that, and since it is Daddy's money, the student decides not to take a chance.

Opened containers require caution and some attention to the question "Why was this discarded?" But in the case of discards from student apartments, the answer may be that the item was discarded through carelessness, ignorance, or wastefulness. This can sometimes be deduced when the item is found with many others, including some that are obviously perfectly good.

Some students, and others, approach defrosting a freezer by chucking out the whole lot. Not only do the circumstances of such a find tell the story, but also the mass of frozen goods stays cold for a long time and items may be found still frozen or freshly thawed.

Yogurt, cheese, and sour cream are items that are often thrown out while they are still good. Occasionally I find a cheese with a spot of mold, which of course I just pare off, and because it is obvious why such a cheese was discarded, I treat it with less suspicion than an apparently perfect cheese found in similar circumstances. Yogurt is often discarded, still sealed, only because the expiration date on the carton had passed. This is one of my favorite finds because yogurt will keep for several days, even in warm weather.

Students throw out canned goods and staples at the end of semesters and when they give up college at midterm. Drugs, pornography, spirits, and the like are often discarded when parents are expected—Dad's day, for example. And spirits also turn up after big party weekends, presumably discarded by the newly reformed. Wine and spirits, of course, keep perfectly well even once opened.

My test for carbonated soft drinks is whether they still fizz vigorously. Many juices or other beverages are too acid or too syrupy to cause much concern provided they are not visibly contaminated. Liquids, however, require some care.

One hot day I found a large jug of Pat O'Brien's Hurricane mix. The jug had been opened, but it was still ice cold. I drank three large glasses before it became apparent to me that someone had added the rum to the mix, and not a little rum. I never tasted the rum and by the time I began to feel the effects I had already ingested a very large quantity of the beverage. Some divers would have considered this a boon, but being suddenly and thoroughly intoxicated in a public place in the early afternoon is not my idea of a good time.

I have heard of people maliciously contaminating discarded food and even handouts, but mostly I have heard of this from people with vivid imaginations who have had no experience with the Dumpsters themselves. Just before the pizza shop stopped discarding its garbage at night, jalapeños began showing up on most of the discarded pizzas. If indeed this was meant to discourage me it was a wasted effort because I am native Texan.

For myself, I avoid game, poultry, pork, and egg-based foods whether I find them raw or cooked. I seldom have the means to cook what I find, but when I do I avail myself of plentiful supplies of beef which is often in very good condition. I suppose fish becomes disagreeable before it becomes dangerous. The dog is happy to have any such thing that is past its prime and, in fact, does not recognize fish as food until it is quite strong.

457

■ *Look carefully at this photograph. What details make you feel this is a family on the edge? How would you describe the expressions of the various family members? What do you consider to be the photograph's focal point? How has Mark set up the image to reinforce the family's separateness from mainstream society? What compositional role does the automobile play in the photograph?*

◀ **Mary Ellen Mark, *The Damm Family in Their Car, Los Angeles, California, 1987.***
Mary Ellen Mark (b. 1940) is one of the most recognized photographers to
document lives along the margins — a recent survey by *American Photo* magazine
ranked her as the most influential woman photographer of all time. After receiving an M.A. at the University of Pennsylvania's Annenberg School of
Communications, Mark began traveling widely to learn about other cultures.
Eventually settling in New York City, doing photojournalism for magazines along
with production stills for Hollywood movies, Mark discovered a way to combine
portraiture and documentary photography when she was trying to capture the
daily lives of women in the mental ward of an Oregon hospital. That series of
photographs was published as a book, *Ward 81*, in 1979. Mark then turned her
attention to another marginalized group, this time from a different culture, publishing *Falkland Road: Prostitutes of Bombay* in 1981. Her photographic series
on street kids in Seattle for *Life* magazine in 1983 led to another highly praised
book, *Streetwise* (1988). Her eleven books also include *Indian Circus* (1993),
Portraits (1995), and a retrospective volume, *American Odyssey* (1999). In
1987 and again in 1994, Mark followed a North Hollywood, California, homeless
family — Dean, Linda, Chrissy, and Jesse — who lived in their car in North
Hollywood at the time this photograph was taken. As a documentary photographer, Mark does not simply shoot and run but gets very close to her subjects,
their families, and their communities: "I'm just interested in people on the
edges. I feel an affinity for people who haven't had the best breaks in society. . . .
What I want to do more than anything is acknowledge their existence."
(Copyright © 1999 by Mary Ellen Mark)

459

COMMENT
"After all these years, I'm still interested in photography because I am constantly
finding new ways to construct an image — to better understand that visual language.
The single image with a metaphoric value appeals to me more than the traditional
photo-essay. I am always trying to discover which photographs work, why they work,
what is necessary to include in a photograph, and what you can leave out. Often the
strongest images are those that exclude elements and leave more to the imagination."

— Mary Ellen Mark

Home leftovers, as opposed to surpluses from restaurants, are very often bad. Evidently, especially among students, there is a common type of personality that carefully wraps up even the smallest leftover and shoves it into the back of the refrigerator for six months or so before discarding it. Characteristic of this type are the reused jars and margarine tubs which house the remains.

I avoid ethnic foods I am unfamiliar with. If I do not know what it is supposed to look like when it is good, I cannot be certain I will be able to tell if it is bad.

No matter how careful I am I still get dysentery at least once a month, oftener in warm weather. I do not want to paint too romantic a picture. Dumpster diving has serious drawbacks as a way of life.

I learned to scavenge gradually, on my own. Since then I have initiated several companions into the trade. I have learned that there is a predictable series of stages a person goes through in learning to scavenge.

At first the new scavenger is filled with disgust and self-loathing. He is ashamed of being seen and may lurk around, trying to duck behind things, or he may try to dive at night.

(In fact, most people instinctively look away from a scavenger. By skulking around, the novice calls attention to himself and arouses suspicion. Diving at night is ineffective and needlessly messy.)

Every grain of rice seems to be a maggot. Everything seems to stink. He can wipe the egg yolk off the found can, but he cannot erase the stigma of eating garbage out of his mind.

That stage passes with experience. The scavenger finds a pair of running shoes that fit and look and smell brand new. He finds a pocket calculator in perfect working order. He finds pristine ice cream, still frozen, more than he can eat or keep. He begins to understand: people do throw away perfectly good stuff, a lot of perfectly good stuff.

At this stage, Dumpster shyness begins to dissipate. The diver, after all, has the last laugh. He is finding all manner of good things which are his for the taking. Those who disparage his profession are the fools, not he.

He may begin to hang onto some perfectly good things for which he has neither a use nor a market. Then he begins to take note of the things which are not perfectly good but are nearly so. He mates a Walkman with broken earphones and one that is missing a battery cover. He picks up things which he can repair.

At this stage he may become lost and never recover. Dumpsters are full of things of some potential value to someone and also of things which never have much intrinsic value but are interesting. All the Dumpster divers I have known come to the point of trying to acquire everything they touch. Why not take it, they reason, since it is all free.

This is, of course, hopeless. Most divers come to realize that they must restrict themselves to items of relatively immediate utility. But in some cases the diver simply cannot control himself. I have met several of these pack-rat types. Their ideas of the values of various pieces of junk verge on the psychotic. Every bit of glass may be a diamond, they think, and all that glistens, gold.

Mary Ellen Mark, *Chrissy Damm and Adam Johnson, Liano, California, 1994.* In an interview that appeared in the winter 1997 issue of *Aperture*, Mary Ellen Mark says of this image: "When I was photographing the Damm family, I would just spend all day. This is Chrissy with her boyfriend, Adam. This is in the house where they were squatting; they were no longer living in a car, but rather a shack without water or electricity. I just hung out with the kids. They were in love. . . . I think Jesse likes us. With Chrissy, it's a little harder to tell. She is more complex. Everything is hidden with her." (Copyright © 1999 by Mary Ellen Mark)

COMMENT
"In its social aspect, [Mary Ellen Mark's] work has become synonymous with how important it is to acknowledge the humanity of those people on the edges of society, and often at the edges of their own lives."

—Andrew Long, photography critic for *Salon* and *The New Yorker*

I tend to gain weight when I am scavenging. Partly this is because I always find far more pizza and doughnuts than water-packed tuna, nonfat yogurt, and fresh vegetables. Also I have not developed much faith in the reliability of Dumpsters as a food source, although it has been proven to me many times. I tend to eat as if I have no idea where my next meal is coming from. But mostly I just hate to see food go to waste and so I eat much more than I should. Something like this drives the obsession to collect junk.

As for collecting objects, I usually restrict myself to collecting one kind of small object at a time, such as pocket calculators, sunglasses, or campaign buttons. To live on the street I must anticipate my needs to a certain extent: I must pick up and save warm bedding I find in August because it will not be found in Dumpsters in November. But even if I had a home with extensive storage space I could not save everything that might be valuable in some contingency.

I have proprietary feelings about my Dumpsters. As I have suggested, it is no accident that I scavenge from Dumpsters where good finds are common. But my limited experience with Dumpsters in other areas suggests to me that it is the population of competitors rather than the affluence of the dumpers that most affects the feasibility of survival by scavenging. The large number of competitors is what puts me off the idea of trying to scavenge in places like Los Angeles.

Curiously, I do not mind my direct competition, other scavengers, so much as I hate the can scroungers.

People scrounge cans because they have to have a little cash. I have tried scrounging cans with an able-bodied companion. Afoot a can scrounger simply cannot make more than a few dollars a day. One can extract the necessities of life from the Dumpsters directly with far less effort than would be required to accumulate the equivalent value in cans.

Can scroungers, then, are people who *must* have small amounts of cash. These are drug addicts and winos, mostly the latter because the amounts of cash are so small.

Spirits and drugs do, like all other commodities, turn up in Dumpsters and the scavenger will from time to time have a half bottle of a rather good wine with his dinner. But the wino cannot survive on these occasional finds; he must have his daily dose to stave off the DTs. All the cans he can carry will buy about three bottles of Wild Irish Rose.

I do not begrudge them the cans, but can scroungers tend to tear up the Dumpsters, mixing the contents and littering the area. They become so specialized that they can see only cans. They earn my contempt by passing up change, canned goods, and readily hockable items.

There are precious few courtesies among scavengers. But it is a common practice to set aside surplus items: pairs of shoes, clothing, canned goods, and such. A true scavenger hates to see good stuff go to waste and what he cannot use he leaves in good condition in plain sight.

Can scroungers lay waste to everything in their path and will stir one of a pair of good shoes to the bottom of a Dumpster, to be lost or ruined in the muck. Can scroungers will even go through individual garbage cans, something I have never seen a scavenger do.

Individual garbage cans are set out on the public easement only on garbage days. On other days going through them requires trespassing close to a dwelling. Going through individual garbage cans without scattering litter is almost impossible. Litter is likely to reduce the public's tolerance of scavenging. Individual garbage cans are simply not as productive as Dumpsters; people in houses and duplexes do not move as often and for some reason do not tend to discard as much useful material. Moreover, the time required to go through one garbage can that serves one household is not much less than the time required to go through a Dumpster that contains the refuse of twenty apartments.

But my strongest reservation about going through individual garbage cans is that this seems to me a very personal kind of invasion to which I would object if I were a householder. Although many things in Dumpsters are obviously meant never to come to light, a Dumpster is somehow less personal.

I avoid trying to draw conclusions about the people who dump in the Dumpsters I frequent. I think it would be unethical to do so, although I know many people will find the idea of scavenger ethics too funny for words.

Dumpsters contain bank statements, bills, correspondence, and other documents, just as anyone might expect. But there are also less obvious sources of information. Pill bottles, for example. The labels on pill bottles contain the name of the patient, the name of the doctor, and the name of the drug. AIDS drugs and antipsychotic medicines, to name but two groups, are specific and are seldom prescribed for any other disorders. The plastic compacts for birth control pills usually have complete label information.

Despite all of this sensitive information, I have had only one apartment resident object to my going through the Dumpster. In that case it turned out the resident was a university athlete who was taking bets and who was afraid I would turn up his wager slips.

Occasionally a find tells a story. I once found a small paper bag containing some unused condoms, several partial tubes of flavored sexual lubricant, a partially used compact of birth control pills, and the torn pieces of a picture of a young man. Clearly she was through with him and planning to give up sex altogether.

Dumpster things are often sad — (abandoned teddy bears, shredded wedding books, despaired-of sales kits. I find many pets lying in state in Dumpsters. Although I hope to get off the streets so that Lizbeth can have a long and comfortable old age, I know this hope is not very realistic. So I suppose when her time comes she too will go into a Dumpster. I will have no better place for her. And after all, for most of her life her livelihood has come from the Dumpster. When she finds something I think is safe that has been spilled from the Dumpster I let her have it. She already knows the route around the best Dumpsters. I like to think that if she survives me she will have a chance of evading the dog catcher and of finding her sustenance on the route.

Silly vanities also come to rest in the Dumpsters. I am a rather accomplished needleworker. I get a lot of materials from the Dumpsters. Evidently sorority girls, hoping to impress someone, perhaps themselves, with their mastery of a womanly art, buy a lot of embroider-by-number kits, work a few stitches horribly, and eventually discard the whole mess. I pull out their stitches, turn the canvas over, and work an original design. Do not think I refrain from chuckling as I make original gifts from these kits.

I find diaries and journals. I have often thought of compiling a book of literary found objects. And perhaps I will one day. But what I find is hopelessly commonplace and bad without being, even unconsciously, camp. College students also discard their papers. I am horrified to discover the kind of paper which now merits an A in an undergraduate course. I am grateful, however, for the number of good books and magazines the students throw out.

In the area I know best I have never discovered vermin in the Dumpsters, but there are two kinds of kitty surprise. One is alley cats which I meet as they leap, claws first, out of Dumpsters. This is especially thrilling when I have Lizbeth in tow. The other kind of kitty surprise is a plastic garbage bag filled with some ponderous, amorphous mass. This always proves to be used cat litter.

City bees harvest doughnut glaze and this makes the Dumpster at the doughnut shop more interesting. My faith in the instinctive wisdom of animals is always shaken whenever I see Lizbeth attempt to catch a bee in her mouth, which she does whenever bees are present. Evidently some birds find Dumpsters profitable, for birdie surprise is almost as common as kitty surprise of the first kind. In hunting season all kinds of small game turn up in Dumpsters, some of it, sadly, not entirely dead. Curiously, summer and winter, maggots are uncommon.

The worst of the living and near-living hazards of the Dumpsters are the fire ants. The food that they claim is not much of a loss, but they are vicious and aggressive. It is very easy to brush against some surface of the Dumpster and pick up half a dozen or more fire ants, usually in some sensitive area such as the underarm. One advantage of bringing Lizbeth along as I make Dumpster rounds is that, for obvious reasons, she is very alert to ground-based fire ants. When Lizbeth recognizes the signs of fire ant infestation around our feet she does the Dance of the Zillion Fire Ants. I have learned not to ignore this warning from Lizbeth, whether I perceive the tiny ants or not, but to remove ourselves at Lizbeth's first pas de bourrée.[1] All the more so because the ants are the worst in the months I wear flip-flops, if I have them.

(Perhaps someone will misunderstand the above. Lizbeth does the Dance of the Zillion Fire Ants when she recognizes more fire ants than she cares to eat, not when she is being bitten. Since I have learned to react promptly, she does not get bitten at all. It is the isolated patrol of fire ants that falls in Lizbeth's range that deserves pity. Lizbeth finds them quite tasty.)

By far the best way to go through a Dumpster is to lower yourself into it. Most of the good stuff tends to settle at the bottom because it is usually weightier than the rubbish. My more athletic companions have often demonstrated to me that they can extract much good material from a Dumpster I have already been over.

---

[1] *pas de bourrée:* A transitional ballet step.

To those psychologically or physically unprepared to enter a Dumpster, I recommend a stout stick, preferably with some barb or hook at one end. The hook can be used to grab plastic garbage bags. When I find canned goods or other objects loose at the bottom of a Dumpster I usually can roll them into a small bag that I can then hoist up. Much Dumpster diving is a matter of experience for which nothing will do except practice.

Dumpster diving is outdoor work, often surprisingly pleasant. It is not entirely predictable; things of interest turn up every day and some days there are finds of great value. I am always very pleased when I can turn up exactly the thing I most wanted to find. Yet in spite of the element of change, scavenging more than most other pursuits tends to yield returns in some proportion to the effort and intelligence brought to bear. It is very sweet to turn up a few dollars in change from a Dumpster that has just been gone over by a wino.

The land is now covered with cities. The cities are full of Dumpsters. I think of scavenging as a modern form of self-reliance. In any event, after ten years of government service, where everything is geared to the lowest common denominator, I find work that rewards initiative and effort refreshing. Certainly I would be happy to have a sinecure again, but I am not heartbroken not to have one anymore.

I find from the experience of scavenging two rather deep lessons. The first is to take what I can use and let the rest go by. I have come to think that there is no value in the abstract. A thing I cannot use or make useful, perhaps by trading, has no value however fine or rare it may be. I mean useful in a broad sense — so, for example, some art I would think useful and valuable, but other art might be otherwise for me.

I was shocked to realize that some things are not worth acquiring, but now I think it is so. Some material things are white elephants that eat up the possessor's substance.

The second lesson is of the transience of material being. This has not quite converted me to a dualist, but it has made some headway in that direction. I do not suppose that ideas are immortal, but certainly mental things are longer-lived than other material things.

Once I was the sort of person who invests material objects with sentimental value. Now I no longer have those things, but I have the sentiments yet.

Many times in my travels I have lost everything but the clothes I was wearing and Lizbeth. The things I find in Dumpsters, the love letters and ragdolls of so many lives, remind me of this lesson. Now I hardly pick up a thing without envisioning the time I will cast it away. This I think is a healthy state of mind. Almost everything I have now has already been cast out at least once, proving that what I own is valueless to someone.

Anyway, I find my desire to grab for the gaudy bauble has been largely sated. I think this is an attitude I share with the very wealthy — we both know there is plenty more where what we have came from. Between us are the rat-race millions who have confounded their selves with the objects they grasp and who nightly scavenge the cable channels looking for they know not what.

I am sorry for them.

465

Margaret Morton, *Mr. Lee*. Morton has gathered photographs and oral histories in *Fragile Dwelling* (New York: Aperture, 2000), a collection that documents the inventive ways in which homeless people create places and communities. This text accompanies several photographs of Mr. Lee, two of which are reproduced here.

MR. LEE

At the crest of the Hill, just before it narrows to a ravine and plummets toward Forsyth Street, stands the curious home of Mr. Lee, an immigrant from Guangdong Province in China, who found his way to the encampment in 1989. He brought few possessions but soon astonished his neighbors by constructing a house without pounding a nail or sawing a board. It is bound together with knots. Bright yellow plastic straps wrap his soft rounded hut, binding old mattresses and bedsprings into walls. The exterior is festooned with red bakery ribbons, paper lanterns, and castoff calendars that celebrate the Chinese New Year. Oranges, symbols of prosperity, have hardened in the bitter cold and hang from the straps like ornaments.

Every morning, Mr. Lee quietly draws Chinese characters on flat sheets of cardboard and lashes them to the outside of his hut: CONGRATULATIONS TO MR. LEE FOR HAVING A BIG COMPANY, HE HAS HUNDREDS OF THOUSANDS OF WORKERS, EACH WORKER GETS PAID $500 A DAY, PROSPERITY TO MR. LEE, MR. LEE THE GREAT INVENTOR. He does not write about the job he once held as a restaurant worker in Queens, or about his last apartment, a walk-up on Mott Street.

At dawn, when Mr. Lee leaves the Hill, he places a stone against his door and secures it with elaborate knots. He slowly wanders the streets of Chinatown with two burlap rice sacks slung over his shoulder, pausing to collect bits of cloth and cord left by morning delivery trucks. In the early evening he returns and, with great ceremony, ties his new treasures to the exterior of his hut. Mr. Lee sometimes binds these objects in such a way that they take on new forms and identities. The majestic cluster of fruit perched atop his roof is in fact a teddy bear, which he found on the street and skillfully transformed.

Much like his house, Mr. Lee is soft and round and held together by knots. Bits of wire twisted through buttonholes fasten his multiple layers of second-hand clothing.

◀ **Margaret Morton,** *Mr. Lee's House, the Hill, 1991.* The photograph of Mr. Lee's house is included in Margaret Morton's book *Fragile Dwelling* (2000), a collection of photographs documenting the various ways New York City's homeless people have constructed their own housing. As her publisher says: "To Morton, these assemblages of crates, scrap wood, broken furniture, and other debris of the modern city are not an eyesore to be quickly dismissed and then forgotten. They are in fact, as she shows us, homes — laboriously and ingeniously built, little by little, piece by piece." Morton spent ten years on this project, taking photographs and recording oral histories. A professor of art at The Cooper Union for the Advancement of Science and Art, Morton, who received her M.F.A. degree from Yale, has published several other books, including *The Tunnel and Transitory Gardens* (1995). Her photographs have been widely exhibited and featured in numerous magazines in the United States and abroad.

Margaret Morton,
Mr. Lee, Chinatown,
1992. (© Margaret
Morton. Reprinted by
permission)

468

■ *What connection does the photographer establish between Mr. Lee and his house? In your judgment, how do the photographs of Mr. Lee and of his house reinforce the connection Morton makes in her verbal description?*

MESSAGE

What lessons does Lars Eighner learn from his experience in the art of Dumpster diving? How do these lead to ethical principles? Are these principles applicable to everyone, even the affluent? What do you think Eighner means when he writes: "I think of scavenging as a modern form of self-reliance"?

METHOD

What characterizes Mr. Lee's method of construction? Where does he find his supplies? How does his method help reveal something about his personal and ethnic identity? How does Margaret Morton's brief "oral history" help you make sense out of Mr. Lee's distinctive style? Can you find any similarities between Mr. Lee's methods and Lars Eighner's craft? In what ways do they both demonstrate "self-reliance"?

MEDIUM

In her afterword to *American Odyssey,* Mary Ellen Mark writes: "Photographs can be enigmatic. They sometimes work because of what is included in the frame, and sometimes because of what is not." This is a principle that can be applied to all works of art, regardless of the medium: we need to observe what the artist has included as well as what he or she has left out. Can you apply Mark's principle to all of the photographs depicting homeless people in this section? After noting what's included—details, postures, expressions, backgrounds, and so on—identify elements you think the photographers omitted. Why do you think those particular elements were omitted?

469

COLOR LINES

In the introduction to his 1903 classic, *The Souls of Black Folk*, W.E.B. Du Bois wrote presciently that "the problem of the Twentieth Century is the problem of the color line." He envisioned a century in which the races would be socially, culturally, and politically divided.

But will Du Bois's prediction hold true for the twenty-first century? In "Race Over," the prominent African American sociologist Orlando Patterson tries to imagine America's racial future. He comes up with a national scenario, based largely on changing demographic patterns, that is both concise and controversial. "By the middle of the twenty-first century," Patterson predicts, "America will have problems aplenty. But no racial problem whatsoever."

Whether today's college generation will ever see such an uplifting future is highly debatable, but it has been noted by many commentators that, as the *New York Times* put it in December 2003, "the under-25 members of Generation Y" represent "the most racially diverse population in the nation's history." The growing attraction to young audiences of what some call "ethnic ambiguity" has not been lost on both the media and the marketing image-makers, who now feature stars, models, athletes, and artists whose ethnic heritages are not readily identifiable. One fashion magazine editor said recently: "We're seeing more of a desire for the exotic, left-of-center beauty that transcends race or class."

Orlando Patterson, *Race Over*. Orlando Patterson, a professor of sociology at Harvard University, specializes in the analysis of slavery in different societies and historical moments, from ancient Greece and Rome to the American South. His work examines slavery as a system of relationships of domination. In this essay, he explores the possibility of a time when race ceases to be a factor in systems of power. "Race Over" appeared in the January 10, 2000, issue of *The New Republic*.

Orlando Patterson
RACE OVER

One can quibble with W.E.B. Du Bois's famous prediction for the twentieth century. This has been not simply the century of the color line but a century of Jim Crow and myriad other persecutions—many within color boundaries. But, if Du Bois's epigraph was only half right, his modern-day disciples, who insist the color line will define the next 100 years as well, are altogether wrong. The racial divide that has plagued America since its founding is fading fast—made obsolete by migratory, sociological, and biotechnological developments that are already under way. By the middle of the twenty-first century, America will have problems aplenty. But no racial problem whatsoever.

For this we can thank four social patterns, each indigenous to a particular region of the country but which together will reshape the nation as a whole. The strongest and clearest might be called the California system. Cultural and somatic mixture will be its hallmark. A hybrid population, mainly Eurasian—but with a growing Latin element—will come to dominate the middle and upper classes and will grow exponentially, especially after the 2020s. Lower-class Caucasians, middle-class racial purists, and most African Americans, under pressure from an endless stream of unskilled Mexican workers, will move away. Those African Americans who remain will be rapidly absorbed into the emerging mixed population. The California system will come to dominate the American and Canadian Pacific Rim.

The second major pattern might be called the Caribbean-American system. Increasingly, the countries of the Caribbean basin will be socially and economically integrated with the United States. As their fragile and already declining economies collapse (most dramatically in post-Castro Cuba), they will swarm the mainland by legal and illegal means. Florida will be the metropolitan center of this system, although Caribbean colonies will sprout all over the Northeast. Caribbean peoples will bring their distinctive concept of race and color to America, one in which people marry lighter and "white" as they move up the social ladder. This system will differ from the California one in that the dominant element will be Afro-Latin rather than Eurasian. Since the Caribbean is much closer than Asia, this system will also create a distinctive social type: genuinely transnational and post-national communities in which people feel equally at home in their native and American locations. Increasingly, people will spend their childhoods and retirements in the Caribbean and their productive years in America. The Caribbean-American system will compete with the African American community not only in the lower reaches of the labor force but as the nation's major source of popular culture, especially in music and sports. But, despite these differences, the Caribbean-American system, like the California one, will render the "one drop" rule obsolete.

The third and most problematic system will be the one now emerging in the Northeast and urban Midwest. Here, the economic situation for all classes of African Americans and native-born Latinos is likely to deteriorate—with the ending of affirmative action, a shrinking public sector, and competition from skilled and unskilled (mainly Caribbean basin) immigrant labor. The rise of workfare without compensating provision for child care, combined with the growing

472

COMMENT

"When I began looking for a job after college, I discovered that being a white Latina made me a nonthreatening minority in the eyes of these employers. My color was a question *only* of culture, and if I kept my cultural color to myself, I was "no problem." Each time I was hired for one of my countless "visiting appointments"—they were never permanent "invitations," mind you—the inevitable questionnaire would accompany my contract in which I was to check off my RACE: CAUCASIAN, BLACK, NATIVE AMERICAN, ASIAN, HISPANIC, OTHER. How could a Dominican divide herself in this way? Or was I really a Dominican anymore? And what was a Hispanic? A census creation—there is no such culture—how could it define who I was at all? Given this set of options, the truest answer might have been to check off OTHER.

"For that was the way I had begun to think of myself."

—Julia Alvarez, from "A White Woman of Color" (*Half and Half*, Random House, 1988)

pattern of paternal abandonment of children, will further undermine traditional family norms among African American, Latino, and, increasingly, the European American lower classes. Reversing the pattern that emerged after World War II, African Americans, Latinos, and the poorest Caucasians will move into the inner and secondary rings of what are now mainly European American middle-class suburbs. The middle classes will move to either gated exurbs or gentrified central cities—leaving a European American underclass that resembles other ethnic underclasses more and more.

But, although these developments will at first exacerbate racial conflict, they will ultimately transform racial frustrations into class ones. Indeed, for the first time in the nation's history, young, poor, and alienated Caucasians, African Americans, and Latinos will find common ground—based on social resentment and a common lumpen-proletarian,[1] hip-hop culture. Even as these young people periodically engage in murderous racial gang fights, intermarriage and miscegenation will escalate as the young poor of all races break away from present gender and racial taboos. In contrast to the California and Florida systems, the growing hybrid population in the Northeast and industrial Midwest will be lower-class, alienated, and out of control. But it will be hybrid nonetheless.

The exception will be in the Southeast, in what may be called the Atlanta pattern. African Americans and European Americans will cling to notions of racial purity and will remain highly (and voluntarily) segregated from each other. Affirmative action will be the bulwark of this system, the price the European American elite willingly pays for "racial" stability and the reassuring presence of a culturally familiar but socially distant African American group and a pliant working class. The old Confederacy will remain a place where everyone knows who is white and who is black and need reckon with no in-between. But, as opposed to the nineteenth and twentieth centuries, when the South defined the terms of racial engagement on which the entire nation interacted (more or less brutally), in the twenty-first century the Southern model will become an increasingly odd and decreasingly relevant anachronism.

For the decline of race as a factor in American life will result not only from immigration, which can perhaps be halted, but also from biotechnology. More and more in the coming decades, Americans will gain the means to genetically manipulate human appearance. The foundations of genetic engineering are already in place. Given the interest of the affluent population in male-pattern baldness, the restoration of hair loss after cancer treatment, and cancer-free tanning, science is likely to create dramatic new methods of changing hair texture and skin color. Indeed, last November, scientists at Columbia University transplanted scalp cells from one person to another. I don't expect many African

473

---

[1] *Lumpen-proletarian.* The word comes from the German and was used by Karl Marx to describe those living on the margins of society, such as homeless, permanently unemployed, etc. —ED.

Americans to choose straight-haired whiteness for themselves or their progeny, but many will opt for varying degrees of hybridity. In a world dominated by mass culture, many will embrace changes that enhance their individuality. Once dramatically manipulable by human action, "race" will lose its social significance, and the myth of racial purity will be laid to rest.

By the middle of the next century, the social virus of race will have gone the way of smallpox. The twenty-first century, relieved of the obscuring blinkers of race, will be a century of class and class consciousness, forcing the nation to finally take seriously its creed that all are created equal. It should be interesting.

COMMENT

"Global marketers like H&M, the cheap chic clothing chain with stores in 18 countries, increasingly highlight models with racially indeterminate features. 'For us the models must be inspiring and attractive and at the same time, neutral,' said Anna Bergare, the company's Stockholm-based spokeswoman. The campaigns contrast notably with the original marketing strategy of Benetton, another global clothing chain, whose path-breaking 1980's ads highlighted models of many races, each very distinct. These days even Benetton's billboards play up the multiracial theme. In a typical campaign, a young man with Asian features and an Afro hairdo is posed beside a blue-eyed woman with incongruously tawny skin and brown hair with the texture of yarn.

"Such a transition — from racial diversity portrayed as a beautiful mosaic to a melting pot — is in line with the currently fashionable argument that race itself is a fiction. This theory has been advanced by prominent scholars like K. Anthony Appiah, professor of philosophy at Princeton, and Evelyn Hammond, a professor of the history of science and Afro-American studies at Harvard. In a PBS broadcast last spring, Ms. Hammond said race is a human contrivance, a 'concept we invented to categorize the perceived biological, social and cultural differences between human groups.'

"More and more, that kind of thinking is echoed by the professional image makers. 'Some of us are just now beginning to recognize that many cultures and races are assimilating,' said John Partilla, the chief executive of Brand Buzz, a marketing agency owned by the WPP group. 'If what you're seeing now is our focus on trying to reflect the blending of individuals, it reflects a societal trend, not a marketing trend.'

" 'For once,' Mr. Partilla added, 'it's about art imitating life.' "

— Ruth La Ferla, From "Generation E.A.: Ethnically Ambiguous" (*New York Times*, 12/28/03)

Derek Jeter, 2003. New York Yankees player Derek Jeter is African American and Caucasian. He and the other celebrities pictured here are just a few of the individuals who represent the generation Ruth La Ferla refers to as "ethnically ambiguous," representatives of America's increasingly multiracial population. (Photo by Evan Agostini/Getty Images)

Jessica Alba, 2003. Actress Jessica Alba is French, Danish, Mexican Indian, and Spanish. (TOM MAELSA/AFP/Getty Images)

Vin Diesel, 2003. Actor Vin Diesel is half Irish and half undisclosed. (Photo by Getty Images)

Christina Aguilera, 2003. Singer Christina Aguilera is half Equadorean. She tweaks her looks often — sometimes blond, sometimes dark. She posed as an Indian Bollywood goddess in the January 2004 issue of *Allure* magazine. (© Stephane Cardinale/People Avenue/Corbis)

MESSAGE

To what forces does Orlando Patterson attribute the vast racial changes that he expects will occur in America within the next half-century? Why do you think he gives no time in his essay to an analysis of legislative or judicial enactments? Do you suppose he thinks that further laws will not be necessary for the changes he envisions? According to Patterson, what will be the twenty-first century's equivalent of the color line?

METHOD

Patterson's case assumes a division of the United States into four geographical areas, each with unique characteristics. Two of these regions, however — the Northeast/urban Midwest and the Southeast — present problems. Why do these regions not fit entirely into Patterson's demographic scenario? How does he acknowledge these exceptions and at the same time try to show that they support his argument? Do you think he succeeds?

MEDIUM

Do you think the presence of celebrities you now see in the media suggests that Patterson is on to something? In what ways does the current marketing of mixed-ethnic personalities support Patterson's case? Do you think this media trend will continue well into the twenty-first century and help make race obsolete? What evidence do you see in the media today that the trend will or will not continue?

ANIMAL RIGHTS

In "Us and Them" (see pp. 417–29) we examined the lines that divide people — those who are "like us" from those who aren't. Sometimes these lines can be ambiguous and at other times crystal clear; nevertheless, they all separate some people from other people. But human beings share the planet with countless other living species: What about these creatures? Is there an unbridgeable gap between humans and nonhumans? Can we rightfully claim dominion over all creatures and do what we want with them? Or are we ethically obligated to treat other creatures kindly and respectfully?

The idea of drawing a clear boundary between humans and nonhuman creatures has led to one of today's most heated intellectual controversies. The challenge also constitutes a major topic of philosophic debate, one that is represented by the following essays and ads, which explore the meaning of "rights" as applied to nonhumans. It's a very practical debate: Are all animals entitled to equal rights, or do some — notably those that most resemble humans — deserve greater rights? In other words, is it permissible to use mice and rats for laboratory testing but not monkeys or apes? Or, as some maintain, is it morally impermissible to subject any creature to scientific experimentation, no matter how noble the goal? Do farm animals require protection from harsh conditions and confinement? Should furriers be abolished, hunting eliminated, hamburgers forbidden? As you can see, the issue raises a multitude of ethical and practical questions — and they aren't as easy to answer as they may at first seem.

Steven M. Wise, *Why Animals Deserve Legal Rights.* Is an ape more of a "person" than a two-year-old human? Any child could tell you that an ape is not — only people are people. But in this essay, Steven Wise argues that it's not that simple, and that science proves that some animals really are people — or at least that they deserve the same rights. Wise (b. 1950) has been a Harvard professor and an animal rights lawyer for over twenty years. He has written two books on the subject of animal rights: *Rattling the Cage: Toward Legal Rights for Animals* (2000) and *Drawing the Line: Science and the Case for Animal Rights* (2002). This essay appeared in the *Chronicle of Higher Education* on February 2, 2001.

Steven M. Wise

WHY ANIMALS DESERVE LEGAL RIGHTS

478

For centuries, the right to have everything that makes existence worthwhile — like freedom, safety from torture, and even life itself — has turned on whether the law classifies one as a person or a thing. Although some Jews once belonged to Pharaoh, Syrians to Nero, and African Americans to George Washington, now every human is a person in the eyes of the law.

All nonhuman animals, on the other hand, are things with no rights. The law ignores them unless a person decides to do something to them, and then, in most cases, nothing can be done to help them. According to statistics collected annually by the Department of Agriculture, in the United States this year, tens of millions of animals are likely to be killed, sometimes painfully, during biomedical research; 10 billion more will be raised in factories so crowded that they're unable to turn around, and then killed for food. The U.S. Fish and Wildlife Service and allied state agencies report that hundreds of millions will be shot by hunters or exploited in rodeos, circuses, and roadside zoos. And all of that is perfectly legal.

What accounts for the legal personhood of all of us and the legal thinghood of all of them? Judeo-Christian theologians sometimes argue that humans are made in the image of God. But that argument has been leaking since Gratian, the twelfth-century Benedictine monk who is considered the father of canon law, made the same claim just for men in his *Decretum.* Few, if any, philosophers or judges today would argue that being human, all by itself, is sufficient for legal rights. There must be something about us that entitles us to rights.

Philosophers have proffered many criteria as sufficient, including sentience, a sense of justice, the possession of language or morality, and having a rational plan for one's life. Among legal thinkers, the most important is autonomy, also known as self-determination or volition. Things don't act autonomously. Persons do.

Notice that I said that autonomy is "sufficient" for basic legal rights; it obviously isn't necessary. We don't eat or vivisect human babies born without brains, who are so lacking in sentience that they are operated on without anesthesia.

But autonomy is tough to define. Kant thought that autonomous beings always act rationally. Anyone who can't do that can justly be treated as a thing. Kant must have had extraordinary friends and relatives. Not being a fulltime academic, I don't know anyone who always acts rationally.

Most philosophers, and just about every judge, reject Kant's rigorous conception of autonomy, for they can easily imagine a human who lacks it, but can still walk about making decisions. Instead, some of them think that a being can be autonomous—at least to some degree—if she has preferences and the ability to act to satisfy them. Others would say she is autonomous if she can cope with changed circumstances. Still others, if she can make choices, even if she can't evaluate their merits very well. Or if she has desires and beliefs and can make at least some sound and appropriate inferences from them.

As things, nonhuman animals have been invisible to civil law since its inception. "All law," said the Roman jurist Hermogenianus, "was established for men's sake." And why not? Everything else was.

Unfortunately for animals, many people have believed that they were put on earth for human use and lack autonomy. Aristotle granted them a few mental abilities: They could perceive and act on impulse. Many Stoics, however, denied them the capacities to perceive, conceive, reason, remember, believe, even experience. Animals knew nothing of the past and could not imagine a future. Nor could they desire, know good, or learn from experience.

For decades, though, evidence has been accumulating that at least some nonhuman animals have extraordinary minds. Twelve years ago, seven-year-old Kanzi—a bonobo[1] who works with Sue Savage-Rumbaugh, a biologist at Georgia State University—drubbed a human two-year-old, named Alia, in a series of language-comprehension tests. In the tests, both human and bonobo had to struggle, as we all do, with trying to make sense of the mind of a speaker. When Kanzi was asked to "put some water on the vacuum cleaner," he gulped water from a glass, marched to the vacuum cleaner, and dribbled the water over it. Told to "feed your ball some tomato," he could see no ball before him. So he picked up a spongy toy Halloween pumpkin and pretended to shove a tomato into its mouth. When asked to go to the refrigerator and get an orange, Kanzi immediately complied; Alia didn't have a clue what to do.

---

[1] Bonobos are great apes, like chimpanzees and gorillas, and are man's closest genetic relative. —ED.

In the forty years since Jane Goodall[2] arrived at Gombe, she and others have shown that apes have most, if not all, of the emotions that we do. They are probably self-conscious; many of them can recognize themselves in a mirror. They use insight, not just trial and error, to solve problems. They form complex mental representations, including mental maps of the area where they live. They understand cause and effect. They act intentionally. They compare objects, and relationships between objects. They count. They use tools—they even make tools. Given the appropriate opportunity and motivation, they have been known to teach, deceive, and empathize with others. They can figure out what others see and know, abilities that human children don't develop until the ages of three to five. They create cultural traditions that they pass on to their descendants. They flourish in rough-and-tumble societies so intensely political that they have been dubbed Machiavellian, and in which they form coalitions to limit the power of alpha males.

Twenty-first-century law should be based on twenty-first-century knowledge. Once the law assumed that witches existed and that mute people lacked intelligence. Now it is illegal to burn someone for witchcraft, and the mute have the same rights as anyone else.

Today we know that apes, and perhaps other nonhuman animals, are not what we thought they were in the pre-scientific age when the law declared them things. Now we know that they have what it takes for basic legal rights. The next step is obvious.

480

Vicki Hearne, *What's Wrong with Animal Rights*. In this essay,   ▶
which originally appeared in *Harper's* magazine and was selected
by Susan Sontag for *Best American Essays 1992*, Vicki Hearne
(1946–2001) argues against organized activism for animal rights.
A professional dog trainer and Yale professor, Hearne spent her
life advocating for animals — and disagreeing with organizations
like PETA (see p. 485). She wrote poetry, prose, and essays,
including *Adam's Task: Calling Animals by Name* (1986) and
Bandit: Dossier of a Dangerous Dog (1992).

[2] Jane Goodall (b. 1934) is an international authority on chimpanzees and the author of many award-winning books such as *Reason for Hope: A Spiritual Journey* (1999).—ED.

Vicki Hearne

WHAT'S WRONG WITH ANIMAL RIGHTS

Not all happy animals are alike. A Doberman going over a hurdle after a small wooden dumbbell is sleek, all arcs of harmonious power. A basset hound cheerfully performing the same exercise exhibits harmonies of a more lugubrious nature. There are chimpanzees who love precision the way musicians or fanatical housekeepers or accomplished hypochondriacs do; others for whom happiness is a matter of invention and variation—chimp vaudevillians. There is a rhinoceros whose happiness, as near as I can make out, is in needing to be trained every morning, all over again, or else he "forgets" his circus routine, and in this you find a clue to the slow, deep, quiet chuckle of his happiness and to the glory of the beast. Happiness for Secretariat[1] in his ebullient bound, that joyful length of stride. For the draft horse or the weight-pull dog, happiness is of a different shape, more awesome and less obviously intelligent. When the pulling horse is at its most intense, the animal goes into himself, allocating all of the educated power that organizes his desire to dwell in fierce and delicate intimacy with that power, leans into the harness, and MAKES THAT SUCKER MOVE.

If we are speaking of human beings and use the phrase "animal happiness," we tend to mean something like "creature comforts." The emblems of this are the golden retriever rolling in the grass, the horse with his nose deep in the oats, the kitty by the fire. Creature comforts are important to animals—"Grub first, then ethics" is a motto that would describe many a wise Labrador retriever, and I have a pit bull named Annie whose continual quest for the perfect pillow inspires her to awesome feats. But there is something more to animals, a capacity for satisfactions that come from work in the fullest sense—what is known in philosophy and in this country's Declaration of Independence as "happiness." This is a sense

---

[1] Secretariat was one of America's greatest racehorses, winner of the Triple Crown in 1973.—ED.

481

of personal achievement, like the satisfaction felt by a good wood-carver or a dancer or a poet or an accomplished dressage horse. It is a happiness that, like the artist's, must come from something within the animal, something trainers call "talent." Hence, it cannot be imposed on the animal. But it is also something that does not come *ex nihilo*.[2] If it had not been a fairly ordinary thing, in one part of the world, to teach young children to play the pianoforte, it is doubtful that Mozart's music would exist.

Happiness is often misunderstood as a synonym for pleasure or as an antonym for suffering. But Aristotle associated happiness with ethics—codes of behavior that urge us toward the sensation of getting it right, a kind of work that yields the "click" of satisfaction upon solving a problem or surmounting an obstacle. In his *Ethics*, Aristotle wrote, "If happiness is activity in accordance with excellence, it is reasonable that it should be in accordance with the highest excellence." Thomas Jefferson identified the capacity for happiness as one of the three fundamental rights on which all others are based: "life, liberty, and the pursuit of happiness."

I bring up this idea of happiness as a form of work because I am an animal trainer, and work is the foundation of the happiness a trainer and an animal discover together. I bring up these words also because they cannot be found in the lexicon of the animal-rights movement. This absence accounts for the uneasiness toward the movement of most people, who sense that rights advocates have a point but take it too far when they liberate snails or charge that goldfish at the county fair are suffering. But the problem with the animal-rights advocates is not that they take it too far; it's that they've got it all wrong.

Animal rights are built upon a misconceived premise that rights were created to prevent us from unnecessary suffering. You can't find an animal-rights book, video, pamphlet, or rock concert in which someone doesn't mention the Great Sentence, written by Jeremy Bentham in 1789. Arguing in favor of such rights, Bentham wrote: "The question is not, Can they *reason?* nor, can they *talk?* but, can they suffer?"

The logic of the animal-rights movement places suffering at the iconographic center of a skewed value system. The thinking of its proponents—given eerie expression in a virtually sadopornographic sculpture of a tortured monkey that won a prize for its compassionate vision—has collapsed into a perverse conundrum. Today the loudest voices calling for—demanding—the destruction of animals are the humane organizations. This is an inevitable consequence of the apotheosis of the drive to relieve suffering: death is the ultimate release. To compensate for their contradictions, the humane movement has demonized, in this century and the last, those who made animal happiness their business: veterinarians, trainers, and the like. We think of Louis Pasteur as the man whose work saved

---

[2] *ex nihilo:* Latin, "out of nothing."—ED.

you and me and your dog and cat from rabies, but antivivisectionists of the time claimed that rabies increased in areas where there were Pasteur Institutes.

An anti-rabies public relations campaign mounted in England in the 1880s by the Royal Society for the Prevention of Cruelty to Animals and other organizations led to orders being issued to club any dog found not wearing a muzzle. England still has her cruel and unnecessary law that requires an animal to spend six months in quarantine before being allowed loose in the country. Most of the recent propaganda about pit bulls—the crazy claim that they "take hold with their front teeth while they chew away with their rear teeth" (which would imply, incorrectly, that they have double jaws)—can be traced to literature published by the Humane Society of the United States during the fall of 1987 and earlier. If your neighbors want your dog or horse impounded and destroyed because he is a nuisance—say the dog barks, or the horse attracts flies—it will be the local Humane Society to whom your neighbors turn for action.

In a way, everyone has the opportunity to know that the history of the humane movement is largely a history of miseries, arrests, prosecutions, and death. The Humane Society is the pound, the place with the decompression chamber or the lethal injections. You occasionally find worried letters about this in Ann Landers's column.

Animal-rights publications are illustrated largely with photographs of two kinds of animals—"Helpless Fluff" and "Agonized Fluff," the two conditions in which some people seem to prefer their animals, because any other version of an animal is too complicated for propaganda. In the introduction to his book *Animal Liberation,* Peter Singer says somewhat smugly that he and his wife have no animals and, in fact, don't much care for them. This is offered as evidence of his objectivity and ethical probity. But it strikes me as an odd, perhaps obscene underpinning for an ethical project that encourages university and high school students to cherish their ignorance of, say, great bird dogs as proof of their devotion to animals.

I would like to leave these philosophers behind, for they are inept connoisseurs of suffering who might revere my Airedale for his capacity to scream when subjected to a blowtorch but not for his wit and courage, not for his natural good manners that are a gentle rebuke to ours. I want to celebrate the moment not long ago when, at his first dog show, my Airedale, Drummer, learned that there can be a public place where his work is respected. I want to celebrate his meticulousness, his happiness upon realizing at the dog show that no one would swoop down upon him and swamp him with the goo-goo excesses known as the "teddy-bear complex" but that people actually got out of his way, gave him room to work. I want to say, "There can be a six-and-a-half-month-old puppy who can care about accuracy, who can be fastidious, and whose fastidiousness will be a foundation for courage later." I want to say, "Leave my puppy alone!"

I want to leave the philosophers behind, but I cannot, in part because the philosophical problems that plague academicians of the animal-rights movement

483

are illuminating. They wonder, do animals have rights or do they have interests? Or, if these rightists lead particularly unexamined lives, they dismiss that question as obvious (yes, of course animals have rights, prima facie) and proceed to enumerate them, James Madison style. This leads to the issuance of bills of rights—the right to an environment, the right not to be used in medical experiments—and other forms of trivialization.

The calculus of suffering can be turned against the philosophers of festering flesh, even in the case of food animals, or exotic animals who perform in movies and circuses. It is true that it hurts to be slaughtered by man, but it doesn't hurt nearly as much as some of the cunningly cruel arrangements meted out by "Mother Nature." In Africa, 75 percent of the lions cubbed do not survive to the age of two. For those who make it to two, the average age at death is ten years. Asali, the movie and TV lioness, was still working at age twenty-one. There are fates worse than death, but twenty-one years of a close working relationship with Hubert Wells, Asali's trainer, is not one of them. Dorset sheep and polled Herefords would not exist at all were they not in a symbiotic relationship with human beings.

A human being living in the "wild"—somewhere, say, without the benefits of medicine and advanced social organization—would probably have a life expectancy of from thirty to thirty-five years. A human being living in "captivity"— in, say, a middle-class neighborhood of what the Centers for Disease Control call a Metropolitan Statistical Area—has a life expectancy of seventy or more years. For orangutans in the wild in Borneo and Malaysia, the life expectancy is thirty-five years; in captivity, fifty years. The wild is not a suffering-free zone or all that frolicsome a location.

The questions asked by animal-rights activists are flawed, because they are built on the concept that the origin of rights is in the avoidance of suffering rather than in the pursuit of happiness. The question that needs to be asked—and that will put us in closer proximity to the truth—is not, do they have rights? or, what are those rights? but rather, what is a right?

Rights originate in committed relationships and can be found, both intact and violated, wherever one finds such relationships—in social compacts, within families, between animals, and between people and nonhuman animals. This is as true when the nonhuman animals in question are lions or parakeets as when they are dogs. It is my Airedale whose excellencies have my attention at the moment, so it is with reference to him that I will consider the question, what is a right?

When I imagine situations in which it naturally arises that A defends or honors or respects B's rights, I imagine situations in which the relationship between A and B can be indicated with a possessive pronoun. I might say, "Leave her alone, she's my daughter" or "That's what she wants, and she is my daughter. I think I am bound to honor her wants." Similarly, "Leave her alone, she's my mother." I am more tender of the happiness of my mother, my father, my child, than I am of other people's family members; more tender of my friends' happinesses than your friends' happinesses, unless you and I have a mutual friend.

Possession of a being by another has come into more and more disrepute, so that the common understanding of one person possessing another is slavery. But the important detail about the kind of possessive pronoun that I have in mind is reciprocity: if I have a friend, she has a friend. If I have a daughter, she has a mother. The possessive does not bind one of us while freeing the other; it cannot do that. Moreover, should the mother reject the daughter, the word that applies is "disown." The form of disowning that most often appears in the news is domestic violence. Parents abuse children; husbands batter wives.

Some cases of reciprocal possessives have built-in limitations, such as "my patient/my doctor" or "my student/my teacher" or "my agent/my client." Other possessive relations are extremely limited but still remarkably binding: "my neighbor" and "my country" and "my president."

The responsibilities and the ties signaled by reciprocal possession typically are hard to dissolve. It can be as difficult to give up an enemy as to give up a friend, and often the one becomes the other, as though the logic of the possessive pronoun outlasts the forms it chanced to take at a given moment, as though we were stuck with one another. In these bindings, nearly inextricable, are found the origin of our rights. They imply a possessiveness but also recognize an acknowledgment by each side of the other's existence.

The idea of democracy is dependent on the citizens' having knowledge of the government; that is, realizing that the government exists and knowing how to claim rights against it. I know this much because I get mail from the government and see its "representatives" running about in uniforms. Whether I actually have any rights in relationship to the government is less clear, but the idea that I do is symbolized by the right to vote. I obey the government, and, in theory, it obeys

485

People for the Ethical Treatment of Animals, *They Called Him Christmas.* ▶
Founded in 1980, PETA is "dedicated to establishing and protecting the rights of all animals." However, philosophers and moralists have discussed animal rights for hundreds of years — the American Society for the Prevention of Cruelty to Animals (ASPCA) was founded as far back as 1866. It was only in the 1970s that the animal rights movement began building an active membership, spearheaded by a highly influential philosophical book, Peter Singer's *Animal Liberation* (1975). Singer's book and his continued publications in the field stimulated a wide-ranging debate of the issue and gave rise to various animal rights organizations throughout the world, one of the most famous being People for the Ethical Treatment of Animals (PETA). Anti–animal testing is one of many messages PETA sends; they also campaign against the use of animals for food and for clothing, cruelty to animals, adopting puppies and kittens, shopping at pet stores, and fishing and hunting. PETA urges people to spay and neuter their pets. (Courtesy of PETAOnline.org)

486

They called him Christmas.
He was cruelly used by Iams.

Life for Christmas was far from a celebration. A severe ear infection was discovered only when a PETA investigator noticed it while giving him a little love and attention, something that he had never had before in the entire six years that he had been confined to his cage in the lab.

Hundreds of dogs were caged in this laboratory in barren steel and cement cells, where many went crazy from intense confinement, turning in endless circles. Iams officials visited this lab, witnessed the suffering, and did nothing. Pleas for a resting board and exercise for the dogs were ignored. The lab director ordered the dogs' vocal cords to be cut because their cries irritated him. And despite Iams' claim that it doesn't deliberately kill animals in its tests, in this Iams contract lab—one of many—at least 27 dogs were killed.

Please join us in calling on Iams to rely on non-animal laboratory-analysis and in-home tests using dogs and cats whose human companions have volunteered them for such tests. Visit IamsCruelty.com to learn how you can help.

PETA   *Bad For Life* IAMDEAD

1–866-TEST-KIND • IamsCruelty.com

me, by counting my ballot, reading the *Miranda* warning to me, agreeing to be bound by the Constitution. My friend obeys me as I obey her; the government "obeys" me to some extent, and, to a different extent, I obey it.

What kind of thing can my Airedale, Drummer, have knowledge of? He can know that I exist and through that knowledge can claim his happinesses, with varying degrees of success, both with me and against me. Drummer can also know about larger human or dog communities than the one that consists only of him and me. There is my household—the other dogs, the cats, my husband. I have had enough dogs on campuses to know that he can learn that Yale exists as a neighborhood or village. My older dog, Annie, not only knows that Yale exists but can tell Yalies from townies, as I learned while teaching there during labor troubles.

Dogs can have elaborate conceptions of human social structures, and even of something like their rights and responsibilities within them, but these conceptions are never elaborate enough to construct a rights relationship between a dog and the state, or a dog and the Humane Society. Both of these are concepts that depend on writing and memoranda, officers in uniform, plaques and seals of authority. All of these are literary constructs, and all of them are beyond a dog's ken, which is why the mail carrier who doesn't also happen to be a dog's friend is forever an intruder—this is why dogs bark at mailmen.

It is clear enough that natural rights relations can arise between people and animals. Drummer, for example, can insist, "Hey, let's go outside and do something!" if I have been at my computer several days on end. He can both refuse to accept various of my suggestions and tell me when he fears for his life—such as the time when the huge, white flapping flag appeared out of nowhere, as it seemed to him, on the town green one evening when we were working. I can (and do) say to him either, "Oh, you don't have to worry about that" or, "Uh oh, you're right, Drum, that guy looks dangerous." Just as the government and I—two different species of organism—have developed improvised ways of communicating, such as the vote, so Drummer and I have worked out a number of ways to make our expressions known. Largely through obedience, I have taught him a fair amount about how to get responses from me. Obedience is reciprocal; you cannot get responses from a dog to whom you do not respond accurately. I have enfranchised him in a relationship to me by educating him, creating the conditions by which he can achieve a certain happiness specific to a dog, maybe even specific to an Airedale, inasmuch as this same relationship has allowed me to plumb the happiness of being a trainer and writing this article.

Instructions in this happiness are given terms that are alien to a culture in which liver treats, fluffy windup toys, and miniature sweaters are confused with

488

◄ **FBR,** *Animal research saves animals.* The Foundation for Biomedical Research produced this poster as part of an educational campaign to "promote public understanding, appreciation and support for the humane and responsible use of animals in medical and scientific research." The Foundation wants to show people that animal research benefits animals as well as humans. (Courtesy of the Foundation for Biomedical Research)

respect and work. Jack Knox, a sheepdog trainer originally from Scotland, will shake his crook at a novice handler who makes a promiscuous move to praise a dog, and will call out in his Scottish accent, "Eh! Eh! Get back, get BACK! Ye'll no be abusin' the dogs like that in my clinic." America is a nation of abused animals, Knox says, because we are always swooping at them with praise, "no gi'ing them their freedom." I am reminded of Rainer Maria Rilke's[3] account in which the Prodigal Son leaves— has to leave—because everyone loves him, even the dogs love him, and he has no path to the delicate and fierce truth of himself. Unconditional praise and love, in Rilke's story, disenfranchise us, distract us from what truly excites our interest.

In the minds of some trainers and handlers, praise is dishonesty. Paradoxically, it is a kind of contempt for animals that masquerades as a reverence for helplessness and suffering. The idea of freedom means that you do not, at least not while Jack Knox is nearby, helpfully guide your dog through the motions of, say, herding over and over—what one trainer calls "explainy-wainy." This is rote learning. It works tolerably well on some handlers, because people have vast unconscious minds and can store complex preprogrammed behaviors. Dogs, on the other hand, have almost no unconscious minds, so they can learn only by thinking. Many children are like this until educated out of it.

If I tell my Airedale to sit and stay on the town green, and someone comes up and burbles, "What a pretty thing you are," he may break his stay to go for a caress. I pull him back and correct him for breaking. Now he holds his stay because I have blocked his way to movement but not because I have punished him. (A correction blocks one path as it opens another for desire to work; punishment blocks desire and opens nothing.) He holds his stay now, and—because the stay opens this possibility of work, new to a heedless young dog—he watches. If the person goes on talking, and isn't going to gush with praise, I may heel Drummer out of his stay and give him an "Okay" to make friends. Sometimes something about the person makes Drummer feel that reserve is in order. He responds to an insincere approach by sitting still, going down into himself, and thinking, "This person has no business pawing me. I'll sit very still, and he will go away." If the person doesn't take the hint from Drummer, I'll give the pup a little backup by saying, "Please don't pet him, he's working," even though he was not under any command.

The pup reads this, and there is a flicker of a working trust now stirring in the dog. Is the pup grateful? When the stranger leaves, does he lick my hand, full of submissive blandishments? This one doesn't. This one says nothing at all, and I say nothing much to him. This is a working trust we are developing, not a mutual congratulation society. My backup is praise enough for him; the use he makes of my support is praise enough for me.

489

---

[3] *Rainer Maria Rilke:* Austrian lyric poet (1875–1926), one of the most renowned poets of the twentieth century. — ED.

Listening to a dog is often praise enough. Suppose it is just after dark and we are outside. Suddenly there is a shout from the house. The pup and I both look toward the shout and then toward each other: "What do you think?" I don't so much as cock my head, because Drummer is growing up, and I want to know what he thinks. He takes a few steps toward the house, and I follow. He listens again and comprehends that it's just Holly, who at fourteen is much given to alarming cries and shouts. He shrugs at me and goes about his business. I say nothing. To praise him for this performance would make about as much sense as praising a human being for the same thing. Thus:

A: What's that?
B: I don't know. [Listens] Oh, it's just Holly.
A: What a goooooood human being!
B: Huh?

This is one small moment in a series of like moments that will culminate in an Airedale who on a Friday will have the discrimination and confidence required to take down a man who is attacking me with a knife and on Saturday clown and play with the children at the annual Orange Empire Dog Club Christmas party.

People who claim to speak for animal rights are increasingly devoted to the idea that the very keeping of a dog or a horse or a gerbil or a lion is in and of itself an offense. The more loudly they speak, the less likely they are to be in a rights relation to any given animal, because they are spending so much time in airplanes or transmitting fax announcements of the latest Sylvester Stallone anti-fur rally. In a 1988 *Harper's* forum, for example, Ingrid Newkirk, the national director of People for the Ethical Treatment of Animals, urged that domestic pets be spayed and neutered and ultimately phased out. She prefers, it appears, wolves—and wolves someplace else—to Airedales and, by a logic whose ulterior structure is both emotionally and intellectually forever closed to Drummer, claims thereby to be speaking for "animal rights."

She is wrong. I am the only one who can own up to my Airedale's inalienable rights. Whether or not I do it perfectly at any given moment is no more refutation of this point than whether I am perfectly my husband's mate at any given moment refutes the fact of marriage. Only people who know Drummer, and whom he can know, are capable of this relationship. PETA and the Humane Society, and the ASPCA and the Congress and NOW—as institutions—do have the power to affect my ability to grant rights to Drummer but are otherwise incapable of creating conditions or laws or rights that would increase his happiness. Only Drummer's owner has the power to obey him—to obey who he is and what he is capable of—deeply enough to grant him his rights and open up the possibility of happiness.

MESSAGE

In 1789 (just around the time the U.S. Constitution was being ratified) British philosopher and social reformer Jeremy Bentham wrote about animals: "The question is not, Can they *reason?* nor, can they *talk?* but, can they suffer?" As Vicki Hearne points out, there's hardly an article, pamphlet, or video supporting the animal rights movement that doesn't cite Bentham's influential question. Why do you think Bentham's question plays such a large role in the animal rights movement? Consider it slowly, carefully. What do you think it means? Do you suppose the statement is so powerful because it is irrefutable? Could the remark also be used to support the position of those who oppose animal rights? Explain your answer.

METHOD

Contrast the two methods of argument employed by Vicki Hearne and Steven Wise. Why do you think Hearne refers at such length to her own experiences as an animal trainer? In your opinion, does that experience make her especially qualified to defend the position she takes? Do you think it strengthens her argument? Does it give her claim more legitimacy than Wise's? How might Wise counter Hearne's claim?

MEDIUM

Hearne maintains that animal rights publications are illustrated with photographs of only two kinds of animals: "Helpless Fluff" and "Agonized Fluff." Why does she use these terms? What do they suggest? In what ways do the advertisements included here support Hearne's opinion? In what ways do they challenge it?

491

Assignment I

This chapter calls our attention to issues that often get pushed to the margins of our society — problems addressed by public awareness groups such as CAIR and PETA, writers such as Maya Angelou and Richard Rodriguez, and photographers such as Joseph Rodriguez and Mary Ellen Mark. Is it useful for groups to educate each other about who they are and what they stand for? As a class, list the memorable public awareness campaigns you can think of. In small groups, choose a topic that you think is worth educating the public about. Design an ad campaign that will best gain the public's attention. What message do you want to get out to the public? What medium will work best — posters, radio, TV, or web site? Finally, your creative team will need to decide what method you will use to get your message across. Will you use a direct, subtle, ironic, serious, or satirical tone? Try to be specific about your target audience as you plan your campaign as a group. A terrific site to explore as you plan your campaign is the Ad Council web site at www.adcouncil.org/campaigns/.

Human Rights Campaign Foundation poster. This is one of a series of ads the Human Rights Campaign Foundation has designed to raise public awareness about issues around civil marriages for gay and lesbian couples. (Courtesy of the Human Rights Campaign Foundation)

Assignment 2

Several of the essays in this chapter call attention to some of the subtle ways discrimination and division occur in everyday conversations. Form three separate
research groups to design a "test" of the issues raised by David Brooks, Jan
Morris, and Lars Eighner. The group working with "People Like Us" might design
a poll about the diversity of their peers' immediate social networks. The group
working with "Herstory" might think of ways to record usage of gendered
language. The group working with "Dumpster Diving" might track the con-
sumption/disposal habits of the people they know. Groups working with the
Morris and Eighner essays might simply track their own uses of gendered language
or their consumer/disposal habits for a two-week period. Once your group has
gathered its data, you should design a visual graph or chart that accurately
describes the trends you've noticed. In a final presentation to the class, analyze
your study results and share your data display.

(Royalty Free/Corbis)

1. Suppose you want to turn Lars Eighner's "On Dumpster Diving" (p. 454) into a documentary film. After rereading the essay carefully, break into small groups. Each group will design a plan for how the essay would be filmed. What details of Eighner's essay would you include? Which ones would you exclude? How would your film convey his ideas? What would be your lead idea? At a panel session, someone representing each group should discuss his or her group's plan.

2. Richard Rodriguez organizes his essay around his response to a photo-essay by Joseph Rodriguez (pp. 430–39) in which the photographer tries to document both the personal and criminal aspects of gang members' lives. Other photographers in this book attempt similar projects: for example, Mary Ellen Mark and Margaret Morton turn their lenses on the homeless in an attempt to make visible a side of society that remains invisible to many. Using Rodriguez's, Mark's, or Morton's pictures as a starting place, write an essay that begins with your response to the photographs themselves and ends with a larger statement about how you respond to the issues they invoke. Do the photographs make it clear how the photographer wants us to respond? Does the desire of the recorder make a difference, or does the record speak for itself? Explain.

3. In most written arguments, the writer will employ two sets of terms — one of words intended to be taken positively that support or reinforce the writer's position, and the other of words intended to have negative meanings. The terms, often left undefined, are not necessarily used as a dictionary would define them. Go through the essays by David Brooks, Orlando Patterson, Steven Wise, and Vicki Hearne, identifying some key terms that you think each author intends to be taken as positive or negative. Then choose a term you think plays a significant role in the argument but should be taken in a different sense from what the author intended. In an essay, discuss how the author uses this term and why you disagree with this usage.

4. David Brooks ends "People Like Us" (p. 422) by saying: "Look around at your daily life. Are you really in touch with the broad diversity of American life? Do you care?" In a short personal essay, craft a response to both questions. Are you personally in contact with diverse groups of people and opinions, or are you usually surrounded by people whose appearance and ideas pretty much resemble your

DIVIDING LINES

own? Then consider the second question: Does it matter to you at all? Don't forget to explain why it does or doesn't matter.

5. After breaking into small groups, use library resources and/or the Internet to discover what you can about Jeremy Bentham and his philosophy of Utilitarianism. Can you establish the full context of his influential remark: "The question is not, Can they *reason?* nor, can they *talk?* but, can they suffer?" Where did the comment first appear, and what did Bentham mean by it? For example, to what extent did he believe that animals possessed inherent rights and deserved to have them granted by the state? Each group should then carefully consider, and prepare a brief report on, the links between the current animal rights movement and Utilitarianism.

6. Practice the art of disputation. Break into small groups. Using Orlando Patterson's "Race Over" (p. 471) as the central issue, each group should prepare a list of points that challenges Patterson's argument that race will no longer be a major concern by the middle of the twenty-first century. The list of points should dispute Patterson's demographic forecast; his discussion of mixed ethnicity; his examples, statistics, and any other elements of

his case that can be called into question. Each group should appoint a speaker who will summarize to the class all the available arguments against Patterson's claim. After listening to all the points, the class as a whole should judge which ones present the strongest case against Patterson's argument.

7. Both Melanie Sumner's "Marriage" and Penelope Scambly Schott's "Report on the Difference between Men and Women" (pp. 442–43) suggest gender stereotypes that are often found in cartoons. After breaking into a collaborative group, members should select either one of these texts, identify the stereotypes, and try transforming the story or essay into a cartoon. The cartoon need not be professionally rendered but should effectively translate the author's miniature narrative into picture and text. Afterwards, groups should compare their productions.

8. Consider Margaret Morton's *Mr. Lee's House, the Hill, 1991* (p. 467) in conjunction with her photograph of Mr. Lee and the oral history she composed about him. Then consider Mr. Lee's house in conjunction with the section titled Home (see pp. 229–42) in Chapter 3, Shaping Spaces. Using Nicole Lamy's memoir as a model, compose a brief

495

personal essay in the voice of Mr. Lee in which he describes his house and what it means to him.

9. Divide into small groups. Each group should consider itself as the creative department of a small advertising agency that is preparing a magazine ad to support the animal rights movement. But each agency director is concerned about Vicki Hearne's claim that too many ads oversimplify animals into two classes, "Helpless Fluff" and "Agonized Fluff." Your group is asked to develop something different that will portray animals in a more complex manner but still persuade people that the animal rights cause is the best one. How will you accomplish this? Each group should try drafting an ad—using both image and text—that is convincing without oversimplifying.

10. How do photographers capture gender differences? How do they express the dividing lines that often exist between men and women? Select about five photographs in this book (or feel free to use material from outside), and consider how the photographers were conscious of gender differences. What common features can you detect? Are men and women (or boys and girls) presented differently? Are they positioned differently? After studying your sample photographs, write an essay in which you analyze at least three ways that men and women tend to be portrayed in photographs according to gender roles. (In preparation, you might review Lauren Greenfield's photo, *Sara, 19*, in the section about photographs that appears in the Introduction on pp. 26–27.)

6

PACKAGING CULTURE

In one of the most remarkable convergences of our time, shopping has now become so closely linked to our entire culture that it is difficult to see where one's social experiences end and one's consumerism begins. We live in a packaging culture; mass consumption has permeated every nook and cranny of American life. As the architect Sze Tsung Leong puts it: "Not only is shopping melting into everything, but everything is melting into shopping." Although consumer culture became a marked characteristic of the second half of the twentieth century, the rapid rise of an all-pervasive commercialism is being felt more powerfully now than ever before.

Critics have recently begun to study shopping as a key social and cultural phenomenon. *The New York Times* in 2003 introduced in its weekly magazine a section called "Consumed," which puts an intellectual spin on the daily experience of buying products. Also in 2003, two college professors published scholarly books on mass consumption: Sharon Zukin's *Point of Purchase: How Shopping Changed American Culture,* and Lizabeth Cohen's *A Consumer's Republic: The Politics of Mass Consumption in Postwar America.* One of the landmark texts in the development of serious study of the subject is the lavishly illustrated *Harvard Design School Guide to Shopping.* Published in 2001, the book examines how "shopping has infiltrated, colonized, and even replaced, almost every aspect of urban life." As the text points out, perhaps "the beginning of the twenty-first century will be remembered as the point where the urban could no longer be understood without shopping."

We constantly witness how the consumer environment has wrapped itself around our lives, blurring distinctions between product and package, marketable item and marketing image, contents and container. On television over the past few years we have grown accustomed to a new version of the old

commercial, the "infomercial." This clever approach imitates a conventional talk show format (often with a studio audience), but in reality it is a long, drawn-out sales pitch. In similar fashion, newspapers now regularly publish "advertorials," ads for products, institutions, or causes roughly disguised as serious editorials. Moreover, glossy magazines have for so long been jam-packed with advertising that just a few years ago publishers decided to go all the way and simply produce subscription and newsstand magazines wholly devoted to products with no independent editorial content: catalogues disguised as magazines. An example is *Lucky,* which bills itself as "The magazine about shopping." On September 16, 2002, David Carr wrote in *The New York Times* that *Lucky* "may be the first consumer magazine in the United States to use advertising motifs to design every page of editorial content. Articles, in the traditional sense, are nowhere to be found."

Indeed, marketing has fused with all kinds of media. When popular films incorporate consumer products into their storylines or background imagery, the technique is called "product placement." For example, when an actor in a film buys a Pepsi or wears a Patagonia vest or sends a package via FedEx, the visibly identified product or company benefits not only from the wide exposure but also from its association with the movie star. In addition, the contrived promotion (which an agency has usually paid for) looks natural; it does not resemble an advertisement. Video games have also introduced product placement. One of the most effective examples of product placement can be seen almost everywhere: brand-name clothing. Instead of being paid by corporations for displaying their products, consumers pay the corporations for the privilege of publicly advertising their brand names and logos, such as Nike, Old Navy, and Tommy Hilfiger. In this way, our own bodies become walking billboards — yet another advertising medium.

Like all other media, the Internet has become a productive channel of consumerism, as shopping joins e-mail as one of the most popular online activities. With their multiple links and pop-up ads, web sites are designed to attract potential shoppers. E-stores have borrowed heavily from the vocabulary of brick-and-mortar retail outlets, and consumers can cruise virtual aisles while filling up their shopping carts or adding to their wish lists. Although many people are happy to avoid the hassles of on-site shopping, some express disappointment that a medium with such far-reaching cultural potential as the Internet has been essentially transformed into a gigantic shopping mall. As the computer guru and software engineer Ellen Ullman wrote in 2000: "It's enormously sad to see the Internet being turned into the world-wide infomercial. The scariest part is the way web site owners speak unabashedly about blurring the lines between editorial content and advertising, eagerly looking forward to the web as a giant product-placement opportunity."

As the boundaries dissolve between shopping and all other activities, how do we separate commercialism and consumerism from everything else? Can valid distinctions still be made? When we view a beautiful landscape, do we instead perceive valuable "real estate"? Do we look solely for "brand name" prestige when we "shop" for a college? Is patriotism so closely tied to shopping today that, as Ian Frazier writes in "All-Consuming Patriotism" (p. 538), "Money and the economy have gotten so tangled up in our politics that we forget we're citizens of our government, not its consumers"? Do we support a politician on the basis of ideas and ideals, or mainly because of a charismatic image created by political consultants? Is the best part of a trip to a famous art museum our visit to the museum store? When we enhance our bodies at the gym, are we really doing it for health purposes

or to become (p. 581) a more desirable "commodity"? When does self-esteem turn into self-promotion? To what degree does our self-identity depend on brand images, consumer satisfaction, and how closely we conform to a marketer's profile?

This chapter will examine the many ways consumer culture shapes our attitudes, values, and expectations. It explores how advertising penetrates all media, sometimes directly but at other times disguised as noncommercial messages. The selections and activities in this chapter examine the phenomenon of "social marketing" and explore how those committed to noncommercial causes and public advocacy nevertheless rely on traditional strategies of product advertising, thus further blurring the line between the exchange of ideas and the consumption of ideas. You will be asked to consider how the way something is packaged — whether a product, a person, or an opinion — affects the way we perceive and relate to it. And throughout the chapter you will be invited to unpack some packages and see what's really inside.

Emphasis

This cartoon explosion, with its flames and capital BLAMM, perfectly illustrates **emphasis** —a force and intensity of expression. Emphasis can be given to one element over another through color or size, or even by simply using **bold-face type**. The materials you will encounter in this chapter all have something to do with advertising and marketing, and in advertising, emphasis is all. As you read through the essays and ads that follow, ask yourself

(Getty Images)

what is being emphasized and how that emphasis is made clear. Is an image or product dominant? Is the headline the biggest feature on the page? Is the company being advertised the most prominent, or does a mood or a feeling get the most emphasis?

 Go to **ix visual exercises** to explore emphasis as it applies to visual texts.

Concept: *Emphasis & Color*

Definition

:: emphasis

For speech or writing, *emphasis* means putting stress on a word or a group of words to give it more importance. In visual texts, it means the same thing; emphasis gives certain elements greater importance, significance, or stress than other elements in a text. In the e-mail shown here, the use of capital letters emphasizes the command to take away personal food.

next ▶

exercise 06

06 · definitions · analysis · assignment

ix visual exercises

HOW TO MAKE AN AD

DIRECTIONS | 2 ESSAYS | PHOTO | AD

Most of the advertising we read in magazines, hear on radio, and see on television is written by copywriters — men and women who have a unique verbal talent, especially for catchy phrases and witty expressions. One of the ways copywriters may become famous is by creating memorable slogans. A **slogan** is a catchy phrase or sentence that is closely linked to the product, used repetitively throughout the ad, and perhaps even continued throughout a series of ads. A famous slogan used for many years to sell Listerine mouthwash has entered the language: "Always a bridesmaid, never a bride." Another was AT&T's "Reach out and touch someone." In this cluster you can read about the creation of one of advertising's most well-known slogans, "Does she . . . or doesn't she?" These slogans differ from certain other well-known slogans in that they do not name a brand. Slogans that do — like "This Bud's for you" — are technically termed "nameonics" because they simultaneously reinforce the brand name. A type of slogan that's set to music and sung on radio and television is a **jingle**. A jingle usually consists of a simple rhymed verse set to an easy tune. As everyone knows, jingles have a way of stubbornly sticking in our minds.

Because advertising can combine so many elements — words, visuals, voice, music, drama, stage settings, etc. — an advertising agency's copywriting team usually works in tandem with graphic artists, designers, music producers, and film makers, all led by an art director, who in turn may report to the marketing chief of the corporation that has hired the agency. As we learn to examine and evaluate advertising, we need to remain aware that advertising in any fashion is a wholly collaborative enterprise, involving the skills of numerous people. We also must always be attentive to the type of advertising under consideration: Is it a print ad intended for newspapers or magazines, a television commercial, a radio spot, a billboard, a direct mail item, a web-page pop-up? All these commercial texts have their own special means of delivering their message.

Adbusters, *How to Create Your Own Print Ad.* The nonprofit organization Adbusters educates people about the dangers of advertising—but it does so by "using the master's tools," that is, by employing the same techniques of advertising that are used in the service of selling material goods. These instructions are a fascinating look into the way advertising companies think about the texts they create. (Image courtesy of www.adbusters.org)

Adbusters

HOW TO CREATE YOUR OWN PRINT AD

1. Decide on your communication objective
2. Decide on your target audience
3. Decide on your format
4. Develop your concept
5. The visual
6. The headline
7. The copy
8. Mistakes to avoid

1. DECIDE ON YOUR COMMUNICATIONS OBJECTIVE

The communications objective is the essence of your message. If you want to tell people not to eat rutabagas because it's cruel, then that's your communications objective. A word of caution: though perhaps the most important of your eight steps, this is also the one that beginners tend to neglect. A precise and well-defined objective is crucial to a good ad. If your objective isn't right on, then everything that follows will be off as well.

2. DECIDE ON YOUR TARGET AUDIENCE

Who is your message intended for? If you're speaking to kids, then your language and arguments will have to be understandable to kids. On the other hand, if you're speaking to high income earners (for example, if you're writing an ad to dissuade people from wearing fur coats), then your language will have to be more sophisticated. So define who your target audience is, because that will decide how your message is conveyed.

3. DECIDE ON YOUR FORMAT

Is it going to be a poster, a half-page magazine ad, or a tiny box in the corner of a newspaper? Make this decision based on the target audience you're trying to reach, and the amount of money you can afford to spend. If you're talking to kids,

504

a poster in one high school will not only cost less, it will actually reach more of your target audience than a full-page ad in the biggest paper in town. When it comes to deciding on the size of your ad, the more expensive it will be to produce and run. Don't let that discourage you. You can do a lot with a small ad so long as it's strong, clear, and properly targeted.

4. DEVELOP YOUR CONCEPT

The concept is the underlying creative idea that drives your message. Even in a big ad campaign, the concept will typically remain the same from one ad to another, and from one medium to another. Only the execution of that concept willl change. So by developing a concept that is effective and powerful, you open the door to a number of very compelling ads. So take your time developing a concept that's strong.

Typically, an ad is made up of a photograph or a drawing (the "visual"), a headline, and writing (the "copy"). Whether you think of your visual or your headline first makes little difference. However, here are a few guidelines worth following.

5. THE VISUAL

Though you don't absolutely require a visual, it will help draw attention to your ad. Research indicates that 70% of people will only look at the visual in an ad, whereas only 30% will read the headline. So if you use a visual, then you're already talking to twice as many people as you otherwise might. Another suggestion is to use photographs instead of illustrations whenever possible. People tend to relate to realistic photographs more easily than unrealistic ones. But whether you choose a photograph or an illustration, the most important criterion is that the image be the most interesting one possible and at least half your ad whenever possible.

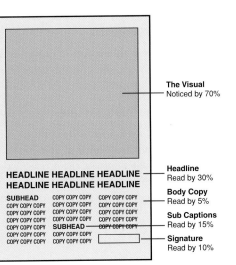

The Visual
Noticed by 70%

HEADLINE HEADLINE HEADLINE
HEADLINE HEADLINE HEADLINE

Headline
Read by 30%

SUBHEAD

Body Copy
Read by 5%

Sub Captions
Read by 15%

Signature
Read by 10%

505

6. THE HEADLINE

The most important thing to remember here is that your headline must be short, snappy and must touch the people that read it. Your headline must affect the reader emotionally, either by making them laugh, making them angry, making them curious or making them think. If you can't think of a headline that does one of these four things, then keep thinking. Here's a little tip that might help: try to find an insight or inner truth to the message that you're trying to convey, something that readers will easily relate to and be touched by. Taking the rutabagas example once again; it might be tempting to write a headline like: "Stop Exploiting These Migrant Workers." However, with a little thought, a more underlying truth might be revealed—that migrant workers are as human as we are, and that our actions do hurt them. From that inner truth, you might arrive at the headline: "Do unto others as you would have them do unto you." Of course, the headline doesn't have to be biblical, though that in itself will add meaning and power for many people. Finally, whenever possible, avoid a headline longer than fifteen words. People just don't read as much as they used to.

7. THE COPY

Here's where you make the case. If you have compelling arguments, make them. If you have persuasive facts, state them. But don't overwhelm with information. Two strong arguments will make more of an impression than a dozen weaker ones. Finally, be clear, be precise, and be honest. Any hint of deception will instantly detract from your entire message. Position your copy beneath the headline, laid out in two blocks two or three inches in length. Only about 5% of people will read your copy, whereas 30% will read your headline. By positioning your copy near your heading, you create a visual continuity which will draw more people to the information you want to convey. Use a serif typeface for your copy whenever possible. Those little lines and swiggles on the letters make the reading easier and more pleasing to the eye.

SUBHEADS

If you have lots of copy, break it up with interesting subheads, as we've done in the graphic [on the previous page]. This will make your ad more inviting, more organized, and easier to read.

THE SIGNATURE

This is where the name of the organization belongs, along with the address and phone number. if you don't have an organization, then think of a name that will help reinforce the message you're trying to convey. Perhaps "Citizens for Fairness to Migrant Rutabaga Pickers" would work for the example we've been using. This isn't dishonest. Your organization doesn't have to be incorporated or registered for it to be real.

8. SOME MISTAKES TO AVOID

The single most common mistake is visual clutter. Less is always better than more. So if you're not certain whether something is worth including, then leave it out. If your ad is chaotic, people will simply turn the page, and your message will never be read. The second most common mistake is to have an ad that's unclear or not easily understood (haven't you ever looked at an ad and wondered what it was for?). The best way to safeguard against this is to do some rough sketches of your visual with the headline and show it around. If people aren't clear about your message, then it's probably because your message is unclear. And however tempting, don't argue with them or assume that they're wrong and that your ad is fine. You'll be in for an unpleasant surprise. Proofread your ad, then give it to others to proofread, then proofread it yet again. Typographical errors diminish your credibility and have an uncanny habit of creeping into ads when you least expect it.

■ Pick any print ad from a magazine or other source. Go through the categories listed here. Does the ad "make mistakes"? Does it have all the elements that are recommended here: a communication objective, an argument, subheads, a signature? Who is the target audience? What format is the ad in? What is the concept?

506

Chris Ballard, *How to Write a Catchy Beer Ad.* Coors Light's "Love Songs" campaign was created by the ad agency Foote, Cone & Belding in Chicago. The concept got its start when the marketing chief of Coors challenged ad agencies to create an anthem for "what guys really like." The campaign has been incredibly popular. This essay appeared in the January 26, 2003, issue of *The New York Times Magazine.*

Chris Ballard

HOW TO WRITE A CATCHY BEER AD

FOOTBALL, GUITARS — AND TWINS — TURNED A COMMERCIAL INTO A PHENOMENON.

John Ferreira, a 35-year-old music producer who is known for television commercials, is adamant about the nature of his signature recording. "It is not," he says with disdain, "a jingle. I hate that word. I mean, I've done the 'Power of Cheese' ads, so I know a jingle. This" — he pauses — "this is rock and roll."

He walks over to a computer in his Chicago recording studio and pulls up a clip of the ad in question, a recent Coors Light spot. Two power chords detonate out of the speakers and an unseen vocalist begins to chant in what could best be described as an inebriated karaoke growl: "I. Love. Football on TV. Shots of Geena Lee. Hanging with my friends. And . . . twins!" The music is accompanied by a montage of young people having what appears to be extraordinary amounts of fun, punctuated by shots of the former "Baywatch" star Geena Lee Nolin and a pair of blond, curvaceous twins emitting soft-porn smiles. For the second stanza, even more guitars kick in and the pace quickens. "I. Love. Burritos at 4 A.M. Parties that never end. Dogs that love cats. And . . . and twins! And I. Love. You. Too!" There is a brief lull, some guitar feedback, and then a group shout of "Here's to love songs!"

If you've watched television in the last nine months, especially any NFL games, chances are you've seen the ad, which is titled "Love Songs." Something of a cultural phenomenon, it has incited sports-bar sing-alongs, turned the (real-life) twins, Diane and Elaine Klimaszewski, into pseudo-celebrities, and become a popular download on the Internet. Though you won't see "Love Songs" during today's Super Bowl — Anheuser-Busch owns exclusive rights to beer advertising

COMMENT

"The sexual exploitation of women in beer ads supports the misperception that women exist for men's pleasure alone; as well, it creates a standard of beauty that is impossible for the average woman to achieve, often resulting in feelings of inadequacy and blah, blah, blah, blah. Does anyone even care anymore?

"That said, there is something uniquely off-color about Coors' latest advertising campaign. The commercial spots, which first aired during the 2002–2003 NFL season, are responsible for Coors' highest-ever ad ratings, predicted increases in product sales, and a newfound relevance with 21- to 25-year-old male consumers. Though the musical odes to stuff guys love — "two-hand touch," "short skirts," "burritos at 4 a.m." — played during the commercials are clever, credit for the campaign's success goes to Diane and Elaine Klimaszewski. Besides being just plain hot, the aesthetically gifted 26-year-old blondes featured in the campaign are twin sisters. Twin sisters whose four blue eyes seem always to be saying, 'Hey boys, anyone up for a three-way?' Sisters in a three-way? Gross."

—Shari Waxman, salon.com

◀ **The Coors Light Twins at *Maxim* Magazine's Circus Maximus Party, January 30, 2004.** Twins Elaine and Diane Klimaszewski have achieved pop-culture celebrity status from their stint as the Coors Light Twins. The "Love Songs" ad campaign featuring the twins has been extended into print ads and into appearances at football games, and it has been spoofed on *Saturday Night Live.* The twins have parlayed their popularity into multimedia success: they have been in *Playboy* and *Maxim* magazines, have appeared in videos, TV shows, and movies, and have their own fanclub and web site, twinship.tv. (Evan Agostini/Getty Images)

for the telecast—the ad has nonetheless become the standard against which all other beer ads are measured.

Companies like Coors don't need focus groups to tell them that for young males, Beautiful Girls + Guitars + Beer = Fun. The age-old problem is how to insert your brand into the equation. Do so and you reach the coveted 21-to-27-year-old male demographic, "the Holy Grail of beer advertising," says Benj Steinman of *Beer Marketer's Insights,* an industry newsletter. How one brewery accomplished this with a jingle—or "anthem," as those who worked on the ad prefer to call it—can be considered a primer on the art of marketing to the *Maxim* generation.

When Ron Askew, 48, became chief of marketing at Coors in October 2001, he directed the company's ad agency, Foote, Cone & Belding, to design a campaign that was "young, music-driven, and full of guy insights." FCB in turn sent off 30 creative teams for six weeks to come up with ideas. They came back with dozens of concepts. A couple, like a montage of frenzied party scenes set to the Fatboy Slim song "Because We Can," made it to the small screen. Most didn't.

The team of Aaron Evanson and John Godsey provided the "Love Songs" idea. Two hours before the meeting, they were driving back from a focus group in Indianapolis when Godsey, 38, came up with the idea of writing a love song for guys. His inspiration was "I Love," a 1974 hit by Tom T. Hall in which the country musician extols the virtues of, among other things, pickup trucks, coffee in a cup, and little fuzzy pups. Knowing that puppies weren't likely to sell beer, they began to compile a list of things they thought would—"sports, supermodels, eating, and hanging out with friends," Evanson says.

In putting it into verse, they started with what Godsey calls a "no-brainer": *football on TV.* Next came the supermodel. "Our first choice was Pamela *Lee,*" says Evanson, 32. "Then came Geena *Lee,* and Jenny McCar-*thy.* And—you have to twist it a bit, Yasmine *Bleeeeeth.*" He pauses. "After all, there are only so many beautiful supermodel iconic women who rhyme with *TV.*"

Originally, Evanson wanted the second stanza to honor dogs that eat rather than love cats, but Godsey talked him out of it. "We needed to show that guys have a soft side," Godsey says. As for the twins, Evanson says, "we were trying to think of what rhymes with *friends,* and then it hit—guys like twins!" Godsey adds, "*Triplets* didn't rhyme." By the end of the ride, they had a basic working version. It was crude. It was simple. It was catchy. It was exactly what Coors wanted.

It was also innovative. The first rule of jingles is that they must trumpet the brand—"This Bud's for you," "The night belongs to Michelob." In the lyrics to "Love Songs," though, there is no mention of Coors Light. The reason, Godsey says, is that they wanted "to make it sound like a real band" so that "people would respond to it as a song, not an ad." That's where Ferreira came in.

A veteran of European funk-rock bands, Ferreira has worked in commercials since 1995, when he founded Genuine Music. His directions from Godsey were to choose a vocalist who had a "young raw voice" so the song wouldn't sound "slick and jingle-y." Ferreira called in 32-year-old Steven Simoncic, who goes by "Slimmy," a former lead singer for a Chicago band called Every Hundredth

510

Monkey. After trying out a Sex Pistols–like delivery, Slimmy switched to what Ferreira calls a "kind of monotone, half-drunk voice" because, as Godsey says, "we wanted there to be a wink in the delivery."

The "band," which consisted of Ferreira on guitar, Slimmy on vocals, and studio musicians, recorded continously over the course of more than 14 hours. Slimmy did more than 40 iterations alone of the final repetition of "and . . . and twins!" "We wanted people to know we didn't take this too seriously, so we made it seem like he was having trouble rhyming," Godsey says. "He goes, 'And, and,'—and then he's like, oh, I'll just go with twins again." Though the final product is seamless, it is actually a compilation of snippets from more than 30 different takes. Genuine's engineer, Mike Tholen, who once worked with the hard-rock band Ministry, took about two months to finish it. For producing the music on an ad like this, companies like Genuine receive $30,000 to $100,000. (With the video, the final production on this ad probably cost between $750,000 and $1 million.)

After recording a rough track of the music in late October, FCB presented the concept to Coors, which approved it. In January, they secured rights to the Hall song, hired a director, and cast actors. "We wanted people you'd felt like you'd known your whole life," Evanson says. It is a fine line beer ads have to tread, to make the people in ads seem just like you, only a bit better — the industry buzz word is *aspirational.* "The women in the party scenes had to look hot but approachable, someone I wouldn't be scared to talk to," Godsey says. The same went for the twins, whom Godsey says they chose because they were "All-American and real."

Once filmed, "Love Songs" went through "post-testing," a series of corporate round tables and focus groups. The spot made it through without any major changes, just a directive to tone down the shots of Geena Lee and the twins because, as Godsey says, "Coors's mantra is to 'show sexy not sex.'" The spot was put on the air in April, and by football season, it had become inescapable. The 26-year-old Klimaszewski sisters sang the national anthem at a Patriots game in November, posed for a *Maxim* spread, and appeared on the game show *Fear Factor.* People called Coors by the dozens asking to buy the "CD," and Web surfers searched for the tune — some chatroom denizens thought it was by the rock band P.O.D.; others thought it was by the Cure.

The key to the ad's success, Godsey says, was the humor: "We've found that a lot of women like the ad because they can see their husband or boyfriend liking those things, and laugh at him."

Now the twins are spawning clones. A new Miller Lite ad — under the guise of being two young men's fantasy commercial — shows two impossibly buxom women getting into a catfight over whether the beer is "less filling" or "tastes great," shedding their clothes in the process. The battle ends — what fight doesn't? — in a vat of wet cement (and in the cable version, one says to the other, "Let's make out"). Shortly after it began appearing, someone who worked on the Coors ad got a call from a friend. Sorry, the friend said, your commercial is now my second-favorite one on TV.

511

James B. Twitchell, *How to Advertise a Dangerous Product.* In this essay, advertising expert and historian James B. Twitchell (b. 1943) examines the origins of the Miss Clairol campaign and explains the thinking behind Shirley Polykoff's verbal and visual strategy, one that artfully transmitted a different message to men than it did to women. A professor of English and advertising at the University of Florida, Twitchell has written extensively on advertising and material culture. He contributes regularly to *Creativity* magazine and has written three book-length studies of advertising, *Adcult USA: The Triumph of Advertising in American Culture* (1997), *Lead Us Into Temptation: The Triumph of American Materialism* (1999), and *Twenty Ads That Shook the World: The Century's Most Groundbreaking Advertising and How It Changed Us All* (2001).

James B. Twitchell
HOW TO ADVERTISE A DANGEROUS PRODUCT

512

Two types of products are difficult to advertise: the very common and the very radical. Common products, called "parity products," need contrived distinctions to set them apart. You announce them as "New and Improved, Bigger and Better." But singular products need the illusion of acceptability. They have to appear as if they were *not* new and big, but old and small.

So, in the 1950s, new objects like television sets were designed to look like furniture so that they would look "at home" in your living room. Meanwhile, accepted objects like automobiles were growing massive tail fins to make them seem bigger and better, new and improved.

Although hair coloring is now very common (about half of all American women between the ages of thirteen and seventy color their hair, and about one in eight American males between thirteen and seventy does the same), such was certainly not the case generations ago. The only women who regularly dyed their hair were actresses like Jean Harlow, and "fast women," most especially prostitutes. The only man who dyed his hair was Gorgeous George, the professional wrestler. He was also the only man to use perfume.

In the twentieth century, prostitutes have had a central role in developing cosmetics. For them, sexiness is an occupational necessity, and hence anything that makes them look young, flushed, and fertile is quickly assimilated. Creating a full-lipped, big-eyed, and rosy-cheeked image is the basis of the lipstick, eye shadow, mascara, and rouge industries. While fashion may come *down* from the couturiers, face paint comes *up* from the street. Yesterday's painted woman is today's fashion plate.

In the 1950s, just as Betty Friedan was sitting down to write *The Feminine Mystique,* there were three things a lady should not do. She should not smoke in public, she should not wear long pants (unless under an overcoat), and she should not color her hair. Better she should pull out each gray strand by its root than risk association with those who bleached or, worse, dyed their hair.

This was the cultural context into which Lawrence M. Gelb, a chemical broker and enthusiastic entrepreneur, presented his product to Foote, Cone & Belding. Gelb had purchased the rights to a French hair-coloring process called Clairol. The process was unique in that unlike other available hair-coloring products, which coated the hair, Clairol actually penetrated the hair shaft, producing softer, more natural tones. Moreover, it contained a foamy shampoo base and mild oils that cleaned and conditioned the hair.

When the product was first introduced during World War II, the application process took five different steps and lasted a few hours. The users were urban and wealthy. In 1950, after seven years of research and development, Gelb once again took the beauty industry by storm. He introduced the new Miss Clairol Hair Color Bath, a single-step hair-coloring process.

This product, unlike any hair color previously available, lightened, darkened, or changed a woman's natural hair color by coloring and shampooing hair in one simple step that took only twenty minutes. Color results were more natural than anything you could find at the corner beauty parlor. It was hard to believe. Miss Clairol was so technologically advanced that demonstrations had to be done onstage at the International Beauty Show, using buckets of water, to prove to the industry that it was not a hoax. This breakthrough was almost too revolutionary to sell.

In fact, within six months of Miss Clairol's introduction, the number of women who visited the salon for permanent hair-coloring services increased by more than 500 percent! The women still didn't think they could do it themselves. And *Good Housekeeping* magazine rejected hair-color advertising because they too didn't believe the product would work. The magazine waited for three years before finally reversing its decision, accepting the ads, and awarding Miss Clairol's new product the "Good Housekeeping Seal of Approval."

FC&B passed the "Yes you *can* do it at home" assignment to Shirley Polykoff, a zesty and genial first-generation American in her late twenties. She was, as she herself was the first to admit, a little unsophisticated, but her colleagues thought she understood how women would respond to abrupt change. Polykoff understood emotion, all right, and she also knew that you could be outrageous if you did it in the right context. You can be very naughty if you are first perceived as being nice. Or, in her words, "Think it out square, say it with flair." And it is just this reconciliation of opposites that informs her most famous ad.

COMMENT

"The question 'Does she or doesn't she?' wasn't just about how no one could ever really know what you were doing. It was about how no one could ever really know who you were. It really meant not 'Does she?' but 'Is she?' It really meant 'Is she a contented homemaker or a feminist, a Jew or a Gentile — or isn't she?' "

—Alix Frick, advertising executive and Shirley Polykoff's daughter

513

514

Does she...or doesn't she?®

Hair color so natural only her hairdresser knows for sure!™

Are mothers getting younger or do they just look that way! She, for one, has the fresh, wholesome quality, the bright, shining hair that just naturally keeps a woman looking prettier, younger—as though she's found the secret of making time stand still. In a way she has. It's with Miss Clairol, the most beautiful, most effective way to cover gray and to revitalize or brighten fading color.

Keeps hair in wonderful condition—so soft, so lively—because Miss Clairol carries the fresh color deep into the hair shaft to shine outward, just the way natural color does. That's why hairdressers everywhere recommend Miss Clairol and more women use it than all other haircolorings. So quick and easy. Try it yourself. Today. **MISS CLAIROL**
HAIR COLOR BATH is a trademark of Clairol Inc. © Clairol Inc. 1963

Even close up, her hair looks natural. Miss Clairol keeps it shiny, bouncy. Completely covers gray with the younger, brighter lasting color no other kind of haircoloring can promise—and live up to!

◀ **Miss Clairol, *Does she . . . or doesn't she?*** Although the Coors Light "Love Songs" jingle is far from subtle, advertising often hinges on *ambiguity*—we tend to look twice at an ad that can be read in more than one way, or that has a "surprise" hidden within it. Advertisements also often promote products that promise us a key into a way of life that we would otherwise not have access to. In the 1950s, people generally kept quiet about what they did to enhance their appearance—for example, "respectable" women would never admit to coloring their hair. Today, when even major league baseball players flamboyantly dye their hair, it may seem peculiar to think that such behavior was once secretive. When an advertising firm decided to market hair coloring to women back in the mid-1950s, the biggest problem was how to persuade women that it was acceptable. The problem was creatively handled by one of the first women to make a name in copywriting.

Shirley Polykoff (1908–1998) designed the "Does she . . . or doesn't she?" campaign, which became one of the most famous and successful in advertising history. Polykoff was born into a Jewish immigrant family from Russia and wrote that as a child, "I remember reading magazine advertisements with special attention. They seemed to be a window opening into a wondering world—the world of mainstream America—that I avidly wanted to be a part of." She details her immigrant background and advertising career in an entertaining autobiography, appropriately titled *Does She . . . Or Doesn't She?: And How She Did It* (1975). The "Does she . . . or doesn't she?" campaign ran for almost twenty years (1956–1972), during which time the number of American women coloring their hair increased from 7 percent to more than 40 percent. (From *Good Housekeeping*, August 1963)

515

■ *Advertisements are a careful combination of words and image. Consider the ad's image. Why do you think Polykoff wanted to focus on mothers? How does the ad's copy reinforce the image? Because the product is called "Miss Clairol," why do you think Polykoff didn't feature younger, single women? Why might that strategy not work? Why do you think she intentionally omitted the presence of a husband? Find a contemporary Clairol print ad, and analyze the relationship between copy and image. How has the message changed from the "Does she . . . or doesn't she?" campaign?*

COMMENT

"There was a time, not so long ago—between, roughly speaking, the start of Eisenhower's Administration and the end of Carter's—when hair color meant something. . . . Between the fifties and the seventies, women entered the workplace, fought for social emancipation, got the Pill, and changed what they did with their hair. To examine the hair-color campaigns of the period is to see, quite unexpectedly, all these things as bound up together, the profound with the seemingly trivial. In writing the history of women in the postwar era, did we forget something important? Did we leave out hair?"

—Malcolm Gladwell, critic

She knew this almost from the start. On July 9, 1955, Polykoff wrote to the head art director that she had three campaigns for Miss Clairol Hair Color Bath. The first shows the same model in each ad, but with slightly different hair color. The second exhorts "Tear up those baby pictures! You're a redhead now," and plays on the American desire to refashion the self by rewriting history. These two ideas were, as she says, "knock-downs" en route to what she really wanted. In her autobiography, appropriately titled *Does She . . . Or Doesn't She?: And How She Did It,* Polykoff explains the third execution, the one that will work:

#3. Now here's the one I really want. If I can get it sold to the client. Listen to this: *"Does she . . . or doesn't she?"* (No, I'm not kidding. Didn't you ever hear of the arresting question?) Followed by: *"Only her mother knows for sure!"* or *"So natural, only her mother knows for sure!"*

I may not do the mother part, though as far as I'm concerned mother is the ultimate authority. However, if Clairol goes retail, they may have a problem of offending beauty salons, where they are presently doing all of their business. So I may change the word "mother" to "hairdresser." This could be awfully good business — turning the hairdresser into a color expert. Besides, it reinforces the claim of naturalness, and not so incidentally, glamorizes the salon.

The psychology is obvious. I know from myself. If anyone admires my hair, I'd rather die than admit I dye. And since I feel so strongly that the average woman is me, this great stress on naturalness is important [Polykoff 1975, 28–29].[1]

■ *In her memo, Shirley Polykoff worries that she might not be able to sell her client on "Does she . . . or doesn't she?" as a hook for the campaign. What obstacle do you think she anticipates? Where do you think the phrase comes from? Do you think Polykoff made it up?*

516

While her headline is naughty, the picture is nice and natural. Exactly what "Does She . . . Or Doesn't She" do? To men the answer was clearly sexual, but to women it certainly was not. The male editors of *Life* magazine balked about running this headline until they did a survey and found out women were not filling in the ellipsis the way they were.

Women, as Polykoff knew, were finding different meaning because they were actually looking at the model and her child. For them the picture was not presexual but postsexual, not inviting male attention but expressing satisfaction with the result. Miss Clairol is a mother, not a love interest.

If that is so, then the product must be misnamed: it should be *Mrs.* Clairol. Remember, this was the mid-1950s, when illegitimacy was a powerful taboo. Out-of-wedlock children were still called bastards, not love children. This ad was far more dangerous than anything Benetton or Calvin Klein has ever imagined.

The naughty/nice conundrum was further intensified *and* diffused by some of the ads featuring a wedding ring on the model's left hand. Although FC&B experimented with models purporting to be secretaries, schoolteachers, and the like, the motif of mother and child was always constant.

■ *Twitchell discusses the ad's ambiguity. What makes the headline ambiguous? In what sense is the ambiguity intentional? From the advertiser's perspective, what positive effects will the ambiguity produce? How might it help sales? Besides the headline, what other ambiguities does Twitchell find in the ad?*

---

[1] Shirley Polykoff, *Does She . . . Or Doesn't She?: And How She Did It* (Garden City, N.Y.: Doubleday, 1975).

So what was the answer to what she does or doesn't do? To women, what she did had to do with visiting the hairdresser. Of course, men couldn't understand. This was the world before unisex hair care. Men still went to barber shops. This was the same pre-feminist generation in which the solitary headline "Modess . . . because" worked magic selling female sanitary products. The ellipsis masked a knowing implication that excluded men. That was part of its attraction. Women know, men don't. This you-just-don't-get-it motif was to become a central marketing strategy as the women's movement was aided *and* exploited by Madison Avenue nichemeisters.

Polykoff had to be ambiguous for another reason. As she notes in her memo, Clairol did not want to be obvious about what they were doing to their primary customer — the beauty shop. Remember that the initial product entailed five different steps performed by the hairdresser, and lasted hours. Many women were still using hairdressers for something they could now do by themselves. It did not take a detective to see that the company was trying to run around the beauty shop and sell to the end-user. So the ad again has it both ways. The hairdresser is invoked as the expert — only he knows *for sure* — but the process of coloring your hair can be done without his expensive assistance.

MESSAGE	METHOD	MEDIUM
In "How to Create Your Own Print Ad" we learn that "the communications objective is the essence of your message." After reading the descriptions of both the Miss Clairol ad and the commercial for Coors Light, how would you describe in one sentence their communications objective?	Compare Adbusters' advice on how to write a print ad with a classic example of such an ad, Miss Clairol's "Does she . . . or doesn't she?" In what ways does the Miss Clairol ad appear to conform to Adbusters' advice on text, layout, target audience, and so on? Can you find aspects of the ad that seem to violate Adbusters' rules?	Consider the descriptions of the creative processes that went into the print ad for Miss Clairol and the commercial for Coors Light. How did a consideration of the medium that would deliver each ad affect the creative processes? Try reversing the advertising assignment: How could the Miss Clairol ad be turned into a TV commercial and the Coors Light commercial into a print ad?

ADVERTISING MORALITY

Newspapers and magazines are usually full of advertisements — for cars, clothing, home furnishing, luxury items, and so on. But mixed in with these ads you will find others that are not trying to sell a product but are instead promoting ideas or opinions — a way to be, live, or act. These opinion ads (or "op-ads" for short) are frequently taken out by organizations or advocacy groups in an attempt to get their message across to a wide public. Because advertising is very expensive to design and place, and because many advocacy groups do not have huge corporate budgets, these ads often appear in black and white and with minimal graphics. Yet some groups budget more than others and launch campaigns that win industry awards for creativity and persuasiveness.

518

    Advocacy advertising falls under the general category of social marketing, which involves all advertising that aims to solve social problems by influencing public perception and behavior. Government agencies and nonprofit foundations often participate in campaigns to promote programs that will benefit the public (e.g., recycling, conservation, health advice). Advocacy ads are often more narrowly targeted and sponsored by nonprofit institutions or activist groups with a particular agenda, and they frequently involve controversial issues. Advocacy ads should be distinguished from another type of social marketing, cause-related marketing, which has become popular with for-profit organizations and corporations seeking to link their name with good causes. The materials that follow explore some of the ways that people use advertising for a moral purpose.

COMMENT

"And then I met the murderers. Murderers who were penitent. Murderers who were catatonic. Murderers who were arrogant, who proclaimed their innocence, or had genuinely forgotten just what they had done to land them on death row. They were as different as their cases, their upbringing, their race, their intelligence. Yet there was something all of them shared. I saw it on my first death row, stepping onto an enclosed, three-tiered cell block, the inmates dressed in hot pink scrub pants and T-shirts, out of their cells for their two-hour recreation.

"It was in the way they noticed us without noticing, making us the intruders. It was in the way they sneered, or hid, or laughed, as if at a joke we could not possibly understand. It was something in their eyes, a light that shone neither outward nor inward, but hung suspended, like a bubble in ice. Something that rendered them diabolic and divine, as if having killed had lurched them into a new plane of being, a plane where nothing could embarrass or confuse them again, where they did not need to know anything they did not already know, where time did not flow but froze, cracking only when one of them was taken from the block to be executed.

"These men, I saw, were different than you and I. Not in what they dreamed of doing, but in what they'd done. Some were pleasant, gangly, floppy-haired boys wishing they could be out on their mountain bikes, some fond, regretful men and women wishing they could be with their children. A few dreamed of taking to the pulpit, where they could preach the dangers of drugs and alcohol and godlessness to all who would listen. Some were charming. Some were soulful. Some were philosophical. All of them, in some ways, inspired pity.

"And then I remember their crimes. The sexual assault and cold-blood-ed assassination of a teenage convenience store clerk for a few hundred dol-lars and three hundred cartons of cigarettes. The torturing and killing of a three-year-old girl. Four women kidnapped, raped, and murdered by the same man over a five-year period. A teenage girl and boy clubbed to death during a robbery. If this had been your daughter, your wife, your brother, your child. . . ."

— Ken Shulman, interviewer of death row inmates

519

Barbara Ehrenreich, *Dirty Laundry: Benetton's "We, on Death Row" Campaign*.
When Benetton, an Italian clothing company, decided to launch a marketing campaign sympathetically featuring death row inmates, the age-old controversy over capital punishment rose to new levels of intensity. Between January and April 2000, Benetton released posters worldwide and took out sizable inserts in such magazines as *Talk*, *Vanity Fair*, and *Rolling Stone*. Outraged by the advertising, victims' rights supporters called for boycotts and conducted a national case against what they considered Benetton's commercial exploitation of human suffering.

The campaign also blurred the distinction between journalism and advertising: Could the 96-page Benetton magazine insert — which included photographs, interviews, and even an essay — be legitimately called a photo essay, or was it primarily a calculated and cynical attempt to sell a product? As the controversy branched out to encompass issues of art, ideology, and commercialism, a serious photography magazine, *Aperture*, invited a prominent journalist and anti–death penalty activist to weigh in on the advertising: in "Dirty Laundry," Barbara Ehrenreich examines the controversial campaign and finds herself caught in a classic "on the one hand . . . on the other hand" perspective.

A leading member of America's Socialist Party and an activist for progressive causes, Barbara Ehrenreich (b. 1941) contributes essays to numerous magazines. Her many books include *The Hearts of Men: American Dreams and the Flight from Commitment* (1983), *The Worst Years of Our Lives: Irreverent Notes from a Decade of Greed* (1990), *Kipper's Game* (1993), *The Snarling Citizen: Essays* (1995), and *Blood Rites: Origins and History of the Passions of War* (1997). She writes regularly for *Time* magazine. This essay first appeared in *Aperture* (Summer 2000).

Barbara Ehrenreich

DIRTY LAUNDRY: BENETTON'S "WE, ON DEATH ROW" CAMPAIGN

You have to be pretty gung-ho anti–death penalty to care about the execution of a serial killer like Darrell Rich, a.k.a. Young Elk, who murdered three women and a little girl during a two-month spree in 1978, adding in some torture, sodomy, and rape. But there are already upwards of five hundred people in the San Quentin parking lot when I arrive on the night of his execution, all but about three of them there to bear solemn, disapproving witness to the execution. Some in the crowd are the usual genderless, vegan, all-purpose Berkeley-based protestors, but a lot more are parishioners of local Catholic churches, holding up flimsy white wooden crosses. A boy of about fourteen offered me a cross as I walked up to the parking lot from the service road, and since crosses do service in all kinds of dubious causes these days, I asked him what it symbolized. "Jesus," he said. "Jesus was a victim of capital punishment."

This is my first execution vigil and there isn't much to do but stand there in the dark, listening to a series of earnest speakers and watching the half-moon try to escape the telephone lines overhead. The Aztecs did a much better job of human sacrifice, I can't help thinking—tearing their victims' hearts out and rolling the bodies down the temple stairs toward the populace massed below. Or the Romans, who, it should be recalled, tossed common criminals to the lions, as well as religious eccentrics and captives of war. At least then the gods got their due and the crowd got its spectacle, unlike the stealthy parody of a medical procedure—lethal injection—being prepared for at this moment inside San Quentin's walls.

Cold and tired of standing, I check my watch: 11:05 P.M., meaning fifty-six minutes to go. Then I realize that this is exactly what I am here for: to try to find out what fifty-six minutes feels like when it contains one's entire future, as allotted by the state.

For better or for worse, there is now an easier way to protest the death penalty than by attending vigils in the chill air late at night. You can buy Benetton. While our vigil will win less than a minute of coverage on local TV news, Benetton's "We, on Death Row" advertising campaign has already attracted international attention, beginning with the company's ninety-six-page insert in the January issue of *Talk* magazine. There are no sweaters or other Benetton products in the insert, and no hint of the chic, only photos and brief interviews with twenty-six Americans awaiting execution, along with some quotes from the Pope and the Dalai Lama calling the death penalty "cruel and unnecessary," "immoral and wrong." That was enough to set off a firestorm, as the expression goes, of protest from the pro–death penalty side. The state of Missouri is suing Benetton for gaining access to its death-row inmates by deceptively claiming to be undertaking an

521

■ *Look carefully at what Ehrenreich says here: How serious is she? In your opinion, would she truly prefer it if, instead of a lethal injection, the prisoner had his heart ripped out or was tossed to the lions? Where do you think she finally stands?*

COMMENT

"When *Life* magazine makes a cover about war, it makes the cover to inform but also to sell the magazine and to sell the advertising pages inside the magazine — Chivas Regal and all the others. So *Time* magazine and all the others make a cover to inform and to sell. To do what I do, I do that to sell but also to inform. And as soon as you inform, people point a finger at you and say, 'You are exploiting!' No. It's the people who don't even inform who are exploiting. It's Prada bullshit, or Gap bullshit, or Chanel."

— Oliverio Toscani

COMMENT

"Toscani is on another planet. . . . I understand the combat he's leading here with these types of images, and I appreciate his iconoclasm, but what's sick here is marrying these high-impact social images with futile consumer products, like sweaters."

— Dominique Anginot, photographer

"international photo-documentary project" unrelated to selling sweaters. Sears, Roebuck has dumped its Benetton line of clothing, claiming that some customers were so outraged by the "We, on Death Row" campaign that they wrote to the company "indicating that they will never buy from Sears again. . . ."

But even the most ardent death-penalty opponent needs two hands to think through the Benetton campaign. On the one hand, you have the fact that Benetton is not only a clothing company, it's an Italian clothing company, and, like most Europeans, Italians take American executions pretty hard. Every time anyone is executed anywhere in the world, the Italian government signals its displeasure by bathing the Colosseum in golden lights at night, and when the news arrived that Texas had executed Odell Barnes on March 2, five hundred Romans gathered at the Colosseum to protest and in some cases weep, never mind that it was 1 A.M. So you can see the Benetton campaign as part of the inevitable cultural blow-back from globalization: U.S. companies export their images of slender, upscale young people engaged in playful acts of consumption; an Italian company replies with images of America's designated sacrificial victims; low-income men, doomed and forgotten; "the least amongst us," in Jesus's phrase.

On the other hand—well, the other hand reaches out for substance, for sincerity, and comes back soiled. In launching its death-row campaign, Benetton isn't just being a "good corporate citizen," as one company spokesman says; it's selling sweaters. If the point were simply to contest the death penalty, the words "United Colors of Benetton" would be buried modestly within the *Talk* magazine insert, for example, instead of being highlighted in bright green on the cover. And surely the faces of the doomed would not be showing up on billboards over the caption "United Killers of Benetton." For one thing, some of them are probably innocent, condemned simply by their inability to afford competent legal defense. But "United Death-Row Inmates, Some Innocent and Some Not, Of Benetton" probably wouldn't work on a billboard.

523

The Benetton campaign is a classic example of what is known in the marketing business as "branding": attaching to one's product a sensibility that, it is hoped, consumers will want to acquire for themselves. Nike isn't just sneakers; it's youth and triumph and Nietzschean[1] overcoming. Marlboro is rugged manliness; Apple, intellectual nonconformity. And Benetton has, over the years, already positioned itself at the edge of the taboo, which is of course precisely where the much-sought-after quality of "edginess" resides. One of the company's past campaigns celebrated interracial love; another featured a man dying of AIDS. Forbidden love, a stigmatized disease, and now state-sponsored, ritual killing. You can wear your Benetton summer cropped-neck T to say "I care," or maybe just "I dare."

But then—did I say you need only two hands to work this out?—there are the photos. It is the photos of the condemned men (and one woman) featured in the Benetton magazine insert that fill my mind as I wait there in the dark at San

---

[1] Friedrich Nietzsche (1844–1900) was the prominent German philosopher, now famous for his theory of the superman, his emphasis on individual will, and his statement that "God is dead." (—Ed.)

"I think people like seeing other people suffer and killed."

—John Lotter,
death row inmate

"It's hard to keep on hoping every day."
— Christopher Simmons,
death row inmate

Quentin. Without Benetton, I would never have seen these faces, and now that I have seen them, no amount of cynicism about corporate motives can protect me from them. There is Joseph Amrine, forty-four years old and fourteen years on death row, looking bruised and wistful. There is Jeremy Sheets, twenty-six, with the straight brows and almond eyes of a medieval saint. There is Kevin Nigel Stanford, who has lived thirty-seven years, eighteen of them on death row, his soft, tan face glowing with religious resignation. Maybe some of them do look "scary," as an acquaintance remarks, and it's hard not to read the accompanying interviews without wondering "guilty or innocent?"—not that the interviews, which are a lot about loneliness and what it sounds like in prison at night, offer any answers to that.

The faces do, though, in their own way. Stare long enough and you see that each of them is saying: Look, violence is not a singular event, it is always a chain. It begins, in these cases, with a childhood of neglect and abuse; moves on to legally recognized crimes; then feeds itself further on the cruelty of imprisonment and capital punishment. One act of violence cannot cancel another; it can only propagate the chain. Capital punishment is just one more link, and a crucial one, because it draws so many more people into the cycle of violence—those who pay for the executions with their tax money, which is almost all of us, and those who fail to raise their voices in protest.

At the vigil I detect some North Face and probably Sears, but no visible Benetton. We have been standing a long time—almost a lifetime, or what's left of it—when a rabbi takes the microphone and recounts Darrell Rich's crimes in almost too much detail: the crushed skull, the bodies covered with bite marks, the little girl hurled from a bridge, already drowning in her own blood. Then he tells us why this matters and why it matters that we're here—because every life is "a whole world"—or, as this bit of Jewish wisdom is sometimes put, "a miracle, a universe." Part of the miracle of Darrell Rich is that, well into his imprisonment, he discovered that he was one-quarter Cherokee and took up Native American spirituality along with the name Young Elk. His last wish—denied by the state—was for a purifying sweat-lodge ceremony as a last rite. Now the hope, apparently shared by all the cross-bearers around me, is that he will be able to hear the music of the Indian drum circle that begins to play a few minutes before midnight, and that the sound will bear him safely into the spirit world.

I am trying, insofar as an atheist can, to invest these last moments with exalted thoughts. Maybe it will make a difference that we are here vigiling, and that Benetton runs its ads. Maybe Young Elk's spirit will manifest itself above the fortress of San Quentin, clean at last and ready to redeem us. Maybe the victims' relatives, who are inside right now watching him twitch as the poison enters his veins, will find peace now and even a wisp of forgiveness in their hearts.

But exaltation eludes me. The last few minutes feel like a demonic mockery of the countdown on New Year's Eve. A ball's going to drop, I can sense it coming, only it's filled with some garbagy mix of regret and sorrow and so much waste. This, I finally decide, is not something you want to get on your clothes.

▶

**Office of National Drug Control Policy, The Partnership for
Drug-Free America, *Father* and *The Enforcer*.** Drug use has been
the focus of one of our most politically charged public debates for
decades. In the early 1980s the message to teens from the Reagan
administration was "Just Say No."

In 1998, with bipartisan support, Congress created the National
Youth Anti-Drug Media Campaign with the goal of preventing and
reducing youth drug use. Unprecedented in size and scope, the
Campaign is the most visible symbol of the federal government's
commitment to youth drug prevention. The Campaign is a strategically
integrated communications effort that combines advertising with
public communications outreach to deliver anti-drug messages and
skills to America's youth (*Father*) and their parents (*The Enforcer*).
The Partnership for Drug-Free America participates in the National
Youth Anti-Drug Media Campaign, which is coordinated by the
Office of National Drug Control Policy. At the core of this multi-faceted
initiative is a paid advertising program featuring messages created by
The Partnership. The Partnership donates all advertising to the National
Youth Anti-Drug Media Campaign on a pro bono basis. (Courtesy of The
Partnership for Drug-Free America®)

528

JOHN AND KAREN WERE STONED AND HOOKED UP. AFTER THEY CAME DOWN, THEY REALIZED THAT IF THEY HADN'T **FATHER** SMOKED THINGS NEVER WOULD HAVE GONE AS FAR AS THEY DID. THE CONSEQUENCES WILL LAST A LIFETIME.

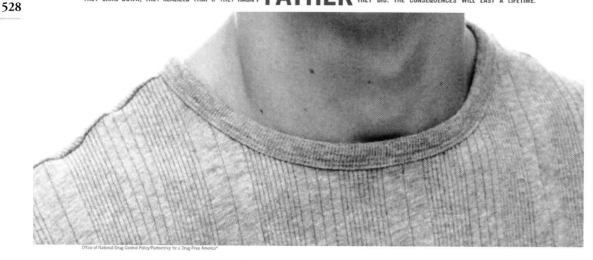

Office of National Drug Control Policy/Partnership for a Drug-Free America®

STONED DECISIONS ARE STILL DECISIONS.
YOUR ACTIONS HAVE CONSEQUENCES, LONG AFTER YOU'VE SOBERED UP.

freevibe.com

k|n|o|w|l|e|d|g|e|
THE ANTI-DRUG.

THE ENFORCER

SHE DOESN'T LOVE BEING TOUGH. SHE'S TOUGH BECAUSE SHE LOVES.

It takes more than a hero to keep kids away from marijuana. It takes parents strong enough to make rules and back them up. A little discipline today could make all the difference tomorrow. **You're more powerful than you know.**

Call 1-800-788-2800 for more information or visit theantidrug.com.

PARENTS.
THE ANTI-DRUG.

HAVE YOU EVER SEEN A REAL INDIAN?

AMERICAN INDIAN
COLLEGE FUND
INVEST IN OUR STRENGTH

American Indian College Fund, *Have You Ever Seen a Real Indian?* The American Indian College Fund (AICF) launched this campaign in 2001 "to challenge the American public's notions about who Indian people are and what they can become." Founded in 1989, the AICF serves approximately 26,000 Indian students across the United States, in the form of scholarships and financial support for tribal colleges. This campaign is geared toward changing public awareness rather than raising funds. (Reprinted by permission)

■ Note the method used to capture your attention in the AICF ad. How are you expected to understand "Have you ever seen a real Indian?" Is it a rhetorical question (a question asked for effect and in which the answer is implied), or is it a question that requires an answer? How can you tell? How would the question be answered?

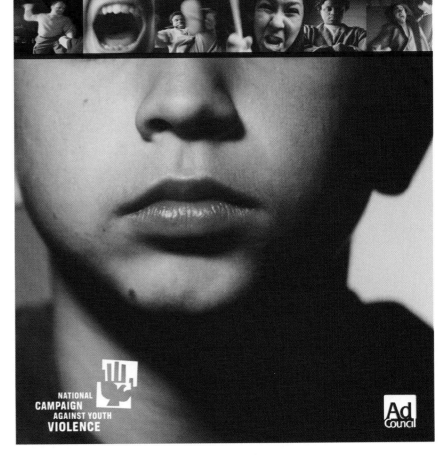

Whether you know it or not, you could be exposing children to violence every day. By losing your temper with a neighbor. Threatening another motorist. Kids learn to deal with difficult situations by watching us. So the next time you're around a kid, think about the message you're sending. To find out what you can do, call 1-888-544-KIDS or visit www.NoViolence.net. Is there any real way to stop youth violence? Try starting with yourself.

CHILDREN AREN'T BORN VIOLENT. BUT YOU CAN CERTAINLY CHANGE THAT.

NATIONAL CAMPAIGN AGAINST YOUTH VIOLENCE

Ad Council

National Campaign Against Youth Violence, *Children Aren't Born Violent.* Founded in 1999, the NCAYV works with U.S. communities to "highlight and strengthen local efforts to reduce youth violence." The Ad Council designed this print ad, which ran nationally. A nonprofit organization staffed by volunteer advertising professionals, the Ad Council is responsible for such memorable public service messages as "Only You Can Prevent Forest Fires," "Friends Don't Let Friends Drive Drunk," "Take a Bite Out of Crime," and "A Mind Is a Terrible Thing to Waste." (National Campaign Against Youth Violence. Compliments of Executive Director, Sarah Ingersoll)

▼ **Nike, *The Most Offensive Boots We've Ever Made.*** Adbusters includes a picture
of this ad on its web site — it shows Nike itself turning the practice of culture
jamming back against groups like Adbusters. The shoe company first designed a
campaign that made fun of the "sweatshop" accusation — and then had fake pro-
testers "deface" billboards like the ones shown here with notices that the new
Nikes gave players an "unfair advantage." Adbusters writes that "it took hard
work to link the words 'Nike' and 'sweatshop' in the public mind, but as that idea
is repeated, it steadily loses freshness. It becomes unfashionable, then clichéd."
(Image courtesy of Nathan Shanahan and www.adbusters.org)

Adbusters, *You're Running Because You Want That Raise.* This spoof ad is one of an ongoing series in
which Adbusters uses the techniques of advertising to target what it sees as particularly egregious
corporate offenders from the fashion, tobacco, alcohol, and food industries. (Image courtesy of
www.adbusters.org)

YOU'RE RUNNING BECAUSE YOU WANT THAT RAISE, TO BE ALL YOU CAN BE. BUT IT'S NOT EASY WHEN YOU WORK SIXTY HOURS A WEEK MAKING SNEAKERS IN AN INDONESIAN FACTORY AND YOUR FRIENDS DISAPPEAR WHEN THEY ASK FOR A RAISE. SO THINK GLOBALLY BEFORE YOU DECIDE IT'S SO COOL TO WEAR

NIKE

533

COMMENT

"I know what you're thinking: that's rich, asking an adman to define truth. Advertising people aren't known either for their wisdom or their morals, so it's hard to see why an adman is the right person for this assignment. Well, it's just common sense — like asking an alcoholic about sobriety, or a sinner about piety. Who is likely to be more obsessively attentive to a subject than the transgressor?

"Everyone thinks that advertising is full of lies, but it's not what you think. The facts presented in advertising are almost always accurate, not because advertising people are sticklers but because their ads are very closely regulated. If you make a false claim in a commercial on network television, the FTC will catch it. Someone always blows the whistle.

"The real lie in advertising — some would call it the 'art' of advertising — is harder to detect. What's false in advertising lies in the presentation of situations, values, beliefs, and cultural norms that form a backdrop for the selling message.

"Advertising — including movies, TV, and music videos — presents to us a world that is not our world but rather a collection of images and ideas created for the purpose of selling. These images paint a picture of the ideal family life, the perfect home. What a beautiful woman is, and is not. A prescription for being a good parent and a good citizen.

"The power of these messages lies in their unrelenting pervasiveness, the 24-hour-a-day drumbeat that leaves no room for an alternative view. We've become acculturated to the way advertisers and other media-makers look at things, so much so that we have trouble seeing things in our own natural way. Advertising robs us of the most intimate moments in our lives because it substitutes an advertiser's idea of what ought to be. . . ."

— Jay Chiat, founder of Chiat/Day, the agency responsible for the Energizer Bunny

■ *In what ways — both graphically and textually — do the ads collected here resemble familiar product ads? Are they "better" or more morally valid than other kinds of advertising?*

534

MESSAGE

When we think of "message," we usually think of information that's been put into words. But advertisers often try to convey their messages through images. Consider the pictures that accompany the many advertisements in this cluster. In how many of these ads does the picture dominate the text? How would you describe the information conveyed by some of these images? Select one advocacy advertisement and focus on the image alone. Do you think it conveys a clear message? To what extent does it depend on a text or headline to convey its information? Would any of these advertisements make sense without accompanying text?

METHOD

In what ways — both graphically and textually — do the cause-related ads included here resemble the product ads we are familiar with in magazines and on television? In your opinion, is selling an idea or a political view the same as selling a Ford truck, a Bud Light, or a Dell computer? Are the methods of persuasion similar? Select any one of the advocacy ads and point out similarities and differences in its persuasive methods as compared to those of the familiar product ad.

MEDIUM

The anti-drug campaign aims to "reach Americans wherever they live, work, learn, and play." This kind of social marketing usually involves finding alternative media for reaching people — using the side of a bus, for example, as advertising space. What media do you think would be most effective for reaching young people who are either active drug users or actively at risk of becoming one? How would you launch a campaign in that media?

535

SELLING AMERICA

Messages put out by governments to stimulate patriotic feeling and to elicit support for national policies or causes usually fall under the communication category of **propaganda**. Although many kinds of one-sided messages (like those in advocacy ads) designed to influence public opinion can be termed "propaganda," the word has taken on a decidedly negative connotation and is often used to suggest the dissemination of misinformation with the intent of indoctrinating the public. One person's propaganda, however, can be another person's truth; for example, those who strongly support or believe in a particular cause (such as anti-tobacco agenda or anti–gun control legislation) tend to see advertising that promotes their cause not as propaganda but as vitally necessary and socially responsible information. The materials that follow include examples of advertising that sells the idea of America and an essay that explores the relationship between selling and loving your country.

To see Joe Citizen's slide show, "Wrapping Ourselves in the Flag," go to bedfordstmartins.com/convergences.

The American flag as merchandising tool. Pizza boxes, bikinis, Little Debbie Snack Cakes, beer bottles, T-shirts, jewelry, ice cream cones: these are just a few of the products whose manufacturers "borrowed" the theme of patriotism and used the American flag to sell in the wake of 9/11. Here you see two examples among thousands of possibilities. (Image Works)

COMMENT

"The problem with the unbridled use of patriotic themes in marketing and advertising is that when this symbolism becomes ubiquitous, the original intent of the message inevitably becomes confused and diluted. When every corporation starts using the flag in its advertising, the patriotic symbolism becomes just another meaningless element of one more gratuitous ad campaign. When the flag is attached as a symbol to otherwise completely unrelated products, the combination starts to look more like a parody done in bad taste, than it does an expression of true patriotism. The danger here is that when the symbolism of the flag starts to completely lose its meaning, it leaves the door open for it to be redefined by whatever market force or political strategy is prevalent at the time."

—Joe Citizen, web site creator

Ian Frazier, *All-Consuming Patriotism*. Was it propaganda when President Bush went on television after 9/11 and encouraged Americans to keep shopping? When the government advises us to shop, do we experience shopping and spending as an act of citizenship? Is loyalty to one's nation the same as "brand loyalty" to a product? In this essay, Ian Frazier combines humor with a serious message as he reflects on how our fears of terrorism have helped transform citizens into customers.

Ian Frazier was born in Ohio in 1951 and was educated at Harvard University, where he wrote for the *Harvard Lampoon*. His writing has appeared in *The New Yorker, The Atlantic Monthly,* and *Harper's,* and he frequently contributes essays to *Outside.* He is the author of two collections of humor pieces, *Dating Your Mom* (1985) and *Coyote v. Acme* (1996), and several award-winning nonfiction books, *Great Plains* (1989), *Family* (1994), and *On the Rez* (1999).

Ian Frazier

ALL-CONSUMING PATRIOTISM

AMERICAN FLAG: $19.95.
NEW YACHT: $75,000.
TRUE PATRIOTISM? PRICELESS.

I think of myself as a good American. I follow current events, come to a complete stop at stop signs, show up for jury duty, vote. When the government tells me to shop, as it's been doing recently, I shop. Over the last few months, patriotically, I've bought all kinds of stuff I have no use for. Lack of money has been no obstacle; years ago I could never get a credit card, due to low income and lack of a regular job, and then one day for no reason credit cards began tumbling on me out of the mail. I now owe more to credit card companies than the average family of four earns in a year. So when buying something I don't want or need, I simply take out my credit card. That part's been easy; for me, it's the shopping itself that's hard. I happen to be a bad shopper—nervous, uninformed, prone to grab the first product I see on the shelf and pay any amount for it and run out the door. Frequently, trips I make to the supermarket end with my wife shouting in disbelief as she goes through the grocery bags and immediately transfers one wrongly purchased item after another directly into the garbage can.

It's been hard, as I say, but I've done my duty—I've shopped and then shopped some more. Certain sacrifices are called for. Out of concern for the economy after the terror attacks, the president said that he wanted us to go about our business, and not stop shopping. On a TV commercial sponsored by the travel industry, he exhorted us to take the family for a vacation. The treasury secretary, financial commentators, leaders of industry—all told us not to be afraid to spend. So I've gone out of my comfort zone, even expanded my purchasing pat-

I Want You for U.S. Army, c. 1917. It was not until World War I that propaganda art came into its own as a powerful tool of mass communication. Each message was carefully crafted—text, color, images, and design—to appeal to a specific audience. The four recruiting tools shown here indicate how the Army's message changed over the last century, even though they share the same purpose: to get people to enlist. Selling the benefits of military service means also selling ideals about god, country, democracy, freedom, and what it means to be an individual. In the best-known American poster of all time, shown here, Uncle Sam challenges you to serve your country. This World War I poster was a self-portrait of the illustrator, James Montgomery Flagg; the pose was taken from a British poster with the headline "Britons Want You." Flagg's poster was so popular that it was used again in World War II. (U.S. Army materials courtesy of the U.S. government, as represented by the Secretary of the Army)

terns. Not long ago I detected a look of respect in the eye of a young salesman with many piercings at the music store as he took in my heavy middle-aged girth and then the rap music CD featuring songs of murder and gangsterism that I had selflessly decided to buy. My life is usually devoid of great excitement or difficulty, knock wood and thank God, and I have nothing to cry about, but I've also noticed in the media recently a strong approval for uninhibited public crying. So now, along with the shopping, I've been crying a lot, too. Sometimes I cry and shop at the same time.

As I'm pushing my overfull shopping cart down the aisle, sobbing quietly, moving a bit more slowly because of the extra weight I've lately put on, a couple of troubling questions cross my mind. First, I start to worry about the real depth of my shopping capabilities. So far I have more or less been able to keep up with what the government expects of me. I'm at a level of shopping that I can stand. But what if, God forbid, events take a bad turn and the national crisis worsens, and more shopping is required? Can I shop with greater intensity than I am shopping now? I suppose I could eat even more than I've been eating, and order additional products in the mail, and go on costlier trips, and so on. But I'm not eager, frankly, to enter that "code red" shopping mode. I try to tell myself that I'd be equal to it, that in a real crisis I might be surprised by how much I could buy. But I don't know.

My other worry is a vague one, more in the area of atmospherics, intangibles. I feel kind of wrong even mentioning it in this time of trial. How can I admit that I am worried about my aura? I worry that my aura is not . . . well, that it's not what I had once hoped it would be. I can explain this only by comparison, obliquely. On the top shelf of my bookcase, among the works vital to me, is a book called *Trials and Triumphs: The Record of the Fifty-Fifth Ohio Volunteer Infantry,* by Captain Hartwell Osborn. I've read this book many times and studied it to the smallest detail, because I think the people in it are brave and cool and admirable in every way.

The Fifty-Fifth was a Union Army regiment, formed in the Ohio town of Norwalk, that fought throughout the Civil War. My great-great-grandfather served in the regiment, as did other relatives. The book lists every mile the regiment marched and every casualty it suffered. I like reading about the soldiering, but I can't really identify with it, having never been in the service myself. I identify more with the soldiers' wives and mothers and daughters, whose home-front struggles I can better imagine. *Trials and Triumphs* devotes a chapter to them, and to an organization they set up called the Soldiers' Aid Society.

The ladies of the Soldiers' Aid Society worked for the regiment almost constantly from the day it began. They sewed uniforms, made pillows, held ice-cream sociables to raise money, scraped lint for bandages, emptied their wedding chests of their best linen and donated it all. To provide the men with antiscorbutics[1]

---

[1] **Antiscorbutics:** Items used to prevent or cure scurvy, an illness caused by a deficiency of vitamin C. (—Ed.)

while on campaign, they pickled everything that would pickle, from onions to potatoes to artichokes. Every other day they were shipping out a new order of homemade supplies. Some of the women spent so much time stooped over while packing goods in barrels that they believed they had permanently affected their postures. When the war ended the ladies of the Soldiers' Aid said that for the first time in their lives they understood what united womanhood could accomplish. The movements for prohibition and women's suffrage that grew powerful in the early 1900s got their start among those who'd worked in similar home-front organizations during the war.

I don't envy my forebears, or wish I'd lived back then. I prefer the greater speed and uncertainty and complicatedness of now. But I can't help thinking that in terms of aura, the Norwalk ladies have it all over me. I study the pages with their photographs, and admire the plainness of their dresses, the set of their jaws, the expression in their eyes. Next to them my credit card and I seem a sorry spectacle indeed. Their sense of purpose shames me. What the country needed from those ladies it asked for, and they provided, straightforwardly; what it wants from me it somehow can't come out and ask. I'm asked to shop more, which really means to spend more, which eventually must mean to work more than I was working before. In previous wars, harder work was a civilian sacrifice that the government didn't hesitate to ask. Nowadays it's apparently unwilling to ask for any sacrifice that might appear to be too painful, too real.

But I *want* it to be real. I think a lot of us do. I feel like an idiot with my tears and shopping cart. I want to participate, to do something—and shopping isn't it. Many of the donors who contributed more than half a billion dollars to a Red Cross fund for the families of terror attack victims became angry when they learned that much of the money would end up not where they had intended but in the Red Cross bureaucracy. People want to express themselves with action. In New York City so many have been showing up recently for jury duty that the courts have had to turn hundreds away; officials said a new surplus of civic consciousness was responsible for the upsurge. I'd be glad if I were asked to—I don't know—drive less or turn the thermostat down or send in seldom-used items of clothing or collect rubber bands or plant a victory garden or join a civilian patrol or use fewer disposable paper products at children's birthday parties. I'd be willing, if asked, just to sit still for a day and meditate on the situation, much in the way that Lincoln used to call for national days of prayer.

A great, shared desire to *do* something is lying around mostly untapped. The best we can manage, it seems, is to show our U.S.A. brand loyalty by putting American flags on our houses and cars. Some businesses across the country even

541

Wake Up, America! This poster, showing a sleeping woman personifying America, was also created by James Montgomery Flagg to get people behind the war effort during World War I. (Bettman/Corbis)

You'll be on the Greatest Team in the World!

YOU'LL hit 'em *hard* and you'll hit 'em *fast* on this All-American team. You'll fly and fight in planes that were built to scorch the sky. You'll wear a pair of silver wings. And, brother, to win those wings you've got to be *good!*

Maybe you'll be the Bombardier, the fellow who presses the button and "lays the eggs." When your ship is over the target, you'll take charge. You'll line up your sights, let go your bombs—and deliver the "knock-out punch."

Maybe you'll be the Navigator, the "quarterback" of the team. With charts and instruments you'll guide your bomber's flight to its objective, and then bring it home again. And if enemy fighters get in your way, you're mighty handy with a .50 caliber machine gun.

Maybe you'll be the Pilot. You'll fly a big, powerful Fortress or Liberator..a fast medium bomber..or a hard-hitting fighter. With hundreds of flying hours behind you, and a fighting crew at your side, no pilot will ever be better prepared for the job that's got to be done.

Do you need a college diploma to be an officer in the

Air Forces? *No!* If you can qualify as an Aviation Cadet, you will be given five months' training (after a brief conditioning period) in one of America's finest colleges. At the same time, you will get dual-control flying instruction to accustom you to the air . . . then go on to eight months of full flight training, during which you will receive a $10,000 life insurance policy paid for by the government.

Will you be thoroughly trained? You'll get training that can't be beat! You'll be instructed by Aces who have been in actual combat in every theater of war . . . men who know how to teach you the "tricks of the trade" that will make you a finer flyer and a better fighter than your enemy.

Will you be well-paid after you've won your wings? If you call $246 to $327 a month good pay, the answer is *yes*. And on graduation you will receive an extra $250 for uniform allowance. Opportunities will exist for rapid advance in rank and pay.

And after the war you will be qualified for leadership in the world's greatest industry—Aviation!

How can you qualify to win your Army wings?

You, too, belong on this fighting team—the U. S. Army Air Forces—as a Bombardier, Navigator or Pilot! And here is what you can do about it right now.

If you are 17 but not yet 18 . . . go to your nearest Aviation Cadet Examining Board . . . take your preliminary examinations to see if you can qualify for the Air Corps Enlisted Reserve. If you qualify, you will receive your Enlisted Reserve insignia . . . but will not be called for training until you are over 18.

If you are 18 but under 27 . . . go to your nearest Aviation Cadet Examining Board . . . see if you can qualify as an Aviation Cadet. If you are in the Army, you may apply through your commanding officer.

If you are under 18 (whether or not you have joined the Air Corps Enlisted Reserve) . . . see your local Civil Air Patrol officers about taking C. A. P. Cadet training—also see your High School adviser about taking H. S. Victory Corps prescribed courses. Both will afford you valuable pre-aviation training.

For complete details—see your nearest Aviation Cadet Examining Board, the commanding officer of the College Training Detachment nearest you or your local Civil Air Patrol.

(Essential workers in War Industry or Agriculture—do not apply).

U. S. ARMY RECRUITING SERVICE

"Nothing'll Stop the Army Air Corps"

◀ *You'll be on the Greatest Team in the World!*, **1943.** This World War II–era recruiting poster emphasizes serving your country as a sport, starting with the line "You'll hit 'em *hard* and you'll hit 'em *fast* on this All-American team."

display in their windows a poster on which the American flag appears as a shopping bag, with two handles at the top. Above the flag-bag are the words "America: Open for Business." Money and the economy have gotten so tangled up in our politics that we forget we're citizens of our government, not its consumers. And the leaders we elect, who got where they are by selling themselves to us with television ads, and who often are only on short loan from the corporate world anyway, think of us as customers who must be kept happy. There's a scarcity of ideas about how to direct all this patriotic feeling because usually the market, not the country, occupies our minds. I'm sure it's possible to transform oneself from salesman to leader, just as it is to go from consumer to citizen. But the shift of identity is awkward, without many precedents, not easily done. In between the two—between selling and leading, between consuming and being citizens, is where our leaders and the rest of us are now.

We see the world beyond our immediate surroundings mostly through television, whose view is not much wider than that of a security peephole in a door. We hear over and over that our lives have forever changed, but the details right in front of us don't look very different, for all that. The forces fighting in Afghanistan are in more danger than we are back home, but perhaps not so much more; everybody knows that when catastrophe comes it could hit anywhere, most likely someplace it isn't expected. Strong patriotic feelings stir us, fill us, but have few means of expressing themselves. We want to be a country, but where do you go to do that? Surely not the mall. When Mayor Giuliani left office at the end of 2001, he said he was giving up the honorable title of mayor for the more honorable title of citizen. He got that right. Citizen is honorable; shopper is not.

544

COMMENT

"When the United States wished to make public its wants, whether for men or money, it found that art was the best medium."

—Joseph Pennell, artist

When was the last time you got promoted?, ▶ **1973.** The U.S. Army slogan in 1973 has become "Today's Army wants to join you," and the copy emphasizes that the Army can help you learn skills and save money; there is no mention of patriotism.

When was the last time you got promoted?

When the only jobs you can get are the jobs anyone can do, they're not very likely to get you anywhere. For example, delivering the office mail, or waiting tables at the local pizza parlor.

Jobs with a future take skill and experience. Today's Army can give you both.

We have over 300 jobs in

fields that offer you a future in the Army or in civilian life. Data processing, intelligence, air operations support, medical, communications, administration, to name a few.

They're jobs we'll pay you to learn. At the same starting salary our men get. With the same opportunity for regular promotions and raises. And the salary you earn in today's Army goes a long way because we provide your meals and housing while medical and dental care are free.

You can save most of your salary, or spend it on the 30 days paid vacation you'll get every year. Or stretch it by buying the things you want at post exchanges where prices are lower than in civilian stores.

And if you would like to continue your education while in the Army, we'll help you. Then help you again after you're out with up to 36 months of financial assistance at the college of your choice.

If you're looking for a job with a future, but want some time off first, we can arrange that too. With our Delayed Entry Option you can sign up for the training you want today, and take up to six months before coming in.

For more information, talk it over with your nearest Army Representative.

Today's Army wants to join you.

goarmy.com, 2001. In January 2001, the U.S. Army replaced its memorable "Be all you can be" campaign with a web, print, and TV campaign that emphasizes individuality and independence: "An army of one." Louis Caldera, who initiated the marketing campaign, says, "They are going to get the ethic of selfless service, duty, honor, and country in basic training . . . but you've got to get them in the door to try selfless service."

COMMENT

"Nearly everything in corporate marketing today is about brand name identification and appealing to a specific segment of the public. But applying marketing 'science' to military recruiting may backfire. . . . The army's new advertising campaign seems likely to fail if it succeeds in recruiting smart, independent-minded young people who find that the army doesn't live up to the image in the ad they saw on *Friends*."

— Lucian K. Truscott IV, 1969 graduate
of West Point and author of *Full Dress Gray*

MESSAGE

In "All-Consuming Patriotism," Ian Frazier says that "out of concern for the economy after the terror attacks, the president said that he wanted us to go about our business, and not stop shopping." Does Frazier regard this presidential mandate as governmental propaganda or not? Do you regard it as propaganda? Do you think the president's advice is comparable to the recruitment posters and ads also included in this cluster? Explain why or why not.

METHOD

An important part of Frazier's essay deals with a little-known Civil War book he cherishes, *Trials and Triumphs: The Record of the Fifty-Fifth Ohio Volunteer Infantry*. Why is this book not only so meaningful to the author but also crucial to the structure of his essay? What does his description of the accounts in the book enable him to accomplish as a writer?

MEDIUM

Since 9/11 the American flag and its multiple depictions have become a ubiquitous presence. Do you think it is appropriate to use the flag for commercial purposes? How do you react when you see it in different commercial contexts? Do you think, for example, that a pizza box or store window is an appropriate medium on which to display the flag? On what grounds do you base your opinion?

THE MALL

COMIC | ESSAY | 4 PHOTOS | MIXED MEDIA

There are many places where Americans can shop — supermarkets, convenience stores or neighborhood stores, car dealerships, downtown shopping centers, flea markets, online retail shops, and specialized discount chains like Home Depot, Toys 'R Us, or Sports Authority (these are known as destination stores because consumers make special trips to shop there). But when the average consumer or the cultural critic thinks about shopping, only one place captures the imagination: the suburban shopping mall.

For many years, people shopped in the "downtown" shopping district of their city, where they could find several competing department stores. But with the enormous demographic shift from the city to the suburbs in the 1950s, and as families became increasingly dependent on automobiles, retailers quickly sensed that the decades-old downtown shopping district was doomed. In 1956, a Jewish immigrant from Austria who had barely escaped the Nazis, Victor Gruen (1903–1980), made the first step toward changing the landscape of America by designing the nation's first entirely enclosed, climate-controlled shopping mall in Edina, Minnesota. In doing so, Gruen not only permanently altered Americans' ideas of public space but also revolutionized traditional patterns of shopping. The following materials explore what the mall has come to mean in American life, both as a place and as a philosophy.

COMMENT

"I am called a retail anthropologist, which makes me uncomfortable, especially around my colleagues in academia who have many more degrees than I do. For whatever combination of reasons,
I've spent my adult life studying people while they shop. I watch how they move through stores and
other commercial environments — restaurants, banks, fast-food joints, movie theaters, car dealerships, post offices, concert halls, malls.

"In fact, you can observe a lot of a community's life in its mall. Families especially tend not to
be on display in many public spaces nowadays. You can find them in places of worship, but they're
on their best behavior, and mostly just standing or sitting. Increasingly, cities are becoming the
province of the rich, the childless, or the poor; I love cities, but America hasn't lived in them for a
long time. The retail arena is the best place I know to learn what people wear and eat and how they
interact with their parents, friends, lovers, and kids.

"We tend to think of the mall as a recent, primarily American phenomenon, and a rather banal
one at that. But the mall has always been with us, in different guises and under other names. Since
virtually the dawn of civilization, we've organized our world in part around the function of shopping. Even the simplest agrarian societies needed places where they might assemble to exchange
goods, and from that basic impulse came everything else — marketplaces, villages, towns, cities.

"Many otherwise fair-minded, intelligent people scorn and despise malls. Some still end up
shopping in them on a regular basis. But they're not proud of it. They may not be swayed by arguments about how the mall is a contemporary version of the souks, bazaars, arcades, bourses, and
markets of old. It's true that malls can harm vulnerable downtowns by drawing shoppers away, and
that they could be much better places — more imaginative, more alive with the human quest for art
and beauty — than they are. But by studying the shopping mall and what goes on there, we can
learn quite a bit about ourselves from a variety of perspectives: economic, aesthetic, geographic,
spiritual, emotional, psychological, sartorial. Just step inside."

— Paco Underhill, founder of a behavioral market research firm, from "Inside the Machine"

549

Peter Bagge, *Malls*. Americans' love/hate relationship with shopping malls is graphically rendered in
Peter Bagge's "Malls," which also succinctly provides a brief history of their evolution. Bagge has served
as editor of R. Crumb's magazine, *Weirdo*, and has published a comic book series, *Hate* (ending in
2001), and graphic novels including *The Bradleys* (1988), *Studs Kirby: The Voice of America* (1989),
Hey Buddy! (1997), *Buddy the Dreamer* (1994), *Fun with Buddy & Lisa* (1995), *Buddy Go Home*
(1998), and *Buddy's Got Three Moms* (1999). His art has appeared in many magazines, including
Details, Spin, Artforum, and Suck.com. This cartoon history first appeared in the August 2002 issue
of *Reason* magazine. (Reprinted with permission from *Reason* magazine. Copyright 2003 by Reason
Foundation, 3415 S. Sepulveda Blvd., Suite 400, Los Angeles, CA 90034. www.reason.com)

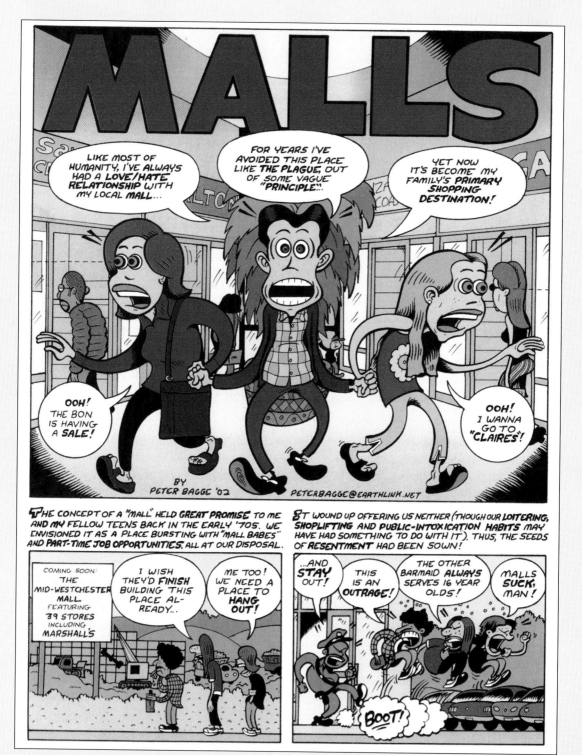

OF COURSE, MALLS WEREN'T DESIGNED SOLELY FOR THE AMUSEMENT OF TEENAGED WASTRELS. THE IDEA BEHIND THEM IS AS OLD AS "SHOPPING" ITSELF: TO PROTECT THE CUSTOMERS AND VENDORS FROM THE ELEMENTS!

OUT! ALL OF YOU!

THIS IS A HOUSE OF PRAYER, NOT A DEN OF THIEVES!

AWW, BUT JESUS, IT'S POURING OUT!

TOSS!

STILL, MOST BUSINESS TRANSACTIONS HAVE ALWAYS TAKEN PLACE WHERE THE MOST FOOT TRAFFIC WAS — THAT BEING IN THE HEART OF CITIES + TOWNS; PLACES THAT ALWAYS APPALLED AGRARIAN SNOBS LIKE TOM JEFFERSON.

... I VIEW GREAT CITIES AS PESTILENTIAL TO THE MORALS, HEALTH AND LIBERTIES OF MAN...

OH THOMAS, GET A GRIP!

WIDESPREAD AUTOMOBILE OWNERSHIP MARKED THE BEGINNING OF THE END OF "MAIN STREET" AND THE RISE OF THE SUBURBAN SHOPPING CENTERS — THE ADVANTAGES OF WHICH WERE LOST ON MANY CRITICS, WHO SUDDENLY WERE FILLED WITH NOSTALGIA FOR THE "OLD WAYS".

...OUR SOCIAL FABRIC IS BEING TORN ASUNDER BY THESE UGLY MONOLITHS!

OVER-RELIANCE ON THE AUTOMOBILE HAS DESTROYED OUR SENSE OF COMMUNITY...

HEY, "MR." COMMUNITY, WANNA CARRY MY GROCERIES HOME FOR ME?

← AN "EGGHEAD"

THESE EARLY SHOPPING CENTERS WERE QUICKLY REPLACED THEMSELVES BY ENCLOSED SHOPPING CENTERS, OR "MALLS". SOON EVERY SUBURBANITE IN AMERICA WAS WITHIN DRIVING DISTANCE OF ONE, WHILE THEIR CRITICS BECOME EVEN MORE VOCIFEROUS IN THEIR CONDEMNATION OF "MALL CULTURE."

LOOK AT ALL THIS SPRAWL!

PRECIOUS FARMLAND IS BEING GOBBLED UP BY PARKING LOTS!

WE'RE RUNNING OUT OF FARMS?

?!?

MALLS CONTINUED TO EXPAND INTO ONE-STOP SHOPPING AND SERVICE DESTINATIONS, RENDERING DOWNTOWNS ALL BUT OBSOLETE — WHILE "SPRAWLBUSTERS" CONTINUE TO RAIL AGAINST THIS NATURAL (OR TO THEM, UNNATURAL) TREND.

...NO MORE MOM 'N' POP STORES...PETITIONERS BANNED... COMPLETE CORPORATE TAKEOVER... IMPROPER DRAINAGE... LIGHT POLLUTION...

HAVE NO FEAR! "GINGER" IS HERE!

IT'S THE ANSWER TO ALL YOUR PROBLEMS!

MEANWHILE, THE OLD "MAIN STREET"S FOUGHT BACK WITH SUCH TOKEN GESTURES AS BRICK SIDEWALKS, PEDESTRIAN ONLY STREETS AND PUBLIC ART PROJECTS — ALL OF WHICH PROVED TO BE MOSTLY IN VAIN, HOWEVER.

...WORKS SUCH AS THESE CONTRIBUTE TO THE SENSE OF "PLACE" THAT TRADITIONAL COMMUNITIES LIKE OURS PROVIDE...

WHO CARES?

I JUST WANT YOU TO GET RID OF THESE GODDAMNED PARKING METERS!

551

MALLS FINALLY MET THEIR MATCH IN THE FORM OF GIANT DISCOUNT "BIG BOX" STORES LIKE **WAL-MART** AND **COSTCO,** WHO WISELY REFUSE TO SHARE REAL ESTATE OR PARKING SPACE WITH ANY POTENTIAL **COMPETITION.**

THESE MEGASTORES HAVE PUT MANY **DEPARTMENT STORE** CHAINS OUT OF BUSINESS, AND THE LOSS OF THEIR "ANCHOR STORES" HAS LED TO A PROLIFERATION OF "DEAD MALLS" —YET EVEN **THOSE** HAVE THEIR NOSTALGIC DEFENDERS!

ONE RESPONSE TO THIS THREAT HAS BEEN TO TURN MALLS INTO **VACATION DESTINATIONS** — SUCH AS THE "MALL OF AMERICA," WHICH FEATURES RIDES, NIGHTCLUBS AND **GUIDED TOURS** TO GO ALONG WITH ITS 400-PLUS SHOPS!

DOWNTOWNS ALSO CONTINUE TO FIGHT BACK BY "MALL-IFYING" THEIR SHOPPING DISTRICTS—AS WELL AS REVIVING AND EXPANDING THEIR OLD "FARMER'S MARKETS," WHICH ALSO DOUBLE AS **TOURIST TRAPS** !

THE WORKING-CLASS APPEAL OF THE MEGASTORES HAS INSPIRED SOME MALLS TO "UPSCALE" IN ORDER TO ATTRACT **MORE AFFLUENT CUSTOMERS** — WHILE SIMULTANEOUSLY **ALIENATING** SHOPPERS WHO DON'T FIT IN WITH THEIR NEW "IMAGE"...

ONE UNIQUE RESPONSE IS THE **CROSSROADS MALL** IN SUBURBAN SEATTLE — A FORMER "DEAD MALL" THAT NOW SERVES AS A BUSTLING **COMMUNITY CENTER** FOR ITS MIXED IMMIGRANT NEIGHBORHOOD, COMPLETE WITH A LIBRARY AND EVEN ITS OWN **POLICE STATION**...

FOR THE LONGEST TIME I WAS A RABID **MALL-HATER.** NOT ONLY DID THEY NOT FIGURE INTO MY CHOSEN "URBAN PEDESTRIAN" LIFESTYLE, BUT THEY ALSO REPRESENTED THE **"SUBURBAN WASTELAND" MENTALITY** THAT I SPENT MY ENTIRE YOUNG ADULTHOOD TRYING TO **ESCAPE** FROM.

BECOMING A **PARENT** CHANGED ALL THAT. SUDDENLY WE **HAD** TO SHOP WITH A CAR JUST TO BE ABLE TO LUG THE **KID** TO AND FRO — AS WELL AS TO HAUL ALL OF OUR **PURCHASES.** PLUS, HAVING A **STROLLER** MAKES THE MALL A VERY **CONVENIENT** PLACE TO SHOP!

I ALSO NOTICED THAT THE MALL WAS FAR MORE CON-VENIENT FOR ANYONE IN A **WHEELCHAIR,** OLD FOLKS WHO DON'T WANT TO BE **HURRIED,** AND ADOLESCENT GIRLS WHO WANT TO HANG OUT WITHOUT BEING **HARASSED...**

NOW WHENEVER I HEAR SOMEONE HOLDING FORTH ON WHAT **EVIL INSTITUTIONS** MALLS ARE I CRINGE WITH EMBARRASSMENT, SINCE IT REMINDS ME OF WHAT A SELF-RIGHTEOUS BLOWHARD I USED TO BE!

RECENTLY MY WIFE AND I DECIDED TO TAKE IN A DINNER AND A MOVIE **DOWNTOWN** FOR THE FIRST TIME IN A WHILE — FORGETTING UNTIL IT WAS TOO LATE WHAT A PAIN **PARKING** AND **STREET PEOPLE** CAN BE DOWN THERE...

MAYBE WE'VE JUST GOTTEN **OLD** AND **SOFT**—AND SO WHAT IF WE **HAVE?** — BUT ON THE WAY HOME WE CAME TO AN **AGREEMENT:** THAT FROM NOW ON WE'D SPEND OUR EVENINGS OUT AT THE **LOCAL MALL!**

553

David Guterson, *Enclosed. Encyclopedic. Endured.: One Week at the Mall of America.* One of the finest essays on the mall experience was written by novelist David Guterson (b. 1956), who spent a week visiting Minnesota's world-famous Mall of America shortly after it opened. Guterson has written for *Sports Illustrated* and *Harper's*, where he is now a contributing editor. His books include *Snow Falling on Cedars*, which won the 1995 PEN/Faulkner Award; a collection of short stories, *The Country Ahead of Us, the Country Behind* (1996); *East of the Mountains* (2003); and *Our Lady of the Forest* (2003). The text reprinted here has been excerpted from a longer version that first appeared in the August 1993 issue of *Harper's*.

David Guterson

ENCLOSED. ENCYCLOPEDIC. ENDURED.: ONE WEEK AT THE MALL OF AMERICA

Last April, on a visit to the new Mall of America near Minneapolis, I carried with me the public-relations press kit provided for the benefit of reporters. It included an assortment of "fun facts" about the mall: 140,000 hot dogs sold each week, 10,000 permanent jobs, 44 escalators and 17 elevators, 12,750 parking places, 13,300 short tons of steel, $1 million in cash disbursed weekly from 8 automatic-teller machines. Opened in the summer of 1992, the mall was built on the 78-acre site of the former Metropolitan Stadium, a five-minute drive from the Minneapolis–St. Paul International Airport. With 4.2 million square feet of floor space—including twenty-two times the retail footage of the average American shopping center—the Mall of America was "the largest fully enclosed combination retail and family entertainment complex in the United States."

Eleven thousand articles, the press kit warned me, had already been written on the mall. Four hundred trees had been planted in its gardens, $625 million had been spent to build it, 350 stores had been leased. Three thousand bus tours were anticipated each year along with a half-million Canadian visitors and 200,000 Japanese tourists. Sales were projected at $650 million for 1993 and at $1 billion for 1996. Donny and Marie Osmond had visited the mall, as had Janet

Jackson and Sally Jesse Raphael, Arnold Schwarzenegger, and the 1994 Winter Olympic Committee. The mall was five times larger than Red Square and twenty times larger than St. Peter's Basilica; it incorporated 2.3 miles of hallways and almost twice as much steel as the Eiffel Tower. It was also home to the nation's largest indoor theme park, a place called Knott's Camp Snoopy.

On the night I arrived, a Saturday, the mall was spotlit dramatically in the manner of a Las Vegas casino. It resembled, from the outside, a castle or fort, the Emerald City or Never-Never Land, impossibly large and vaguely unreal, an unbroken, windowless multi-storied edifice the size of an airport terminal. Surrounded by parking lots and new freeway ramps, monolithic and imposing in the manner of a walled city, it loomed brightly against the Minnesota night sky with the disturbing magnetism of a mirage.

I knew already that the Mall of America had been imagined by its creators not merely as a marketplace but as a national tourist attraction, an immense zone of entertainments. Such a conceit raised provocative questions, for our architecture testifies to our view of ourselves and to the condition of our souls. Large buildings stand as markers in the lives of nations and in the stream of a people's history. Thus I could only ask myself: Here was a new structure that had cost more than half a billion dollars to erect—what might it tell us about ourselves? If the Mall of America was part of America, what was that going to mean?

I passed through one of the mall's enormous entrance ways and took myself inside. Although from a distance the Mall of America had appeared menacing—exuding the ambience of a monstrous hallucination—within it turned out to be simply a shopping mall, certainly more vast than other malls but in tone and aspect, design and feel, not readily distinguishable from them. Its nuances were instantly familiar as the generic features of the American shopping mall at the tail end of the twentieth century: polished stone, polished tile, shiny chrome and brass, terrazzo floors, gazebos. From third-floor vistas, across vaulted spaces, the Mall of America felt endlessly textured—glass-enclosed elevators, neon-tube lighting, bridges, balconies, gas lamps, vaulted skylights—and densely crowded with hordes of people circumambulating in an endless promenade. Yet despite the mall's expansiveness, it elicited claustrophobia, sensory deprivation, and unnerving disorientation. Everywhere I went I spied other pilgrims who had found, like me, that the straight way was lost and that the YOU ARE HERE landmarks on the map kiosks referred to nothing in particular.

Getting lost, feeling lost, being lost—these states of mind are intentional features of the mall's psychological terrain. There are, one notices, no clocks or windows, nothing to distract the shopper's psyche from the alternate reality the mall conjures. Here we are free to wander endlessly and to furtively watch our fellow wanderers, thousands upon thousands of milling strangers who have come with the intent of losing themselves in the mall's grand, stimulating design. For a few hours we share some common ground—a fantasy of infinite commodities and comforts—and then we drift apart forever. The mall exploits our acquisitive

Mall spaces. These mall spaces capture a sense of the historical continuity of the spaces humans create to shop within. (*The Markets of Trajan, Rome*, Scala/Art Resource, NY; *The Crystal Palace, London, 1851*, © Historical Picture Archive/Corbis; *The Houston Galleria*, © Lowell Georgia/Corbis; *The Mall of America, Bloomington*, Mark Erickson/Getty Images)

instincts without honoring our communal requirements, our eternal desire for discourse and intimacy, needs that until the twentieth century were traditionally met in our marketplaces but that are not met at all in giant shopping malls.

On this evening a few thousand young people had descended on the mall in pursuit of alcohol and entertainment. They had come to Gators, Hooters, and Knuckleheads, Puzzles, Fat Tuesday, and Ltl Ditty's. At Players, a sports bar, the woman beside me introduced herself as "the pregnant wife of an Iowa pig farmer" and explained that she had driven five hours with friends to "do the mall party scene together." She left and was replaced by Kathleen from Minnetonka, who claimed to have "a real shopping thing—I can't go a week without buying new clothes. I'm not fulfilled until I buy something."

Later a woman named Laura arrived, with whom Kathleen was acquainted. "I *am* the mall," she announced ecstatically upon discovering I was a reporter. "I'd move in here if I could bring my dog," she added. "This place is heaven, it's a *mecca*."

"We egg each other on," explained Kathleen, calmly puffing on a cigarette. "It's like, sort of, an addiction."

"You want the truth?" Laura asked. "I'm constantly suffering from megamall withdrawal. I come here all the time."

Kathleen: "It's a sickness. It's like cocaine or something; it's a drug."

Laura: "Kathleen's got this thing about buying, but I just need to *be* here. If I buy something it's an added bonus."

Kathleen: "She buys stuff all the time; don't listen."

Laura: "Seriously, I feel sorry for other malls. They're so small and *boring*."

Kathleen seemed to think about this: "Ridgedale Mall," she blurted finally. She rolled her eyes and gestured with her cigarette. "Oh, my God, Laura. Why did we even *go* there?"

There is, of course, nothing naturally abhorrent in the human impulse to dwell in marketplaces or the urge to buy, sell, and trade. Rural Americans traditionally looked forward to the excitement and sensuality of market day; Native Americans traveled long distances to barter and trade at sprawling, festive encampments. In Persian bazaars and in the ancient Greek agoras the very soul of the community was preserved and could be seen, felt, heard, and smelled as it might be nowhere else. All over the planet the humblest of people have always gone to market with hope in their hearts and in expectation of something beyond mere goods—seeking a place where humanity is temporarily in ascendance, a palette for the senses, one another.

But the illicit possibilities of the marketplace also have long been acknowledged. The Persian bazaar was closed at sundown; the Greek agora was off-limits to those who had been charged with certain crimes. One myth of the Old West we still carry with us is that market day presupposes danger; the faithful were advised to make purchases quickly and repair without delay to the farm, lest their attraction to the pleasures of the marketplace erode their purity of spirit.

In our collective discourse the shopping mall appears with the tract house, the freeway, and the backyard barbecue as a product of the American postwar years, a testament to contemporary necessities and desires and an invention not only peculiarly American but peculiarly of our own era too. Yet the mall's varied and far-flung predecessors—the covered bazaars of the Middle East, the stately arcades of Victorian England, Italy's vaulted and skylit gallerias, Asia's monsoon-protected urban markets—all suggest that the rituals of indoor shopping, although in their nuances not often like our own, are nevertheless broadly known. The late twentieth-century American contribution has been to transform the enclosed bazaar into an economic institution that is vastly profitable yet socially enervated, one that redefines in fundamental ways the human relationship to the marketplace. At the Mall of America—an extreme example—we discover ourselves thoroughly lost among strangers in a marketplace designed to serve no community needs.

In the strict sense the Mall of America is not a marketplace at all—the soul of a community expressed as a *place*—but rather a tourist attraction. Its promoters have peddled it to the world at large as something more profound than a local marketplace and as a destination with deep implications. "I believe we can make Mall of America stand for all of America," asserted the mall's general manager, John Wheeler, in a promotional video entitled *There's a Place for Fun in Your Life.* "I believe there's a shopper in all of us," added the director of marketing, Maureen Hooley. The mall has memorialized its opening-day proceedings by producing a celebratory videotape: Ray Charles singing "America the Beautiful," a laser show followed by fireworks, "The Star-Spangled Banner" and "the Stars and Stripes Forever," the Gatlin Brothers, and Peter Graves. "Mall of America . . . ," its narrator intoned. "The name alone conjures up images of greatness, of a retail complex so magnificent it could only happen in America."

Indeed, on the day the mall opened, Miss America visited. The mall's logo—a red, white, and blue star bisected by a red, white, and blue ribbon—decorated everything from the mall itself to coffee mugs and the flanks of buses. The idea, director of tourism Colleen Hayes told me, was to position America's largest mall as an institution on the scale of Disneyland or the Grand Canyon, a place simultaneously iconic and totemic, a revered symbol of the United States and a mecca to which the faithful would flock in pursuit of all things purchasable.

561

COMMENT

"Not only is shopping melting into everything, but everything is melting into shopping. Through successive waves of expansion — each more extensive and pervasive than the previous — shopping has methodically encroached on a widening spectrum of territories so that it is now, arguably, the defining activity of public life. Why has it become such a basic aspect of our existence? Because it is synonymous with perhaps the most significant and fundamental development to give form to modern life: the unfettered growth and acceptance of the market economy as the dominant global standard. Shopping is the medium by which the market has solidified its grip on our spaces, buildings, cities, activities, and lives. It is the material outcome of the degree to which the market economy has shaped our surroundings, and ultimately ourselves."

—architect Sze Tsung Leong, from ". . . And Then There Was Shopping."
in the *Harvard Design School Guide to Shopping*

562

Barbara Kruger, *I shop therefore I am.* One of the main features of contemporary art is the way it has absorbed commercial media for its own aesthetic and political purposes. A leader in this movement is the artist Barbara Kruger (b. 1945), who mixes text and image in a mesmerizing fashion that resembles the slogans and graphics of mass persuasion, yet with surprising twists and juxtapositions. She has taken issues of feminism and social justice into unaccustomed territories: billboards that say "We need health care and housing," matchbook covers that read "Your comfort is my silence," T-shirts that claim "Don't Die for Love: Stop Domestic Violence," and shopping bags with Kruger's now-famous slogan, "I shop therefore I am." Kruger has playfully adopted the famous statement made by French philosopher René Descartes (1596–1650), "I think, therefore I am," and placed her revised statement of being on a card that has the exact dimensions of a credit card. Since the mid-1970s, Kruger has had numerous individual and group exhibits. In 2000, she received a comprehensive retrospective at the Museum of Contemporary Art in Los Angeles and at the Whitney Museum of American Art in New York City. *I shop therefore I am* was taken from the book *Thinking of You* (1999). (Barbara Kruger, "Untitled" (I shop therefore I am). 111" × 113", photographic silkscreen/vinyl, 1987. Courtesy Mary Boone Gallery, New York)

563

COMMENT

"Direct address has motored my work from the very beginning. I like it because it cuts through the grease. It's a really economic and forthright approach to the viewer. It's everywhere and people are used to it. They look at each other when they talk (most of the time). They watch TV. Talking heads and pronouns rule, in the best and worst sense of the word. I'm interested in how identities are constructed, how stereotypes are formed, how narratives sort of congeal and become history."

— Barbara Kruger

564

MESSAGE

The architect Sze Tsung Leong notes that "Not only is shopping melting into everything, but everything is melting into shopping." In what ways does David Guterson's essay on the Mall of America reinforce that observation? What kinds of experiences does Guterson find that demonstrate this two-way melting process?

METHOD

Consider Paco Underhill's comment on "retail anthropology." What do you think a retail anthropologist studies? What methods does he or she employ to study shopping patterns and behavior? What academic disciplines would be most useful for someone who undertakes such studies? Would a retail anthropologist look at shopping malls differently than David Guterson or Peter Bagge? Why or why not?

MEDIUM

Sze Tsung Leong calls shopping a medium. Do you agree? What do you think he means? Consider the various media you are familiar with. How is shopping similar to any of these media? In Guterson's descriptive essay and Bagge's comic, can you see any indications that shopping could correctly be called a medium? Explain why or why not.

CELEBRITY

ESSAY | 2 PHOTOS | 2 ADS | MAGAZINE COVER

What makes a celebrity? As the historian Daniel J. Boorstin wryly puts it, celebrities are people known for their "well-knownness." That is, to become a celebrity, your attainments or accomplishments matter less than the extent of media coverage you receive — being well known in itself will suffice to turn anyone into a celebrity. An obscure young White House intern with very few personal achievements can by virtue of a scandal become more universally known than, say, the president of Harvard University or 95 percent of the U.S. Senate. This is largely because mass media coverage generates more mass media coverage until it becomes nearly impossible to escape the blitz of stories, interviews, photographs, video clips, talk show gossip, and editorials. But such "instant" celebrities like Monica Lewinsky are still rare compared to the more common celebrities — movie stars, recording artists, and athletes — spawned by the various entertainment industries and supported by a wide network of publicity channels, from magazines like *In Style* or *People* to such TV shows as *Larry King Live* or *The Tonight Show with Jay Leno*.

Neal Gabler's essay deals with celebrity in its most ordinary fashion — the ongoing life stories we follow in magazines, tabloids, and television shows. But celebrity can reach a more transcendent level where the personality achieves a mythic significance. Often — but not always — such celebrity is reserved for those who die young or in mid-career (Elvis Presley, John Lennon, Marilyn Monroe, John F. Kennedy, Diana, princess of Wales); living mythic celebrities include Michael Jackson and Muhammad Ali. At this level the celebrity becomes an **icon**. Originally a term that referred to the image of a holy person, "icon" derives from the ancient Greek *eikon*, meaning a likeness or image. The word, however, has grown into a key term of popular culture studies, referring to such personalities as those above who have achieved a superabundance of fame and are so universally known that their names never need appear with their photos for identification.

Neal Gabler, *Our Celebrities, Ourselves.* Do celebrities represent something essential to American life, more significant than the fact of simply being well known? In this essay the cultural historian Neal Gabler attempts to move beyond Boorstin's comment by suggesting a new way to interpret the powerful role of celebrities in our culture. For Gabler, "one may have to think of celebrity in an entirely new way — not as a status that is conferred by publicity, but as a narrative form, written in the medium of life." Gabler has taught at the University of Michigan and Pennsylvania State University. A commentator on ABC's *Good Morning America,* he has published widely; his most recent book is *Life the Movie: How Entertainment Conquered Reality* (1998). This essay appeared in the March 14, 2003, issue of *The Chronicle of Higher Education.*

Neal Gabler

OUR CELEBRITIES, OURSELVES

It has been more than 40 years since the historian Daniel Boorstin, in a now famously clever turn of phrase, defined a celebrity as someone who is known for being well known. If he were writing about celebrity today, Boorstin might describe it less flippantly as one of America's most prominent cottage industries and one of television's fastest-growing genres — one in which spent entertainers can find an afterlife by turning their daily existence into real-life situation comedy or tragedy. Anyone caring to stargaze can see *The Osbournes, The Anna Nicole Smith Show, Star Dates, The Surreal Life,* and the network prime-time celebrity interviews conducted by Barbara Walters, Diane Sawyer, Jane Pauley, and others. A reality series for VH1 capturing the life of the former star Liza Minnelli was derailed by a spat between the network and the principals. Meanwhile, cable networks continue to troll for celebrities eager to expose their lives to the public. Programs on the drawing boards include one in which over-the-hill stars spend the weekend with typical families, and another in which stars return to their hometowns and revisit their roots.

When Boorstin was writing in the early '60s, celebrity was one of those absurdities of contemporary culture — a large and ever-growing class of public figures for which there had been no precedent. Celebrities existed not to entertain, though they usually were entertainers, but rather to be publicized. Their talent, as Boorstin put it, was to grab the spotlight, whether or not they had done anything to deserve it. Now they have not only become an entertainment themselves, a kind of ambulatory show, but are also a cultural force with tremendous appeal, though exactly what that appeal is has been hard to determine. Most conventional analysts, from the popular historian Barbara Goldsmith to the pundit Andrew Sullivan, find celebrity a form of transport—a vicarious fantasy that lifts audiences out of the daily grind. Others, like Joshua Gamson in *Claims to Fame: Celebrity in Contemporary America,* see celebrity-watching as a ritual of empowerment through deconstruction. The audience doesn't seek to be elevated; it seeks to bring the celebrities back to earth. Still others, notably the rulers of the media, attribute the rapid rise of celebrity to mundane financial considerations, like the cheapness of programming real-life celebrities as opposed to fictional stories, and to the power of celebrities to sell magazines and tabloids by appearing on the cover.

There is no doubt some truth to each of those explanations—particularly the last one—but none of them fully expresses the range and power of celebrity in contemporary America, or its rampant march through the culture. None really gets to the root of the matter. To do that, one may have to think of celebrity in an entirely new way—not as a status that is conferred by publicity, but as a narrative form, written in the medium of life, that is similar to narratives in movies, novels, and television.

The only difference, really, is that since it is written in the medium of life, it requires another medium, be it television or print, to bridge the gap between the narrative lived and the narrative watched. In fact, celebrity narratives are so pervasive, with so many being generated, that they have subordinated other narratives and commandeered other media, until one could argue that life itself has become the dominant medium of the new century, and celebrity its most compelling product. Though purists will blanch at the thought, celebrity may even be the art of the age.

When you think of celebrity as a form of narrative art—the romances and divorces, the binges, the dysfunctions, the triumphs, the transgressions—you can immediately appreciate one of its primary appeals, which is the appeal of any good story. Boorstin was wrong: Celebrities aren't known for being well known. They are known for living out real-life melodramas, which is why anyone from Elizabeth Taylor to Joey Buttafuoco can be a celebrity. All one needs is a good story and a medium in which to retail it, and the media, always in desperate need of a story, are only too happy to oblige. And so we get the saga of Ozzy Osbourne, one-time Goth-rock star now stumbling through life as an addled dad to his own teenagers, or Whitney Houston insisting that she isn't addicted to drugs even as she crumbles before our eyes, or Mariah Carey telling us how she has rebounded from a nervous breakdown (she was really just exhausted) and a series of career disasters.

Of course, conventional narratives can provide equally riveting tales, but celebrity has advantages over fiction, not the least of which is novelty. Traditional narrative forms are so familiar to us now, especially with the proliferation of television programs and the staggering number of books published—well over 100,000 each year—that they have become exhausted, attenuated, predictable. We feel as if we've seen it all before. Celebrity is an antidote to that sense of

567

Jeff Koons, *Michael Jackson and Bubbles.* *Michael Jackson and Bubbles* (1988) forms part of a series of works Koons calls *Banality.* The auction house Sotheby's estimated that the ceramic statue of the pop star and his pet monkey would sell for $3 to 4 million; an anonymous buyer spent a record-breaking $5.6 million to take it home. (Image courtesy of the San Francisco Museum of Modern Art. Purchased through the Marian and Bernard Messanger Fund)

■ *The art critic Christopher Knight has written about Jeff Koons: "He turns the traditional cliché of the work of art inside out. Rather than embodying a spiritual or expressive essence of a highly individual artist, art here is composed from a distinctly American set of conventional middle-class values." In your opinion, how well does that comment apply to* Michael Jackson and Bubbles? *How can a piece of sculpture, like this one, be said to be composed from middle-class values? How can an artist use subject matter, style, technique, or other factors to present complex ideas?*

COMMENT

"Jeff Koons can say more in a single piece of art than most writers could say in a novel. Pop culture and high art collide in his artwork to reveal the truths of modern culture — especially its emphasis on materialism, celebrity, and consumerism. Nowhere is his genius for subverting reality more apparent than in his groundbreaking 1988 porcelain sculpture, *Michael Jackson and Bubbles*. Taking as his subject the undisputed King of Pop and his chimpanzee companion, Koons created a work that comments not only on Jackson's unique celebrity but on the very issues of identity and idolatry. The medium is very much the message in this sculpture, as porcelain's slick and seamless surface mimics the impenetrable public image that Jackson created for himself. Koons has created a commentary on the pop star that is at once impenetrable and inherently fragile, an icon made of clay, glazed and gilded to perfection."

—Sotheby's press release, New York, April 3, 2001

exhaustion. Though celebrity narratives themselves have certain conventions — already, the idea of a famous eccentric displaced into normal life, which *The Osbournes* introduced a year ago, has been stolen by Anna Nicole Smith — they also have a *frisson*[1] that so-called imaginative narratives lack.

Part of that *frisson* is the intensification of one of the staples of any form of storytelling: suspense. Readers or viewers always want to know what's going to happen next, and there are some readers for whom that tension is so excruciating that they race to the end of the book for the outcome so that they can then read comfortably and without anxiety. Celebrity, playing out in real time, obviously has suspense, since there is no author to imagine the finish, only life itself to devise the next scene. One never knows what will happen. Who knew that Sharon Osbourne would be diagnosed with cancer? Who knew that Michael Jackson would dangle his infant son from a hotel balcony, or that his nose would erode into a nub after multiple plastic surgeries? Who knew whether Winona Ryder would be convicted or acquitted of her shoplifting charges, or what the sentence would be? Who knows whether Jennifer Lopez and Ben Affleck will be wed or whether something will happen to spoil their idyll? No one knows. The scenes just keep unspooling, and we wait, like Dickens's 19th-century readers eagerly snatching the next installment of his new novel, or like the moviegoers in the '30s watching the weekly chapters of a serial — only it is not just the *what* that we anticipate, it is the *when* or even the *if*. Fictional narratives have closure. They end, and the characters are frozen in time. Celebrity narratives resist closure. They go on and on and on.

569

---

[1] *Frisson:* French word meaning a moment of excitement; here the author uses it to mean the intense thrill experienced in the climax of a suspenseful narrative. (—Ed.)

Celebrity has another advantage over conventional narratives. All narratives depend on our emotional connection to the material—not only on our anticipation of what will happen, but also on our caring about what happens. In the case of fictional tales, we must, in the timeworn phrase, suspend our disbelief, because we know that what we are watching or reading is not real, although to be conscious of the unreality would seriously undermine, if not destroy, our sense of engagement. We must believe that these are not fictional creations but people, and that there is something at stake in the outcome of their story. That is one reason Henry James insisted on "felt life" as his aesthetic standard.

Great works still compel us to suspend our disbelief and convince us that we are watching life itself, but that is a harder and harder sell at a time when many Americans, particularly younger ones, are aware of narrative manipulations and regard all imaginative fiction as counterfeit. Celebrity, on the other hand, doesn't require one to suspend disbelief, because it is real, or at least purports to be. The stakes are real, too. Sharon Osbourne may eventually die of her cancer. Kelly Clarkson would get a record contract if she won *American Idol.* The various celebrities who beam at us from the cover of *People* each week will find romance or will recover or will succeed—or they won't. Either way, something is at stake. There are consequences that we will be able to see down the road. It matters.

Finally, there is the appeal of voyeurism that is heightened precisely because celebrity is unavoidably contrasted with the fictional narratives in which most celebrities find themselves. For many fans today, the roles that celebrities play, both on television and in movies, and the roles they assume as they project themselves in the media, operate as a kind of disguise. They obscure the real person. Celebrity purportedly allows us to peek behind the disguise and see the real person in real joy or torment. This has resulted in an odd reversal that further underscores the power of celebrity. There was a time when celebrities, with a few exceptions, interested us only because of the work they did; their movies, books, albums, TV shows piqued our curiosity. We wanted to know more. But the ratio of interest in the work to interest in the personalities within the work has changed. Now the work they do serves as a curtain that celebrity draws, but since celebrities almost always have a larger appeal than that work—more people certainly know about the Osbournes

570

Timothy Greenfield-Sanders, *Jeff Koons.* Celebrity seems the goal of every career—athlete, artist, actor, activist. Here artist Jeff Koons poses with a backdrop of his own choosing for a *GQ* spread. Koons was born in York, Pennsylvania, in 1955 and studied at both the Maryland College of Art and the Art Institute of Chicago. In the late 1970s he traded on the New York Stock Exchange to support his career as an artist, which from the start concentrated on popular culture and such everyday commodities as vacuum cleaners and inflatable toys. This portrait appeared in the September 2001 issue of *GQ* magazine. (© Timothy Greenfield-Sanders)

than buy Ozzy's albums, just as more people are following the exploits of J. Lo and Ben Affleck than watch their movies—the work is almost an excuse for the celebrity. In effect, you need a curtain so that you can reveal what is behind it. Celebrity, then, is the real narrative—the real achievement.

After the terrible events of 9/11, some predicted that the days of celebrity obsession were over, and that Americans would prefer the comforts of closure to the roilings of reality. It hasn't turned out that way. If anything, 9/11 itself delivered a narrative of such extraordinary impact that it was impossible for fictional narratives to equal or approximate it, and it may even have created a new aesthetic divide—not between good stories and formulaic ones, but between real stories and imagined ones. In that context, celebrity, for all its seeming triviality and irrelevance, survives and thrives because it still has the mark of authenticity.

That element of authenticity is critical in understanding the public's attraction not only to the text of celebrity, but also to its subtext, without which celebrity would just be a bundle of melodramatic, albeit real, stories. The deeper appeal of these narratives is that they address one of the central tensions in contemporary America: the tension between artifice and authenticity, between the image and the reality.

The celebrity narrative is especially well suited to reify that issue. One is likely to think of celebrities as creatures of artifice. They wear makeup and costumes (even when they are not before the cameras, the hottest ones are dressed by designers), they rely on public-relations stunts and gossip to promote themselves, and they play roles and affect attitudes. That isn't just the public's view. Celebrities often think of themselves in the same way. Cary Grant was once quoted, perhaps apocryphally, as having said that it wasn't easy being Cary Grant. Presumably he meant that the persona was vastly different from the person who inhabited it, and that the latter was always having to work to become the former.

That idea—of a distance between the celebrity as public figure and the person within the celebrity narrative—is, indeed, the basis for almost every celebrity narrative that features an entertainer, as opposed to narratives, like those of Joey Buttafuoco or John Wayne Bobbitt or Kato Kaelin, that create the celebrity in the first place, out of notoriety. As I wrote in *Life the Movie,* virtually every celebrity profile, be it in *People, Vanity Fair, The New Yorker,* or on *Entertainment Tonight* or *Access Hollywood,* focuses on the celebrity's battle to find himself or herself, to achieve some genuineness, to understand what really constitutes happiness instead of settling for the Hollywood conception of happiness.

These stories are all chronicles of self-discovery. Now that she is rid of Tom Cruise, Nicole Kidman can find herself. Having broken up with her boyfriend, Justin Timberlake, Britney Spears is flailing about trying to find herself. Winona Ryder's shoplifting was a cry for help to enable her to find herself. Whitney Houston is now in a state of denial, but she will eventually have to find herself or perish. Lost in romance, drugs, abuse, failure, breakdowns—you name it—

celebrities must fight through the layers of image to discover who they really are. Whether that is just more public-relations blather or not, those are the stories we read and see every day.

It is the same process that is charted on the new celebrity television shows. Ozzy Osbourne may be brain-fried and distracted, but his life, for all its oddities and even freakishness, is touchingly ordinary in its emotional groundedness. Ozzy has found himself in his family, which makes the program remarkably old-fashioned and life-affirming. Next to the F-word, the word most often used on the program is "love." Similarly, Anna Nicole Smith, the former *Playboy* center-fold now overweight and bovine and searching for love, may be a moron, but there is something attractive in her almost pathetic ordinariness beneath all her attempts at grandeur. Watching her and Ozzy and the minor stars from old sit-coms now looking for love on *Star Dates,* one is reminded not how different these celebrities are from us but how similar they are once they have recognized the supposed falsity of the celebrity way of life.

All of that may seem a very long way from the lives of those who read and watch the celebrity narrative—us. Not many Americans, after all have had to struggle with the sorts of things, like romantic whirligigs, drug detoxification, and sudden career spirals, that beset celebrities. And yet in many respects, celebrity is just ordinary American life writ large and more intense. In an image-conscious society, where nearly everyone has access to the tools of self-invention and self-promotion—makeup, designer clothes, status symbols, and quirks of behavior, language, and attitude—people are forced to opt for a persona or else to find out who they really are. That is the modern condition. Each of us, to a greater or lesser degree, is fighting the same battle as the celebrities, which is why celebrity, for all its obvious entertainment value, resonates psychically in a way that few modern fictional narratives do. Celebrity doesn't transport us from the niggling problems of daily life. It amplifies and refines them in an exciting narrative context.

And so we keep watching as we might watch any soap opera, engaged by the melodrama, or any sitcom, amused by the comedy. We watch not because, as Boorstin wrote, we are too benumbed by artifice to recognize the difference between celebrities and people of real accomplishment who are more deserving of our attention. Rather we watch because we understand, intuitively or not, that these celebrities are enacting a kind of modern parable of identity, with all its ridiculousness and all its tragedy. We watch because in their celebrity—Ozzy's and Anna Nicole's and Whitney's and Winona's and J. Lo's and Mariah's and even Jacko's—we somehow manage to find ourselves.

573

L'Oréal

Official Partner of the Cannes Festival.

Laetitia Casta Jennifer Lopez Virginie Ledoyen Claudia Schiffer

Andie MacDowell Milla Jovovich Kate Moss Gong-Li

L'Oréal has always had a
passion for beauty, film stars
and their unforgettable faces.
Today we offer the best
in beauty to all
the women of the world.
Because they're worth it.

L'Oréal, *Celebrity Beauty,* **2000, and Georges Marciano,** *Anna Nicole Smith,* **2001.**
Companies often use celebrities to advertise their products. Anna Nicole Smith, the cover girl of the Guess/Georges Marciano ad, is famous for nothing much more than her life and her ability to market herself as interesting. The celebrity actresses and models in the L'Oréal ad don't necessarily use L'Oréal products — but the company hopes that we associate their "unforgettable beauty" with L'Oréal. (The Advertising Archive, Ltd.)

576

Time **cover, September 8, 1997.** Not all celebrities occupy the same level of public esteem. Some — like Marilyn Monroe, Jacqueline Kennedy Onassis, or Elvis Presley — become cultural icons, their images instantly recognized and their status often ensured by attention that extends far past the monthly magazine or TV interview. All such icons are celebrities, but few celebrities can be called icons; reaching that level requires more than being well known. An icon assumes mythic proportions and usually epitomizes some special era or a major aspect of the culture and society. The late Princess Diana, whose untimely death made her a celebrity-martyr, is one such icon — and someone who died trying to escape photographers. (Reprinted by permission of TimePix)

COMMENT

"Diana, Princess of Wales, became skillful at constructing the images of herself that she wanted people to see. I recall a British newspaper editor telling me how Diana composed the famous shot in which she sat, alone and lovelorn, in front of the world's greatest monument to love, the Taj Mahal. She knew, he said, exactly how the public would 'read' this photograph. It would bring her great sympathy, and make people think (even) less well of the Prince of Wales than before. Diana was not given to using words like 'semiotics,' but she was a capable semiotician of herself. With increasing confidence, she gave us the signs by which we might know her as she wished to be known. Some have been saying that her 'collusion' with the media in general, and with photographers in particular, must be an important mitigating factor in any discussion of the paparazzi's role in her death. Perhaps so; but one must also consider the importance a woman in her position attaches to controlling her public image. The public figure is happy to be photographed only when she or he is prepared for it, 'on guard,' one might say. The paparazzo looks only for the unguarded moment. The battle is for control; for a form of power."

—Salman Rushdie from "Crash," *The New Yorker*, September 15, 1997

577

COMMENT

"Our celebrity culture has become so greedy and wild that it overwhelms and consumes the writer's individual voice. It feels, sometimes, like the writer gives up, thinks of the rent bill, and types on a kind of automatic pilot, giving the magazine or the reader or the movie publicists what they want — and nothing more. Our appetite for the same photograph of a movie star in a spaghetti-strap dress is insatiable, and so, it seems, is our appetite for the same article. But why do we continue to read it over and over, why are we interested in it when we could generate it from thin air as easily as Tom Kummer? It may be because the celebrity profile is not about information, it is not about journalism, it is not about words; it is a ritual."

— Katie Roiphe from *Brill's Content,* Dec 00/Jan 01

578

MESSAGE

Katie Roiphe has argued that the public craves information about celebrities because "we are interested in fame: its pure, bright, disembodied effervescence." Do all the materials in this section send the same message about fame? Do the Koons sculpture or Peyton's portraits or the cover of *Time* say something different about the individuality of celebrities?

METHOD

Neal Gabler wants readers to think of celebrity in "an entirely new way." How does he go about presenting that new way? What sort of examples does he offer to support his argument that celebrity is a narrative, a story? Of what importance to his essay is the historian Daniel Boorstin's rather dismissive definition of celebrity? Do you think Gabler provides a more accurate view of why people are so fascinated by celebrities' lives? Do you find any problems with his method of argument?

MEDIUM

Gabler writes that "life itself has become the dominant medium of the new century." Think about this statement carefully. What do you think it means? In what sense can life itself be considered a "medium"? Radio, television, and newspapers are all media — but how is life in any way analogous to other types of media?

THE BODY

ESSAY | 2 ADS | BOOK COVER | 2 PHOTOS

In his defense of slavery, the ancient Greek philosopher Aristotle argued that
one reason some men are intended to be slaves is that "it is the intention of
nature to make the bodies of slaves and free men different from each other."
Slaves have "robust" muscular bodies that enable them to carry out heavy
physical labor, unlike the bodies of Athenian citizens, who are useless for "such
servile labors, but fit for civil life." Aristotle's stereotype prevailed in the western
world for centuries, long after the institution of slavery ended, as people assumed
a muscular male body belonged mainly to farmers, blacksmiths, and common
laborers. The muscular body became so identified with labor and the working
classes that not having one could signify a superior social standing.

A similar phenomenon occurred with respect to suntans. A tanned individual
was presumably someone who had to work outdoors in the hot sunshine. Thus,
a deeply tanned body was generally considered unappealing and the sign of inferior social status. A thin body with a fair complexion (as can be seen in many
eighteenth- and nineteenth-century portraits) indicated a higher social standing
and suggested what was then valued as "gentility." Good looks, therefore,
were not inseparable from socioeconomic factors. The American poet Walt
Whitman — the "Poet of Democracy" — was one of the first individuals to praise
manual labor, sunbathing, and robust bodies; throughout his work he celebrated
the physical attributes of his fellow working-class Americans. The materials that
follow explore the evolution of beauty and ask you to consider current attitudes
in a broader perspective.

Eric Tyrone McLeod, *Selling Out: Consumer Culture and Commodification of the Male Body*. In this carefully researched essay, McLeod explores the ways in which the ideals of masculinity changed considerably in the twentieth century, especially in its last decades, as male musculature took on significance it never had before. McLeod surveys the social evolution of the "ideal" body, the growth of body-building, the present glorification of enormous muscles, and "what it means to be a 'man' in the consumerist mentality." This essay first appeared in *Post Road* (Nov. 6, 2003). Eric Tyrone McLeod recently graduated Arizona State University's Barrett Honors College with a degree in Exercise Science. He also holds a degree in Russian from Arizona State University.

Eric Tyrone McLeod

SELLING OUT: CONSUMER CULTURE AND COMMODIFICATION OF THE MALE BODY

581

The human body, particularly within the last half of the 20th century, has been transformed into something to buy, something to work on as a supreme testament to one's self-worth. The result of a cultural preoccupation with the body is the rise of a self-obsessed public—once seen as predominantly female, now certainly male as well—fearful of any indication of aging or physical flaw. The body, female and more recently male, is one of the primary means for marketers to move product; within consumer culture the body "is proclaimed as a vehicle of pleasure: it's desirable and desiring" (Featherstone). D. Kirk puts it this way: "Media representations of bodies are, in a sense, re-constructing bodies by repackaging the associations between bodies and values that people make in their everyday lives." The bodies that represent the values marketed as desirable are clearly difficult for the vast majority of the population to achieve—or, if achieved, to maintain. And even if the "ideal" body is attained, there is nothing stopping the industry from changing that ideal to maintain discontent. Scholar Susan Bordo maintains in her 1999 book *The Male Body:* "ideals of beauty can be endlessly tinkered with . . . remaining continually elusive, requiring constant new purchases, new kinds of work on the body." Because contentment is anathema to a consumer culture, it is against the best interests of the culture to have a satisfied and content consumer base.

Varda Burstyn, in his book *The Rites of Men,* articulates that the key to selling "lies in activating a series of sometimes irrational associations geared to stimulate the emotions that drive people to buy, notably desire and anxiety." If the market depends on the permanent dissatisfaction of its customers, how is that condition fostered in the public? Mike Featherstone sees certain themes, "infinitely revisable, infinitely combinable," that "recur within advertising and consumer culture imagery: youth, beauty, energy, fitness, movement, freedom, romance, exotica, luxury, enjoyment, fun." The buyer is led to believe that life is improved via commodity in ways unrelated to functional purpose. Promoting anxiety about appearance, then, generates desire for transfiguration: "Body image industries make money off your bodily insecurities, and they're not going to make a profit by telling you that you look fine already."

Americans largely believe a significant measure of their worth as individuals is determined by their ability if not to actually *perform* as athletic and/or sexual dynamos, then at least to *look* as if they could. The effect that the body-as-commodity mindset has had upon women has been studied for some time now, but only in the past ten to twenty years has attention been paid to the effect of these same messages on men. Marketers have come to realize that men can be made to feel just as insecure about their physical appearance as women have been for decades. Economically, the growing parity of women has meant the erosion of one of the primary means American men cling to in defining masculinity: a role as primary breadwinner. "The development of capitalism after World War II saw a continued erosion of traditional means of male expression and identity due to . . . women's continued movement into public life," writes critic Michael Messner. As a result, women have increased freedom to be discriminating in their romantic and sexual choices, and corporations have been quick to jump on the insecurities these changes have engendered in men, aiming to instill preconceived notions of idealized male beauty and sexual performance. The early 20th-century ideal of the genteel, morally upstanding male has given way to a more aggressive, competitive ideal: the notion of the "hypermasculine" male. Varda Burstyn defines this as a cultural "shift in emphasis from 'character' to 'sex appeal.'"

Before World War II, American men were largely unexposed to any uniform notion of personal worth through attainment of a physical ideal. What defined masculinity was *internal* character; external appearance had little to do with perceptions of worth in men. Health of the male population was associated with spirituality and high morals, often linked to a sense of nationalistic pride via the efforts of President Theodore Roosevelt in his attempt to link physical fitness with national security. Roosevelt imagined that the physical robustness of American men was a key factor in repelling national threats. The rising fear of increased immigration at that time led to the depiction of foreign peoples as scrawny, malnourished, and sickly. In contrast, a corpulent (white) man was seen as a success, someone that had the financial means to provide for himself and his family many times over.

By the 1920s, with the rise in popularity of the flapper's androgynous look, the perception of health had virtually reversed itself: now immigrants were depicted as being fat and slovenly, gluttonous invaders capable of taking over the country. The early years of the 20th century also witnessed the beginnings of a national obsession with sport at the collegiate level. The meaning and importance of organized sport transcended mere physical activity and began to take on an importance connected to national pride: "Empire and nation became identified with team sports," Toby Miller asserts of the era. By the end of the 1940s, Hollywood and public sports had helped to set the stage for the revision of the masculine ideal. All that was missing was an efficient means to transmit this new ideal to an ever-growing population; with the advent of television in the 1950s, this was swiftly rectified.

The rise of consumer culture in America began in earnest shortly after World War II: once the industrial might of the country was transformed from military to domestic concerns. The rise of factory farming and scientifically engineered agriculture meant that the United States was blessed with a surplus of food, and innovations in labor-saving technology ensured that Americans would be exerting less physical effort to ensure themselves a piece of the "good life." In the 1950s the very idea of *physical* labor (and, by extension, physical exertion of any sort) carried a negative class connotation; if you worked with your hands, you had not advanced in the pursuit of the American Dream. Yet as early as 1953, *Time* magazine announced that the U.S. was becoming a nation of "fatties"; physical health was still largely a non-issue for the American population at this time. According to the magazine's calculations, half the women and a quarter of the men in America were overweight. For the diet industry in America—still in its infancy—the focus was primarily on women. A woman's worth was determined by how close she came to achieving the socially constructed notion of the *female* American dream: Susan Bordo sees that "women, for their part, were expected not only to provide a comfortable, well-ordered home for men to return to but to offer beauty, fantasy, and charm for a man to 'escape' to and restore himself with after the grim grind of the working day." The health, too, of men was also considered the responsibility of their wives, since wives maintained the household. A middle-class man told by his doctor to lose a little weight by "cutting back" subsequently shifted the burden of responsibility onto his wife, who might encourage him to leave something behind on his dinner plate—or to skip his evening cocktail. Diets for men revolved around the vilification of carbohydrates (a trend currently in revival) with the sole exception of alcohol ("Drinking Man's Diet" plans, allowing generous alcohol intake, were introduced in the 1950s).

President Dwight Eisenhower initiated campaigns to "fight the flab" in the name of patriotic opposition to communism; physical fitness once again became tied to national security and pride when studies showed children of Eastern European and Asian nations were in better health than their American counterparts. Yet exercise prescriptions and programs in the 1950s were concerned with seeing results with as little exertion as possible. Devices were invented to shake, roll, jiggle, and shock one's body loose of unwanted fat. As early as 1951 machines were invented to electrically stimulate muscles to tone and shape (we have seen the return of these devices on the market, promising a "hardbody" with little to

Robert Cameron, *The Drinking Man's Diet*, 1964. The anti-carb movement has been around for a while: here is a pamphlet, written by Robert Cameron in 1964, that told men they could drink their martini and eat their steak and still lose weight. It breezily started with the promise of dieting the fun way: "Did you ever hear of a diet which was fun to follow? A diet which would let you have two martinis before lunch, and a thick steak generously spread with Sauce Béarnaise, so that you could make your sale in a relaxed atmosphere and go back to the office without worrying about having gained so much as an ounce? A diet which allows you to take out your favorite girl for a dinner of squab and broccoli with hollandaise sauce and Chateau Lafitte, to be followed by an evening of rapture and champagne?" (Courtesy of Cameron & Company Publishers, San Francisco)

584

THE ORIGINAL LOW-CARB DIET

The
Drinking Man's Diet

New Revised Edition

**HOW TO LOSE WEIGHT
WITH A
MINIMUM
OF
WILLPOWER**

Also Recommended for Teetotalers

no effort). In this period, too, American life began to shift in the mid-century to a culture increasingly based on the cultivation of self-esteem. The necessities of life had been secured by a majority of Americans; manufacturers began to look for ways to create desire and perceived need for luxury items. The end of the 1950s witnessed the beginnings of unchecked consumerism and the rise of its relationship to self-importance and the concept of self-development.

By the 1960s, not only had television become a primary influence in American social life, but the patriarchal status quo faced its greatest challenge to date with the social upheavals of the age. While the seismic shifts in the cultural paradigm are too great to discuss here, it is important to note the result of this atmosphere on perceptions of masculinity within the social structure. Taking stock of their political and social situation as never before, women judged it lacking. The American male's ironclad role as provider began to show cracks in its foundation, and certainly one important factor influencing the crisis of masculinity was "the increasing involvement of women in traditionally male-dominated social arenas" (White and Gillett). The birth control pill was introduced to the public in May 1960, and the patriarchal structure received a jolt. More than a few male scholars began to worry that women would become lascivious, seeking out mates and partners based not on ability to provide economic security, but to explore "carnal fulfillment." Pressure was on men to perform sexually. With the arrival of women's liberation came the suggestion, and more often the understandable demand, that men had a role to play in the sexual satisfaction of their partners. Men were required not only to be fertile providers for their mates but also to be skilled and attractive while doing it. As Burstyn points out, "The *Playboy* man became the ideal representative of 1960s capitalism and its world political order. For such men, the sexual practices of the 'new virility' and the consumer-pornographic culture could deliver on two important levels: they valorized 'uninvolved' sexual exchange, and . . . provided symbolic confirmation of men's difference from and superiority to women."

But for the physical fitness of the American population, the dominant theme remained the link between national security and pride with the health of the common man. As a way of fighting the ever-present threat of communism, President Kennedy, like Eisenhower before him, promoted nationwide fitness programs in the schools. These programs often consisted of little more than group calisthenics performed half-heartedly, but the impetus for the collective health of the population was there: a new context for fitness was emerging. The 1960s produced a profound sense of anxiety: the American military fiasco in Vietnam left men with little sense of what was reliable in society, and government officials lost public credibility and trust. As a result, individuals began to look more within themselves for a sense of stability and purpose. "Attention to the self offered refuge from a world that was becoming darkly unpredictable," as Lynne Luciano puts it. America had seen a decline in its prestige and influence on a global scale, and economic stagnation further eroded any sense of security and direction within the nation. With this shift came increasing importance placed on the image men presented to the world as a marker of their worth. In targeting men, the fitness and diet industries no longer played to the idea of "health" so much as to the ideal of *transforming* one's physical self as a medium of expressing oneself to others. Physical appearance and the image one presented to the world were now the focus of the newly instituted cult of youth and self-expression.

The 1970s, then, widely valorized the acquisition and preservation of a youthful, sexy body; for men, the emphasis was on a gradually increasing ideal of muscularity. This emphasis on physical appeal manifested in the nation's growing number of health clubs, which began to replace singles bars as opportunities to meet the opposite sex. As Sam Fussell puts it in "Bodybuilder Americanus": "Yesterday's muscle pits [are] today's fern bars. And in the continuing decline or outright absence of spirituality in their lives, many men began to look towards physical development and exertion as a means towards spiritual fulfillment. This was a particularly strong sentiment of the "jogging boom" of the 1970s. The

585

concept of the long-distance runner as pseudo-ascetic, coupled with the activity's chemical euphoria (brought on by the infamous "endorphin-high"), presented running as much a spiritual quest as a means of keeping the cardiopulmonary system in good working order. Men lagged behind women in consumption of beauty products, diet aids, and exercise equipment, but the gap was closing.

As Lynne Luciano sees it, "washboard stomachs and bulging pectorals [are] the 1980s version of the 1950s house or a new station wagon." Toby Miller, author of *Sportsex,* claims that in the 1980s, "The traditional ways of understanding consumers—race and class—were supplanted by categories of self-display." Wages and salaries for the working class declined in the 80s, heightening public anxiety and increasing the need for men to discover a means of self-identity and expression other than their earning power. This means lay in the presentation of the physical self. Health became of secondary importance in the 1980s; it was OK if you felt ill or depressed, according to the popular Billy Crystal character on *Saturday Night Live,* so long as you "looked mahvelooos." The embarrassment over national fiascoes like the Vietnam War and the Iran hostage crisis, coupled with the shrinking role of men as sole provider in the average household, meant society began to look increasingly in directions other than economics and politics for signifiers of masculinity. One signifier was muscle. The body became a predominant symbol of male power and strength after decades of seismic cultural changes in traditional views of masculinity. The book *Sport and Postmodern Times* glosses the shift the following way: "The Reagan administration capitalized on the logic of will by redeploying an amplified individualism and will that located America's decline and uncertain status of bodies and historical movements that it marked through the lack of will: the social and countercultural movements of the 1960s and the feminized Carter administration" (Rail).

Hollywood accelerated this shift with the promotion of action-adventure movies portraying actors such as Arnold Schwarzenegger, Sylvester Stallone, and Jean-Claude Van Damme. "United States national popular culture became saturated with images of hard, addicted, cyborg bodies," as Cheryl Cole puts it in *Sport and Postmodern Times.* As little as ten years prior, weight lifters were seen as unusual: a subculture that exercised but with seemingly little athletic purpose for it. Weight lifting now took on new status in the eyes of the "common man"; by the mid-80s it was the physical activity in which most middle class men engaged. Associated with the growing obsession with muscularity was a hysteric fear of fat. A 1987 study showed that among MBA graduates, workers could expect to lose $1000 a year in annual salary for every excess pound they carried. Being out of shape became firmly entrenched in the national psyche as a major character flaw. In the workforce it was no longer sufficient to be qualified for a job, one had to look qualified for it. A study by Kathleen Martin et al. observing the effects of exercise on image impression found that people tended to regard a subject who exercised as "A harder worker, more confident, [having] more self-control than both . . . nonexercising and control targets." Being overweight branded one lazy and out of control; being thin was a sign of ambition and vitality. "Major corporations frequently require executives to tailor their body shapes to the company ethos," Miller points out. Older men seeking new opportunities in an era of middle management downsizing began to turn to plastic surgeons in record numbers for facelifts and other elective procedures. Bordo quotes a cosmetic surgeon: "'A youthful look,' as one says, 'gives the appearance of a more dynamic, charging individual who will go out and get the business.'" Burstyn sees that the 1980s, a time of remasculinization and remilitarization after the defeat of Vietnam and the stagnant economy of the 1970s, represent "a vast proliferation of men's cultural genres as well as an expansion in the world of sport."

By the 1990s millions of Americans participated in some form of weight training, which by and large had nothing to do with health and fitness and everything to do with improving self-image. Muscularity took on an importance for American men on an unprecedented scale, pushed along by corporations anxious to capitalize on men's insecurities over failing to measure up to a media-driven ideal. The effects are clear even in toy making, where action figures such as G.I. Joe went through a remarkable transformation. In its original incarnation, had the G.I. Joe doll been 5'10" tall (the male average), his dimensions would have included a 32-inch waist, a 44-inch chest, and 12-inch biceps (an attainable physique for adult males). But as one study observes, "earlier Joes are shamed by the . . . figure introduced in 1991. His waist had shrunk to 29 inches, and his biceps are up to 16½ inches—approaching the limits of what a lean man might be able to achieve without steroids" (Pope et al.). Where children had been receiving messages as to the impossible standards of desirable female body types through Barbie dolls in the past, they were now receiving equivalent messages about male bodies.

Although the 1990s saw a slight decline in the portrayal of heavily muscled actors in leading roles, the emphasis on muscles and leanness still clearly exists today, and we are currently subject to public admiration and criticisms of our physical selves like never before; fat continues its leading role as the "Great Satan" of the American psyche. In *Seven* (1995) actor Kevin Spacey portrayed a chilling serial killer whose victims embodied the seven deadly sins of the Catholic Church. For the sin of gluttony, he forced a morbidly obese man to eat until he burst. The killer describes the victim to police as "an obese man, a disgusting man, a man you would point out to your friends so you could join together in mocking him, a man who if you saw him while you were eating, *you wouldn't be able to finish your meal.*" Spacey went on to portray a character in the film *American Beauty* whose mid-life crisis compels him to seek exercise advice from his neighbors in order to "look better naked." Bordo, an academic feminist, comments that the male torso has become the most utilized body part, male or female, to sell commodities:

> Feminists might like to imagine that Madison Avenue heard our pleas for sexual equality and finally gave us "men as sex objects." But what's really happened is that women have been the beneficiaries of what might be described as a triumph of pure consumerism—and with it, a burgeoning male fitness and beauty culture—over homophobia and the taboos against male vanity, male "femininity," and erotic display of the male body that have gone along with it.

587

As more and more images of male bodies are made available by popular culture for public consumption, we need to interrogate what it means to be a "man" in the consumerist mentality. The male body is often depicted in film and advertising as heavily muscled, hairless, and oiled, more a machine than organic entity. The projected power of masculinity is the primary goal, often through actual or metaphoric display of the phallus as a "yardstick" of masculinity. Our culture "encourages men to think of themselves as their penises," Bordo says; it still "conflates sexuality with something we call 'potency.'" Taking their cue from a project that tracked the bodily dimensions of *Playboy* centerfolds over the years to show they were getting steadily thinner, Pope et al. applied the same scrutiny to the male centerfolds in *Playgirl.* What they observed is consistent with the depiction of ideal males in most other arenas of popular culture: "The average *Playgirl* centerfold man has shed about 12 pounds of fat, while putting on approximately 27 pounds of muscle over the last twenty five years."

The cultural obsession with muscularity is also a preoccupation with size, and this even includes the size of commodities males consume. Witness the rise of the macho cigar culture (as though one phallus on the male weren't enough); the entertainment industry's continued focus on lean, muscled actors paired with large-breasted women; and the design and production of ever-bigger sport utility vehicles (SUVs) that can barely keep up with consumer demand. Men's magazines, too, have exploded in their diversity and proliferation over the last ten years. *Men's Health* magazine alone jumped in circulation from 250,000 in 1990 to 1.5 million in 1997. These publications mirror their counterparts marketed to women in that they offer diet and exercise tips, along with articles offering sexual advice. Headlines of the June 2001 issue scream such promises as "Pack on Muscle!" "Drop those last 10 pounds!" "Instant Sex—Touch Her Right Here" "Your Perfect Sex Partner—Find Her on p. 125!" Interestingly enough, when one turns to the latter article it actually concerns trying to find ones perfect spouse—but it is the sexual aspect of marriage that is the article's focus.

To correct bodily flaws and stave off future degeneration, Americans throw a staggering amount of money at the fitness and beauty industries. The authors of *The Adonis Complex,* Pope et al., state that in 1999 Americans spent $4 billion on gym memberships and home exercise equipment. In addition, "men received 690,361 cosmetic procedures, including 217,083 hair transplantations or restorations, 65,861 chemical peels, 54,106 liposuctions, and 28,289 treatments to remove varicose veins" (Pope et al.). This total does not include face lifts, rhinoplasty, pectoral and calf implants, and penis augmentations. The authors go on to cite a study conducted in 1997 by Euromonitor that estimated American men spent $3.5 billion annually on men's toiletries, and estimate that billions more are spent yearly on supplements, protein products, and herbal extracts. Pope et al. note that "male body-image industries—purveyors of food supplements, diet ads, fitness programs, hair-growth remedies, and countless other products—now prey increasingly on men's worries, just as analogous industries have preyed for decades on the appearance-related concerns of women."

In the current role that sports plays in America we can see the deleterious effects of hypermasculine ideals. Over the course of a century sport has become something more than a popular pastime; it is akin to a religious experience. Baron Pierre de Coubertin, founder of the modern Olympic games, wrote in 1929 that the Olympics were to be revived and modernized under the concept that "modern athletics is a religion, a cult, an impassioned soaring" (Burstyn). "In industrial society," Burstyn notes, "sport has overtaken many of the previous functions of an established patriarchal church and organized religion: the moral instruction of children, the ritual differentiation of men and women, the worship by both of a common divinity forged in the masculine model." Hence NBA all-star Charles Barkley's infamous statement in the early nineties that "I am not a role model" is nothing short of heresy.

"Sport and its associations have become the great cultural unifiers of the nineteenth and twentieth centuries," affirms Burstyn; yet still, "sport is a religion of domination and aggression constructed around a male godhead." Sports provide an anchor for traditional concepts of masculinity in a world where these concepts constantly undergo challenge and change by the prevailing zeitgeist. Within the realm of sport, men have a refuge free from the encroaching equality of women, a space where they can compete, display aggression, and engage in zero-sum competition that produces clear winners and losers. Burstyn writes, "In a gender arrangement of compulsory heterosexuality such as the one that has prevailed in capitalist societies, surplus masculinity is produced through a creation of a feminine-phobic, overcompensating masculinity that tends to domination and violence." Nowhere in society is this more evident than in professional sports.

African American professional athletes suffer the dual burden of providing a male ideal to the general public, as well as an example of the black male to a white public. Michael Jordan was transformed from a black athlete to the white public's notion of a model African American, characterized by his unthreatening demeanor and decided reluctance to comment on anything remotely political. "Michael Jordan . . . exemplified the healthy body, the athletic body . . . the body distanced from the threatening black masculinity inscribed on that other predominant inner-city figure—the addict" (Rail). As a result Jordan has achieved nearly messianic stature in the white media, crossing racial lines as the epitome of grace and genteel mannerism off the basketball court (but still driven by hypermasculine notions *on* the court). In contrast, athlete O.J. Simpson represents the black pariah, having betrayed the trust and adoration of the white public, which collectively feels he got away with the murder of his wife Nicole Brown Simpson in 1995. Mike Tyson is the representation of masculinity (and in particular the African American male) gone horribly wrong; aggression lashing out uncontrollably through rape/violence against women, biting off the ear of Evander Holyfield during a match, and other psychotic outbursts both verbal and physical. "Commercial discourse has also tended to . . . heighten reactionary ideas about black men. It has done so primarily by exploiting the hypersexuality and violence embedded in the racist cultural legacy" (Burstyn). For many whites, Simpson and Tyson reaffirm their darkest fears about the black male. As Bordo points out, "When a white boy acts like a thug, he proves he's not a sissy to the other white boys in his group; when a black boy engages in the same behavior, the same white boys may regard it as proof that he's a jungle brute after all."

With professional sports as the vanguard of masculine ideals, the use of drugs and other potentially hazardous methods to attain the perfect body in the general populace is assured. "The public health problem of steroid use would be minor if the victims were only a few professional athletes and actors. But millions of boys and men have looked to these men as role models, and have longed to have bodies like theirs" (Pope et al.). Yet resistance training, or weight lifting, represents perhaps the most universal means men employ in attempting to realize the hyper-masculine ideal. Former bodybuilder-turned social critic Sam Fussell notes "steroids or not, a natural bodybuilder is an oxymoron. Bodybuilding is to flesh what origami is to paper." Bodybuilding has its own lifestyle and code, but unlike most subcultures, it also strives to align itself with traditional cultural values. The leaders of the bodybuilding industries have done their utmost—with varying degrees of success—to integrate bodybuilding into mainstream culture. "They strive to gain respect by projecting a persona of wholesomeness. . . . Three values are heavily projected to the public via the leading publications: health, heterosexuality, and rugged individualism" (Yiannakis et al.). Accompanying the enhanced body image bodybuilders acquire through larger muscles is pride in the implication that they have extraordinary discipline: while anyone can accumulate material goods, striving for and attaining an almost freakish level of muscularity requires not only physical *effort* but a strong work ethic.

The desire to modify the body in such a drastic way is indicative of the changing ideals of masculinity in society. The recent explosion of interest in body-building is related to the growing threat to male privilege represented by female gain in social arenas like the workplace and/or family: "The resurgent cultural ideal of the muscular body in contemporary culture and the increased popularity of bodywork practices are symptomatic of a trend in our culture seeking to reestablish an ideology of gender difference in the face of emancipatory forces" (White and Gillett). Once seen as deviant and somehow sexually suspect by the general populace, bodybuilding has become a legitimate means of self-transformation in a 21st-century consumer culture. As one critic puts it: "Body-building, then, *stands to gain cultural acceptance by being what was previously most reprehensible,* that is, self-indulgent, narcissistic, excessive, and sexually exotic" (Yiannakis et al., italics mine).

Calvin Klein Pro Stretch, *Fredrik Ljungberg*. The most recent face — and body— of Calvin Klein is U.K. soccer player Freddie Ljungberg. He was chosen, accord-ing to Calvin Klein, because he represents "the ideal" of Calvin Klein Pro Stretch, a new performance-inspired men's underwear that combines designer style with athletic flexibility. Swedish-born Ljungberg plays as midfielder for Arsenal FC in the English Premier League, and in 2002 he was voted player of the year in England. (The Advertising Archive)

FREDRIK LJUNGBERG

591

In and of itself bodybuilding provides little by way of genuine societal power to its devotees: bodybuilder Fussell argues that muscle symbolically replaces the financial or political power he lost, or never had: "the reconstructed, pumped-up male body promises control, control over your every muscle fiber, control over your immediate environment." Further, "it's materialism incarnate, *with muscles replacing money as numerical gradations, as incremental units of self-worth.* It's as American as conspicuous consumption, with status the goal, envy the motivation" (Fussell, italics mine). With strength and power over self and others the only legitimate social currency, the net effect of the bodybuilding culture is a reaffirmation of the dangerous hypermasculine ideal. Strength, aggression, and size are reinforced as societal markers of positive masculinity, and traditional gender roles are glorified: Fussell sees bodybuilding producing "the romantic idealization of . . . natural man, untrammeled by thought, by knowledge of good and evil, by, in fact, knowledge. Intellect is held to be effete, essentially feminine and suspect."

Obsessive bodybuilding—as with other factors like steroid use, and extreme dieting—can also contribute to body image disorders in males: "The emergence of 'megarexia,' a condition in which male bodybuilders obsessively perceive themselves as too fat or too thin regardless of how muscular they become, is highly conducive to the rationalization of steroid abuse" (White and Gillett). As men are convinced of the need to adhere to a media-driven ideal in order to feel successful, they become prey to the same false promises that the diet industries have made to women. Bordo mentions that, despite the reigning cultural perception that by and large only women are affected by eating disorders, by 1999 *one million men had been diagnosed with an eating disorder* (compared to eight million women). Male reluctance to admit to having a "female disease" means that men are reluctant to seek treatment.

Liposuction is now performed on almost as many men as women to get rid of stubborn fat. A particular form of liposuction is now practiced which sucks the fat from around the abdominal wall, thereby producing the coveted "six-pack" abdominal definition. Chin reshaping (which may involve reshaping the existing bone structure or inserting a plastic implant) can deliver "lantern jaw" looks. Pectoral and calf implants can increase the size of those body parts resistant to training. Penile augmentation (which involves severing ligaments holding the penis to the abdominal wall—so that it hangs lower and appears longer—and the injection of fat into the shaft of the penis) promises that no man need be ashamed of his "endowments." Cosmetic surgery has experienced a surge in male patients only in the last thirty years or so, and procedures aimed at men are now as diverse as procedures for women (for instance, hair transplantation/restoration usually involves scalp grafts, hair plugs, or even a bizarre set of titanium anchors screwed into the skull into which to snap hairpieces).

Psychology Today ran a poll in 1997 that found that 43% of men surveyed were unsatisfied with their overall appearance. Of these, 63% did not like their abdomens, 52% their weight, 45% their overall muscle tone. 17% of the men polled would subtract three years from their life if it meant they could achieve their ideal body. Bordo emphasizes the dilemma women have faced in attempting to emulate media notions of beauty: "We try to accomplish the impossible, and often get into trouble. Illusions set the standard for real women, and they spawn special disorders and addictions: in trying to become as fat-free and poreless as the ads, the fleshy body is pushed to achieve the impossible." The recent emphasis on male beauty ideals has ensured that men are no longer relatively immune to the sting of this paradox. Bordo notes further that "I never dreamed 'equality' would move in the direction of men worrying more about their looks rather than women worrying less." Socially conditioned to possess a natural reluctance to discuss emotions and anxiety, the majority of mainstream American men are without significant support for their bodily insecurities. "And so this 'feeling and talking taboo' adds insult to injury: to a degree unprecedented in history, men are being made to feel more and more inadequate about how they look — while simultaneously being prohibited from talking about it or even admitting it to themselves" (Pope et al.). But as Varda Burstyn sees it, if we can reclaim "physical culture *from* corporate culture, we can balance, 'masculine' with 'feminine' in our culture and within ourselves."

Bibliography

Bordo, Susan. *The Male Body: A New Look at Men in Public and in Private.* New York: Farrar, Straus, and Giroux, 1999.

Burstyn, Varda. *The Rites of Men: Manhood, Politics, and the Culture of Sport.* Toronto: University of Toronto Press, 1999.

Featherstone, Mike, ed. *The Body: Social Process and Cultural Theory.* London: Sage Publications, 1991.

Fussell, Sam. "Bodybuilder Americanus." *Michigan Quarterly Review,* 32(4), 1993.

Loland, N. W. "Some Contradictions and Tensions in Elite Sportsmen's Attitudes Towards Their Bodies." *International Review for the Sociology of Sport,* 34/3, 1999.

Luciano, Lynne. *Looking Good: Male Body Image in Modern America.* New York: Hill & Wang, 2001.

Messner, Michael A. "Sports and Male Domination: The Female Athlete as Contested Ideological Terrain." *Sociology of Sport Journal,* 5, 1988.

Messner, Michael A., and Don F. Sabo. *Sex, Violence, and Power in Sport: Rethinking Masculinity.* Freedom, CA: Crossing Press, 1994.

Miller, Toby. *Sportsex.* Philadelphia: Temple University Press, 2001.

Pope, Harrison G., K.A. Phillips, and R. Olivardia. *The Adonis Complex: The Secret Crisis of Male Body Obsession.* New York: The Free Press, 2000.

Rail, Genevieve, ed. *Sport and Postmodern Times.* New York: State University of New York Press, 1998.

Rowe, David. "Accomodating Bodies: Celebrity, Sexuality, and 'Tragic Magic.'" *Journal of Sport and Social Issues,* February, 1994.

Sharp, M., and D. Collins. "Exploring the 'Inevitability' of the Relationship Between Anabolic Steroid Use and Aggression in Human Males." *Journal of Sport & Exercise Psychology,* 20, 1998.

White, P. G., and J. Gillett. "Reading the Muscular Body: A Critical Decoding of Advertisements in *Flex* Magazine." *Sociology of Sport Journal,* 11, 1994.

Yiannakis, Andrew, and Merril J. Melnick, eds. *Contemporary Issues in Sociology of Sport,* Champaign, IL: Human Kinetics, 2001.

COMMENT

"Medieval noblewomen swallowed arsenic and dabbed on bats' blood to improve their complexions; 18th-century Americans prized the warm urine of young boys to erase their freckles; Victorian ladies removed their ribs to give themselves a wasp waist. The desire to be beautiful is as old as civilization, as is the pain that it can cause. In his autobiography, Charles Darwin noted a 'universal passion for adornment,' often involving 'wonderfully great' suffering.

(Rhydian Lewis/Getty Images)

"The pain has not stopped the passion from creating a $160 billion-a-year global industry, encompassing make-up, skin and hair care, fragrances, cosmetic surgery, health clubs, and diet pills. Americans spend more each year on beauty than they do on education. Such spending is not mere vanity. Being pretty — or just not ugly — confers enormous genetic and social advantages. Attractive people (both men and women) are judged to be more intelligent and better in bed; they earn more, and they are more likely to marry.

"Beauty matters most, though, for reproductive success. A study by David Buss, an American scientist, logged the mating preferences of more than 10,000 people across 37 cultures. It found that a woman's physical attractiveness came top or near top of every man's list. Nancy Etcoff, a psychologist and author of 'Survival of the Prettiest,' argues that 'good looks are a woman's most fungible asset, exchangeable for social position, money, even love. But, dependent on a body that ages, it is an asset that a woman uses or loses.'

"Beauty is something that we recognize instinctively. A baby of three months will smile longer at a face judged by adults to be 'attractive.' Such beauty signals health and fertility. Long lustrous hair has always been a sign of good health; mascara makes eyes look bigger and younger; blusher and red lipstick mimic signs of sexual arousal. Whatever the culture, relatively light and flawless skin is seen as a testament to both youth and health: partly because skin permanently darkens after pregnancy; partly because light skin makes it harder to hide illness. This has spawned a huge range of creams to treat skin in various ways.

(SW Productions/Getty Images)

594

"Then again, a curvy body, with big breasts and a waist-to-hip ratio of less than 0.8 — Barbie's is 0.54 — shows an ideal stage of readiness for conception. Plastic surgery to pad breasts or lift buttocks serves to make a woman look as though she was in her late teens or early 20s: the perfect mate. 'Mimicry is the goal of the beauty industry,' says Ms. Etcoff.

"Basic instinct keeps the beauty industry powerful. In medieval times, recipes for homemade cosmetics were kept in the kitchen right beside those used to feed the family. But it was not until the start of the 20th century, when mass production coincided with mass exposure to an idealized standard of beauty (through photography, magazines, and movies) that the industry first took off."

— *The Economist* Special Report, "The Beauty Business," May 24, 2003

MESSAGE

Eric Tyrone McLeod's essay deals with the "commodification" of the male body. In what sense has the body become a commodity? What exactly is a commodity? Do you think regarding the body as a commodity is a good thing or a bad thing? Explain your response.

METHOD

McLeod's essay is heavily dependent on his research of the topic. Do you think he could have written his essay without reference to other published sources of information? Suppose he had simply visited gyms and weight rooms to make observations and take notes: Would he have arrived at similar conclusions? What if he had based his essay on personal experiences alone? Look at McLeod's research methods more closely. Which studies does he seem most dependent on? Can you find information in the essay that the author doesn't source? Provide some examples of these, and explain why you think they don't require sources.

MEDIUM

Using McLeod's essay as your source of information, consider how once the human body — both male and female — becomes a commodity, it can also become subject to all other forms of packaging and marketing. Can muscles be thought of as packaging? Can displaying the body be considered a form of marketing? What is the merchandise, and what is being marketed? Explain some of the media implications of bodily commodification.

Assignment 1

As the photo selections in Selling America point out, and as Ian Frazier's essay supports, the American flag has become a tool to motivate consumers to shop in the name of patriotism. While this is certainly not the first time in our history that the flag has been used to inspire patriotic duty, it may be, as Frazier points out, the first time that duty has been defined as a call to unbridled consumerism as opposed to sacrifice. Now that the image of the flag has been used as consumer motivator through rampant advertising, do you think that it can be resurrected as a cultural symbol? Or is it destined to become yet another over-exploited icon thrown at us by advertisers? To help answer this question, break into small groups to discuss possible ways of solving the problem that Blizzard raises. How can the image of the flag be reclaimed,

(S. Meltzer/Getty Images)

and does it need to be? Using the Adbusters "How to Create Your Own Print Ad" guidelines (p. 504), create an ad for a non-profit patriotic organization that attempts to reclaim the image of the American flag. In your group, you will need to carefully construct your objective in order to decide whether you want to shame the companies that have manipulated the image, or if you want simply to remind the American public of the flag's real symbolism.

Assignment 2

The clusters Celebrity and The Body in this chapter seem to mutually define each other in many ways. As Neil Gabler points out in his essay on celebrities, many of them are dressed by designers even when they are not in front of the cameras, further positioning celebrities as models of the unattainable perfect body, perfect look, and perfect overall image that we should strive for. To investigate the issues raised in these two sections, collect a variety of celebrity tabloids to analyze in small groups. Look at the composition of the covers first — how have the designers used color and layout to emphasize the most important items in the publication? What images appear regularly on the covers? What do the headlines say about our purposes for reading these tabloids? Do the images and text on the covers indicate how we should measure up to these celebrities?

(© Tim Graham/Corbis)

After carefully analyzing the tabloid covers, collect a variety of popular magazines that are not completely devoted to celebrities but that feature them on their covers (*Good Housekeeping, Glamour,* etc.). Analyze the function of the celebrity on the covers of these magazines — how does the treatment of the celebrity on these covers compare to their treatment on tabloid covers? Do the celebrities on the covers of these magazines relate to the subjects of the magazines? What messages are being sent about how we should measure up to the celebrity in question based on the cover? How would the feel of the magazine change if the cover photo were of an anonymous model? Finally, analyze the mission of one of your magazines to determine what sort of information it is trying to share with its readership. As a group, decide how to redesign the magazine cover to better communicate the overall mission of the magazine without a celebrity cover. In a presentation, your group will need to provide a rationale for your new design, as well as articulate why the celebrity cover is not the best choice.

1. Break into several groups and, using Adbusters' "How to Create Your Own Print Ad" (p. 504) as a guide, create a rough draft of a print ad either for a product you invent or for something familiar that you seldom see advertised—perhaps your college or a local hang-out. Afterwards, groups should compare their creations and discuss what advertising elements and strategies seem most and least effective.

2. After reading Eric Tyrone McLeod's essay on the commodification of the body (p. 581), break into small groups and discuss how both men and women can be adversely affected by striving for media ideals of physical perfection. Then imagine your group has formed an organization against such media ideals that could inform the public about resisting extreme alterations to the human body. Create a name for your organization (check the entry on abbreviation in the glossary) and then, after studying some of the examples of opinion ads, prepare a rough draft of an advertisement that promotes your cause. Try to think of a catchy headline; also be sure to offer in the body of your ad's copy some reasons why attempting to achieve certain physical ideas could actually be harmful.

3. Write a sci-fi essay. Architects, city planners, and retailing experts are beginning to see a decline in the popularity of the giant shopping mall, but at present no one has a vision of what might replace it. Using your imagination, in a short essay try to visualize the next new shopping experience. Describe what the new architecture would look like and—on the basis of your own shopping experiences—what improvements the mall replacement would offer to consumers.

4. By the time we reach college, most of us have had experiences shopping, hanging out, or even working at a mall or shopping center. After reading David Guterson's essay on the Mall of America (p. 554) and Paco Underhill's comment about working as a "retail anthropologist" (p. 549), write an essay that describes your personal response to the mall experience. Do you find it an exciting, fun place to be, where you can socialize, flirt, see the latest fashions and trends; or is it an impersonal space, designed to encourage unnecessary consumerism and social anxiety? Or is it both, or neither, of these? Regardless of your viewpoint, be sure to enliven your essay with concrete details so that readers can see your mall as a real place.

5. As mentioned in the book's Introduction, the eminent literary critic Raymond Williams once observed that the biggest problem with advertising is not, as most people imagine, that it promotes a materialistic view of the world (p. 29). The prob-

lem, he argued, is that advertising is not materialistic enough. After breaking into small groups, discuss what you think Williams meant by this apparently paradoxical comment. Then each group should collect from various sources (this book included) examples of product ads — for automobiles, appliances, food, electronic gadgets, and so on — that support his opinion. After surveying the ads, each group should select a single print ad that best exemplifies Williams's point about lack of materialism. One person from each group should then present this example to the entire class and point out how and why the particular ad fails to be sufficiently materialistic. A key question to ask is: What is being sold?

6. Write a pop culture research paper. Quite a few movies have featured shopping malls in a significant role. Using your own memory and resource tools at your school's library or on the Internet, compile a list of films that have featured malls. Use this list as the basis of a research essay on the way the film industry has depicted the shopping mall. Can you find some of the earliest examples? Can you detect changes in the way malls have been presented over time? How do films generally portray malls? This research paper can either be constructed as a historical overview or focus on one film in which the mall is of special significance. Either way, your paper must cite sources and criticism.

7. In "Our Celebrities, Ourselves" (p. 566), Neal Gabler speaks of the "medium of life." The architect Sze Tsung Leong maintains that shopping is a medium (p. 562). If this is the case, what isn't a medium? Of course, this is a difficult question. But do your best thinking. In a short reflective essay, consider the general concept of a medium (see also the book's Introduction, p. II) and make a case for either position: (A) No human experience can exist outside of or separate from some kind of medium, or (B) Human beings can and do have unmediated experiences.

8. The advertising campaign for the American Indian College Fund (p. 530) asks, "Have you ever seen a real Indian?" Think about the ad's full intentions; it might help to look at a picture of historical Indians like the Cheyenne and Arapaho chiefs pictured on page 325. What is the ad attempting to do with stereotypes? After breaking into small groups, each group should follow the AICF's lead and design a nonstereotypical ad along the lines of "Have you ever seen a real _____?" If someone in the group can do a rough sketch of the ad, that's fine; if not, the group can provide a verbal description of its message and design.

9. As an artist, Barbara Kruger (p. 563) chooses unusual canvases for delivering her message: billboards, buses, magazines, plaques, bus stops. Does her work fit your definition of art? In an essay, discuss how Kruger's work relies on familiar types of advertising and yet is not in itself advertising. What does she borrow from the advertising world, and how does she transform it? You may want to use the Internet and reference library to learn more about Kruger's life and art.

10. Many Americans tend to think that political propaganda is a thing of the past, associated with Nazi Germany or the Soviet Union, for example. Consider, however, the role of propaganda in our own nation's two-party system today. After forming several small groups to discuss and develop a working definition of "propaganda," each group should research several current newspapers, news magazines, or networks (the Internet can be a resource) and examine statements issued by both Democrats and Republicans on leading issues of the day. Given your group's definition, how do the statements you find suggest the techniques of propaganda? How one-sided are the statements? Can you find examples demonstrating how one political party claims that its statements are true and accurate but that the rival party's are false and propagandistic? Do you see any indications of the newspaper, news magazine, or network that provided the source of the statements participating in propaganda or favoring one side? Each group should summarize its findings and report to the class as a whole on the extent of propaganda evident in current politics.

PACKAGING CULTURE

abbreviation: The shortening of a word or phrase, usually for convenience, efficiency, or memorability. Nicknames are a common form of abbreviation (Bob for Robert, Sue for Susan). Many shortenings become standard or common words in themselves (phone = telephone, abs = abdominal muscles). In communications, two important forms of abbreviation are **initialisms** and **acronyms.** Initialisms consist of the first or key letters of words and the letters are pronounced individually: ACLU (American Civil Liberties Union), WNBA (Woman's National Basketball Association), UFO (unidentified flying object). Initialisms have become popular in e-mail and in live chat rooms, where commonly used phrases are often abbreviated: BRB (be right back), GTG (got to go). Although many people refer to such abbreviation as acronyms, that word technically applies only to abbreviation that are pronounced as words or that form new words: AIDS (acquired immune deficiency syndrome) and RAM (random-access memory) are examples of the former; laser (*l*ight *a*mplification by *s*timulated *e*mission of *r*adiation) is an example of the latter. Since acronyms can be rhetorically effective, many organizations adopt them to reinforce their message: NOW (National Organization for Women), MADD (Mothers Against Drunk Driving).

abstract art: Art that focuses on form, structure, and patterns of color (rather than concrete images) to evoke broad or general ideas and emotions. Abstract art often lacks a recognizable subject, which allows for different perceptions and opinions.

acceptance: Positive reception or response from an audience. In constructing arguments, writers usually estimate the degree of acceptance their message is likely to have from a particular audience. In rhetoric, delivering a message to an audience that already accepts your position is often called preaching to the converted. Thus, if you are advocating an antiregulation policy for firearms, it is far easier to address your message to the National Rifle Association than to a pro–gun control group. In consumer behavior theory, acceptance measures the reception of a message by an individual. Advertisers hope for optimum acceptance through the use of positive imagery. "You deserve a break today" was a popular McDonald's advertising slogan designed to put the consumer in an accepting mood.

action: In narrative, the leading events. The action of a story or essay might be a small part of the whole piece. In advertising, the word "action" refers to the process of moving individuals to think of a product or service in a favorable light and to behave accordingly.

advertisement: A public announcement that promotes a product, service, business, or event to increase awareness and sales. Advertisements are present in nearly every form of media and are powerful means of communication. Advertisements in broadcast media are known as commercials. Advertisers in print media buy space, whereas those in broadcast media buy time.

advertising photography: The use of photographs to promote and sell products. Advertising photographs are powerful because they increase memorability.

advertorial: A combination of advertisement and editorial designed to promote an interest or opinion. Advertisements created by special interest groups that lobby for legislative change often take the form of advertorials.

advocacy advertisement: An advertisement that aims to raise consciousness, gather support, or speak in favor of a specific social cause. Among these types of advertisements are public service announcements and political ads. Advocacy advertising is also sometimes referred to as "cause marketing."

aerial photography: Photographs taken from the sky, sometimes using infrared film, at a great distance from the subject. This method of photography is useful in landscape photography, archaeological surveys, military reconnaissance, or any other area that deals with a large distant subject.

allegory: Artistic work in which elements (characters, places, images, etc.) are understood to represent something else, often spiritual, moral, or political. George Orwell's novel *Animal Farm* is an allegory in which farm animals represent humans in a workers' rebellion. The book gives a symbolic depiction of problems with government, caste, and injustice in society.

alliteration: Repetition of consonant sounds, generally at the beginning of words but also at key or successive syllables. Alliteration is widespread in poetry (Shakespeare: "When to the sessions of sweet silent thought / I summon up remembrance of things past") and in prose that strives for impact (Tom Paine: "These are the times that try men's souls"). Advertising copy frequently makes use of alliteration, especially when the desire is to create a memorable or catchy slogan.

ambiguity: The condition that exists when a term or statement can be interpreted in several different ways, leaving the audience unsure as to which meaning is correct. Quite common in ordinary communication, ambiguity is often the unintentional result of a semantic or grammatical error. In literary works, authors sometimes intentionally use ambiguous expressions to create multiple meanings or uncertainty. Deliberate ambiguity is also frequently found in advertisements.

analogy: A comparison made between two similar subjects to clarify a meaning. Analogies are used in speech, writing, and art to give an example or show how two or more things are alike. An analogy can be drawn between children fighting on a playground and countries going to war.

architecture: The art and science of designing and constructing buildings. The word "architecture" can also denote the structure of something created; the framework or structural makeup of a piece of writing or a web page can be considered its architecture.

argument: The use of logical reasoning to support a particular point of view. Also, a form of discourse that attempts to convince an audience that a specific claim or proposition is true wholly because a supporting body of logically related statements is also true.

audience: A group of people who will see, hear, or otherwise experience a performance, a work of art, or any other form of written or verbal communication. Since everyone perceives information differently, audience is a major consideration in rhetoric and writing. An author can make a piece of work more effective by keeping in mind the particular group being addressed. An audience can be a literal group attending a performance or an anonymous widespread group reading or watching broadcasts. Martin Luther King Jr.'s "I Have a Dream" speech had a literal audience (those who attended the speech), an implied audience (the American people), and an anonymous cumulative audience (any person that has since heard or read the speech).

blog: Short for "weblog," blog refers to a page with hyperlinks to other pages, often with short bits of accompanying text telling surfers about where the links are going.

campaigns: In marketing and advertising, the strategies that companies implement in television, radio, and print media to attract consumers to buy their products.

caption: Written information accompanying an image that explains to the viewer what he or she is looking at.

cartography: The science or process of making maps.

causation: The act of making something occur or the process of bringing something into being. Causation presupposes the belief that every action or state of being is the result of a previous action. In media or art, causation refers to that which evokes a reaction from an audience. In writing, it is a key element of explanation and plot development.

classification: The categorization of items in groups according to type. Classification is a procedure for identifying and organizing the parts of a subject.

cliché: Once a word or phrase enters the common vernacular as a widely accepted way of describing something, it becomes a cliché. Drab and unimaginative, clichés are the work of a lazy mind. They weaken the overall quality of a speech or text. Examples include a critic referring to a new movie as a "tour-de-force," or a poet writing a line such as "his eyes were as blue as the ocean."

collage: A picture made by adhering various images or objects onto a surface. A collage can consist of bits of paper, pieces of cloth, photographs, and other various objects randomly or purposefully arranged.

color: Reflected light that is perceived by human beings as variations of the primary shades—red, blue, yellow. Color is used to meet or break a convention in art, or to evoke an emotion. In advertising, color is often used to attract and keep the consumer's attention. In writing, the word "color" is used to describe the use of elaborate detail; vivid descriptions are said to "add color" or make a scene more visual for the reader.

comic: Words and drawing arranged sequentially to tell a story or joke. Comic strips syndicated in newspapers and comic books are two of the most familiar genres, though recently writers / illustrators have merged the comic book with serious fiction to produce the graphic novel, one of the best-known being Art Spiegelman's *Maus*.

comparison: A search for similarities between two or more subjects drawn from the same class or general category. Comparing two subjects is often an effective way to construct an argument or provide an opinion.

composition: A term that can be applied to many types of expression, including writing, music, art, architecture, photography, film, design, typography, and advertising. Composition essentially refers to the way something is made or made up (the word means literally putting together), particularly the way in which its parts are arranged and how they relate to the whole.

computer art: Pictures created or altered using digital technology. Each dot of light on the computer screen is called a pixel (from "picture" + "element"). The combination of pixels in a sequence creates a visible image. Computer artists can alter the order of pixels to enhance or even change the image.

content: The meaning or message behind a work of art. Every photograph, painting, novel, essay, or movie usually has a theme or idea that it tries to convey to its audience. The content of a painting that shows an African American man standing beside chains might be the idea of slavery, while the content of a particular news report might be the presidential election.

context: Context can be understood in two distinct ways: Most immediately, the term refers to whatever surrounds a word, image, passage, or text—where the text was taken from. Knowing the immediate context of an excerpt (a magazine or a Web site or an article about slavery, what the text before and after said, etc.) helps explain its full meaning. In a larger sense, context can refer to the historical, social, or economic moment from which a text emerged.

contrast: A process that highlights the differences between two or more subjects. Showing differences often magnifies the pros and cons of like subjects.

contrivance: An artificial device that makes an object or event appear clever and spontaneous, though it is actually planned and affected. "Contrived" carries a negative connotation, suggesting that the subject aspires to be genuine but ultimately appears unrealistic or unconvincing to the audience.

convergence: Diverse things coming together at a single point from different directions.

cyberspace: A term coined by novelist William Gibson in 1984 to describe the invisible networking system of computers and digitized data throughout the world. The word "cyberspace" is often used to describe the Internet and virtual reality.

definition: The meaning of a word (as in a dictionary or a glossary). As a rhetorical term, definition refers to the practice of exploring the full meaning of a concept in an extended essay. Definition also pertains to other media: in visual areas such as photography or television, it denotes an image's degree of clarity. In recordings, definition relates to the sharpness of the sound.

demographics: Statistical information about the consumer population, including size and growth, based on factors such as age, sex, occupation, and family size. Advertisers often determine their target market on demographic information. (See also *target market*.)

description: A verbal or visual account or representation of a person, place, object, or state of mind. Detailed description can often make information clearer or more manageable for an audience. Objective description is primarily factual and excludes mention of the writer or artist's personal evaluation or response. Subjective description includes attention to both the subject described and the writer or artist's response to it.

digital imaging: The conversion of an analog photograph to a digital image through the use of a computer scanner.

digital photography: The process of creating or altering photographs through the use of digital technology and computer graphics. (See *digital imaging*.)

documentary photography: The use of photographs to record information. Documentary photography can inform the viewer, conjure an emotional response, or convey a socially conscious message through the use of visual stimuli. Judicial photography, medical photography, photojournalism, biographic photography, scientific photography, war photography, and travel photography are some examples.

draft: A drawing or sketch, usually of a preliminary nature; also a preliminary version of any kind of writing. A finished work is usually preceded by several drafts.

emphasis: A means of ascribing more importance to an issue by way of drawing special attention to its message.

feminism: A term that is generally used to refer to the belief in securing women's rights and privileges equal to those of men for employment. It is also specifically used to refer to a political movement and organization that actively seeks such rights, especially active in the 1970s.

format: The physical dimensions or components of something. In photography, the dimensions of photographic film, traditionally measured in millimeters or inches. The photographer chooses a specific film format for aesthetic reasons, depending on the type of photos he or she wishes to take. In book publishing, the format of a textbook would refer to all the components that make up that book—the different colors used, the margins, the arrangement of pictures and written text.

frame: The limit of what is recorded in a painting, photograph, or image at a given time. In photography, this refers to the size and extent of an image on a negative. In film and video, the frame is the area covered by the camera and is what we see on the screen. Framing is especially important in photography in that the photographer can usually choose how to frame the picture so that certain images are included and others excluded. Framing is applied to many different kinds of expression: one frames an argument by putting it a certain way or constructing specific limits.

genre: Any of the categories existing within each creative discipline that allow for the organization of specific forms or methods of expression. Magical-realism, fantasy, and romance are three examples of genres found in fiction.

hyperbole: Exaggerated expression used for emphasis or persuasion. Hyperbole makes up a large portion of everyday speech, where words like "terrific," "great," or "super," are commonly used, along with extreme expressions: "I'm starving" instead of "I'm hungry." When deliberately used in advertising or publicity purposes to promote excitement, such exaggerations are popularly known as "hype." Movie ads will try to stimulate public interest through superlatives conveniently supplied by reviewers: "The most breathtakingly gorgeous film of the year."

hypermedia: Multiple forms of media (text, graphics, etc.) processed through computer applications. Hypermedia is concerned with not only relaying information but also reminding users of the medium itself.

hypothesis: An unproved theory that is tentatively accepted as true in order to provide a basis for further investigation or argument. In an essay we often first state our idea about a subject as a hypothesis, which we then examine, develop, support, and restate it as a conclusion.

illustration: In writing, a process in which authors select examples to represent, clarify, and support ideas, statements, and principles. Also the visual elements used to clarify or supplement a text, such as the illustrations in a dictionary or encyclopedia.

informative essay: An essay whose purpose is to educate readers on a given topic using research, facts, and a logical structure.

installation: The arrangement of a work (or works) of art in a gallery or exhibition. The art is placed or hung in a specific order so the audience will most likely view each piece according to the artist's wishes.

irony: A kind of antithesis created through the use of words that suggest the opposite of their literal meaning or through a situation in which the results do not match the intentions or expectations. Countries going to war in the hope of obtaining peace is an example of irony. In written expression, irony often depends on understanding the context and inferring the tone of voice.

jingle: A catchy, easily recognizable piece of music associated with a product or service, played during a television or radio advertisement. A mnemonic device, the jingle is successful when it persuades a consumer to purchase the advertised product or service.

kitsch: A defining fashion, media, or product design from a particular era whose cultural value is renewed after a period of obsolescence. Kitsch tends to connote items of dubious sophistication and includes arcana as diverse as shag carpeting, busts of Lenin, and reruns of *The A-Team.*

media: Technically, the plural of *medium*. In common use, though, refers to various means of mass communication such as newspapers, television, and radio.

medium: A means of conveying ideas or information. Includes all forms of mass communication (television, radio, newspapers) as well as personal and interactive forms of communication (audio and video recordings, the Internet, letters, and e-mail).

memoir: Personal writing reflecting on a person's contributions to the world. Autobiographical yet different from autobiography, the memoir documents life as remembered by the author.

message: A term that refers to *what* a text is saying. A message can be a discrete unit of communication, a condensed moral or organizing concept, or a strong signal or gesture that delivers a clear idea.

metaphor: A verbal or visual image used to represent or symbolize something else. Metaphors are often used in literature to expose the reader to a theme or idea without being obvious or overbearing. In Mary Shelley's *Frankenstein,* the monster is viewed by many as a metaphor for the rebels of the French Revolution: both monster and rebels became too powerful to control, even by their creators.

method: A term that refers to *how* a text is put together— generated, expressed, structured, and put to purpose.

modernism: A style of art that rejects the artistic styles and restrictions of the past. Because artistic expression changes with time, it is difficult to describe the modernist style at any given point. However, modernists usually have a radical new attitude about both past and present that affects their entire concept of art.

montage: A work of art that consists of overlapping images or themes, often borrowed or appropriated from other works. In film, a montage is a display of overlapping visual images, often fading in and out of focus and set to music. Writers can achieve a montage effect by describing in detail a number of different images at once, giving the reader a layered mental picture.

mundane: Ordinary, commonplace. In literature, many writers use mundane aspects of life to project a larger concept. Arthur Miller's play *Death of a Salesman,* whose main character is the "everyman" Willy Loman, deals with the difficulties of family relationships and failure to live up to expectations.

narration: A way of telling what happened by linking a succession of events together into a meaningful sequence. In writing, narration refers to the main voice, which often speaks directly to the reader.

narrative art: Art that represents a story or events taking place. Many paintings depict scenes in progress and thus allow the viewer to infer what has happened or is about to happen. (See also *narration.*)

opinion essay: A composition in which the author advances his or her personal beliefs in a persuasive and well-reasoned manner with the intention of convincing readers of the expressed opinion's importance or veracity.

parallelism: The arrangement of words, phrases, sentences, paragraphs, and sections of a composition so that similar elements are given equal emphasis or form. Parallelism is a basic principle in both grammar and rhetoric.

parody: A deliberate imitation, usually for comic or satirical purposes, of any written, artistic, or musical work or expression. For example, the Beatles routinely parodied other musical styles. A successful parody depends on the audience's understanding that the imitation is done purposefully—thus much parody is exaggerated so that the point is unmistakable.

pattern: A series of images or pieces of information that, when considered as a whole, conveys a certain message or agenda. The emergence of patterns in literature and visual arts contributes to the formation of different styles and genres.

personal essay: A composition that focuses on the author's individual experience.

perspective: A particular way of seeing, literally or figuratively. An individual's perspective is affected by his or her personal history and experiences, character, mood, circumstances, and any other qualities that makes a person unique. In fiction, perspective is synonymous with *point of view*.

photo-essay: A magazine item that combines text and photography. The photographs provide a visual reference and add clarity to the text.

photojournalism: Photographic images that accompany text dealing with news coverage. The photographs give the audience a visual reference of what is occurring and often relay as much information about the story as the written article does.

photo-realism: A painting style in which the artist imitates the precision and objective qualities of a photograph. Computer photo-realism is the process of making digital images that resemble photographs.

plot: The closely linked sequence of events in a story. In literature, plot refers to the things that "happen" in the story.

point of view: The vantage point from which a piece of writing is presented. In expository prose, the author's point of view might be compared to a light illuminating an object: the strength, color, and position of that light not only determine what aspect of the object we see but also affect what kind of response we have to it.

Polaroid: A camera that passes exposed film between rollers that release chemicals needed for development. With this apparatus, photos can be shot and developed automatically, within minutes. (The word is also applied to the resulting photograph: "a Polaroid picture.")

pop art: Contemporary art that appeals to a wide (popular) audience. Andy Warhol is perhaps the most famous pop artist. His unusual artworks, such as paintings of Campbell soup cans and sculptures of Brillo cartons, made him internationally known.

portraiture: The making of a painting or photograph of a person's face or body. Portraiture focuses on the human form, with particular attention to physical detail. Leonardo DaVinci's Mona Lisa is a famous portrait.

postmodernism: An artistic and literary movement that resists the concrete images of modernism. In fiction, postmodern writers often create unusual effects through the use of disjointed and nonlinear plots, bizarre characters, and metafiction (writing about writing). Postmodernist painters tend to paint unrecognizable subjects to elicit emotion from the viewer and call attention to the artwork itself rather than to create a definitive picture. Where the modernist impulse grew out of seeing works (paintings or poems) as isolated objects or texts, much of postmodernism depends on viewing a work in an expanded or unexpected context; for example, the museum space itself will become an element of the exhibited work. Postmodernist artists often blur traditional boundaries between high and low culture, different media, or art and commerce. Despite an enormous amount of attention, the term has received no fully successful definition: some influential critics believe the movement is over, while others think it never existed in the first place.

premise: A statement given as the basis of an argument. Etymologically meaning "to place before," premises are the assumptions from which deductive reasoning proceeds.

propaganda art: Art publicized by a government or other organization to promote a policy, idea, doctrine, or cause.

public art: Art produced for and by the community.

purpose: The overall goal or aim of a work, the effect it hopes to achieve, the agenda or cause it promotes, or the response it expects to receive from an audience.

representation: A depiction of a person, place, thing, or idea. Representational art contains a recognizable subject and a clear objective.

résumé: A document that summarizes for prospective employers the skills, job objectives, and past experience of an individual. A résumé can also refer to a summary of events.

rhetoric: The art of effective or persuasive expression. Rhetorical methods have been taught since antiquity and still remain a central ingredient of most writing courses. The term has recently been expanded to include elements of visual persuasion as well.

search engine: A term that refers to a program that searches web documents for specified keywords and returns a list of documents where the keywords are found. Search engines like Google, Alta Vista, and Yahoo! also offer services like chat rooms and other functions that will keep users coming back to their site.

self-portrait: A visual image or verbal description in which the artist and subject are the same. Many artists photograph, paint, and write about themselves to gain perspective on or insight into their own identity.

sensationalism: An emphasis on the most lurid and shocking aspects of a subject. Many gossip magazines sensationalize the lives of celebrities in order to attract an audience.

sequence: The arrangement of images, objects, or words in a series. See Scott McCloud's illustrations on page 137 for an innovative look at sequence.

simile: An explicit comparison of two things normally not considered alike, usually brought together by the word "like" or "as." Thoreau compared grass to a ribbon: "The grass-blade, like a long green ribbon, streams from the sod into the summer." Dickens drew a simile between a character and a cannon: "He seemed a kind of cannon loaded to the muzzle with facts, and prepared to blow them clean out of the regions of childhood at one discharge."

slogan: A phrase, often copyrighted, that attempts to encapsulate an organization's defining principle in a manner that is both memorable and efficient. For instance, think of Nike's simple, effective "Just Do It."

staged photography: Photographs in which the subject plays a fictional role with a specific costume and pose. Most staged photographs are used for advertisements—a picture of people sunbathing on a beach could advertise a summer resort.

story: A fictional or nonfictional representation of an experience or series of events.

surreal: Having strange and irrational qualities. In surrealist art, the artist strives to render a dreamlike rather than a concrete effect. Writing, movies, and television can also have a surreal effect when tone, plot, and character do not conform to the audience's expectations. The term is commonly used to suggest real experiences that seem unreal; many eyewitnesses of the September 11, 2001, World Trade Center attacks repeatedly said in interviews that the experience seemed "surreal."

syllogism: A formal deductive argument composed of a major premise (All human beings are mortal), a minor premise (Joe is a human being), and a conclusion (Therefore, Joe is mortal).

tabloid: A popular, small-format newspaper or magazine with an emphasis on sensationalism and gossip. Tabloids often give personal information about celebrities, recount bizarre occurrences, and display unusual or sometimes even altered photographs.

target market: A group of consumers for whom a company creates a product or to whom it advertises a product. The target market is the group identified as most likely to buy a specific product.

war photography: Photographic coverage of a war or other conflict. Many war photos are considered art and are on display in museums and galleries. Often dramatic and emotional, war photography gives the viewer a sense of the destructive nature of war.

Acknowledgments

Introduction

Barbara Kruger. *Untitled* (*Love is something you fall into*), 1990. From *Thinking of You* by Barbara Kruger (Cambridge: MIT Press, 1999). Courtesy of the Mary Boone Gallery, New York. (p. 3)

Rigo 95, *Innercity Home.* © Rigo 95, courtesy of Gallery Paule Anglim, San Francisco, California. Reprinted by permission. (p. 4)

Ron English. *Camel Jr's.* Copyright © Ron English. Reprinted by permission of Ron English. (p. 6)

Weegee. *Car Crash Upper Fifth Ave., July 13, 1941.* Courtesy of Weegee/ICP/Getty Images. (p. 8)

Tibor Kalman. *True Stories,* 1987. Courtesy of M&Co., New York. Reprinted by permission. (p. 11)

Audience Wearing 3-D Glasses, February 5, 1953. Copyright © Bettmann/CORBIS. (p. 14)

Maya Lin. *Vietnam Veterans Memorial.* Courtesy of Maya Lin Studio. (p. 16)

cnn.com. "Day of Terror." © Cable News Network, LP, LLLP. (p. 18)

Stephen Jay Gould. "A Time of Gifts." From *The New York Times,* September 26, 2001. Copyright © 2001 by Stephen Jay Gould. Reprinted by permission of Rhonda Roland Shearer, on behalf of the Art Science Research Lab. (pp. 22–23)

How to Erase a Skater. From Ivan Amato, "Lying with Pixels." *Technology Review,* July/August 2000. Infographic Betsy Hayes. Photos Sarnoff Corp/IOC/ USOC. (p. 25)

Lauren Greenfield. *Sara, 19.* Copyright © 2004 by Lauren Greenfield. (p. 26–27)

Negative Population Growth. "Remember when this was heavy traffic?" Courtesy of Negative Population Growth. Reprinted by permission. (p. 30)

Chapter 1

Interior view showing art galleries of the Kulturforum in Berlin, 2003. © Ludovic Maisant/Corbis. (p. 42)

Judith Ortiz Cofer. "Silent Dancing," "Lessons from the Past," and book cover are reprinted with permission from the publisher of *Silent Dancing: A Partial Remembrance of a Puerto Rican Childhood* (Houston: Arte Publico Press–University of Houston, 1990). (pp. 43–54)

Hulton Deutsch. *Woman collaborators are punished in Cherbourg.* © Hulton Deutsch Collection/Corbis. (p. 55)

John D. Freyer. Introduction to *All My Life for Sale* by John D. Freyer. © 2002 by John D. Freyer. All text and images are reprinted with permission from the publisher (London: Bloomsbury, 2002). (pp.56–67)

eBay homepage. URL: www.ebay.com. These materials have been reproduced with the permission of eBay Inc. Copyright © eBay Inc. All rights reserved. (p. 68)

Dorothy Allison. "What Did You Expect?" From *Allure* Magazine, April 1998. Copyright © 1998 by Dorothy Allison. Reprinted by permission of Conde Nast Publications. (pp. 71–78)

Childhood portrait of Dorothy Allison reprinted from her memoir, *Two or Three Things I Know for Sure,* 1995. Copyright © 1995 by Dorothy Allison. (p. 72)

Book cover from *Bastard Out of Carolina,* by Dorothy Allison. Copyright © 1992 by Dorothy Allison. Used by permission of Dutton, a division of Penguin Group (USA) Inc. Photo by Elizabeth DeRamus. (p. 75)

Film still of Jena Malone from *Bastard Out of Carolina.* Photofest. (p. 77)

Anne Sexton. "Résumé, 1965." From *Anne Sexton: The Last Summer* (2000) by Arthur Furst. Reprinted by permission of the Harry Ransom Humanities

Research Center, The University of Texas at Austin. (pp. 80–83)

Arthur Furst. Portraits of Anne Sexton from *Anne Sexton: The Last Summer* by Arthur Furst. © 2000 by Arthur Furst. (pp. 84, 87)

Anne Sexton. "Self in 1958". From *Live or Die,* by Anne Sexton. Copyright © 1958 by Anne Sexton. Reprinted by permission of Houghton Mifflin Company. All rights reserved. (pp. 85–86)

Sally Mann. *Jessie Bites* (1985); *Blowing Bubbles* (1987); *Emmett, Jessie and Virginia* (1990); and *Candy Cigarette* (1989). © by Sally Mann. Courtesy: Edwynn Houk Gallery, New York. (pp. 90, 93, 96, 98)

Janet Malcolm. "The Family of Mann." From *Diana & Nikon: Essays on Photography* by Janet Malcolm. Copyright © by Janet Malcolm. Reprinted by permission of the author. (pp. 91–95)

Melissa Harris. "Daughter, Model, Muse Jessie Mann on Being Photographed." From *Aperture 162* (Winter 2001). Copyright © 2001 by Melissa Harris. Reprinted by permission of the publisher (New York: Farrar Straus & Giroux, 2002). (pp. 97–101)

Leonardo Da Vinci. The *Mona Lisa.* Réunion des Musées Nationaux/Art Resource, NY. (p. 104)

Joseph A. Harriss. "Seeking Mona Lisa." From *Smithsonian Magazine,* May 1999. Copyright © 1999 by Joseph Harriss. Reprinted by permission of the author. (pp. 105–116)

Dean Rohrer. *The New Yorker* cover (February 1999). © 1999 by Condé Nast Publications. Reprinted by permission. All rights reserved. (p. 107)

Marcel Duchamp. *L.H.O.O.Q.* (1930). Cameraphoto/Art Resource, NY. (p.110)

Vik Muniz. *Mona Lisa (Peanut Butter and Jelly)* (1999). Art © Vik Muniz/Licensed by VAGA, New York, NY. Courtesy of the Brent Sikkema Gallery, New York, NY. (p. 112)

Andy Warhol. *Mona Lisa: 1963.* © 2004 by Andy Warhol Foundation for the Visual Arts/ARS, New York. Photo: Peter Schalchli, Zurich. (p. 115)

Lillian Feldman Schwartz. "The Mona Lisa Identification." From *Visual Computer* by Lillian Feldman Schwartz. Copyright © 1987 by Lillian Feldman Schwartz. Reprinted by permission of Springer Verlag New York, Inc. (pp. 117–23)

Lillian Feldman Schwartz. *Mona/Leo.* Copyright © 1987 by Lillian Feldman Schwartz. All rights reserved. (p. 119)

Lillian Feldman Schwartz. *Leonardo Morphed to the Mona Lisa.* Copyright © 1995 by Lillian Feldman Schwartz. All rights reserved. (pp. 120–21)

Soundportraits.org homepage. Courtesy of Sound-portraits.org. (p. 126)

Portrait of a Boy Soldier. Library of Congress, neg. # B8184-10573. (p. 127)

Chapter 2

Scott McCloud. From *Understanding Comics.* Copyright © 1993, 1994 by Scott McCloud. Reprinted by permission of HarperCollins Publishers Inc. (p. 137)

David Sedaris. "Ashes." From *Naked* by David Sedaris. Copyright © 1997 by David Sedaris. Reprinted by permission of the publisher (New York: Little, Brown & Company, Inc., 1997). (pp. 139–49)

David and Amy Sedaris. © Scott Gries/Getty Images. (p. 148)

Danny Lyon. *Ernst; Four Generations;* and *Raphe at Seventeen, 1992.* All images found in *Knave of Hearts* (1999) by Danny Lyon. Courtesy Magnum Photos, Inc., © Danny Lyon. (pp. 150–53)

Gary Trudeau. *Doonesbury* cartoons. From *Buck Wild Doonesbury* (Andrews McMeel Publishing, 2000). Copyright © G.B. Trudeau. Reprinted with permission of Universal Press Syndicate. All rights reserved. (pp.156–57)

Jennifer Ringley. Two screen shots from jennicam.com. Reprinted courtesy of jennicam.org. (p. 158)

Sara Tucker. "Introduction to Diller + Scofido's *Refresh.*" Reprinted by permission of Dia Art Foundation. (pp. 160–63)

Diller + Scofido, *Refresh,* 1998. A project for Dia Art Foundation at www.diaart.org/dillerscofidio/. (pp. 161–62)

Lee Siegel. "Reality in America." From *The New Republic,* June 23, 2003. Copyright © 2003 by *The New Republic.* Reprinted by permission of *The New Republic.* (pp.166–75)

Mr. Personality contestants. Photofest. (p. 167)

American Idol contestants at *Swimfan* premiere. © Reuters NewMedia Inc./CORBIS. (p. 169)

Extreme Makeover Before and After. Photofest. (p. 172)

Casting call, *Fear Factor,* March 6, 2003. © Christopher Smith/CORBIS. (p. 174)

Anthony Jaffe. "It's a Real, Real, Real, Real, Real World." From *Mother Jones, Mojo Wire,* January 2001. Copyright © 2001. Reprinted with permission from

MotherJones.com. Mother Jones Magazine website. (pp. 176–78)

Z poster. Reprinted by permission of the Everett Collection Inc. (p. 181)

Louise Erdrich. "*Z*: The Movie that Changed My Life." From *The Movie That Changed My Life,* edited by David Rosenberg. © 1993 by Louise Erdrich. Reprinted by permission of Janklow & Nesbit Associates. (pp. 182–86)

Fox's *X-Men 2* poster (2003), Metro-Goldwyn-Mayer's *The Wizard of Oz* poster (1939), New Line Cinema's *The Lord of the Rings*: *The Return of the King* poster (2003), Newmarket Films' *The Passion of the Christ* poster (2003). All images reprinted by permission of Photofest. (pp.187, 188, 190, 191)

Warner Brothers' *The Matrix* poster (1999). Reprinted by permission of the Everett Collection Inc. (p. 189)

Weegee. *Newsboy, Mulberry Street Café, Dancing,* and *Car Crash Upper Fifth Ave., July 13, 1941.* All photographs courtesy of Weegee/ICP/Getty Images. (pp. 194, 197–99)

Wendy Lesser. "Weegee." From *Threepenny Review* 56 (Winter 1994). Copyright © 1994. Reprinted by permission of Wendy Lesser and *The Threepenny Review.* (pp. 195–98)

Nora Ephron. "The Boston Photographs." From *Scribble, Scribble: Notes on the Media* by Nora Ephron. Copyright © 1978 by Nora Ephron. Reprinted by permission of International Creative Management. (pp. 200–05)

Stanley Forman. *The Boston Photographs* (1975). © Stanley J. Forman. (pp. 202–03)

Bronston Jones. *Missing,* 2001. From the exhibit *Missing: Last Seen at the World Trade Center.* © Bronston Jones. All rights reserved. (pp. 206–07)

Don DeLillo. "Videotape." From *Antaeus,* No. 75/76, Autumn 1994, edited by Daniel Halpern. Copyright © 1994 by Don DeLillo. "Alternate ending to 'Videotape'" from *Underworld* by Don DeLillo. Copyright © 1997 by Don DeLillo. Reprinted by permission of the author. (pp. 210–14)

Film stills from Artisan Entertainment's *The Blair Witch Project* (1999), Miramax Films' *Sex, Lies, and Videotape* (1989), and Dreamworks Films' *American Beauty* (1999). All courtesy of Photofest. (pp. 212, 214, 215)

Jeff Wall. *Man with a Rifle* (2000). © 2002 Jeff Wall Studio. (p. 216)

Book cover for *Lord of the Rings*: *The Two Towers,* by J.R.R. Tolkein (Boston: Houghton Mifflin, 1988). Reprinted by the permission of the publisher. All rights reserved. (p. 219)

DVD case for *Lord of the Rings*: *The Two Towers.* © New Line Productions, Inc. (p. 219)

Chapter 3

Nicole Lamy. "Life in Motion." From *The American Scholar,* volume 69, no. 4, Autumn 2000. Copyright © 2000 by the author. Reprinted by permission of the publisher and the author. (pp. 230–36)

Nicole Lamy. *Life in Motion.* Copyright © 2002 by Nicole Lamy. Reprinted by permission of Nicole Lamy. (pp. 232–33)

Bill Bamberger. *Nancy and Alejandra Camarillo, Plaza Florencia, 2002; Ada Bennett and daughter Faith, San Antonio, 2002; Christopher McDonald at home in Orchard Village, 1994; Charles Evans Hughes, Mountainview Courts, Chattanooga, 1995; The Mobile Gallery, 2002.* All photographs © Bill Bamberger (p. 237–241)

John Edgar Wideman. "First Shot." From *Hoop Roots* by John Edgar Wideman. Copyright © 2001 by John Edgar Wideman. Reprinted by permission of Houghton Mifflin Company. All rights reserved. (pp.244–54)

Paul D'Amato. *Jump Shot/Tiro con salto* (1994). © Paul D'Amato. (p. 245)

Brad Richman. *Silver Springs, Maryland—August 1993; Portland, Maine—October 8, 2000;* and *Washington, D.C.—July 10, 1999.* © Brad Richman. Courtesy of Lee Marks Fine Art. (pp. 248–49)

Dana Lixemberg. *Tamika Catchings.* From *The New York Times* magazine, May 25, 2003. © Dana Lixenberg. (p. 251)

Nicholas Howe. "Fast-Food America." From *The Kenyon Review,* Summer/Fall 2002. Reprinted by permission of the author. (pp. 257–61)

Horn & Hardart. *Automat.* © Bettmann/CORBIS. (p. 258)

Ray Kroc Standing outside McDonald's (1963). © Bettmann/CORBIS. (p. 259)

David Butow. *Traffic along U.S. Highway 412* (2001). © David Butow/CORBIS. (p. 261)

Lauren Greenfield. *Penny Wolfe and daughter Jessica, Santa Monica Place; Hot Dog on a Stick employees Dominique King and Wendy Recinos at Baldwin Hills Crenshaw Plaza; Keum Ja Chung and Hyung Hee Im* in the Koreatown Plaza; and *Baldwin Hills Crenshaw Plaza.* All photographs are © 2004 Lauren Greenfield. (pp. 262–63)

Pico Iyer. "Nowhere Man." From *The Utne Reader,* May/June 1997. Copyright © 2002 by Pico Iyer. Reprinted by permission of the author. (pp.266–68)

Sylvia Otte. *Airport Lounges.* © Sylvia Otte/Photonica. (p. 268)

CD cover for *In What Language?* © Nick Zlonis. (p. 269)

N. Scott Momaday. "The Way to Rainy Mountain." From *The Way to Rainy Mountain.* Copyright © 2001 by N. Scott Momaday. Reprinted by permission of the publisher (Tucson, Arizona: University of Arizona Press, 1996). (pp. 272–76)

Joan Frederick. *Rainy Mountain, Kiowa Holy Place, Oklahoma.* © Joan Frederick. (p. 272)

Jesse DeMartino. *Jason and Mike at the Cabin Near Huntsville, Texas, 1996.* © Jesse DeMartino. Reprinted by permission. (p. 277)

Stephen Dunn. "The Sacred." From *Between Angels.* Copyright © 1997 by Stephen Dunn. Reprinted by permission of W.W. Norton & Company, Inc. (p. 278)

Mitch Epstein. *Cocoa Beach, Florida, 1983.* Found in *Architecture,* December 1999. Copyright © 1983 by Black River Productions, Ltd./Mitch Epstein, courtesy of Brent Sikkema, New York. (p. 279)

Black Rocket/Yahoo. "Yahoo! A Nice Place to Stay on the Internet." Appeared in *Print: America's Graphic Design* magazine, November/December 2000. Reproduced courtesy of Vincent Soyez/Oliver Piro Inc. (p. 282)

Jonathan G.S. Koppell. "No 'There' There: Why Cyberspace Isn't Anyplace." From *The Atlantic Monthly,* August 2000. Copyright © 2000 by Jonathan G.S. Koppell. Reprinted by permission of the publisher. (pp. 283–86)

SimCity™*4* and *The Sims*™*2* images. © 2003 Electronic Arts Inc. SimCity is a trademark or registered trademark of Electronics Arts Inc. in the U.S. and/or other countries. All rights reserved. (pp. 284, 288)

Noah D. Zatz. "Mapping Physical and Electronic Space." From "Sidewalks in Cyberspace" from *Harvard Journal of Law & Technology,* volume 12, no. 1, Fall 1998. Copyright © 1998 by Noah D. Zatz. Reprinted by permission of the publisher. (pp. 287–90)

Google screen shot. Courtesy of Google Inc. (p. 290)

Steve Satushek. *Boy Running in Field.* Courtesy of iconica image bank, A0018-000109. (p. 292)

Federal Home Loan Bank of Seattle, *Report on lending initiatives.* Design and photo: Methodologie, Seattle. (p. 293)

Chapter 4

Official Program, *Woman Suffrage Procession,* 1913. Courtesy of the Library of Congress, digital id #CPH3A21392. (p. 302)

"Freeze" Altoids advertisement. Reprinted with permission of Callard & Bower-Suchard, Inc. (p. 302)

Declaration of Independence. Draft: Library of Congress, negative #LC-MSS 27748-i. Broadside: Courtesy of The Massachusetts Historical Society. Calligraphy: The National Archives. (pp. 304–05, 309, 310, 312)

Thomas Starr. "The Read Declaration." From *The Boston Globe,* June 29, 2003, p. D5. Copyright © 2003 by Thomas Starr. Reprinted by permission of the author. (pp. 306–07)

James Munves. "Going to Press." From *Thomas Jefferson & the Declaration of Independence,* by James Munves. (New York: Charles Scribner's Sons, 1978). Copyright © 1978 by James Munves. Reprinted by permission of the author. (pp. 308–13)

Gettysburg Address. Lithograph: Rare Books and Special Collections Division, McGill University Libraries, Montreal, Canada. (p. 314)

Peter Norvig. *PowerPoint Presentation for the Gettysburg Address.* Peter Norvig. (p. 315)

The Texas Chainsaw Massacre. 1973 poster. Photofest. (p. 319)

Sherman Alexie. "The Texas Chainsaw Massacre." First published in *The Kenyon Review New Series,* Summer 1992, Vol. XIV, No. 3. Copyright © 1992 by Sherman Alexie. Reprinted by permission of the author. (pp. 320–21)

Verlyn Klinkenborg. "Sand Creek." From *Mother Jones,* November/December 2000. Copyright © 2000 Foundation for National Progress. Reprinted by permission of *Mother Jones.* (pp. 322–27)

Colonel John M. Chivington; Cheyenne and Arapaho chiefs; and *Troops storming the Sand Creek.* Images courtesy of the Denver Public Library, Western History Collection. (pp. 324, 325, 328)

Brian Callahan. *Map of Sand Creek.* Originally printed in *Mother Jones,* November/December 2000. (p. 329)

Wayne F. Miller. *Rabbits for Sale, 1948; Two Girls Waiting Outside a Tavern; One-Room Kitchenette;* and *Three Teenagers in Kitchenette Apartment.* All photos from *Chicago's South Side: 1946–1948* by Wayne F. Miller (2000). Copyright © by Wayne F. Miller. Courtesy of Wayne F. Miller/Magnum Photos, Inc. (pp. 332–36)

Gwendolyn Brooks. "Kitchenette Building." From *A Street in Bronzeville,* by Gwendolyn Brooks. Copyright © 1945 by Gwendolyn Brooks. Reprinted by permission of the author. (p. 335)

Gordon Parks. "Speaking for the Past." From *Chicago's South Side: 1946–1948,* by Wayne F. Miller. Copyright © 2000. Reprinted by permission of the University of California Press. (pp. 337–38)

Plastic Man. Cover from "Police Comics" #38. Copyright © 1945 DC Comics. Interior cells from "Police Comics" #1. Copyright © 1941 DC Comics. All rights reserved. Used with Permission. (pp. 340, 346)

Art Spiegelman. "Forms Stretched to Their Limits: What Kind of Person Could Have Dreamed Up Plastic Man?" From *The New Yorker,* April 19, 1999. Copyright © 1999. Reprinted by permission of Condé Nast Publications. (pp. 342–53)

Jack Cole. *True Crime.* Courtesy of Benjamin S. Samuels. (p. 350)

Jack Cole. *Murder, Morphine, and Me.* All frames courtesy of Benjamin S. Samuels. (pp. 351-352)

Superman. From "Action Comics" #1. Copyright © 1938 DC Comics. All rights reserved. Used with Permission. (p. 354)

Green Lama, August, 1945. Courtesy of Benjamin S. Samuels. (p. 355)

Ms. Magazine, July 1972. Reprinted with permission of *Ms.* Magazine. (p. 357)

Vietnam Veterans Memorial. Image courtesy of Maya Lin Studio. (p. 359)

Maya Lin. Proposals and sketches. Courtesy of the Library of Congress. Copyright © Maya Lin. (pp. 363–65)

Maya Lin. "Between Art and Architecture." From *Boundaries* (New York: Simon & Schuster, 2000). Copyright © 2000 by Maya Lin Studio, Inc. Reprinted by permission of Simon & Schuster. (pp. 36–383)

Aerial View of Vietnam Veterans Memorial. Courtesy of the National Park Service. (pp. 372–73)

Detail of Names and *Vietnam Veterans Memorial in Winter.* Courtesy of the Maya Lin Studio. (pp. 378–81)

Michael Arad and Peter Walker. "Reflecting Absence." Proposal reprinted by permission of the Lower Manhattan Development Corporation. Images copyright © 2004 LMDC. Rendering by dbox. (pp. 384–86)

United States Holocaust Memorial Museum. "Forgetting Would Be a Second Abandonment." Created to promote the National Days of Remembrance, April 30–May 7, 2000. Courtesy of the U.S. Holocaust Memorial Museum, Washington, D.C. (p. 387)

Susan Sontag. "Watching Suffering from a Distance." Excerpted from *Regarding the Pain of Others,* by Susan Sontag. Copyright © 2003 by Susan Sontag. Reprinted by permission of Farrar, Straus & Giroux, LLC. (pp. 391–93)

Alexander Gardner. *A Harvest of Death, Gettysburg, July 1863.* Library of Congress, negative #LC-B8184-7964-A. (p. 395)

Ron Haviv. *Bijeljina, Bosnia, 1992.* © Ron Haviv/VII. (p. 396)

Ronald L. Haeberle. *My Lai villagers before and after being shot by U.S. troops.* Reprinted by permission of Ronald S. Haeberle/TimePix. (pp. 398–99)

Physicians Against Land Mines. Advertisement. Leo Burnett/Physicians Against Land Mines (PALM). By permission of the Center for International Rehabilitation. (p. 404)

Laurent Rebours. *Statue of Iraqi President Saddam Hussein Being Pulled Down in Downtown Baghdad,* Wednesday, April 9, 2003. © 2003 AP/Wide World Photos. (p. 406)

Human Rights Watch. *Remembering Rwanda: Africa in Conflict, Yesterday and Today.* © 2004 Corinne Dufka/Human Rights Watch. (p. 407)

Chapter 5

Roz Chast. *Deconstructing Lunch.* © The New Yorker Collection 2000 Roz Chast from cartoonbank.com. All rights reserved. (p. 416)

Dennis McDonald. *Burlington County Times,* Berkeley, New Jersey, 2003. From *America 24/7* (NewYork: DK Publishing, 2003). © 2003 Dennis McDonald, Affiliation for America 24/7. (p. 418)

Kurt Wilson. *St. Ignatius, Montana, 2003.* From *America 24/7* (NewYork: DK Publishing, 2003). © 2003 Kurt Wilson, Affiliation for America 24/7. (p. 419)

Maya Angelou. "Human Family." From *I Shall Not Be Moved* by Maya Angelou (New York: Bantam Books, 1991). Copyright © 1991 by Maya Angelou. Reprinted by permission of Random House, Inc. (pp. 420–21)

Danielle P. Richards. *Teaneck, New Jersey, 2003.* From *America 24/7* (NewYork: DK Publishing, 2003). © 2003 Danielle P. Richards, Affiliation for America 24/7. All rights reserved/Affiliation for America 24/7. (p. 421)

David Brooks. "People Like Us. From *The Atlantic Monthly,* September 2003. Copyright © 2003 by David Brooks. Reprinted by permission of *The Atlantic Monthly.* (pp. 422–28)

Gary Fandel. *West Des Moines, Iowa, 2003.* From *America 24/7* (NewYork: DK Publishing, 2003). © 2003 Gary Fandel, Affiliation for America 24/7. (pp. 424–25)

CAIR. "We're All Americans." Courtesy of the Council on American-Islamic Relations. (p. 427)

Richard Rodriguez. "Gangstas." From *Mother Jones* (Special Issue on guns), January/February 1994. Copyright © 1994 by Richard Rodriguez. Reprinted by permission of Georges Borchardt, Inc., Literary Agency. (pp. 431–38)

Joseph Rodriguez. *Chivo; Members of Florencia 13 gang outside school; Mike Estrada holds a photo of his father who is in prison;* and *Funeral of two-and-a-half-year-old Thomas Regalado III.* All photos courtesy of Joseph Rodriguez/Black Star. (pp. 432, 434, 436–37)

Roger Ressmeyer. *Crying Infants, 1984.* © Roger Ressmeyer/ CORBIS. (p. 441)

Penelope Scambly Schott. "Report on the Difference between Men and Women." From *Fourth Genre,* Fall 1999. Copyright © 1999 by Penelope Scambly Schott. Reprinted by permission of the author. (p. 442)

Melanie Sumner. "Marriage." From *Harper's Magazine,* October 2003. Copyright © 2003 by Melanie Sumner. Reprinted by permission of *Harper's Magazine.* (p. 443)

Eric James. *School Bus, 2003.* © 2003 by Look-Look Magazine/Eric James. (pp. 444–45)

Jan Morris. "Herstory." From *Forbes* magazine, October 4, 1999. Copyright © 1999 by Jan Morris. Reprinted by permission of A.P. Watt as agent for the author. (pp. 446–48)

Todd Goldman. *Boys Are Stupid.* Courtesy of David & Goliath, Inc. (p. 449)

Jacob Riis. *Homeless Boys, New York City* (titled *Street Arabs in Their Sleeping Quarters, circa 1890*) and excerpt from the text. From Jacob A. Riis, *How the Other Half Lives* (Canada: Dover Publications, 1971).

Copyright Museum of the City of New York; part of the Jacob A. Riis Collection (image 121). (pp. 452–53)

Lars Eighner. "On Dumpster Diving." From *Threepenny Review,* Fall 1991 by Jan Morris. Copyright © 1991 by Lars Eighner. Reprinted by permission of the author. (pp. 454–65)

Mary Ellen Mark. *The Damm Family in Their Car.* First appeared in *Life* magazine 1987. *Chrissy Damm and Adam Johnson.* First appeared in *Aperture,* Winter 1997. Both images copyright © 1999 by Mary Ellen Mark, collected in *Mary Ellen Mark: American Odyssey 1963–1999* (New York: Aperture, 1999). Reprinted by permission. (pp. 458, 461)

Margaret Morton. *Mr. Lee's House, the Hill, 1991, Mr. Lee, Chinatown, 1992,* and text, "Mr. Lee." All from *Fragile Dwelling* by Margaret Morton (New York: Aperture, 2000). Copyright © Margaret Morton. Reprinted by permission. (pp. 466–68)

Orlando Patterson. "Race Over." From *The New Republic,* January 10, 2000, pp. 6–8. Copyright © 2000 by Orlando Patterson. Reprinted by permission of *The New Republic.* (pp. 471–74)

Derek Jeter, 2003. Photo by Evan Agostini. © Getty Images. (p. 475)

Jessica Alba, 2003. © Tom Maelsa/AFP/Getty Images. (p. 475)

Vin Diesel, 2003. © Tom Maelsa/AFP/Getty Images. (p. 475)

Christina Aguilera, 2003. © Stephane Cardinale/People Avenue/Corbis. (p. 475)

Steven M. Wise. "Why Animals Deserve Legal Rights." From *The Chronicle of Higher Education,* February 2, 2001. Copyright © 2001 by Steven M. Wise. Reprinted by permission of the publisher. (pp. 478–80)

Vicki Hearne. "What's Wrong with Animal Rights." From *Harper's Magazine,* 1991. Copyright © 1991 by Vicki Hearne. Reprinted by permission of *Harper's Magazine.* (pp. 481–90)

People For the Ethical Treatment of Animals. "They called him Christmas." Courtesy of PETAOnLine.org. (p. 486)

FBR. "Animal research saves animals." Courtesy of the Foundation for Biomedical Research. (p. 487)

Human Rights Campaign Foundation poster. "Why are 'Pro-Family' Groups Attacking This Family?" Courtesy of the Human Rights Campaign Foundation. (p. 492)

Bar graph. Royalty Free/CORBIS. (p. 493)

Chapter 6

Blamm. Getty Images. (p. 502)

Adbusters. "How to Create Your Own Print Ad." Reprinted by permission of Adbusters Media Foundation. (pp.504–06)

Chris Ballard. "How to Write a Catchy Beer Ad: Football, Guitars—and Twins—Turned a Commercial into a Phenomenon." From *The New York Times Magazine,* January 26, 2003. Copyright © 2003 by Chris Ballard. Reprinted by permission of *The New York Times Magazine.* (pp. 507–11)

The Coors Light Twins at *Maxim* Magazine's Circus Maximus Party, January 30, 2004. Evan Agostini/ Getty Images. (p. 508)

James B. Twitchell. "How to Advertise a Dangerous Product." From *Twenty Ads That Shook the World: The Century's Most Groundbreaking Advertising and How It Changed Us All.* Copyright © 2000 by James B. Twitchell. Used by permission of Crown Publishers, a division of Random House, Inc. (pp. 512–17)

Miss Clairol. "Does she . . . or doesn't she?" From *Good Housekeeping,* August 1963. Copyright © 1960/2001 Clairol Inc. Reproduced with the permission of Clairol Inc. (p. 514)

Barbara Ehrenreich. "Dirty Laundry: Benetton's 'We, on Death Row' Campaign." From *Aperture* 160, Summer 2000. Copyright © 2000 by Barbara Ehrenreich. Reprinted by permission of the publisher. (pp. 519–27)

"Father" and "The Enforcer" are courtesy of The Partnership For a Drug-Free America®. (pp.528–29)

American Indian College Fund. "Have You Ever Seen a Real Indian?" Reprinted by permission. (p. 530)

National Campaign Against Youth Violence. "Children Aren't Born Violent." National Campaign Against Youth Violence. Compliments of the Executive Director, Sarah Ingersoll. (p. 531)

Nike. "The Most Offensive Boots We've Ever Made." Image courtesy of Nathan Shanahan and www.adbusters .org. (p. 532)

Adbusters. "You're Running Because You Want That Raise." Courtesy of www.adbusters.org. (p. 533)

Amy Sancetta. Photo of pizza box in garbage. AP/Wide World Photo. (p. 537)

Sondra Dawes. Photo of patriotic bikinis. © Sondra Dawes/The Image Works. (p. 537)

Ian Frazier. "All-Consuming Patriotism." From *Mother Jones,* March/April 2002. Copyright © 2002 by Ian Frazier. Reprinted by permission of *Mother Jones.* (pp. 538–44)

"I Want You for U.S. Army." Smithsonian American Art Museum, Washington, DC/Art Resource, New York. (p. 539)

"Wake Up America!" © Bettmann/CORBIS. (p. 542)

"You'll be on the Greatest Team in the World!," "When Was the last time you got promoted?" and www.goarmy .com. U.S. Army materials courtesy of the U.S. Government, as represented by the Secretary of the Army. (p. 543, 545, 546)

Peter Bagge. *Malls.* Reprinted with permission from *Reason* magazine. Copyright © 2003 by Reason Foundation, 3415 S. Sepulveda Blvd, Suite 400, Los Angeles, CA 90034. www.reason.com (pp. 550–53)

David Guterson. "Enclosed. Encyclopedic. Endured.: One Week at the Mall of America." From *Harper's Magazine,* August 1993. Copyright © 1993 by David Guterson. Reprinted by permission of Georges Borchardt, Inc. for the author. (pp. 554–61)

The Markets of Trajan, Rome. Scala/Art Resource, NY. (p. 556)

The Crystal Palace, London, 1851. © Historical Picture Archive/CORBIS. (p. 557)

The Houston Galleria, 1971. © Lowell Georgia/CORBIS. (p. 558)

The Mall of America, Bloomington. Mark Erickson/Getty Images. (p. 559)

Barbara Kruger. *Untitled* (*I shop therefore I am*), 1987. From *Thinking of You* (1999). 111″ × 113″ photographic silkscreen/vinyl, 1987. Courtesy Mary Boone Gallery, New York. (p. 563)

Neal Gabler. "Our Celebrities, Ourselves." From *The Chronicle of Higher Education,* March 14, 2003. Copyright © 2003 by Neal Gabler. Reprinted by permission of the publisher. (pp. 566–73)

Jeff Koons. "Michael Jackson and Bubbles," 1988. Porcelain; 42″ × 70.5″ × 32.5″. San Francisco Museum of Modern Art. Purchased through the Marian and Bernard Messenger Fund. (p. 568)

Timothy Greenfield-Sanders. *Jeff Koons.* From *GQ* magazine, 2001. © Timothy Greenfield-Sanders. (p. 571)

L'Oréal. *Celebrity Beauty,* 2000. The Advertising Archive, Ltd. (p. 574)

Georges Marciano. *Anna Nicole Smith,* 2001. The Advertising Archive, Ltd. (p. 575)

Cover of *Time* Magazine, September 7, 1997. Courtesy of TimePix. (p. 576)

Charles Atlas. "How Joe's Body Brought Him Fame Instead of Shame," 1944. Image is under license from Charles Atlas Ltd. NY, NY (www. Charles Atlas.com). For over 75 years the Charles Atlas "Dynamic Tension®" health and fitness course continues to help students train without the use of weights. (p. 580)

Eric Tyrone McLeod. "Selling Out: Consumer Culture and Commodification of the Male Body." From *Post Road Magazine.* Copyright © 2002 by Eric McLeod. Reprinted by permission of the publisher. (pp. 581–93)

Robert Cameron. *The Drinking Man's Diet,* 1964. Courtesy of Cameron & Company Publishers, San Francisco. (p. 584)

Calvin Klein Pro Stretch. *Fredrik Ljungberg.* The Advertising Archive Ltd. (p. 591)

Two women with mirror and lipstick. Rhydian Lewis/ Getty Images. (p. 594)

Spilled pink nail polish. SW Productions/Getty Images. (p. 594)

Handful of small American flags. S. Meltzer/Getty Images. (p. 596)

Magazine covers featuring Princess Diana. © Tim Graham/CORBIS. (p. 597)

615

Action Comics #1, *Superman,* 354

Ada Bennett and daughter Faith, San Antonio, 2002 (Bamberger), 238

Adbusters, "How to Create Your Own Print Ad," 504
You're Running Because You Want That Raise, 533

Airport Lounges (Otte), 268

Alexie, Sherman, "The Texas Chainsaw Massacre," 320

"All-Consuming Patriotism" (Frazier), 538

Allison, Dorothy, *Bastard Out of Carolina* (book cover), 75
Bastard Out of Carolina (film still), 77
Dorothy Allison, 1958 (photo), 72
"What Did You Expect?," 71

"All My Life for Sale" (Freyer), 57

allmylifeforsale.com (Freyer), 57

"Alternate Ending" (DeLillo), 214

American Beauty (film still), 215

American flag as merchandising tool (2 photos), 357

American Idol (photo), 169

American Indian College Fund (AICF), *Have You Ever Seen a Real Indian?,* 530

Angelou, Maya, "Human Family," 420

Animal research saves animals (Foundation for Biomedical Research), 487

Anna Nicole Smith (Guess/Georges Marciano), 575

Anne Sexton, Summer 1974 (Furst), 84

Anne Sexton, two photographs (Furst), 87

Arad, Michael, and Peter Walker, "Reflecting Absence," 384

"Ashes" (Sedaris), 139

Atlas, Charles, *How Joe's Body Brought Him Fame Instead of Shame,* 580

Audience Wearing 3-D Glasses (photo), 14

Automat (Horn & Hardart), 258

Bagge, Peter, *Malls,* 550

Baldwin Hills Crenshaw Plaza (Greenfield), 263

Ballard, Chris, "How to Write a Catchy Beer Ad," 507

Bamberger, Bill, *Ada Bennett and daughter Faith, San Antonio, 2002,* 238
Charles Evans Hughes, Mountainview Courts, Chattanooga, 1995, 240
Christopher McDonald at home in Orchard Village, 1994, 239
The Mobile Gallery, San Antonio, 2002, 241
Nancy and Alejandra Camarillo, Plaza Florencia, 2002, 237

Bastard Out of Carolina (book cover, Allison), 75

Bastard Out of Carolina (film still, Allison), 77

"Between Art and Architecture" (Lin), 368

Bijeljina, Bosnia, 1992 (Haviv), 396

Blair Witch Project, The (film still), 212

Blowing Bubbles (Mann), 93

"Boston Photographs, The" (Ephron), 200

Boston Photographs, The (Forman), 202

Boy Running in Field (Satushek), 292

Boys Are Stupid (Todd Goldman), 449

Brooks, David, "People Like Us," 422

Brooks, Gwendolyn, "Kitchenette Building," 335

Burlington County Times (McDonald), 418

Butow, David, *Traffic along U.S. Highway 412,* 261

Callahan, Brian, *Map of Sand Creek,* 329

Calley, William L., "Court Martial Transcript," 402

Calvin Klein Pro Stretch, *Fredrik Ljungberg,* 591

Camel Jr.'s (English), 6

Cameron, Robert, *The Drinking Man's Diet,* 584

Candy Cigarette (Mann), 98

Car Crash Upper Fifth Ave. (Weegee), 8, 199

Celebrity Beauty (L'Oréal), 574

Charles Evans Hughes, Mountainview Courts, Chattanooga, 1995 (Bamberger), 240

Chast, Roz, *Deconstructing Lunch,* 416

Cheyenne and Arapaho chiefs (photo), 325

Children Aren't Born Violent (National Council Against Youth Violence) 531

Chivo (Rodriguez), 432

Chrissy Damm and Adam Johnson (Mark), 461

Christina Aguilera (photo), 475

Christopher McDonald at home in Orchard Village, 1994 (Bamberger), 239

cnn.com, 18

Cocoa Beach, Florida, 1983 (Epstein), 279

Cofer, Judith Ortiz, "Lessons of the Past," 53

    "Silent Dancing," 44

    Silent Dancing: A Partial Remembrance of a Puerto Rican Childhood (book cover), 52

Cole, Jack, *Murder, Morphine and Me,* 351, 352

    True Crime, 350

Colonel John M. Chivington (photo), 324

Coors Light Twins (photo), 509

Council on American-Islamic Relations (CAIR), *We're All Americans,* 427

"Court Martial Transcript" (Calley), 402

Crying Infants (Ressmeyer), 441

Crystal Palace, London (photo), 557

Da Vinci, Leonardo, *Mona Lisa,* 104

Da Vinci Timeline (Schwartz), 120

D'Amato, Paul, *Jump Shot/Tiro con salto,* 245

Damm Family in Their Car, The (Mark), 458

Dancing (Weegee), 198

"Daughter, Model, Muse Jessie Mann on Being Photographed" (Harris), 97

David and Amy Sedaris (photo), 149

Declaration of Independence (draft, print, calligraphy), 304–305

    Declaration of Independence (broadside detail), 310

    Declaration of Independence (calligraphy detail), 311

    Declaration of Independence (draft detail), 309

Deconstructing Lunch (Chast), 416

DeLillo, Don, "Alternate Ending," 214

    "Videotape," 210

DeMartino, Jesse, *Jason and Mike at the Cabin Near Huntsville, Texas, 1996,* 277

Derek Jeter (photo), 475

Deutsch, Hulton, *Women Collaborators Are Punished in Cherbourg,* 55

Diana, Princess of Wales (*Time* magazine cover), 576

Diller + Scofidio, *Refresh,* 161–62

"Dirty Laundry: Benetton's 'We, On Death Row' Campaign" (Ehrenreich), 519

Does she . . . or doesn't she? (Miss Clairol), 514

Doonesbury (Trudeau), 156, 157

Dorothy Allison, 1958 (photo), 72

Drinking Man's Diet, The (Cameron), 584

Duchamp, Marcel, *L.H.O.O.Q.,* 110

Dunn, Stephen, "The Sacred," 278

ebay.com, 68

Ehrenreich, Barbara, "Dirty Laundry: Benetton's 'We, On Death Row' Campaign," 519

Eighner, Lars, "On Dumpster Diving," 454

Emina's Story (Physicians Against Land Mines), 404

Emmett, Jessie, and Virginia (Mann), 96

"Enclosed. Encyclopedic. Endured.: One Week at the Mall of America" (Guterson), 554

Enforcer, The (Office of National Drug Control Policy), 529

English, Ron, *Camel Jr.'s,* 6

Ephron, Nora, "The Boston Photographs," 200

Epstein, Mitch, *Cocoa Beach, Florida, 1983,* 279

Erdrich, Louise, "*Z:* The Movie That Changed My Life," 182

Ernst (Lyon), 150

Extreme Makeover (2 photos), 172

"Family of Mann, The" (Malcolm), 91

Fandel, Gary, *West Des Moines, Iowa, 2003,* 424–25

"Fast-Food America" (Howe), 257

Father (Office of National Drug Control Policy), 528

Fear Factor (photo), 174

Federal Home Loan Bank of Seattle, *Report on lending initiatives,* 293

"First Shot" (Wideman), 244

Forgetting Would Be A Second Abandonment (United States National Holocaust Memorial Museum), 387

Forman, Stanley, *The Boston Photographs,* 202–203

"Forms Stretched to Their Limits" (Spiegelman), 342

Foundation for Biomedical Research (FBR), *Animal research saves animals,* 487

Four Generations (Lyon), 152

Frazier, Ian, "All-Consuming Patriotism," 538

Frederick, Joan, *Rainy Mountain, Kiowa Holy Place, Oklahoma,* 272

Fredrik Ljungberg (Calvin Klein Pro Stretch), 591

Freyer, John, "All My Life For Sale," 57

Funeral of two-and-a-half-year-old Thomas Regalado III (Rodriguez), 437

Furst, Arthur, *Anne Sexton, Summer 1974,* 84
    Anne Sexton, two photographs, 87

Gabler, Neal, "Our Celebrities, Ourselves," 566
"Gangstas" (Rodriguez), 431
Gardner, Alexander, *A Harvest of Death, Gettysburg, July 1863,* 395
Gettysburg Address (calligraphy), 314
Gettysburg Address (PowerPoint), 315
goarmy.com, 546
"Going to Press" (Munves), 308
Goldman, Todd, *Boys Are Stupid,* 449
google.com, 290
Gould, Stephen Jay, "A Time of Gifts," 22
Greenfield, Lauren, *Baldwin Hills Crenshaw Plaza,* 263
    Hot Dog on a Stick employees Dominique King and Wendy Recinos at Baldwin Hills Crenshaw Plaza, 262
    Keum Ja Chung and Hyung Hee Im in the Koreatown Plaza International Food Court, 263
    Penny Wolfe and daughter Jessica, Santa Monica Place, 262
    Sara, 19, 26–27
Greenfield-Sanders, Thomas, *Jeff Koons,* 571
Green Lama, The (comic), 355
Gries, Scott, *David and Amy Sedaris,* 149
Guess/Georges Marciano, *Anna Nicole Smith,* 575
Guterson, David, "Enclosed. Encyclopedic. Endured.: One Week at the Mall of America," 554

Haeberle, Ronald L., *My Lai villagers before and after being shot by U.S. troops,* 398, 399
Harris, Melissa, "Daughter, Model, Muse Jessie Mann on Being Photographed," 97
Harriss, Joseph A., "Seeking Mona Lisa," 105
Harvest of Death, Gettysburg, July 1863 (Gardner), 395
Have You Ever Seen a Real Indian? (American Indian College Fund), 530
Haviv, Ron, *Bijeljina, Bosnia, 1992,* 396
Hearne, Vicki, "What's Wrong with Animal Rights?," 481
"Herstory" (Morris), 446
Homeless Boys, New York City (Riis), 452
Horn & Hardart, *Automat,* 258
Hot Dog on a Stick employees Dominique King and Wendy Recinos at Baldwin Hills Crenshaw Plaza (Greenfield), 262
Houston Galleria (photo), 558
How Joe's Body Brought Him Fame Instead of Shame (Charles Atlas), 580

"How to Advertise a Dangerous Product" (Twitchell), 512
"How to Create Your Own Print Ad" (Adbusters), 504
How to Erase a Skater (photo), 25
"How to Write a Catchy Beer Ad" (Ballard), 507
Howe, Nicholas, "Fast-Food America," 257
"Human Family" (Angelou), 420
Human Rights Campaign Foundation, *Why Are "Pro-Family" Groups Attacking This Family?,* 492
Human Rights Watch, *Remembering Rwanda: Africa in Conflict, Yesterday and Today,* 407

I shop therefore I am (Kruger), 563
I Want You for U.S. Army (poster), 539
Innercity Home (Rigo 95), 4
"Introduction to Diller + Scofidio's *Refresh*" (Tucker), 160
In What Language? (Iyer and Ladd), 269
"It's a Real, Real, Real, Real, Real World" (Jaffe), 176
Iyer, Pico, "Nowhere Man," 266
Iyer, Vijay, and Mike Ladd, *In What Language?,* 269

Jaffe, Anthony, "It's a Real, Real, Real, Real, Real World," 176
James, Eric, *School Bus,* 444–45
Jason and Mike at the Cabin Near Huntsville, Texas, 1996 (DeMartino), 277
Jeff Koons (Greenfield-Sanders), 571
jennicam.com (Ringley), 158
Jessica Alba (photo), 475
Jessie Bites (Mann), 90
Jones, Bronston, *Missing,* 206, 207
Jump Shot/ Tiro con salto (D'Amato), 245

Kalman, Tibor, *True Stories,* 11
Keum Ja Chung and Hyung Hee Im in the Koreatown Plaza International Food Court (Greenfield), 263
"Kitchenette Building" (Brooks), 335
Klinkenborg, Verlyn, "Sand Creek," 322
Koons, Jeff, *Michael Jackson and Bubbles,* 568
Koppell, Jonathan G. S., "No 'There' There," 283
Kruger, Barbara, *I shop therefore I am,* 563
    Untitled (Love is something you fall into), 3
Kulturforum (photo), 42

Lamy, Nicole, "Life in Motion," 230
    Life in Motion, 232–33
Lesser, Wendy, "Weegee," 195
"Lessons of the Past" (Cofer), 53

L.H.O.O.Q. (Duchamp), 110
"Life in Motion" (Lamy), 230
Life in Motion (Lamy), 232–33
Lin, Maya, "Between Art and Architecture," 368
    "Proposal and sketches," 363
    Vietnam Veterans Memorial, 16, 359, 372–73, 378–81
Lixemberg, Dana, *Tamika Catchings,* 251
Lord of the Rings: The Return of the King, The (book cover and DVD case), 219
Lord of the Rings: The Return of the King, The (film promo), 190
L'Oréal, *Celebrity Beauty,* 574
Lyon, Danny, *Ernst,* 150
    Four Generations, 152
    Raphe at Seventeen, 153

Malcolm, Janet, "The Family of Mann," 91
Mall of America, Bloomington (photo), 559
Malls (Bagge), 550
Man with a Rifle (Wall), 216
Mann, Sally, *Blowing Bubbles,* 93
    Candy Cigarette, 98
    Emmett, Jessie, and Virginia, 96
    Jessie Bites, 90
Map of Sand Creek (Callahan), 329
"March 16–18, 1968" (Partsch), 401
Markets of Trajan, Rome, (photo), 556
Mark, Mary Ellen, *Chrissy Damm and Adam Johnson, Llano, California, 1994,* 461
    The Damm Family in Their Car, Los Angeles, California, 1987, 458
"Marriage" (Sumner), 443
Matrix, The (movie poster), 189
McCloud, Scott, *Understanding Comics,* 137
McDonald, Dennis, *Burlington County Times,* 418
McLeod, Eric Tyrone, "Selling Out: Consumer Culture and Commodification of the Male Body," 581
Members of Florencia 13 gang outside school (Rodriguez), 434
Michael Jackson and Bubbles (Koons), 568
Mike Estrada holds a photo of his father who is in prison (Rodriguez), 436
Miller, Wayne F., *One-Room Kitchenette,* 334
    Rabbits for Sale, 332
    Three Teenagers in Kitchenette Apartment, 336
    Two Girls Waiting Outside a Tavern, 333
Miss Clairol, *Does she . . . or doesn't she?,* 514
Missing (Jones), 206, 207
Mobile Gallery, San Antonio, 2002, (Bamberger), 241

Momaday, N. Scott, "The Way to Rainy Mountain," 272
Monal Leo (Schwartz), 119
Mona Lisa (da Vinci), 104
Mona Lisa: 1963 (Warhol), 115
"Mona Lisa Identification, The" (Schwartz), 117
Mona Lisa (Peanut Butter and Jelly) (Muniz), 112
Morris, Jan, "Herstory," 446
Morton, Margaret, "Mr. Lee," 466
    Mr. Lee, Chinatown, 1992, 468
    Mr. Lee's House, the Hill, 1991, 467
Most Offensive Boot We've Ever Made, The (Nike), 532
"Mr. Lee" (Morton), 466
Mr. Lee, Chinatown, 1992 (Morton), 468
Mr. Lee's House, the Hill, 1991 (Morton), 467
Mr. Personality (photo), 167
Ms. magazine cover (*Wonder Woman for President*), 357
Mulberry Street Café (Weegee), 197
Muniz, Vik, *Mona Lisa (Peanut Butter and Jelly),* 112
Munves, James, "Going to Press," 308
Murder, Morphine and Me (Cole), 351, 352
My Lai villagers before and after being shot by U.S. troops (Haeberle), 398, 399

Nancy and Alejandra Camarillo, Plaza Florencia, 2002 (Bamberger), 237
National Campaign Against Youth Violence (NCAYV), *Children Aren't Born Violent,* 531
Negative Population Growth, "Remember when this was heavy traffic?", 30
New Yorker, The (magazine cover), 107
Newsboy (Weegee), 194
Nice Place to Stay on the Internet, A (Yahoo!), 282
Nike, *The Most Offensive Boot We've Ever Made,* 532
Norvig, Peter, *PowerPoint Presentation for the Gettysburg Address,* 315
"No 'There' There" (Koppell), 283
"Nowhere Man" (Iyer), 266

Office of National Drug Control Policy (ONDCP), The Partnership for a Drug-Free America, *The Enforcer,* 529
    Father, 528
"On Dumpster Diving" (Eighner), 454
One-Room Kitchenette (Miller), 334
Otte, Sylvia, *Airport Lounges,* 268
"Our Celebrities, Ourselves" (Gabler), 566

Parks, Gordon, "Speaking for the Past," 337
Partsch, Thomas R., "March 16–18, 1968," 401

Passion of the Christ, The (film promo), 191

Patterson, Orlando, "Race Over," 471

Penny Wolfe and daughter Jessica, Santa Monica Place (Greenfield), 262

People for the Ethical Treatment of Animals (PETA), *They Called Him Christmas,* 486

"People Like Us" (Brooks), 422

Physicians Against Land Mines (PALM), *Emina's Story,* 404

Plastic Man (comics), 341, 346

Portland, Maine—October 8, 2000 (Richman), 249

Portrait of Boy Soldier (photo), 127

PowerPoint Presentation for the Gettysburg Address (Norvig), 315

"Proposal and sketches" (Lin), 363

Rabbits for Sale (Miller), 332

"Race Over" (Patterson), 471

Rainy Mountain, Kiowa Holy Place, Oklahoma (Frederick), 272

Raphe at Seventeen (Lyon), 153

Ray Kroc Standing outside McDonald's, 1963 (photo), 259

"Real Declaration, The" (Starr), 306

"Reality in America" (Siegel), 166

Rebours, Laurent, *Statue of Iraqi President Saddam Hussein Being Pulled Down in Downtown Baghdad,* 406

"Reflecting Absence" (Arad and Walker), 384

Refresh (Diller + Scofidio), 161–62

"Remember when this was heavy traffic?" (Negative Population Growth), 30

Remembering Rwanda: Africa in Conflict, Yesterday and Today (Human Rights Watch), 407

Report on lending initiatives (Federal Home Loan Bank of Seattle), 293

"Report on the Difference between Men and Women" (Schott), 442

"Résumé 1965" (Sexton), 80

Ressmeyer, Roger, *Crying Infants,* 441

Richards, Danielle P., *Teaneck, New Jersey, 2003,* 421

Richman, Brad, *Portland, Maine—October 8, 2000,* 249
    Silver Springs, Maryland—August 1993, 248
    Washington, D.C.—July 10, 1999, 249

Rigo 95, *Innercity Home,* 4

Riis, Jacob, *Homeless Boys, New York City,* 452

Ringley, Jennifer, jennicam.com, 158

Rodriguez, Joseph, *Chivo,* 432
    Funeral of two-and-a-half-year-old Thomas Regalado III, 437
    Members of Florencia 13 gang outside school, 434
    Mike Estrada holds a photo of his father who is in prison, 436

Rodriquez, Richard, "Gangstas," 431

"Sacred, The" (Dunn), 278

"Sand Creek" (Klinkenborg), 322

Sara, 19 (Greenfield), 27

Satushek, Steve, *Boy Running in Field,* 292

School Bus (James), 444–45

Schott, Penelope Scambly, "Report on the Difference between Men and Women," 442

Schwartz, Lillian Feldman, *Da Vinci Timeline,* 120
    Mona/Leo, 119
    "The Mona Lisa Identification," 117

Sedaris, David, "Ashes," 139

"Seeking Mona Lisa" (Harriss), 105

"Self in 1958" (Sexton), 85

"Selling Out: Consumer Culture and Commodification of the Male Body" (McLeod), 581

Sex, Lies, and Videotape (film still), 213

Sexton, Anne, "Résumé 1965," 80
    "Self in 1958," 85

"Sidewalks in Cyberspace" (Zatz), 287

Siegel, Lee, "Reality in America," 166

"Silent Dancing" (Cofer), 44

Silent Dancing: A Partial Remembrance of a Puerto Rican Childhood (book cover, Cofer), 52

Silver Springs, Maryland—August 1993 (Richman), 248

SimCity 4 (2 screen shots), 284

Sims, The (2 screen shots), 288

Sontag, Susan, "Watching Suffering From A Distance," 391

Soundportraits.org, 126

"Speaking for the Past" (Parks), 337

Spiegelman, Art, "Forms Stretched to Their Limits," 342

Starr, Thomas, "The Real Declaration," 306

Statue of Iraqi President Saddam Hussein Being Pulled Down in Downtown Baghdad (Rebours), 406

St. Ignatius, Montana, 2003 (Wilson), 421

Sumner, Melanie, "Marriage," 443

Superman (Action Comics #1), 354

Tamika Catchings (Lixemberg), 251

Teaneck, New Jersey, 2003 (Richards), 421

"Texas Chainsaw Massacre, The" (Alexie), 320

Texas Chainsaw Massacre, The (movie poster), 288

They Called Him Christmas (People for the Ethical Treatment of Animals), 486

Three Teenagers in Kitchenette Apartment (Miller), 336

Time magazine cover (*Diana, Princess of Wales*), 576

"Time of Gifts, A" (Gould), 22

Traffic along U.S. Highway 412 (Butow), 261

Troops storming the Sand Creek (illustration), 328

Trudeau, Gary, *Doonesbury,* 156

True Crime (Cole), 350

True Stories (Kalman), 11

Tucker, Sara, "Introduction to Diller + Scofidio's *Refresh,*" 160

Twitchell, James B., "How to Advertise a Dangerous Product," 512

Two Girls Waiting Outside a Tavern (Miller), 333

Understanding Comics (McCloud), 137

United States National Holocaust Memorial Museum, *Forgetting Would Be A Second Abandonment,* 387

Untitled (Love is something you fall into) (Kruger), 3

"Videotape" (DeLillo), 210

Vietnam Veterans Memorial (Lin), 16, 359, 372–73, 378–81

Vin Diesel (photo), 475

Wake Up, America! (poster), 542

Wall, Jeff, *Man with a Rifle,* 216

Warhol, Andy, *Mona Lisa: 1963,* 115

Washington, D.C.—July 10, 1999 (Richman), 249

"Watching Suffering from a Distance" (Sontag), 391

"Way to Rainy Mountain, The" (Momaday), 272

Weegee, *Car Crash Upper Fifth Ave.,* 8, 199
    Dancing, 198
    Mulberry Street Café, 197

Newsboy, 194

"Weegee" (Lesser), 195

We're All Americans (Council on American-Islamic Relations), 427

West Des Moines, Iowa, 2003 (Fandel), 424–25

"What Did You Expect?" (Allison), 71

"What's Wrong with Animal Rights?" (Hearne), 481

When was the last time you got promoted? (poster), 545

"Why Animals Deserve Legal Rights" (Wise), 478

Why Are "Pro-Family" Groups Attacking This Family? (Human Rights Campaign Foundation), 492

Wideman, John Edgar, "First Shot," 244

Wilson, Kurt, *St. Ignatius, Montana, 2003,* 421

Wise, Steven M., "Why Animals Deserve Legal Rights," 478

Wizard of Oz, The (movie poster), 188

Woman Suffrage Procession, Official Program (illustration), 302

Women Collaborators Are Punished in Cherbourg (Deutsch), 55

Wonder Woman (*Ms.* magazine cover), 357

X-Men 2 (movie poster), 187

Yahoo!, *A Nice Place to Stay on the Internet,* 282

You'll be on the Greatest Team in the World! (poster), 543

You're Running Because You Want That Raise (Adbusters), 533

Zatz, Noah D., "Sidewalks in Cyberspace," 287

Z (movie poster), 181

"*Z*: The Movie That Changed My Life" (Erdrich), 182

INDEX OF AUTHORS AND TITLES

www.bedfordstmartins.com/convergences

Visit the *Convergences* companion web site for online materials to supplement the text. When you see a "go to" bar > go in *Convergences*, it means that there's a particularly interesting connection between what's in the book and what's online. You'll find lots of stuff to explore: annotated links to sites that extend each of the clusters in the book as well as collections of online magazines and museums. For instructors, the complete text of *Resources for Teaching CONVERGENCES* is available, downloadable in PDF format.

CONVERGENCES
MESSAGE • METHOD • MEDIUM   SECOND EDITION
Robert Atwan

CONVERGENCES

Welcome to the book companion site for *Convergences: Method Message Medium*, by Robert Atwan, Second Edition.

Log on

E-mail address:

Password:

Go

Forget your password?

I am not registered. Sign me up as a(n):

Student
Instructor

View Content by Cluster

Chapter 1: Staging Portraits
Chapter 2: Telling Stories
Chapter 3: Shaping Spaces
Chapter 4: Making History
Chapter 5: Dividing Lines
Chapter 6: Packaging Culture

Instructor Resources

● Instructor's Manual

Student Resources

● Links by Cluster

Other Resources at Bedford/St. Martin's

● Diana Hacker's Research and Documentation Online

● Mike Palmquist's Research Activities and Checklists

● Mike Palmquist's Guided Tutorials on Research Processes

● Mike Markel's Web Design Tutorial

● Model Documents Gallery

Bedford/St. Martin's | Composition | About This Book | Order a Book | Contact Us | Tech Support